INTRODUCTION TO EARLY CHILDHOOD EDUCATION

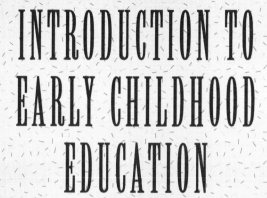

EVA ESSA
UNIVERSITY OF NEVADA-RENO

ROSEMARY YOUNG
BROCK UNIVERSITY

Nelson Canada

International Thomson Publishing
The trademark ITP is used under licence

© Nelson Canada,
A Division of Thomson Canada Limited, 1994

Published in 1994 by
Nelson Canada,
A Division of Thomson Canada Limited
1120 Birchmount Road
Scarborough, Ontario M1K 5G4

All rights reserved. No part of this work covered by the copyrights hereon may be reproduced or used in any form or by any means—graphic, electronic or mechanical, including photocopying, recording, taping or information storage and retrieval systems—without prior written permission of the publisher.

To show your appreciation for the time and effort that the author and publisher have invested in this book, please choose **not** to photocopy it. Choose instead to add it to your own personal library. The investment will be well worth it.

Every effort has been made to trace ownership of all copyrighted material and to secure permission from copyright holders. In the event of any question arising as to the use of any material, we will be pleased to make the necessary corrections in future printings.

Canadian Cataloguing in Publication Data

Essa, Eva
        Introduction to early childhood education

1st Canadian ed.
Includes bibliographical references and index.
ISBN 0–17–604175–3

1. Early childhood education – Canada. 2. Early childhood education – Canada – Aims and objectives. 3. Early childhood educators - Training of – Canada. I. Young, Rosemary Elaine. II. Title.

LB1139.3.C3E77 1994   372.21'8'0971   C94–930189–2

Acquisitions Editor   Charlotte Forbes
Editorial Manager   Nicole Gnutzman
Developmental Editor   Heather Martin
Art Director   Bruce Bond
Designer   Sue Peden
Cover Illustration   Ljuba Levstek

Printed and bound in Canada
3 4 5 BBM 98 97 96 95

To my son, Daniel Shattuck,
who is always teaching me
about early childhood

CONTENTS

CHAPTER 3   EARLY CHILDHOOD EDUCATION PROGRAM MODELS   54

CHAPTER 4   EARLY CHILDHOOD EDUCATION IN CANADA   84

PREFACE

It is almost with a sense of disbelief that I am writing the preface for the first Canadian edition of *An Introduction to Early Childhood Education* by Eva Essa from the University of Nevada in Reno. I have thought about this project for many years, and, like my students, have been frustrated by the dearth of published Canadian material on early childhood education.

In the summer of 1967, I had my first experience working with 3- and 4-year-old children from disadvantaged homes in an early childhood program designed to give them a "head start" before they entered the public school. At that time, we turned to our neighbours in the United States for resources, guidelines, and materials because they had gained valuable experience and insights through their federally funded Head Start program. However, since that period the early childhood education profession has grown considerably in every province and territory. Despite this growth, most Canadian students enrolled in introductory courses in early childhood education have been using American texts. At best, these texts include an appended chapter or two on Canadian issues. Consequently, college and university instructors in this country have had to assemble supplementary Canadian materials for their early childhood education courses.

But why? Early childhood education in Canada has its own proud history dating back to the 19th century, its own professional organizations, and its own legislation and practices. Early childhood educators in Canada also face unique challenges, ranging from planning outdoor play during a lengthy winter, to offering educational programs for early childhood professionals in our northern reaches, to persuading politicians to make high-quality early childhood programs accessible and affordable for all Canadians. I have tried to capture the uniqueness of early childhood education in Canada in this book.

While the organization and material in a number of chapters owe much to Eva Essa's first edition, much of the book is new. My own analysis of the field and of student needs, coupled with the ideas and insights of my reviewers, led me not only to add Canadian material, but also to make a number of organizational and substantive changes. Notwithstanding these changes, the book's underlying philosophy remains the same: early childhood educators are entrusted with the responsibility of designing a program that fosters development and provides the nurture and care that all young children need.

As an introductory text, this book is intended to provide an overview of the field of early childhood education, its historical and, this book is theoretical origins, and the day-to-day work of professionals working in early childhood programs. In keeping with current definitions of early childhood, the book now focuses on children between birth and 8 years of age. The text can be used in full courses in three- and four-year university programs, in two-year community college programs, and in in-service courses for elementary school teachers who want to transfer into the early childhood division. Chapters 1 to 9 would be appropriate for a one-semester overview course, while Chapters 10 to 18 are suitable for a subsequent half-course on methods in early childhood education.

ORGANIZATION OF THE TEXT

The book is organized into six sections. Part 1, "The What of Early Childhood Education," provides an overview of the field, its history, current models, and early childhood education in Canada. Chapter 1, "The Scope of Early Childhood Education?," examines changes in Canadian society that have shaped the scope of the field, the variety of programs that exist for young children, and some factors that influence the quality of these programs. In Chapter 2, "The History of Early Childhood Education?," we consider the historical and theoretical foundations of the field, with reference to the works and ideas of important educators and theorists who have shaped early childhood education as we know it today. The links between theory and practice become clearer in Chapter 3, "Early Childhood Education Program Models." In this chapter, five program models are examined in detail, and more eclectic models are briefly discussed. The latest research on the effectiveness of these models is provided so that students can better evaluate their short- and long-term effectiveness. In Chapter 4, "Early Childhood Education in Canada," we consider the history and scope of early childhood education in each province and territory, as well as current regulations governing ECE programs. We then look at the strengths and weaknesses of the field from a national perspective, and consider its future.

Part 2, "The Who of Early Childhood Education," focuses on the various people involved in early childhood education—the children, their families, and their teachers. Chapter 5, "Children and Their Families" examines the characteristics of young children—the things they have in common and the things that make each child unique. Then we look at parents and other family members with whom early childhood teachers share the responsibility for raising young children. Chapter 6, "Teachers," considers the different roles of those who work in early childhood programs. We review early childhood education as a Canadian profession, our national organizations, and some of the issues facing teachers in the field today.

In Part 3, "The How of Early Childhood Education—The Basics," we examine several fundamental components of high-quality early childhood education programs. Chapter 7, "Goals, Objectives, and Evaluation," provides information about setting appropriate goals and objectives for young children. We also consider the role of evaluation as a means of matching the program with the developmental level of the children in it. In addition, we discuss the important cautions and concerns associated with the increasing use of standardized tests in Canada.

Chapter 8, "Programming for the Whole Child," addresses some of the basic constructs in early childhood education programs. We review play and its importance in early childhood education as well as the implementation of developmentally and individually appropriate practices. The importance of an anti-bias curriculum that does not encourage stereotypes is also discussed. Finally, some basic components of that curriculum and planning guidelines are addressed. Environmental considerations for providing a good early childhood program are raised in Chapter 9, "The Physical Environment." Just where is it that children and their teachers play and work? Which settings, materials and equipment best enhance and support young children's development throughout the year?

Part 4, "The How of Early Childhood Education—Curriculum," examines the program in more detail. Although the book emphasizes the integration of different subject areas, we examine four developmental areas in this section in some detail because many beginning teachers—and their instructors—find this approach valuable. Chapter 10, "Creative Development through the Curriculum," looks at enhancing children's creativity in an environment where children are free to experiment and create. It also touches on aesthetic appreciation and factors that decrease creativity. The young child's need to be active in order to learn and develop is the focus of Chapter 11, "Physical Development through the Curriculum." In this chapter, we consider movement, the senses, health, and safety in the early childhood program. We then look at various aspects of enhancing children's thinking in Chapter 12, "Cognitive Development through the Curriculum." Here we turn to mathematics and science for examples. In Chapter 13, "Language Development through the Curriculum," we concentrate on the many informal and formal ways in which language is encouraged in the early childhood program. We also consider second-language learning, the ways in which experience with stories supports children's development, and emergent literacy. We end this section with a look at how a good early childhood program can facilitate the young child's burgeoning social skills. Chapter 14, "Social Development through the Curriculum," examines a wide range of issues, including theories of social development, social competence, racial and cultural awareness, moral development, and social types of pretend play.

In Part 5, "The How of Early Childhood Education—Guidance," we discuss the principles and techniques that teachers might use to guide the social behaviour of young children in their programs. Chapter 15, "Guiding Routines and Group Activities," looks at two important aspects of the preschool day—routines and group activities. Guidance suggestions for routines (e.g., meals and naps) and group activities (e.g., circles and meals) are provided to help the beginning teacher work effectively in the early childhood program. In Chapter 16, "Guiding Behaviour," we consider several approaches to handling behaviour. We also examine some general principles that are important in helping children meet appropriate expectations. We conclude this section by addressing a topic that teachers of young children increasingly face. In Chapter 17 "Helping Children Cope With Stress," we look at different sources of stress and ways of helping children cope with it.

Part 6, "The future of Early Childhood Education," ends the book. In Chapter 18 of this final section, "Issues and Dilemmas in Early Childhood Education," we consider questions that become pertinent as we approach the 21st century. What issues and challenges will the profession face? What does the future hold for early childhood education in Canada? How can we ensure the availability of affordable, high-quality child care for very young Canadians?

STUDENT-FRIENDLY FEATURES

I have tried to keep the learning needs of adult students in mind while writing this book. Each chapter begins with an overview of the material that will be discussed. Three types of high-interest boxes are included in the text. The Canadian Professional Speaks Out boxes contain contributions from Canadian professionals on topics of interest to students in the field. Through these boxes, students are introduced to issues of concern to professionals on both coastlines, in urban and rural settings, and in the Far North. The Parents and Professionals boxes link the chapter material to parents' needs and interests, while the Closer Look boxes examine specific topics in greater detail. All three boxes contain material that encourage classroom discussion and thinking about practical concerns that students confront in field placements.

Each chapter ends with a series of key questions that are designed to encourage critical thinking and discussion of the issues raised in the chapter. **Key terms** are presented in the text in **boldface type** and definitions of every key term are found not only in the text but also in the **glossary** at the end of the book. In addition, each chapter concludes with a list of the key terms used in the chapter, along with the **key points** that have been covered.

The text also includes up-to-date research on early childhood education. Publications that were released as this book was being prepared have been included, and Canadian research has been emphasized.

TERMINOLOGY

The choice of terminology is complicated by the fact that it is not consistent across all provinces and territories. For example, the definitions of *infant* and *toddler* vary from one Canadian jurisdiction to another. Similarly, a *teacher* in one jurisdiction would be a *caregiver* in another and a *child care worker* in yet another location. I have chosen to use the terms *early childhood teacher* and *early childhood educator* synonymously in this text. *Caring for a Living (Canadian Child Day Care Federation [CCDCF], 1992)*, a Canadian study of individuals working in child care settings, found that there is a high level of training among these individuals, even in those Canadian jurisdictions where it is not required. Similarly, individuals working in elementary schools also have considerable training. Consequently, I have chosen the term "teacher" for all of those who work with young children. The term has a positive connotation among the public and better reflects the professionalism of caring, early childhood teachers.

SUPPLEMENTAL MATERIALS

An instructor's guide prepared by the author contains suggestions for course planning, recommended class discussion topics and activities, and suggested assignments. The guide also includes, from each province and territory, additional data, that can be made into transparencies or slides.

ACKNOWLEDGMENTS

This book would not have been completed if others had not been generous with their knowledge and their time. To all of them, I owe a great deal of thanks. While I cannot thank everyone who has helped, several individuals deserve special recognition. Don Rutledge, Ian Begg, and Glenn MacDonald have influenced my thinking about many issues over the years. John Novak, Patricia Cranton, and Ralph Connelly, my colleagues, introduced me to everything that goes into writing a book, and they humoured me throughout the process. Kris Kirkwood and Terry Boak supported my application for a sabbatical leave that would give me a year to work on the book, and Brock University granted the leave. Cynthia Peterson worked on references and, along with Tracy Biernacki and Lisa Hom, printed and copied multiple drafts of the manuscript. Billy Sun helped to prepare the index.

Polly Richardson, a former coordinator of the early childhood education program at Mohawk College and former president of the Association for Early Childhood Education—Ontario, taught me much about working with young children and about the profession when I was a student, a teacher in the "lab school," and an instructor in the program. Polly came to Ontario from Winnipeg, has extensive knowledge of Hamilton's war time day nurseries, and was active in the NEAO's training programs for early childhood educators in Ontario, as well as in the founding of ECE programs in Ontario's community colleges. She remains a source of inspiration.

The students I have taught at Brock University and, some years ago, at Mohawk College helped me formulate ideas about the field and taught me a great deal about teaching. They also emphasized their need to know the Canadian story of early childhoood education. The many children I have worked with—both as a teacher and a psychologist—at the Mohawk College Laboratory Preschool, the Laneway School, and the Toronto and Peel Boards of Education challenged my thinking and broadened my understanding. Thanks are also due to the many teachers who welcomed me into their classrooms.

Many talented Canadian professionals with an interest in early childhood education enriched the book with their contributions to the Canadian Professional Speaks Out boxes. The children and teachers at Power Glen Cooperative Nursery School, Hillfield-Strathallan College, and Wheatley School of Montessori education allowed me to take photos in their classes.

It has been a great pleasure to work with the many people at Nelson Canada who have been involved in the production of this book. Charlotte Forbes, Acquisitions Editor, deserves special mention for her unflagging guidance, support, and friendship. Heather Martin, Developmental Editor, has been involved in almost everything; among other things, she coordinated the Canadian Professional Speaks Out contributions and helped with permissions. Nicole Gnutzman, Editorial Manager, has been a great help in the latter stages of the book. Jim Leahy, a thoughtful freelance editor, knows the manuscript almost as well as I do. Sue Peden, a talented composition analyst/designer, transformed the manuscript into a wonderful looking book.

My family helped in less obvious, but equally important ways. They saw me in front of a computer for many months, and they pitched in with each successive deadline. Don Shattuck, my husband, has solved computer problems, worked on photos, and was a creative dad on many occasions. Daniel, our son, was just over 2 when I started, and now, at 3 1/2, he says "What? Aren't you finished yet?" My parents, Catharine and Harold Young, drove Daniel to preschool many times and helped in countless other ways. Pat, David, Barbara, Martin, Erin, and Heather Young also deserve thanks.

Finally, I am grateful to the following reviewers for their comments, criticisms, and suggestions.

Jan Kubli Carrie	Camosun College
Betty Exelby	Loyalist College
Joan Kunderman	Red River Community College
Laurie Papas	Kwantlen College
Lois Rennie	Capilano College
Sina Romsa	Red River Community College
Heather Sloan	Niagara College
Alice Taylor	Holland College
Judy Wainwright	Mount Royal College
Marilynn Yeates	St. Lawrence College

Part

1

THE WHAT OF EARLY CHILDHOOD EDUCATION

Each section of this book focuses on a different aspect of early childhood education (ECE), beginning with a definition of just what this field is. Part 1 addresses the what of early childhood education in the following ways:

- In Chapter 1, "The Scope of Early Childhood Education," we will delve further into what is involved in this field. We will examine the many variations that exist today in programs for young children. As part of this examination, we will look at the need for such programs, particularly the social factors that have shaped the scope of the field.

- In Chapter 2, "The History of Early Childhood Education," we will examine some of the historical and theoretical foundations of the field by considering the works and ideas of important predecessors of early childhood education today.

- In Chapter 3, "Early Childhood Education Program Models," we will consider the links between theory and practice as we review several model programs based on specific theories.

- In Chapter 4, "Early Childhood Education in Canada," we consider the history and scope of early childhood education in the provinces and territories, as well as legislation and teacher training.

THE SCOPE OF EARLY CHILDHOOD EDUCATION

Early childhood education—this is the field you are exploring through this text and the course in which you are enrolled. What is early childhood education? Is it the same in all the provinces and territories, or does it vary like other aspects of Canadian education? And just when is early childhood, or does that also vary from one location to the next? What place does early childhood education have in Canadian society? What are its roots? What is its future?

As you begin learning about this field of study, the answers to some of these questions will gain greater significance and become more focused. This chapter presents an overview of the field of early childhood education, while later chapters introduce new topics and issues. The following outline provides you with a summary of the chapter.

1. A number of social factors have contributed to the expansion of early childhood programs and brought early childhood education into the public consciousness. We will examine three factors:

   - changes in family life such as an increased number of two-earner families and single parents;
   - growing evidence of the benefits of early education for children from disadvantaged backgrounds, children who are physically or mentally challenged, and other children at risk; and
   - child advocacy, which has helped bring the needs of young children and their families to public and legislative prominence.

2. There is considerable diversity in the types of early childhood programs both within and between the provinces and territories. We will look at the following ways in which programs may differ:

   - purposes of programs
   - program settings
   - ages of the children
   - sources of funding support

3. A most important factor in describing early childhood programs is quality. We will examine the following elements that contribute to the quality of early childhood programs:

   - child–adult ratio
   - group size
   - mixed-age grouping
   - developmental appropriateness of the program
   - quality of child–adult interaction
   - staff qualifications
   - staff consistency
   - respect and concern for the staff
   - ongoing professional development
   - quality of the physical environment
   - family involvement
   - quality as a combination of factors

THE GROWTH OF EARLY CHILDHOOD EDUCATION

Although the importance and value of education in the early years of life have been acknowledged for more than 2000 years (Carter, 1987), relatively recent factors have brought early childhood education to the forefront of public awareness. Fundamental changes in the economy, family life, public awareness, and public support have had a profound effect on early childhood education. You have undoubtedly seen recent newspaper headlines and national magazine covers that have directed a spotlight on child care. Much of their focus has been on changes in family life that have brought about the need for child care outside the home. These changes result from an interplay of many complex factors including the rising cost of living, a growing number of dual-income families, an increase in single-parent families, an increased number of teenage parents, greater family mobility, and a decrease in the impact of the extended family.

But the needs of working families are not the only reason that early childhood education has been in the public eye. Over the past quarter-century, the success of some publicly funded early childhood programs in Canada and the United States has shown us that high-quality early educational intervention can combat poverty and dysfunction. There has also been increased attention to the needs of special populations of young children and how to bring them into the mainstream of society; for instance, children who are physically challenged, mentally challenged, abused, or culturally different have benefited from such programs.

Finally, many professionals are outspoken and eloquent advocates for the rights of children. They continue to lobby for governmental changes that will improve the lives of young children.

CHANGES IN FAMILY LIFE

"Typical" family life has changed considerably since the end of World War II. Demographic information indicates that increasing numbers of women are entering the workforce (e.g., Statistics Canada, 1985; Women's Bureau, 1990). No longer do most mothers stay at home to rear their young children. In some families, both parents work because of the desire for personal and professional development rather than for economic reasons. In other cases, economic need forces families to rely on two salaries because one simply does not provide for all of their financial needs. And in some families, both parents work for both personal and economic reasons.

Whereas in 1951, only 11 percent of Canadian married women worked, that figure had risen to 44 percent in 1975, 56 percent in 1987, 60 percent in 1989, and almost 70 percent in 1993 (Doxey, 1990; Women's Bureau, 1970a, 1970b, 1990; Statistics Canada, 1993). Unfortunately, government studies of women in the workforce in the 1950s and 1960s had an unusual definition of working mothers: in addition to having children under 14, they had to have been married at some time (e.g., Women's Bureau, 1970a). Of course, that definition of a working mother eliminates single parents from consideration, and it makes comparisons with more recent studies of working mothers, which include all mothers regardless of marital status, somewhat difficult. Nevertheless, it is clear that there has been a steady increase in the number of married and unmarried women in the workplace since 1975. A look at Exhibit 1-1 will give you some idea of the number of Canadian children 9 years and younger, who do not require supplemental care, and the arrangements of those who do need it.

There is some regional variation in these figures that is related, at least in part, to employment opportunities. Nevertheless, women in all areas of the country are far less likely to be home rearing their children in the 1990s than they were in the 1950s. Both parents in two-parent families with children 5 years and younger work in about 50 percent of the cases. They are even more likely to work if their children are 6 years or older. The pattern is similar for single parents. About 40 percent of single parents with children aged 5 and under work, as do over 60 percent of those with school-aged children.

Recent projections (e.g., Jones, Marsden, & Tepperman, 1990) suggest that the number of women in the workforce will continue to increase, and that, by the year 2000, their rate of participation in the workforce will approach that of men. (In 1989, 77 percent of Canadian men were in the workforce [Women's Bureau, 1990].) In fact, in the 1990s, Canada Employment and Immigration Centre publications across the

Exhibit 1-1 NUMBER OF CANADIAN CHILDREN 0–9 YEARS OF AGE: CAREGIVING NEEDS AND CAREGIVING ARRANGEMENTS

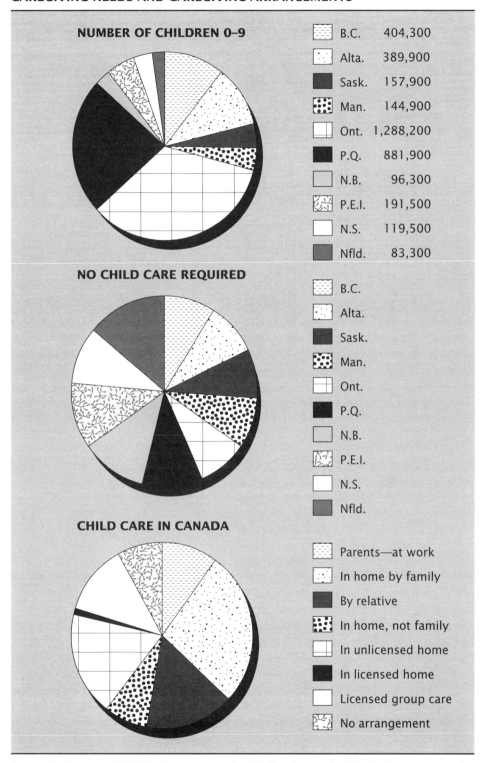

NUMBER OF CHILDREN 0–9

B.C.	404,300
Alta.	389,900
Sask.	157,900
Man.	144,900
Ont.	1,288,200
P.Q.	881,900
N.B.	96,300
P.E.I.	191,500
N.S.	119,500
Nfld.	83,300

NO CHILD CARE REQUIRED

B.C.
Alta.
Sask.
Man.
Ont.
P.Q.
N.B.
P.E.I.
N.S.
Nfld.

CHILD CARE IN CANADA

Parents—at work
In home by family
By relative
In home, not family
In unlicensed home
In licensed home
Licensed group care
No arrangement

Source: A. Pence et al. (1992). "An overview of NCCS data for British Columbia." In A. Pence (Ed.), *Canadian child care in context: Perspectives from the provinces and territories* (pp. 67, 83). Ottawa, ON: Statistics Canada and Health and Welfare Canada.

country (see Employment and Immigration Canada, 1992) project that child care will be one of the top ten high-demand occupations throughout the decade. Even in economically depressed regions (the Niagara region in Ontario, for example), they predict that the number of child care workers in the workforce will increase by 23 percent between 1992 and 1999.

Another family change that has increased the demand for child care is the rise in the number of single parents. Prior to changes in Canada's divorce laws in 1968, divorces were rare—only 1.6 married women per 1000 divorced in 1961 (Ram, 1990). That figure jumped to 6.1 in 1971 and 11.3 in 1981 to 12.4 in 1986 (Ram, 1990). While the divorce rate has been levelling off after the flurry of activity that followed the 1968 Divorce Act, the marriage rate also has steadily declined. In 1961, 93.1 per 1000 single women over 15 married in Canada (Ram, 1990). By 1986, that figure had dropped to 71.9 per 1000. While the majority of single-parent families are created through divorce, there also is a growing number of never-married parents, some still finishing their high-school education, and some older who choose to remain single. The percentage of single-parent families varies somewhat by province and territory, from a low of 11 percent in Saskatchewan, Ontario, and Newfoundland and to a high of 30 percent of the parents of preschoolers in the Yukon.

The divorced single parent with custody of the children, most frequently the mother, typically experiences a significant decrease in income and standard of living. In addition, the single parent usually has to work (or work longer hours) to support the family. Of course, to work outside the home, the single, divorced parent, male or

female, needs to find appropriate child care. Single parents who have never married face similar challenges when it comes to child care. A number of them, however—teenage mothers who have chosen to keep a child, for example—do not have the skills required to enter the workforce. As the National Council of Welfare's 1990 report, *Women and Poverty Revisited*, indicates, many of these mothers have not completed even Grade 11. If they are to find alternatives to relying on social assistance for their livelihood, they must return to school. For this reason, child care facilities attached to secondary schools are becoming more common.

A third change in family life is the increasing mobility of many of today's families. Work demands cause some families to move away from relatives who might otherwise provide support. Family mobility, involving only the small **nuclear family**, has contributed to the declining influence of the **extended family**, that network of relatives such as grandparents, uncles, and aunts, or adult brothers and sisters beyond the immediate family.

Traditionally, the most prevalent form of child care was having a relative look after the children. Many parents seem more comfortable leaving a young child with a relative than with a stranger, and relatives may charge little or no money, making this a financially attractive alternative. While relatives are still a frequently used source of care, the **Canadian National Child Care Study (CNCCS)** (Pence, Read, Lero, Goelman, & Brockman, 1992) found that non-relatives now are more likely than relatives to care for Canadian children. Quite often, female relatives, who traditionally would have been home, are working (Wash & Brand, 1990).

Changes such as increasing numbers of dual-income families and single-parent families, and a decline in the impact of the extended family, have dramatically raised the demand for child care and brought early childhood education to the forefront of public attention. "Child care is now as essential to family life as the automobile or the refrigerator" (Scarr, Phillips, & McCartney, 1990, p. 26). In A Canadian Professional Speaks Out, Karen Troughton describes how the need for child care is as pronounced in rural Saskatchewan as it is in more urban areas.

BENEFITS OF EARLY CHILDHOOD EDUCATION

The need of working parents for child care makes early childhood education a topic of national prominence, but this is not the only reason for its increasing importance. A great deal of research, which we will discuss later in this chapter, has shown that high-quality child care programs have positive effects on the development of young children. On a parallel though separate track, much discussion and research has centred on the benefits of early education for special populations of children and families. Thus, children from poverty backgrounds, children with disabilities, and children at risk for other reasons have been enrolled in publicly funded programs. Since the mid-1960s, financial support has increased as a result of mounting evidence that high-quality early childhood programs can and do make a long-term difference that carries into adulthood. Researchers have concluded that good early childhood programs not only improve the lives of the children and families involved, but also result in substantial economic benefits for society. Although early intervention programs are expensive, their cost is more than recovered in subsequent years through greater schooling success, decreased need for special education, lowered delinquency and arrest rates, and decreased welfare dependence (Berrueta-Clement, Schweinhart, Barnett, Epstein, & Weikart, 1984; Wright, 1983).

A CANADIAN
PROFESSIONAL SPEAKS OUT

Rural Child Care:
A Saskatchewan Perspective

What is it like to live on a farm and experience a lack of child care services? Nettie Wiebe from Laura, Saskatchewan, is the Women's President of the National Farmer's Union. She knows all too well what lack of child care services is like. She and fellow farm women have experienced many stressful situations in regard to child care arrangements. Nettie, who has four young children, has had to take the children along with her on the grain truck out to the field. Other farm mothers have had to leave their children alone napping in the farm house while they are in the field summer fallowing. Regular trips have to be made back and forth to the house to check on the children. This makes for very anxious times for parent and children.

Another farm mom went through *six* different child care arrangements in a short period of time. Flexible child care could not be found.

Farm children are exposed to many dangerous situations. Heavy equipment is a part of farm life, as are various kinds of chemicals. Many parents have no option but to leave children by themselves. In 1991–92, 41 Saskatchewan children under the age of 15 were hospitalized due to farm accidents.

Other problems that hinder rural families are distance and relative cost. Families must travel long distances for child care services. In the 1989–91 Federated Women's Survey, which questioned 1740 rural families across Canada with at least one child, more than 50 percent of the respondents had to travel 15 km or more to the child care centre. In Saskatchewan, some parents have to travel more than 100 km to a centre. The population density is often too small to support the urban type of child care program; therefore, smaller, more flexible programs are needed.

Farm families have seasonal fluctuations in their income. Paying for child care services requires a regular monthly income. Therefore, farm families cannot obtain child care services at certain times because of irregular income. With low grain prices, many families cannot afford child care at any time of the year.

Rural parents may often need child care on a seasonal basis. Activities such as calving, planting, cultivating, haying, and harvesting occur at different times of the year. At these times flexible child care is needed. For example, full day care is needed in April, May, June, August, and September.

In November 1992 the National Conference on Farm Women Employment was held in Quebec. The following is a summary of their proposal for rural child care:

Needs and Services:

- Recognition and development of child care services at the farm residence as well as local, community-based, diversified child care services.
- Assurance of children's safety through the recognized training of child care workers.
- Recognition of the farm as the place of residence and work.

Financial Support:

- Recognition by Revenue Canada that child care expenses are farm business expenses.
- Subsidized child care reciprocally based on the net income of farm families.
- Subsidies for sparsely populated regions.
- Recognition of subsidization for in-home as well as financial support for local community-based child care centres.

Decision-makers must now recognize the needs of rural child care. They have the reports and recommendations. Now they must implement them so that families like Nettie Wiebe's will have quality child care.

Karen Troughton
Instructor, Early Childhood Development Program
Kelsey Institute, Saskatchewan Institute of Applied
Science and Technology
Saskatoon, Saskatchewan

CHILD ADVOCACY

A third factor that has brought early childhood education into the public consciousness is the urgency with which many professionals view the plight of increasing numbers of children and families. Of particular concern are the many families that face extreme poverty, lacking the most basic necessities.

In Canada, on average, one in five children lives in circumstances that fall below the poverty line; in some regions of the country (the Atlantic region, for example), that figure is higher, while it is lower in other areas. Yet the social problems reach beyond the needs of the poor, to working parents with moderate incomes who are beset by the scarcity of affordable, high-quality care. A report from the **National Day Care Study (NDCS)**, *Status of Day Care in Canada 1990* (National Child Care Information Centre, 1991), suggested that available licensed child care settings may serve less than 8 percent of Canadian children under 3 years who need child care and only 27 percent of children between 3 and 5 years who need child care. Organizations such as the Childcare Advocacy Association of Canada and the Canadian Child Care Federation, as well as many provincial organizations, actively campaign for high-quality early childhood programs.

The needs of children and families have become political concerns. They have come to the attention of both political leaders and the public at large through the astute efforts of children's rights advocates, including early childhood professionals. But there is a continuing need to promote a common concern for the welfare of all children.

WHEN IS EARLY CHILDHOOD?

If you were to ask several individuals to define the term *early childhood*, it is likely that you would receive a different answer from each person. In fact, even early childhood educators have difficulty using terms consistently. Some of this uncertainty stems from the fact that the definition of early childhood has widened over the past 30 years, as has the range of early childhood programs (Doxey, 1990). In this text, the term **early childhood** refers to the period from birth to age 8, and most current works would agree with this definition.

WHAT IS INCLUDED IN EARLY CHILDHOOD EDUCATION?

We have looked at some of the historical roots of early childhood education and reasons for the rapid growth of the field. But **early childhood education** is a broad term and includes a variety of approaches and programs. Nursery schools and child care centres (formerly referred to as day care centres), parent cooperative preschools and infant stimulation programs, and junior kindergartens and kindergartens are but a few of the early childhood programs that exist in Canada. Toy-lending libraries, home-based child care, and employer-sponsored child care centres also fall within the definition of early childhood education programs. Winnipeg's Assiniboia Downs Race Track Child Care Centre Winnipeg as well as the Edmonton Hospital Workers' Day Care are early childhood programs that are offered by the workplace. Other programs include the Pairiviq

Child Care Centre, an Inuit child care centre in Iqaluit, Northwest Territories, and Gizhaadaawgamik, a day care centre for Indian children in Toronto, which derives its name from the Ojibwa word that means "a place to care for children." Some early childhood programs, such as drop-in centres, do not have explicit educational goals, while other programs such as babysitting cooperatives and drop-off child centres do not have formal programs. All of these programs, however, aim to provide an experience for young children that they would not ordinarily receive from their parents at home.

Clearly, the term early childhood education refers to a wide variety of programs. The programs may vary across a number of dimensions, and just some of them are shown in Exhibit 1-2.

Other variations will become evident in later chapters. We will now examine some of the classifications into which programs can be grouped.

EXHIBIT 1-2 SOME DIMENSIONS OF ECE PROGRAMS

SETTING	AGE OF CHILDREN	SOURCE OF FUNDING	PURPOSE
Child's own home —babysitter —nanny —relative Someone else's home/family child care homes —licensed —not licensed Centre-based programs —full day —part day —nursery school —cooperative —before- and after-school program	Infants < 18 months Toddlers 18–35 months Preschoolers 3–5 years Kindergarten children—5 years Primary level children 6–8 years	For-profit Non-profit Employer-supported University & college-affiliated Publicly supported	Care Enrichment Compensation Religious education

PURPOSE OF PROGRAMS

We have already touched on some basic differences in programs that stem from their underlying thrust. The major purpose of many programs is to care for children while their parents work. The rapid rise in recent years in the numbers of children in full day care, either in child care centres or in family child care homes, has paralleled the increasing prevalence of working mothers. The primary goal of child care programs is to provide safe and nurturing care in a developmentally appropriate setting for children.

Enrichment, a second aim, particularly prevalent in part-time preschools. Such programs usually include specific activities to enhance socialization, cognitive skills, or overall development of young children. The underlying notion is that children will benefit from experiences that they may not receive at home, for instance, participating in group activities, playing with a group of age-mates, or learning specific concepts from specially trained teachers.

One phenomenon that has been growing recently is that of the **hurried child** or **hothousing**, apt terms that have become popular. Hothousing is aimed at accelerating

some aspect of young children's development and is of considerable concern to many early childhood professionals (e.g., Elkind, 1981b, 1987; Gallagher & Coche, 1987; Hills, 1987; Sigel, 1987). It differs from enrichment by the nature of its activities and by its lack of developmental appropriateness. Such programs are generally designed to meet the expectations of "upwardly mobile 'yuppy' [sic] parents, who want designer diapers and designer degrees in Greek, Suzuki, and computer programming for their infants" (Clarke-Stewart, 1988, p. 147).

A third major purpose, found particularly in publicly funded programs, is compensation. Compensatory programs aim to make up for some lack in children's backgrounds. The basic philosophy of compensatory programs, such as Mary Wright's (1983) University of Western Ontario Preschool, is to provide experiences that will help children enter the mainstream of society more successfully. Such experiences sometimes include a range of services, encompassing early childhood education, nutrition, and parent education.

An additional purpose of programs like the Gizhaadaawgamik Centre mentioned above, is the preservation and transmission of cultural traditions and languages. Similarly, some but by no means all church-based schools aim to provide educational programs in a religious context.

These categories, although descriptive of some underlying differences among programs, are not mutually exclusive. Few child care centres are concerned with only the physical well-being and care of children. Most also provide enriching experiences that further children's development. At the same time, preschool programs have to be concerned with appropriate nurture and safety while the children are in their care. Similarly, compensatory programs are also concerned with enriching experiences and caring for children, while child care or preschool programs may serve to compensate for something lacking in the backgrounds of some of the children.

PROGRAM SETTINGS

Programs for young children can be divided into home-based and centre-based settings. The Canadian National Child Care Study (CNCCS) (Pence et al., 1992) examined the types of caregiving arrangements Canadian parents reported using for children between 0 and 9 years of age.

The results, shown in Exhibit 1-3, clearly show that home-based care is more frequent than centre-based care. However, parents favour different types of care for children of different ages, with centre-based care being most frequent for preschoolers.

Centre-Based Programs

Centre-based programs include full-day **child care centres** and **nursery schools** or **preschools**; more children are usually enrolled in them than in home-based programs. Typically, child care centres are located in either a separate building of their own, or any variety of buildings that have extra space available and a need for child care or the desire to offer it. Schools, churches, colleges and universities, hospitals, YWCA and YMCA buildings, and office towers are among the many locations with child care centres. Nursery schools and preschools are less likely than centres to be in a building of their own. Nursery schools or preschools are usually part-day programs with *primarily* an educational orientation, that serve children from 2 to 5 years of age. Colleges and

EXHIBIT 1-3 CANADIAN'S CHILD CARE ARRANGEMENTS: PERCENTAGE OF TOTAL NUMBER OF CHILDREN IN EACH CAREGIVING SETTING BY AGE

TYPE OF CARE	AGE			
	0–17 MONTHS	18–35 MONTHS	3–5 YEARS	6–9 YEARS
Parents—at work	10.0	11.2	10.7	9.3
Parents—at home	20.0	15.6	17.5	24.6
Sibling(s)	[1]	[1]	[1]	6.9
Self	[2]	[2]	[1]	5.3
Relatives in child's home	10.4	7.5	7.5	5.9
Relatives not in child's home	14.3	11.8	8.3	6.5
Non-relative in child's home	9.3	10.5	8.0	6.0
Non-relative not in child's home—licensed	[1]	2.7[3]	1.7[3]	0.83
Non-relative not in child's home—unlicensed	26.3	25.1	18.7	12.7
Preschool	[2]	[2]	2.8	[1]
Kindergarten	[2]	[2]	6.0	[1]
Child care centre	5.4	12.5	13.9	1.6
Before-/after-school program	[2]	[2]	1.13	4.7
No arrangement	[1]	[1]	2.4	15.6
Total	223 300	269 600	570 200	862 600

[1] too small a sample   [2] nil   [3] estimate

SOURCE: A. Pence et al. (1992). "An overview of NCCS data for British Columbia." In A. Pence (Ed.), *Canadian child care in context: Perspectives from the provinces and territories* (p. 83). Ottawa, ON: Statistics Canada and Health and Welfare Canada.

universities often have attached to them nursery schools that are used as demonstration centres for teacher education courses, and as laboratories for research on child development and education. **Parent-cooperative** nursery schools, which emerged in Toronto in the 1930s, and in Victoria, Saskatoon, Montreal, and Vancouver in the 1940s (Stevenson, 1990), are another type of nursery school created and controlled by parents. The parents employ the teachers, and historically have had to assist in the program.

Child care centres, in contrast with nursery schools, offer full-day programs for infants and children of working parents, so the custodial aspect of child care must be included as *one* of their purposes. However, child care centres and nursery schools are by no means mutually exclusive. The better nursery schools emphasize education and care as do the better child care centres. Moreover, child care centres often have half-day options, and nursery schools sometimes have before- and after-school options. Nevertheless, the child care centre typically is open for a minimum of ten hours a day. Consequently, child care programs must provide meals and opportunities for naps or quiet times, and must deal with the realities of diaper changes, toilet training, and toothbrushes and combs. Historically, many child care centres provided only custodial care, but there has been a gradual shift in focus and it probably would be difficult to find a Canadian child care centre in the 1990s that did not at least express an interest in the education of the children. Frequently, the interest is not just expressed, but is clearly exemplified in child care centres offer a comprehensive program that aims to encourage development in all areas. For example, Jane Wilson, a Canadian ECE professional, describes an unusually flexible child care centre, located in a small Manitoba community, that does meet rural families' needs for child care.

 # A CANADIAN PROFESSIONAL SPEAKS OUT

Rural Child Care — A Manitoba Perspective

For decades farm families have had to cope with balancing farming and raising a family. Years ago, a "hired girl" or the extended family made it possible for the farm wife to go into the field to work. In 1993 most farms can only survive with the help of an "off farm income." This income supplements the declining price of agricultural produce and the increasing costs of machinery, fuel, repairs, and so on. The question arises: If one parent is in the field and one parent works off the farm, where are the children? The grim reality is that a lot of the time they are left unsupervised for hours on end, playing with the livestock or on tractors. Parents do not admit, even to themselves, that their children are at risk — what type of parent would knowingly place [his or her] child in danger?

In defence of the farm lifestyle, there is no better place to raise children than on a farm. We left an urban centre and moved back to the farm to raise our children. To go to the barn, to feed the livestock, to go for a ride on a tractor may be great, but to have your child with you while you work hour after hour is courting disaster. Parents have to concentrate on their job and not worry about their children's safety. After all, doctors and plumbers do not and cannot take their children to work. Why is it expected and accepted that farm children go to work with their parents? Because it has been done for the past 60 years! Why then are farm children put at risk in 1993? What can be done to help farm families remove this stress factor from their lives and not add to their existing burden?

The rural municipality of Lakeview, with a total population of 468 people, contains the small village of Langruth (population 160). Langruth can proudly call itself the home of Lakeview Children's Centre, a licensed facility with 28 spaces upstairs for infants and preschool and 10 spaces in the basement for school-age children. The centre began in 1988 as the dream of four women who had a vision for a rural child care centre that would

- offer quality care (trained child care professionals);
- be affordable (provincial subsidies available);
- be accessible (open to all children);
- be accountable (non-profit);
- be flexible to meet farmers' needs.

Lakeview Children's Centre has succeeded admirably on all five points. We have met the needs of our community's parents and children. Our hours of operation are from 6:30 a.m. to 10:30 p.m. (upon prior arrangement). Our enrolment can vary greatly: 5 children one day and 18 the next. The staff ratios fluctuate according to the number of children at the centre on any given day. If we have a number of children cancel, a staff member takes a day off without pay. This type of arrangement works for us — we all come from farms and there is plenty of work to do at home.

Governments, both federal and provincial, should use Lakeview as a model of quality rural child care. Everyone is aware of the economic climate in Canada in 1993, but the bottom line is farm children are being hurt, disabled, and even killed at their parents' worksite. It is the responsibility of parents, government, and society as a whole to say we do not want our children at risk; we want a comprehensive system that will ensure the safety of the next generation of farmers.

Jane Wilson
Director,
Lakeview Children's Centre
Langruth, Manitoba

In Canada, centre-based programs have increased more than any other type of child care. While in 1971, only 17 000 Canadian children were cared for in centre-based settings, close to 300 000 Canadian children were in licensed child care settings in 1990 (National Child Care Information Centre, 1991). Over that same period, the number of children cared for in licensed family child care homes increased from 600 to 38 000 (National Child Care Information Centre, 1991).

Home-Based Settings

In Canada, like the United States (Hofferth & Phillips, 1987), when all ages of children are considered, the largest number are cared for in homes. Some children are cared for in their own homes, while others are in family child care homes. A **family child care home** is someone else's home where a caregiver provides child care. As we will see below, these homes may or may not be licensed, and the quality of care ranges from excellent to atrocious. Canadian infants and toddlers in particular are cared for in family child care homes (Pence et al., 1992). In some cases, this is because parents of very young children prefer a more intimate, homelike setting. Parents with several children often prefer this setting, as it means that they do not have to drop off three children, for example, at three different locations on their way to work. Still other parents choose this arrangement for very young children as they do not want them exposed to the many illnesses one may encounter in a large centre. But for many parents, the main reason they choose family child care is that it is readily available and often considerably cheaper than centre-based care. In Saskatchewan and Newfoundland, centre-based care for infants is still not permitted, so family child care may be the only alternative in those areas.

Most provinces require licensing or registration of family child care homes that receive government funding, but the vast majority of homes are unlicensed (Halpern, 1987; Pence, 1992). Certainly, the vast majority of Canadian children in family child care are in unlicensed facilities (see Exhibits 1-1 and 1-3). While licensing does not ensure quality, it does provide some safeguards. For example, the building must be safe and pass fire regulations, and there are limits on the number and ages of children who can be in the home at any given time. Moreover, licensed homes are inspected on a regular basis. Later, in our discussion of the scope of child care in each province, you will note that the number of licensed spaces—particularly for infants and toddlers—across the country is consistently low in both family- and centre-based child care programs. While it may be like trying to determine if the chicken or egg comes first, it is possible that parents would choose licensed centre-based care for the very young more frequently, if more spaces were available.

Exhibit 1-3 also shows that many Canadian children under 5 years are cared for in their own homes, by a relative or non-relative, but this arrangement is less frequent for school-aged children. A small number of these homes may be family child care homes where caregivers look after their own children and several others. Frequently, however, parents arrange to have a **nanny** come into the home on a daily basis or a live-in basis. Nannies have become an attractive child care option for families where both parents work and/or have schedules that do not conform to centre-based programs. Some nannies have training in child care, and they may attend to other household tasks, like cooking and light cleaning. In 1993, Canada's immigration policies required that nannies from abroad must have Grade 12 education and six months of on-the-job-training to enter the country.

AGES OF CHILDREN

The classification of early childhood spans from birth to age 8, which includes infants, toddlers, and children in kindergarten and the primary grades. Needless to say, working parents need care for children of varying ages.

Infants and Toddlers

One of the most dramatic increases in recent years has been in infant and toddler programs. But what is an infant and what is a toddler? The answer is not as clear as it might be. In seven of the twelve provinces and territories, **infants** are defined as being between 0 and 18 months of age, so we will use the majority's definition. Canadians seem to have more difficulty with the term toddler, so we will use the most common definition: **toddlers** range from 19 to 35 months of age.

Not all infant/toddler programs fall under the heading of child care, however. A number of compensatory programs, such as **infant stimulation programs** for infants at risk for developmental delays, enrol children from infancy. Programs for infants and toddlers with special needs, such as a visual or hearing impairment, also start early parent–child education programs as soon as possible. Other programs with a compensatory focus involve infants and toddlers and their families in programs as a way of intervening in the poverty cycle.

Preschoolers

The largest segment of children in licensed Canadian early childhood programs are between 3 and 5 years of age (Pence et al., 1992). About 22.5 percent of the parents in the CNCCS indicated they used nursery schools, child care centres, and kindergartens for their 3- to 5-year-old children. Another 20.3 percent of children in this age group were in family child care homes, while 15.5 percent were cared for in their own homes by a relative or non-relative. The 1991 NDCS suggested that the available licensed child care spaces would serve only 27.7 percent of Canadian working women, and about 24 percent of the CNCCS sample reported using these facilities. Again, these numbers suggest that there are simply not enough licensed spaces to meet parental needs.

There are many different types of preschool programs, some more developmentally appropriate than others. A number of different models will be discussed in later chapters.

Kindergarten and Primary Children

Most definitions of early childhood include children up to age 8. Thus, directions for curriculum, teaching strategies, and the environment in kindergartens and primary classrooms derive (or should) from what is known about the development and mode of learning of young, school-aged children.

Developmentally appropriate practice for this age group, just as for earlier ages, involves an integrated approach. An **integrated curriculum** acknowledges the importance of all aspects of human development—social, emotional, physical, cognitive, language, and creative—rather than focusing primarily on the cognitive. It also involves learning experiences that promote all aspects of development and does not segment the day into separate times, such as for math, reading, physical education, or social studies. Through the use of learning centres (to be discussed in Chapter 9) and themes (Chapter 8), such subjects are fully integrated and considered an inseparable part of each other (Bredekamp, 1987).

Before- and After-School Care

Young school-aged children whose parents work full time also require care when they are not in school. This is often provided through before- and after-school programs and full-day holiday and summer care. Such programs generally focus on recreation and care rather than education, and particularly on self-directed and self-initiated activities, since the children spend the bulk of their day in school (Alexander, 1986). The 1991 NDCS indicated that school-aged child care is growing faster than any other kind of program in Canada. However, the NDCS also indicated that there were only spaces for 5.56 percent of the children of all Canadian working women. In fact, the CNCCS (see Exhibit 1-3) found just under 5 percent of school-aged children in these programs.

The parents of 15.6 percent (134 900) of Canadian 6-to 9-year-olds in the CNCCS had made no child care arrangements (Pence et al., 1992). In another 5.3 percent or 45 800 cases, the parents said the children looked after themselves.

Children without formal before- and after-school programs are often labelled **latch-key** or **self-care children**. They arrive at school with the "latch-key" around their necks and return to an empty home after school. Concerns about the safety, vulnerability, and lack of judgment of young school-aged children have prompted an increase in before- and after-school programs. Relatively little research, however, has been carried out to measure the long-term effects of various arrangements for the school-aged children of working parents (Powell, 1987a).

SOURCES OF SUPPORT FOR PROGRAMS

One way of grouping early childhood programs is by the base of their support, especially financial. Many early childhood programs are privately owned, for-profit businesses, whereas others are not-for-profit enterprises operated through public funds or sponsored by an agency or church. A growing number of early childhood programs are also supported by employers.

For-Profit Programs

In Canada, only 35 percent of all licensed child care centres are operated for profit (National Child Care Information Centre 1991). The number of Canadian profit-making centres has dropped sharply since 1968, when 75 percent of all the licensed Canadian child care spaces were in for-profit centres. However, there is considerable regional disparity in these figures. Presumably, government incentives for non-profit centres have played a significant role in this decline. In Saskatchewan, for example, only non-profit centres were eligible for government funds until 1990, and there were no profit-making centres in the province then. However, one might expect to see a change in the distribution of centres there, now that funding is available. Other provinces, Manitoba and Ontario, for example, give non-profit centres subsidies that allow them to increase teacher salaries.

The Canadian figures stand in sharp contrast to those for the United States, where about 60 percent of all child care programs are operated for profit, either as a

single, independently owned business or as part of a regional or national chain (Wash & Brand, 1990). This is a rapidly rising figure in the United States, and it is expected to continue to increase. For many years, the majority of child care in most American communities was provided by local owners who operated one or two centres. Over the past two decades, however, child care chains, which have experienced tremendous growth—increasing by as much as a thousandfold—have moved into virtually every metropolitan area (Neugebauer, 1988). There is some concern that they may want to move into the Canadian market in the future. Child care chains are big business! Some even sell stock that is traded on the New York Stock Exchange, deal in mergers and takeovers, and utilize sophisticated marketing strategies.

In both Canada and the United States, a series of concerns about the quality of for-profit child care have emerged (e.g., Baynham, Russell, & Ross, 1988; Kagan & Newton, 1989; McIntosh & Rauhala, 1989; Meisels & Sternberg, 1989; National Child Care Staffing Study, 1989; Neugebauer, 1991; West, 1988). A poorer quality of care, lower salaries and poorer benefits, less educated teaching staff, and more frequent licensing violations in for-profit centres have been documented in both Canada and the United States. Without question, some of these difficulties stem from these centres' need to make a profit. In Canada, the National Council of Welfare (1988) has clearly outlined the source of the difficulties:"Profits are made by keeping costs down—paying low salaries to caregivers, raising child–staff ratios or compromising health, safety or nutritional standards—all of which hurt children" (p. 27).

This is not to say that every for-profit centre does this, and that every non-profit centre does not. In the United States, Neugebauer (1991) found that there was a wide range of quality in for-profit centres as in other types of centres. Kagan and Newton (1989) reported similar findings about overall quality, but noted that non-profit centres had more favourable teacher–child ratios, more services, better management, and more child-centred environments. The controversy continues, and, more and more in Canada, there is a tendency for provincial and territorial governments to provide subsidies only to non-profit centres.

Non-Profit Programs

In for-profit early childhood programs, what is left over after expenses are paid is profit that goes back to the owner or stockholders. In non-profit programs, such monies generally are incorporated back into the program or are returned to the sponsoring agency. Some of you may wonder about the difference between returning the money to the non-profit sponsoring agent versus the owner of a profit-making centre; undoubtedly, in some cases, there is no major difference. However, if the profits are returned to the program, this is likely to have a positive effect on all aspects of the program.

Non-profit centres gain their status through incorporation or sponsorship from an entity that is itself not operated for profit. Groups such as parent-run organizations, social service agencies, churches, YMCAs, YWCAs, municipalities, hospitals, colleges, and universities are the most common sponsors of non-profit early childhood programs. However, you probably can find non-profit schools where the operators are paid very large salaries and little profit returns to the program.

Nonetheless, non-profit child care centres in Canada generally have been founded by groups sincerely interested in providing affordable, high-quality child care. In the 1970s and 1980s, when the need for child care for working parents became a more pressing social concern, many groups like churches and the YMCA/YWCA responded to that need by opening their facilities during the week or offering them to non-profit groups. Often, YMCA, YWCA, and church buildings included nursery, preschool, or recreational rooms that were used primarily on weekends. Some church programs are affiliated with and incorporate the religion of their churches, but many are secular. Not all church-based programs are non-profit, however. Sometimes an enterprising member of a congregation arranges to rent the facilities to a for-profit centre.

A unique form of non-profit early childhood program is the **parent-cooperative**. Parent-cooperatives, usually part-day preschool programs, are based on a staffing structure that includes a paid professional head teacher and a rotating staff of parents. As part of enrolling their children in the program, parents are required to assist a specified number of days in the classroom. This arrangement serves both a staffing and a parent education function. With increasing numbers of parents entering the workforce full time, however, fewer parents have the time to participate in cooperative programs. Nonetheless, they continue to be popular with families with a stay-at-home parent, and with those who work part-time. Cooperative groups are also finding ways of offering full-day child care programs, and having working parents involved in fundraising and maintenance activities.

Publicly Supported Programs

Another significant supporter of early childhood programs is the public sector, whether it be the federal, provincial, or territorial governments, or the municipalities. Although there was some activity in the field of early childhood during the war years, the **Canada Assistance Plan (CAP)**, enacted in 1966, was the first piece of federal legislation that had a significant impact on child care arrangements in the provinces and territories (Clifford, 1992; Townson, 1985). The long-term aim of the CAP was to alleviate the effects of poverty and it included provisions regarding social assistance or "welfare" as well as child care services, rehabilitation and homemaker services, and counselling for those who qualify for social assistance. CAP permitted the federal government to share 50 percent of the costs of child care with the provinces and territories, but *only for those persons in need.* There is still considerable variation between the provincial and territorial definitions of "in need."

The federal government also provides some support for child care on Indian reserve lands through Indian and Northern Affairs Canada (Child Care Resource, 1990). Some provinces and territories (e.g., Ontario and the Yukon) also fund Indian and Inuit programs, while others do not (e.g., Manitoba and Newfoundland).

Similarly, it is worth noting that the provinces and territories as well as many municipalities in Canada make significant financial contributions to early childhood programs. In fact, some provinces provide more support for early childhood programs than CAP requires, and many municipalities provide early childhood programs for their residents. Some ministries of education also are involved in providing child care to school-aged children when they are not in school.

Employer-Supported Programs

One of the fastest-growing groups with a stake in early childhood programs are employers. Many companies maintain that their interest in the needs and concerns of parent-employees has resulted in a more productive and stable workforce. For the working parents of young children, work and family are not separable and, in fact, often overlap. Child care, in particular, is not just a family issue but also a concern to employers. Employees with young children, compared with other workers, more often are late for work, leave work early, miss work altogether, and deal with personal issues while at work. When employers support child care in some way, they often report that the result is lower absenteeism, greater stability and loyalty, better morale, decreased stress, and less distraction among their employees (Fernandez, 1986; Mayfield, 1990; Milkovich & Gomez, 1976; Rothman Beach Associates, 1985). However, research has not yet fully documented these claims.

There are many ways in which employers can support their workers' child care needs. Some large companies have created child care centres in or near the place of work. For example, Statistics Canada in Ottawa, the National Film Board in St. Laurent, and Nanisivik Mines in the Northwest Territories have established workplace child care centres. In some instances, employers also make arrangements with community child care centres, such as offering vouchers or direct subsidies. Such an arrangement can ensure that employees are given priority when child care openings are available. Another way in which employers help their workers is by banding together with several other employers to support a child care centre that meets the joint needs of their employees. The Edmonton Hospital Workers Day Care, for example, is run by a consortium of employers. As part of a strike settlement, several Edmonton hospitals banded together to form a non-profit child care facility that includes family-based child care for shift workers and young infants as well as a child care centre for older children and day workers. Larger corporations also are expressing a greater interest in employee child care—and elder care. In July 1992, twelve large American companies, including giant corporations such as IBM, AT&T, Xerox, and Kodak, announced they were committing millions of dollars to build and expand facilities for the care of their employees' children and elderly relatives (U.S. Firms, 1992).

Not all employers, however, operate on such a large scale. Some provide referral services to help match employees' needs with available resources in the community. Other companies have helped develop and train a community network of family child care homes to meet their workers' needs. A growing trend among employers is to provide more responsive scheduling options, for instance, job sharing or flextime. Child care is increasingly becoming a benefits option as companies rather than provide a common benefits package for all allow their employees to select from a menu. Some companies, recognizing the significant problem posed by children who are ill, have begun to explore sick-child care options (Friedman, 1989; NAEYC Information Service, 1990).

University- and College-Affiliated Programs

A sizable group of early childhood programs are linked to higher education. The institution in which you are enrolled may, in fact, have such a program. Some are specifically laboratory or training programs that support student practice-teaching experiences and provide subjects for research; others serve primarily as campus child care centres for the young children of students, staff, and faculty. Many combine these two functions, offering child care to the campus community while utilizing the children and families for practicum and research purposes.

Some programs are operated as a joint campus venture, others are affiliated with a specific department or unit, and others only rent space from the university or college. Campus programs that are laboratory schools are generally high-quality, incorporating what has been learned about young children and early childhood programs through research, theory, and professional practice. However, not all campus programs are high-quality. In some cases, universities and colleges simply rent space to child care programs so that there will be some child care on campus.

Public-School Involvement

A relatively recent development in early childhood program sponsorship is the involvement of public schools. A few provinces have provided services to young children below kindergarten age for a number of years, and more public schools are considering extending their programs to preschoolers. Some provinces have appropriated monies for prekindergarten programs and others have placed early childhood programs high on their agendas.

In addition, public schools have, for many years, provided early childhood centres as part of high-school or vocational training programs. Recent additions of secondary courses on the family are accelerating this trend.

Although many early childhood educators feel that public-school involvement is a natural and inevitable step, some persistent issues surround this move. One of the most serious concerns is that prekindergarten programs in public schools will focus on school readiness rather than on developmental appropriateness, simply offering a downward extension of the kindergarten and first-grade curriculum and methods (Elkind, 1988; Morado, 1986).

A recent U.S. study of public-school prekindergartens provides support that such fears may, in many instances, be legitimate. "We saw some wonderful programs, full of child-centred and interesting activities. Others were rigid and boring. Still others sounded good on paper, but observations revealed that classroom practice in no way resembled written philosophy" (Mitchell & Modigliani, 1989, p. 57). The authors of this report go on to say, however, that their finding of a mix of good and inappropriate practice in public school programs was not so different from what they saw in community-based early childhood programs.

Public-school sponsorship of early childhood programs is, of course, subject to the same limited supply of money that constrains other publicly supported programs. Typically, therefore, existing programs serve a limited group of children, and they are most likely to be available in large urban centres.

DEFINING QUALITY IN EARLY CHILDHOOD PROGRAMS

Up to this point, we have discussed early childhood programs in fairly concrete, descriptive terms, looking at characteristics by which programs can be grouped. Programs can and should also be examined in terms of how they best meet the needs and consider the well-being of children. Such considerations are related to quality.

Current research is, in fact, focusing on identifying factors that create good early childhood programming for young children. The old questions about whether child care is good or bad for children or what type of care is best are now obsolete; today's research questions seek to find out how to make child care better for young children (Phillips, 1987). Current research is attempting to determine which variables make a program a "good program." The emerging picture tells us that quality in child care is not dependent on single, separable factors but is a result of the presence and interaction among a variety of complex elements (Clarke-Stewart, 1987a). Of course, as a student with interest in the field, you will be pleased to know the knowledge you acquire in your courses has been found to lead to better teaching, as you will see below.

TEACHER QUALIFICATIONS

Research has given us some indication about teachers who are most likely to provide a high-quality early childhood program. Earlier we discussed how the National Day Care Study (Ruopp et al., 1979) found group size to be one of two important quality variables. The other significant variable that emerged from this study was the importance of a staff with *specific training in early childhood education and development.* Such teachers engaged in more interactions with the children, and the children showed greater social and cognitive abilities compared with those whose teachers lacked such training. These findings, particularly in relation to children's more advanced cognitive and language ability, have been supported in other research (Clarke-Stewart, 1987a; Clarke-Stewart & Gruber, 1984; Howes, 1983). In addition, teachers with early childhood training were rated as more positive and less punitive, employing a less authoritarian style of interaction with the children (Arnett, 1987).

TEACHER–CHILD RATIO

It has generally been assumed that when caregivers are responsible for large numbers of children, the quality of care is affected adversely. A number of studies have addressed this assumption and found that the ratio significantly affects children's behaviour and teacher–child interactions (Phillips & Howes, 1987).

Ratio is a concept that people have difficulty defining by the terms "high" and "low." If you convert a ratio to a decimal, it becomes straightforward. A teacher–child ratio of 1:4 would give you 0.25, while a ratio of 1:8 would give you 0.125, a lower ratio. A *high* ratio means there are fewer children per teacher, while a *low* ratio means there are more children.

Researchers have found that when there are larger numbers of children per adult, there is less verbal interaction among adults and children than when the **teacher–child ratio** is higher. Conversations are brief and routine and contain more prohibitions (Smith & Connolly, 1981). A significant factor in providing quality care has to do with giving children individualized attention, confirming their unique identity and worth as individuals. When an adult is responsible for a large number of children, that adult is less able to provide such attention and more concerned instead with controlling and managing the group. Teachers also spend more time in activity centres with children when the teacher–child ratio is lower (Ruopp et al., 1979). Moreover, children are more likely to show interest in activities and to persist at an activity when the teacher–child ratio is lower (Ruopp et al., 1979).

What is an appropriate teacher–child ratio? There is no definitive answer, although there are some suggested guidelines. The recent *National Statement on Quality Child Care* (Canadian Child Day Care Federation, 1991), developed by experts from across the country, has suggested guidelines for teacher–child ratios and **group size** for centre-based programs (see Exhibit 1-4). Keep in mind, however, that

EXHIBIT 1-4   RECOMMENDATIONS FOR TEACHER–CHILD RATIOS WITHIN DIFFERENT GROUP SIZES

GROUP SIZE[1]	AGE						
	0–12 MONTHS	12–24 MONTHS	2 YEARS	3 YEARS	4–5 YEARS	5–6 YEARS	6–9 YEARS
6	1:3[2]	1:3					
8		1:4	1:4				
10			1:5	1:5			
12				1:6			
14				1:7			
16					1:8	1:8	
18					1:9	1:9	
20							1:10
22							1:11
24							1:12

[1] In mixed-age groupings, the teacher–child ratio and group size should be based on the age of the majority of children in the group. However, if there are infants, ratios and group sizes for infants should be maintained at all times.

[2] The ratios assume that the teachers are full-time in the program. If they have other duties such as administration or parent interviewing, an additional teacher should be present to maintain the ratios.

SOURCE: Canadian Child Day Care Federation. (1991). *National Statement on Quality Child Care* (p. 9). Ottawa, ON: Canadian Child Day Care Federation.

teacher–child ratio is one variable that interacts with other factors, such as group size and teacher qualifications. "We should avoid blanket statements about high teacher–child ratios being good and low ratios being bad until we check out the *limits* beyond which a low ratio is bad and the *outcome* for which a high ratio is good" (Clarke-Stewart, 1987a, p. 114; italics in original).

GROUP SIZE

In the late 1970s, the large-scale U.S. National Day Care Study (Ruopp et al., 1979) published its findings, and Canadians have found the report quite relevant to our early childhood programs. The study showed that group size was one of two consistently important variables that define quality of care for young children. In smaller groups, children were more cooperative, innovative, and verbal; they showed less hostility and conflict than children in larger groups; and they made greater gains over time on cognitive and language tests. The association between test gains and group size was particularly marked in centres serving low-income children. Children in smaller groups were also less likely to be uninvolved in activities, and to be observed wandering aimlessly. Furthermore, teachers in smaller groups spent more time interacting with children and less time in detached observation. Another study found more elaborate play, including more pretend play, among children in smaller rather than larger groups (Bruner, 1980). One recent study summarized that with a moderate number of children in a group, children seem to demonstrate greater social competence (Clarke-Stewart, 1987b). When teachers are in charge of large groups of children, on the other hand, they tend to be less responsive to the children, and they provide less social stimulation (Howes, 1983). As group size increases beyond eighteen children, teachers spend more time in management activities and show a marked increase in the time they spend passively observing activities and interactions (Ruopp et al., 1979).

Ideal group size cannot really be defined because other variables, including the parameters of the physical environment, need to be considered. As Exhibit 1-4 indicates, the recommended group size varies with the age of the children.

MIXED-AGE GROUPING

Only in relatively recent times has our society stratified children into narrow groups defined by age, particularly in the educational context. "Although humans are not usually born in litters, we seem to insist that they be educated in them" (Katz, Evangelou, & Hartman, 1990, p. viii). Many theorists and researchers have expressed concern about the increasing separation of people into age-segregated groups in education, housing, recreation, work, and other aspects of life (Bronfenbrenner, 1971). It is more natural, they say, that people of all ages interact and share various aspects of their lives. Throughout history, socialization was facilitated because people of all ages learned from and helped each other.

Early childhood education programs are also often segregated into narrow, homogeneous age groups, with the 3-year-olds in one class, 4-year-olds across the hall in another, and the mature 5-year-olds in their own environment. But many educators suggest that heterogeneous or **mixed-age grouping** will benefit both younger and older children. Positive social behaviours such as sharing, turn-taking, and helpfulness are encouraged in mixed-age groups. Similarly, older children have more opportunities to practise leadership skills, and young children become involved in more complex forms of pretend play. Children also appear to reap cognitive benefits from mixed-age grouping (Katz, Evangelou, and Hartman, 1990). In addition, children in some mixed-age settings stay with the same teacher for several years and this stability can be reassuring. Recently, a few public schools have been organizing mixed-age classes at the primary level, and teachers in those classes talk enthusiastically about the experience. However, other teachers, accustomed to single-age classes, pale at the suggestion that mixed-age classes may become more common.

As we have already mentioned, quality in early childhood programs depends on many factors. There are certainly many outstanding, high-quality programs in which children are grouped by narrow age criteria; other equally good programs utilize a mixed-age model. Nonetheless, research suggests that children receive some unique benefits from being placed in groups that contain a wider age range of children. For this reason, mixed-age grouping is included as a criterion of quality.

DEVELOPMENTAL APPROPRIATENESS OF THE PROGRAM

Child development theory and research have given us a good understanding of what young children are like and under what conditions they thrive and learn best. From such information, we are able to plan environments, develop activities, and set expectations that match children's needs and characteristics (Bredekamp, 1987). Throughout this book—particularly Chapter 8, which considers how to structure an appropriate environment; Chapters 9 through 14, which examine how various components of the curriculum reinforce development; and Chapters 15 through 16, in which we consider guidance principles—we will focus on developmentally appropriate practice.

In recent years, there has been increasing concern that public education is not adequately preparing children for the challenges of the future. This concern, expressed by those in the **back-to-basics movement**, has led to a push to return to "the basics" in education. Some have interpreted this to include young children, with the idea that an earlier introduction to academics will result in better-prepared and better-educated children. But, as we will consider in various contexts in this book, early childhood professionals and researchers have expressed grave apprehensions about this trend, aptly termed hothousing, which pushes preschoolers into inappropriate tasks for which they are not developmentally ready (Gallagher & Coche, 1987). Young children can learn a lot of material in a mechanistic, rote manner, but if these experiences are meaningless, such information has little relevance (Sigel, 1987). Thus, for an early childhood program to meet quality criteria, it must respect the emerging abilities of young children without imposing inappropriate expectations.

TEACHER–CHILD INTERACTION

Although many factors contribute to the quality of an early childhood program, perhaps the most important factor on which quality depends is the interaction between the teachers and the children. In a good program, teachers are involved with children,

they are nurturing and responsive, there is ample verbal exchange, and interactions aim to teach, not just to control (Clarke-Stewart, 1987a). A wonderful physical facility, an exemplary teacher–child ratio, and a favourable group size would all be negated by uncaring and unresponsive teacher–child interaction. It is, after all, the teachers who determine the tone and the character—in effect, the quality—of a program.

TEACHER CONSISTENCY

A serious concern among professionals and parents alike is the high rate of teacher turnover in early childhood programs. The low wages of professionals in the field, documented by a current Canadian study, *Caring for a Living* (Canadian Child Day Care Federation [CCDCF], 1992), have been identified as a significant factor in this turnover. Nevertheless, many young children spend the bulk of their waking hours in child care, with adults other than their parents, and consistency in caregivers is important. One important task of the early years is forming a secure attachment relationship to adults. Although primary attachment is with parents, research has shown that young children certainly do become attached to their teachers. But when children lose a teacher with whom they have formed such an attachment, the loss can be profound (Phillips & Howes, 1987).

One study found that there is less teacher–child interaction in centres with a high teacher-turnover rate (Phillips, Scarr, & McCartney 1987). This is not surprising when interaction is dependent in part on establishing a relationship, something that takes time to develop. In general, research supports the finding that children seem to be better adjusted, less dependent, less anxious, and more sociable in programs with a low staff-turnover rate (Clarke-Stewart, 1987a).

RESPECT AND CONCERN FOR TEACHERS

As we have discussed, a nurturing, well-trained, and consistent staff is important to a quality program, but a reciprocal concern for the well-being of the teaching staff is also needed. Working with young children is a demanding, challenging job. Thus, it is in the best interests of the children, the families, and the employer if staff members receive appropriate pay and benefits, and work in a satisfying environment. In such a setting, the needs of the staff are seriously considered, an atmosphere of camaraderie is fostered, autonomy is encouraged in planning an appropriate program for the children, and the physical environment includes space for adults (Jorde-Bloom, 1988). Chapter 6 will discuss some of the parameters and some of the issues associated with providing such an environment for the staff.

PHYSICAL ENVIRONMENT

Even though we will discuss this topic in greater detail in Chapter 9, it is necessary to note here that the physical facility is another important factor that contributes to program quality. According to research, children demonstrate higher cognitive skill levels and greater social competence in schools that are safe and orderly, contain a wide variety of stimulating equipment and materials, and are organized into learning centres on the basis of similar materials and activities when compared with children in programs that lack these features (Clarke-Stewart, 1987b).

A child-oriented environment conveys to children that this place is meant for them. There are interesting and worthwhile things to do in a child-oriented

environment because it was designed with the characteristics, ages, and abilities of the children in mind. A child-centred environment also requires fewer restrictions and prohibitions because it was fashioned specifically for children. This helps to create a positive and pleasant atmosphere. In short, a good environment conveys to children that this is a good place to be, that people here care about them, that they are able to satisfy their desire to learn and their innate curiosity, and that it is safe engage in activities without fear of failure.

FAMILY INVOLVEMENT

With increasing numbers of children spending many hours per day in child care, parents and teachers are more than ever partners in many aspects of child rearing and socialization. Studies have shown that the children benefit when parents and the early childhood staff share a common commitment to acting in the best interests of the children, communicate openly, and have mutual respect. On the other hand, if there is a lack of communication so that parents do not know what happened at school and teachers are not informed of significant events in the child's home life, there is lack of continuity for the child. In Chapter 5, we will explore this home–school link in much greater detail.

QUALITY AS A COMBINATION OF FACTORS

For the purposes of discussion, we have isolated a number of components that contribute to quality early childhood programming, including teacher–child ratio, group size, teacher qualifications, mixed-age grouping, developmental appropriateness of the program, teacher–child interaction, staff consistency, concern for staff, the physical environment, and family involvement. It is important to keep in mind, however, that quality can best be understood and studied as a combination of components (Phillips, 1987). As you further your understanding and knowledge of the field of early childhood education, remember that quality is not defined by a single factor, but rather depends on the complex interaction of a variety of elements in which you, as an early childhood professional, play a key role.

At this point, you have a broad overview of early childhood education and the factors that define quality programs. In the next chapter, we will examine the field's historical roots. Where did our ideas about the field come from and where were the methods developed?

KEY POINTS OF CHAPTER 1

THE GROWTH OF EARLY CHILDHOOD EDUCATION

▲ 1. Increasing numbers of women are entering the workforce. More than 50 percent of mothers of preschoolers now work and require child care for their youngsters.

▲ 2. There are significantly more single parents today than ever before, mostly because of the increase in the divorce rate. These parents need care for their children while they work.

▲ 3. Families today move more than families did in the past. Migration within the country and immigration to Canada from other countries mean that many Canadian children are far away from relatives who might have been available to provide child care while the parents work.

BENEFITS OF EARLY CHILDHOOD EDUCATION

▲ 4. Research has shown that good early childhood education programs have a lasting effect on children from disadvantaged backgrounds.

▲ 5. Investment in such programs has substantial social and financial benefits for society.

▲ 6. Some professionals participate in child advocacy, bringing to public and legislative attention the needs of children and families in poverty as well as the need for affordable child care for families with moderate incomes.

WHAT IS INCLUDED IN EARLY CHILDHOOD EDUCATION

▲ 7. Early childhood programs can be defined by their purpose. The main purpose of many programs is child care; the goal of others is enrichment. A third category includes programs whose main aim is compensation for some lack in the children's backgrounds.

▲ 8. Programs are either home-based, such as family child care homes, or centre-based, located in a school facility and usually serving larger groups of children.

▲ 9. Programs are specially designed for children of varying ages, such as infants and toddlers, preschoolers, and school-aged children.

KEY TERMS

back-to-basics
  movement
Canada Assistance Plan
  (CAP)
Canadian National Child
  Care Study (CNCCS)
centre-based program
child–adult ratio
child advocacy
child care centre
  early childhood
early childhood
  education
employer-supported
  program
extended family
family child care home
for-profit program
group size
hothousing
hurried child
infant
infant stimulation
  program
integrated curriculum
latch-key or self-care
  children
mixed-age grouping
nanny
National Day Care Study
  (NDCS)
not-for-profit program
nuclear family
nursery school
parent-cooperative
parent-cooperative
  nursery school
preschool
teacher–child ratio
toddler

▲10. Centre-based infant/toddler programs are one of the fastest-growing types of programs today.

▲11. Centres that serve school-aged children before and after school are an alternative to leaving these children, termed latch-key children, alone at home. They are increasing at a faster rate than any other child care program in Canada.

▲12. The majority of early childhood programs are operated on a non-profit basis. However, limited government funding for child care may mean that some of the U.S. child care chains will continue to expand across the border, particularly in metropolitan areas where there often is a shortage of spaces.

▲13. A number of non-profit organizations and agencies can sponsor early childhood programs.

▲14. Another type of early childhood program is sponsored or supported by an employer for the children of employees. Child care as a work benefit is thought to increase worker productivity and loyalty.

▲15. Early childhood programs affiliated with institutions of higher learning provide training for students and child care for student, parents, faculty, and staff.

▲16. The Canada Assistance Plan requires the federal government to share child care funding with the provinces on a 50-50 basis. Increases in federal funding seem unlikely at this time, but the more affluent provinces and municipalities are likely to increase their contributions to child care.

▲17. School boards across the country are beginning to offer programs for preschoolers, and to provide child care services. This trend seems likely to continue.

DEFINING QUALITY IN EARLY CHILDHOOD PROGRAMS

▲18. When an adult is in charge of too many children, the behaviour of both the children and adult are adversely affected by this low child–adult ratio.

▲19. Research has shown that a moderate group size results in children who are more socially and intellectually competent than those who spend their day in large groups.

▲20. Grouping children of varying ages together has benefits for both younger and older children in many developmental areas.

▲21. High-quality programs have developmentally appropriate expectations and activities and do not push children into inappropriate, accelerated activities.

▲22. Frequent and responsive interaction between adults and children is a necessity in high-quality programs.

▲23. Research shows that teachers with specific early childhood training are important in a high-quality program.

▲24. Staff consistency is important, because high staff turnover has a negative impact on young children.

▲25. A good staff, which provides an appropriate program for young children, has to be respected and nurtured.

▲26. A child-oriented environment and family involvement also contribute to the quality of a program.

KEY QUESTIONS

1. Interview several parents whose preschool-aged children are enrolled in an early childhood program. Why are their children in such a program? How did the parents select the program? What program criteria were important to them?

2. If you have a local compensatory education program, arrange to visit it. What benefits do you see for the children? Talk to a teacher member and find out what services are provided for the children and their families.

3. If you were given "three wishes" to bring about changes for young children and their families, what would these be? Share your choices with others in your class. From a combined list, develop several child and family issues that you think child advocates might address.

4. Visit an early childhood program in your community and share your experience with other members of your class who have visited different programs. Classify the programs according to their characteristics, for instance, purpose, setting, age of children served, and source of support. Does your community have a variety of programs? Which types predominate? What family needs do these programs meet?

5. If you were asked by the parent of a young child, "How do I find a good child care program?" what would you answer? How can you help a parent recognize quality indicators?

6. Projections for the future, as we have discussed, indicate an increased need for good early childhood programs. What changes do you think are needed to bring about improvements for children and for early childhood professionals?

THE HISTORY OF EARLY CHILDHOOD EDUCATION

How we approach the education and care of young children in the 1990s depends, to a great extent, on the work of many people over many centuries. Current ideas about children and how they should be treated can be traced back through history. Plato, for example, thought that adults should observe children's play and organize village play-groups, and Quintillian, a Roman, thought that play would foster intellectual development in the young child (Caplan & Caplan, 1974).

Learning about the historical roots of early childhood education is important for several reasons. First, it valuable to know that our current practices are based on a blend of ideas and traditions that have evolved over centuries. At times, ideas become unfashionable, but they often re-emerge in a slightly altered way. Understanding these cycles of change will make it easier for you to accept and explain the ongoing changes in early childhood education that you will experience as a professional, a parent, and/or an interested observer. Second, if you are a professional in the field, you will find that your knowledge of the history of early childhood education can be a source of support, pride, and inspiration. Many of the early educators and thinkers in the field were driven to improve the quality of young children's lives, and they persisted in their efforts, even when they paid a personal toll. Finally, knowing the theories that explain *why* you do things in a certain way can be empowering. If you are questioned about your practices, you can confidently explain the theoretical basis and developmental appropriateness of what you do.

We will examine several aspects of the history of early childhood education:

1. Early childhood education, although relatively new as a formal system, has antecedents that reach far back in history when many ideas about children and how they should be treated were shaped. We will discuss some of these ideas at the beginning of this chapter.

2. We will explore the writings and work of many individuals through history who have contributed to our ideas about young children and early childhood education.

3. We will also look at the theories that have influenced the field. Particularly in this century, a number of individuals have formulated theories that help us understand the nature of young children and how best to meet their needs.

   • Some theorists—in the **nature** camp—believe that children's development follows an inborn plan.

- Others—in the **nurture** camp—contend that children's development is affected primarily by external factors.
- Still others—the **interactionists**—think that children's development is determined by an interaction of inborn and external factors.

A LOOK BACK—CHILDREN THROUGH TIME

Interest in the care and education of young children goes back thousands of years. Our Western tradition is traced to ancient Greece, where the writings of philosophers such as Plato and Aristotle reflected a keen sensitivity to the needs of children and the importance of appropriate education in shaping their character (deMause, 1974; Greenleaf, 1978). These educated Greeks saw human development as a transformation from the imperfect state of childhood to the ideal of adulthood, and the Greek tradition included education for girls as well as for boys (Sameroff, 1983). Unfortunately, however, this sensitivity to the needs of young children was not shared by all, and infanticide was also common in this era (deMause, 1974). Infanticide was more likely to occur with females, and estimates suggest that the male-to-female ratio was 4:1 (deMause, 1974). Harsh discipline, beatings, and extreme isolation produced by locking children in closets and drawers persisted for centuries, even though laws against infanticide emerged as early as the 4th century A.D. (deMause, 1974). Children of the wealthy were rarely cared for by their own parents, but rather by hired wet nurses and teachers. Children of the poor were less fortunate, and were sent to be apprentices, servants, and slaves at an early age.

By the Middle Ages, even the concept of childhood seemed to have been lost. Children became little more than property and were put to work, for instance, in the fields or tending animals, just as soon as they were big enough. "The typical man or woman emerged straight out of his babyhood into a sort of junior adult status" (Braun & Edwards, 1972, p. 6). Schools and formal education as a way of passing on cultural traditions had virtually disappeared in Europe except in a few places, notably Islamic Spain, where learning was highly valued.

The Renaissance led to slight improvements in the child's lot in life, but the period from 0 to 7 years was still viewed as an unfortunate waiting period for entry into the adult world. Education became more common, but it generally was limited to the sons of the wealthy. The children of the poor went to work, not school. The 17th century saw little improvement: the Puritans' children in the Old and New Worlds were born "ignorant and sinful" (Borstelmann, 1983, p. 15). Puritan parents, as well as the Quakers, often resorted to restraint, harsh discipline, and "the rod" to ensure their children became holy. The Enlightenment was to bring welcome changes. John Locke, the child of strict Puritans, and Rousseau, a product of Geneva's strict Calvinism, became children of the Enlightenment, and emphasized the importance of the early years. Since their time, there have been slow but steady improvements in views about the young child and early childhood education.

Significant changes in attitudes about children began to take shape in the 19th century, and kindergarten programs became part of the educational system in some locations by the middle of the century. In fact, one of the first public **kindergartens** in North America was established in Toronto in 1873 by Dr. J.L. Hughes (Young, 1981). Hester Howe, a school principal, became concerned that the school children had to bring their preschool-aged siblings to school with them as their mothers were working. Hughes suggested opening a crèche for these preschool children, and in 1892, the crèche, which is now Victoria Day Care Services in Toronto, was opened. Other significant events in early childhood education in Canada soon followed, especially in the more populated provinces.

The 20th century, while a relatively short period in time, represents a very active time for the field of education. For one thing, education for all children came to be increasingly accepted, and this reinforced the idea that childhood was a separate period in life. Education in North America, in the eyes of such progressive educators as John Dewey, was a training ground for democracy, a way of equalizing social inequities by imbuing children from a young age with democratic ideals. Philosophers and scientists, who proclaimed the early years as specially relevant, also contributed to the field. Among these, Sigmund Freud focused unprecedented attention on earliest experiences as the foundation of personality.

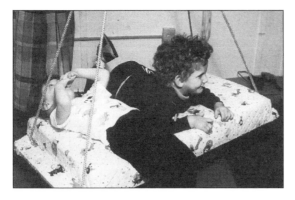

The 20th century also has seen the development of scientific methods of observation that led to the **child study movement,** out of which grew many university preschool laboratory programs designed to facilitate the careful study of young children. For example, the University of Toronto's Institute for Child Study was opened in 1926, and the St. George's Nursery School was an integral part of the Institute (Young, 1981).

Still another contribution to today's field is the notion of early childhood education as a means to social reform. Important programs were developed throughout this century with the idea of rescuing the poor from poverty. A common purpose motivated those who helped move young children out of factories into schools at the turn of the century, and those who developed Canadian and American compensatory programs in the 1960s. The 1960s compensatory programs, often known as Head Start programs, were designed to give young children from poverty backgrounds an "edge" or "head start" the summer before they entered school, as the research showed they typically were less successful in school than their more affluent peers.

Finally, another change that has profoundly affected early childhood education today is the steadily increasing need for child care, which we will discuss below. Although recent changes in the economy and family life have brought the proliferation of child care programs available today, such programs are not new. During World War II, many women were required to work and needed arrangements for care of their young children (Braun & Edwards, 1972; Carter, 1987; Greenberg, 1987; Siegel & White, 1982; Stapleford, 1976; Weber, 1984). Child care centres were established in Canada and the United States for mothers employed in the defence industries during that time, but most were closed after the war. Nursery schools seem to have been concentrated in affluent, urban areas in the 1950s. However, the compensatory education movement of the 1960s, coupled with the steadily increasing number of women in the workforce since that time, has led to the rapid growth of the field during the past thirty years.

VIEWS OF CHILDREN

Traditionally, the way people view young children has been determined by the intellectual, social, and economic context of each period. Because children are vulnerable and dependent, their image and treatment tends to be shaped by the needs of the times. When needs have changed, influential thinkers and writers like Locke and Rousseau have shaken the very foundation of thoughts about children.

Today, at least in the developed world, we view children much more benignly than in the past, although many would maintain we still do not place a high enough value on the care of the very young. Nevertheless, we at least acknowledge that the childhood years are unique and important, we provide children with special environments, and we promote education as a social and personal necessity. Today's view of children is based to a greater extent on theory and research rather than on the religious or political ideas that, in part, dictated the image of children in the past. However, children in underdeveloped countries are not so fortunate, and child labour is not a thing of the past. Well-organized protests in India in 1993, for example, highlighted the plight of child carpet makers who "are not fed properly, seldom paid, and often beaten if they make mistakes while weaving" (Kids Freed, 1993, p. C10). Similar problems are common in many areas of Africa, Central America, and Asia. Closer to home, over one million children of migrant farm workers are thought to be working illegally in the United States (Morrison, 1991). Obviously, many children are still waiting to benefit from the more benign view of childhood that has evolved over the centuries.

Let us now turn to some of the important figures in our historical account of early childhood education and see how their ideas have shaped our thinking. After that, we will then review the work of influential theorists whose conceptualizations have further refined our ideas of young children.

INFLUENTIAL PEOPLE IN THE HISTORY OF EARLY CHILDHOOD EDUCATION

Individuals have contributed to our current view of young children and their care and education. We will touch on the works of only a few of them in this text. Some developed their ideas because of their direct work with children, often the poor and underprivileged; others' theories emerged out of political and philosophical concerns about the problems of society and how reforms could be brought about.

The Renaissance and Reformation periods led to profound changes in thinking about education and young children. Philosophers, writers, and church leaders of this time generated many new ideas that have influenced thinking in the field of early childhood education.

MARTIN LUTHER (1483–1546)

The name Luther is usually associated with the Protestant Reformation, but he also wrote extensively about education. During Luther's time, education had been restricted to the sons of the wealthy, who were tutored in the Latin language. Luther believed that education should be accessible to all, and to further that aim he recommended that teaching should be done in one's native language. He thought that the way to salvation was through reading the bible, and he translated it into German so that it would be readily available for German families.

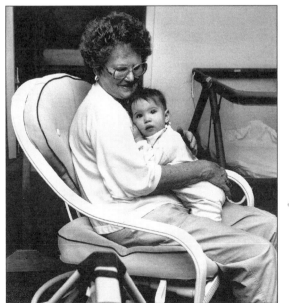

JOHN AMOS COMENIUS (1592–1670)

Comenius, like Luther, was involved with the church. He was a bishop in Moravia, later Czechoslovakia, and an advocate of universal education. Perhaps more than any of his predecessors, Comenius understood and stressed the importance of the early years. In *The Great Didactic* (1667), he wrote:

It is the nature of everything that comes into being, that while tender it is easily bent and formed, but that, when it has grown hard, it is not easy to alter. … A young plant can be planted, transplanted, pruned, and bent this way or that. When it has become a tree, these processes are impossible (p. 58).

Comenius also emphasized the value of active learning, hands-on experiences, and the involvement of parents in their children's education, especially before they were 6 years of age. His 1658 publication *Orbis pictus (The World of Pictures)* is viewed as the first picture book for children, and it reflects his commitment to providing tangible learning materials that are appealing to the senses. Comenius, like Montessori and Piaget centuries later, also maintained that a child's development followed an internal timetable, and that teachers needed to work with that natural order. He was perhaps the first critic of "hothousing" in arguing that education would succeed only "if the mind be duly prepared to receive it ... [and] if the pupil be not overburdened by too many subjects" (Comenius, 1967, p. 127).

JOHN LOCKE (1632–1704)

John Locke was an English physician and philosopher who spent time in exile in Holland because of his opposition to the throne. Locke proposed that children were born as *tabula rasa* (blank slates), and that experience would determine what the infant became. Locke maintained that education should be pleasant for the young child rather than devoted to rote drills and learning. He also encouraged parents to abandon harsh discipline procedures as well as restrictive practices like swaddling babies in fabric and constraining their physical activity.

JEAN-JACQUES ROUSSEAU (1712–1778)

Rousseau was not an early childhood educator, but his ideas have certainly influenced the field. As a philosopher writing in the context of the corrupt French society of his time, Rousseau developed the idea that society actually hindered human beings from developing according to their nature. Society, with its hierarchy of the few who were rich and powerful, imposed only misery on the masses, a state that is not natural. Rousseau, in fact, considered anything natural and primitive to be good. Thus, he argued, if children could develop without the artificial trappings of civilization, they would be able to achieve their true potential of being moral and good.

According to Rousseau, young children are innately pure and noble, but they need to be protected from the evil influences of society. In a protected rural environment, they learn from what is concrete and natural, through trial and error and experimentation. Rousseau recognized that children's mode of thinking and learning is different from that of adults and considered *good education to be based on the stage of development of the child*, not on *adult-imposed criteria*. A child-centred, uncorrupted education will, eventually, result in adults who are moral and interested in the common good of society.

Rousseau never worked with children—in fact, he actually abandoned all of his own children to foundling homes—but he wrote extensively about his philosophy in his novels and essays. Today, we agree with Rousseau that children have a unique nature that needs to be nurtured and protected in an appropriate environment. Although his highly idealistic view of childhood and human nature was never fully adopted by his followers, Rousseau nonetheless had a great influence on later early childhood educators, as we shall soon see (Braun & Edwards, 1972; Carter, 1987; Grimsley, 1967; Weber, 1984).

JOHANN PESTALOZZI (1746–1827)

Pestalozzi, a native of Switzerland, was deeply influenced by Rousseau's educational ideas. He felt that all people, even the poorest, had the right to an education as a way of helping them develop their moral and intellectual potential. He believed in

education according to nature and considered that learning for young children is intricately tied to concrete experiences and observation. Unlike Rousseau, however, he stressed the important role of the mother in children's earliest years.

Also unlike Rousseau, Pestalozzi actually worked with children, developing educational methods that are still used today. For instance, he stressed the importance of recognizing individual differences among children and the relevance of children's self-activity rather than rote as the basis of learning. One of the schools he established became world-famous, drawing visitors and students from all over Europe. He is considered to be the first to actually teach young children of preschool age, marking the beginning of the kindergarten movement (Braun & Edwards, 1972; Ulich, 1967; Weber, 1984).

ROBERT OWEN (1771–1858)

Robert Owen, a disciple of Pestalozzi, was a British industrialist, philosopher, philanthropist, and social reformer (Pence, 1990; Weber, 1971). When he began to manage a textile mill in New Lanark, Scotland, he became concerned about the plight of young children who typically began to work in the mill at 6 years of age. Owen disliked the image of dark, satanic mills, which Dickens so aptly painted, and wanted life in New Lanark to be better both for children and their parents. Owen quickly changed the minimum age for employment to 10 years, improved housing, opened a low-cost company store, and set up schools for children and their parents.

In 1816, Owen's **infant school** was opened for the young children in New Lanark who attended once they could walk. Owen had visited Pestalozzi, and had read his works as well as Rousseau's, but he adopted Locke's view of the child as a *tabula rasa*. Singing, dancing, outdoor experiences and play were major components of his program; Owen wanted learning to stem from the child's natural curiosity rather than from rigid lessons. Corporal punishment was not permitted and there was no fixed schedule. Rousseau's emphasis on learning from nature was evident in Owen's program, which highlighted learning from gardens, animals, woods, and orchards.

FRIEDRICH FROEBEL (1782–1852)

Friedrich Froebel, a German, was one of the visitors at Pestalozzi's school, observing it with some mixed feelings. He greatly admired Pestalozzi's skills but was concerned about his inability to articulate his methods. Froebel, however, was better able to put into words his educational principles. Like his predecessors, Rousseau and Pestalozzi, Froebel believed in the interrelatedness of nature and the child's developing mind. He also advocated that education should harmonize with the child's inner development, recognizing that children are in different stages at various ages. He saw childhood as a separate stage that was not just a transition to adulthood but a stage with great intrinsic value in its own right.

Froebel also stressed the important role of play in young children's development—play was a pure and natural mode of learning through which children achieve harmony (Braun & Edwards, 1972; Carter, 1987; Ulich, 1947, 1967; Weber, 1984). Froebel developed a carefully programmed curriculum and specific materials that are described by Barbara Corbett in A Canadian Professional Speaks Out.

A CANADIAN
PROFESSIONAL SPEAKS OUT

Froebel Education in Canada

As a Canadian I am grateful that our ancestors had the foresight to incorporate Froebel's kindergarten in our public education system. Planted into our thinking by that act were Froebel's theories and practices of *education through child development.* Friedrich Froebel (1782–1852) was the German educator who invented the kindergarten for children from ages 3 to 7—the time when the educational foundation for learning is formed. His first kindergarten was in Bad Blankenberg, Germany, in 1837. Toronto has the distinction of having the first public kindergarten in Canada (1883), and Ontario, in 1887, was the first government system to give grants to Froebel's kindergarten as part of the public school system.

The word *kindergarten* reveals Froebel's thought. The children are individual plants tended and cultivated by a kindergartner (gardener) in the social setting, called *the garden of children.* Froebel's kindergarten provides for a five-year bridge from the home where cultivation for the 3-year-old is individual, to the school, from Grade 3 on, where the groupings are larger and socially more complex. His kindergarten combines the intimate family grouping—where the ratio can be one to eight for the youngest children, increasing to one to twelve for 6- or 7-year-olds—with the more relaxed plays of children whereby the seeds of all future learning are planted. The Froebel Gifts, which are toys consisting of solid geometrical shapes, tablets, lines, and points, allow the child to objectively build her inner world as well as to imitate the outer environment in which she lives and moves every day. These planned plays are pleasant as well as informative and creative for the child who is in the process of becoming.

In becoming, children are educated to be thinkers. It is not enough to know the known. In Froebel's view the child must also be encouraged to think creatively as he or she learns the known. Thus, on becoming an adult, he or she will be able to use the known in new, creative ways. Children so educated will become the leader who that will take us into the 21st century.

Since we opened our Froebel Kindergarten in 1970, and seven years later expanded to include to grade to eight, we have seen this leadership emerging. It is evident in our graduates who have gone on to high school and university as well as in children who [currently] attend our Froebel Education Centre in Mississauga, Ontario. It is the rare child who ever says, "What shall I do now?" Most of our children have so many ideas that it takes all the teachers' skills to guide each one through the process of self-education. For the child, that process requires concentrated effort, and for the kindergartner it is the process of helping a child develop the God-given potential from within. Isn't that what education is—leading the child out of him- or herself into all his relationships with his fellow human beings and the natural world?

Barbara E.Corbett
The Froebel Education Centre
Mississauga, Ontario

Froebel's view of children differed from Locke's *tabula rasa* notion. While Locke emphasized the importance of *nurture* or the environment, Froebel leaned toward the *nature* or maturational side of this centuries-old controversy. Like plants, children arrived in the world with some predetermined traits that the teacher in the garden for children should help to unfold. However, just as a seed of corn could not grow into a rose even with the best gardener, so the teacher could not fundamentally alter the child's inborn characteristics.

JOHN DEWEY (1859–1952)

John Dewey, the father of **progressive education**, led the American attack on traditional forms of public schooling. In the late 1800s, schools in the United States were very teacher-centred and subject-centred, and the curriculum, rather than the individual child's needs, determined what happened on any day. Harsh punishment and rote learning were the norm, and students were passive receptacles to be filled with knowledge by the teacher.

Dewey studied under G. Stanley Hall, who had introduced child study and, ultimately, developmental psychology to North America (Cairns, 1983). Clearly, public education was not geared toward the child in Dewey's and Hall's time, and they both warned parents and teachers about the negative consequences of traditional instruction (Borstelmann, 1983; Dewey, 1897, 1900, 1902). Dewey advocated that educators should use the child's interests and that education should emphasize active learning through real experiences; activity would lead to knowledge. He ran a model early childhood program at the University of Chicago, and demonstrated in his work, a child-centred approach rather than a subject-centred approach.

The principles of progressive education influenced a number of developments in early childhood education. For example, the Open Education model in Britain and some areas of Canada, which we will discuss in the next chapter, grew out of Dewey's work (e.g., Weber, 1971). The nursery school movement, with its emphasis on play and parent education, also can be traced to Dewey (Fein & Clarke-Stewart, 1973). Dewey's work also had an impact on the popularity of the programs of other educators, including Froebel and Maria Montessori (Hunt, 1968).

MARGARET MCMILLAN (1860–1931)

Margaret McMillan (1919, 1930) and her sister Rachel were born in the United States, but moved to Britain when they were children (Braun & Edwards, 1972; Gardner, 1949; Weber, 1971). Margaret became a social activist, and in the late 19th century, as a member of a school board, she became an outspoken advocate for poor children in the schools. Many children had significant medical and social problems that festered in urban slums, and although 80 percent of newborns were healthy at birth, only 20 percent of them were still healthy when they entered school at age 5. Margaret, with Rachel's assistance, set up a medical clinic in Deptford, a London slum, in 1902, and it soon expanded to include an "open-air" camp. In 1911, the McMillans opened their play-oriented, open-air nursery school. In addition to teaching self-care and hygiene, the McMillans experimented with open-air sheds. The shed was a shelter in a garden playground, and the children could wander freely from the indoors to the outdoors. Creativity was highly valued, and clay, drawing, block play, and movement were an integral part of these play-based programs.

Rachel died in 1917, but Margaret worked in nursery education until her death in 1931. Chiefly because of Margaret's ongoing advocacy, the British government agreed to fund nursery schools for 3- to 5-year-olds in 1918, but the war and the economic devastation it brought slowed their spread until the 1930s. Margaret's work also influenced developments in North America, and most of the nursery schools founded in the 1920s and 1930s were modelled after the open-air nurseries. Of course, the term "nursery school" also comes from the McMillans, and their program remains one of the first models for compensatory education programs (Gardner, 1949; McMillan, 1919, 1930; Weber, 1971).

MARIA MONTESSORI (1870–1952)

A true feminist of her time, Maria Montessori was the first woman to become a medical doctor in Italy. Her psychiatric interest led her to work with children with cognitive disabilities, who, in her era, were placed in psychiatric institutions. Montessori thought their problems were often educational more than medical, and she proved her point when a number of these institutionalized children easily passed regular school

exams after she had worked with them. In 1907, the city of Rome asked Montessori to take charge of a children's day nursery that was attached to a housing tenement for the poor. The housing authorities wanted someone who would keep the children off the stairs and prevent them from dirtying the newly painted walls. But Montessori found in this **casa dei bambini (children's house)** the opportunity to explore her teaching methods with normal children.

Montessori's methods, which we will discuss in Chapter 3, were based on the principle that young children learn in a way that is fundamentally different from how adults learn. She was particularly impressed with the great capacity of children to learn so much during the first few years of life. She called this capacity the **absorbent mind**, similar to a sponge soaking up liquid. If children's absorbent minds are exposed to appropriate learning experiences in the developmental stages, their minds will grow. This is especially true during **sensitive periods**, times when children are most receptive to absorbing specific learning.

Montessori's curriculum takes advantage of these sensitive periods by making appropriate experiences available to children at times when they are most ready to learn from them. She used the term **prepared environment** to describe this match of the right materials to children's stages of development.

Much of Montessori's philosophy and approach, particularly her **self-correcting materials** and strong sense of respect for children, have had an enduring impact on early childhood education. Whether by design in contemporary Montessori schools or by common acceptance in other programs, Montessori's influence is still strongly felt today (Braun & Edwards, 1972; Carter, 1987; Chattin-McNichols, 1992; Elkind, 1983; Gettman, 1987; Simons & Simons, 1986).

INFLUENTIAL THEORISTS OF CHILD DEVELOPMENT

Although many of the predecessors of early childhood education developed a theoretical or philosophical viewpoint about how children develop, it was not until our century that such ideas were founded on a more systematic base through observations and research. The **human development theory** is a way of describing what happens as individuals move from infancy through adulthood, identifying significant events commonly experienced by all people, and explaining why changes occur as they do. It is useful to have a grasp of different theories as you develop your own professional identity and beliefs. This not only gives you a way of assessing your personal values but offers some alternative views about how children develop and should be treated (Thomas 1990a). We will now look at an overview of just a few of the most influential developmental theorists whose ideas have contributed, directly or indirectly, to the field of early childhood education today. Separate texts and courses on development consider these theorists and others in considerably more detail, and they are invaluable for those planning a career in early childhood education.

SIGMUND FREUD (1856–1939)

Freud, the founder of **psychoanalytic theory**, proposed a way of viewing development that radically challenged many of the previously held ideas about childhood. Even if many of Freud's students and followers altered a number of his ideas, his influence on early childhood education has nonetheless been significant. Freud was the first to emphasize the importance of the early years as a foundation for later development. His work with adults who suffered psychological problems led him to the conclusion that

the roots of their ills lay in their early experiences of childhood. Today, we acknowledge the significance of the early years, although we recognize their value not just in personality formation but in all areas of development.

Freud described stages of development centred on the part of the body from which the child derives most pleasure at that time (see Exhibit 2.1). Freud's notion of stages is still considered valid by many observers.

According to Freud, all behaviour is motivated by the **pleasure principle**, a desire to maximize what is pleasant. Three facets of personality are involved in this search for pleasure.

Exhibit 2-1 ERIKSON'S AND FREUD'S DEVELOPMENTAL SEQUENCES

ERIKSON'S PSYCHOSOCIAL STAGES	FREUD'S PSYCHOSEXUAL STAGES	DEVELOPMENTAL TASK	POSITIVE INFLUENCES
Trust vs. mistrust (0–18 months)	**Oral stage** (0–18 months)	Developing trust in the world (negative outcome is suspicion)	Warm and caring caregivers, especially the primary ones
Autonomy vs. shame and doubt (18 months–3 years)	**Anal stage** (18 months–3 or 4 years)	Developing a positive sense of autonomy (negative outcome is shame, doubt, and low self-confidence)	Allow the child to be independent and to explore
Initiative vs. guilt (3–5 years)	**Phallic stage** (3 or 4 years–6 years)	Developing a positive view of one's own actions and wishes (negative outcome is guilt over own actions)	Allow the child to form own ideas, plans, and desires. Have supportive parents and caregivers.
Industry vs. inferiority (6 years–puberty)	**Latency stage** (6 years–puberty)	Developing confidence in one's own accomplishments (negative outcome is sense of inadequacy)	Parents, teachers, and caregivers who support child's efforts and do not constantly compare child to others
Identity vs. identity diffusion (adolescent years)	**Genital stage** (puberty on)	Developing a sense of identity (negative outcome is role confusion and aimlessness)	
Intimacy vs. isolation (early adulthood)		Development of close, rewarding relationships (negative outcome is flight from close ones)	
Generativity vs. stagnation (middle age)		Developing responsibilities to help others, including children (negative outcome is being self-absorbed)	
Integrity vs. despair (old age)		Developing a sense of satisfaction with one's life (negative outcome is a sense of bitterness and failure)	

1. The first is the **id**, which is dominant during the earliest years and seeks immediate pleasure in any way possible through the satisfaction of needs.

2. The **ego**, the rational part of the personality, operates on the **reality principle**, and helps the id find appropriate ways to achieve pleasure.

3. The **superego**, conscience, develops during the preschool years, and is based on the moral norms of society that are passed on by parents and other adults.

Freud maintained that the ego mediates between the id and the superego in the manner described in Exhibit 2-2.

Freud's influence on thinking about children was marked during the first half of the 20th century. He also influenced the thinking of many neo-Freudians who continue to shape our views of the young child (Douvan, 1990; Weber, 1984; Zimiles, 1982).

EXHIBIT 2-2 THE EGO MEDIATES

Three-year-old Cassie sees her classmate, Tito, riding the new tricycle that the school has just purchased.

"I WANT that trike and I WANT it now! It's bright red. It's shiny. It's faster that any other trike in the world! I WANT it!" clamours Cassie's id.

"But," whispers her superego, "you can't just grab that tricycle. Remember the rule. Tito has it so it is his until he is finished playing with it."

Having to deal with the conflicting id and superego, the ego tries to mediate: "Look, if you just grab that tricycle, you will get in trouble. Why not go to Tito and ask him if you can ride it when he is done?"

Thus, Cassie compromises. She can't have the tricycle immediately, but she will get it through conventional channels and will not suffer the consequences of breaking the school's rules.

JEAN PIAGET (1896–1980)

One of the most influential forces in early childhood education today is Jean Piaget. Piaget's **cognitive developmental theory** presents a complex picture of how children's intelligence and thinking abilities emerge. Piaget did not suggest specific educational applications of his work, but educators have transformed his theory, more than any other, into actual models.

Piaget, a biologist by training, thought cognitive development was similar to how all organisms function physiologically, adapting to and organizing the environment around them. A common example illustrates our own biological adaptation to the physical environment. If the temperature becomes too warm or too cold, we sweat or shiver to adapt. In a way similar to this physiological adaptation, we also adapt mentally to changes in the environment. At the same time that we adapt, we mentally organize what we perceive in our environment so that it makes sense to us.

In a cognitive sense, **adaptation** is involved any time new information or a new experience occurs. The person must adapt to incorporate any new information or experience into the psychological structure. When something new presents itself, however, the existing mental structure is "upset" or put into **disequilibrium** because this new information or experience does not exactly fit into the old structures. To return to balance, or **equilibrium**, adaptation takes place through the complementary processes of assimilation and accommodation. **Assimilation** occurs when the person tries to make the new information or experience fit into an existing concept or schema. **Accommodation** takes place when the schema is modified or a new concept is formed to incorporate the new information or experience. A Closer Look illustrates how these two types of adaptation operate through a group of preschoolers on a field trip to the zoo.

 A CLOSER LOOK

Assimilation and Accommodation at the Zoo

Many of the children have often visited this zoo, and they are familiar with the animals. Raymond, for example, has always enjoyed the cats and can identify the lions, tigers, leopards, lynxes, and ocelots. Before Raymond visited this time, the zoo acquired a pair of panthers, animals Raymond had not seen before. "Look!" he exclaims, "there are two black leopards!" Raymond fit the new animals into an existing mental structure that told him that the new cats were leopards of a different colour. After all, his pet cat, Fluffy, is multicoloured and his other cat, Eclipse, is black, indicating that cats of all sorts come in different colours. Raymond is using assimilation, making the new information fit into what he already knows.

For Monique, who has recently moved to the area, this is the first time she has ever visited a zoo. There are many novel experiences for her, because before her visit she had seen some wild animals only in books and on television. Seeing the llamas, Monique considers what these animals might be. They somewhat resemble horses, but she immediately dismisses this category because she knows that horses have smooth hair and shorter necks. She has seen pictures of camels, but the animals she sees now do not have humps on their backs. She finally decides that these must be animals she does not know; after all, she has seen many other new animals today. Monique goes to one of the teachers, who tells her about llamas, thus helping her in the process of accommodation, creating a new concept into which this new information can be fitted.

Organization is a process that is complementary to adaptation. While adaptation allows for new information and experiences to be incorporated into existing mental structures, organization defines how such information and experiences are related to each other. Consider a pedal. By itself it is a small, flat, rectangular item made of red plastic. However, in proper context, fitted on a tricycle, the pedal takes on an entirely different meaning as it allows the child to turn the wheels that, in turn, make the tricycle move. Organization allows us to expand the visual cues about the pedal to include information about its function as part of a whole.

Piaget called the cognitive structures into which we adapt and organize our environment **schemata** (schema is the singular form). Schemata are concepts or mental representations of experiences that we constantly create, refine, and reorganize. One popular analogy of schemata is an index card file. Babies are born with only a few "index cards," but, with experience, they create new cards and "dividers" as their store of information becomes more complex. As a **stage theorist**, Piaget conceived of qualitatively different characteristics and accomplishments in cognitive ability during the four stages of development shown in Exhibit 2-3. Each stage is built on and incorporates the accomplishments of the previous one. **Maturation**, which interacts with experiences to determine the course of development, sets limits on when children are capable of achieving specific cognitive abilities. (You might note that Piaget acknowledges

EXHIBIT 2-3 PIAGET'S PERIODS OF COGNITIVE DEVELOPMENT

STAGE 1: **Sensorimotor Period** (0–2 years)

The first period is characterized by motor behaviour through which schemata are formed. The child does not yet represent events mentally but relies on coordination of senses and movement, on **object permanence** development, on learning to differentiate means from ends, and on beginning to understand the relationship of objects in space in order to learn about the environment.

STAGE 2: **Preoperational Period** (2–7 years)

Language and other forms of representation develop during this period, although thinking is not yet logical. Children's internal mental representations, which allow them to think of objects even if these are not physically present, is the major accomplishment of this period. Children have an egocentric view of the world, in terms of their own perspective. Early classification, seriation, and role play begin.

STAGE 3: **Concrete Operations Period** (7–11 years)

The child has internalized some physical tasks or operations and no longer depends only on what is visible, but can apply logic to solving problems. The child is now able to reverse operations (for instance, $5 - 3 = 2$ is the same as $3 + 2 = 5$). The child can also practise **conservation**—recognize that an object does not change in amount even if its physical appearance changes (stretching a ball of clay into a snake).

STAGE 4: **Formal Operations Period** (11–15 years)

The final period, rare even in adults, is characterized by sophisticated, abstract thinking and logical reasoning abilities applied to physical as well as social and moral problems.

the importance of experience as well as maturational factors, in contrast to other theorists who undermine the role of experience.)

Thus, the infant, dependent on movement and the senses, learns through those avenues. By age 2, however, there emerges the ability to engage in **representation** of objects. This ability opens up a world of new possibilities, but this age group is still limited by the observable characteristics of objects. Reasoning is not yet logical, although by about age 7 children begin to apply **logical thinking** to concrete problems. Finally, by adolescence, the young person may be able to apply logic and **abstract thinking** to a wide range of problems.

Early childhood teachers are concerned primarily with children in the preoperational period, but they need to be aware of developments in preceding and subsequent periods. An understanding of the characteristics, abilities, and limits of young children is vital to appropriate teaching (Ginsburg & Opper, 1969; Lavatelli, 1970; Piaget, 1983; Saunders & Bingham-Newman, 1984; Thomas, 1990a, 1990b; Tribe, 1982; Wadsworth, 1984).

J.B. WATSON (1878–1958)

Many of the theorists and educators we have considered to this point believed that there is an inborn plan according to which children develop. Rousseau, Pestalozzi, Froebel, and Montessori all felt that, given an appropriate environment and understanding adults, children would develop according to nature's plan into healthy, responsible, intelligent adults. Freud and Piaget likewise believed that development is predetermined and will follow the same stages in each person. John Locke, on the other hand, strongly disagreed with the maturational or growing plants view of development. In this sense, Locke could be seen as the forerunner of **behaviourism**. Locke maintained that children were like blank slates at birth, and that their experiences would determine their development. The behaviourists of the 20th century would agree with Locke; they maintain that children are shaped by external, environmental forces, rather than internal ones.

The father of behaviourism was John Broadus Watson, an American psychologist, who "shook the house of psychology to its foundations" (Kessen, 1965, p. 228) between 1913 and 1920 with his behavioural theory (Watson, 1925a, 1925b, 1928). At that time, psychology emphasized the contents of the mind, and the introspective method was considered the appropriate way to study the mind. Watson maintained that results based on the introspective method were unreliable, especially in the study of young children and animals. He argued that the observation of behaviour was the correct way to gather information; the effect of his theory was that psychology changed from a discipline that studied the mind using introspective methods to one that studied **observable behaviours** and responses.

Watson used the techniques of **classical conditioning** to study fear in young children; today, however, many of his studies are seen as unethical (Kaplan, 1991). For example, in his famous (but now infamous) studies of Albert, a 9-month-old baby in hospital, he and a colleague (Watson & Rayner, 1920) conditioned Albert to fear rats by showing him a rat and following that with a loud noise. Albert eventually began to fear all furry objects. Watson did not decondition him even though he knew a month in advance that Albert would be leaving hospital. The success that Watson and his followers had in changing children's behaviour in such studies led them to argue that development was environmentally determined, and parents had an important role to play.

B.F. SKINNER (1904–1990)

Certainly, Watson's view of development emphasizes the importance of early experience and education, and some of his followers have applied behaviourist principles to parenting and teaching. B.F. Skinner, the most famous of Watson's followers, both popularized and extended behaviourism so that it was the dominant force in psychol-ogy until at least the 1980s. Skinner's writings and those of his many followers have had a widespread influence on all aspects of education, including the early childhood years. The application of his theoretical and experimental work can be seen in **behaviour modification**, which operates on the underlying principle that behaviour can be changed or modified by manipulating the environment, which includes both physical and social components.

Skinner emphasized that almost all behaviours are learned through experience and can be increased or decreased in frequency as a function of what follows them. In other words, if something pleasant or enjoyable consistently happens after the child engages in a specific behaviour (the teacher smiles when Jeremy helps to put away the blocks), he is likely to repeat that behaviour. Conversely, if something unpleasant or painful follows a behaviour (Larissa burns her finger when she touches the stove), she is likely not to repeat it. Deliberately attempting to increase or decrease behaviour by controlling consequences is called **operant conditioning**.

Skinner used the term **reinforcement** to describe the *immediate consequence of behaviour* that is likely to strengthen it. Reinforcement can be either positive or negative: positive reinforcement entails providing something rewarding for the behaviour, while negative reinforcement entails the removal of something unpleasant or aversive.

Whether consciously using the behavioural approach or not, early childhood educators frequently use **positive reinforcement** because of its powerful effect on children's behaviour. For example, teachers of young children are most likely to use **social reinforcers**—for instance, a smile, a hug, attention, or involvement—when they see a child engaging in a behaviour they consider desirable. Teachers may also provide **negative reinforcement**; for example, if Don Lon is hitting Rana, and the teacher intervenes at Rana's request, Rana would be reinforced for the behaviour, assuming that Don Lon stopped hitting once the teacher intervened. Reinforcement of both types is a very effective way of controlling behaviour.

Punishment, an unpleasant or aversive consequence that *immediately* follows a behaviour is likely to weaken that behaviour. According to Skinner (and almost all early childhood professionals), punishment is not a very effective way of controlling behaviour. Like reinforcement, punishment can be either positive or negative. As with reinforcement, positive punishment entails adding an unpleasant stimulus, while negative punishment entails the removal of a pleasant one. Assuming that Don Lon in the above example likes to be with other children, the teacher would be using **negative punishment** if she removed him from the group for hitting. Alternatively, if Rana had hit him back, she would have been giving **positive punishment** for his behaviour (and then the teacher would have a greater challenge). Exhibit 2-4 summarizes Skinner's view of positive and negative reinforcement and punishment.

In addition, other techniques such as systematic attention to behaviour and its consequences can be used to encourage new behaviours or eliminate undesirable ones. However, we will leave discussion of these units until we consider children's behaviour. Teachers in many programs frequently use a number of behavioural techniques, even if they do not strictly adhere to behaviour theory (Braun & Edwards, 1972; Bushell, 1982; Neisworth & Buggey, 1993; Peters, Neisworth, & Yawkey, 1985; Sameroff, 1983; Skinner, 1969, 1974; Weber, 1984).

Exhibit 2-4 SKINNER'S VIEW OF REINFORCEMENT AND PUNISHMENT

	POSITIVE (+ FOR ADDING)	NEGATIVE (– FOR REMOVING)
Reinforcement—strengthens frequency of the behaviour	Add something pleasant (e.g., candy, smile, praise, etc.)	Remove something unpleasant (e.g., hitting child, etc.)
Punishment—reduces frequency of the behaviour	Add something unpleasant (e.g., hitting, etc.)	Remove something pleasant (e.g., candy, friends, praise, etc.)

ARNOLD GESELL (1880–1961)

Gesell, like John Dewey, was a student of G. Stanley Hall, and has had a major influence on early childhood education as well as developmental psychology in the 20th century (Cairns, 1983). Gesell initially worked in the field of education, and then returned to school in the middle of his career to pursue a degree in medicine at Yale. In 1911, after completing his M.D., he founded the Gesell Institute, a child study institute that still exists at Yale, where he worked until his death. Unlike Dewey, Gesell (and Montessori) accepted Hall's view that development is predetermined and that intelligence is fixed (Hunt, 1968). However, by Gesell's time that notion had been altered somewhat, and Gesell used the term *maturation* to describe how children unfold in predetermined patterns.

Gesell studied the regularities in children's development for over 40 years, often with the assistance of his colleagues, Francis Ilg and Louise Bates Ames. They observed large numbers of children and studied their motor and language development, as well as their adaptive behaviours and personal-social skills. They recorded their observations of each child, and averaged them for each age group so that they could present an overview of the typical child at different age levels. In 1928, Gesell published *Infancy and Human Growth*, a report on growth in infants, and by his death he had studied children through to 10 years of age. The overviews of infants and children at different ages, outlined in Chapter 5, follow Gesell's approach, and are referred to as **norms**. Gesell found the norms to be so orderly that, in the same year Watson wrote his polemic on early stimulation, he wrote about "the inevitableness and surety of maturation" (1928, p. 378).

The growth of the nursery school movement in the 1920s was partly the result of Gesell's emphasis on the importance of the early years as "biologically the most important period in the development of the individual" (1923, p. 3). Moreover, Gesell's child study institute as well as the University of Iowa's Child Welfare Research Station and their laboratory schools became models for other institutes that were established in Canada and the United States in the 1920s and 1930s. As noted above, the Institute for Child Study, founded in 1925, was the first Canadian centre, but child study was soon a focus in a number of centres across the country—in Montreal, Saskatoon, and Winnipeg, for example (Northway, 1973). Advanced degrees in the study of early childhood became available at these institutes, and many of the professionals who have shaped the field in Canada as well as the United States were trained in these facilities (Northway, 1973).

Other lasting contributions of Gesell include the perhaps archaic, but persistent notion of school readiness. With his belief that maturation is predictable and orderly, Gesell discouraged parents and teachers from interfering with a child's development in most areas. According to him, only social development was subject to environmental influences, and as a consequence, most early childhood programs from the 1920s until the 1960s emphasized social growth and did not tamper with or try to stimulate growth in the other spheres of development. If a child did not seem ready for a program (kindergarten, for example), the child was kept home for an additional year of unfolding, rather than given stimulation to encourage development in the areas where there was a lag.

ERIK ERIKSON (1902–)

One of Freud's followers, Erik Erikson, modified and refined Freud's stages of development with **psychosocial theory** in a way that is much more acceptable to us today. Like Freud, Erikson sees each stage defined by conflict, but he sees such conflict as healthy, resulting in opportunities for personal growth. Each stage and its attendant conflict are centred not just on the person alone but also on his or her relationships with others. Although Freud's five stages ended with adolescence, Erikson's theory includes eight stages that span infancy through adulthood. Erikson believes these stages, which are summarized in Exhibit 2-1, occur in all human beings in the described sequence at the time in life when their emergence is most critical. The first four stages are particularly important to early childhood education because they describe significant tasks that occur in the young child's life. Stages occur at critical times in development, but never completely disappear. Thus, trust is still important beyond infancy; children continue to struggle with the balance between autonomy and dependency; and initiative and industry are relevant even beyond the early years, though in a more mature form. Erikson emphasizes the importance of play in meeting the tasks of autonomy and initiative during the preschool years. Erikson's stages highlight some of the important issues for young children and the balance we must provide to help them achieve healthy development (Erikson, 1963; Maier, 1965, 1990; Tribe, 1982; Weber, 1984).

INFLUENTIAL EVENTS IN EARLY CHILDHOOD EDUCATION

With the exception of the flurry of activity during World War II, there was little change in early childhood education from the 1920s until the 1960s. Dewey and Hall's emphasis on child-centred programs became popular, and criticisms of the teacher-centred approach of Froebel led to the demise of his model in North America. Similarly, Montessori programs, which were popular in the United States between 1910 and 1918, were attacked by William Heard Kilpatrick in his 1914 work, *The Montessori System Examined.* Kilpatrick was a lecturer at Teachers College in New York, where he was known as "the million-dollar professor" (Hunt, 1968, p. 108). Kilpatrick was an ardent follower of Dewey, and was "compelled to say that in the content of her [Montessori's] doctrine, she belongs to the mid-nineteenth century, some fifty years

behind the present development of educational theory" (Kilpatrick, 1914, pp. 62–63). Kilpatrick's work was circulated widely to both students and educators, and led to the demise of Montessori programs until the 1960s.

Gesell's emphasis on maturation seemed to govern thinking about education in the early years until the 1960s: there was little to do with young children other than wait for them to unfold, except in the area of social development. Thus, most early childhood programs, which were patronized by middle-class families, emphasized social growth and avoided interfering with cognitive development. Allowing the child to flourish in a supportive environment was sufficient. While day care centres were available, they had a welfare orientation (except during the war) and were a service to those families who needed daytime care for their children (Young, 1981).

During the late 1940s and throughout the 1950s, there was strong pressure on families to have the mother stay at home with children, at least until they were 3 years of age. Studies of infants and young children who were reared in orphanages where there was little human contact and virtually no stimulation had repeatedly found significant delays in the development of these unfortunate youngsters (Skeels, 1966; Spitz, 1945). Moreover, these problems persisted through adolescence when personality problems also were apparent (Goldfarb, 1943). These studies culminated in John Bowlby's now classic 1951 monograph, *Maternal Care and Mental Health*. Bowlby, after reviewing the orphanage studies, concluded that the best environment for a child, at least until age 3, was at home with his or her mother or permanent mother substitute. While this guiding principle was accepted in the 1950s, partly because it was consistent with the social and political climate of the times, it was quickly debunked in the 1960s (Caldwell 1968, 1971, 1973a, 1973b). At that time, many researchers (Casler, 1961; Yarrow, 1961) realized that the sensory deprivation experienced by institutionalized infants and children bore no resemblance to short-term intermittent separations from a mother.

SPUTNIK AND EDUCATIONAL UPHEAVAL

In 1957, the Russians launched the first space missile, *Sputnik*. The success of the Soviet space program and, conversely, the failure of the Americans to be the first in space also launched an attack on the school system in the United States that soon filtered up to Canada. Outmoded teaching techniques, dull curricula, and too little emphasis on the sciences were seen as part of the reason the Americans lagged behind the Russians. The U.S. civil rights movement in the 1950s and 1960s spawned further examinations of the school system. The schools were seen to be failing the middle classes and not producing the desired rocket scientists; poor children did worse in school than their middle-class counterparts; and black children in the U.S. South were the poorest in terms of their educational accomplishments (see Coleman, 1966; Riessman, 1962). While the school system could be held accountable for the performance of children of poor families, marked differences between poor children and their more advantaged peers were found at the time of school entry. These latter differences pointed to the importance of experience in the preschool years.

RESEARCH AND THE REDISCOVERY OF THE EARLY CHILDHOOD YEARS

A number of important advances in psychological knowledge, which were critical for our understanding of the early childhood years, also occurred shortly after *Sputnik* was launched. Interestingly, these new psychological understandings were remarkably in tune with the political and educational pressures of the time. Perhaps the most important psychological advance was the replacement of the maturational view of development with the interactional view, which said that development is determined by both environmental and genetic factors. J. McVicker Hunt, in his 1961 book, *Intelligence and Experience*, systematically presented evidence from studies showing the relationship between experience and development in humans and animals. (Much of the research Hunt discussed had been completed at Canadian universities, especially at McGill where Donald Hebb and his students studied the effects of early experience on the neural development and behaviour of animals.) Hunt concluded that "the assumption that intelligence is fixed and that its development is predetermined by the genes [was] no longer tenable" (p. 342).

The early childhood years were identified as the period when intelligence was most susceptible to the effects of experience. Benjamin Bloom reviewed a number of longitudinal studies of intelligence in his 1964 text, *Stability and Change in Human Characteristics*, and concluded that "marked changes in the environment in the early years can produce greater changes in intelligence than will equally marked changes in the environment at later periods of development" (pp. 88–89). The work of Bloom and Hunt clearly had different implications for early childhood educators than did Gesell's maturational theory.

Another advance in psychological knowledge of children was North America's belated discovery of Piaget's extensive investigations into the origins of intelligence in the young child. An eminent Canadian psychologist with a behaviourist background, Dr. Daniel Berlyne, from the University of Toronto, can be credited with helping North America to discover Piaget (Rowland & McGuire, 1968). Piaget's work had been ignored in North America for two reasons: (1) His clinical method was unorthodox in the hey-day of behaviourism, and (2) "the lack of adequate translations into English of his elegant but difficult French" (Rowland & McGuire, 1968, p. 145) meant that his works were unavailable to the English-speaking world. Berlyne was among the first to recognize the severity of this problem and act upon it.

In 1950, Berlyne, in collaboration with M. Piercy, translated Piaget's *Psychology of Intelligence* into English. In that book, Piaget outlined his theory of mental development. Berlyne spent time with Piaget in Geneva and continued to disseminate Piaget's thinking in North America and to integrate it into his own work. The post-*Sputnik* discovery of Piaget forced psychologists like Burton White (1968) and educators to realize that "if we pay little attention to the events occurring in the first years of life, much of the story may be over by the time we begin to 'educate' the child, even if we start as early as age 3, let alone age 6" (145).

A third factor that influenced North Americans' view of the young child in the 1960s was, in Ira Gordon's (1967) somewhat satirical words, the "rediscovery in sociology that language learning begins in the home" (p. 20). The theoretical work of Basil Bernstein in England indicated that social class had a profound effect on the type of language and the cognitive style ultimately developed. Bernstein's work emphasized the significance of language learning in the early years and spawned considerable North American research in this area (e.g., Hess & Shipman 1965a, 1965b, 1968).

The "rediscovery" of infancy and early childhood created a new series of challenges, at least for politicians, educators, psychologists, and sociologists, if not for society at large. Gordon (1968) summarized the challenge:

> Our old norms are shaken. ... Our present theory of the child as competent, as active, as individual ... requires that we intervene, that we do something during this period. ... We cannot sit idly by and let [the child] flower, because he [she] will not. We have to find and define the optimum environment and then we have to convince our public that it needs to provide it (p. 20).

Now that you have some appreciation for the historical roots of early childhood education, we will examine some current program models that have been used in the past century. Several of the program models described in Chapter 3 were developed in response to the challenges Gordon summarizes above, while others, like Montessori's model and Open Education, were rediscovered and refined in response to these same challenges.

KEY TERMS

absorbent mind

abstract thinking

accommodation

adaptation

anal stage

assimilation

autonomy vs. shame
  and doubt

behaviourism

behaviour modification

casa dei bambini (chil-
  dren's house)

child-centred approach

child study movement

classical conditioning

cognitive developmental
  theory

concrete operations
  period

conservation

disequilibrium

ego

equilibrium

formal operations
  period

genital stage

human development
  theory

id

industry vs. inferiority

infant school

initiative vs. guilt

interactionist

kindergarten

latency stage

logical thinking

maturation

nature

negative punishment

negative reinforcement

norms

nurture

object permanence

observable behaviour

operant conditioning

KEY POINTS OF CHAPTER 2

A LOOK BACK—CHILDREN THROUGH TIME

▲ 1. Interest in the education and care of young children can be traced back to ancient Greece, but attitudes toward education and child care practices have changed many times over the centuries.

VIEWS OF CHILDREN

▲ 2. The concept of childhood and treatment of children through history has always been tied to economic, religious, and social factors. During the 20th century, the view of early childhood as an important part of human development was particularly promoted.

INFLUENTIAL PEOPLE IN THE HISTORY OF EARLY CHILDHOOD EDUCATION

▲ 3. Luther was an advocate of universal education. Comenius extended Luther's ideas so that universal education would include the very young. John Locke maintained that the very young were like empty slates, so the quality of early experience became critical. Robert Owen, his follower, founded the first infant school in Scotland in 1816.

▲ 4. Rousseau advanced the notions that children are innately noble and good, that their way of learning is different from that of adults, and that they should be removed from the corrupting influences of society.

▲ 5. Pestalozzi believed that young children learned actively, from concrete experiences, a philosophy he implemented in the schools he established.

▲ 6. Froebel, who is credited with beginning the kindergarten, placed great emphasis on the importance of play.

▲ 7. John Dewey, the father of progressive education, emphasized child-centred methods in democratic schools.

▲ 8. The McMillan sisters founded the first open-air nurseries that gave rise to the British infant nursery schools and infant schools.

▲ 9. Montessori, working with slum children in Rome, developed a successful method of early education that is still widely followed today.

INFLUENTIAL THEORISTS OF CHILD DEVELOPMENT

▲10. Freud's psychoanalytic theory places great importance on the early years. He proposed a structure of personality in which conscious and unconscious elements operate to balance the child's continual goal of maximizing pleasure.

▲11. Piaget's cognitive developmental theory, one of the most influential in early childhood education, describes how children's thinking is unique in each of four stages.

▲12. Watson and Skinner, two important proponents of behavioural theory, emphasized that almost all behaviour is learned and can be increased by positive consequences and decreased by negative consequences.

oral stage
organization
phallic stage
pleasure principal
positive punishment
positive reinforcement
preoperational period
prepared environment
progressive education
psychoanalytic theory
psychosocial theory
punishment
reality principle
reinforcement
representation
schemata
school readiness
self-correcting material
sensitive periods
sensorimotor period
social reinforcer
stage theorist
superego
trust vs. mistrust

▲13. Gesell, a maturationist, was the father of normative psychology and the child-study movement.

▲14. Erikson refined Freud's theory and proposed eight stages of psychosocial development.

INFLUENTIAL EVENTS IN EARLY CHILDHOOD EDUCATION

▲15. *Sputnik* unleashed a chain of political and social events that led to a dramatic rise in both research and interest in the early childhood years during the 1960s.

KEY QUESTIONS

1. Historic events have a great impact on our view of children and how we treat them. What social and political events have taken place during your life that have had an impact on young children and their education? Also ask this question of a relative or friend who was born in an earlier era.

2. What was your earliest school experience? How does it compare with the type of programs you see for young children today?

3. Observe an early childhood program. What evidence do you see of the influence of one or more theorists, for instance, Piaget, Erikson, or the behaviourists? Ask one of the teachers if he or she draws on any particular human development theories and compare them with your observations.

4. Observe a Montessori school in your community. How does it differ from other early childhood programs you have seen? How is it similar? What elements of Maria Montessori's original program do you see?

5. Read Spitz's or Skeels's accounts of the orphans they studied during the 1930s and 1940s. What changes would you make to the institutions if you were the director? Design a compensatory early childhood education program for the orphans.

EARLY CHILDHOOD EDUCATION PROGRAM MODELS

How we approach the education and care of young children depends, to a great extent, on what we believe children are like. Programs for preschoolers are often structured around some underlying assumptions about the nature of children. For instance, a belief that children learn actively by exploring their environment would result in a different type of early education program than one based on the idea that children learn passively by being taught specific information and skills. Similarly, a belief that children are basically unruly and need strict control would result in a different approach than the notion that children generally strive toward social acceptance.

A number of **early childhood education program models** founded on particular theoretical perspectives have emerged over the years. These program models describe typical goals, materials, roles, and schedules, and they often specify a particular theoretical stance (e.g., behaviourist, maturationist, etc.). We will consider some of these models in this chapter when exploring the following questions:

1. What theories of development have been applied to the development of early childhood education programs and what are some of the models that have evolved? We will examine five of these models:

   - Montessori programs
   - Open Education
   - Project Head Start
   - Cognitively Oriented Curriculum
   - Bereiter-Engelmann model

   These models differ in a number of ways, including their view of development. As you study the models, try to determine if they have a *nature*, *nurture*, or *interactionist orientation*, and see which theories of development you would associate with them.

2. What does the research tell us about the effectiveness of these models? We will examine the available research on these models, as well as the research on programs that follow an **eclectic model.** These eclectic programs have selected ideas and practices from different models, and blended them into a composite program.

APPLICATION OF THEORIES IN EARLY CHILDHOOD EDUCATION

Theories of human development are important to early childhood education when they influence program practices and methods. This has happened over the years as a number of early childhood education program models, founded on a particular theoretical view, were developed. Such models represent a coherent approach to working with young children, and they may specify a philosophical and theoretical base, goals, instructional practices, methods, and materials. In some cases, models also are quite specific about the role of teachers, children, and parents in the program, while others are less rigid.

There was a great proliferation of early childhood models in the 1960s and 1970s when educators and researchers were encouraged (and funded) to develop alternative approaches for Head Start programs. Most of these models were designed to examine different ways of helping children, at risk for later academic failure, to improve school performance. But the research on these models has implications for all children (Evans, 1982).

Roopnarine and Johnson (1993) have described fourteen early childhood education models, including home-based and centre-based ones. The centre-based models could be placed in one of three categories: (1) Montessori models, (2) behaviourist models, and (3) interactionist models. We should not, however, assume that all early childhood programs conform to one of these carefully prescribed views. Quite frequently, programs are very eclectic in their approach. In fact, if you asked a number of teachers in early childhood programs to describe their program's philosophical foundations, you would likely find that many adhere only to a vaguely recognized theory.

Nevertheless, it is beneficial to examine how some specific models have taken the views of a particular theorist (or theorists) and transformed these into program application. We will examine only five models here, although many alternative approaches exist. These five were selected to illustrate how particular views of child development can be implemented in practice. Included will be a brief overview of Montessori programs as they exist today. We will also consider the Open Education approach, which is derived from the works of Dewey and Freud among others and was developed first in the British infant schools. The U.S. Project Head Start has been influential and has led to the development of several alternative models, so it merits discussion. The Cognitively Oriented Curriculum (COC), based, in part, on Piaget's principles, and developed as a variant of Project Head Start, also is included. We will also consider a behaviourist model, the Bereiter-Engelmann model, which also was developed in the 1960s. Betty Exelby describes the more eclectic Reggio Emilia curriculum in the Canadian Professional Speaks Out section.

   # A CANADIAN PROFESSIONAL SPEAKS OUT

The Reggio Emilia Approach

In Reggio Emilia, northern Italy, there exists a comprehensive and exceptional program of child care services (13 infant/toddler and 22 preschool programs). In this approach to child care, children are viewed as rich, powerful, full of the desire to learn, and able to construct their own knowledge. Children's interests direct program content and time-lines. Teachers are dedicated observers/recorders, analyzers, researchers, and a resource for children and parents.

Extensive observation notes, audio and video tapes, slides, photographs, albums, the children's creative efforts, and statements of explanation are referred to as *documentations.* These are reviewed to better understand the children's experience and learning path, and are aesthetically prepared and strategically positioned throughout the centre to be visited and revisited by children, teachers, and parents. From this process new discoveries emerge.

An emphasis on experiences in the arts and symbolic representations permit self-expression, observable learning, and further explorations. Short- and long-term projects in small or large groups of children are explored. Other daily activities are similar to those in most programs.

Pairs of teachers work with a group of children for a three-year period. The result is a secure, stable environment with close parent–teacher relationships and extensive parent involvement.

The Reggio centres have an astonishing visual appeal and are warm and welcoming. Attention is paid to aesthetics. Displays of children's works and teacher documentation are everywhere, bathed in natural and artificial light. All areas are furnished and equipped creatively, economically, and with loving attention to detail. The environment is affectionately viewed as the "third teacher."

Teachers meet frequently to discuss and be challenged by their documentation and that of others. In this collegial atmosphere the curriculum is co-constructed with an educational coordinator acting as mentor and facilitator.

Play space is augmented by a central workshop where materials of every type are stored attractively, even in glass containers. An artist-in-residence assists children and teachers in their explorations. The workshop is home for project development and is completed according to the child's time-line and needs.

Scholars and educators the world over have come to Reggio Emilia and have experienced professional admiration, envy, and awe. Their interest and determination to revisit, compare, question, contemplate, review, integrate and/or disregard Reggio's program characteristics and components will bring unique changes to their own schools and their efforts to create developmentally appropriate programs.

Bibliography

Benham, H. (1992). Reggio Emilia: The power and value of the child. *Scholastic, Pre-K Today* 7(2):5.

Department of Early Education, City of Reggio Emilia (1987). *The hundred languages of children.* Catalogue of the exhibit. U.S. distributor: Pamela Houk, Dayton Art Institute, P.O. Box 941, Dayton, Ohio, 45401.

Edwards, C.P., L. Gandini, and G.E. Forman, eds. (1993). *The hundred languages of children: The Reggio Emilia approach to early childhood education.* Norwood, NJ: Ablex.

Gandini, L. (1984). Not just anywhere: Making child care centers into "particular" places. *Child Care Information Exchange* 78 (1991):5–9.

Gandini, L. (1988). Early childhood integration of the visual arts. *Gifted International* 5 (2):14–18.

Katz, Lilian G. (1990). Impressions of Reggio Emilia preschools. *Young Children 45* (6):11–12.

LeeKeenan, D., and C.P. Edwards (1992). Using the project approach with toddlers. *Young Children 47*(4).

New, R. (1990). Excellent early education: A city in Italy has it. *Young Children 45*(6).

Newsweek (1991). The 10 best schools in the world, and what we can learn from them. December 2.

Scholastic, Pre-K Today (1992). Reggio Emilia: A model of creativity. *7* (2): 81–84.

Video

City of Reggio Emilia (1987). *To make the portrait of a lion.* Early Childhood Educational Exchange C/O Pat Corsaro, 12 Walker Rd. #10, North Andover, MA 01845.

The long jump: a video analysis of a small group project at school in Reggio Emilia, Italy. Performance Press, 19 The Hollow, Amherest, MA 01002.

Newsletter

Innovations in Early Education: The International Reggio Exchange.

The Merrill Palmer-Institute, 71A East Ferry Ave., Detroit, MI 48202.

Betty Exelby
Loyalist College
Belleville, Ontario

For each model, we will describe the environment, the children and teachers, the role of parents, and the materials and curriculum. Then, after reviewing the models, we will discuss the available research on these five models and several eclectic ones.

MONTESSORI PROGRAMS

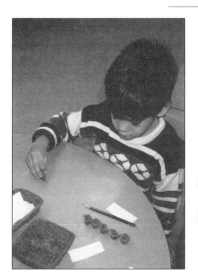

Maria Montessori's ideas and methods found a receptive audience in the 1920s in the United States, where Montessori programs briefly flourished (Hunt, 1968). In the 1960s, when early childhood programs were multiplying rapidly, Montessori was "rediscovered," and programs based on her model proliferated (Chattin-McNichols, 1992; Hunt, 1968; Spitz, 1986). Many of the programs established in the 1960s still exist in the 1990s, and, in some communities, many additional ones have also been established.

Montessori might best be considered as an eclectic, rather than a human development theorist per se. Her model was based on some carefully considered ideas about how young children learn and a clearly articulated philosophy of education. Montessori maintained that children were inherently good and insisted that **respect for the child** was the cornerstone of successful educational programs. Her ongoing belief in the goodness of the child can be traced to Rousseau, but her emphasis on the vital importance of early experience—and her attempts to teach those who had been labelled as "idiots"—place her clearly in the Lockian tradition. The heavy emphasis on **sensory education** in Montessori's program stems from her fascination with Jean-Marc-Gaspard Itard's work with a **feral child**, the so-called wild boy of Aveyron. (*Feral children* are children who, lost or abandoned by their parents, were thought to have been reared by animals in the wild.) She also studied the work of Edouard Séguin, a disciple of Itard. She visited his programs for "idiots" in London and Paris, and, feeling the need for a period of quiet meditation, translated over 1000 pages of Itard's and Séguin's works into Italian so she could "weigh the sense of each word, and ... read the *spirit* of the author" (Montessori, 1965, p. 41). Some of her materials were adapted from Séguin, but she developed many on her own. Her philosophy of education was unique.

Montessori, like Piaget, maintained that children's thinking was different from adult's, and she saw the years from 0 to 6 as critical for development. During those years, children had an *absorbent mind* that allowed them to learn without direct instruction. Between 3 and 6 years, children were in *a sensitive period*, a period when they were especially receptive to learning certain things—language skills, for example. Montessori maintained that children learn best in *a prepared environment*. The teacher's role is to prepare the environment by selecting and arranging materials that will interest children. Then, the process of **self-education** or **auto-education** will occur; that is, the child will educate herself or himself by activity in the prepared environment.

Today, a wide range of Montessori programs can be found. Some adhere quite rigidly to the original techniques, whereas others follow an approach that has been adapted to better fit the current social context (Chattin-McNichols, 1992). It is interesting to note that although Montessori devised her program to meet the needs of impoverished children and to help them learn important life skills, Montessori programs today are, for the most part, attended by children from more affluent homes.

The Environment

If you visit a traditional Montessori classroom, you will soon observe some of the prominent features of such a program, some similar to other types of early childhood settings, some unique to Montessori. You will quickly notice the sense of order inherent in the room. In addition, you may find the noise level in the class to be quite low, relative to programs like the Cognitively Oriented Curriculum described below.

You will not see a teacher's desk at the front of the classroom and rows of desks for the children. While this is not surprising in the 1990s, it was highly unusual (and threatening for some) when Montessori originated her program at the turn of the century. Child-sized equipment and movable furniture was even more unusual in her time, but Montessori saw it as a sign of respect for the child. Child-sized, movable furniture, rather than fixed rows of desks, are now in every early childhood program, and this is part of Montessori's legacy. The materials are clearly organized on shelves that are easily accessible to the children. There are distinct areas, each containing materials unique to promoting the tasks to be mastered in that area. The environment is also set up to be aesthetically pleasing, with plants, flowers, and attractive furnishings and materials. The logic, order, and beauty are all integral to the Montessori philosophy.

The Children

You will also note that children of different ages, mostly from affluent homes, are involved in individual activities, as Montessori believed in multi-age groupings in classrooms. Generally, Montessori programs are designed to include children who span at least a three-year age-spread. Typically, children from 2 1/2 or 3 to 5 years of age are found in one classroom, while the 6- to 9-year-old children would be in another class. The individualized nature of the Montessori program also will be apparent to you on your visit. Children initiate activities and are free to engage in whatever projects they choose, defining a work space for their selected activity on a mat on the floor or a tabletop. Children are self-directed, and the younger ones usually work independently, although, at times, you will see them working in pairs or small groups. Younger children may be learning how to participate in specific activities by observing and imitating their older classmates.

The Teachers

There appears to be little adult control in a Montessori class. The teacher's involvement is unobtrusive and quiet. In fact, Montessori saw the teacher as a **director** of activities, and in many programs the teachers are known by that term. You are unlikely to see a Montessori teacher leading a large group activity or lesson. However, you probably would see the teacher both observing children carefully and demonstrating the use of materials to children who have not used them before. The teacher does not reinforce or praise children for their work since the activities are intended to be self-rewarding and *intrinsically motivating*, so the children do not have to be persuaded or cajoled to use them.

Montessori teachers usually learn about the methods and curriculum through an intensive course of study after they have completed a first degree. However, some postsecondary school programs are available too. The teacher education programs are usually supervised by either the American Montessori Society (AMS) or the Association for Montessori Internationale (AMI).

The Parents

Parents are rarely involved in more traditional Montessori programs as classroom helpers. While they may visit in some classes, generally they are asked to sit and be *unobtrusive observers*. In responding to criticisms about the lack of parent involvement in Montessori programs, Chattin-McNichols (1992) comments: "Some parents can't seem to resist walking around, following their child, or *even interrupting other children* to ask them about their work, praise them, or pat their heads. Needless to say, this is not welcomed by Montessori teachers" (p. 20; italics added).

The Schedule

Most Montessori programs allow periods of time for indoor and outdoor activities and for snacks. However, the focus is on the individual versus the group, and group "lessons" would not occur every day. Rather, in this child-centred program, children

determine when they will use the different materials, and they may have five- to ten-minute group times one or two times a week.

The Materials

As you look more closely at the materials, you will see that they have some special characteristics. Montessori materials are *didactic*, each designed to teach a specific lesson. In addition, they are *self-correcting* so the child gets immediate feedback from the material after correctly (or incorrectly) completing a task. Materials are graduated from the simple to the more complex; therefore, children are challenged by progressively more difficult concepts. The materials are carefully and attractively constructed, usually made of natural materials such as varnished wood.

The Curriculum

Different materials fit into each of the three distinct areas of the curriculum. When children first enter a Montessori program, they are introduced to the **daily living** component, in which practical activities are emphasized. Such activities focus on self-help and environmental care skills such as buttoning, brushing hair, watering plants, washing windows, and sweeping.

The second set of activities and materials are **sensorial**, helping children develop, organize, broaden, and refine sensory perceptions of sight, sound, touch, smell, and taste. To foster visual discrimination, for instance, children use the **pink tower**, ten cubes increasing in regular increments of one centimetre, stacked from largest to smallest. A more complex visual discrimination task is involved with the set of **colour tablets**, which require the child to arrange hues of one colour from the darkest to the lightest; an even more advanced task might require the child to find the second darkest hue of each of the seven graded colours when all of the tablets are placed out at random. Other children might be using materials that are designed to encourage auditory discrimination. The **sound boxes**, for example, consist of two sets of cylindrical boxes that are filled with materials like salt and rice, and children match the boxes on the basis of the sounds they make. Similarly, the **tonal bells**, two sets of bells that vary only in colour, are matched by sound. In addition to being self-correcting, **isolation of a single quality** also is a characteristic of the sensorial materials; they vary in tone, colour, or size, for example, but not on all three dimensions, and this allows the child to use the materials with minimal adult assistance.

The third aspect of the program involves **conceptual** or **academic materials**. The practical and sensorial skills learned in the first two areas have laid the groundwork on which writing, reading, and mathematics are built. Conceptual learning activities are concrete, multisensory, and actively involve the child. Thus, children use their fingers to trace letters cut out of sandpaper, trace letters in cornmeal, or use the **movable alphabet** to manipulate letters to form words. Many of the math materials are based on a decimal system; for instance, the **golden beads** come singly or in units of 10, 100, and 1000. Other activities, including maps and animal and plant pictures to identify and classify, promote cultural understanding.

You may notice that some traditional early childhood activities are absent in the Montessori school. Montessori maintained that children under 6 were not able to handle fantasy, so you are not likely to find a dramatic play area in most traditional programs. Research suggests that Montessori teachers vary considerably in their tolerance (or intolerance) of disruptions caused by children using materials for fantasy play (Chattin-McNichols, 1992). Some stop it immediately, while others allow it to continue, especially if the materials are being used constructively.

Montessori's emphasis on reality also means that many programs will not have a creative art corner, or other activities that invite children to freely use their imagination. If you look carefully, you also might be puzzled by the fact that children do not combine materials in their play; this is because there usually is a restriction on how children may use materials. As David Elkind (1983) points out, once children have mastered the use of a particular material in the established manner, they should be free to act on the material and use it freely, in a more experimental way. However, the Montessori method typically allows materials to be used only in the prescribed procedure. For example, a child would not be permitted to use the pink tower and colour tablets together to build a castle or yard.

You may also note less emphasis on encouraging language learning. The emphasis is placed on showing children how to do things, rather than telling them, and then letting them complete tasks on their own. However, in Montessori programs for culturally deprived and language-delayed children, it is likely that you would notice a much greater emphasis on language. Critics also suggest that you would not see enough activities that foster social development in a Montessori program, but if you carefully observe children in the program over several days, you will see opportunities for cooperation, collaboration, and playful social interaction in most programs.

OPEN EDUCATION

Many American textbooks on education and curriculum (e.g., Lay-Dopyera & Dopyera, 1987b; Lawton, 1988; Schwarz & Robison, 1982) discuss the **Bank Street Model**, developed at the Bank Street College of Education in New York, but fail to acknowledge that its roots and earlier history can be traced to Britain where **open education** was developed in the **British Infant School** (Weber, 1971). In fact, as a number of American authors note (e.g., Feeney, Christensen, & Moravcik, 1991; Gordon & Browne, 1993; Evans, 1975; Morrison, 1984; Weber, 1971), North Americans showed little interest in open education until the 1960s. Then, school reformers in Canada and the United States flocked to Britain to study the infant schools.

Lillian Weber (1971) visited British nursery and infant schools in the mid-1960s. Her book, *The English Infant School and Informal Education*, provides an excellent description of open education, its philosophical roots, and its refinement during the 20th century.

Susan and Nathan Isaacs, a husband–wife team who taught at Cambridge and the University of London, formulated the rationale for the open model. They drew heavily upon the works of Dewey, Piaget, and Freud, and upon Susan's own observations and studies at her famous nursery school, the Malting House School in Cambridge. Susan's work at Malting House became known to and emulated by a whole generation of teachers who studied under her at the University of London, and this helped to ensure the success of the open model. To fully appreciate the richness of her program (and to find an abundance of program ideas), consult Isaacs' (1933) vivid description of her school in *Intellectual Growth in Young Children*.

Of course, the roots of the open model predate the Isaacs by at least a century. They can be traced to Owen's 1816 infant school in New Lanark, as well as to the McMillans' 1911 open-air nursery. Nevertheless, the Isaacs formally defined the open model and successfully fostered its application on a national level, something that has not happened in any other country.

The open model was applied in both the nursery schools for 3- to 5-year-olds and the infant schools for 5- to 8-year-olds. Nursery schools as well as infant schools were funded through the Department of Education and Science as early as 1918, a fact that may be surprising for some Canadians, especially residents of New Brunswick, who have just seen publicly funded kindergartens established in the 1990s. Unlike Canada, there is a remarkable continuity between the methods used in the British nursery and infant schools. While many of our early childhood programs in Canada would compare favourably with those Weber (1971) visited in Britain, we are far less likely to have comparable programs for our children between 5 and 8 years of age. Consequently, in reviewing the features of open education, you might try to keep in mind a typical primary-level class in your community for comparison.

Open programs are **child-centred**, the different subjects are integrated into **activities,** and children learn through **discovery**. For example, children in an open program might visit a fire hall. Upon return to the classroom, some might become firefighters in the dramatic play area, while others draw firetrucks, and still others dictate or write stories and poems about the experience. The next day, some might make a papier-maché model of the fire hall and the firetrucks, while others go to the library and find additional resources on firefighting. Three weeks later, one or two children might still be pursuing the fire hall theme, but others would have moved on to new topics.

Children's ability to learn through play and to choose experiences that interest them underlie learning in the open model. The school, in turn, must foster and maintain this boundless curiosity by providing a rich environment that allows the children to learn; the child determines how that learning will occur.

The Environment

If you were to visit an open classroom, you would quickly observe many features that are shared by quality early childhood programs, but it is likely that a number of practices would vary greatly from the primary-level classrooms in your community. Perhaps the most striking feature would be the gradual admission time; some children enrol in September, others in January, and others in April. This eases the difficulties that are so often associated with school entry. In fact, you may also see children who will enrol in the program only after several months of visiting with a parent; this gradual introduction to the school setting is encouraged. You also may wonder at the fact that in the open nursery schools, children arrive over a lengthy period of time, and leave at quite different times.

As in the Montessori program, multi-age or family groupings are a standard feature of the open model; the 5- to 8-year-old children are grouped in the infant school and the 3- to 5-year-old children are in the nursery. You also might be puzzled by the **integrated day**: there are no lessons at prescribed times, but there are many **activity centres**. In addition, some of the children might not be in the classroom, but out of the room, working on several different projects. For example, three of them might be in the garden, with a senior citizen from the community, while others are in the library. In addition, you see several children playing at the water table and the carpentry bench that are in the corridor. You also see some large blocks and two easels there. Open schools use space beyond the classroom, and there is freedom of movement in and out of the class for older children that is rare on this side of the Atlantic. The emphasis on the outdoors as a learning resource also is a striking feature that can be traced back to the McMillan sisters. Quite frequently, North American children at the primary level see the outdoors only at recess; even in warm weather, it is an undervalued resource in Canada, but that is not the case in the open class. You are almost overwhelmed by the number of available materials, many of them home-made. Teachers see this profusion of materials as necessary for sustaining the child's curiosity.

The Children

The children in open programs come from widely differing backgrounds just as children in our neighbourhood-based elementary schools do. If you visit an open class, you would not find the children in rows and the teacher at a desk. However, you would find more collaborative activity and probably a higher noise level than you would in a Montessori program. You would undoubtedly notice that children are free to use materials in the way they want, and that they enjoy their freedom of movement. Children initiate projects, and the teacher serves as a resource person. Older and younger children may be playing together, and a variety of things are happening at the same time.

The Teachers

The teachers in open schools see themselves as being there to support the child's interests. Teachers in the open class have to keep careful records on each child as they have to know what each child understands and how he or she arrived at that understanding. Consequently, the teacher's notes do not just include final accomplishments—being able to count to 5, for example—but they also include information on the activities the child engaged in that led to this accomplishment.

In the infant schools, in particular, teachers traditionally have not shared their North American colleagues' concerns about covering certain topics before the children go to the next grade. Children in Britain have been moved from one to another group on the basis of age, not achievement. Two factors seem to account for this difference: (1) until the 1990s, the curriculum was determined at a local level (unlike Canada where the curriculum has been set down by the provinces since schools began), and (2) children in open classes do not receive regular report cards, which are more common in this country.

The Parents

Parents are frequent visitors and volunteers in the open classroom, as are other members of the community. During her year-and-a-half of visits, Weber notes that she never found a school that did not have some parents present. The gradual arrival and admission procedures described above facilitate the development of positive relationships between teachers and parents.

Britain's history also helped to forge the warm bond that exists between parents and teachers in the open schools. During World War II, many children in England had to be evacuated from their homes because of the frequent bombings. While the conditions were not as extreme as those in the orphanages we discussed in Chapter 2, the great void in the lives of the evacuated children who were separated from their homes and neighbourhoods was evident. Teachers were frequently the people who had to care for the children if they were evacuated from their homes. In so doing, their understanding of the importance of the home to the child grew so that they were more likely to encourage a close relationship with the home. North Americans do not have that history, and too often, teachers, especially at the primary level, are reluctant to foster that closeness.

The Schedule

While there usually is a meeting time when all children in the school gather together several days a week, you will not find a set schedule in an open school. The entire group of children is never the focus of a set lesson; teachers work with small groups and there are many different activities in progress at one time—and often, they are occurring in several different locations. However, there typically are set times for movement and physical education, and lunch.

The Materials

As noted above, materials are abundant in the open class. Sand, water, and clay are in every class, as are materials for movement in the nursery classes and physical education in the infant classes. A wide range of painting supplies is available, both in the classes and the corridors, and workbenches and stoves are plentiful. Dramatic play areas and musical instruments are found in every class. Blocks, "beautiful junk" for assembling things, and manipulative toys like puzzles and Lego also are in every class. Many of the materials are home-made or donated, and you seldom see materials prepared for use on just one occasion.

The Curriculum

Britain has not had a history of a government-prescribed curriculum or the fixed standards for each grade that characterize North American programs. In an excellent Canadian guidebook about how to introduce the open model in Canadian classrooms, *Change: One Step at a Time*, Lois Napier-Anderson (1981) warned Canadians that the provincially dictated curricula made open education more difficult to implement here. Weber issued similar cautions to her American audience, and noted that Dewey's progressivism never became a reality in the United States because of a standardized curriculum.

PROJECT HEAD START

In 1964, with the Economic Opportunity Act, the United States government launched the largest, most significant early childhood education project the world has seen. Project Head Start was a response to both the civil rights movement and the post-*Sputnik* educational crisis facing the United States. The project aimed to break the poverty cycle by providing children and their families with the educational, medical, dental, nutritional, psychological, and social services they required to escape from poverty. Rather than a model per se, Head Start might be better viewed as the grandparent of a number of model early childhood programs. In fact, the remaining three models we will discuss in this chapter all originated in response to the availability of funds to develop variants of the Head Start program and to evaluate their effectiveness.

Canadians and Head Start

Head Start is relevant to Canadians in the field of early childhood education for several reasons. First, the scope of the project and the emphasis it placed on the importance of the early years had an impact that was felt far beyond the U.S. boundaries. Second, much of the significant research on the effectiveness of early childhood programs has been completed because Head Start emphasized an evaluation component, and researchers acknowledged the importance of this activity. Finally, many Canadians were seeing generic Head Start programs in their own communities, including at least one in Nova Scotia that predated the U.S. project.

Canadians also were hearing legislators talk about making funds available for Head Start projects in the 1960s (a time when funds were available!). For example, in 1965, inspired by Head Start, Ontario's minister of education, William G. Davis, spoke in the legislature of his concerns about early childhood education.

Not surprisingly, generic Head Start programs soon became available in larger urban centres in Ontario. Some were junior kindergartens, funded by school boards and the province (e.g., Toronto and Hamilton). Canadian university students, administrators, and alumni also founded a number of programs in the 1960s, the decade of social concern. The University of Western Ontario's Community Action Project (CAP), for instance, was initiated by students who received funding from the university, various levels of government, and donations from corporations. The Varsity, Downtown Education Project (VDEP) in Toronto was somewhat larger in scope, and included two different centres. VDEP was funded for several years by contributions from a charitable foundation (Atkinson Foundation) and from the University of Toronto's Students' Administrative Council, Board of Governors, and alumni. VDEP then turned into a full-time alternative school, primarily for "graduates" of the summer program, that relied on self-raised funds at first, and later on funds from the Toronto Board of Education.

The East Coast also saw a flurry of activity, as did the Far North. Nova Scotia perhaps saw the greatest increase in Canadian Head Start projects in the 1960s, as the provincial government made funds available for disadvantaged communities (Irwin & Canning, 1992b). Some programs also received federal and provincial funding, while others searched for local funds. A number the programs were interracial and aimed to improve relations between whites, blacks, and Natives in communities like Halifax, Truro, and Hants County. In fact, one program, the Brunswick-Cornwallis Pre-school Program, predated Project Head Start by two years. Alexa McDonough, in Nova Scotia, supervised nine such programs with a staff of thirty. In Newfoundland, the St. John's Club of the Canadian Federation of University Women initiated an eleven-week pilot program that drew on the university and community volunteers for staff and evaluations (Glassman, 1992a). The program was extended and eventually received federal funding as a demonstration project. It continues today as a parent cooperative. The Skookum Jim Society in Whitehorse, Yukon, also started a generic Head Start program in 1968 with funding from the Department of Indian Affairs and a lot of volunteer efforts (Johnson & Joe, 1992).

When the federal government made Local Initiatives Program and Opportunities for Youth funding available in the early 1970s, the number of generic Head Start programs in certain areas of the country multiplied rapidly. Many of those programs continue to serve young children in the 1990s.

The Environment

There is no one Head Start Program, but many variants that are developed at the local level to be consistent with broad national goals. Children are to experience a learning environment that fosters development in all areas, and parents are to be involved in the program. Some programs are full-day ones, while others are half-day. Typically, medical, dental, and nutritional services are made available for children in the program. Children receive at least one hot meal a day, regular medical and dental examinations are provided, and immunizations are kept up-to-date. The early identification of developmental delays and learning problems is encouraged, and referrals to psychologists for complete assessments are made if a problem is suspected. An individual who helps families obtain needed social services is also part of the program.

The Children

Family income is the main criterion for admission to a Head Start program. At least 90 percent of the children in a program must come from families that meet the federal government's defined poverty level. In addition, federal guidelines require that a minimum of 10 percent of the children in the program must have disabilities.

The Parents

Parenting education and parent involvement are also integral elements of Head Start. Teachers in Head Start, like teachers in open models, recognize that parents are the dominant influence in a young child's life. If the child's life is to improve, so must that of the parent. Many parents have found employment through the program because it gives them priority for any available non-professional Head Start jobs. Consequently, parents usually work as bus drivers, cooks, and teacher assistants. Parents also are involved with the advisory council for the programs.

The Teachers

Minimum standards for U.S. early childhood teachers are determined at the state level. Some states require little or no training for those working in early childhood programs, including Head Start, but others have stringent criteria.

The **Child Development Associate** (CDA) program, a competency-based program, was developed in the United States during the 1970s to facilitate in-service training of early childhood professionals. Approximately 80 percent of the recipients of a CDA have come from Head Start programs. The program has been a model for

Canadian jurisdictions, which are in the process of introducing teacher-training requirements for early childhood educators. A program like the CDA tries to credit an untrained teacher with extensive experience for the knowledge and skills obtained on the job, and then requires the person to fill in the missing knowledge and skill gaps.

The CDA has been described as an alternative avenue toward professionalism for people who traditionally have been excluded from higher education, specifically those from low-income backgrounds (Peters, 1988). The CDA model may also be relevant in those areas of Canada where travel to postsecondary institutions is a problem. In the Yukon, the Northwest Territories, Newfoundland, and northern British Columbia, for example, attending an early childhood education training program located far from one's home can be major hardship. Similarly, moving to a major urban centre from a reserve in order to study can be very difficult, and many students fail to complete the programs as the cultural adjustment process, coupled with the demanding program, can be simply too great.

The Schedule

Just as there is no standard Head Start environment, scheduling varies from one program to another. A Montessori Head Start program would follow the Montessori scheduling pattern, while a Head Start program following the Cognitively Oriented Curriculum would have a schedule similar to that program's.

The Materials and Curriculum

There are no standard materials in Head Start programs, nor is there a national curriculum. Some Head Start programs follow a Montessori approach, while the open model, as exemplified by the Bank Street College of Education (Gilkeson & Bowman, 1976), can be found in others.

COGNITIVELY ORIENTED CURRICULUM (COC)

A number of programs based on the theoretical precepts of Jean Piaget have evolved over the last several decades. One of these, the Cognitively Oriented Curriculum (Weikart & Schweinhart, 1993), was developed by the High/Scope Foundation of Ypsilanti, Michigan, under the leadership of David Weikart. This approach was initially designed in the early 1960s as a program for children from impoverished backgrounds, but has since been adopted more widely, partly through the publication of its carefully outlined curriculum manual, *Young Children in Action* (Hohmann, Banet, & Weikart, 1979). Mary Wright (1983) adopted this model in her University of Western Ontario (UWO) preschool, and it also has been adopted by many preschools and some primary programs in Canada. The Niagara South Board of Education, for example, has programs for 4-year-olds that are directly based on the COC model. Some preschool settings in Nova Scotia also follow the COC model, which is even cited in the 1990 provincial guidelines.

In line with Piagetian theory, the cognitively oriented model is based on the premise that children are active learners who construct their own knowledge from meaningful experiences. If you were to visit a cognitively oriented class, you would observe this philosophy in the environment, schedule, and activities, and in the children's and teacher's behaviour.

The Environment

The environment is designed to be stimulating but orderly, a place where children can independently choose from a wide variety of interesting materials and use them in the manner they choose, as long as they do not hurt themselves or the environment. The classroom is divided into clearly defined work areas, each with a specific set of materials appropriate to that area. A cognitively oriented classroom contains housekeeping, block, art, quiet, and large-group areas, although there might also be construction, music and movement, sand and water, and animal and plant work areas as well. There is an emphasis on real materials, such as dishes and tools, rather than toy versions. Accessible, uncluttered storage spaces in each work area are clearly labelled with silhouettes or pictures, facilitating clean-up and promoting a sense of order.

The Children

Weikart's original program was designed for children from extremely deprived backgrounds. In addition to being deprived, most of the children were black and from single-parent families. The model has been adopted by many others, and is as likely to include middle-class children from advantaged homes and ethnic minority children as well as disadvantaged children. There is considerable interaction between children in a COC, and the encouragement of social skills is stressed in some applications of this model, such as Wright's UWO program.

The Teachers

Teachers in the COC have a more structured role than those in the open and Montessori classes as the schedule described below suggests. Large-group circle times as well as small group lessons are structured into the program every day. In contrast to the Montessori classes, however, teachers let children use materials in the manner they wish.

The teachers work in teams, and the teacher–child ratio in Weikart's programs has varied from 1:5 to 1:8. However, Weikart and Schweinhart (1993) maintain that a ratio of 1:10 and a group size of 20 would be safe with trained teachers and 3- to 4-year-olds. The teachers are expected to become familiar with each child's developmental level, and to plan the child's program accordingly. Traditionally, the teachers' emphasis has been on intellectual challenges that will further development, rather than on social development. However, in Wright's UWO program, social development was seen as equally important.

The Parents

In Weikart's original program, parents were involved in biweekly sessions with a teacher and their child (or children) in their homes. During these sessions, the teachers aimed to show parents new ways to approach their children, and demonstrated how simple activities like cooking could be learning experiences. In addition, they tried to learn more about the child's family and culture in these visits so they could better meet the child's needs. Some adaptations of the COC, Wright's UWO project, for example, have not followed Weikart's parent program, and this may be a significant omission.

The Schedule

The daily schedule is integral to the philosophy of the cognitively oriented program. Consistency helps children gain gradual understanding of time. The day is begun with a **planning time**, when children decide what activities they would like to participate in during the ensuing work time. A teacher helps each child individually think through what he or she plans to do, and then records the child's plans. A large block of time is then set aside for **work time**, during which children engage in self-selected activities, supported and assisted by the teachers.

After work time comes **recall time**, usually carried out in small groups, where children review their work time activities. This **plan-do-review cycle** is the heart of the cognitively oriented curriculum, helping children make deliberate, systematic choices with the help of the teacher. Additional daily periods include clean-up, considered a learning opportunity; small-group time, which typically includes a teacher-planned activity that reinforces a cognitive concept; large-group time for stories, music, games, and other whole-group activities; outside time; and meals and nap, as appropriate to the length of the program day.

The Materials

While there is no prescribed list of materials for a COC program, certain areas or centres are considered to form the core of the program: the block area, the house area, the art area, the quiet area, the construction area, the sand and water area, the music and movement or large-group area, the animal and plant area, and finally, the outdoor play area (Hohmann et al., 1979). Each of these areas is richly furnished, much like the open class.

The block area, as an example, would include building materials, things to take apart and put together, and materials for filling and emptying. You might see blocks of several different sizes, tubes and boxes, Tinkertoys, interlocking materials, trucks and trains, small and large cars, and people and animals in the centre. Typically, the block area is located next to the housekeeping area; role play is common in both areas, and children often want to use materials from each. The quiet area is filled with small manipulative materials and books. Some materials (e.g., beads, cubes, dominoes, and sound boxes) can be used for sorting and building, while others (e.g., pegs and pegboards, Lego blocks, Tinkertoys, and puzzles) are things that fit together and pull apart. Still other materials in the quiet area (e.g., nesting boxes and rings, and plastic pipe fittings) can be used for ordering and building.

The Curriculum

Throughout the day, teachers focus on extending the cognitively oriented curriculum's **key experiences**, a set of eight concepts based on the characteristics and learning capabilities of preoperational children, as discussed by Piaget. (We will consider some of these concepts when we discuss cognitive development and the early childhood curriculum.) The key experiences give the teachers a framework within which to observe each child's individual performance as well as support and extend children's self-initiated activities. Following is a brief description of these eight concepts.

1. *Active learning* takes place when activities are initiated and carried out by children themselves. It involves learning through all the senses, manipulating and combining materials as a way of discovering their relationships, self-selecting activities and materials, and learning to use equipment and tools.

2. *Using language* is strongly stressed and encouraged through talking with others about meaningful experiences, describing, expressing feelings, having language written down by a teacher, and playing with language.

3. *Representing experiences* and ideas, according to Piaget the hallmark of the preoperational period, allows children to represent the world in non-verbal ways. Key

experiences include such activities as recognizing objects through the senses, imitating actions and sounds, role playing, and drawing or painting.

4. **Classification** begins during the preoperational period as children note similarities and differences between objects. Children are encouraged to investigate and describe the attributes of things, sort and match objects, use objects in different ways, talk about characteristics that some things do not have, and distinguish between "some" and "all."

5. **Seriation,** the ability to arrange objects along some dimension, is promoted by having children make comparisons, arranging objects in order, and matching.

6. **Number concepts** are the basis for mathematical understanding and are built on many concrete experiences. To promote this concept, experiences are planned to encourage children to compare, count, and engage in one-to-one correspondence.

7. **Spatial relationships** are encouraged through assembling and taking things apart, rearranging and reshaping objects, observing and describing things from different perspectives, working with shapes, experiencing and representing the child's own body, locating objects in the environment, and experiencing and describing relative positions and distances.

8. **Time** is a gradually acquired concept involving both understanding of time units and sequencing of events in time. Experiences that help children learn such concepts include signals for stopping and starting actions, experiencing and describing different rates of speed and time intervals, observing seasonal changes, discussing future events, planning, representing past events, and describing the order of events (Hohmann et al. 1979).

The cognitively oriented curriculum provides one illustration of how Piaget's theory has been put into practice. Central is the idea that children are active learners who develop appropriate concepts through interaction with the environment. Through a carefully prepared environment and the guidance of knowledgeable teachers, children attain a deeper understanding of the rules that govern the physical and social world.

THE BEREITER-ENGELMANN MODEL— DISTAR

During the height of Head Start program development, several models based on behavioural theory evolved. One was developed by Carl Bereiter and Siegfried Engelmann in the 1960s, and it was labelled DISTAR. Like many of the models developed during that era, it was designed primarily to help children from poverty backgrounds gain some successful experiences that would diminish the likelihood of failure once they started elementary school. The Bereiter-Engelmann model is noticeably different from the other programs we have described because it is based on some very different premises, both about how children learn and about how to best meet their needs.

DISTAR programs for children without special needs have not been plentiful in the 1980s and 1990s. However, DISTAR methods are increasingly being adopted by "hothousing" programs, and educational critics, like *The Globe and Mail's* Andrew Nykoforuk, refer to the DISTAR research more and more frequently in their push for work-oriented, academic-based programs. Consequently, students and teachers in the 1990s need to be familiar with the model and the research on it, so they can respond to parents' queries and engage in the current educational debate in Canada.

Bereiter and Engelmann maintained that disadvantaged children, who were behind their more fortunate peers, needed not just enrichment activities, but a program that would *accelerate* their rate of learning. Such a program would not be well-rounded. Rather, the DISTAR program would emphasize the areas of development Bereiter and Engelmann thought were most relevant to school, and it would ignore other areas of development. Thus, the Bereiter-Englemann program was designed to meet very specific, teacher-determined learning goals rather than to meet the needs of the whole child.

The Environment

In addition, the environment of the Bereiter-Engelmann model is quite different from that of other early childhood programs. The facility is arranged into small and large classrooms. Direct teaching activities are carried out in the small rooms, and the large room is used for less structured, large-group activities. A model floor plan suggested by Bereiter and Engelmann (1966) includes three small classrooms—named the Arithmetic Room, the Reading Room, and the Language Room—each furnished with five small chairs facing a chalkboard (and, presumably, the teacher). The most important feature of these small study rooms should be their acoustic properties, ensuring that they filter out any noise that would distract from lessons. They recommend that the rooms should also be plain, to minimize distraction from the task at hand. A larger "homeroom," furnished with tables, a piano, and a chalkboard, provides a place for snack and music times.

Bereiter and Engelmann also suggest that there be very few materials available to the children, mainly ones that will reinforce concepts taught in the lessons. They assume that the richness and variety of peer play and games, for example, will be readily available in the child's normal environment.

The Children

Traditionally, the children in the Bereiter-Engelmann programs came from very deprived homes and were eligible for Head Start programs. Subsequently, DISTAR methods have been adopted in some elementary schools in both Canada and the United States, and they serve children from more diverse backgrounds. The DISTAR

materials are now marketed for special education programs for children with language delays and disabilities, cognitive delays, and learning disabilities. These latter children come from a broad range of socioeconomic and ethnic groups.

The Teachers

Bereiter and Engelmann (1966) suggest that elementary school teachers are more suited to teach in this model than are teachers trained to work with young children. They comment on the training of early childhood educators: "[It] has provided them with a deeply ingrained bias against 'forcing' the child in any way; the intensive preschool is premised on 'forcing' the child" (p. 69).

The Parents

Typically, parents were not involved in the DISTAR model. However, in some of the special education applications of DISTAR methods, parents are asked to do supplementary work at home.

The Schedule

The daily schedule revolves around three fast-paced, no-nonsense, intensive 20-minute lessons in language, math, and reading, each involving five children and one teacher. These small-group periods are interspersed with functional times for eating and toileting and a 15- to 20-minute music period. Music is also a direct-instruction activity because it is used to reinforce language. Three teachers work with the children, each teaching one of the three subjects to each of the three groups of children.

The Materials

As noted above, there are few materials available to the children in a DISTAR program. Bereiter and Engelmann (1966) maintain that:

> sterilizing the environment is a firm requirement of the work-oriented preschool. Toys should be limited. ... Paper, crayons, and chalk (but no paint) should be available. ... Motor toys ... are not necessary (p. 72).

The materials that are available reinforce concepts learned in lessons. There are no housekeeping areas, no block areas, no creative art areas, and no practical life activities in this model. It is assumed that the richness and variety of peer play and games, for example, will be readily available in the child's normal environment.

The Curriculum

The core of this highly structured preschool curriculum is daily lessons conveyed through a direct-instruction approach. The teacher presents carefully planned lessons, drills, and exercises designed to meet very specific goals. As noted above, these lessons are offered in just three academic areas—language, math, and reading. Precise teacher questions, which require specific verbal answers from the children, are presented in a carefully sequenced order.

The teacher's enthusiasm is important in implementing this approach. Each lesson is designed to help the children master specific skills related to program goals. For example, language goals related to the use of plurals might be stressed one day in a language lesson, while the use of complete sentences, if–then statements, affirmative and negative statements, and polar opposites (big/little, up/down) would be covered in later lessons. Other topics in this prescribed curriculum include colour recognition and naming, counting to twenty, recognition of letters, ability to rhyme, and development of a sight-reading vocabulary. Constant reinforcement, both in the form of praise and food, is used to motivate and encourage the children.

RESEARCH AND EVALUATION OF PROGRAM MODELS

After learning about some of the program models in early childhood education, you are probably wondering if one model is better than another or if it makes any difference. We will review the research on the five models, as well as more recent research on eclectic models and long-term follow-up studies, but first, several cautions are in order. While there have been many attempts to compare the effectiveness of different program models, unfortunately, the results are not conclusive. A great number of variables can affect the outcome of these comparisons, and they have rarely been controlled in the available studies (Clarke-Stewart & Fein, 1983; Johnson, 1993).

To a valid comparison of program models, you could not study, for example, children in existing programs who entered on a first-come, first-served basis; those children almost certainly would differ on a number of dimensions (e.g., family background, age, sex, ethnicity, etc.) other than the program model, and that would make the interpretation of results very difficult. What you would need to do for the study to be valid would be more like a lottery. You would have, for example, from a given community a list of 4-year-olds whom you would randomly place in the different program models. Of course, that is unlikely to happen as families have preferences about the location and type of program they select. Historically, such preferences as well as limited research funds have meant that most research on program models has been less than ideal.

Decisions about what to measure when you are comparing models also are difficult and subject to well-founded criticism. For example, if you measured children's achievement in reading and mathematics, you might expect to see the DISTAR model favoured as it provides direct instruction in those areas. If, on the other hand, you were measuring creativity or social development, you probably would not think DISTAR "graduates" would be favoured in these areas. A more general problem is the difficulty of ensuring that the children in each program model are comparable in every way (e.g., family environment, age, temperament, sex, ethnicity, etc.). To date, there have been very few studies of even a single model that have successfully controlled these variables, and none that have compared the preceding five models. In fact, much of the research in the field is addressing more fundamental questions, such as "Does early education matter?" and "For how long?" Nevertheless, there is some information available about the effectiveness of the different models and their relative strengths.

COMPARISONS OF PROGRAM MODELS

While there are no studies that directly compare the five models you have considered, each model has been compared with some other programs. Some familiarity with these limited findings is worthwhile, especially for professionals who are frequently asked for advice on program selection.

Cognitively Oriented Curriculum, DISTAR, and Traditional Nursery School Models

Weikart and Schweinhart (1993) describe a study that compared the effects of three program models—the DISTAR model, the Cognitively Oriented Curriculum, and the traditional nursery school model. The study is remarkable, not just because of its excellent methods, but also because it followed the children until they were 15 years old. All of the children were from extremely disadvantaged families, and most of them were black. After one year in the program, the IQs of the children in all three program models rose 27 points, from the below-average level to average. The DISTAR group made slightly greater gains only in the first year.

At age 15, however, the graduates of the programs did differ on self-reported delinquent acts. The DISTAR youths had higher rates of juvenile delinquency than those youths who had been in the other programs. In trying to account for this difference, the authors of this study speculated that children in the teacher-centred DISTAR program did not develop as great a sense of responsibility and initiative as those in the child-centred programs (Schweinhart, Weikart, & Larner, 1986b). Not surprisingly, proponents of the direct instructional approach have questioned these conclusions, and criticized the follow-up study's research procedures (Bereiter, 1986; Gersten, 1986). Additional research would be needed to see if this is a persistent finding, but you would have to question the ethical issues involved in such a study in view of the available results.

Montessori, DISTAR, and Traditional Head Start Models

Several studies, all initiated during the Head Start era, have compared Montessori, DISTAR, and Head Start programs that follow a traditional nursery school program (Chattin-McNichols, 1992; Lazar & Darlington, 1982; Lindauer, 1993). Because these

studies were an outgrowth of Head Start, all the children were from low-income homes, many were black, and many of the families had just one parent.

Louise Miller and her colleagues (Miller & Dyer, 1975; Miller & Bizzell, 1983) randomly assigned 4-year-old children to one of the model programs within their neighbourhood. After a year in these programs, children in all of the programs made gains on verbal intelligence scores. The gains of the DISTAR group were the greatest, not only on the verbal intelligence scores but also on a test of receptive language skills and on academic achievement measures. However, once the children entered school, the DISTAR group had the largest decline in IQ scores. By second grade, the Montessori children had the highest IQ, reading, and mathematics scores. Some of these gains were still present in sixth grade, and even in Grade 10. Changes in self-esteem and attitude may be relevant to these findings, but the reason why such gains would be more persistent for Montessori graduates remains a topic for discussion. The same study found that the levels of curiosity and inventiveness of the DISTAR children seemed lower than those of youngsters from the other programs, while the Montessori graduates had high curiosity scores until Grade 2 (Miller & Dyer, 1975; Miller & Bizzell, 1983).

Montessori, DISTAR, and Traditional Nursery School Models

Dr. Merle Karnes compared 4-year-old lower-class children who attended Montessori, DIS-TAR, traditional nursery school, and community-integrated programs (Karnes, 1969; Karnes, Shwedel, & Williams, 1983). The community-integrated programs placed children eligible for Head Start funding into middle-class preschools. The 4-year-old DISTAR children made greater gains than Montessori graduates on mathematics tests after one year, and they continued to gain in their early school years. The children in DISTAR and nursery school programs also made greater gains on language measures than children in Montessori programs. However, after a year in grade school, the Montessori children made additional gains on IQ tests, and they were more successful in school, up to their Grade 10 year.

DISTAR and Montessori Models

Bereiter (1967) studied the academic achievement of 3- to 4-year-old middle-class children in Montessori and DISTAR programs. The DISTAR children made significantly greater gains on reading, spelling, and arithmetic than did the Montessori children during the one-year program.

Montessori Programs, Open Model, and Regular Public School

Banta (1969) compared children from four different preschool/primary school combinations: (1) Montessori preschool/Montessori primary, (2) Montessori preschool/Open primary, (3) Head Start preschool/regular primary, and (4) no preschool/regular primary. While there was a trend for the children in the two Montessori combinations to do better on verbal memory tests, the results were not significant. However, both Montessori groups had higher scores on a creativity test than did children in the other program combinations.

Open and Formal Models

Several British studies have compared the development of children in open programs with that of children in structured, teacher-centred, formal programs. Much of the research is observational and does not focus on test scores. However, Silberman (1970) found that children from the open models did better than children in formal programs on measures of spoken and written language, drawing and painting, attention and memory, "neatness," ingenuity, and breadth and depth of extra-school interests. The general level of reading achievement also rose in Britain as the number of open classes increased.

Observational studies (Evans, 1975) have consistently noted the inventiveness and excellence in the arts in children in open programs. They also have noted high reading and free-writing skills, and similar strengths in mathematics. Nevertheless, the observational studies need to be supplemented with more empirical evidence for the superiority of the open model.

EVALUATIONS OF INDIVIDUAL MODELS

Montessori Evaluations

Montessori schools today vary considerably. Many, in fact, are a blend of the Montessori method and elements of traditional early childhood programs. Some studies have shown that Montessori children display greater task persistence and more independence than children from other programs; others report they score lower on tests of creativity and language development (e.g., Chattin-McNichols, 1981, 1992; Elkind, 1983; Gettman, 1987; Lillard, 1973; Lindauer, 1993; Miezitis, 1972; Simons & Simons, 1986). Generally, there are no strong, consistent differences between children in Montessori programs and those in more traditional ones. However, several longitudinal studies reported above have found differences—favouring Montessori graduates—that persist into secondary school.

Open Model Evaluations

There has been very little controlled research on the open model, and most of it has been observational in nature. Critics of open education, like Andrew Nykoforuk in *The Globe and Mail*, point to the abundant research on direct, formal models at the elementary level and suggest that proponents of the open model need to document the model's effectiveness.

Head Start Evaluations

You have already considered some of the Head Start evaluations that involved comparison studies of different program models. Typically, the research showed that children in the program made gains in IQ and academic achievement scores. However, the so-called Westinghouse Report (Cicirelli 1969), a national study of the impact of Head Start, soon dampened the enthusiasm that greeted the early results. Apparently, these gains were short-lived, and disappeared soon after entry into elementary school when control children, who had not attended Head Start, caught up with the program graduates. Many criticisms of the Westinghouse report followed (Lazar & Darlington, 1982) pointing to the inadequacies of the design, the measures, and the control groups used in the report. One group of critics, who formed the Consortium for Longitudinal Studies in 1975 (Lazar & Darlington, 1982), had been involved in high-quality, research Head Start programs in the 1960s. They decided to pool their results from the 1960s and to conduct a long-term follow-up of the graduates who were between 8 and 18 years of age when the follow-up started.

In 1982, *Lasting Effects of Early Education: A Report from the Consortium for Longitudinal Studies* (Lazar & Darlington, 1982) reported that early education programs had lasting effects on low-income children in at least four areas:

1. Children who had attended these programs did better in elementary school, and were less likely than matched controls to fail a grade or to be placed in special education.

2. Children who attended the programs had higher IQs and did better than their controls on achievement tests in their early school years.

3. In 1976, children who attended the programs up to ten years before were more likely than controls to cite their school and work accomplishments as reasons for being proud.

4. Participation in the programs had lasting effects on maternal attitudes. The mothers of program children were prouder than control mothers of their children's school accomplishments, even when actual school performance was controlled, and had higher aspirations for them.

Of course, these results were welcomed by those who had supported early education, and they have had an ongoing, positive impact on the willingness of governments and foundations to support early childhood education.

Cognitively Oriented Curriculum Evaluations

The Perry Preschool Project, launched by Weikart in 1962 in Ypsilanti, Michigan, followed the Cognitively Oriented Curriculum, and it was one of the studies included in the Consortium's database. As of the summer of 1993, the 123 children in the project followed until they were 27, and the results provide unequivocal support for the efficacy of early education (Berrueta-Clement et al., 1984; Schweinhart & Weikart, 1985, 1993; Weikart & Schweinhart, 1993). At 19 years, graduates of the program were significantly better than matched controls in a number of ways. They were more likely to graduate from high school, attend postsecondary institution, and be self-supporting at age 19. They were less likely to have been classified as mentally impaired, to have been arrested, or to be on public assistance. In addition, literacy levels were higher in graduates than controls, and the graduates spent significantly fewer years in school programs for children with cognitive disabilities.

A series of calculations looked at the initial cost of the preschool versus future money saved because of the reduced need for special education, welfare, and crime, as well as the future taxes the graduates would pay (Weikart & Schweinhart, 1993). Estimates suggest that the investment of $5000 per child per year in the preschool program resulted in a return of $28 000 per graduate to the taxpayers who would pay for special education, criminal justice, and welfare. Hence, the return from a high-quality program like the Cognitively Oriented Curriculum more than justifies the initial cost.

More recent results (Schweinhart & Weikart, 1993) report on the program graduates versus no-program controls at age 27 years, and these data are consistent with earlier findings. Schweinhart and Weikart were still able to find 95 percent of the graduates and matched controls at age 27, which is quite remarkable in itself. A series of interviews with the 27-year-old program graduates and their controls revealed the following statistically significant results:

1. Graduates have higher monthly salaries than controls. About 30 percent of the graduates earn over $2000 a month, but only 7 percent of the no-program controls do.

2. While 71 percent of the graduates completed Grade 12, only 54 percent of the no-program controls did.

3. Between ages 17 and 27, 59 percent of the graduates received some type of social service, while 80 percent of the no-program controls did.

4. By age 27, 35 percent of the no-program controls had five or more arrests, while only 7 percent of the graduates did.

DISTAR Evaluations

As you saw above, the DISTAR model has been included in a number of comparative studies that sought to examine the impact of this approach. Initial evaluations typically find that DISTAR children gain more than other children on IQ and achievement test scores. However, those gains decline quickly over the next few years. The only longitudinal data on the DISTAR graduates (Miller & Dyer, 1975; Weikart & Schweinhart, 1993), discussed in the section on comparisons between models, raised three concerns about them: (1) their greater drop in scores upon entry to public school, (2) their higher rate of adolescent delinquency, and (3) their lower curiosity and inventiveness scores. If these results are reliable, it would seem that the graduates pay a fairly high cost for the rapid, but short-lived gains they make on IQ and achievement tests. When these negative results are coupled with the impressive results of the long-term follow-ups on graduates of child-centred programs, it seems likely that programs like DISTAR may induce dependence on the teacher and a need for ongoing external reinforcement. In contrast, the less teacher-centred programs seem to be associated with children who have developed an intrinsic motivation to learn.

We have explored some different early childhood education models, and we have discussed the research on the effectiveness of these models. Most of this research has been done in U.S. programs that enrolled low-income, mostly black children. Follow-up studies such as these provide evidence that high-quality early childhood intervention programs can and do make a difference. Let us now briefly examine what additional research tells us about the effectiveness of some other programs—some Canadian programs, some eclectic programs, and some programs for low-risk children.

ADDITIONAL RESEARCH ON EARLY CHILDHOOD EDUCATION

Mary Wright's (1983) UWO preschool was based on preserving "the best in the traditional Ontario preschool program, which had been developed in the 1940s at the University of Toronto's Institute for Child Study" (p. 353), and combining it with aspects of more recent Piagetian programs, like the Cognitively Oriented Curriculum. Wright's program included both high- and low-income children, but financial constraints resulted in the presence of only the low-income children in the school follow-up study. All children made gains on ability, achievement, and social skill measures when they were in the program, and the gains were greater if they were enrolled for two years. In grade school, the low-income preschool graduates were less likely to fail and less likely to be placed in special education classes relative to matched controls. Moreover, they were viewed by their teachers as better adjusted than matched controls. Finally, there was a tendency for those low-income graduates who had spent two years in the program to do better than those who had only one year in a high-quality program.

Goelman and Pence (1990) have conducted a series of studies in British Columbia. They examined centre-based and family child care, the quality of the child's care at home and in the child care setting, and language development as a function of these variables. In the Victoria study, parents developed higher levels of friendship with family-based caregivers, but they had fewer negative concerns about centre-based care. This is consistent with the higher turnover rates that were found in family-based care. The providers of family child care generally had lower educational levels than centre-based teachers, but they were able to be more flexible about caregiving arrangements. Nevertheless, most of the home-based providers would have preferred to be employed in a different capacity.

The unlicensed family homes were more likely to be of low quality than the licensed homes and centres in Victoria. In the low-quality homes, children watched more television than in the higher-quality settings, and their language development lagged behind that of children in licensed homes. However, caregiver training and the mothers' educational levels also were positively related to the language development scores. Moreover, those families with limited resources (e.g., single-parent families and ones with low income, little education, and lower-paying jobs) were more likely to have their children in low-quality, unlicensed settings.

The Vancouver study followed the Victoria one, and concentrated on family-based care. Both the child's home and the care home were rated for quality, as were the parents and providers. The children's language was studied in both settings. The analyses confirmed the trends in Victoria. As you might predict, the quality of language and cognitive stimulation in both the child's own home and the care home was related to the child's own language development. The socio-emotional climate of the child's own family was also directly related to cognitive stimulation in the child's home and the care home, and to language development.

Several studies in the United States that involved more eclectic programs have also added to our knowledge about the effects of early childhood education. For example, adolescents who had participated in the Syracuse University Family Development Research Program (FDRP) during their infant and preschool years were much like those who had participated in the Perry Preschool's Cognitively Oriented Curriculum. Most impressive was the highly significant difference in involvement in the juvenile justice system between these teenagers and a comparable (control) group that had not participated in an early intervention program. Not only had far fewer of the FDRP youngsters been involved in juvenile delinquency, but the severity of the offences, the number of incidents, and the cost of processing were far lower (Honig, 1993; Lally, Mangione, & Honig, 1988). In addition, early intervention resulted in better school performance and lower absenteeism during adolescence for centre graduates—especially females—than for matched controls. The teachers also rated the FDRP girls, relative to controls, as higher in self-esteem and self-control (Lally, Mangione, & Honig, 1988).

Additional studies have provided information on the effects of an early childhood program on middle-class children. Some studies have found that middle-class children in high-quality early childhood programs exhibit greater cognitive, language, and social competence than children without such experience (Clarke-Stewart, 1984; Howes and Olenick, 1986); others, however, have found greater levels of aggressiveness among children with child care experience (Haskins, 1985).

A study of infant day care, conducted in Toronto by William Fowler (1971, 1972, 1973, 1974, 1978; Fowler & Khan, 1974), found that middle-class infants and toddlers made very significant gains on ability measures. In fact, their gains were even greater than those of the lower-class children.

A recent U.S. study (Larsen & Robinson, 1989) followed children from advantaged families, those who had attended a high-quality preschool program, into third grade and compared them with children who had not had a similar early childhood experience. Results showed that, particularly for males, the early childhood program experience seems to be related to higher school achievement scores. Another study (Tietze, 1987), using a sampling of the general elementary school population of one state in Germany, found that children who had attended an early childhood program experienced greater school success than children who had not been in a preschool program (measured by retention and special education placement information).

One interesting variation of such investigations evaluated a sample of middle-class 8-year-olds in a state with *minimal child care standards.* The researchers (Vandell & Corasaniti, 1990) compared parents' and teachers' ratings of children who had been in full-time child care since infancy with those of children who had experienced part-time or no child care. The youngsters with full-time child care histories were considered to have poorer peer relations, work habits, emotional health, and academic performance, and to be more difficult to discipline. The authors contrasted these findings to the positive results found in Sweden for children who had extensive child care histories in *high-quality settings.*

Clearly, more research can help us better assess the impact of early childhood education on all children, not only those in Canada and the United States. Many factors, including home experience and environment, quality of the program and teachers, and program philosophy, need to be taken into account. All such information will help us to better understand how we contribute to the lives of young children and to maximize their chance of success in the future. This information can also help us assist those parents seeking advice on selecting a child care program.

PARENTS AND PROFESSIONALS

When Parents Ask for Advice about Choosing a School

When parents look for an early childhood program for their young child, their final decision may be based on a variety of criteria. For some parents struggling to make ends meet, affordability may be the most important consideration. Others may want a program that is convenient, near their home or place of employment. The major concern of some may be that their children are in a clean and safe environment where basic needs are met by caring adults. Other parents may be looking for an early childhood program that will lay the groundwork for later school success.

At some time, you may well be asked for advice by a parent who is trying to select the right school for her child. How do you advise a parent who asks, "Where do you think I should enrol Wendy?" It is generally best not to recommend one specific school to a parent because different programs meet different needs. You can, however, help the parent identify priorities to find a program that best meets both the child's and the family's needs. Which criteria are most important and which are not important? Parents may be concerned about cost, location, hours of operation, the credentials of the adults, the school's philosophy, the provision of lunch, and other such matters. Some telephone calls can then help the parent gather this information and develop a list of several potential programs.

Once the parent has some possible schools in mind, encourage her to visit them and spend some time observing. Help the parent identify quality indicators by which to evaluate each program. These should include a careful examination of child–adult interactions, activities, schedule, and the environment. Help the parent discriminate between a program that "looks" good and one that aims to meet the needs of each individual child.

Setting priorities, finding out which programs best fit these priorities, and observing will help parents in their decision-making process. Although such a process is time-consuming, spending a few hours to select the right program can save considerable time later. Such a process can help ensure that the child is in a program that is right for her.

KEY POINTS OF CHAPTER 3

APPLICATION OF THEORIES IN EARLY CHILDHOOD EDUCATION

▲ 1. A number of human development theories have been applied to early childhood education through specific models.

▲ 2. Today there is great variation among Montessori programs. The traditional Montessori environment and materials include some unique features; the role of the teacher and the children's activities differ from those in other types of early childhood programs.

▲ 3. Open education was developed in Britain and incorporates the ideas of Dewey, Piaget, and Freud. Teachers in the open model use the child's natural curiosity as the starting point for all learning. Open programs are child-centred and encourage discovery learning through activity centres.

▲ 4. Project Head Start was launched in 1964 and is the most ambitious, far-reaching early childhood program to date.

▲ 5. The cognitively oriented curriculum, based on the theory of Piaget, revolves around activities that help children learn specific cognitive concepts.

▲ 6. The Bereiter-Engelmann model, DISTAR, based on behavioural theory, uses a direct-instruction approach in which the teacher presents carefully planned lessons in three academic areas.

RESEARCH AND EVALUATION OF PROGRAM MODELS

▲ 7. Research on early intervention programs such as Head Start has shown that they result in long-term positive effects and cost benefits. DISTAR graduates usually make the greatest gains initially, but they experience the greatest decline in scores when they enter school.

▲ 8. Montessori graduates have retained gains in IQ and mathematics scores through to Grade 10.

▲ 9. Children in open programs have high reading and independent writing skills, and excel in the arts relative to children in formal models.

▲10. There are no consistent differences between Montessori graduates and graduates of more traditional programs.

▲11. Long-term follow-up studies of Head Start and COC graduates show significant benefits that persist into adulthood.

▲12. The higher delinquency rate of DISTAR graduates remains a source of concern.

ADDITIONAL RESEARCH ON EARLY CHILDHOOD EDUCATION

▲13. The UWO project has shown that similar positive changes in IQ and achievement scores, and in measures related to school success, are seen in Canadian children who attend high-quality preschool programs.

▲14. In Victoria, children in unlicensed family child care homes watched more television and had lower language scores than did children in licensed homes.

▲15. Although there is far less research about the benefits of early childhood programs on middle-class children, some evidence indicates that high-quality programs can have a positive effect. For example, Fowler's Toronto-based study found that middle-class infants and toddlers made greater gains in a high-quality child care centre than did their lower-class peers.

KEY QUESTIONS

1. What are the strengths/weaknesses of the five program models? Which program would you select for your children and why?

2. Visit a program in your community that conforms to one of the five models with a view to sharing your observations with your classmates. Does the program follow the model closely or is it somewhat eclectic? What three features of the program did you like the best?

3. Roopnarine and Johnson (1993) described fourteen early childhood education models, including home-based and centre-based ones. The centre-based models could be placed in one of three categories: (1) Montessori models, (2) behavioural models, and (3) interactionist models. Where do the five models you have considered fit in this categorization and why? Which theorists have influenced each model?

4. In the discussion of DISTAR, the higher delinquency rates of DISTAR graduates versus those in the COC and traditional nursery schools were noted. Bereiter and Engelmann say the finding is unreliable because the original study had a poor technical design. You would have to do additional research to see if this result is reliable (i.e., reproduceable). Discuss the ethical issues involved in conducting such a study in view of the available results.

5. In the Victoria study of family child care settings, children in low-quality homes watched more television and had lower language development scores than did children in higher quality homes. However, the children in low-quality settings also had more troubled, less affluent homes and their parents had less education. To what extent do you think television was a factor in their delayed language development? What other factors contributed to this delay? What recommendations would you make to the parents of the children in low-quality homes?

EARLY CHILDHOOD EDUCATION IN CANADA

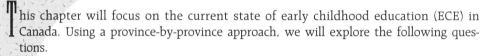

This chapter will focus on the current state of early childhood education (ECE) in Canada. Using a province-by-province approach, we will explore the following questions.

1. How and when did early childhood education evolve in each province and territory?

2. What regulations cover early childhood programs in each jurisdiction? After considering the historical roots of ECE and its regulation in each province and territory, we will examine the similarities and differences in the legislation in these jurisdictions.

3. When was child care first legislated? Are child–teacher ratios specified in the legislation? Are there maximum group sizes or centre sizes? What are the ratios, group sizes, and facility sizes for (1) infants, (2) toddlers, (3) 3- to 5-year-olds, and (4) school-aged children? What are the space requirements in each jurisdiction?

4. When, if ever, were teacher-training requirements introduced? What teacher education programs are available? The research reviewed in Chapter 1 indicated that teachers with specific training in early childhood education and child development provided higher-quality care. Are we responding to this research in Canada?

5. What is the scope of licensed care in Canada? Are there enough licensed facilities to meet parental child care needs?

6. What role should government play in child care as we approach the 21st century?

As a student in an introductory course, you will probably be most interested in the section on your own province or territory. However, you may want to see how the services, legislation, and/or teacher education programs in your area compare with others. Perhaps you plan to enter the profession, or have young children requiring care, or are thinking about relocating after you graduate. If that is the case, you perhaps are interested in learning about practices and alternatives in other parts of the country.

Assembling the information for this chapter was less challenging than seemed likely at first because of the publication of *Canadian Child Care in Context: Perspectives from the Provinces and Territories* (Pence, 1992), a two-volume work of almost 1000 pages. As part of the government-funded Canadian National Child Care Study (CNCCS), teams of authors from each province, the Yukon, and the Northwest Territories were asked to compile articles on their province or territory, the history of

early childhood education there, and current ECE regulations and practices. In addition, information on the scope of licensed child care and parents' child care needs and use was compiled for each province and territory. Those documents are a valuable resource, but could not be fully covered in most ECE courses. Hence, they will be summarized below.

In addition to Pence's invaluable volumes, most institutions in the country that offer ECE courses willingly responded to the author's 1991 requests for information about their programs. In addition to their published data (Child Care, 1990), the Child Care Resource and Research Unit at the University of Toronto also shared unpublished data on child care in Canada that were presented at the third National Child Care Conference in May 1993 (Child Care, 1993). Governments from across the country also responded to the author's requests for information about their legislation for ECE programs. Thus, it was only through the collaborative efforts of ECE professionals and government officials across the country that this chapter, based on Young (1993), could be assembled. As students in ECE courses, you gain a much broader perspective on the field in this country than virtually all of your predecessors. That perspective may subsequently influence your decision about where to pursue your career either as an ECE professional and/or as a parent of children requiring a high-quality program.

THE ROOTS OF EARLY CHILDHOOD EDUCATION IN CANADA AND REGULATION IN THE FIELD

BRITISH COLUMBIA

Ritch and Griffin (1992) provided an overview of British Columbia, the third most populous province in Canada, for the CNCCS. Over half of B.C.'s 3 million people live in urban centres, and 50 percent of the people are concentrated in the Greater Vancouver area. The province has been ethnically diverse since the Canadian Pacific Railway was built in the 1880s; even in the early 1900s, Vancouver had the largest Chinese community in Canada.

In recent years, B.C. has seen a large influx of immigrants from the Pacific Rim as well as from the rest of Canada. Over 50 percent of the children in Vancouver come from homes where English is not the first language.

Traditionally, B.C. had a resource-based economy with forestry, fishing, mining, and agriculture being its mainstays. However, the service-based industries now employ 70 percent of the workforce. Average incomes are high in B.C., and it continues to be one of the more affluent provinces.

Historical Overview

Linda McDonell's 1992 article, "An Historical Overview of Child Care in British Columbia," provides an excellent summary of developments in early childhood in B.C. from 1910 to the present. In 1910, the only early childhood facility was the City Crèche, located in a hospital in downtown Vancouver. The crèche was a facility where working mothers could leave their children for the day when they found work as domestics. The crèche closed at the onset of the Depression, and nursery schools and private kindergartens did not appear until the 1940s. There were some family day care homes available to working mothers in the interim, mainly in Vancouver, where there was some concern about having high-quality substitute care. World War II led to an increase in day care facilities, but B.C. did not have enough women working in war-related industries to qualify for federal funds.

B.C. led the country when it initiated the licensing of child care facilities in 1937. By 1939, the province had twenty licensed programs. The nursery school movement became visible in the 1940s, as did cooperative preschools, which steadily multiplied. Some private kindergartens also were established. There were 170 licensed programs in B.C. by 1945, and concern was expressed about the need to establish standards for these facilities. In 1955, the province, responding to mounting pressure, added training requirements to the legislation, and the Faculty of Education at the University of British Columbia (UBC) began to offer these courses. Trained early childhood educators became the norm in urban areas. However, despite considerable effort to offer courses in rural areas, few teachers in the remote areas of B.C. were qualified, even in 1975. Training programs became more widely available during the 1970s and the early 1980s, and courses in infant and toddler care also were established.

In 1989, the regulations were revised so that centres could have programs for infants under 18 months of age (Griffin, 1992). Training requirements were also clarified. In addition, the maximum number of hours a child could spend in a centre per day was increased from ten to thirteen. A review of the regulations was initiated in 1993 and changes are to be finalized in 1994 (Child Care, 1993).

Regulation

Early childhood programs in B.C. are regulated by several different bodies (Child Care, 1990, 1993; Griffin, 1992; McDonell & Griffin, 1992). School-based programs, including kindergartens (now known as Primary I classes), fall under the Ministry of Education. Non-school-based early childhood programs are governed by three ministries (Child Care, 1990; McDonell & Griffin, 1992). The Ministry of Advanced Education, Training and Technology is responsible for teacher training, while funding of those eligible for assistance under the Canada Assistance Plan comes from the Ministry of Social Services and Housing. The licensing of programs, inspections, certification of teachers, and approval of early childhood training programs all fall in the hands of the Ministry of Health. One does not have to have had many dealings with governments to suspect that this tri-ministerial involvement brings additional challenges to the field.

The 1979 Community Care Facility Act and the British Columbia Child Care Regulations, as amended in 1990, specify requirements for early childhood programs in the province (Child Care, 1990, 1993; Griffin, 1992; McDonell & Griffin, 1992). Teacher–child ratios, group size, facility size, and teacher qualifications are regulated, but we will leave these issues until later in the chapter when we consider them from a national perspective. The revised regulations also contain an extensive account of appropriate programming for the young child's physical, intellectual, language, social, and emotional development.

ALBERTA

The population of Alberta has almost quadrupled from 1921 to the time of the 1986 census, and that growth seems to have occurred primarily in the urban areas (Greenwood-Church & Crozier-Smith, 1992). While over two-thirds of the province's population were in rural settings in the 1930s, 80 percent lived in urban settings in the 1980s (Greenwood-Church & Crozier-Smith, 1992). A large number of European immigrants moved to Alberta prior to World War I, giving the province a long tradition of ethnic diversity. While Alberta's fluctuating oil market has led to waves of immigration and emigration, the province has not experienced the significant increases in foreign immigrants witnessed by British Columbia and Ontario, for example.

Historical Overview

"An Historical Overview of Child Care in Alberta" (Read, Greenwood-Church, Hautman, Roche, & Bagley, 1992) traces the development of early childhood education in Alberta until 1988, while Read (1992) discusses developments from 1988 until 1990. Child care has a comparatively brief history in Alberta where it was not generally available until the late 1960s. Until that time the few child care centres that existed were privately owned and received little attention from the government beyond routine fire and health inspections. With the advent of CAP in 1966, and Alberta's Preventive Social Service Act in the same year, the onus was on the province to provide preventive, rather than custodial services, including child care. The province provided 80 percent of the funding to any municipality that opened a non-profit child care centre, and the cities of Edmonton and Calgary quickly took advantage of the new funding agreement. Similar growth occurred in smaller urban centres, but the two major cities provided a model for ensuring high-quality programs. However, the municipal centres were primarily for children from low-income and single-parent families. As a consequence, profit-making child care continued to predominate in Alberta, and child care chains and franchises found the province a receptive home.

The first training programs for ECE teachers within the province were not instituted until 1970 when several two-year diploma courses and some extension courses were established. The demand for graduates of these programs increased after 1973 when the province finally agreed to provide funding for kindergarten programs offered by either the school boards or private non-profit organizations.

Legislation governing child care licensing was not introduced until 1978, and only after the Alberta Association for Young Children (AAYC) had applied consistent pressure on the government to adopt and enforce standards. Interestingly, the standards were lower than those that Edmonton and Calgary had adopted from the Child Welfare League of America in the 1960s, and actually led to a decline in ECE standards, if not quality, in these two cities. Nonetheless, requirements for physical facilities and child–teacher ratios were stated in the Social Care Facilities Licensing Act. Training requirements were not included, however, much to the dismay of the AAYC.

Group-size requirements were added to the legislation in 1980, and teacher–child ratios were improved.

Inspections of child care facilities in Alberta after the 1978 Licensing Act seemed to be inconsistent and often cursory. Concerns about the inspection procedures and the continued lack of training requirements were expressed by a number of groups and resulted in a commission of inquiry into child welfare during the 1980s. Moreover, the failure of the government to tie financial subsidies for child care centres to the quality of care in those centres was subject to criticism. Making subsidies contingent on strict conformity to the regulations typically is an effective method of ensuring compliance with the legislation.

The ongoing barrage of criticism of the government's policies (and lack of policies), led by groups like the AAYC, finally led to the 1990 publication of *Alberta Day Care Reforms.* In that document, the province outlined training requirements that are to be fully implemented by 1995 (Read, 1992). By September 1995, all supervisors of child care facilities must have completed a two-year diploma in ECE, or have equivalent education and experience. By September 1992, one in six teachers in an ECE centre was to have completed a one-year ECE certificate program. In 1994, the ratio changes to one in five, and in 1995, one in six. Teachers without those certificates will have to complete an orientation course. Centres that provide care for school-aged children have to be licensed. However, they still do not have to conform to the teacher–child ratios set down in the regulations.

Regulation

Because of ECE's recent history in the province, many of the current regulations in Alberta have been discussed above. In 1990, new regulations regarding teacher–child ratios, group size, and teacher qualifications were added to the Social Care Facilities Act (Read, 1992). Teacher–child ratios and group size are not regulated for school-aged children. According to the new regulations, the program must meet the children's physical, social, intellectual, creative, and emotional needs. The new requirements for teachers have been discussed above and, especially in view of the research on quality of care and teacher education, these regulations are welcome.

SASKATCHEWAN

Jean Nykyforuk (1992b) provides an excellent overview of this province in a 1992 article, "A Socio-Geographic Overview of Saskatchewan." The province is vast, but its population is just over one million. While it is seen as a primarily rural province, over 60 percent of the population lived in urban centres at the time of the 1986 census. Like Alberta, Saskatchewan had a large wave of immigrants in the first decades of the 20th century, and it again experienced growth after World War II. However, since 1987, with the slump in its economy, Saskatchewan has experienced a net loss in population. The province continues to be ethnically diverse, and also includes a large aboriginal population. The province's economy is still tied to agriculture and mineral production, and manufacturing is secondary. Weather also remains a critical factor for Saskatchewan's well-being. The drought in the late 1980s had a marked effect on the province's economy.

Historical Overview

Nykyforuk (1992a) also detailed the history of child care for the National Child Care Study in her article "An Historical Overview of Child Care in Saskatchewan." World War II did not have an impact on child care in Saskatchewan as there were too few war-related industries for the province to qualify for the federal government's funding. It was not until the 1960s that a substantial number of women entered the workforce and began to need child care facilities. This growing need for child care, coupled with the financial assistance offered under CAP in 1966, led to a steady increase in the number of unregulated centres. Most were privately owned and operated as business ventures.

In 1969, the province enacted child care legislation, passing the Child Welfare Act. All advertised centres were to be inspected by a social worker who had the authority to close a centre; apparently this provision was not very effective. Several advocacy groups, including the Saskatchewan Day Care Development Committee, the Saskatoon Steering Committee, and the People for Child Care Action, were relentless in pressuring the government for improved legislation, more accessible child care, and larger government grants. In 1974, the government announced its intention to implement a new program and to increase funding. In 1975, new Day Care Regulations were passed; significantly, they required that all licensed facilities (except those already in existence in 1975) be non-profit organizations, run by a board that includes more than 50 percent of parent users of the centres.

The regulations also included procedures and standards for licensing, requirements for centre size, and details of financing. Training requirements, however, were minimal, consisting of a 42-hour in-service program for centre-based teachers and nothing for

family child care providers. Interestingly, nursery schools were exempt from the act and are not regulated by the province. Nykyforuk reports that 97 percent of all facilities were non-profit by 1987.

A number of difficulties with the parent-board model have occurred, perhaps mainly because the boards did not have business training. In fact, the preschool-cooperative movement has found it necessary to develop training programs, which they offer each year for incoming board members.

The 1980 provincial review of child care services reported a number of difficulties, including the lack of any in-province training programs, other than the 42-hour government course. Both one- and two-year programs in early child development (initially, it was called the Child Care Worker Program) were established in 1981 at the Kelsey Institute in Saskatoon, which followed an out-reach system to make programs available across the province through the community colleges.

Advocacy groups were active in Saskatchewan in the 1980s, seeking both expanded services and increased funding for child care. They also successfully lobbied against the Grant Devine government's 1984 intent to allow profit-making child care. A provincial organization, the Saskatchewan Child Care Association (SCCA) was formed in 1988 to express concerns about the profession as well as advocacy issues. Nykyforuk (1992a) suggests that the advocacy groups were needed as the government had not been increasing the number of licensed spaces, even though demand was increasing. As a consequence, a number of unlicensed, unregulated facilities sprung up, and the 1975 legislation did not limit the number of children who could be cared for in an unlicensed facility. While the unlicensed centres received no government funding, they also were not subject to the regulations.

In 1989, the Child Care Act was passed, replacing the 1975 regulations (Dill, 1992). Under the new act, profit-making centres can be established, but they must have parents on their boards. The legislation also insists that all centres be licensed, and it restricts the number of children who can be cared for in family child care homes whether or not they are licensed (Dill, 1992). In addition, the act permits centre-based care for infants. The regulations that accompany the act now require supervisors of child care centres to have completed a one-year certificate program.

Regulation

The 1990 regulations noted above introduced new requirements for centre size and group size as well as for the care of infants under 18 months (Child Care, 1993; Dill, 1992; Truemner, 1992). Nursery schools, however, are still not regulated. The new act requires programs to provide a developmentally appropriate environment. As noted above, supervisors now have to hold a certificate or its equivalent, but teachers only have to be over 16 and to take an orientation course within six months of being hired.

MANITOBA

Manitoba's population of 1 063 015 people in the 1986 census, 75 percent of whom live in urban settings, makes it the fifth most populous province (Stevens, 1992). Stevens (1992) provided an overview of the province for the CNCCS that helped to place child care in Manitoba in context. Manitoba's economy has shifted from its total reliance on native resources in the 19th century to an economy dependent on the service industries (Stevens, 1992). Manitobans have a history of ethnic diversity, but they have not experienced significant immigration waves in recent years.

Historical Overview

Friesen, Humphrey, and Brockman (1992b) prepared an article, "An Historical Overview of Child Care in Manitoba," for the CNCCS that provided much of the following information on the development of the child care profession, facilities, and policies in Manitoba. Child care has a lengthier history in Manitoba than it does in the other Prairie provinces, and can be traced back to the turn of the century when the Mothers' Association started advocating on behalf of the children of immigrants in Winnipeg. Several day care centres were established prior to World War I, and crèches sprung up over the years in communities where mothers worked for long shifts and volunteers identified a need for care. Church-based day cares were also involved in founding day nurseries when they perceived a need.

After World War II, child care services continued to evolve, and Friesen et al. (1992b) identify three periods of development that will be outlined below: (1) 1945–1974, (2) 1974–1981, and (3) 1982–present. Between 1945 and 1974, there was a steady increase in the number of child care facilities, and their growth was more marked when federal funds became available under CAP in 1966. Part-day nursery

schools that offered enrichment opportunities for more affluent children and compensatory programs for the less fortunate also grew in number beginning in the early 1940s. A laboratory nursery school was established at the University of Manitoba in 1943, during the period when the child study movement was flourishing. Licensing of centres was a municipal responsibility during this time, and the requirements focused on issues of health and safety, rather than curriculum, teacher education, group size, and teacher–child ratios. A series of government studies and briefs submitted to the government pointed to problems with the lack of consistent licensing standards as well as the lack of training programs in the province. A pilot training program was established at Red River Community College in the late 1960s. Then, in 1970, the University of Manitoba began a four-year program in Family Studies, while the University of Winnipeg introduced a three-year degree program in Developmental Studies in 1971.

Friesen et al. (1992b) identify the years from 1974 to 1981 as the second period of development of child care services in the province. In 1974, the government began to fund its Child Day Care Program, and in the first year about 1500 spaces were included in this non-profit program that was available to families eligible for subsidies. The new program apparently had more of a social-service orientation than the previous programs, which had a welfare bias. While private centres that been in operation from 1974 through to 1977 were permitted to take subsidized children, up to 50 percent of their capacity, as of 1977, non-profit spaces and family child care were generally favoured by the government's funding policies.

Licensing and inspections did not become uniform in Manitoba until 1982 when the new government introduced the Community Child Day Care Standards Act and Regulations (Friesen et al., 1992b). The act also included standards for teacher training, teacher–child ratios, programming, equipment, health and safety, and behaviour management as well as requirements for the physical facility and fire safety. Funding for non-profit organizations that had a parent-elected board was also outlined in the act, and capital grants were made available. Teacher training standards that had to be implemented in full by 1988 led to a rapid increase in the number of teachers who were knowledgeable in the area of child development. Between 1984 and 1988, the number of teachers who had completed a two-year diploma in ECE rose from 17 percent to 62 percent. The availability of funding for substitute teachers, while untrained teachers upgraded their training in intensive programs, presumably was a significant factor facilitating this rapid change. A competency-based assessment procedure also was introduced for people with experience in the field, but no formal training. Salary enhancement grants (SEGs) for eligible non-profit centres were introduced in 1986, partly in recognition of the educational requirements teachers had to meet, and partly in recognition of the negative effects of low salaries.

During the period 1982 to 1988, the integration of children with exceptionalities also expanded, and funds for the additional teachers required were made available. School-based child care also received capital allowances. In addition, the government demonstrated its interest in child care by working with the federal government to try to develop a comprehensive national system of child care.

The 1988 Manitoba Child Care Task Force demonstrated a continuing interest in the quality child care system the NDP government had begun to implement, and a number of the Task Force's recommendations were adopted. Although SEGs had been increased, teachers staged a one-day walk-out from their centres in October 1989 to protest the still inadequate salaries (Friesen et al., 1992a). The Manitoba Child Care Association, founded in 1974, accepted the government's plan to have a working group study the salary complaints, and in February 1990, the group's recommendations for short-term changes were adopted. SEGs were increased, as was funding. Non-profit workplace child care centres also became eligible for capital grants. A number of groups, including the Assiniboia Downs Race Track Child Care Centre discussed in Chapter 1, have taken advantage of the available funding.

Regulation

Non-school-based ECE programs fall under the Ministry of Family Services in Manitoba, and the Community Child Day Care Act and Regulations mentioned above are the relevant pieces of legislation (Child Care, 1990, 1993; Friesen, 1992; Friesen et al., 1992a). The legislation on group size and teacher–child ratios is extremely strict and perhaps the best in the country, at least for centre-based care. A play-based program is described in the legislation, and, as noted above, teachers must meet training requirements.

ONTARIO

Ontario, with close to 10 million people, is the most populous province in Canada. Over 80 percent of the population is urban; and 90 percent of the residents live in the small area of southern Ontario that makes up less than 10 percent of the province's land mass (Kyle, 1992d). Kyle (1992a) sketched an overview of social and demographic trends in Ontario that will help you place child care in its provincial context. Immigration to Ontario has been steady since World War II, and less than 50 percent of Ontario's population have British ancestors (Kyle, 1992d). In major urban centres like Toronto, as many as 40 percent of children in educational settings may not have English as a first language, and in some neighbourhoods there may not be any children with English as their native tongue (Kyle, 1992d). The needs of immigrant families, coupled with a high percentage of two-working-parent families, has led to a proliferation of early childhood programs: often both parents in immigrant families must work, and the families frequently require language classes.

Ontario also has close to 100 000 aboriginals, more than any other province. However, aboriginals constitute only 10 percent of the province's population. Special early childhood programs have been developed to meet the needs of aboriginal children living on reserves and in some urban centres.

Historical Overview

Young (1981) traced the development of early childhood education in Ontario through to the 1980s, and Irene Kyle (1992b), in her article "An Historical Overview of Child Care in Ontario," discussed more recent developments.

ECE has had a long but fragmented history in Ontario. One of the first public kindergartens in North America, if not the first (Morrison, 1991), was established in 1871 in Ontario by Dr. J.L. Hughes (Stapleford, 1976). Dr. Hughes, who provided the impetus for the optional kindergartens, later became interested in child care as a consequence of discussions with Hester Howe, a public school principal (Stapleford, 1976). Howe had many pupils in her school who brought their preschool-aged siblings to school because their widowed or deserted mothers were working and unable to care for their children during the day. Hughes suggested the establishment of a crèche to care for these preschoolers and thus, the crèche, which is now known as Victoria Day Care Services in Toronto, was opened in 1892. Unfortunately, the subsequent history of early childhood education programs in Ontario has not been marked by the coordinating force of people such as Dr. Hughes.

In 1885, Ontario again established itself as a pioneer in education when it passed legislation making kindergartens for 5-year-olds an integral part of the public school system (Fleming, 1971). However, it was not until after World War II that kindergartens became virtually universal in Ontario schools. Junior kindergartens are a more recent phenomenon in Ontario. In 1943, the first junior kindergarten for 3- to

4-year-old children was established by the Ottawa Public School Board (Young, 1981). Dr. McGregor Easson, the chief inspector of Ottawa public schools at the time, cited the positive effects that British and American nursery schools had on children's development as an explanation for these programs. Four years later, the Toronto Board of Education introduced a junior kindergarten program that was made available only to children from deprived environments (Young, 1981). Although the 1950 *Report of the Royal Commission on Education in Ontario* recommended that half-day, optional programs for 3- and 4-year-old children be established by the public school boards, the increase in the number of junior kindergarten programs throughout the 1950s was minimal (Young, 1981).

The establishment of early childhood education programs for children under 5 years of age, including nursery schools and child care centres, was much more sporadic and subject to the political and social pressures of the time than the establishment of kindergartens. Although the number of child care centres increased after the 1892 establishment of the crèche and peaked during World War I, the 1920 Ontario Mother's Allowance Act, which provided unsupported mothers with sufficient funds to remain at home, resulted in a declining need for child care (Stapleford, 1976). In 1926, however, the St. George's School for Child Study, now the Institute for Child Study, was established under sponsorship of the Department of Psychology at the University of Toronto with funds from the Laura Spelman Rockefeller Foundation (Fleming, 1971,; Northway, 1973; Stapleford, 1976). The introduction of the study of child development at the university seemed to prompt a recognition of the educational aspects of care for children under 5. A number of half-day nursery schools that catered to middle-class children were established in subsequent years, and child care centres began to offer both education and care.

World War II marked a period of significant and rapid change for child care in the province (Stapleford, 1976). Mothers were needed to staff the war-related industries, and thus the provision of extensive child care services became an urgent matter. A number of child care facilities were opened in response to this demand during the early war years (Stapleford, 1976). Early in 1942, a report by the Welfare Council of Toronto and District indicated that the available child care services were inadequate (Stapleford 1976). Consequently, the Council pressured the provincial and federal governments to provide appropriate care for the children of employed mothers. By July 1942, the Dominion-Provincial Wartime Day Nursery Agreement, a cost-sharing arrangement, was negotiated and Ontario established an advisory committee to direct efforts aimed at the rapid provision of day care. A wartime day nursery, which doubled as a demonstration and training centre for teachers, was in operation within two months (Stapleford, 1976). Parents paid fees covering approximately a third of the centre's costs, and the federal and provincial governments shared the remaining expense.

The province established a Day Nursery Branch in the Department of Public Welfare to promote and administer the establishment of additional "day nurseries," as they were called at the time. Dorothy Millichamp, the Assistant Director of the Institute for Child Study, was appointed to head the newly created Day Nursery Branch (Stapleford, 1976). By the end of the war, twenty day nurseries with 1200 children between the ages of 2 and 5 had been established throughout the province. Moreover, an additional 42 child care centres had been established in the public schools for 3000 children ranging from 6 to 14 years (Stapleford, 1976). These facilities for some 4200 children reflected an unusually strong commitment to the full development of each child, especially given the haste with which the centres were conceived and opened (Stapleford, 1976). In large part, the developmental nature of these centres is attributable to the influence that Millichamp and her colleagues at the Institute had on ideas of appropriate day care. However, many of the unsupervised day nurseries that opened during the early war years, in response to the demand for child care facilities, did not have the same commitment to high-quality care (Stapleford, 1976).

The end of the war marked the end of federal government support for child care centres in the province. Contrary to popular expectation, the return of the veterans to the workforce did not mean that all the working mothers wanted to return to the home. Consequently, in 1946, the government passed the Day Nurseries Act and became one of the first jurisdictions in North America to have both licensing and inspection of child care centres, and provincial and municipal sharing of the operating costs. By the end of 1947, there were 146 licensed centres in the province, including 25 full-day and 139 half-day programs. Growth was slow throughout the 1950s, which is not surprising in view of Bowlby's assertion (discussed in Chapter 2) that short-term separations from the mother were comparable to being placed in a sterile orphanage. Once Bowlby's work was reassessed, confidence in child care grew, and by 1960 there were approximately 360 licensed day nurseries in the province (Stapleford, 1976).

The growth of preschools and child care centres in Ontario during the 1960s and 1970s was particularly rapid. By September 1980, a total of 66 998 children were enrolled in 1400 centre-based facilities licensed under the Ontario Day Nurseries Act (Young, 1982). Most spaces were for children 3 years and older; only 910 infants under 18 months and 2474 toddlers, ranging from 18 to 30 months, were in such centres in 1980. Junior kindergartens also multiplied in the 1960s and 1970s, and kindergartens were available in all school boards by the 1970s.

Given the lengthy history of ECE in the province, it is perhaps surprising to find that teacher education continues to be fragmented. Fleming (1971, vol. 5, p.1), comments that Ontario has never been noted for the importance it has placed on the formal preparation of teachers. With the exception of the Institute for Child Study's graduate education and training program for nursery school and child care teachers, there were no facilities for the preparation of preschool teachers prior to the war. The provincially operated demonstration and training child care centre, established in 1942 to meet wartime needs, ceased operations shortly after the expiry of the War Measures Act.

In the years that followed the war, the primary impetus for the establishment of education and training programs for preschool teachers came from the Toronto Nursery Education Association (TNEA) (now the Association for Early Childhood Education, Toronto [AECET]) and subsequently the Nursery Education Association of Ontario (NEAO) (now the Association for Early Childhood Education, Ontario [AECEO]), which were founded in 1946 and 1950 respectively. The first success these associations had

was in persuading the government and Ryerson Polytechnic Institute to establish an ECE program. Shortly afterwards the NEAO succeeded in convincing several universities to offer three-part extension courses for preschool teachers (Fleming 1971; Stapleford, 1976). Following successful completion of the first two sessions of these courses, students were given a letter of standing "recommending the holder as a student assistant" (Fleming, 1971, vol. 5, pg. 17). Students who demonstrated their competence as teachers in a nursery school or child care setting for a period of a year, and who completed the third part of the course, were eligible to apply for NEAO certification. The NEAO, a voluntary professional organization, had instituted a voluntary system of certification to regulate the competence of the members of the profession. NEAO certification provided prospective employers with an effective means of identifying competent staff.

Since 1960 there have been a number of significant developments in terms of the availability of teacher education and training programs for early childhood educators in the province. In 1965, when the Ontario

Colleges of Applied Arts and Technology were proposed, the NEAO saw them as educational institutions that could meet the growing demand for competent early childhood educators to staff the rapidly increasing number of child care centres and preschools in the province (Young, 1981). Early in 1966, NEAO representatives and Department of Education personnel began to prepare a series of guidelines for the development of ECE programs in the colleges. In September of the same year, the first program opened at Centennial College and attracted far more applicants than enrolment capacity would allow. In 1967, an additional eight colleges offering the ECE program were opened, and all had a capacity enrolment that year.

Despite the availability of trained teachers, the government continued to see child care as a welfare service, and professionals in the field grew more vocal (Kyle, 1992b). In the early 1980s, the Ontario Federation of Labour organized a child care conference, which led to the establishment of the Ontario Coalition for Better Day Care (now Child Care). The Coalition was very active in the 1980s, and eventually the Conservative government, in a pre-election package, announced a program that would increase funding and child care spaces. The defeat of that government in 1985 was followed by a Liberal/NDP coalition, then a Liberal majority in 1987 and subsequently an NDP government in 1990. These frequent changes in government have meant that some policies developed by one party were later questioned and their implementation delayed by another party. Nonetheless, there have been some significant developments in this period.

The Liberal/NDP coalition developed a child care plan that became a reality in 1987 when New Directions for Child Care was included in the new government's throne speech. This policy injected over $165 million into child care, which was clearly recognized as a public service rather than a welfare benefit. School-aged programs were made a priority, and capital funding for child care centres in all new schools became available. Direct operating grants (DOGs) were given to all non-profit centres in 1988 in an effort to improve teacher salaries; later, 50 percent of the DOGs were given to profit-making centres.

Concerns about the quality of care, especially in profit-making centres, emerged during this period. A series of articles in *The Globe and Mail* (McIntosh &, Rauhala, 1989) and the provincial auditor's report in the same year pointed to inadequate enforcement of the regulations across the province; subsequent government initiatives have tried to rectify this situation. A shortage of trained teachers, due primarily to the rapid turnover of underpaid teachers in the field, is a continuing concern.

In 1990, funding for full-day kindergartens became available, and school boards were given a 1994 deadline for implementing junior kindergarten programs. In 1992, the Peel Board of Education, having hastily established junior kindergartens in 1990, ended them when cuts in provincial funding were announced. Other school boards suggested they would follow Peel's example, and in the spring of 1993, the impoverished Ontario government revoked its deadline that would have made all school boards offer junior kindergarten programs by September 1994. However, reports of a leaked cabinet document suggested that universally available school-based programs for all children between 3 and 5 years will become available, and they will conform to the Day Nurseries Act, not the Education Act (Critics Challenge, 1993).

Regulation

Kyle (1992c, 1992d) outlined the Ontario regulations for child care for the CNCCS. Two ministries are involved in early childhood education. School-based programs, including junior and senior kindergartens, are regulated by the Ministry of Education. However, child care centres housed in schools and all non-school-based child care settings, including nursery schools and parent–child resource centres, are regulated by the Ministry of Community and Social Services (COMSOC). The Day Nurseries Act and Ontario Regulation 143/88, discussed above, specify requirements for centre-based and family child care in Ontario. The legislation outlines minimum requirements for the physical setting, teacher qualifications, teacher–child ratios, group size, nutrition, and safety in licensed facilities. The legislation also specifies that centres must provide appropriate programs that enhance motor skills, language, and cognitive and socio-emotional development.

The Education Act does not have comparable requirements regarding group size, teacher–child ratios, and indoor and outdoor space; teachers do not have to have a background in ECE. This leads to some serious discrepancies in the program requirements for 4- and 5-year-old children in the province. For example, a 4-year-old in a junior kindergarten may be in a class of 25 children with a teacher who has minimal experience with children of this age, while a 4-year-old in a child care centre would not be in a class with more than sixteen children and two teachers, at least one of whom has studied young children in depth.

QUEBEC

Carrière's (1992) article, "A Socio-Geographic Overview of Quebec," provides an overview of this distinct province in which more than 90 percent of its 6.5 million inhabitants are of French origin. While Quebec is the largest province physically, most of its population lives in the St. Lawrence Valley and 80 percent were in urban centres during the 1986 census. While pulp and paper production, mining, and hydroelectric power generation remain factors in the economy, manufacturing and the service sector have become major forces in Quebec. The province continues to be a destination point for a number of immigrants, especially native French speakers. Of course, all immigrant children must enrol in francophone schools.

Historical Overview

Desjardins (1992) provides a detailed account of the lengthy history of child care in Quebec, which dates back to the first half of the 19th century. Families moving into the cities to find work in new industries led to the creation of facilities to care for their children. As factory work by children under 12 did not become illegal until 1885, parents could not rely on older siblings or neighbours for child care as they were working. Children's shelters, run by the Grey Nuns and Sisters of Providence, were established in Montreal and some smaller locations as early as 1858. Over 60 000 preschoolers attended these centres between 1858 and 1922, but they in no way came close to meeting the need for child care in the province. Children under 2 years were not permitted to attend the shelters, and, typically, the eldest girl in a family left school at 10 or 11 to care for the younger children in her family. A labour journalist for *La Presse*, Jean-Baptiste GagnePetit, campaigned against this practice and day care centres eventually received some provincial government funding in the 1890s. English-speaking mothers had even more difficulty finding care. Desjardins reports that the Montreal Day Nursery, founded in 1887 by wealthy volunteer women, was the only centre for English children in the 19th century.

Many of the shelters were closed early in the 20th century, while others became orphanages. With the advent of World War I, however, several child care centres were established, but orphanages became the more common form of care for single parents.

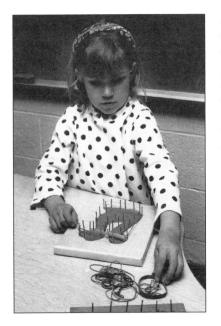

Apparently, only a tenth of the children in orphanages in Quebec were real orphans. Despite recommendations by the Liberal government that child care facilities and junior kindergartens be funded during the Depression, the Duplessis government firmly opposed women who worked outside the home and refused to assist them. World War II forced the government to abandon, at least temporarily, its view of working women as immoral, and six centres were opened in Montreal with federal funding. The Catholic Church, a potent force in Quebec society, denounced the child care centres, and most francophone women who worked during the war relied on informal methods of care. Duplessis closed the centres as soon as the war ended despite considerable protest, and unregulated, unsubsidized child care was the norm in the province throughout the 1950s. The city of Montreal had 27 private centres at that time, and a number of them offered a five-day residential program for children with working parents, so they could return to their homes each weekend. The Montreal Day Nursery also continued its service, and several religious groups offered help to needy children.

Despite the advent of CAP in 1966, the Quebec government remained steadfast in its opposition to child care by anyone other than parents, and it was not until the 1970s that any significant changes occurred. Federal government funding came through the Local Initiatives Program (LIP), a federally funded job creation program that provided "start-up funds" for many child care programs throughout the country. In addition, the Perspectives Jeunesse or Focus on Youth program another federally funded job creation program targeted at youths, led to the creation of around 70 child care centres in Quebec, much to the dismay of the provincial government. When the funding stopped in 1973, occupations of government offices and street protests followed, pressuring Bourassa's Liberal government to develop a child care policy. The Bacon Plan, implemented in 1974, allowed needy children to be subsidized, but favoured for-profit centres as non-profit centres no longer received any public funds. Desjardins notes that 54 of the 70 non-profit centres had to close for financial reasons several months after the Bacon Plan was implemented.

Pressure on the government to play a role in child care continued throughout the 1970s, and, finally, in 1978, the government issued a policy statement on child care. The policy favoured parent choice of services, joint parent–government funding of child care, and additional options such as family child care and school-aged care facilities. In 1979, the government passed the Child Care Services Act and created a new government office, the Office of Child Care Services (Office des Services de Garde à l'Enfance [OSGE]), that now falls under the Minister for Women's Issues (i.e., Ministre Déléguée à la Condition Féminine), to deal with children's issues. The OSGE, among other responsibilities, was to ensure that quality child care was available, to monitor centres, and to improve teacher training.

The Act Respecting Day Care recognized five types of child care: the group child care centre (Garderie), family child care homes (Milieu familial), drop-off centres (Halte garderie), school-aged child care (Milieu scholaire), and nursery schools. The new legislation set standards for these facilities that have undergone several revisions in recent years. Teacher training, teacher–child ratios, group sizes, and centre sizes were regulated, as were health and safety, equipment, and the physical plant.

Regulation

The OSGE, a unique institution in Canadian child care, is a semi-autonomous body that has the power to set standards and regulations for child care and to ensure that the legislation is followed (Child Care, 1990; Fullum, 1992a, 1992b). The Ministère de la

Main-d'Oeuvre et de la Sécurité du Revenu (MMS) et l'Information Professionnel and the Ministère de l'Éducation (ME) are also involved in child care (Fullum, 1992a, 1992b). The MMS administers the subsidy program for child care for the OSGE. The ME administers the start-up and operating grants that are available for school boards that want to establish child care in their schools. The ME also is responsible for the university and college programs that are available for teacher training. Teacher–child group size are regulated, as is centre size. Teacher qualifications are also specified in the legislation. While centres must outline their developmental objectives in order to receive a licence, the legislation does not contain information about a prescribed curriculum.

NEW BRUNSWICK

New Brunswick's population of 709 445 in the 1986 census made it the third smallest province in the country (Gamble, 1992b). Joan Gamble (1992b), an ECE professor at the University of Moncton, prepared "A Socio-Geographic Overview of New Brunswick" for the Canadian National Child Care Study. In the article, she provides an outsider with a picture of the province's economy and people. Almost two-thirds of New Brunswick's population are English speaking, while a third of the population is French speaking. The province also has close to 5000 Micmac and Maliseet Indians. The population is evenly split between urban and rural settings. While fishing, logging, trapping, and other resource-based occupations used to be the mainstay of the New Brunswick economy, industries like tourism, education, information technology, and governments also are important employers. The province is one of the poorer ones, and many young people have moved away during periods when jobs were plentiful in places like Alberta and Ontario. Women have moved into the workforce in increasing numbers, but the unemployment rate is chronically high.

Historical Overview

Gamble (1992a) also prepared "An Historical Overview of Child Care in New Brunswick" for the CNCCS. The history of child care in New Brunswick, as in many provinces, is brief. During the first half of the century, the extended family was responsible for child care in the province. If one could not call on that informal network, the only option was to turn to the child welfare services. Prior to the 1950s, that usually meant allowing one's children to be placed in an orphanage, and those institutions were underfunded and of very questionable quality. Many served both children and adults who needed care. Large institutions for children in New Brunswick remained in existence until the mid-1970s, even though the research showing their negative effects on development had been available since the 1940s.

A number of unregulated child care centres were established in the 1960s and early 1970s in New Brunswick, and professionals in the field were becoming concerned about the quality of care in these centres. The formation of the Garde de Jour NB Day Care Association in 1973 was significant and the Association helped to accelerate changes in child care policies. In September 1974, the government proclaimed the Day Care Act, and teacher–child ratios and health and safety requirements finally became a reality. However, as we have seen in so many other jurisdictions, enforcement of the act was sporadic as there was only one supervisor to inspect all centres in the province. More comprehensive regulations were included in the 1980 Child and Family Services and Family Relations Act. The new legislation also differed in tone: child care was seen as a child development service, rather than a welfare issue.

Since 1974, excellent degree programs in education with a specialization in ECE have been available at the University of New Brunswick and the Université de Moncton, and some of the key experts in the field were graduates of these programs. However college programs were needed. The Garde de Jour NB Day Care Association and other interested groups persistently urged the government to establish teacher-training programs. Finally, several college-based training programs were established in the early 1980s. Subsequently, a competency-based program was developed for teachers with experience but no formal training, so that they became eligible for an equivalency certificate. Then, in 1987, the Canada Employment Centre agreed to fund teachers in a part-time, formal training program, and many have taken advantage of this opportunity.

A number of significant developments in ECE have occurred in the early 1990s. For example, kindergartens have become part of the school system, and government-funded early intervention programs are available. "Excellence in Education," a 1992 provincial government report, also recommends significant changes in teacher education. Although the province still does not have any training regulations, a review of the child care legislation was initiated in 1992 (Child Care, 1993). Subsequently, a working group was established by the government in 1993 (Child Care, 1993). Teacher training, standardization of regulations, and wage enhancement grants are being discussed by the group.

Regulation

Lutes (1992) and Lutes and Gamble (1992) outlined New Brunswick's regulations for the CNCCS. School-based ECE programs fall under the Department of Education, while non-school-based programs are under the Department of Health and Community Services. The 1980 Family Services and Family Relations Act and the 1983 Regulations 83–85 for the act contain regulations for non-school-based ECE programs. The 1985 Day Care Facilities Standards also apply to these programs. Centre size, teacher–child ratios, and group sizes are regulated in centre- and family-based ECE programs. The legislation does require centres to provide stimulating, developmentally oriented programs; but there are still no requirements for teachers, other than that they be 16 or older and willing to take training. Primary staff must be 19 as of 1993 and supervise staff under that age (Child Care, 1993).

PRINCE EDWARD ISLAND

Mullen (1992) provides an overview of P.E.I., Canada's smallest but most densely populated province. The 1986 census found that close to 50 000 of the island's almost 130 000 people live in urban settings, while 70 000 live in rural, non-farm settings. The economy of P.E.I. has become far more service-based in the past 30 years, and service industries now employ two-thirds of the labour force.

Historical Overview

Flanagan-Rochon and Rice (1992) documented the history of child care in the province for the CNCCS. Orphanages and informal mechanisms of child care, often involving relatives, were the norm in P.E.I. until the late 1960s when unregulated kindergartens developed, especially in the urban areas. Social workers saw these programs as potentially beneficial for disadvantaged children, and soon wanted full-day programs. Some federally funded, unregulated, unlicensed full-day programs were developed for children from impoverished families, and private operators opened centres in urban areas like Charlottetown.

Significant growth in centre-based child care in P.E.I. was not seen until the mid-1970s. Nevertheless, concern mounted about the crowding, inadequate ventilation and lighting, and poor programming that characterized a few available settings in Charlottetown. In 1971, the provincial Department of Social Services assumed responsibility for regulating and funding child care. The province continued to fund several of the Head Start-type programs that had been federally funded until 1971, as well as the University of P.E.I. and Charlottetown child care centres. Moreover, they established a two-year ECE program at Holland College. Then, in 1973, the Child Care Facilities Act was enacted, but it addressed only basic concerns like health and safety. However, the government initiated discussions about additional regulations with child care centre operators, who, in turn, formed the Early Childhood Development Association (ECDA).

The ECDA gained prominence through a variety of public education programs and through ongoing submission of proposals for better regulations and training requirements to the government. They were instrumental in having the government undertake its 1983 *Study of Child Care Services in Prince Edward Island*, which led to the introduction of teacher-training requirements and other far-reaching revisions to the regulations for the act. The revised regulations were introduced in 1986 and the Child Care Facilities Act and the regulations were revised in 1987. The province, with the assistance of the federal government, funded a part-time program in ECE at Holland College for teachers seeking to upgrade their qualifications. The University of P.E.I. also introduced extension courses in ECE. As well, the government issued a long-range policy paper on child care and increased available funding. The Direct Funding Program, announced in 1987 and improved in 1990, not only allocates maintenance funds for centres, but it also provides operating grants with a portion designated for teachers' salaries (Flanagan-Rochon & Rice, 1992; Flanagan-Rochon, 1992a, 1992b). Consequently, salaries have increased substantially since 1987.

Regulation

The Ministry of Health and Social Services is responsible for non-school-based ECE programs, including kindergarten, in P.E.I., while the Department of Education oversees school-based ECE programs (Flanagan-Rochon, 1992a, 1992b). The five-member, multidisciplinary Child Care Facilities Board, which, by law, includes two ECDA members, is responsible for licensing and enforcement of the Child Care Facilities Act. The Coordinator of Early Childhood Services, the Assistant Coordinator, and their administrative assistant are resources for the board, and they act as inspectors in the province. They ensure that the regulations related to group size, teacher–child ratios, centre size, and teacher training are followed. The curriculum must include group and individual activities, active and quiet play, and developmentally appropriate activities.

NOVA SCOTIA

Canning and Irwin (1992) prepared "A Socio-Geographic Overview of Nova Scotia" for the CNCCS. In 1986, 46 percent of Nova Scotia's 880 000 people lived in rural settings, but a large proportion of them live adjacent to urban areas where they work. Forestry, construction, mining, and fishing remain important in Nova Scotia's economy, but the service sector provides two-thirds of the available jobs. Unemployment rates are typically higher than the national average in Nova Scotia, even if they are lower than in the rest of the Atlantic region. The lack of employment opportunities forces many people to move to central and western Canada during economically bleak times, and this accounts for the relatively slow population growth. While more ethnically diverse than the other Maritime provinces, almost 90 percent of Nova Scotians are of British or French origin.

Historical Overview

Irwin and Canning (1992b) documented the history of child care in Nova Scotia for the CNCCS. Child care was not regulated until 1967 when the Day Nurseries Act was proclaimed, and CAP funding did not become available until 1972. However, there were child care programs in the province before that time. Several centres were established in Halifax in 1910 for the children of working women, and orphanages became common institutions in the following decades. A centre for underprivileged children that charged ten cents a day for milk and snack was established by the Protestant Orphans' Home in Halifax in 1946, perhaps in an attempt to keep the children from becoming residents of their home. In addition to the child care centres opened by several orphanages, there were some generic Head Start programs, some parent-run programs, and a student-run child care centre that operated on a non-profit basis before licensing became a reality. In addition, some profit-making centres had been founded, sometimes by mothers who could not find adequate child care for their own children. Part-day preschool programs with an educational, rather than custodial, orientation also were available for those who could afford them.

The 1967 Day Nurseries Act emphasized the importance of the physical environment for licensing, and did not address teacher training or curriculum. However, a government committee looking at child care in the province just prior to the act suggested that training programs were needed. The committee also suggested that CAP assistance be available only if children were in non-profit centres, and that was adopted as policy. Part-time summer and evening ECE courses, organized by professionals in the field, were offered as early as 1968, and the program has continued since then, both with and without provincial funding. A Child Study option was established in Dalhousie University's Faculty of Education in 1970, and soon after, Mount St. Vincent

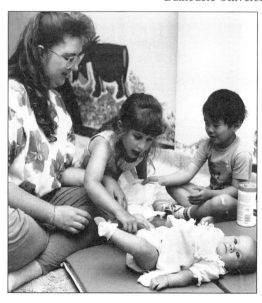

University began a one-year diploma program in ECE and then a four-year degree program. The Nova Scotia Teachers' College also offers a two-year diploma course in child development through its Froebel Institute.

A number of child care centres were established in the early 1970s with the federal funding that was available through the Local Initiatives Program (LIP). Citizens involved in these centres pressured the province to continue funding these centres when LIP ended, and eventually received limited assistance. While additional assistance was offered in 1974 by the newly elected Liberals, they soon put a freeze on subsidized places that remained in effect until 1989. Centres were permitted to extra-bill on several occasions between 1975 and 1979 to keep solvent, and this led to an outcry about the lack of support for child care in the province. A task force was appointed in 1979 to look at financing, and improved funding, including yearly increments to the available subsidies, became a reality. Subsequently, a 1983 task force made far-reaching recommendations about teacher training,

funding, infant care, and ECE-trained government employees. The teacher-training recommendations, which required two-thirds of centre teachers to have ECE training by 1989, were accepted. Many of the other recommendations were accepted in principle, subject to the availability of federal approval of a cost-sharing plan. However, the federal approval did not materialize, and issues such as separate infant care standards and subsidies continue to be discussed. Nonetheless, the recommendations from government continued through the following years and the advocacy groups extracted firm promises only from the losing parties in the 1988 election.

Rural areas remained underserviced, subsidized spaces remained frozen, teachers remained underpaid, and protest grew. Finally, in March 1990, 80 percent of the province's non-profit centres closed. Teachers filled the legislative gallery, and the media focused on parental and community support for their demands for increased wages and better funding (Irwin & Canning, 1992a). Salary-enhancement grants were announced within days, and the government created a Round Table on Day Care that was to review salaries, legislation, training, certification, and involvement of the private sector in child care by 1991. The Round Table was released its interim report in April 1991, and 100 new subsidized spaces, fewer than were recommended, were created in 1992. The Round Table was still meeting regularly in 1993, while the need for more quality child care continued.

Regulation

The Day Care Services Section of the Department of Community Services is responsible for child care in Nova Scotia. All facilities with four or more children are required to have licences. The 1978 Day Care Act and Regulations, amended in 1984 and 1987, outlines requirements for licensed, non-school-based centres. Centre size, teacher–child ratios, and group size are regulated for some ages, but not all. The act specifies that the program must be designed to stimulate all areas of development, and the 1990 *Guidelines for Operating a Day Care Facility for Children in Nova Scotia* notes that a variety of models, including Montessori, the Cognitively Oriented Curriculum, and thematic approaches are acceptable. Two-thirds of the teachers in a centre must have ECE training or the equivalent combination of experience and courses for those teachers working in centres prior to the change in the act.

NEWFOUNDLAND

Marc Glassman (1992a, 1992b) provided an overview of Newfoundland's sociogeographic features for the CNCCS, and traced the history of child care in that context. In the 1986 census, 60 percent of the province's 568 349 people were found to be in urban areas. Only 2 percent of Newfoundland's population have non-British, non-French origins. A small percentage of the population is aboriginal, although the government has relocated Inuit communities in Labrador because of hydroelectric developments. Fishing, mining, logging, and their related industries remain important in the province's economy, but the 1992 and 1993 moratorium on the fishery has been devastating for the province. While the service sector accounts for a larger portion of the economy, it, in turn, depends heavily on federal transfer payments and government employment. The ongoing but troubled Hibernia oil fields project and the Churchill

Falls hydroelectric project are viewed as possible means of enriching the economy of one of the poorest provinces.

Like the other Atlantic provinces, Newfoundland had many people leave during the early 1980s, the boom years in central and western Canada, as employment was difficult to find at home. Newfoundland has had the dubious distinction of leading the country in unemployment rates and poverty statistics throughout the 1970s and 1980s.

Historical Overview

As noted above, Glassman (1992a) has compiled the history of child care in Newfoundland. The Day Care and Homemaker Services Act was not passed until 1975 when licensing and regulations for child care were introduced. Moreover, kindergarten was not available across the province until the 1973–1974 school year. Several accounts suggest that a group of nuns operated a child care centre at the turn of the century in Renews, and unregulated kindergarten programs were available at least by the mid-1920s. Private preschool and kindergarten programs for fee-paying parents became more plentiful in St. John's between the 1940s and 1960s, and workplace child care grew in St. John's in the 1960s. Play groups and generic Head Start programs also multiplied in the capital city during the 1960s. In addition, several child care centres and preschools were established in Labrador. It is interesting that the government prohib-ited care for children under 2 years in any licensed facility as of 1968, even though they did nothing about licensing existing facilities until 1975.

After a review of 1971 census data pointed to the great shortage of child care in Newfoundland, the province launched a review committee in 1974. The committee's recommendations led to the enactment of the aforementioned child care act in 1975 as well as the Day Care and Homemaker Services Regulations in 1976. Although the act seemed to emphasize the custodial aspects of child care and ignore teacher education, it did bring standards and licensing into being before more affluent provinces, Alberta, for example. Until 1980, subsidies were available only if children were in non-profit child care, but it was then extended to include up to 50 percent of the spaces in any private child care centre in the province. Centres became more common in the St. John's area, but concerns still remain about the lack of facilities in the rural areas.

The Early Childhood Development Association (ECDA), founded in 1971, persisted in asking the government to implement regulations, teacher education programs, and funding policies that would enhance the quality of child care in the province. Many of their recommendations have been accepted, although the waiting period was often extended. As of 1989, supervisors of child care centres must have a one-year ECE certificate and a year of experience, or a two-year diploma or a degree in ECE, or a related degree (e.g., child development) and a year of experience. In addition, one teacher in programs with less than 25 children (two if there are more than 25) must have a year of supervised experience or training. The ECDA convinced Memorial University to offer a nine-course certificate program in ECE in the early 1970s, and it was extended to include a Corner Brook location. In 1980, however, the university cancelled the

program, assuming that what is now Cabot College and the Faculty of Education at Memorial would soon be offering respectively two-year and four-year degree programs in ECE. Finally, in 1983, a year-long certificate program was established with Canada Employment and Immigration funding; the long-awaited two-year diploma program did not come into being until 1986. In 1988, both certificate and diploma programs were established in Corner Brook, some eight years after the university had cancelled the original program, fearing redundancy.

The issue of junior kindergarten was raised several times during the 1980s, both by teachers and government committees concerned about how unprepared many children are for kindergarten. The teachers were successful in reorganizing kindergarten programs to be more play-based and child-centred, but junior kindergartens are still not a reality in most school boards. Infant care, or the lack thereof, also remains a concern; the province still does not permit licensed care for children under 2 years. The Association of Early Childhood Educators of Newfoundland and Labrador, founded in 1989, seems to have replaced the ECDA, and they, along with several child care advocacy groups, aim to ensure that affordable, high-quality child care is available in the province. In the Canadian Professional Speaks Out section, Joanne Morris describes some very significant developments in teacher education that were initiated in 1991.

Regulation

The Department of Social Services is responsible for ECE programs in the province, and a ten-member Provincial Licensing Board oversees licensing and subsidies (Randell, 1992a, 1992b). Nursery schools and preschools in private schools also fall under the Day Care and Homemaker Services Act, which means that ECE programs receive equal treatment lacking in some provinces, such as Ontario. The Department of Education oversees the curriculum in kindergartens and primary programs, and is represented on the Licensing Board. A full-time ECE consultant with the Department of Social Services develops programming standards and may inspect centres to see if they comply with

A CANADIAN
PROFESSIONAL SPEAKS OUT

Current Regulations on Teacher Education in Newfoundland

An exciting new initiative in the province of Newfoundland and Labrador is the development of a certification process for all staff of licensed centres, accompanied by an individualized program of study toward the diploma in Early Childhood Education. This is a joint venture of the Department of Social Services as the licensing body, the Department of Education, which approves curriculum, and Cabot College of Applied Arts, Technology and Continuing Education as the lead institute that is developing the provincially approved curriculum into distance education, including summer institutes. Primary funding for this initiative has been provided by the Child Care Initiatives Fund, Health and Welfare Canada.

It was recognized several years ago that there were approximately 450 to 500 practising early childhood educators, of whom only a small percentage had formal training. The diploma program is offered on-site in two locations within the province for full-time studies. Evening courses had been tried unsuccessfully due to the cost-recoverable nature of these offerings. Limited access to training led to this program design in order to address the vast geographic distances that exist between communities. Training through distance education methodologies makes it accessible, and quality is built in through qualified advisers/tutors, regular performance evaluation, and summer institutes for practical and group work. Participants are able to continue their employment and upgrade at their own pace toward certification levels that recognize various levels of academic education.

A challenging component of this program is to evaluate each participant's experiential learning in order to award advanced standing in their studies. Participants develop a comprehensive portfolio through a credit course, documenting their learning, which is further verified by identified individuals and through a performance evaluation. This enables participants to begin their studies in areas they need to work on and to avoid repeating learning in areas in which they can already demonstrate competence.

Until now the legislation governing certification has not been enforceable due to the absence of accessible training. This initiative is viewed as having widespread significance in upgrading the quality of existing service delivery. Supervisors and lead staff of centres will be priorized as having to meet certification standards. Provincial orientation courses will become available for those not wanting to pursue lead positions within a centre and will satisfy entry level certification. As the pool of qualified individuals grows throughout various regions within the province, others in training will gain the benefits of qualified advisers and field supervisors in their communities. It is also anticipated that education and certification will lead to a greater sense of professionalism within the field and greater public awareness of the importance of quality child care.

Joanne Morris
Cabot College
St. John's, Newfoundland

them, at the request of the Licensing Board. The Department of Health is represented on the Licensing Board and is responsible for building, fire, health, and electrical code inspections. Finally, the Department of Education, Post-Secondary Studies, is responsible for postsecondary ECE programs. Teacher–child ratios, group size, and centre size are regulated. Minimal teacher qualification requirements are in place in a province that saw the first ECE graduates only in 1988.

YUKON TERRITORY

Mauch (1992c) describes this territory in "A Socio-Geographic Overview of the Yukon." Almost 75 percent of the territory's 30 000 residents are likely to live in Whitehorse, Faro, Dawson City, or Watson Lake. There is a large aboriginal population, of whom the Inuvialuit are the best known. Around 25 percent of the population are Native Canadians; in rural settings, they are usually the majority group. Mining and tourism are the major industries, and both are quite susceptible to fluctuations in the economy. Mining and tourism also attract a transient labour force that leaves the territory after earning high wages for a while. Single-parent families are especially common in the Yukon; 30 percent of all preschoolers, for example, live in single-parent families. The birth rate is high, exceeded only by that in the Northwest Territories. Moreover, over 70 percent of working-age females are employed. These characteristics of the Yukon's population have a number of implications for child care.

Historical Overview

Linda Johnson and Mary Jane Joe (1992) have documented the history of child care in the Yukon and include a fascinating overview of Yukon life before the gold rush, which would be good supplementary reading material. Prior to the influx of people that came with the discovery of gold, most aboriginal and Native peoples led a traditional life, living in small bands and supporting themselves through hunting and fishing. The extended family was a reality, there were few non-Natives, and major urban centres did not exist. The 1896 rush to the Klondike quickly ended the tranquillity. Schools were established in the Yukon with the arrival of non-Native parents, but Natives were excluded from them. In addition, they became foreigners in their own land, the wildlife and resources being disrupted by the newcomers. The rush came to a fairly abrupt halt in 1904, but the practices of the foreigners had become part of life for many in the Yukon. Native children were frequently sent to boarding schools run by missionaries (some of which are currently under investigation because of accusations of abuse), and uprooted from their families, language, and customs. In 1942, with the construction of the Alaska Highway, the population multiplied to almost six times its prewar size with the arrival of construction crews. Wildlife disruption, social disorder, and epidemics of non-Native diseases were pronounced. While growth slowed after the war, the population of 9000 was double what it had been in pre-highway years, and urban centres started to spring up along the highway, further disrupting traditional ways of life.

Federal funding for schools was provided on the condition that Native children be allowed to attend them, and these children were slowly integrated into public schools. Nonetheless, many schools were still residential because they were concentrated in larger towns and cities, and racism was a reality for most Native students (and adults) in these urban centres. Kindergartens were not available in the 1960s in the Yukon, but a generic Head Start kindergarten was opened in Whitehorse in 1968 with the aim of more gradually introducing Native children to English and school. The first child care centre opened the same year in Whitehorse. A subsequent boom that accompanied the opening of a zinc mine at Faro led to more demand for child care, and a number of child care centres and preschools opened in the early 1970s. However, there was no legislation, and any government funding for child care programs was on an ad hoc basis. Finally, in 1974, the Yukon Child Care Association (YCCA) was formed, at the government's suggestion, and, in conjunction with the Department of Welfare, it began to draft legislation, arrange for inspections, draft funding policies, and lobby the politicians. While their proposals were ready by 1975, it took five years of persistent work before the government finally adopted the Day Care Act and Regulations. The legislation required centres with more than seven children to be licensed, and it set out teacher–child ratios and maximum centre sizes. Funding for new centres had not been provided and standards for teachers had not been included, but some form of regulation was welcome.

In 1979, the Yukon attained a fully elected Cabinet and responsible government, and the politicians became more responsive and better able to respond to concerns. This change in governing procedures was associated with a number of improvements for child care in the Yukon, including a new subsidy program and a half-time staff position to help enforce legislation. The election of the NDP government in 1985 led to further changes. Standards were improved in revised legislation, a full-time coordinator for child care services was hired, and funding was increased. Start-up grants and improvement funds also became available for group and family child care. Nevertheless, concerns remained. Most children in the Yukon were not in licensed child care and there were only three trained teachers in the territory. Most centres were in Whitehorse, while 50 licensed spaces were all to be found in other communities in 1987. A series of discussion papers followed the flurry of legislation and, in January 1989, the government released its policy paper, *Working Together: A Child Care Strategy for the Yukon*. Substantial funds were made available, subsidies were increased, training programs were established, and new legislation was promised. The new Child Care Act was passed in 1990.

Regulation

Mauch (1992a; 1992b) outlined the relevant legislation for the CNCCS. All of the senior kindergartens fall under the Ministry of Education in the Yukon, as do primary programs. Other ECE programs are under the jurisdiction of the Ministry of Health and Human Resources. The legislation covers teacher–child ratios, but not group size. It also specifies that centres should provide experiences for children that will encourage development in all areas, but it does not yet regulate teacher qualifications.

NORTHWEST TERRITORIES

Cairns, Moore, Redshaw, and Wilson have described the socio-geography of the N.W.T. (1992d), documented the historical roots of child care there (1992b), and reviewed legislation and training programs for the CNCCS (1992a, 1992c). The territories are a vast expanse of land, covering four time zones, yet the total population was just over 53 000 in 1988. While 25 percent of the people live in Yellowknife, and almost 50 percent in the small communities around Great Slave Lake close to Fort Smith, the rest of the population is in very small communities and fluctuating locations. The aboriginal people, including the Inuit, the Dene, and the Métis, comprise 58 percent of the territories' population. Hunting, trapping, and fishing are important both as sources of food and cash for the aboriginal people, but municipal, provincial, and federal government positions account for 80 percent of the 18 561 employed people. Mining and oil production also are significant forces in the economy. The cost of living is high, especially in areas north of Yellowknife, where supplies are brought by air once a year.

Historical Overview

The Dene and Inuit followed a traditional hunting and gathering way of life into the 1950s and 1960s, and child care, as we know it, was not an issue. However, moving to communities where their children could attend school has meant an end to that way of life for most of the aboriginal people. Residential schools, established at the turn of the century, also disrupted life, as many children forgot their Native language and some of their traditions and never learned others, such as parenting.

The first child care centres were not established until the 1970s, and government regulation and funding was not firmly in place until 1987. Limited subsidies were available from 1971, but funding centres were not seen as a government concern. Short-term funds, including the federal LIP grants, were often used to set up centres, and parents and communities struggled to keep budgets low and the centres affordable. In one centre, "bare-bones" budgeting meant that teachers even brought bones from home to make soup each day! The Pairivik centre in Iqaluit (then Frobisher Bay) was established in 1971 by Inuit women who were working and returning to school. The centre was bilingual, and children attended on a drop-in basis, which was consistent with community needs; sometimes they would attend for several months, then leave to visit relatives in another area, and then return for several months again. A similar facility opened in Baker Lake, but received less government funding. Organizations like the YWCA and companies such as the Nanisivik Mine also opened centres to meet the needs of working parents. A number of centres also were established in the early 1970s with LIP funding in far-ranging locations, including Fort Simpson, Pangnirtung, Inuvik, and Coppermine.

In 1976, the government adopted a subsidy policy, but avoided regulating and licensing policies. In 1980, the policy was changed so that funds were made available to eligible families, rather than centres with eligible children. This revision would make child care services more readily available to families in small communities that did not have centres. While this did allow parents to find family child care homes and babysitters, it led to the closing of the Yellowknife YWCA centre, which had previously received deficit funding. A group of parents took over the centre, which continues to operate. Several private facilities were opened in the early 1980s, and a prekindergarten centre was opened in Fort Norman with funding from the National Native and Drug Abuse Program.

The second national child care conference in Winnipeg in 1982 was a significant event for child care in the N.W.T. A number of delegates from the territory attended, and ultimately they formed the N.W.T. Child Care Association (NWTCCA). They were concerned about the lack of regulations, but knew that strict rules would prevent centres from opening in many small communities. They developed voluntary standards for Yellowknife and shared them with small communities. Subsequently, a discussion paper stimulated the government to fund a family child care program in Yellowknife and eventually to review child care needs, as public demand for services was growing in small communities as well as Yellowknife. Finally, in 1988, the Northwest Territories Child Day Care Act and the Child Day Care Standards Regulations became law (Cairns et al., 1992a, 1992c), and all of Canada had child care legislation. The act covered licensing, health and safety, teacher–child ratios, nutrition, and space. Teacher education was not covered as there were no available programs. However, significant progress has been made in this area since 1988, discussed below.

Since the late 1980s, professionals in the N.W.T. were emphasizing the development of culturally appropriate child care practices and culturally appropriate teacher education

practices for people in that vast expanse. The geography of the N.W.T. poses special problems for inspection and monitoring, and for professional development, as many communities are accessible only by plane. In 1989, the government introduced start-up, maintenance, and operating grants for non-profit centres and homes, and Cairns et al. (1992a) report there were requests for funding for over 400 new spaces.

Regulation

The Department of Education, Culture, and Employment's Child Day Care Section administers the Northwest Territories Child Day Care Act and two inspectors are responsible for all licensing and monitoring of group and centre sizes, and teacher–child ratios. Programs are to facilitate development and reflect the ethnic and cultural backgrounds of the children. Currently, teachers are only required to be 19 years of age, and they must supervise any support staff under 19. The children's cultural background also is to be reflected in staffing patterns.

CURRENT PRACTICES AND FUTURE DIRECTIONS IN EARLY CHILDHOOD EDUCATION IN CANADA

Clearly, there are many differences in the history of early childhood education across Canada. Some of these variations in early childhood programs reflect the sociogeographical and political differences that mark the country. For example, the "have-not" provinces generally have been slower to fund programs. However, that is not always the case. Alberta, for example, despite its wealth, was most reluctant to acknowledge early childhood education as a provincial responsibility. If it were not for the persistent demands of professionals, parents, and other advocates for regulations and training, that province would likely still be without legislation.

In some jurisdictions, early childhood programs have been available for over a century, while they are quite recent developments in others. The provinces with more progressive legislation (e.g., Manitoba) generally have had early childhood programs in place for a long time. This lengthy history generally leads to higher standards for teacher education. In addition, the regulations for early childhood programs differ greatly between jurisdictions, and sometimes even within them. Nevertheless, at least every province and territory now has some form of regulation. However, professionals in the field will have to continue to advocate uniform national standards for early childhood programs.

TEACHER–CHILD RATIOS, GROUP SIZE, AND CENTRE SIZE IN CANADA

The research on quality in early childhood programs, discussed in Chapter 1, pointed to teacher–child ratios and group size as important variables in defining high-quality programs. The specific group and centre sizes and the teacher–child ratios for each Canadian jurisdiction are discussed below . As you know from Chapter 1, legislative definitions of terms like "infant," "toddler," and "preschooler" vary across the country, but some generalizations are possible. Exhibit 4-1 summarizes the Canadian legislation. As you can see, the legislation does not yet ensure the best ratios and the most favourable group sizes throughout the country. Group size is still not regulated in Nova Scotia, Newfoundland, and the Yukon. The required teacher–child ratios in some locations are also quite low. The regulations on teacher–child ratios, group size, and centre size are anything but consistent across the country. In Exhibit 1-4 on page 23 of Chapter 1, you saw the teacher–child ratios recommended in the National Statement on Quality Child Care (Canadian Child Care,

EXHIBIT 4-1 LEGISLATION OF CHILD CARE, AND COVERAGE OF RATIOS AND GROUP SIZE IN THE CURRENT REGULATIONS

PROVINCE OR TERRITORY	DATE OF FIRST LEGISLATION	ARE RATIOS REGULATED?	GROUP SIZE REGULATED?
B.C.	1937	✓	✓
Alta.	1978	✓	✓
Sask.	1969	✓	✓
Man.	1982	✓	✓
Ont.	1946	✓	✓
P.Q.	1979	✓	✓
N.B.	1974	✓	✓
P.E.I.	1973	✓	✓
N.S.	1967	✓	–
Nfld.	1975	✓	–
Yukon	1975	✓	–
N.W.T.	1988	✓	✓

✓ yes
– no regulations in place in 1993

SOURCES: Cairns et al. (1992b), Child Care (1990, 1993), Desjardins (1992), Friesen et al. (1992b), Gamble (1992a), Glassman (1992a), Irwin & Canning, (1992b), Kyle (1992b), McDonell (1992), Nykoforuk (1992a), Read et al. (1992), Stapleford (1976), and Young (1981, 1993).

1992). If you look at Exhibit 4-2, you will see that only five of twelve jurisdictions conform to the recommendations for infants.

EXHIBIT 4-2 TEACHER–CHILD RATIOS AND GROUP SIZE FOR CENTRE-BASED CARE—BREAKDOWN BY PROVINCE FOR INFANTS[1]

PROVINCE OR TERRITORY	RATIOS FOR INFANTS	GROUP SIZE	CENTRE SIZE
B.C.	✓ 1:4	12	36
Alta.	2:6[2], 2:8	6[2]–8	80
Sask.	✓ 1:3	6	90
Man.	1:3[2], 1:4	6[2]–8	70
Ont.	3:10	10	NA
P.Q.	1:5	15	60
N.B.	✓ 1:3	9	60
P.E.I.	✓ 1:3	6	50
N.S.	1:4[3]	25	50
Nfld.	NA	NA	50
Yukon	1:4	NA	NA
N.W.T.	✓ 1:3[2], 1:4	6[2]–8	30

[1] In seven of the twelve provinces and territories, infants are defined as being between 0 and 18 months of age (see Chapter 1 for definition).
[2] Infants under 12 months.
[3] Recommended, not yet legislated.
NA: Not applicable.

SOURCES: Cairns et al. (1992c), Canning et al. (1992), Child Care (1990, 1993), Flanagan-Rochon (1992b), Friesen (1992), Fullum (1992b), Hautman et al. (1992), Kyle (1992c), Lutes (1992), Mauch (1992b), McDonell & Griffin (1992), Randell (1992b), Truemner (1992), and Young (1993).

EXHIBIT 4-3 TEACHER–CHILD RATIOS AND GROUP SIZE FOR CENTRE-BASED CARE—BREAKDOWN BY PROVINCE FOR TODDLERS[1]

PROVINCE OR TERRITORY	RATIOS FOR TODDLERS	GROUP SIZE	CENTRE SIZE
B.C.	1:4	12	36
Alta.	1:4–1:6	8–12	80
Sask.	1:5–1:10	10–20	90
Man.	1:4–1:6	8–12	70
Ont.	1:5–1:8	15–16	NA
P.Q.	1:8	30	60
N.B.	1:3–1:5	9–10	60
P.E.I.	1:3–1:5	6–10	50
N.S.	1:7	NA	60
Nfld.	1:6	NA	50
Yukon	1:6	NA	NA
N.W.T.	1:4–1:6	8–12	30

[1] Canadians seem to have difficulty with the term *toddler*; there are three different definitions across nine jurisdictions, and another four avoid the term. We will use the most common definition: toddlers range from 19 to 35 months of age. When there are several entries in a column, it is because that jurisdiction has cut-offs that do not conform to the definitions.
NA: Not applicable.

SOURCES: Cairns et al. (1992c), Canning et al. (1992), Child Care (1990, 1993), Flanagan-Rochon (1992b), Friesen (1992), Fullum (1992b), Hautman et al. (1992), Kyle (1992c), Lutes (1992), Mauch (1992b), McDonell & Griffin (1992), Randell (1992b), Truemner (1992), and Young (1993).

The situation is not much better for Canadian toddlers. As Exhibit 4-3 shows, in some locations, the regulated group size is two to three times greater than the recommended size. Similarly, the teacher–child ratios are twice as high as those suggested in the National Statement on Quality Child Care. The teacher–child ratios specified in the regulations for 3- to 5-year-olds (see Exhibit 4-4) are closer to those being advocated in most areas, but the regulated group sizes are considerably higher in a number of provinces. Moreover, group size, which has such a pronounced impact on the quality of care, is still not regulated at all in Nova Scotia and the Yukon.

Exhibit 4-4 TEACHER–CHILD RATIOS AND GROUP SIZE FOR CENTRE-BASED CARE—BREAKDOWN BY PROVINCE FOR CHILDREN 3 TO 5 YEARS[1]

PROVINCE OR TERRITORY	RATIOS	GROUP SIZE	CENTRE SIZE
B.C.	1:8–1:10	20–25	60–75
Alta.	1:8–1:10	16–20	80
Sask.	1:10	20	90
Man.	1:8–1:10	16–20	70
Ont.	1:8	16	NA
P.Q.	1:15	30	60
N.B.	1:7–1:12	20–24	60
P.E.I.	1:10	30	50
N.S.	1:7	NA	60
Nfld.	1:8	NA	50
Yukon	1:8	NA	NA
N.W.T.	1:8–1:9	16–18	30

[1] Some jurisdictions have different requirements for children of the same age, depending on the type of facility they attend.

Sources: Cairns et al. (1992c), Canning et al. (1992), Child Care (1990, 1993), Flanagan-Rochon (1992b), Friesen (1992), Fullum (1992b), Hautman et al. (1992), Kyle (1992c), Lutes (1992), Mauch (1992b), McDonell & Griffin (1992), Randell (1992b), Truemner (1992), and Young (1993).

When you study Exhibit 4-5, you will have comparable concerns about the ratios and group sizes for children who are 5 years and older. Similarly, inspection procedures and the regulations related to the physical facility are highly variable across the country. For example, there is a wide range of requirements regarding the actual amount of space each child needs. You may wonder why 2.75 m² is adequate indoor space in some locations (see Exhibit 4-6), while others need 5m² per child. The situation is comparable for outdoor space.

While we have made great strides in improving the quality of licensed early childhood programs in the country, especially with the advent of CAP in 1966 and the wider availability of licensed child care that accompanied CAP funding, our regulations still have a distance to go. Advocates for young children across the country continue to express their concern about this failure to provide the optimum environment for young children.

REGULATION OF TEACHER TRAINING AND PROGRAM AVAILABILITY

The research we discussed in Chapter 1 found that teacher training and knowledge of child development were excellent predictors of high-quality care. However, the Canadian legislation governing child care does not consistently reflect this research finding. Exhibit 4-7 summarizes the regulation of teacher qualifications and the

EXHIBIT 4-5 TEACHER–CHILD RATIOS AND GROUP SIZE FOR CENTRE-BASED CARE—BREAKDOWN BY PROVINCE FOR CHILDREN 5 YEARS AND OLDER[1]

PROVINCE OR TERRITORY	RATIOS FOR OVER 5-YEAR-OLDS	GROUP SIZE	CENTRE SIZE
B.C.	1:10–1:15	20–25	60–75
Alta.	NA	NA	80
Sask.	1:10–1:15	20–30	90
Man.	1:10–1:15	20–30	70
Ont.	1:12–1:15	24–30	NA
P.Q.	1:15–1:20	NA	60
N.B.	1:12–1:15	24–30	60
P.E.I.	1:12–1:15	36 & NA	50
N.S.	1:15	NA	60
Nfld.	1:15	25	50
Yukon	1:8 & NA	NA	NA
N.W.T.	1:10	20	30

[1] Some jurisdictions have different requirements for children of the same age, depending on the type of facility they attend.

NA: Not applicable.

SOURCES: Cairns et al. (1992c), Canning et al. (1992), Child Care (1990, 1993), Flanagan-Rochon (1992b), Friesen (1992), Fullum (1992b), Hautman et al. (1992), Kyle (1992c), Lutes (1992), Mauch (1992b), McDonell & Griffin (1992), Randell (1992b), Truemner (1992), and Young (1993).

EXHIBIT 4-6 SUMMARY OF SPACE REQUIREMENTS IN CHILD CARE SETTINGS IN CANADA

PROVINCE OR TERRITORY	INDOOR SPACE	OUTDOOR SPACE
B.C.	3.7 m²	7 m²
Ont.	5 m²	5.6 m² & fence
Alta.	3 m²	fence & 2 m² <19 months, 4.5 m² > 19 months
Man.	3.3 m²	7 m² & fence
Sask.	3.7 m²—infants 3.25 m²	7 m²
P.Q.	2.75 m²	4 m² & fence
N.B.	3.25 m²	fenced & drained
N.S.	2.75 m²	5.46 m² & fence
P. E. I.	3.5 m²	7 m² or park near
Nfld.	3.3 m²	drained & safe
Yukon	4 m²	5 m², fenced & drained
N.W.T.	2.75 m²	5 m²

SOURCE: Young (1993).

availability of training programs in the country, while Exhibit 4-8 shows the types of available training programs, and the legislative requirements for knowledge of child development and experience. By 1989, teacher education programs were in place in all of Canada, but some jurisdictions still do not require teachers to be trained. Furthermore, many do not require knowledge of child development.

Of course, the regulation of teacher qualifications and the availability of programs are closely related, as Exhibit 4-7 suggests. In some locations (e.g., B.C., Manitoba, and P.E.I.), changes in legislation seem to have stimulated the provision of ECE training programs on a broader basis. In other locations—Alberta and Quebec, for example—teacher training programs have predated legislation by a number of years. In these latter cases, a lengthy history of governmental reluctance to be involved in child care—if not fully opposed to it—seems to have been a factor in the long wait for legislation. In yet other locations like Newfoundland, the Yukon, and the Northwest Territories, however, programs did not become "readily available" until the late 1980s—and "readily available" in these locations may still be thousands of kilometres away. These jurisdictions have been reluctant to implement training requirements when local programs have just recently become available. Presumably, initiatives like those seen in Manitoba, coupled with a gradual phasing in of teacher training requirements, would encourage the maximum number of individuals to enrol in the courses.

EXHIBIT 4-7 LEGISLATION OF TEACHER QUALIFICATIONS AND AVAILABILITY OF TEACHER TRAINING

PROVINCE OR TERRITORY	WHEN WAS TEACHER TRAINING REQUIRED?	WHEN WAS TEACHER TRAINING AVAILABLE?[1]
B.C.	1955	1955
Alta.	1990 regulations to be in effect by 1995	1970
Sask.	1989	1981
Man.	1982	Late 1960s
Ont.	1960	AECEO programs—1960; College programs—1967
P.Q.	1989	1960s
N.B.	–	early 1980s
P.E.I.	1986	1987
N.S.	1989	early 1970s
Nfld.	1989	Short-lived program—1970s; widely available programs—1986
Yukon	–	1989
N.W.T.	–	1988

– no requirements in place in 1993
[1] The founding dates of the few Canadian university-based programs (e.g., Institute for Child Study, 1926), founded during the era of the child study movement (see Chapter 1), are not included here.

SOURCE: Young (1993).

You probably are surprised, especially as a student in the field, to see in Exhibit 4-8 that five of twelve Canadian jurisdictions do not require teachers to be knowledgeable about child development, despite the available research. Moreover, the failure of many legislators to recognize the value of experience is a concern. In three jurisdictions, no one in an ECE program has to be experienced in the field. In another three provinces, only the supervisor has to have experience in the field. While the supervisor is important in a program, quite frequently she or he spends a large proportion of time doing administrative tasks and relatively little in direct contact with the children. Clearly, we still have to make a number of changes in our legislation if we want high-quality programs to be the norm in this country.

EXHIBIT 4-8 SUMMARY OF TEACHER EDUCATION PROGRAMS IN CANADA

PROVINCE OR TERRITORY	ONE-YEAR CERTIFICATE AND/OR TWO-YEAR	DEGREES	CHILD DEVELOPMENT	EXPERIENCE
B.C.	Both	Yes	1 teacher per group & supervisor	Supervisor & 1 teacher per group
Alta.	Both	Yes	Supervisor & 1 of 6 teachers	Supervisor & 1 of 4 teachers by 1993
Sask.	Both	Yes	Supervisor	Supervisor only
Man.	Both	Yes	Supervisor and 1/2–2/3 of the staff	Supervisor
Ont.	Two-year only	Yes	1 teacher per group & supervisor	Supervisor & 1 teacher per group
Quebec	Both	Yes	1/3 of the staff	1/3 of the staff
N.B.	Both	Yes	None required	None required
P.E.I.	Two-year only	No	Supervisor & 1 teacher	Supervisor
N.S.	Both	Yes	Supervisor & 2/3 of the staff	Supervisor & 2/3 of the staff
Nfld.	Both	Yes	Supervisor	Supervisor & 1 teacher per 25 children
Yukon	Two-year with distance education	No	None required	None required
N.W.T.	Both	No	None required	None required

SOURCE: Young (1993).

SCOPE OF LICENSED CHILD CARE IN CANADA AND PARENTAL NEEDS

Another challenge emerges when you look at the number of licensed child care spaces in Canada (National Child Care, 1991; Pence et al., 1992). The information for each jurisdiction is summarized in Exhibit 4-9. Those numbers are small compared with the number of 0- to 9-year-olds requiring some form of care, as the CNCCS demonstrated (see Exhibit 1-1, p. 5). Nonetheless, even more Canadian children are expected to need care in the future. As we approach the year 2000, with more women entering the workforce, fewer children will be cared for at home. A corresponding increase in the availability of licensed programs would be welcome, but a national child care policy may be required before we see more readily available licensed early childhood education programs and fewer latch-key children in this country. While licensed care is expensive, many parents want the assurances that licensing brings with it. They know that a licensed program in a centre or home is inspected, and that it must conform to a set of regulations. They want some guarantee that their children are receiving high-quality care and education while they work.

EXHIBIT 4-9 SCOPE OF CHILD CARE IN CANADA AND NEEDS OF PARENTS

PROVINCE OR TERRITORY	NUMBER OF CHILDREN 0–9 YEARS IN SOME FORM OF CARE[1]	NUMBER OF LICENSED CENTRE-BASED SPACES[1,2,3]	NUMBER OF LICENSED FAMILY CHILD CARE SPACES[1,2,3]
B.C.	283 300	41 331	7155
Alta.	272 300	50 120	6962
Sask.	112 600	3795	1980
Man.	103 000	16 939	2623
Ont.	909 400	102 762	11 762
Yukon	NA	564	84
P.Q.	569 400	77 801	7273
N.B.	59 300	5568	96
P.E.I.	12 300	1913	35
N.S.	79 600	5977	123
Nfld.	44 900	3264	0
N.W.T	NA	694	66

NA: Not available.

SOURCES: [1] Pence et al. (1992).
[2] National Child Care Information Centre (1991).
[3] Young (1993).

And they do not want to spend their time at work worrying about the well-being of their children.

The *National Statement on Quality Child Care* (Canadian Child Day Care Federation, 1991) sees child care as a partnership between parents, professionals (and their associations), training institutions, and all levels of government. That statement provides an outline of the role government should play in child care in this country. Government:

- encourages a variety of flexible delivery models to meet the diverse needs of families;
- recognizes current research and social policy issues as the foundation on which licensing standards are built;
- employs individuals within the licensing body who have completed recognized advanced professional training and experience related specifically to the field;
- provides information to enable parents to make meaningful choices regarding quality care;
- ensures that quality care is accessible and affordable; and
- coordinates various departments and levels at the municipal, regional, provincial/territorial and national levels to ensure quality child care (p. 15).

In light of the current state of affairs in Canada, which you have considered in this chapter, it would be difficult not to conclude that governments at all levels have a major challenge ahead if they hope to meet these objectives. As professionals entering the field, you will have to keep legislators reminded of and concerned about these objectives.

KEY QUESTIONS

1. Compare the history of ECE in your province or territory with that of two other jurisdictions. Then relate those differences to any corresponding differences in the regulations and training programs in each location.

2. State your recommendations for improving the quality of ECE in your province or territory as we approach the 21st century.

3. Review the CNCCS findings on the child care options parents report using in your province or territory. If you were in government, what changes would you recommend? Which child care arrangements concern you and why?

4. Pence's (1992) publication, *Canadian Child Care in Context: Perspectives from the Provinces and Territories*, contains bibliographies for each province and territory that lists publications relevant to ECE. Study the bibliography for your location and select one article for study.

Part 2

THE WHO OF EARLY CHILDHOOD EDUCATION

Early childhood education is made up of different people. In Part 2 we will explore the who of this field by examining the characteristics and needs of the children, their families, and their teachers.

- Chapter 5, "Children and Their Families," looks at the characteristics of young children—the things they have in common and the things that make each child unique. Then we will turn our attention to parents and other family members. They are the ones with whom early childhood teachers share the responsibility for raising young children.

- Chapter 6, "Teacher," examines the different roles of those who work in early childhood programs. We will also focus on early childhood education as a profession, and consider some of the issues teachers in the field face today.

CHILDREN AND THEIR FAMILIES

At the heart of early childhood education are young children. All the topics we will discuss in the following chapters are aimed at gaining a better understanding of children and how, together with their families, we can best meet their needs. Although our focus will be on children, it is always important to keep in mind that they must never be seen in isolation, but rather as part of a family system that provides context and identity through its lifestyle, culture, heritage, and traditions.

Knowing the families of children in an early childhood education program often is as important as knowing the children. Children are integral members of their family systems, and, conversely, family values and culture are an inseparable part of children. Families that choose an early childhood education program are sharing some of the responsibility for socializing their children with the teachers in the program they select. Children need to feel there is continuity between their home and school experiences, and that continuity can best be assured through a carefully fostered partnership between the family and the early childhood program (Powell, 1989).

In this chapter we will take a closer look at children, their families, and the techniques that help cement a strong bond between home and school by considering the following topics:

1. In what ways are young children alike? We will examine three issues in the discussion of similarities between children:

    • "profiles" that identify typical traits shared by the majority of children of different ages;

    • the need of all children for positive self-esteem; and

    • the need of all children for play as a way of learning about the world.

2. We will examine factors that contribute to the wonderful diversity among children. Inborn traits such as temperament will be discussed, and external factors that contribute to differences between children, including culture, language and dialect, and social class, will be considered.

3. We will take a brief overview of family systems theory as a way of viewing the family as a dynamic unit.

4. The Canadian family has undergone many changes recently. We will consider some of these changes by looking at the following:

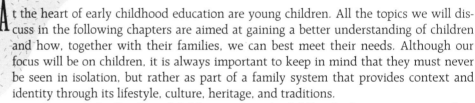

- variety in family forms;
- other factors that contribute to family diversity; and
- families in poverty.

5. Families have specific needs that the early childhood program can address. We will consider issues related to family needs, including:
    - the needs of adults in a unique stage of development, separate from their children's development;
    - the need of families to feel empowered, in control of their lives; and
    - coordination of the needs of the family with the early childhood program.

6. Two-way communication between families and the early childhood program is an important element in providing consistency for children. We will examine the following methods of communicating with parents:
    - communicating with individual parents informally, on a day-to-day basis, and formally, through conferences and home visits; and
    - communicating with groups of parents, through written communiqués, bulletin boards, and meetings.

7. Families can be involved in the early childhood program in a number of ways—as resources, in the classroom, and as decision-makers.

8. One function of the early childhood program is parent education, which can take a variety of forms.

CHILDREN

CHILDREN—SIMILARITIES

Children are generally wonderfully engaging and winning, in part because of the freshness with which they approach all experiences. Most children possess a sense of trust that the world and the people in it are friendly and kind, and they will tackle that world with joy and enthusiasm. The amount of information that children learn in the first few years of life is unparalleled in later learning. At no other time in life will there be such zest and liveliness toward acquiring skills and knowledge.

Our task in working with young children is to provide an environment in which this enthusiasm is nurtured and sustained rather than subdued or even destroyed. Preschoolers are eager to learn, but such eagerness can be battered down if they are frequently overwhelmed by developmentally inappropriate experiences. This is an awesome responsibility on the shoulders of early childhood educators, which can be met through careful and sensitive study and understanding of the characteristics and needs of young children.

AGE-RELATED SIMILARITIES AMONG CHILDREN

Although children are each unique, they nonetheless have much in common. All children share the need for nurturing and trustworthy adults, for stability and security, for increasing autonomy, for a sense of competence and self-worth. Similarly, there are common attributes and skills that characterize children at different ages during the preschool years. In the course of normal development, children reach developmental milestones in a fairly predictable manner and within a reasonable time range (Allen & Marotz, 1989). For that reason, you can make checklists or normative tables that describe the typical features of children at different ages. Arnold Gessell (see Chapter 2), in fact, spent his life developing normative tables. More recently, Allen and Marotz

(1989) published a book, with profiles of typical children from birth to 6 years, that you may wish to consult. The Toronto Board of Education's *Observing Children*, which looks at the typical child from 2 to 13 years, also is a valuable resource.

While a comprehensive summary of developmental norms is beyond the scope of this text, a brief overview of some developmental characteristics of children in the early childhood period is appropriate. This text emphasizes programs for children between 2 and 5 years of age, but also provides an overview of infant and toddler programs as well as primary school programs. However, students interested in working with infants, toddlers, and primary school children will need to seek additional resources that discuss the development of children of these ages and programs for them in more depth.

The First Year (0 to 12 Months)

Early childhood programs for infants under 1 were rare until the 1960s when a number of research-oriented programs were established to determine the effect of high-quality programs on infant development (Fox & Fein, 1990). While there still is considerable controversy about some of the findings (Clarke-Stewart, 1990), the weight of the evidence suggests that high-quality programs are beneficial, even in the first year of life, especially for those from disadvantaged homes. There are excellent materials available for those who want to become caregivers in programs that serve the very young (Maxim, 1989; Morrison, 1988), including *Every Child Is Special* (Shimoni, Baxter, & Kugelmass, 1992), a Canadian text on the topic.

The first year of life is characterized by constant change and many significant firsts (Fogel, 1991). Infants grow very rapidly and develop many physical skills in a short period of time. They learn to control their heads, they begin to smile and sit, and then to crawl and creep. At birth, they are unable to manipulate objects, but by their first birthday, their caregivers are kept busy "childproofing" the environment by placing dangerous objects out of reach. In fact, the first year is quite challenging for caregivers as their charges have developmental needs that alter almost from one day to the next.

Differences in temperament become evident early in the first year of life (Thomas, Chess, & Birch, 1968). Some infants are active and regular, while others are much quieter and still others have an unpredictable schedule. Infants also differ on the approach–withdrawal dimension. Some approach new people, foods, and experiences with enthusiasm, while others tend to withdraw from or be upset by novelty. Some are very adaptable and responsive. Others may scream at any schedule disruption, but sleep through a parade. In a group setting in particular, you will notice that some infants seem to fuss and cry much of the time, while others seem happy most of the time. These inborn characteristics demand that those caring for infants learn about the temperaments of those in their care and adapt their behaviours to meet the individual's needs. A "regular" baby may adapt to a schedule that has some consistency, but the "irregular" baby will need a highly flexible schedule. A more active baby will respond to a program that offers a wide range of activities, but the tranquil, quiet baby will not try all of the activities.

The Second Year (1 to 2 Years)

While the first year of life is characterized by many rapid changes, the second year of life has its own excitement. Usually, children begin to take their first toddling steps between 12 and 15 months of age; this is a major event as walking on two feet, or bipedal locomotion, is a characteristic that differentiates human beings from other members of the animal kingdom. Moreover, language begins to emerge and develop rapidly during this time; the productive use of language is another characteristic that makes humans unique. The fact that these two major human traits develop *without direct teaching* often makes people take these accomplishments for granted, but it would be difficult to find a youngster who was not delighted with these new skills. Suddenly, with hands free, the world is there to explore with extra zeal, and any pleasure or displeasure becomes easier to communicate.

In the second year, the child is quite egocentric, and relates to adults better than children. Early in the second year, children are usually willing to agree to adult requests and to receive adult assistance, but as they approach their second birthday, refusals to cooperate and a strong desire "to do it myself" become more frequent. It is important to remember, no matter how hurried we become, that the child's need and desire to master a task alone must be honoured if we hope to foster self-esteem and a developing sense of autonomy.

Usually, one sees the beginnings of pretend play during the second year, and it becomes more complex as the child's abilities to communicate with others and to understand their requests improve. Storybooks become of greater interest, and the child's attention span slowly increases, even if it remains very short by adult standards. Most play is action-oriented, and a sense of ownership, often expressed by a loud "Mine!", becomes apparent. Building with blocks, scribbling, and matching objects interest the child in the second year, and most activities are approached with vigour and delight.

Two-Year-Old Children

This period is often referred to as "the terrible twos," but this label is not fully deserved. It is true that 2-year-olds, with their limited self-control, may well express their growing independence and self-assertiveness by grabbing a desired toy from a peer or by throwing a tantrum. Tantrums, in fact, are common among 2-year-olds, and reflect, in part, their limited verbal skills, which often do not allow them to express what they want. Two-year-olds are also not adept at delaying gratification; they do not have the ability to wait for something they want "right now" (Allen & Marotz, 1989; Ames, Gillespie, Haines, & Ilg, 1980; Bredekamp, 1987). Moreover, they are just beginning to acquire some social skills, and tend to play side-by-side with peers rather than interact with them.

While these characteristics are typical of 2-year-olds, there also is a brighter side. Curiosity is boundless in 2-year-olds, and the world is their oyster to explore, savour, and enjoy. Two-year-olds undertake many activities for the sheer pleasure rather than to reach a goal. Running is enjoyed in itself rather than seen simply as a means of getting somewhere fast; painting means involvement in a sensory process rather than an interest in producing a picture. Activities are also undertaken with enormous enthusiasm. Two-year-olds wholeheartedly throw themselves into activities, whether painting, squishing play dough, pouring sand and water, or reading books. They particularly enjoy sensory experiences, using touch, taste, and smell, as well as sight and sound. Two-year-olds are notorious for their desire to repeat, using new-found skills over and over again. This desire is normal and should be encouraged, for it builds competence and allows children to fully assimilate skills before moving onto new ones.

During this year, most children increasingly gain body control: they are more self-assured about walking, their running no longer has a baby stagger, and their new-found finger control allows them to put together simple puzzles or paint with a brush. At the same time, they experience tremendous language growth. Their growing vocabulary, sentence length, and grammatical forms open up all sorts of possibilities because of this increased communicative competence. Self-help skills are also improving, including the achievement of toilet training for the majority of children during this year. Just as important as learning motor, language, and self-help skills is the process of gaining independence through this mastery.

Teachers of 2-year-olds need to provide a supportive, consistent, and safe environment in which rapidly growing skills can be practised and mastered. Frequent and enthusiastic praise conveys that adults value the acquisition of skills. Gentle guidance acknowledges children's growing sense of self while helping them develop self-control in relation to others (Bredekamp, 1987).

Three-Year-Old Children

Three-year-olds have truly left babyhood behind, not only in appearance—with the loss of baby fat—but also in added skills. Increased balance and control are evident in large motor, fine motor, and self-help areas. Three-year-olds like to use their new skills by being helpful and wanting to please adults. Their added competence does not mean, however, that they won't occasionally have accidents or revert to earlier behaviours

when upset. Overall, however, their characteristic way of responding to school experiences is with enthusiasm and enjoyment.

By age 3, children's speech is intelligible most of the time and consists of longer sentences. Language becomes much more of a social and cognitive tool. Three-year-olds engage in more extensive conversations, talking *with* and not just *to* people, and they delight in answering questions as well as asking them. In fact, 3-year-old children are usually bursting with questions, constantly asking "Why?", "What for?", and "Where?" about everything imaginable. Three-year-olds can ask questions on topics the encyclopedia, the *Guinness Book of Records*, and *The Farmers' Almanac* never thought of covering! Vocabulary continues to increase dramatically, and grammar becomes more accurate.

This greater language facility helps increase peer interaction among this age group. Three-year-olds are much more socially aware than younger children, and their make-believe play, which they began in the previous year by imitating simple personal and home routines, at times includes several children. Short-lived friendships begin to form, and children will play *with* each other as well as *near* each other. Social problem-solving skills are just beginning to emerge. With guidance, 3-year-olds may share and take turns, but they still find such behaviours difficult (Allen & Marotz, 1989; Ames et al., 1980).

Teachers of 3-year-olds need to respect the growing skills and competencies of their charges without forgetting just how recently they acquired them. It is important to maintain patience and good humour, remembering that the enthusiasm with which 3-year-olds use these skills is not always matched by accuracy and speed. Because 3-year-olds enjoy helping as well as practising self-help skills, such behaviours should be promoted and valued. The emerging social skills of 3-year-olds should be encouraged in an atmosphere where social exploration is safe and where playing alone or not having to give up a favourite toy is also acceptable (Bredekamp, 1987).

Four-Year-Old Children

Four-year-olds have achieved a maturity and competence in motor and language development that leads them to assume a general air of security and confidence, sometimes bordering on cockiness. "It is a time of constantly testing limits in order to practice self-confidence and firm up a growing need for independence" (Allen & Marotz, 1989, p. 87).

Four-year-olds seem to be in perpetual motion, throwing themselves wholeheartedly into activities. They have mastered the basics of movement and now eagerly embellish on these. Climbing, pedalling, pumping on a swing, jumping over and off objects, and easily avoiding obstacles when running are routine, and all contribute to greater flexibility and exploration in play. Showing off new physical stunts—or trying to—is a favourite pastime. Improved muscle coordination is also evident in more controlled use of the fingers, such as in buttoning, drawing, and cutting with scissors. In addition, many self-care activities have become routines rather than the challenges they were at earlier ages.

If increased competence leads to noticeable embellishments in motor activities, this is even more evident in the language area. By age 4, most children's language usage has become remarkably sophisticated and skilled. This accomplishment seems to invite new uses for language beyond communication. The 4-year-olds love to play with language, using it to brag, engage in bathroom talk, swear, tell tall tales, and make up silly rhymes. And, if you can imagine, 4-year-olds are even more persistent than 3-year-olds in asking questions.

For 4-year-olds, peers have become very important. Play is a social activity more often than not, although 4s enjoy solitary activities at times as well. Taking turns and sharing become much easier because 4-year-olds begin to understand the benefits of cooperation. Their imaginative variations of movement and language skills extend into group play, which is usually highly creative and ingenious, touched by their sense of humour.

Teachers of 4-year-olds need to provide an environment in which children have many opportunities for interactions with each other, with adults, and with a wide selection of appropriate and stimulating materials. Because of their heightened social involvements, 4s need consistent, positive guidance to help them develop emerging social skills, for instance, in sharing, resolving conflicts, and negotiating (Allen & Marotz, 1989; Ames et al., 1980; Bredekamp, 1987).

Five-Year-Old Children

Five-year-olds are much more self-contained and controlled; they have replaced some of their earlier exuberant behaviours with a calmer, more mature approach. They are competent and reliable, taking responsibility seriously. They seem to be able to judge their own abilities more accurately than at earlier ages, and they respond accordingly.

Five-year-olds' motor activities seem more poised, their movement more restrained and precise than ever before. There is also greater interest in fine motor activities as children have gained many skills in accurate cutting, gluing, drawing, and beginning writing. This interest is spurred by the new desire to "make something" rather than merely to paint, cut, or manipulate the play dough for the sheer enjoyment of these activities. The self-reliance of 5-year-olds extends to assuming considerable responsibility for self-care as well.

Language has also reached a height of maturity for 5s, exhibited through a vocabulary that contains thousands of words, complex and compound sentence structures, variety and accuracy in grammatical forms, and good articulation. Language increasingly reflects interest in and contact with a broadening world outside the child's intimate family, school, and neighbourhood experiences. The social sphere of 5-year-olds revolves around special friendships, which take on more importance. By age 5, children are quite adept at sharing toys, taking turns, and playing cooperatively. Their group play is usually quite elaborate and imaginative, and it can take up long periods of time (Allen & Marotz, 1989; Ames et al., 1980).

Teachers of 5-year-olds, after providing a stimulating learning environment and setting reasonable limits, can expect this age group to take on considerable responsibility for maintaining and regulating a smoothly functioning program. The 5-year-olds need to be given many opportunities to explore their world in depth and assimilate what they learn through multiple experiences. One way in which children can discuss, plan, and carry out ideas stimulated by their experiences is through group projects (Katz, 1989).

Primary or School-Aged Children

Children from 6 through 8 years of age usually are in Grades 1, 2, and 3 respectively. These grades are known as the primary grades in most provinces, and attendance at a formal school or an approved alternative is no longer an option at this stage in a child's life. Unfortunately, the years from birth to 5 seem to receive more attention from the early childhood field, despite the fact that primary grade children still share many of the developmental needs evident in the earlier years.

The pressure-cooker, skill-oriented primary programs that have become more common in recent years fail to recognize the need of children aged 6 to 8 to play and to experience success. Moreover, such programs do not reflect an understanding of the developmental unevenness that typifies children of this age. Just because Jimmy's gross motor skills are at a 7-year-old level does not mean that his fine motor skills and language skills are at the same level. The situation can be even worse for those primary grade children who have late birthdays relative to the majority of children in their class. Too often, subject- and skill-oriented teachers forget that some children in the class may be almost a year younger than others. At this stage in development, a year is a very long time, and it is unreasonable to assume that children who vary in age by almost a year should be achieving at the same level. Susie may be working at a beginning Grade 1 level in reading, while Mario is at a late Grade 1 level; even though Susie may seem behind to the teacher, the fact that Susie is one year minus a day younger than Mario needs to be considered. The fact is that both Susie and Mario may be working at an *age-appropriate* level.

Certainly, physical growth has slowed down in 6- to 8-year-olds, relative to preschoolers, but basic skills still need to be refined, and children of these ages need active play on a regular basis. Primary-level children are boisterous and enjoy roughhousing, even though there is a risk of injury. Balancing stunts, including riding a two-wheeler and acrobatics, are challenges that are tackled with enthusiasm, but fatigue and hunger may follow.

Peer pressure and a need to be accepted become more marked during these years, and play has a highly social quality. While the 6-year-old has "best friends" for short periods of time, friendships become more enduring and more important for the 7- and 8-year-olds. However, 6-, 7-, and 8-year-olds have rigid gender-role stereotypes, are quite discriminatory, and rarely form close friendships with a member of the opposite sex. Nonetheless, they begin to test behaviours, things, and ideas with friends that they will later have to test in the wider world. The peer group will slowly increase in importance up to the adolescent years, when it will become a more important reference group than the family.

Simple competitive sports become a possibility during the primary years, but they are not without friction. Impatience, a lack of persistence, and complaints are not infrequent, but sensitivity and cooperation also increase during these years. As children approach 7 and 8 years of age, they become less egocentric and logical thinking processes begin to emerge. A sense of morality also starts to develop along with an increasing understanding of rules.

Children in the primary grades like to chatter, but they talk *with* people rather than *to* them. Vocabulary growth is slower than it was during the preschool years down, but it still increases steadily. The mechanical aspects of speech are not fully mature, and irregularities should not be a concern. However, the ability to appreciate the subtleties and the humour of language increases rapidly during this period as many parents and teachers know. Riddles, puns, and "knock, knock" jokes are shared with delight.

Reading and writing usually begin—and are sometimes mastered—during this period, but reversals of letters and numbers are common. Mathematical concepts

proliferate, and sequencing skills and storytelling abilities improve dramatically. Planning, sorting, classifying, and collecting are enjoyed, as are "real" things like radios and cameras. Attitudes toward school as well as toward oneself are being formed at this time, so teachers and parents must ensure that primary level children experience success on a regular basis.

NEED FOR SELF-ESTEEM

One thing shared by all children is the need to feel good about themselves. Young children are beginning to form a **self-concept**, perceptions and feelings about themselves gathered largely from how the important people in their world respond to them. One aspect of self-concept is **self-esteem**, children's evaluation of their worth in positive or negative terms (Essa & Rogers, 1992; Marshall, 1989; Samuels, 1977). Such evaluation can tell children that they are competent, worthwhile, and effective or, on the other hand, that they are incapable, unlikable, and powerless. It is particularly noteworthy that children who feel good about themselves seem to be more friendly and helpful toward peers (Marshall, 1989).

A healthy self-concept is vital to all areas of a child's development. Although readiness in the natural progression of development is triggered internally and furthered by appropriate external stimuli, successful mastery of new learning also depends on a child's feelings of competence and ability to meet new challenges. **Perceived competence** reflects the child's belief in his or her ability to succeed in a given task (Marshall, 1989). Successful experiences result in self-confidence, which, in turn, boosts self-esteem. Thus, many appropriate yet challenging experiences help the child feel successful, confident, and capable (Essa & Rogers, 1992).

The child needs to feel competent and able to face challenges as well as have a sense of **personal control**—the feeling of having the power to make things happen or stop things from happening. When children generally feel that what happens to them is completely out of their hands, particularly if what happens is not always in their best interest, they cannot develop this sense of control and will tend to see themselves as helpless and ineffective. All children need opportunities to make appropriate choices and exercise autonomy to begin to develop the perception that they have control, which also contributes to their emerging sense of responsibility for their own actions (Marshall, 1989).

The early years are crucial in the development of self-concept, since it forms and stabilizes early in life and becomes increasingly resistant to change (Samuels, 1977). Above all, children's positive concepts of themselves reflect healthy parent–child relationships that are founded on love, trust, and consistency. Then, when early childhood teachers enter young children's lives, they also contribute to the formation of that concept.

At the same time, if a child comes to school with a history of abuse or neglect, the teacher's contribution of offsetting positive experiences can help nurture self-esteem. Teachers strengthen children's positive self-esteem if they are sensitive to each child as an individual and to the needs of children for affection, nurture, care, and feelings of competence. Thus, teachers who understand children, know their characteristics, respond to them, and know how to challenge them in a supportive manner contribute to this positive sense of self. In essence, everything the early childhood teacher does has an impact on children's self-concept.

NEED FOR PLAY

Another thing that children have in common is the need for play, which serves as a means of learning about and making sense of the world (Rubin, Fein, & Vandenberg, 1983). But more than that, play is essential to all aspects of children's development. "It is an activity which is concerned with the whole of his being, not with just one small part of him, and to deny him the right to play is to deny him the right to live and grow" (Cass, 1973, p. 11). Play promotes mastery as children practise skills; it furthers cognitive development as thinking abilities are stretched; it involves language, encouraging new uses; it involves physical activity; it helps children work through emotions; its inventive nature makes it creative; it is often a socializing event; beyond all that, however, it provides a way for children to assimilate and integrate their life experiences. In no way is play a trivial pursuit, but rather it is a serious undertaking necessary to healthy development for all children (Almy, Monighan, Scales, & Van Hoorn, 1984).

Although the different types of play will be discussed in more detail in a later section on the "how" of early childhood education, it is worth noting at this point that, with age, children develop increasing social and cognitive skills that influence their play. If you are aware that play changes with age, it helps you to have appropriate expectations for young children in an early childhood program and to engage in their play. For instance, a 10-month-old engages in simple games like "Peek-a-boo!", whereas several 5-year-olds may collaborate to build a rocket ship in the block centre. As a teacher, you are more likely to initiate play sequences with infants and toddlers. With older children, however, you probably will not initiate many play sequences; rather, you would structure the environment to facilitate the child's play. Children between 3 and 5 years, for example, need sizable blocks of time to engage in self-selected play and

many open-ended materials that lend themselves to exploration and mastery (for instance, play dough, sand and water, building blocks). In addition, time, space, and materials that lend themselves to social play should always be available (including dolls, dress-up clothes, blocks). However, organized games with rules, particularly competitive games, are beyond the ability of most preschoolers to understand and should not be part of the early childhood program.

CHILDREN—DIFFERENCES

Infants and young children have many characteristics in common and certainly share basic needs for affection, acceptance, consistency, respect, and appropriate challenges, yet there are many variations among children. The "profiles" of infants, toddlers, preschoolers, and primary-level children presented earlier reflect many common characteristics of these ages, but they rarely describe any one child. While falling within the normal range of development, each child possesses a unique blend of attributes that makes him or her one of a kind.

Children's differences reflect both inborn and external factors that have moulded who they are. Some children are born with an easygoing temperament; for instance, they have a moderate activity level, predictable schedule of sleeping and eating, and a positive attitude toward, and curiosity about new experiences. Other children have more difficult temperaments and, for example, are more irritable, unpredictable, and more difficult to calm down (Thomas, Chess, & Birch, 1968). Although children are born with such temperamental characteristics, these gradually tend to affect the adults around them so that parents and teachers may begin to think of children as "difficult" or "easy" and expect and reinforce their behavioural traits. In turn, then, adults' perceptions of children contribute to children's self-perceptions.

A child's individuality is also shaped by the family—in most cases, the family is the most potent force in the young child's life. Consequently, it is important that early childhood educators endeavour to learn as much as possible about the families of young children. Let us now briefly examine family functioning from a theoretical perspective, and see what educators can do to forge a strong bond between the home and the school. Later in the text, we will consider how to develop programs that respect and value the differences in the cultural, ethnic, religious, linguistic, and economic backgrounds of children's families. At this point, however, it is important to note that early childhood teachers need to be sensitive to family diversity and genuinely value different cultures and backgrounds. Children mirror their primary environment—their home and family—as, of course, they should. If teachers, whether consciously or unconsciously, put down what children experience and learn at home, they will convey that the family, including the child, is in some way inferior and undesirable. What a detrimental impact this would have on children's self-concepts!

THE CHILDREN'S FAMILIES

While children are central in early childhood education, their families have to be considered equally important. Children are integral members of their family systems, and, conversely, family values and culture are an inseparable part of children.

FAMILIES—A THEORETICAL PERSPECTIVE

Family systems theory provides a useful approach to understanding the family as an ever-developing and changing social unit in which members constantly have to accommodate and adapt to each other's demands as well as to demands from outside the family. This theory provides a dynamic rather than static view of how families function.

From the perspective of family systems theory, the influence that family members have on each other is not one-way but rather interactive and reciprocal. Furthermore, it is impossible to understand the family by gaining an understanding of its individual members because there is more to the family than the "sum of its parts." It is necessary to view its interaction patterns and the unspoken "rules" that govern the members' behaviours. Healthy families work well together, communicate often, are able to make effective decisions, and can handle change. In addition, understanding the family means looking at its functioning within the larger context, for instance, the extended family, the community, and the neighbourhood. The early childhood centre becomes part of that larger context in which families function (Bronfenbrenner, 1986; Walker & Crocker, 1988).

Each individual's development occurs in a broader ecological context, within different but overlapping systems. The **microsystem** is the most immediate system that affects the individual; it includes the family, classroom, or workplace. These components of the microsystem are linked together in the **mesosystem** through such relationships as parent–teacher interaction or employment practices that affect the family (for instance, employer-supported child care or maternity-leave benefits that make up any difference between the employee's regular salary and what unemployment insurance pays).

The **exosystem** includes broader components of the neighbourhood and community that affect the functioning of the family, for example, government agencies or mass media. Finally, the broadest system to affect families is the **macrosystem**, which includes cultural, political, and economic forces (Bronfenbrenner & Crouter, 1983).

From such an ecological perspective, the child and family are seen more clearly as part of and affected by many other systems, each of which influences their development and functioning.

Viewing children and families as parts of various systems helps us to avoid seeking simple explanations and to acknowledge the complex interactions that often underlie children's and parents' behaviours. We must take time to look at the many factors affecting behaviour before jumping to conclusions. It is also important to recognize that family and school interact to affect children's development in myriad possible directions (Goelman, 1988). This perspective makes good communication between home and school an imperative, not a choice. Finally, a systems approach helps us see the interrelatedness of all aspects of children's lives. We simply cannot assume that the child's home exists in one isolated "compartment," while the school is in another. In the same way, we cannot presume that families' lives can be segmented into isolated facets.

THE CHANGING CANADIAN FAMILY

The family is and always has been the most important element in most children's lives. The family is where children experience the emotional and physical care and sustenance vital to their well-being. But the family has no simple definition or boundaries. Several decades ago most Canadian children might have been part of a "traditional" family—working father, housewife mother, and two or three children. However, as we saw in Chapters 1 and 4, that image of the traditional family is the exception, rather than the rule in Canada in the 1990s. Douglas Powell (1989) summarized this change well in a recent monograph on families and early childhood programs:

> Early childhood educators increasingly serve families characterized by single-parent households, cultural diversity and ethnic minority status, dual-worker or dual-career lifestyles, reconstituted ("blended") family arrangements, struggles with real or perceived economic pressures, and geographic mobility that decreases access to support traditionally available from extended family members (p. 15).

FAMILY FORMS

A family may be made up of one parent and one child, or it may be part of an extended family of grandparents, uncles, aunts, cousins, and many other relatives who are in frequent, close contact. Families may have one, two, or more parents; these may be the biological parents, step-parents, adoptive parents, or emotionally rather than legally related caregivers. A single parent may have never been married or may be divorced, separated, or widowed; as part of this group, an increasing number of young children live with single fathers (Briggs & Walters, 1985).

If the family has undergone a divorce, children may live with the same single or remarried parent all of the time, may alternate between two parents who have joint custody, or may see one parent for brief times during weekends or holidays. For some children, grandparents or other relatives take on the function of parents. Some divorced parents find alternate living arrangements, perhaps moving back in with their own parents, sharing housing with another adult or single parent, or joining a group housing arrangement. Because of divorce and remarriage, today's children may also acquire various natural and adoptive brothers and sisters, as well as half-siblings,

step-siblings, or unrelated "siblings" in less formal family arrangements. In larger urban communities, in particular, it is also becoming more common to find children living with a gay or lesbian parent, the parent's current mate, and often the children of that mate. While most individuals would not have been open about such a relationship two decades ago, they are becoming a more visible segment of society.

Whatever the family form, a wide range of people can make up a child's network of significant family members, as defined by emotional as well as legal ties. It is necessary, as a teacher of young children, that you also consider and acknowledge these persons as part of a child's family. Anyone who is important in the child's mind should be considered as important by you as well.

It is also important to be aware of legal restrictions that might affect children's relationships with adults in their lives. You should also ensure that such information is accurately and promptly recorded in your files. During some divorce proceedings, for example, one parent may file a **restraining order** against the other, legally limiting or forbidding contact with the child. Although such situations are usually upsetting for everyone involved, it is necessary to be aware of and make appropriate provisions for complying with any legal action. As a professional, you are bound by the restraining order, even if you are not in agreement with it. Having a release form on file at the school is one important way of ensuring that only authorized persons pick up the child. After all, the majority of child kidnappings are committed by a divorced parent who does not have custody of the child (Sheldon, 1983). In A Canadian Professional Speaks Out, Barbara Young, a Vancouver-based lawyer, describes the experiences she has had with "abductions" of children from an early childhood program by the non-custodial parent, and outlines some cautionary measures.

A CANADIAN
PROFESSIONAL SPEAKS OUT

Custody Disputes and Pick-Up Authorization

Most students reading this book will recall hearing or reading about at least one incident of child abduction either by strangers to the child or by a relative or parent of the child.

As early childhood educators you will have children in your centre whose parents are either separated from each other or who are divorcing. This is a stressful and unhappy time for everyone in the family and it will raise concerns for you as the professional responsible for the security of the child during school hours.

There are unfortunate incidents in which parents may give more priority to their legal disputes than to their concerns for the well-being of their children. There have been situations in which a parent not entitled to visit a child has taken that child without the other parent's knowledge or consent by convincing the teacher that it is alright for him or her to do so. This unauthorized removal of the child may place the child at risk and will, of course, cause a great deal of anxiety for everyone until the child is returned.

Your centre must have a policy for ensuring that each child leaves the centre with a person authorized to transport him or her. Under normal circumstances both parents have that authority and can legally assign another person such as a nanny, grandparent, or friend to pick their child up from school.

In a divorce situation the concept of legal authority over the child is complicated somewhat. When parents live together and raise children together they both have equal legal authority to make decisions about a child's upbringing, physical care, and control. Once parents have separated, they may have a written separation agreement or court order that grants "custody" of the child to one parent, which means that the parent has the legal right to make decisions related to the child's physical care and well-being. If the parents have "joint custody," then the situation is much like it was before their separation and they both have the authority to make decisions about the day-to-day care of the child.

The parent who does not have custody of the child will almost always have the legal right to visit with the child and to obtain information about the child's schooling and health. The right to visit the child is called "access." This parent may also have the rights of "joint guardianship," which does not enable that person to make the day-to-day decisions about the child's care but does permit that parent to have access to information about the child's health care, education and religious upbringing and to be consulted by the other parent on decisions related to those and other major issues affecting the child's upbringing.

The ECE centre should have a policy of only allowing the child to leave the centre with a parent or authorized person known to the teachers or with a person who has the parents' written authority to remove the child from the centre. As a policy of registration, the centre should have signatures of the child's parents or guardians on file, and it would be preferable to have a photograph of the parents or people usually responsible for transporting the child. In this way temporary teachers and new staff will have a way of knowing whether or not the adult who comes to get the child is authorized to take the child with him or her.

To be on the safe side the ECE should always rely on the advice of the custodial parent regarding the transporting of children and the giving out of any information about the child.

A good rule of thumb when setting up a policy for the security of your children in the ECE is to err on the side of caution. No responsible parent will begrudge your taking a little more time to ensure that his or her child is safe and is leaving with a person with authority.

As professionals interested in the child's education development and security, you will find it advisable to remain neutral with respect to the matrimonial disputes of your students' parents whenever possible. You may decide to have a policy, as many schools do, of denying requests for letters supporting one parent's parenting ability over that of the other. These requests will certainly be made and do compromise your professional neutrality as the child's educator, which is our prime area of responsibility. In addition, it exposes you to the risk of being subpoenaed to court to be a witness in a custody trial.

There is, of course, an exception to this general rule of remaining neutral, and that is when you believe that a child is in danger of either physical or sexual abuse. You have a legal responsibility to report your concerns to the authorities and if necessary to complete your obligation by testifying at a trial investigating the complaints of abuse.

Barbara Young
Barrister and Solicitor
Young, Noble, & Wirsig
Vancouver, British Columbia

OTHER FAMILY VARIATIONS

Not only is there great variation in family form and composition, but other characteristics differentiate families as well. Some of these include economic, racial, cultural, ethnic, religious, language, and geographic factors. The many ways in which families vary can affect not only family customs and traditions, but also more fundamental issues, such as defining values and relationships (Jenkins, 1987). In some cases, a family's uniqueness includes a mixture of cultures, religions, races, and generations. The teacher can learn about characteristics of various cultural, racial, or religious groups by reading, but it is very important to avoid making large-scale generalizations about a family based on group traits. Families are complex, and only through genuine interest can a teacher get to know them well. Effective and frequent communication helps the teacher become aware of family attributes that can affect the child and family as participants in the early childhood program. (Note that we will discuss in later chapters how the early childhood program can promote understanding of cultural, language, ethnic, and other variations in children and families.)

FAMILIES IN POVERTY

Poverty, as one factor in the lives of many families, bears closer scrutiny. You already are aware of the significant regional variations in poverty rates, discussed in the previous chapter. Canada's aboriginals stand out as being among the poorest people in the country. Poverty is also far more frequent in single-parent families (Pence, 1992).

As you know, a number of Canadian early childhood education programs have been aimed at helping economically disadvantaged families. Children who live in poverty often—but not always—have greater needs than children from more advantaged homes, as do their parents. Poverty is not a problem for children who have competent, stable parents who meet their needs. However, a variety of problems, including psychological instability, marital breakdowns, violence, and alcoholism, for example, are more common in poverty homes. Children from troubled poverty homes are likely to exhibit delays in their cognitive and language skills, in their socio-emotional functioning, and in their physical development. They present a special challenge to early childhood educators. Nevertheless, as you saw in Chapters 1 and 3, teachers in high-quality early childhood programs can have a significant and lasting impact on the lives of disadvantaged children and their families.

Teachers in quality settings also have an impact on the lives of families that are more fortunate. Many affluent families also have a series of concerns and difficulties, such as illness, marital discord, substance abuse, and work-related problems. Other families are faced with fewer difficulties, but still welcome and profit from a supportive relationship with their children's teachers.

THE NEEDS OF FAMILIES

The fact that a child is enrolled in an early childhood program indicates that the family has a need that the program is able to meet. The most common and certainly the most obvious family need is provision of child care while the parents are at work. The growth of child care centres and family child care homes over the past three decades has been in response to the dramatic increase in the number of working single-parent and dual-income families.

But beyond the overall need for responsible and knowledgeable adults to provide care for children while their parents work, families have other needs that the early childhood centre can help meet. Some of these needs concern helping the parents, as individuals, meet the demands of their multiple roles. Others revolve around coordination of home and school routines and practices. One note to keep in mind: although it is an ideal to consider that early childhood teachers can meet everyone's needs—children's, parents', co-workers'—sometimes this is just not possible in actuality. Setting realistic goals within the particular early childhood education work setting can help establish priorities.

PARENTHOOD

We typically view parenthood from the perspective of children's development and how parents facilitate, support, and promote it. Rarely is parenthood seen from the viewpoint of parents and their needs. Erik Erikson (1963), whose theory of human development was one of the first to span adulthood as well as childhood, considers that the most important need of the mature adult in the stage of **generativity** is to care for and nurture others. The tasks of this stage are often carried out in parenthood, through which the adult is concerned with meeting the needs of the next generation. Implied in this process is growth of the adult as an individual that is separate from the nurturance extended to children. This acknowledgment of adulthood as a period of continued development has been advanced in recent years by other writers (for instance, Gould, 1978; Levinson, 1978; Sheehy, 1976).

Parenthood as a distinct process has also been examined in greater depth. Ellen Galinsky (1981), after intensive research and interviews with scores of individuals, suggests that parents change and develop in their roles just as children do, by moving through six stages of parenthood. Each stage involves issues to be faced and a crisis that the parent has to resolve successfully. For instance, the parents of a young preschooler are enmeshed in the **authority stage**, defining rules and their own roles. Toward the end of the preschool years, parents enter the **interpretive stage** in which they are confronted with the task of explaining and clarifying the world to their children. The other stages deal with parents of children at different ages.

Galinsky is particularly concerned with the "images" that parents create, images of what they expect the child to be like before it is born, images of how they and their children will act and interact, or images of the loving relationship they expect. These images, especially what they wish to recreate or what they would like to change, emerge from parents' past experiences. Often, however, images and reality are different. Growth occurs when parents modify images so they become more consistent with reality or adjust their behaviour to come closer to the image.

Galinsky emphasizes that parents frequently feel their responses and emotions are unique, and are unaware that other parents also experience them. Yet, as she points out, during each of the stages of parenthood, parents face predictable issues and strong emotions. It helps parents to discuss and recognize their shared experiences as well as to have opportunities to observe the behaviours of others' children. It is also helpful when professionals explain common reactions and feelings, for instance, to a child's first day at school. In working with children, then, it is very important to acknowledge that parents undergo personal development that parallels their children's growth but that has separate issues and conflicts that need to be resolved.

EMPOWERMENT

When parents feel confident and competent in their abilities as mothers and fathers and members of the larger community, their children benefit. Unfortunately, some

parents feel that they are powerless in controlling what happens to them and to their children. An important role that early childhood programs can serve for families is to promote **empowerment**, a sense of control or power over events in their lives. This is particularly important as families deal with a variety of agencies and professionals, for instance, school, welfare, and political systems.

Parental empowerment has been a direct aim or an unexpected outcome in some programs designed for low-income families (Cochran, 1988; Ramey, Dorvall, & Baker-Ward, 1983; Seitz et al., 1985). As cited in one report of such a program, "Intangible but crucial shifts in attitude took place in parents who were often severely demoralized at the start" (Nauta & Hewett, 1988, p. 401). Parents began to see that they could have an impact. Professionals can use a wide variety of techniques to help parents attain this sense of control, including approaches described in a number of excellent publications, for instance, Alice Honig's *Parent Involvement in Early Childhood Education* (1979).

One of the forces behind the concept of parental empowerment has been the move toward viewing parents and teachers as equals. Not too many years ago, the pervasive attitude was that professionals were experts, whereas parents were the passive recipients of their expertise (Powell, 1989). Such a view does not provide parents with the security that they know their child best and that they should be full participants in any decisions that affect the child. Parents need to be treated with respect, their opinions should be asked for and taken seriously, and they must be involved in decisions about the child. In addition, when early childhood professionals give parents child development information, parents have tools with which to make informed decisions about their children's needs. Thus, involving, consulting with, and providing relevant education for parents can have a far-reaching impact by helping parents recognize their own importance and competence.

COORDINATING FAMILY NEEDS AND THE PROGRAM

Helping parents reach their potential as effective adults may be a goal in some programs that work extensively with families, particularly those from impoverished backgrounds. In all early childhood programs, there are additional points of contact between parents and teachers, at times revolving around seemingly mundane matters, but nonetheless important. A flexible, good-humoured attitude can help establish and maintain positive home–school relationships.

Parents' busy lives, or unforeseen events, are sometimes at odds with the schedule and routine of the early childhood centre. For instance, one mother expressed concern that the centre's afternoon snack, provided at 3:30, was served too late and that the child was not interested in dinner at 5:30. Another parent preferred that her child not take a nap at school, because when he slept during the day, he was just not ready to sleep at home until quite late in the evening. Other problems may keep a parent from arriving until after the centre has closed, for instance, car trouble, a traffic snarl, or unexpected overtime at work.

All of these situations can cause conflict but also provide an opportunity to evaluate what is best for the child, the parents, the other children, and the teachers. Sometimes such predicaments can be resolved fairly easily, but there are times when the needs of the child, the parent, or the school directly conflict. There is no simple answer, for instance, to deciding whether a child should take a nap, particularly when he appears to need it, or not take a nap because a delayed evening bedtime keeps his mother from getting the sleep she needs. Teachers must carefully weigh their own professional judgment of what is best for the child and take into account the child's need for sleep, the potential effect of being sleepy and cranky on the ability to function well at school, and the fact that the child would be treated differently from the other children by not napping (Ethics Commission, 1987). One way of resolving such conflicts—whether it is a matter of discussing naps, snacks, or pick-up time—is communication, our next topic.

COMMUNICATING WITH FAMILIES

Effective, positive communication with families is vital to providing a consistent and congruent experience for young children, but there is no simple formula for assuring that such contact does indeed take place. Each family is unique and brings to the early childhood program distinctive strengths and needs. Just as the teacher deals with each child as a unique individual by employing a variety of teaching and guidance methods, so must a flexible approach be maintained in communicating with families to meet their individual requirements.

Communication with families should not be viewed as simply an opportunity to report inappropriate behaviour, but rather as a way to foster between the program and the family a bond that enhances the child's experiences in both settings. Even if inappropriate behaviour is among the topics discussed, meetings and case conferences about individual children should be supportive and affirm the child's and family's strengths. Parents should leave such meetings feeling they have learned something and they would like to return.

Of course, formal meetings and conferences are not the only way to communicate. There are many bits of information that need to be shared by teachers and the family. For instance, both sides will benefit from discussing the child. In addition, there is often more general information about various aspects of the program that must be shared with families. The type of information to be conveyed often determines the communication method used. Communication, as we will discuss, can be carried out using both individual and group methods. Most early childhood centres utilize a combination of these approaches.

INDIVIDUAL METHODS OF COMMUNICATING WITH FAMILIES

The best way to get to know each family is through individual interaction and contact. Informally, such contact can take place daily, for instance, when children are dropped off and picked up from school. More formally, scheduled conferences between teacher and parents or other family members provide an avenue for exchange of information.

Informal Contact with Families

At the beginning and end of each day, at least one teacher should be available to exchange a few words with family members who drop off or pick up their children. Such informal interactions can make teachers more sensitive to the needs of children and families, can establish a mutual trust, can convey a feeling of caring and interest to parents, and can heighten parents' involvement in the program. "By being open, receptive, and chatty, teachers encourage parent interest and commitment" (Reiber & Embry, 1983, p. 162).

Because frequent school–family contacts are important, it makes sense to structure the schedule so that staff are free to participate in such exchanges (Tizard, Mortimer, & Burchell, 1981). The informal dialogues at the start and end of the day tend to be the most pervasive form of family involvement in early childhood programs (Gestwicki, 1987), especially those primarily involving working parents. In programs where children arrive by bus or come in car pools, the teacher needs to make an extra effort to maintain contact with parents, for instance, through notes or telephone calls (Gestwicki, 1987).

Another informal means of contact with parents is through occasional telephone calls. These provide a comfortable way of talking to parents, particularly if the calls are made often enough so they do not signal "a problem." Some schools send home "happy notes," brief, personalized notes that share with the parents something positive that happened during the day (Bundy, 1991).

Formal Contact with Families

Informal daily contacts between teachers and family members can create a mutually respectful and non-intimidating atmosphere. When teachers and parents feel comfortable with each other, communication will more likely be honest. In addition to such day-to-day encounters, more formal opportunities should be structured, when a sizable block of uninterrupted time is set aside for in-depth discussion. Such formal contacts can take the form of a parent–teacher conference or a home visit.

A **parent–teacher conference** is a regularly scheduled meeting that can satisfy different objectives. It can focus on getting acquainted; sharing information about the child and presenting a "progress report"; or, at the initiation of either teacher or parents, solving problems or discussing specific issues (Bullock, 1986; Reiber & Embry, 1983). Conferences often have negative connotations for the participants, who may view them as a time to share complaints and problems, even as a "last resort" when all else fails. But routinely scheduled conferences should be positive, affirming, and supportive.

A conference should never be an impromptu event. The teacher needs to be well prepared ahead of time, reviewing relevant information and thinking about how best to present it. In fact, preparing for conferences should be an ongoing process, beginning when the child first enters the program (Bjorklund & Burger, 1987). It is helpful if the teacher is ready with some anecdotes to support what the parents are told as well as to convey to them that the teacher knows the child well. It is also important to think through what questions you might want to ask of the parents to help the teacher better understand and work with the child.

At the same time, the teacher should facilitate a relaxed and easy forum for conversation. Sometimes sharing something with the parents, for instance, a picture painted by the child or a favourite recipe for play dough, contributes toward creating a positive atmosphere. The Parents and Professionals box (p. 140) presents some helpful strategies, suggested by Carol Gestwicki (1987) in her book *Home, School, and Community Relations: A Guide to Working with Parents*, to use when conducting a parent–teacher conference.

Another type of formal individual contact between teachers and family is the **home visit**. Home visits share some of the same objectives and procedures with parent–teacher conferences, but they contribute some added benefits as well. A

PARENTS AND PROFESSIONALS

Helpful Strategies for Parent–Teacher Conferences

1. Use common, not technical, terms. Avoid jargon that is not readily understood by someone unfamiliar with child development terminology. Don't tell the parents, "Halie functions one standard deviation below her age norm in fine motor development," when you could convey the message by saying, "Halie is still learning to cut with scissors and string small beads; we've been working on such tasks."

2. Use an egalitarian, not an authoritarian, approach. Parents can easily be put off when confronted with a teacher who is the expert and knows it all, telling them what they "should," "have to," or "must not" do. An authoritarian approach conveys that only the teacher is right and, by implication, the parents are wrong. Nothing prevents give-and-take discussion more quickly!

3. Provide an objective evaluation of the child. Teachers have to be sensitive to how closely parents' self-esteem is tied to their children. When a teacher seems critical of the child, the parents may quickly feel hurt and defensive. This does not mean that you should avoid sharing your concerns about the child. This can be better accomplished, however, by providing the parents with objective descriptions of the child's behaviour rather than by using labels and negative words. Examples of words to avoid include "problem," "immature," "hyperactive," and "slow."

4. Provide privacy and maintain a professional tone in conversations. It is important to ensure confidentiality in all information about children and families. A parent–teacher conference should never include discussions about other children and parents. Such talk can only make the parents wonder what the teacher might say about them.

5. Provide alternatives rather than answers. Problem situations, shared by parents, are seldom simple and easily solved because the teacher cannot know all the complexities. Furthermore, there are usually many possible ways of dealing with problems. It is important to ask the parents what they have tried and what has worked for them. In addition, it is helpful to provide alternatives for parents. You might provide several suggestions that have "worked for other parents" or that "we've tried in the classroom" as ideas for the parent to consider. When parents come to their own conclusions and chart a course of action, these suggestions are much more likely to be effective.

6. Take your time in approaching solutions. It is not realistic to expect that complex problems can be solved during a parent–teacher conference. The teacher may suggest that both she and the parents take time to observe before jumping to premature conclusions (Gestwicki, 1987).

7. Be sure to check back with the family to see if the suggestions are working. If they are not effective, meet again and formulate new strategies. If they are working, continue to provide support and feedback.

teacher who visits a family at home conveys a sense of caring and interest in the child's world beyond the classroom. Children are usually delighted to introduce their room, toys, pets, and siblings to the teacher and are made to feel very special that the teacher is visiting them at home. Parents can observe first-hand the interaction between the child and the teacher, and may become more relaxed with the teacher who has shown this special interest. In addition, teachers can observe first-hand the family's home environment and parent–child interactions as a way of better understanding the child's behaviour. In some instances, especially once a sense of trust has been established, home visits can become an extremely important source of support, for instance, for teenaged parents.

Although there are very important benefits in conducting home visits, they are also quite time-consuming and may (though certainly not inevitably) intimidate the parents. On the other hand, a young teacher from a suburban home may be intimidated by visiting an inner-city home. Other factors may be involved as well. A graduate student of one of the authors was, as a junior kindergarten teacher, expected to visit every child's home at the beginning of the school year. When she learned that the child's father was a convicted murderer, she was quite apprehensive about making the visit, even though she had made many during the previous fifteen years. After discussing her concerns with her supervisor, she had the school principal accompany her to the home (the father was out). A teacher's commitment to learning as much as possible about the children in the class and their families must be weighed against other factors, including perceived risks to the teacher, comfort level of the parents and teacher, and time. There are times when meeting at the centre or school, for example, is preferable.

Problems Between Parents and Teachers

Ideally, parents and teachers cooperate fully to provide positive experiences for children at home and at school. Unfortunately, there are times when this ideal is not always realized. In fact, parent–teacher disharmony is quite common (Galinsky, 1990). Parents and teachers may disagree, particularly when they feel rushed and tired or when they are preoccupied with other aspects of their lives. In addition, both may harbour some unacknowledged negative feelings, for instance, disapproval of working mothers, jealousy or competition for the child's affection, or criticism of the other's child guidance approach (Galinsky, 1988, 1990). Although the child is the common bond between parents and teachers, there are many other factors that affect their moods and impinge on their interactions. The job stress experienced by parents as well as by teachers can certainly spill over into the brief contact between them as children are dropped off or picked up at school during what Ellen

Galinsky calls the "arsenic hour" (1988). In addition, teachers sometimes resent certain parents. For example, there may be parents who convey the impression they do not value the teacher and his or her work. In other cases, the teacher may feel that she or he is the only person who really is an advocate for the child. There also is the case of the parent who is always late picking up the child from the centre.

Galinsky (1988) offers some concrete suggestions for working more effectively with parents. She suggests that when teachers become upset with parents, it is often because teachers' underlying expectations are somehow not realized; teachers need to examine whether what they expect is realistic or not. Similarly, teachers should scrutinize their attitudes toward the parents, looking for hidden resentments or prejudices. Teachers also need to make an effort to see the situations from the parents' point of view, asking themselves how they might feel if they were in the parents' shoes.

It can be very helpful for teachers to develop a support system, whether within their own program or even outside of it, that allows them to express and explore their feelings in an accepting and safe atmosphere. Teachers must also recognize and convey to parents the limits of their role. This includes being familiar with community resources to which parents can be referred when a problem is beyond the scope of the teacher's role and expertise.

There is no simple formula for effective parent–teacher communication. The parent–teacher relationship is founded on trust and respect, which grow out of many small but significant daily contacts. Greeting parents by name, writing personalized notes, making phone calls to parents whom the teacher does not see often, being sensitive to parents' needs, and sharing brief, positive anecdotes about their children all contribute to a good relationship (Morgan, 1989).

Group Methods of Communicating with Families

In addition to personalized, individual contact between parents and teachers, early childhood programs generally also utilize other communication methods for getting information to the parents as a group. These methods can serve a functional purpose, for instance, to let parents know that the school will be closed the day after Canada Day when it falls on a Thursday. They may also take on an educational role, for example, to give parents insight into an aspect of child development. We will review three such methods: written communiqués, bulletin boards, and meetings.

Written Communiqués. Newsletters, memos, or other written material can be an effective way of getting information to all families. In addition, they provide parents with an overview of current happenings in the program and thus facilitate parent–child discussions about the program. It is, of course, important to match written information to the reading abilities of the parents. If many or all of the families in the program are non-English-speaking, for instance, communiqués should be written in the parents' primary language. In larger communities, with a high percentage of immigrants, translation services, if not available through a parent, are often available through an ethnic group's cultural association. Community social workers and psychologists also have access to a list of translators. It is also important that all such materials be neat, attractive, and accurately written. A sloppy, misspelled, and ungrammatical letter conveys that the teacher does not care enough about the families to produce a thoughtful document. Today, many schools have access to a computer, which makes it simpler than ever to compose attractively arranged letters or newsletters, to check the grammar and spelling, and to incorporate graphics.

Many programs produce a regular newsletter that may contain announcements, news of what the teachers have planned for the upcoming time period, new policies, relevant community information, child development research summaries, columns by local experts, and other information of interest to families. A newsletter is only effective if it is read. Thus, its length, the information included, and the writing style need to be carefully considered.

Another form of written communication that can convey a great deal of information to parents is a school handbook, which parents are given when they enrol their children in the early childhood program. Such a handbook should contain relevant information about school policies and procedures, fees, hours of operation, holidays, sick child care, birthday routines, and other important matters. At the same time, it should include a clear statement of the school's philosophy (Bundy, 1991).

Bulletin Boards. Bulletin boards can either be a useful means of conveying information, or a cluttered mass of overlaid memos that no one bothers to look at. To be effective, a bulletin board should be attractively laid out, its contents need to be current, and posted items should not compete with each other for attention. Further, if family members know that only current and important items will be posted on a specific bulletin board, they are more likely to pay attention to it.

Bulletin boards can be used for a variety of purposes. They can be informative, for instance, letting parents know that the children will be taking a field trip the following week or that a child in the group is home with the chicken pox. Many centres include a notice of the day's activities on a bulletin board, which lets parents know the highlights of their child's day. Bulletin boards can also be educational, conveying relevant information in a way that appeals to those who look at it.

At one centre, for instance, the teachers wanted to follow up on comments from several parents that their children were just scribbling rather than drawing something recognizable. The teachers wanted to help parents understand that children's art follows a developmental pattern. They matted selections of the children's pictures, arranged them attractively on bulletin boards organized by the children's ages, and interspersed the pictures with quotes from experts on children's art. The pictures supported the quotations, thus conveying the messages that children gradually move toward representational art and that there are common steps children go through in their development of art. Many parents commented on how helpful they found this bulletin board message. It proved to be a most effective teaching tool!

In another centre, a Canadian cooperative nursery school, the teacher became concerned when she noticed that some parents were not using seat belts for their children when on a trip to the sugar bush, even though they are mandatory. An inviting bulletin board display on the merits of seat belts was her diplomatic approach to this concern.

Meetings and Other Group Functions. Group gatherings can provide another effective way of reaching family members. Such functions can take the form of meetings, the traditional forum for formal parent education, or they can be social. In addition, parent discussion groups may be part of the early childhood program. When planning any kind of group function, however, keep in mind that family members are busy people who will weigh the benefits of attending a school program against other demands on their time. In fact, for some parents the pressure of one more thing to do might be so stressful that it would outweigh the advantages of the program. Because each family's needs are different, the early childhood program must facilitate communication with parents in many different ways and be prepared to individualize ways of meeting these needs.

If the supervisor and staff feel that parent meetings can serve a positive function in meeting the needs of some of the families, they must ensure that what they plan will interest potential participants. One way to assess what might be relevant to parents is to conduct an interest survey. A brief form can solicit preferences about topic choices, time and day, and type of meeting (see Exhibit 5-1 for a sample form). If the teachers or the director plan parent functions without input from the parents, these functions may well fail to match the interest of the parents and result in very low attendance (Gestwicki, 1987). Also, parents are often more likely to come to a meeting if a meal or snack is included and if child care is provided. On the other hand, keep in mind that if children have already spent nine or ten hours at the centre, adding two evening hours may be more than is reasonable.

Parent get-togethers may feature a speaker with expertise on a topic of common interest, or they may revolve around discussion led by a facilitator. It is important to remember that parents' shared experiences are a valuable source of information and support (Kelly, 1981). Thus, if the main part of the program includes a speaker, time should also be allocated for discussion.

EXHIBIT 5-1 PARENT INTEREST SURVEY

DEAR PARENTS:

We would like to plan some family events for this year and want your suggestions. Please help us by sharing your preferences about the following:

(Please rate these as follows: A = yes, definitely interested; B = moderately interested; C = not at all interested.)

1. **Type of event:**
   ____ Parent meeting on a specific topic (topic choice below)
   ____ Parent discussion groups on specific topics
   ____ Family social function (picnic, dinner, party, etc.)
   ____ Fundraiser to benefit your child's class

2. **Topic choice** (for meetings or discussion groups):

____ Child behaviour/guidance	____ Television
____ Child nutrition	____ Good toys for children
____ Learning to read	____ Balancing family/work
____ Self-esteem	____ Working mothers
____ What happens at school?	____ _____
____ _____	____ _____

3. **Best day** (circle your choices): M T W Th F Sa

4. **Best time:**

____ Lunch time	____ Afternoons
____ After work	____ 7:30–9:00 p.m.

5. **Other matters:** Will your attendance be influenced by
   ____ Provision of child care   ____ Provision of meals/snack

Thank you for your help!

One particularly enjoyable way of presenting some topics is to illustrate them with slides or videotapes taken of the children at the school. Such subjects as children's play, social development, or developmentally appropriate toys can be enhanced with such visuals. In addition to gaining insight into an aspect of their children's development, parents will feel great pride in seeing their youngsters depicted on the screen.

Small groups are generally more effective than large groups in encouraging participation (Gestwicki, 1987). A common interest can also create a more intimate atmosphere for a meeting, for instance, involving parents whose children will enter kindergarten the following year or just the parents of children in one class rather than those from the entire early childhood centre.

Some centres generate considerable enthusiasm for social events during which parents and teachers have the opportunity to exchange information in a relaxed atmosphere. These can include holiday parties, meals, or an open house, and they can involve all family members. One university program sponsored a potluck dinner for families, staff, and student-teachers each semester. Prearranged seating assured that students sat with the families of children they were observing. This event attracted almost all of the families and proved to be enjoyable as well as valuable for all involved.

FAMILY INVOLVEMENT

We have been discussing various ways in which communication between teachers and families can be maintained. However this communication takes place, it implies involvement on the part of the family. Let's look at family involvement in more detail now.

Family involvement in the early childhood program is a multifaceted concept, embracing a wide range of options and levels. It can mean, on the one hand, that parents and other family members are passive recipients of information; parents may be more intensely engaged by serving as volunteers in the program; or, at an even more complex level of involvement, they can be participants in the decision-making process of the program (Honig, 1979). Whatever the level, however, ample research has shown that such involvement has positive benefits for children as well as for families (Becher, 1986; Powell, 1989).

There is a reciprocal relationship between the family and the early childhood program, each providing support and help to the other as they are able. Family involvement will vary according to each family's ability to contribute and to its needs. Some families invest a great deal of their time and energy in the program, whereas others need all their resources to cope with the stresses they face. Some families support the program by participating in and contributing time to various school activities; others seek support from the program in facing their personal strains. As a teacher in an early childhood program, you will need to be flexible to be able to recognize each family's capabilities and needs and to set expectations or provide support accordingly. While this may seem like a formidable task early on in your studies, the qualities that drew you to the early childhood profession, coupled with the knowledge and experience you acquire during your studies, will help you to be sensitive to each family's needs.

You will also find that you can involve families in your program in a variety of ways. For example, you might involve family members as resources, as volunteers in the classroom, and/or as decision-makers. A Closer Look (p. 146) presents an interesting example of how a group of parents became involved in their children's program.

FAMILIES AS RESOURCES

Family members have many talents and abilities to contribute to the program. Many early childhood programs invite parents or relatives to participate on occasions when their job skills, hobbies, or other special expertise can augment and enrich the curriculum. For instance, a teacher may invite Ronnie's mother, who is a dentist, to help the children understand the importance of good dental hygiene and care; the teacher may take the children to visit the bakery owned by Annie's uncle, because the class is discussing foods; she can ask Carmelo's father to show the children how he makes pottery; or she may invite Ivan's mother and new baby brother when the class talks about babies and growing up. All family members—parents, siblings, grandparents, other relatives, even pets—can be considered part of the program, extending its resource base.

A Closer Look

The New Playground Equipment

One afternoon, when Linda picked up her two sons from the child care centre, she found herself a participant in a conversation with a teacher and the director. They were concerned about how the centre's tight budget could possibly replace some of the worn-out playground equipment. Linda gave this conversation a lot of thought as she tried to come up with some ideas for a fundraising project. The following week she shared her brainstorm with the director, who was very impressed with her idea for a "children's art auction."

Over the next several months, about two dozen parents, spurred on by Linda's enthusiasm, became involved in this project. A plan evolved for a Saturday evening program that was to begin with a cheese and wine tasting (products donated by local merchants), followed by an auction of artwork with at least one piece from each child. The parents obtained donated mats and frames from local art stores to frame each picture. The resulting products were astounding, as paintings, collages, finger paintings, drawings, and other artwork were attractively set off by the frames. On the day of the art auction, a community meeting hall was transformed into an art gallery filled with the work of promising young artists!

More than 250 people, including parents, grandparents, uncles, aunts, neighbours, and supporters from the community, came to the auction. Each family had been asked to sell a book of ten reasonably priced tickets for the event. In addition, publicity through local media brought a number of people to the auction because they were interested in children's art. A "catalogue" listed the displayed pictures with the names and ages of the artists. A volunteer auctioneer made the evening lively with his comparisons to works by Picasso, the cubists, and other artists. "I saw one almost exactly like this in a museum, and you can bet they paid a lot more for it than this one is going to sell for ... So, what's the opening bid?"

To everyone's delight, the proceeds from ticket sales and the auction were almost $5000. Within two months, the playground included some new equipment. The art auction became an annual event for this centre, and the school's coffers were expanded through the volunteer efforts of parents.

Although this event took time out of their busy lives, parents became committed to the project for a number of reasons. Working with their children's artwork engendered in many of the parents a sense of pride and enjoyment. They also discovered a camaraderie and mutual support in this project as they got to know each other. In addition, they were able to experience the benefits of their time investment when they saw their children using the new equipment. Finally, the success of the event more than matched their expectations, and the pride in their accomplishment was very rewarding.

Family members can also help out with maintenance and construction tasks that are part of the program. In some early childhood programs, especially parent cooperatives (see Chapter 1, page 12), parents routinely take home the dress-up clothes and other classroom items to wash or clean. In others, regularly scheduled clean-up days bring teachers and family members to the centre on specified weekends to deep clean the facility, materials, and equipment. Family members with carpentry skills may construct or repair equipment. Others may develop learning materials and games at home that will expand the activity options available to the children.

There are other ways in which family members can serve as program resources. For instance, they can help orient new families to the early childhood program, serve as role models, and provide support to other families. Their suggestions and ideas can enrich the program. Family members can also be extremely effective in providing local and provincial support for legislation that affects children and families. They can help provide program visibility in the community if the school is seeking outside funding. Family support can be a potent force in maintaining a high-quality early childhood program.

FAMILY MEMBERS IN THE CLASSROOM

Family members may also volunteer as teacher aides. Programs such as parent-cooperative preschools require parent involvement on a regular basis. Some programs modelled after Project Head Start also have required that parents spend time in the classroom, although forced participation can be counterproductive (Honig, 1979). In most programs, particularly child care centres, parents participate occasionally or not at all because parents are usually working while their children are at school. Some teachers relish such involvement; others feel sceptical and reluctant, fearing a clash with the parents' child-rearing practices, feeling stress about being under constant observation, or worrying that the children will get overexcited (Gestwicki, 1987).

Having parents in the classroom can have many benefits for children, parents, and teachers. Children can benefit from having their parents participate in the classroom, feeling pride and a sense of security "as they see parents and teachers working together cooperatively, each respecting the other's contribution" (Gestwicki, 1987, p. 205). For parents, such first-hand experience can provide insight into how their children spend their time at school, a basis for observing their own children in relation to age-mates, and a chance to note guidance techniques used by teachers. Teachers can benefit from the support parents offer, the added pair of hands that can expand activity possibilities, and the opportunity to gain insight into parent–child interactions (Gestwicki, 1987). There are, however, some consequences of having parents in the class that teachers and parents should expect.

The full-time teachers in parent cooperatives perhaps have the most experience with parents in the classroom as the staffing schedule includes a rotating staff of parents. Teachers in cooperatives find that most children behave differently when their own parents are there as teachers, although this change is most pronounced on the first few occasions when a parent is present. It is important to let parents know that children's behaviour tends to be different when a parent is present, as they often become concerned about their children's behaviour in the program. For example, some children become aggressive and loud with a parent present, while others, who are independent most days, might cling and whine.

FAMILY MEMBERS AS DECISION-MAKERS

Some programs ask parents to serve on an advisory or policy board. Some university-based programs, for instance, invite parents to participate in parent advisory councils. Many not-for-profit child care or preschool centres also require a governing board of which parents are members. Effective decision-making boards can promote a true partnership between families and the school program (Dunst & Trivette, 1988), providing support for the school, empowerment of parents, and increased mutual understanding.

PARENT EDUCATION

All forms of family involvement potentially serve an educational function, as parents have the chance to gain insights into their children's development and the school's program. Often, however, early childhood programs provide specific **parent education** aimed at enhancing parent–child relations and improving parenting competence. Given the numbers of children who grow up in abusive homes and in poverty, some professionals even consider that high-quality parent education programs should be mandatory to prevent needless impairment of children through abuse, neglect, and deprivation (Anastasiow, 1988). Evaluation of many parent education programs aimed at economically disadvantaged families has indicated that such programs can be very effective, although much still remains to be learned through systematic research (Clarke-Stewart, 1983; Powell, 1986). In addition, there is limited evidence that parent education enhances the parenting skills of media-class families as well (Harris & Larsen, 1989).

The scope of parent education programs is not easy to capture in a single definition because there is great diversity in the field. Douglas Powell (1986) spells out some of the contrasts in parent education:

> Some programs focus on family–community relations while others teach parents how to stimulate a child's cognitive development. Some programs prescribe specific skills and styles in relating to young children. ... Some programs are highly structured while others let parents select activities they wish to pursue. In some programs the staff serve as child development experts while other programs adhere to a self-help model with staff in non-directive facilitator roles. There are important differences in the use of professionals, assistants, or volunteers, program length (weeks versus years), and program setting (group- versus home-based) (p. 47).

Parent education can take many forms. Often informal, one-to-one interactions at pick-up and drop-off times are valuable, especially because they are tailored to the individual. Parent get-togethers or meetings are another frequently used forum. The content of such programs can vary widely, depending on parents' interests and needs. Christine Cataldo, in her book *Parent Education for Early Childhood* (1987), suggests a wide variety of subjects. Popular topics often revolve around children's development, including characteristics and common problems of various ages. Other topics can focus on various aspects of caring for children, for instance, nutrition, health and fitness, self-care and protection, and selecting child care services. Family composition, challenges, and crises offer many program possibilities as well. Children's play and appropriate toys provide other topic choices of interest to parents. In addition, most parents are concerned with issues related to children's behaviours, discipline, guidance, fears, sexual development and interest, personality development, and self-esteem. Finally, the family's involvement in and promotion of children's education includes many areas of interest to parents.

Programs can be presented by the early childhood staff based on their own expertise, or by local resource persons. It is important that presenters be well informed on the topic chosen and that they provide accurate information. In addition, a variety of packaged parent education materials are also available. Such packages may include extensive manuals and provide the facilitator with all the necessary resources to conduct the program. Two popular examples of such parent education programs that focus on development of child guidance skills are Parent Effectiveness Training (P.E.T.) (Gordon, 1976) and Systematic Training for Effective Parenting (STEP) (Dinkmeyer & McKay, 1976).

KEY POINTS OF CHAPTER 5

CHILDREN—SIMILARITIES

▲ 1. The early childhood educator's understanding of child development is vital in providing a supportive and developmentally appropriate program for young children.

▲ 2. Positive self-esteem is a need shared by all children and is fostered by adults who convey to children that they are competent and worthwhile.

▲ 3. Children's perceived competence reflects their belief in their own ability to be successful; such self-confidence contributes to positive self-esteem.

▲ 4. Children who have a sense of personal control and a feeling that they can make things happen see themselves as effective, which also contributes to self-esteem.

▲ 5. Play provides many opportunities for children to practise skills, stretch thinking abilities, work through emotions, socialize, and be creative.

CHILDREN—DIFFERENCES

▲ 6. Children have inborn temperaments that contribute to individual differences. Some children are basically easygoing, whereas others are difficult.

▲ 7. Children's uniqueness also derives from the cultural, ethnic, religious, or economic background of their families. These differences will be discussed in greater detail in Chapters 8, 13, and 14.

FAMILIES—A THEORETICAL PERSPECTIVE

▲ 8. Family systems theory views the family as a dynamic, constantly changing system that interacts with other systems, for instance, those within the community.

THE CHANGING CANADIAN FAMILY

▲ 9. There is no simple or single definition of the family because families come in many forms.

▲ 10. Families also differ based on economic, racial, cultural, ethnic, religious, language, and geographic factors.

▲ 11. An estimated one-fifth of Canadian children grow up in poverty, a relevant factor in many early childhood programs.

THE NEEDS OF FAMILIES

▲ 12. One of the most important needs of working parents is for high-quality, reliable care for their young children.

▲ 13. Many parents are part of Erikson's stage of generativity, in which care and nurture of children is important.

▲ 14. Galinsky identifies stages of parenthood that are distinct from but overlap with children's stages of development.

▲ 15. A goal of some early childhood programs is to promote empowerment of the parents, to help them achieve a sense of control over their lives.

KEY TERMS

authority stage
autonomy
empowerment
exosystem
family involvement
family systems theory
generativity
home visit
interpretive stage
macrosystem
mesosystem
microsystem
parent education
parent–teacher
    conference
perceived competence
personal control
restraining order
self-conceptself-esteem

▲16. Coordinating the needs of parents with the needs of the children and the program can pose a challenge for early childhood teachers.

COMMUNICATING WITH FAMILIES

▲17. Effective home–school communication is important to parents, teachers, and children.

▲18. Parents and teachers often use the beginning and end of the day as a time for brief, informal communication.

▲19. More formal parent–teacher communication takes place through parent conferences and home visits. Both should be planned to facilitate a positive exchange of information.

▲20. There are some strategies that can help when problems arise between parents and teachers.

▲21. Effective methods of communicating with groups of parents include newsletters, memos, bulletin boards, and group meetings.

FAMILY INVOLVEMENT

▲22. Family involvement in the early childhood program has positive benefits for children, families, and the school.

▲23. Family members may serve as resources to the program by contributing special talents, interests, and abilities; as volunteers; or as members of a policy board, in a decision-making capacity.

PARENT EDUCATION

▲24. Parent education can take many forms to meet the many differing needs of families.

KEY QUESTIONS

1. Observe several children of the same age. These might be children you work with and know well or children you are observing for the first time. What traits do they share? How are they similar? Can you draw some conclusions about children of that particular age?

2. Think about these same children and describe what makes each unique. How do they differ? Do you have any indications about what factors underlie these differences?

3. As you observe children, identify a child who appears to be self-confident. How does the child express this confidence? Do you see a difference between this child and another who seems less assured?

4. Think of your own family history. How has your family changed over the past two (or three or four) generations? Consider maternal employment, divorce, closeness to extended family, and other factors. Compare your family with that of other members of your class.

5. Sometimes the needs of families conflict with those of the program. Which elements of the early childhood program could pose a potential conflict? How might these be resolved? Read the Ethics Commission's "Ethics Case Studies: The Working Mother" in *Young Children* (November 1987, p. 16) for insight into the suggestions of professionals to resolve such a conflict.

6. Visit an early childhood program. What evidence of communication with parents do you see? Look at bulletin boards, notes, pictures, and other written material. What kind of interaction do you notice between parents and teachers? What "messages" about the school's concern for parents do parents get from this communication?

7. Ask several parents whose children are enrolled in an early childhood program about their contacts with the teachers and the program. What is their overall attitude about contact between home and school? Do they feel it is important or not important, positive or negative, present or absent, supportive or lacking in support? What do they expect from the teachers? Do they feel that communication between parents and teachers is important for their children?

8. How can parent involvement benefit the early childhood program? List some concrete ways in which parents might contribute to the program.

6 TEACHERS

This chapter brings us back to that all-important person in early childhood education—the teacher. What does it take to be a teacher? In addition to the training requirements discussed in Chapter 4, most early childhood teachers find they have to be a "jack-of-all-trades." One day, the teacher is a fundraiser and an expert on caring for the frogs someone brought to the centre, and the next day, the job requires a specialist on diaper rash and someone to fill in for the cook who went home sick. Two days later, the teacher is a carpenter, fixing the outdoor shed, and a professional, attending a conference on children with special needs. The list of roles and tasks the teacher is expected to assume probably is infinite, and no text or course can begin to anticipate what you may be called upon to do.

This chapter will focus on teachers not only as teachers but as individuals, as teachers, and as members of a profession. Nonetheless, everything discussed in this book is relevant to an early childhood teacher. Teachers in early childhood programs are the ones who integrate knowledge about the development of children, about the importance of families, about creating a healthy and stimulating environment, about child-centred curriculum planning, and about appropriate and nurturing guidance to provide the best possible care and education for young children. Thus, in this chapter we will explore the following important aspects of teaching and the profession of early childhood education:

1. Early childhood teachers can be described by certain identifiable personal qualities. In addition, we will discuss some predictable stages in their development.

2. We will also look at how the staffs of early childhood programs can include individuals in a variety of roles, including the director, teaching staff, volunteers, support staff, board of directors, and community professionals.

Later, in the final chapter of the book, when you have a deeper understanding of the Canadian early education field, we will look at current issues confronting the profession. We will also consider the face of ECE in this vast land as we approach the 21st century.

THE EARLY CHILDHOOD TEACHER

Before beginning a discussion of early childhood teachers, it is important to make some distinctions in terminology. Unfortunately, no universally accepted categories and titles define those who work with young children, although some have been proposed, as we will discuss later. Often labels conjure up stereotypes and do not reflect different educational and experiential backgrounds found in the field (Phillips & Whitebook, 1986).

Throughout this book the terms **early childhood teacher** and **early childhood educator** will be used interchangeably. Other terms, particularly **caregiver** and **child care worker** can also be used. Traditionally, a caregiver has meant someone who cares for the physical and emotional needs of the child, whereas a teacher serves an educational function. "However, this distinction is not a particularly clear one, for the line between education and nurture in the early years is not a distinct one" (Spodek & Saracho, 1982, p. 401). Moreover, given the high level of training that is required in most Canadian jurisdictions, the term "teacher" has a more positive connotation among the public and better reflects the professionalism of caring, early childhood teachers.

Certainly the early childhood teacher "cares for" and the caregiver "teaches" young children. Which teacher has not tied shoelaces, wiped noses, or dried tears? And which caregiver has not helped children learn how to zip a coat, assemble a puzzle, or share the tricycle? Teaching and caregiving functions seem not only inherent but also integrally related in both roles to the point where a distinction is impossible to make (Willer, 1990).

Lilian Katz (1972), in fact, includes these among the four roles she outlines as functions of teachers of young children: caretaking, providing emotional support and guidance, instructing, and facilitating. The caregiving role, similar in many ways to the role of the mother, diminishes as the child gets older (Katz, 1980).

The distinction between the teacher and the caregiver, then, is more than a general description of what they do, for their roles certainly overlap. What does distinguish teachers, according to Katz (1984b), is their professionalism, the way they use

their knowledge and standards of performance. Teachers possess advanced knowledge in child development and early childhood education that they apply when they have to make judgments and decisions on a moment-by-moment basis. At the same time, they also share with other professionals a commitment to maintaining the high standards set by the profession through its organizations. But there really is no simple or single definition of a good teacher of young children. In a summary of six in-depth interviews that searched for a definition of the "good preschool teacher," Ayers (1989) concludes that there is a "kaleidoscope of possibility, for there are endless good preschool teachers" (p. 141).

QUALITIES OF THE GOOD EARLY CHILDHOOD TEACHER

If asked what qualities a good teacher of young children should have, most of us would come up with an intuitive list of characteristics such as warmth, sensitivity, energy, sense of humour, flexibility, and patience. Research, however, is not particularly clear-cut in showing a consistent relationship between teacher effectiveness and personal qualities. This is partly due to problems in the methodology of such research, inconsistency in what is being measured, difficulty in distinguishing between teaching style and teaching techniques, and even lack of agreement about what constitutes "good" teaching (Feeney & Chun, 1985; Katz, 1984a).

Some clues about what makes a good teacher of young children can be gleaned from early childhood educators and researchers based on their experience and insight. Millie Almy (1975) lists some attributes, including patience, warmth, nurturance, and energy. She also describes maturity, openness to new ideas, and tolerance for a certain amount of ambiguity as necessary qualities. In addition, she finds it particularly important that the early childhood teacher be able to move easily between the concrete level of thinking of the child and the abstract level of the adult, at which theoretical information is translated into appropriate decisions. As Almy summarizes it,

> The early childhood educator role may be seen as that of "double specialist" in a variety of ways: In teaching young children and in assessing their development and learning; in working with children and in working with adults; in thinking concretely (maintaining insight into the child's thought) and thinking formally, in practice as well as in theory (p. 28).

TEACHERS' DEVELOPMENTAL STAGES

Although the idea of developmental stages is commonly understood and used by teachers of young children, the notion of sequenced steps of development among teachers is not as readily considered. Yet Katz (1977) concludes that teachers also undergo a series of stages, each with unique developmental tasks and training needs. It is helpful to realize that others begin their teaching experiences with similar feelings of inadequacy or anxiety and that these evolve into more advanced stages as competence develops.

- *Stage 1: Survival*—The beginning teachers' main concern through the first year or so of teaching is usually focused on whether they will survive. The realization of the great responsibility they have for the group of children, as well as the discrepancy between the success they expect and the reality of the classroom, results in anxiety and feelings of inadequacy. In general, they are acquiring information about what children are like and what can be expected of them. At this stage, the teacher's main need is for support, encouragement, and guidance, provided on-site, as required.

- *Stage 2: Consolidation*—Having recognized that they can indeed survive, teachers begin to focus on specific tasks. As they consolidate the information gained from their first year or two, they move their attention more specifically to problem children or to situations that deviate from the general norm. Their needs at this time are for continued on-site training that supports exploration of alternatives to deal with the problem situations.

- *Stage 3: Renewal*——By now, teachers in their third or fourth year begin to seek some new approaches and ideas as they tire of the way they have been doing things for the past several years. The search for renewal can be met through meetings with colleagues, professional organizations and conferences, professional books and journals, and visits to other programs.

- *Stage 4: Maturity*——This final stage is reached by different teachers at different points and represents a coming to terms with themselves and their profession. Now they ask deeper and more abstract questions, looking at the broader implications of their work in the context of the larger society. Their experience makes these questions more meaningful. Mature teachers need opportunities to read widely, interact with others, and participate in seminars and other forums where such questions are addressed by others searching for similar insights.

 PARENTS AND PROFESSIONALS

Parent Support for Early Childhood Educators

In the last chapter, we discussed the role and responsibility of early childhood teachers toward parents. As indicated, the teacher–parent relationship is a reciprocal process. While teachers provide many services for parents, parents can also be extremely effective advocates for the early childhood education profession. One of the more effective lobbying efforts to promote increased funding allocation for early childhood programs in Quebec was the appearance of a large group of parents who spoke about the importance of that funding to their lives. The legislators found the taxpayers who came to promote this funding quite convincing!

Parental support, however, does not begin in the political arena. First and most important, parents must have a sound appreciation of early childhood educators and a clear understanding of the issues they face. Such understanding is promoted in a high-quality program in which teachers act professionally and are articulate about their field. When parents recognize that the quality of education and care their children receive is inextricably tied to improving the status and working conditions of their children's teachers, they will be better able to help bring about changes.

STAFFING IN EARLY CHILDHOOD PROGRAMS

The early childhood teacher, of course, works within a system along with others who share the tasks of the program. Staff members, from the supervisor or director to the custodian, contribute toward making the program successful. There can be a variety of staffing patterns depending on the type, size, and philosophy of the program as well as on its funding source. A half-day preschool attended by 15 children may, for instance, be staffed by one owner/teacher and one additional teacher. On the other hand, a non-profit child care program in which 160 children are enrolled might involve a board of directors, a director, a curriculum coordinator, a parent coordinator, 12 senior teachers, 28 full- and part-time assistants, a variable number of volunteers, a secretary, a cook, a custodian, a list of substitute staff, and various community professionals who serve as resource persons. Exhibit 6-1 illustrates the staffing patterns of these two hypothetical programs.

EXHIBIT 6-1 STAFFING PATTERNS

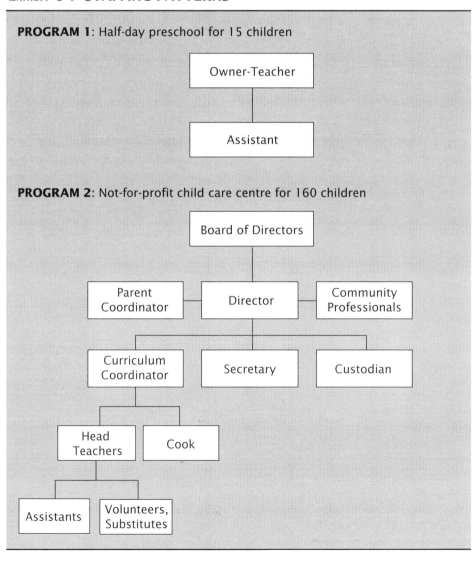

PROGRAM 1: Half-day preschool for 15 children

- Owner-Teacher
- Assistant

PROGRAM 2: Not-for-profit child care centre for 160 children

- Board of Directors
- Parent Coordinator — Director — Community Professionals
- Curriculum Coordinator — Secretary — Custodian
- Head Teachers — Cook
- Assistants — Volunteers, Substitutes

The distribution and allocation of responsibility also varies in different programs. Some have a hierarchical structure, fashioned as a pyramid, where power trickles down from the top and each layer in the structure defers to those above. Thus, in some classrooms that follow this model, one teacher is designated as the senior teacher or teacher supervisor and other teachers work under her or him, following the senior teacher's direction and guidance.

Yet, in the early childhood field there is often an alternative to this pyramid structure because of the strong interdependence and interconnectedness between teachers, who frequently make decisions by consensus. This can be depicted as a web that allows for more flexible and dynamic relationships than the hierarchical model in which the power structure tends to be static and individuals' responsibilities depend on their position in the structure (Dresden & Myers, 1989).

In other programs, classes are co-taught by team teachers who share responsibilities. **Team teaching** is based on a relationship of trust and communication between the two teachers, something that takes time to build. A good team finds many bonuses in this relationship through added flexibility, creativity, problem-solving capabilities, and focus on what each member of the team enjoys most or does best. In addition, the collaboration between the two provides the children with a model for cooperative behaviour (Thornton, 1990).

Whatever the structure, it is sensible to find out ahead of time what the lines of responsibility are in terms of providing direction, feedback, evaluation, and resources. By learning the lines of authority and communication, teachers in a program will know whom to seek out for instructions and information, with whom to discuss problems, and where ultimate responsibility for various decisions lies. Whatever the program's organizational structure, smooth functioning depends in part on a clear understanding of responsibilities and lines of communication and on cooperation among the staff. We will now briefly examine some of the positions and their responsibilities held by staff members in early childhood programs (Click & Click, 1990; Sciarra & Dorsey, 1990; Seaver & Cartwright, 1986).

DIRECTOR AND/OR SUPERVISOR

Directors and/or supervisors perform a variety of tasks, depending on the size and scope of the program. Very large centres may have both an administrative director and teacher supervisor; while the director would play an administrative role, the supervisor would have more direct involvement with the children as well as some supervisory responsibilities. In smaller programs, the director may double as a teacher and supervisor for part of the day. The director is usually responsible for financial, personnel, policy, and facility decisions; provides community linkages; handles licensing and regulation; and is the ultimate decision-maker in the chain of responsibility in all matters that pertain to the program. In addition, the job description often involves staff selection, training, monitoring, and evaluation. In programs that depend on grants and other outside sources of funding, the director may spend much time writing proposals and meeting with influential decision-makers. But a director is often also a plumber, carpenter, and counsellor because he or she holds the ultimate responsibility for whatever needs to be taken care of!

A teacher supervisor, working under a director, usually works with the children, has some administrative duties, and does some staff supervision. Larger programs even have assistant supervisors, whereas smaller programs seldom need one.

TEACHING STAFF

Those who work directly with children may hold a variety of titles, and they vary from one Canadian jurisdiction to another. They also vary greatly with the actual physical layout of a program and group size. As you know from Chapter 4, group size varies greatly across the country, and it affects the staffing structure. In locations that have strict group size regulations, you would usually find two teachers per room. In another setting, however, you may find a large open room with four or five teachers present, while only one teacher may be in yet another program. Nevertheless, there are certain roles that are relatively common across the country. We will look at two common teaching positions in more depth—the senior teacher and the assistant teacher. We will also examine a team teaching approach to the role of the teacher.

The Senior Teacher

In many jurisdictions that require teacher training, the teacher with more education and experience acts as the **senior teacher** when there are two teachers in a room. However, the titles used vary greatly not only from province to province, but even within cities. Typically, the more senior teacher or lead teacher is responsible for planning and implementing the daily program. This involves knowing each child and family well and individualizing the program to meet each one's specific needs. The senior teacher usually also takes responsibility for the physical environment of the classroom, setting up equipment, rotating materials, and ensuring a good match between what is available and the children's skill levels. The senior teacher generally maintains records for the children in the class; is usually involved in parent interactions, both informally at the start and end of each day and formally through conferences or meetings; and takes charge of other staff members who work in the class by providing direction, guidance, and feedback.

The Assistant Teacher

In many settings, one or more teachers function in an **assistant teacher** role. Assistants have a variety of titles within a municipality, and the range of titles is greater when you cross provincial and territorial boundaries. Some terms that are used include auxiliary teacher, associate teacher, small-group leader, aide, and helper. In the assistant role, the teacher works with the senior teacher to provide a high-quality program for the children in the class and their families. Frequently, the assistant has less education and experience than the senior teacher, but this is not always the case. Depending on the assistant's skill level and experience, this teacher may share many of the senior teacher's responsibilities, for instance, participating in curriculum planning, leading large- and small-group activities, being involved in parent interactions, and arranging the environment. Because of the assistant teacher's close working relationship with the head teacher, open and honest communication and mutual respect are vital between the two. In some schools, an assistant teacher may serve as a "floater," moving among classrooms to help with special activities or during specific times of the day.

Team Teaching

In many settings, the "senior teacher" position does not exist; teachers work as a team, under the direction of the program supervisor and/or director. In Mary Wright's (1983) University of Western Ontario program, for example, there was a program director (Wright), who also had teaching responsibilities at the university level, and four highly qualified teachers. One of the teachers was the supervisor of the school, while a second one was the assistant supervisor. The four teachers rotated through four different

teacher timetables, one per week, which Wright describes in great detail in her very readable text.

The team teaching approach allows each teacher to interact with all the children, and to work in all areas of the program. It also maximizes the children's flexibility as each area is covered by a teacher, and the children are free to move from one activity to another. Finally, the teachers experience more variety in their work with this approach, and no one individual is always "stuck" with the less appealing duties (e.g., paint clean-up and washroom duty).

VOLUNTEERS

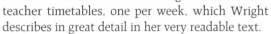

Some centres use volunteers to help with various aspects of the early childhood program. Volunteers can include parents, student teachers or interns, members of volunteer organizations,

foster grandparents, and other interested community members. To use volunteers most effectively, however, there has to be a well-planned orientation, training, and monitoring component that helps the volunteer understand the program, its philosophy, and its operation. Although volunteers can provide a wonderful additional resource to a program, the reality is that volunteers are not as plentiful as the potential need for them.

SUPPORT STAFF

Again, depending on the size and scope of the centre, usually some persons serve in a support capacity. These might include (although they certainly are not limited to) persons involved in food preparation, maintenance, and office management. Large programs often have a cook who is in charge of meal preparation, shopping, and sanitation and maintenance of the kitchen. The cook may also plan meals, if that person has an appropriate background in nutrition, or may participate in classroom cooking projects. A dietician may serve as a consultant to the program to ensure that children's nutritional needs are appropriately met through the program's meals. In smaller programs, particularly those not serving lunch or dinner, the teaching staff or director may take responsibility for snack planning and preparation.

One of the most important yet difficult tasks of any centre serving busy and active young children is maintenance. Daily cleaning, sweeping, vacuuming, sanitizing, and garbage disposal are vital though usually unpopular functions. Large programs may have a custodian as part of the staff, whereas others hold contracts with a janitorial service. Often the expense of a maintenance crew or custodian has to be weighed against other important needs, and the teaching staff finds that its responsibilities include many maintenance chores. Most centres compromise by having the staff maintain a modicum of cleanliness and order, while a cleaning service is responsible for intermittent deep cleaning of the facility.

Other support staff take care of office needs. Large programs often have a secretary who maintains records, answers phone calls, manages typing needs, and may handle some accounting tasks. In smaller programs, such tasks may fall to the director. Some programs may employ a part-time accountant or have a receptionist in addition to the secretary. Programs that are part of or housed with other agencies may share custodial and secretarial staff.

BOARD OF DIRECTORS

Particularly in non-profit centres, some type of policy-making, governing board holds the ultimate responsibility for the program. This board of trustees or **board of directors** may be a very powerful force, making all pertinent decisions that the director then carries out, or it may be only a nominal group that gives the director responsibility to make these decisions. Ideally, a board of directors' role falls somewhere between these extremes (Sciarra & Dorsey, 1990).

Boards of directors are usually made up of program parents and community persons who come from a variety of spheres of expertise and influence, most of which are not likely to be related to early childhood education. It is wise, however, to include one child development expert on the board. The director serves as a liaison, helping the board understand the rationale for decisions made based on child development knowledge, while utilizing their expertise in areas in which the director is not as well versed. Boards can be very effective, for instance, in fiscal management, fundraising, construction and expansion projects, or lobbying for children's rights.

COMMUNITY PROFESSIONALS

The resources of a centre can be expanded through other professionals in the larger community, for instance, health and mental health professionals, social workers, speech therapists, and physio- and occupational therapists. In some programs, especially those involving subsidized children, families may be referred to the early childhood program by a community agency. In these cases, the program and referring agency frequently work together to maximize the help provided to the child and family. In other cases, the early childhood program may help connect families with community agencies and professionals to provide needed services. It is important for teachers to recognize the "boundaries of their own professional expertise" and know when other professionals need to be consulted (Sciarra & Dorsey, 1990, p. 369).

TRAINING AND REGULATION IN EARLY CHILDHOOD EDUCATION

As we have discussed, many individuals contribute toward providing a good early childhood program through their levels and types of expertise. Such expertise stems from different types of training. In addition, a variety of regulations and quality controls apply to early childhood programs and the personnel who staff them. As you know from Chapter 4, the range of training options and requirements varies greatly across the country, as do the regulations governing early childhood programs.

ACADEMIC TEACHER TRAINING PROGRAMS

Because you are reading this text, you are most likely involved in an academic early childhood program whose aim is to prepare qualified teachers and directors of programs for young children through a combination of course work and practicum experiences. Such programs exist at the college level, and at the university and postgraduate levels. In more advanced programs, greater depth and more theoretical and research knowledge become increasingly important variables.

It is interesting to note that Canadians working with young children are relatively well educated. In 1991, the Canadian Day Care Advocacy Association and the Canadian Child Day Care Federation (CCDCF) jointly sponsored *Caring for a*

Living (CCDCF, 1992), a study of the wages and working conditions of teachers working in licensed child care centres across the country. The report found that over 84 percent of administrative directors have diplomas and degrees, while about 87 percent of the teacher supervisors do. Over 70 percent of the senior teachers have diplomas or degrees. Assistant teachers are also well qualified—about 40 percent of them have a diploma or degree. The situation is comparable in the U.S. where two-thirds of teachers and more than one-half of assistant teachers have taken at least some early childhood or child development course work (Whitebook, Howes, & Phillips, 1989). With such a highly trained group of individuals working in the early childhood field, you would expect the profession to be viewed with considerable respect. However, early childhood teachers do not feel their work is held in high regard by the Canadian public, and they are trying to better this situation, as the following section indicates.

PROFESSIONALISM

This book stresses the importance of the early childhood years, early education, and your role as an early childhood educator. To fully realize that importance, however, you must see yourself as a member of a profession. A profession is different from a job by virtue of certain characteristics, for instance, a defined code of ethics, a specialized knowledge base involving theoretical principles, specialized training founded on that knowledge base, and universal standards of practice that stem from that knowledge base (Katz, 1988; Vander Ven, 1986).

Those who have written at great length about early childhood professionalism, recognizing that there are many inconsistencies and problems to be faced, do not always agree on the degree to which the field meets the criteria of a profession. Increasing dialogue through conferences and written works has helped to sharpen the focus more sharply on

relevant issues, for instance, low pay and shortage of qualified early childhood teachers, as well as on strategies for combatting these (we will discuss some of these in Chapter 18). Nonetheless, the expanding concern about professionalism, evident at both national and local levels, should propel early childhood education toward its goals, which include a better definition and greater focus.

Although in many ways the early childhood field has moved toward professionalization, there is concern that professional status is not universally acknowledged by those who work in the field or by the public at large (Dresden & Myers, 1989; Radomski, 1986; Silin, 1985). The *Caring for a Living* (CCDCF, 1992) study found that seven out of ten early childhood teachers had postsecondary degrees or diplomas, as opposed to four of ten workers in the general Canadian workforce. However, the salaries of the teachers were well below the average wage for Canadian industrial workers. In fact, the report indicated that someone working in a warehouse, a position that clearly requires less skill, education, and responsibility, earned 58 percent more than the average teacher in a non-school-based early childhood program! *Caring for a*

Living reported that teachers in the Northwest Territories did very well in a relative sense, but Gillian Moir from Artic College, cautions us about interpreting that finding in A Canadian Professional Speaks Out (p. 162).

Most of the Canadian teachers surveyed (84 percent) felt that their profession was not valued by the general public. "It's a bit of a Catch-22: for not only are staff paid poorly, they believe the value of the work they perform is neither acknowledged nor appreciated. And until they are paid higher wages, these perceptions are unlikely to change" (CCDCF, 1992, p. 1). Changes in salary levels and the public perception of the

 # A CANADIAN PROFESSIONAL SPEAKS OUT

ECE Teacher Salaries in the Northwest Territories

Many Canadians consider the north to be a romantic land of the midnight sun where fortunes are easily made. They anticipate working in the north for a few years, earning a large salary, and returning to the south with a substantial bank account. While it is true that incomes in the north are typically higher than those in the south, living and working in the isolation of northern Canada involves a variety of different factors that affect the cost of living. Any discussion of salary levels for people employed in the north must take into account these factors.

In 1991, the Canadian Child Care Federation and the Canadian Day Care Advocacy Association completed a joint project entitled "Caring for a Living." Their recently published report included salary averages of early childhood educators for four different position levels across the country based on studies from 1990–91. The Northwest Territories ranked first in average salaries for the positions of Assistant Teacher and Administrative Director and second only to Ontario for the positions of Teacher and Teacher Director. What this report fails to indicate are the differences in the cost of living across the country that make higher salaries necessary for residents of the north.

Ignorance of the conditions and difficulties faced by residents in Canada's north is widespread. Few people are aware that the Northwest Territories accounts for almost half of Canada's land mass and yet is inhabited by less than 60 000 people. Moreover, the majority of the inhabitants are located in small communities of less than 3000 people spread across three time zones. In fact, only 15 of approximately 66 communities have year-round access by road; although some communities can be reached by ice road in winter, most communities can only be accessed by plane. This means that all the supplies for these communities (food, building materials, clothes, toys, furniture) must be brought in by plane or via the once-a-year sea lift. Imagine putting together your grocery list and having to plan for an entire year. Imagine living in Iqaluit on Baffin Island and paying over $12 for four litres of milk. Even in Yellowknife, which is accessible by road virtually all year, people are expected to pay 66 cents for a litre of gas and $800 a month for a one-bedroom apartment. Secondary expenses add to the cost of living. To visit family or to go on vacation, residents of Yellowknife face airfares topping $1800 to Toronto. People living in the more remote communities face even higher travel costs.

In an effort to counterbalance these differences in costs, the Northwest Territories government has two minimum wages to accommodate the cost of living in a remote community without road access. Moreover, many salaries include housing allowances to help offset the high cost of housing in the Northwest Territories.

Statistics Canada considers the cost of living in the north to be roughly 25 to 30 percent higher than in southern Canada, the percentage increasing for more remote and isolated settlements. If one were to subtract 25 to 30 percent from the reported average wages for child care workers in the Northwest Territories, perhaps a more accurate comparison of wages with southern child care workers could be made.

So don't cast an envious eye on the salaries paid to the northern child care worker. While "income" is higher, "outgo" is also substantially higher. In the end, when compared with salaries paid in southern Canada, the real income earned by northern child care professionals may, in fact, be less.

Gillian Moir
Arctic College
Yellowknife, NWT

profession are definitely needed, and students entering the profession are most likely to effect these changes.

Students embarking on a career in early childhood education are in a unique position to develop from the start a sense of professionalism that is furthered by every course they take, every day they spend with children, and every conference they attend. Their competence and recognition of the importance of their role will enhance not only their work with children and families, but also their contributions to the early childhood profession. Teachers of young children who have a clear concept of who they are, what they do, and the importance of their role are quite effective in educating the public. Certainly, the Canadian public chose to support the Manitoba and Quebec teachers in their protests against low wages.

ETHICS

One of the hallmarks of a profession is its recognition of and adherence to a **code of ethics**. Such a code embodies guidelines for behaviour, facilitates decision-making, and provides the backing of like-minded professionals when the practitioner takes a "risky but courageous stand in the face of an ethical dilemma" (Katz, 1988, p. 77). In recent years, a number of provincial organizations have developed codes of ethics governing the profession. For example, the Ontario code of ethics, developed by the Association for Early Childhood Education—-Ontario, (AECEO) is shown in Exhibit 6-2.

Codes of ethics recognize that many of the day-to-day decisions made by those who work with young children are of a moral and ethical nature. Early childhood teachers, for instance, may find themselves in situations with conflicting values in which it is not clear whether the rights of the child, the parents, the school, other children in the program, or the teachers are most important (Feeney, 1988). A code of ethics provides common principles for dealing with such dilemmas, principles based on the value of childhood as a unique stage of life, on knowledge of child development, on appreciation of the importance of family and cultural ties, on respect for the dignity and value of children and adults, and on helping individuals reach their potential through trusting, positive relationships.

Because children are particularly vulnerable, those who work with them have an important responsibility that is supported and defined by a code of ethics (Feeney & Kipnis, 1985). As you enter the early childhood profession, it is important to learn about the code of ethics followed in your area. If you are in a jurisdiction that does not yet have a code, you should familiarize yourself with one or more from other jurisdictions, and perhaps help the professional association in your province or territory to develop one.

PROFESSIONAL ORGANIZATIONS

One sign of a profession is the existence of organizations to which members belong and of professional journals that members read. Such organizations and their literature provide members with support and a sense of common interest and purpose. In Canada, early childhood educators have several pertinent organizations and journals at the national level; many more are found at the provincial and territorial levels. In addition, numerous organizations focus on more specialized groups, for instance, those involved in for-profit child care, Montessori, church-sponsored programs, home-based care, early childhood special education, and others. We will briefly discuss the two major national organizations, as well as one influential American organization. The 1992 CNCCS, *Canadian Child Care in Context: Perspectives from the Provinces and Territories*, contains an extensive list of the professional organizations in each Canadian jurisdiction. Some of these are summarized in the following list.

EXHIBIT 6-2 AECEO CODE OF ETHICS

OBLIGATIONS TO CHILDREN

As persons working with and for young children, we are committed to promoting developmental care and education for each child in cooperative relationships with the family and the community. Early Childhood Education programs enable children to participate fully in environments carefully planned to serve individual needs and to facilitate the child's progress in the social, emotional, physical and cognitive areas of development. A person working with young children is obligated to:

1. Maintain and promote each child's self esteem.
2. Recognize and respect the uniqueness and the potential of each child.
3. Be accepting of all children, respecting race, belief system, gender, national origin, and socioeconomic status.
4. Accept and integrate into regular programs the child with special needs when such integration is advisable and sufficient support is available.
5. Be familiar with the knowledge base of Early Childhood Education and demonstrate this knowledge in program practices.
6. Create and maintain a safe and healthy setting that supports the positive growth and welfare of children.
7. Refrain from the physical punishment, verbal abuse (e.g., sarcasm, ridicule) and psychological abuse (e.g., threats, encouraging fear) of children in interactions with them.
8. Maintain the confidentiality of information obtained in the course of professional dealings with children and families. However, when concerned about a child's welfare, it is permissible to reveal confidential information to agencies and individuals who may be able to act in the child's interest.
9. Involve all individuals (colleagues and parents) in decisions concerning the child.
10. Recognize symptoms of child abuse and know and act on law pertaining to child abuse. Involve all individuals (colleagues and parents) in decisions concerning the child.
11. Report in a responsive manner and through the appropriate channels instances of non-compliance with laws and regulations to those who will take corrective action.
12. Advocate and contribute to the extension of public information and education about children's needs for quality services, and
13. Advocate for policies and laws that promote the well-being of children and their families.

OBLIGATIONS TO FAMILIES

Families are of primary importance in children's development. (The term family may include others besides parents, who are responsibly involved with the child.) Because the family and the Early Childhood Educator have a common interest in the child's welfare, we acknowledge a primary responsibility to bring about collaboration between the home and early childhood program in ways that enhance the child's development. A person working with families is obligated to:

1. Develop relationships of mutual trust with families they serve.
2. Respect the dignity of each family.
3. Respect families' child rearing values and their right to make decisions for their children.
4. Interpret each child's progress to guardians within the framework of a developmental perspective and help families understand and appreciate the value of developmentally appropriate early childhood programs.
5. Help family members improve their understanding of their children and to enhance their skills as parents.
6. Participate in building support networks for families by providing them with opportunities to interact with program staff and families.
7. Inform families of program philosophy, policies, and personnel qualifications, and
8. Enable and encourage families to play an active role in their child's program.

OBLIGATIONS TO COLLEAGUES

Early Childhood Education is a profession that relies on a team approach. The relationship of colleagues within a profession influences the status of the profession and the quality of service provided. Colleagues in E.C.E. must act with integrity in supporting one another and adopting professional attitudes and behaviours in their work as models and teachers for young children. An E.C.E. in the profession is obligated to:

1. Present professional qualifications, experience and affiliations honestly.
2. Speak or act on behalf of an association or organization only when duly authorized, and then to do so accurately.
3. Establish and maintain cooperative relationships with colleagues and other professionals providing service to the child.
4. Exercise care in expressing views on the disposition and professional conduct of colleagues, confining such comments to matters of fact which arise out of first-hand knowledge and which relate to the interest of children.
5. Respect the confidentiality of views expressed in private by colleagues.
6. Provide opportunities for professional development and advancement of staff.
7. Support a climate of trust and forthrightness in the work place that will ensure that colleagues are able to speak and act in the best interest of children without fear of recrimination.
8. Present concerns about the professional behaviour of a colleague, first to that person, and attempt to resolve the matter collegially.
9. Participate in the development and implementation of teaching methods that will effectively address the stated educational principles and goals of programs, and

10. Be a willing participant in the training process by articulating concerns constructively and by providing opportunities for students to practise professional skills under knowledgeable supervision.

OBLIGATIONS OF LEADERS

Recognition that persons in leadership positions can substantially influence the quality of programs for young children, a code of ethics must specify additional guidelines for the professional competence and special duties of supervisors, consultants, administrators and training personnel. Persons in leadership positions are accountable for the programs and services provided. An Early Childhood Educator working in a leadership role is obligated to:

1. Develop and state clearly a philosophy toward the care and education of children and adhere to practices that are consistent with the goals inherent in this philosophical approach.
2. Provide a written job description and personnel policies that define program standards.
3. Conduct each staff and student evaluation impartially, basing it on first-hand observations of performance in accordance with the duties and responsibilities contained in the job description or student placement guidelines. Employees who do not meet program standards shall be informed of the areas of concern and when possible assisted in improving their performance.
4. Support professional development and advancement of personnel.
5. Act promptly and decisively in situations where the well-being of children is compromised, ensuring that the best interests of children supersede all other consideration.
6. Inform an employee in advance of the reasons for dismissal, referring only to evidence of unsatisfactory performance which is accurate, documented, current and available to the employee.

7. Exercise utmost discretion when providing information or recommendations about children, families or personnel when such information is solicited by authorized persons. Obtain consent from the parties concerned whenever practical, especially when such information may be prejudicial.
8. Make use of community and professional services when appropriate and provide parents with information about resources that will support and strengthen family life, and
9. Hire, promote and provide training in accordance with Human Rights Legislation.

OBLIGATIONS TO PROFESSIONAL COMPETENCE

Early Childhood Educators have a commitment to ensure their own continuing professional competence and to further the field of Early Childhood Education. A person working in the field of Early Childhood Education is obligated to:

1. Keep professional knowledge up to date.
2. Recognize critical self reflection as an important part of professional development.
3. Engage in self care activities which help avoid conditions (e.g., burnout, substance abuse) which could result in impaired judgement and interfere with their ability to benefit others, and
4. Further the professional development of the field of Early Childhood Education and to strengthen its commitment to realizing its core values as reflected in this Code.

In preparing the revision of the AECEO CODE OF ETHICS, we acknowledge the use of the following resources:

1. Katz, L. and Ward, E., *Ethical Issues on Working with Young Children*. NAEYC, 1991.
2. E.C.E., B.C.–Ethics Project.

SOURCE: Revised 1994 Code of Ethics, Association of Early Childhood Educators, Ontario. Reprinted with permission.

1. *The Canadian Child Care Federation (CCCF)* (formerly the Canadian Child Day Care Federation) or *Fédération Canadienne des services de garde à l'enfance (FCSGE)*, has a recent history. Although the idea for a national organization was formulated in 1983, it was not until 1987 that the CCDCF received federal funding and opened an office in Ottawa. The Federation aims to improve the quality of child care in Canada by providing services to those in the field. It supports provincial and territorial organizations, and aims to provide information and services to professionals in the field. National conferences, regional workshops, a quarterly magazine (*Interaction*), information sheets, and a speakers' bureau are among the services the Federation offers.

   The CCDCF also developed the national statement on the quality of child care. In addition, it is addressing issues related to the training and education of people entering the field. In the fall of 1992, the CCDCF received federal funding for a three-year research project that aims to make Canadian resources widely available and to develop resources on topics where they do not exist. In 1993, the CCDCF changed its name to the Canadian Child Care Federation (CCCF).

2. *The Canadian Childcare Advocacy Association (CCAA)* (formerly Canadian Day Care Advocacy Association), founded in 1983, aims to make high-quality, affordable, non-profit child care accessible to all Canadians who need it. Funded by the Secretary of State and run by a non-profit volunteer board, the Association publishes two journals—*Vision* and *Bulletin*—on a quarterly basis.

3. *The National Association for the Education of Young Children (NAEYC)*, the largest early childhood organization, is a powerful voice for children, families, and teachers in the United States. Its goals are (a) to improve professional practice and working conditions, and (b) to increase public understanding of and support for high quality in early childhood education (Smith, 1990). The Association has a growing membership (77 000 in 1991) that represents a diverse group of individuals. In addition, NAEYC holds an annual conference that is attended by more than 20 000 early childhood professionals yearly. The NAEYC also has an extensive series of publications that are invaluable to professionals in the field, including the bimonthly journal, *Young Children*, and more than 80 books and other resources. At present, our Canadian organizations are not as well developed as the NAEYC and do not yet have a comparable range of publications. Canadians frequently turn to the NAEYC for additional resources they require.

As a student entering the early childhood profession, you should consider becoming a member of a professional organization. Most of the organizations have a student membership option, which costs considerably less than the regular membership. By becoming a member, you can keep abreast of new developments, have the opportunity to meet and participate in a support network with others in the same field, and attend workshops and conferences at the local, provincial, or national level. In fact, you may even be eligible for the CCCF's travel subsidy that would help you attend their national conference (and if you attend the conference, you can suggest to the instructor who assigned this text that you will do a conference report and/or seminar in place of another course assignment). The contacts you make as a student also can be very helpful when you are seeking a position in the field; professionals hiring in the field typically prefer to hire someone they know has been active in their association rather than a total stranger. If you need additional information about the organizations in your community and province, ask your instructor or professionals you know to elaborate on the available associations.

TEACHER SATISFACTION

Canadian early childhood teachers, on average, find great job satisfaction in their profession, which compensates for some of the dilemmas facing the field, which we will address in the final chapter. *Caring for a Living* (CCDCF, 1992) noted that "the nature of the work and the opportunity to make a difference in the lives of children is the silver lining" (p. 1) in early childhood education. The opportunity to contribute to and observe the development of their young charges provides a great source of pleasure to early childhood teachers. In addition, they find other aspects of the job gratifying. Satisfaction with co-workers is very high—8.6 out of 10 for over 7000 Canadian teachers. Undoubtedly, those of you who are planning to enter this profession will be happy to know it brings such rewards to its members.

KEY TERMS

assistant teacher
board of directors
caregiver
child care worker
code of ethics
early childhood educator
early childhood teacher

KEY POINTS OF CHAPTER 6

THE EARLY CHILDHOOD TEACHER

▲ 1. A professional early childhood teacher is distinguished by professionalism, knowledge and standards, judgment, and ability to translate theoretical information into practical application.

▲ 2. Teachers evolve through several stages that are related to their level of experience.

STAFFING IN EARLY CHILDHOOD PROGRAMS

▲ 3. The size and complexity of a program will affect the size and complexity of the staffing pattern.

▲ 4. Early childhood programs can have various structures of staff authority and responsibility.

▲ 5. The role of the director will depend on the size and nature of the program.

6. In many programs, senior teachers and assistants, each with distinct responsibilities, are identified.

▲ 7. Most early childhood programs, depending on their size and scope, have some support staff who help with the maintenance and functioning of the program.

▲ 8. Some programs utilize volunteers, have a board of directors that is involved in the decision-making process, and call on community professionals to expand the services of the program.

KEY QUESTIONS

1. Talk to several teachers of young children. What do they view as the most rewarding parts of their jobs? What most frustrates them? Compare their answers with your own goals and expectations.

2. Review the section on team teaching. What are the advantages of such an approach? What are the disadvantages? Compare this approach with the one used in the program(s) where you have observed and/or had a practice teaching placement.

3. What are the advantages of belonging to a professional early childhood organization? Review several issues of professional journals like *Interaction*, *Vision*, and *Young Children* to gain a sense of what organizations like the CCCF, the CCAA, and the NAEYC have to offer.

4. Professional organizations like the AECEO have been active in developing codes of ethics for the profession and in advocating improved salaries and working conditions. Review their newsletters to see what kind of issues are being discussed.

5. Visit two child care centres in your community and compare them.

THE HOW OF EARLY CHILDHOOD EDUCATION—THE BASICS

We will now turn our attention to the basic "hows" of early childhood education. In Part 3 we will examine the following fundamental components of high-quality early childhood education programs:

- Chapter 7, "Goals, Objectives, and Evaluation," will provide information about setting appropriate goals and objectives for young children. We will also examine the role of evaluation as a means of matching program development with the children in the program.

- Chapter 8, "Programming for the Whole Child," will examine some of the basic constructs in early childhood education programs, including:

  1. The role of play and its importance.
  2. The implementation of developmentally appropriate practices.
  3. The importance of a curriculum that does not encourage bias or stereotypes.

  Some basic components of that curriculum and planning guidelines will then be addressed.

- Chapter 9, "The Physical Environment," will present an overview of environmental considerations for providing a good early childhood program. Just where is it that children and their teachers play and work? What elements do we have to keep in mind as we consider the appropriate environment for programs for young children? Both indoor and outdoor space are important. We will examine the materials and equipment that best enhance and support young children's development throughout the year.

GOALS, OBJECTIVES, AND EVALUATION

orking with young children and planning a program for them requires a sense of direction and purpose, expressed in a set of broad goals and more specific objectives. Goals and objectives provide the "road map" for the early childhood program "journey." But not just any map will provide the specific information needed for your specific program. Goals and objectives should reflect the individual character and uniqueness of your class. One way of identifying that individuality is through systematic evaluation. This chapter, therefore, will cover these two discrete but closely related topics—goals and objectives, and evaluation—by exploring the following points.

1. Goals provide a general overview of what is expected of the children.

2. Objectives are a more specific interpretation of goals. There are different types of objectives.

3. Evaluation is an important element in early childhood education and helps assess whether goals and objectives are being met.

   - One of the most widely used methods of evaluation is observation.

   - Teacher-designed instruments such as checklists and rating scales are another type of evaluation.

   - Many commercially produced standardized tests are used for different purposes.

   - Although evaluation instruments are widely used, there is also considerable concern about their use.

   - Information from evaluations and assessments can be used in different ways.

GOALS

A **goal** provides a general overview of what you expect the children to gain from the program. Goals should be based on a sound understanding of children's development and needs, reflecting age-appropriate expectations and practices. Goals are often based on facilitating and encouraging healthy development in the social, emotional, cognitive, and motor domains and acquisition of related skills. Goals also reflect the theoretical rationale on which the program is based, such as those discussed in Chapter 3, for instance, the Piagetian philosophy as reflected in the cognitively oriented curriculum (Hohmann, Banet, & Weikart, 1979).

Another way of identifying goals, related to a developmental approach, can focus on important processes that children begin to acquire in the early years. Frazier (1980) suggests that these might include:

- *communicating*—expressing, taking in, responding
- *relating* to others
- *finding out*—inquiring, investigating
- *discovering*
- *making*—constructing, creating, inventing
- *choosing*—seeking, preferring, holding on to
- *controlling*—directing, leading, managing
- *persisting*—staying with, enduring.

Keep in mind that there is no one way of wording goals and objectives. Exhibit 7-1 lists a few examples of goals that might be included for a group of young children, and some more specific objectives related to these goals.

OBJECTIVES

An **objective** is a more specific interpretation of a general goal, and it provides a more practical and direct tool for day-to-day program planning. Goals can be identified at the beginning of the program year to provide direction; objectives are useful for short-term

EXHIBIT 7-1 SAMPLE GOALS AND OBJECTIVES

Sample Goal 1: The children will increase their fine motor skills, gaining better control in tasks requiring use of the hands.

Sample Objectives in Support of Goal 1:

- The children will thread 1-inch beads on shoelaces.
- The children will use scissors to cut pictures of their choice from magazines.

Sample Goal 2: The children will improve their language skills, acquiring larger vocabularies, longer sentence lengths, and more complex sentence structures.

Sample Objectives in Support of Goal 2:

- The children will use three new words in discussions and dramatic play related to bread baking after the visit to the bakery (for instance, yeast, rising, kneading).
- The children will retell the story with the flannel board pieces, reflecting the sequence of the story read earlier by the teacher.

Sample Goal 3: The children will gain greater social skills, forming friendships, engaging in more cooperative play, and developing empathy and concern for the feelings of others.

Sample Objectives in Support of Goal 3:

- The children will participate in the cooperative game version of "musical chairs."
- The children will discuss the emotions displayed in the "feeling pictures."

Sample Goal 4: The children will increase their understanding of themselves, their families, and the community in which they live.

Sample Objectives in Support of Goal 4:

- The children will name two functions of the heart, after examining the model of the heart and hearing Dr. Herbert discuss the heart.
- The children will explain the role of the emergency operator and will demonstrate how to dial 911 in case of an emergency.

planning and should be an integral part of unit and lesson planning, identified for planned activities (discussed in more detail in the next chapter). Objectives will differ, depending on whether they are developed for the group as a whole or for an individual child. We will examine three types of objectives commonly used in early childhood education: developmental, content, and behavioural objectives.

DEVELOPMENTAL OBJECTIVES

The purpose of activities is often to promote specific aspects of physical, cognitive, social, or emotional development, each identified as a **developmental objective**. By specifying which developmental domain will be particularly enhanced by each activity, you can ensure that your program provides a good balance of activities that encompass all areas.

Experienced teachers often develop a sense for this type of balance in program planning. For a beginning teacher, however, it can be very helpful to identify which area(s) of development will be promoted by each activity. This might be done through abbreviations, for instance, letters that identify the area of development (FM = fine motor; L = language). On completing a lesson plan, the teacher, with a quick review of developmental objectives, can ensure that all areas are adequately covered.

[handwritten margin notes: Assess all areas of playgroup MUSIC — DRAMATIC PLAY — MANIPULATIVE — organize each area into developmental areas. Gross Motor, Fine Motor etc. Balanced program]

CONTENT OBJECTIVES

Objectives are also identified for the content or subject matter of the curriculum (Essa & Rogers, 1992; Lawton, 1988; Peters, Neisworth, & Yawkey, 1985). A **content objective** relates to what an individual activity is conveying, which, in turn, is tied to a unit's topic or theme. Appropriate topics can be drawn from meaningful aspects of the children's environment to expand their understanding of the world.

Content objectives can be met through a variety of activities, although how they are met will depend on the developmental objectives that have been identified (Essa & Rogers, 1992). For instance, to help children learn about body parts, you can develop any number of activities, such as a language activity (reading a story on the topic), a motor activity (playing a game of "Hokey-Pokey"), or a perceptual activity (gluing cutout body-part shapes). Generally, you will plan a variety of activities, with different developmental objectives, to help reinforce a specific content objective.

A content objective also gives direction to the teacher carrying out an activity. Assume the lesson plan indicates that you will help the children make fruit salad (Essa & Rogers, 1992). What direction does this activity description give you? What will you discuss with the children? Where do you focus? Do you talk about the colour of the fruit, its texture, its sweetness? Do you help children label the individual fruits? Do you relate the fruit salad to what might be served in a restaurant? What about at home? Do you discuss the fact that chefs, or mothers and fathers, make fruit salad? Do you focus on safety and health? Or should you incorporate measurement and math concepts? The objectives will determine the focus and purpose of the activity and will help guide your teaching style and handling of the activity.

BEHAVIOURAL OBJECTIVES

Although developmental and content objectives usually apply to planning for the total group, a **behavioural objective** is generally used in planning for an individual child. Behavioural objectives are very specific, based on what is observable. As an example, a behavioural objective for a 4-year-old might state, "When shown a row containing four blocks—one red, one blue, one yellow, and one green—Simon will point to the red block, when asked, in three out of four trials." The objective does not tell you how to teach red, only how to measure the objective's acquisition (Hendricks, 1986); therefore, it will presumably be tested after a period of time in which Simon will use red play dough, paint, blocks, and Legos, and the teacher will frequently verbalize and encourage Simon to verbalize the colour.

Behavioural objectives, because of their precise nature, are often used in working with children who have special needs. This provides a way of pinpointing a weakness (Simon cannot identify colours yet); breaking down behaviours into small and manageable steps (we'll start with the colour red); documenting progress (it will be clear when Simon points to the red block three times out of four); and providing accountability (Simon has learned the colour red!). When you have young, handicapped children in your program who receive additional government funding, for example, accountability becomes particularly important, and behavioural objectives can help you to document your work and the child's progress.

Notice that the behavioural objective for Simon uses a verb that describes action. When Simon points to the red block, there is no guesswork involved on your part; his pointing is observable. Words such as *label*, *name*, *identify*, *match*, *sort*, *classify*, or *order from largest to smallest* relate to a child's actions that you can observe. On the other hand, words such as *think*, *enjoy*, *consider*, *appreciate*, or *be aware of* describe an internalized process. If, for instance, the objective had stated that Simon will *understand* the colour red, you would have no way to measure this because you cannot "see" Simon understanding the concept of redness (Deiner, 1983).

Behavioural objectives are useful, particularly in planning for an individual child in an area needing attention. Such objectives have also been criticized, however. Because they specify how a child will behave, they eliminate spontaneity, creativity, and playfulness; they ignore a child's internal motivation to master a topic or skill by spelling out and directing the content of activities; they demand a great deal of work from the teacher because each identified behaviour will require developing a list of objectives; and, because they are broken into such small components, it is sometimes difficult to keep in touch with the larger goals for the child (Lawton, 1988).

EVALUATION

Evaluation is closely tied to goals and objectives as a beginning, an ending, and an ongoing process. To set appropriate goals and objectives, we need to know something about our group of children, and **preassessment** can help us learn about them. Later, to find out whether the children have met our goals and objectives, we conduct a **summative evaluation** at the ends of units, for example. In addition, ongoing **formative evaluation** is characteristic in good early childhood programs as it allows us to determine if our planned activities, methods, and topics are accomplishing what we want them to.

Evaluation can be carried out in many ways, but not by all people. We will discuss both informal and formal types of assessment, the applicability of different approaches, and the qualifications the evaluator needs. More specifically, we will examine observational techniques, teacher-developed rating scales and checklists, and standardized tests. We will also address the potential for misusing evaluation instruments, the need for sensitivity and care in using them, and the selection of appropriate measures.

OBSERVATION

One of the most effective informal methods of evaluation is focused observation. Early childhood teachers use observation as a primary method of gaining insight into the various facets of children's development, at different times and in different contexts (Wortham, 1990). Observation can provide us with detailed information about behaviour, can help us understand it, and can provide the basis for predicting behaviour (Richarz, 1980). One of the most appealing features of observation is that it is unobtrusive and natural. It does not interfere with the child's ongoing activity and behaviour, in contrast with more formal tests that require that the child perform specified tasks in an isolated setting.

Types of Observations

Observation can take a variety of forms. One of the most often used is the **anecdotal record**, a brief description or "word picture" of an event or behaviour (Cartwright & Cartwright, 1974). A collection of well-written and accurate anecdotes can provide a very descriptive characterization of a child. **Anecdotal records** come only from direct observation, are written down promptly and accurately, describe the context of the behaviour, are factual rather than interpretive, and can focus either on a typical or unusual aspect of the child's behaviour (Wortham, 1990).

A **running record** is a more detailed account of a child's behaviour over a period of time (Wortham, 1990). Whereas the anecdote focuses on a single event, the running record keeps track of everything that happens in a specified time period, whether it is a half-hour or several months.

Such a record can be very useful when you are trying to pinpoint the source of a problem. It was most helpful in getting a handle on the disruptions in one class, where

3-year-old Erin seemed to be always at the centre of aggressive outbursts. A careful running record, kept over a period of three days, helped the teachers see that Erin was responding to rather subtle taunts from two other children.

One helpful device in keeping a running record is the **ABC analysis**, in which three columns identify the antecedent, behaviour, and consequence of incidents (Bijou, Peterson, & Ault, 1968). This helps you focus not only on the child's behaviour, but also on what precipitates and what follows it as well.

Time sampling provides a way of measuring the frequency of a behaviour over a period of time (Wortham, 1990). Time sampling is a quantitative method of observation, in that you count how often the behaviour occurs at uniform time intervals (Genishi, 1982). You may, for instance, want to know just how often the adults in the classroom attend to Yanik, because you suspect he is often overlooked and neglected. Since you don't have time to observe Yanik all day long, you might determine that every half-hour you will spend five minutes watching Yanik, noting every time a teacher attends to or interacts with him. Over a period of a week, you should have a representative sampling of the attention Yanik receives from adults. You might also decide, for purposes of comparison, to observe Brittany at the same time because Brittany appears to get frequent adult attention.

When you want to observe a less frequent behaviour, **event sampling** can be used (Genishi, 1982; Wortham, 1990). In this case, you wait until a given behaviour occurs and then write a descriptive record of the event. Event sampling can be useful if you have noted that Kareem has periodic crying spells, and you have trouble pinpointing the cause. Thus, each time Kareem engages in this behaviour, one of the teachers stands back and records carefully what is happening. The ABC method can be very useful in recording such an event because you are trying to get a sense of its causes and consequences (Wortham, 1990).

Characteristics of Good Observations

One of the requirements of good observation is that it be *objective*. Your role as observer is to be as impartial as possible, to stand back and record what you see rather than what you think the child is feeling or experiencing. Compare the two records in A Closer Look. What distinguishes the two? The first observation tells you how the observer is interpreting the incident; the second describes what is happening. Can the first observer really know that Letitia does not like Erica? Can she be certain that the teacher is angry and that Letitia made a conscious decision to pick on Erica?

Another characteristic of good observation is that it is *adequately descriptive*. Cohen and Stern (1978) provide some helpful suggestions to beginning observers in the

---

 A CLOSER LOOK

Observations

Observation #1

Letitia comes into the classroom and immediately decides to pick on Erica, whom she doesn't like. She approaches Erica and, in her usual aggressive way, grabs the doll that Erica is playing with. Letitia doesn't really want the doll, she just wants what Erica has. When the teacher sees what has happened, she gets upset with Letitia and makes her give the doll back to Erica. Because of this, Letitia gets really angry and has one of her nasty tantrums, which makes everyone in the class mad.

Observation #2

Letitia marches into the classroom. She looks around for a few seconds, then ambles to the dramatic play area, where Erica is putting a doll into the cradle. Letitia stops two feet in front of the cradle, standing with her legs apart and hands on hips. She watches Erica put a blanket on the doll, then steps right up to it, grabs the doll by an arm, and pulls it roughly out of the cradle. She runs with the doll into the block area and turns around to look back at Erica. As Letitia is running off, Erica yells, "No! I was playing with the doll." Erica looks at Mrs. Wendell, whose eyes move toward the dramatic play area. Erica's shoulders drop and she says in a softer whimper, "Letitia took the doll I was playing with," then starts to cry. As Mrs. Wendell walks toward Letitia, Letitia drops the doll and darts to the art area. Mrs. Wendell catches up with Letitia, holds her by the arm, and urges her back to the block area. She picks up the doll. "Letitia, we need to give this doll back to Erica. She was playing with it." Letitia, her lips pressed together over clenched jaws, pulls away from Mrs. Wendell and throws herself on the floor, kicking her feet and screaming.

use of descriptive vocabulary. The verb *run*, for instance, has many synonyms that can evoke a clearer image of what is being described. Examples include stampede, whirl, dart, gallop, speed, shoot across, bolt, fly, hippety-hop, or dash. Adding descriptive adverbs, adjectives, and phrases will also enliven an anecdote. Although synonyms can add authenticity and life to your observational anecdote, be sure to use the dictionary to ensure that the word means what you intend. What descriptive words in the second example in A Closer Look make the incident come alive?

Good observations also describe **non-verbal cues**, some of the nuances of body language as well as voice inflection that can give deeper meaning to an anecdote. Children, like adults, share subtle movements of face and body and shadings of voice that describe common feelings and reactions. Izard (1982), for instance, uses common facial nuances in infants and children to measure emotion. Body language is not easy to read, requiring experience and practice to interpret accurately. Again, in A Closer Look, do you see some descriptions of such non-verbal signs?

Interpreting Observations

As we have indicated, observational information must be gathered objectively, without inserting personal bias. But there comes the point, once you have gathered a collection of anecdotes, when you can look for patterns (Cohen & Stern, 1978). Interpretations, however, should always be kept clearly separate from observations (Cartwright & Cartwright, 1974). In reviewing observations that span a period of time, you should be able to find clues to children's unique ways of behaving and responding. When a set of observations shows repeatedly that a child reacts aggressively to conflict, or becomes pleasurably involved in messy media, or talks to adults far more than to other children, you can see a characteristic pattern for that child.

But interpretation should be undertaken cautiously. Human behaviour is complex, not easily pigeonholed, and there is the danger of overzealous interpretation when a pattern is more in the mind of the observer than representative of the child.

Some Observational Techniques

Finding time to observe can be challenging for the busy teacher. Cartwright and Cartwright (1974) recommend developing a pattern and time-frame for carrying out observations. Hymes (1981) further suggests setting a goal, a fixed number of anecdotes to record each day. It is helpful to carry a pencil and pad in your pocket while working with children so you can jot down some quick notes, and to set aside a few minutes at the end of the day to write up the records. Keeping such records can also pinpoint children who are being overlooked when, over a period of time, you find very few or no records on some youngsters (Hymes, 1981).

Early childhood student-teachers and, in some programs, teachers, may be asked specifically to record observations for a period of time. If you are assigned a role as an outside observer rather than as a teacher, try to be as unobtrusive as possible so that children's behaviour is minimally affected by your presence. If children come to you to ask what you are doing, as invariably they will, give a simple answer that does not invite further conversation, for instance, "I am writing."

TEACHER-DESIGNED INSTRUMENTS

Other frequently used, informal methods of evaluation include **checklists** and **rating scales** designed by the teacher (Wortham, 1990). A simple check mark or numerical evaluation rather than a lengthy verbal description is used with both checklists and rating scales. The primary difference between these two is that checklists simply note the presence or absence of a skill or concept, whereas rating scales evaluate the level of attainment (Wortham, 1990). Both are quick and easy to use, flexible, and very specific to the needs of your situation.

Checklists for Children

A checklist lists behaviours, skills, concepts, or attributes and is followed by a space for noting their presence or absence. Checklists can be devised for individual children (Exhibit 7-2) or for the entire class (Exhibit 7-3). Some checklists include space for recording multiple observations that can be repeated over a period such as a year (Exhibit 7-2); others are taken at one point in time (Exhibit 7-3). The teachers at the University of Western Ontario preschool in London, Ontario, for example, used a series of checklists that were developed for the program and are readily available in Wright's (1983) text. After assessing each child's developmental level on a series of skills, the teachers could "tailor-fit" the program to each child's developmental needs. Of course, even though they had checklists for each child, they would not post *confidential* results in the centre!

Rating Scales for Children

Rating scales provide more qualitative information than checklists because they indicate to what extent the child engages in or has mastered a behaviour. For example, as a student, you are judged on a rating scale that usually takes the form of letter grades ranging from A (excellent) to F (unsatisfactory).

EXHIBIT 7-2 CHECKLIST OF SELECTED GROSS MOTOR TASKS (TO BE COMPLETED FOUR TIMES DURING THE YEAR)

CHILD: _____

Instructions: Mark with an "X" when task has been mastered.

BEHAVIOUR	DATE OF OBSERVATION 1) _____	2) _____	3) _____	4) _____
Hops on one foot				
Balances on one foot for 5 seconds				
Walks 8 cm balance beam				
Jumps across 24 cm and lands with both feet				
Throws 20 cm ball 2m				
Catches 20 cm ball with both arms				
Pumps on swing				
Pedals tricycle				

EXHIBIT 7-3 CHECKLIST OF SELECTED GROSS MOTOR TASKS FOR THE ENTIRE CLASS

DATE: _____

Instructions: Mark with an "X" when task has been mastered.

NAME	HOPS	BALANCE 5 S	8 CM BEAM	24 CM BROAD JUMP	THROW BALL	CATCH BALL	PEDAL TRIKE	PUMP ON SWING

The dimensions of ratings applied to children will depend on what you want to measure. You may, for instance, want to determine the frequency of each child's participation in various types of activities. In that case you might graph the children on a continuum that goes from "always" to "never" (Cartwright & Cartwright, 1974; Wortham, 1990) as Exhibit 7-4 shows.

Rating scales can also be used to show where a child is in the process of mastering certain tasks. You could, for instance, take the checklist of gross motor skills used in Exhibit 7-2 and turn it into a rating scale by rating each behaviour as follows:

EXHIBIT 7-4 RATING SCALE OF CHILDREN'S FREQUENCY OF PARTICIPATION IN VARIOUS CLASSROOM ACTIVITY AREAS

DRAMATIC PLAY

Instructions: Rate each child's frequency of participation in the dramatic play area.

NAME	FREQUENCY OF INTERACTION				
	ALWAYS	FREQUENTLY	OCCASIONALLY	SELDOM	NEVER

1. performs task all the time;

2. performs task sometimes;

3. performs task rarely; and

4. never performs task.

It may be appropriate to add a "not observed" category to differentiate between a child who cannot perform a task and one who chooses not to engage in the specific behaviour while the teacher is observing.

STANDARDIZED TESTS

Whereas observations and teacher-devised instruments are informal methods of gathering information about children, standardized tests are considered formal assessments. Such instruments are developed by professionals and are distributed commercially. Standardized tests are developed, tested, and refined so that they have **validity** and **reliability**. Validity means that tests measure what they purport to measure. Reliability means they are stable and consistent; you know that when a child's score changes, it is because the child has changed, not the test (NAEYC, 1988). When standardized tests are administered, specific standards for testing conditions are required to ensure uniformity. Over the past few years, the use of standardized tests to evaluate caregiving environments and young children's development has increased. While a comprehensive overview of standardized tests may be offered in advanced courses you will take, we will just briefly examine some general test categories and consider several sample instruments.

Environmental Checklists and Rating Scales

Several standardized rating scales and checklists have been developed and published that help in the evaluation of early childhood programs. The *Early Childhood Environment Rating Scale*, developed by Harms and Clifford in 1980, is perhaps the best known. The *Family Day Care Home Rating Scale* (Harms, Clifford, & Padan-Belkin, 1983) and the *Infant/Toddler Environment Rating Scale* (Harms, Cryer, & Clifford, 1990) are useful for evaluating family child care and infant programs respectively. John Novak and Pamela Rogers, who discuss invitational education in A Canadian Professional Speaks Out (p. 182), have developed a scale to assess how inviting ECE settings are.

These rating scales are helpful both when you are evaluating a program and when you are comparing several programs. The results can help programs to pinpoint areas that need improvement. The results also are useful if you are doing research related to early childhood education. Goelman and Pence (1990), for example, used the Early Childhood Environment Rating Scale and the Family Day Care Home Rating Scale in the Victoria and Vancouver studies you read about in Chapter 3.

Goelman and Pence also used Caldwell and Bradley's (1979) **Home Observation for Measurement of the Environment** (HOME) in the Vancouver study. HOME is used to assess the quality of stimulation in the home environment and this makes it useful for home-based child care. A number of studies (e.g., Bradley & Caldwell, 1984; Gottfried, 1984) have demonstrated that HOME scores are highly correlated with child development. A mother or caregiver who scores highly on HOME would have the following characteristics:

1. She is verbally and emotionally responsive.

2. She does not restrict the child's activity and does not punish the child.

A CANADIAN PROFESSIONAL SPEAKS OUT

Inviting Success in Early Childhood Education

Of the many things young children learn, perhaps the most important is the picture they develop of who they are and how they fit into the world. This highly personal portrayal of existence and possibilities is called the self-concept. We see it as key in the development of each child's intellectual, psychological, social, moral, and physical potential. Children who believe in their personal worth and possibilities are more likely to engage in and sustain activities and relationships that call forth a greater realization of their potential. A vital question then for educators of young children is, "What can we do to promote the development of a positive self-concept?"

We believe that we do not have direct access to another's self-concept. Rather, because an individual's self-concept is personally constructed through the messages received, interpreted, acted upon, and evaluated, our role as educators is to be message designers and implementers. Thus, if we take self-concept to be the core of future development, our educational responsibility is to construct and extend signal systems that invite children to see themselves as valuable, able, and responsible learners who can behave accordingly. We call such an approach to child development *invitational education* and feel that it offers a systematic and morally defensible approach for working in early childhood education.

Invitational education is a perceptually based self-concept approach to teaching, learning, and caring that is centred on the following five principles:

1. People are able, valuable, and responsible and should be treated accordingly.

2. Education should be a cooperative activity.

3. Process is the product in the making.

4. People possess untapped positive potential in all areas of human endeavour.

5. Potential can best be realized by places, policies, processes, and programs specifically designed to invite development, and by people who are intentionally inviting with themselves and others personally and professionally.

Educators using these principles as an operating stance work together to make their centre or school "The Most Inviting Place in Town." Focusing on the development of caring interpersonal practices, nurturing environments, person-centred policies, and engaging programs, invitational educators aim to create an institutional culture that enables all involved to more fully relate, assert, invest, and cope. To assist educators in developing and sustaining inviting environments, several books have been written, an International Alliance for Invitational Education (with a Canadian Centre) has been formed, and a rating scale for early childhood education constructed.

John M. Novak and Pamela Rogers
Brock University
St. Catharines, Ontario

---

3. She provides age-appropriate play materials.

4. She arranges the environment so it is safe and organized.

5. She is involved with the child, and usually is within sight.

6. She provides variety in the available stimulation. In addition to reading to the child several times a week, she takes the child on outings and arranges for the child to eat meals with the family at least once a day.

Of course, these behaviours also can be found in good teachers in centre-based programs.

Screening Tests

Screening tests provide a quick method of identifying children who may be at risk for a specified condition, for instance, developmental delay. Screening is not an end in

itself but *is meant to be followed by more thorough diagnostic testing* if screening shows a possible problem. Because most screening tests are quick and easy to administer, they can be used by a wide variety of people who may have no specialized training.

One widely used screening instrument is the **Denver Developmental Screening Test (DDST)** (Frankenburg, Dodds, Fandal, Kajuk, & Cohr, 1975), which is used with infants and children up to age 6. This test, often used by medical as well as early childhood professionals, examines the child's functioning in self-help, social, language, fine motor, and gross motor areas. If a 3-year-old child, for example, completes the DDST, the child's test scores are compared with **norm-referenced** scores. The norm-referenced scores for 3-year-olds were obtained by having a large group of 3-year-olds complete the test. Similar norms are available for children of the other ages the DDST covers. By testing a large number of children at each age, the test developers were able to determine what the "average child" of each age could do—or what the norm was for each age. For each item on the test, you can determine if the child is functioning around the norm or average level, or above or below average. If a child appears to be well below or above average, then more testing might be recommended.

The DDST has some problems that may limit its value. While the reliability and validity of the test are adequate for a screening device, the norms are questionable. The test was normed on 543 boys and 493 girls from Colorado who did not have known, serious disabilities. A larger norming sample, drawn from a wider geographic area, probably would provide more accurate norms. Ideally, a Canadian norming population would be preferable. Thus, you should view results from the DDST with some caution.

Another widely used screening test is the **Developmental Indicators for the Assessment of Learning—Revised (DIAL-R)** (Mardell-Czudnowski & Goldenberg, 1983), which provides a quick look at development in the motor, concepts, and language areas. This test, normed for children between the ages of 2 and 6, has separate norms for white children and children of visible minorities. Like the DDST, this test is easily used with some practice and does not take long to administer. The DIAL-R had a larger norming sample than the DDST, and the sample was drawn from six states rather than one.

Developmental Tests

Frequently, a screening test will indicate the necessity for more complete assessment and is then followed by a more thorough and time-intensive **developmental test**. Such tests usually measure the child's functioning in most or all areas of development. Developmental assessments are usually **criterion-referenced** rather than norm-referenced. Thus, children are measured against the test developer's educated understanding of what children, at various ages, can be expected to achieve.

One widely used developmental test is the **Brigance Diagnostic Inventory of Early Development** (Brigance, 1978). With some training, early childhood teachers can use this test. It contains subtests for fine motor, gross motor, language, cognitive, and self-help areas for children from birth to age 7. Testing of many of the items can be incorporated into the curriculum. However, the lack of reliable data on the Brigance remains a concern (Salvia & Ysseldyke, 1991).

Intelligence or IQ Tests

One of the oldest types of standardized assessments is the intelligence test. Such tests have stirred considerable controversy, much of it loaded with emotion because it raises the question of whether intelligence is a fixed biological trait or whether it is malleable and can be raised through an enriched environment (Jensen, 1985; Woodrich, 1984). Another volatile controversy about such tests has been the concern over culture bias (Goodwin & Goodwin, 1982)—that tests are slanted to white, middle-class norms and experiences.

One of the major applications of intelligence tests with young children has been to identify those who fall well below or above the normal range. Children who have intellectual disabilities and ones who are gifted have usually been classified on the basis of their IQ scores. One of the concerns with IQ testing in the early childhood years is that the test scores are less reliable (i.e., more likely to change on retesting) at younger ages than at older ages. Infant IQ scores are quite likely to undergo major changes (Salvia & Ysseldyke, 1991), but the IQ scores become more reliable as children approach school age. Nevertheless, more extreme scores are more reliable: infants and toddlers with extremely high or low scores are likely to have very high and low scores respectively on retesting. By 3 or 4 years of age, however, the reliability of overall IQ scores on individually administered intelligence tests is satisfactory (Salvia & Ysseldyke, 1991).

Such tests are highly structured and must be administered by a person *specifically trained in their use*, usually a registered psychologist. The fourth edition of the **Stanford-Binet Intelligence Scale** (Thorndike, Hagen, & Sattler, 1985) is a single test with varying tasks for different ages ranging from 2 through adulthood. The new Stanford-Binet is well-normed, reliable, and valid. However, it is a lengthy test, and other individually administered IQ tests take less time to administer. The Wechsler **Preschool and Primary Scale of Intelligence—Revised (WPPSI-R)** (1989) is another commonly used test for 3- to 7-year-old children. The **Wechsler Intelligence Scale for Children—III (WISC-III)** (1991) is also available for use with children from 6 to 16 years of age. Both Wechsler tests have been revised recently, and the norms are current. The WPPSI-R is less reliable than the WISC-III, especially for 7-year-olds, so the WISC-III should be the test of choice at that age. On all three tests, a score of 100 is average.

Individuals in early childhood education welcomed the 1972 publication of the **McCarthy Scales of Children's Abilities (MSCA)** (McCarthy, 1972), designed for children aged 2 1/2 to 8. The test was much easier and more appropriate for young children than others available at that time. However, the norms are now more than 20 years old, and would be misleading. Unless there is a revision of the MSCA, a more recent test should be selected.

Readiness Tests

The specific purpose of readiness tests—to determine whether a child is prepared to enter a program such as kindergarten or first grade—differentiates them from other types of assessments. Such tests should not be used to predict school success because they merely measure a child's level of achievement of specified academic tasks at the time of testing (Meisels, 1986). A recent study, in fact, found that the **predictive validity** of one widely used readiness test when compared with first-grade teacher judgment and report cards, was very modest, raising questions about the usefulness of the test and about the potential harm to the many children misidentified as not ready for school (Graue & Shepard, 1989).

Success on readiness tests, as you might suspect, depends on the child's having been exposed to the concepts, not on innate ability. Unfortunately, readiness tests do not distinguish between a child who has had limited exposure and the child who has actual learning difficulties. The use of these tests has driven many prekindergarten programs to incorporate activities designed to prepare children for readiness testing, often at the expense of other appropriate activities, particularly exploratory, hands-on experiences (Schickedanz, Hansen, & Forsyth, 1990). Moreover, virtually all of the available readiness tests have technical problems in the areas of reliability and predictive validity (Salvia & Ysseldyke, 1991). Unless the appropriate research is conducted to determine the ability of these tests to predict school achievement, they should not be used to make major educational decisions.

CONCERNS ABOUT USE OF EVALUATION INSTRUMENTS

All of these informal and formal evaluation instruments can give us useful insights into the environments we provide and the children in our care. But although using a variety of methods to better understand children has always been an important part of early childhood education, there is a growing concern about potential misuses, particularly of standardized evaluations. The 1980s brought an increased emphasis on testing, particularly as a way of proving that educational goals are being met (Wortham, 1990). The back-to-basics movement has become a powerful lobby group, and they are asking for more frequent standardized testing, especially for school-aged children. In the 1990s, the provincial and territorial ministers of education have been meeting on a regular basis to develop a national testing program. Pilot testing of selected grades across the country began in the 1993–94 school year.

One major concern involves the misuse of readiness tests. With increasing frequency, such tests are being used to decide children's placement. For instance, a test is used to decide which children will be allowed to move on to first grade, which ones will be placed in a transitional class, and which ones will be retained in kindergarten (Wortham, 1990). Thus, children are often labelled as failures when, in fact, they are expected to conform to inappropriate expectations (NAEYC, 1988). How devastating such practices are on children's self-concepts! Read the eloquent discussion of these concerns in NAEYC's "Position Statement on Standardized Testing of Young Children 3 through 8 Years of Age," which was published in *Young Children* in 1988.

Tests are also being used by prestigious (and expensive) private schools, not just in large cities like New York but also in smaller cities in Canada, to determine which children will be given places. A corollary to this testing trend is that many early childhood programs have adopted curricula whose main aim is to prepare children for readiness tests (Bredekamp & Shepard, 1989). Thus, preschool and kindergarten programs promote developmentally inappropriate methods to meet such goals, intensifying the problem of "failures" and children who are "unready" (NAEYC, 1988). In fact, the NAEYC became so concerned about this that it had Constance Kamii, an eminent early childhood educator, edit a book on the topic. *Achievement Testing in the Early Grades: The Games Grown-ups Play* (Kamii, 1990) is a book you will want to consult if testing becomes a problem in your community.

It has long been acknowledged that standardized tests have a variety of limitations. For instance, a test cannot ask every possible question to evaluate what a child knows on a topic. Another criticism of standardized tests is that they are culture-biased. However, test designers have found it impossible to devise tests that are completely culture-free (Wortham, 1990). In addition, it is very difficult to establish reliable and valid instruments for young children, given the rapid changes that occur in development as well as the normal individual variations among children (NAEYC, 1988). This also calls into question the use of norm groups against which individuals are compared.

In addition to the potential problems with a test itself, there are difficulties in evaluating young children that can affect the accuracy of test results. These might include the child's attention and interest, the familiarity (or unfamiliarity) with the surroundings, the trust the child has in the adult tester (or whether the child has even seen this person before), the time of day, the fact that the child slept poorly the night before, or the fact that the mother forgot to kiss the child good-bye. In too many instances, tests are given to young children in large groups, a practice that further decreases reliability (NAEYC, 1988).

In a number of Canadian settings, there also is concern that tests are *not* always administered and interpreted by individuals with the qualifications to do so. Even some major school boards (but by no means all) in some Canadian jurisdictions rely upon unqualified individuals to complete the testing process, much to the chagrin of Canadian psychologists. An unqualified tester is likely to obtain misleading, unreliable results that might still be used in educational decisions regarding a young child. Parents frequently are upset if testing is recommended, and tend to be overwhelmed by the testing process. They often do not know—or feel they know—what cautions and questions are appropriate, and are reluctant to seek a second opinion, which can be invaluable.

If so many problems are inherent in standardized tests, what is the answer to the dilemma of their increasing use with young children? NAEYC (1988) recommends that the relevance of tests be carefully evaluated by administrators: Will results from the test contribute to improving the program for the children? Will the children benefit from the test? If the benefits are meagre in relation to the cost (expense and time), perhaps the test should not be used. Furthermore, it is recommended that:

- tests be carefully reviewed for reliability and validity;
- tests match the program's philosophy and goals;

- only knowledgeable and qualified persons administer and interpret results;
- testers be sensitive to individual and cultural diversity;
- tests be used only for the purpose for which they were intended; and
- no major decision related to enrolment, retention, or placement in a remedial program be made based on only one test, but that multiple sources of information be used for this purpose.

It is important to keep in mind that any information gathered about children and their families—whether from test results, observations, or something a parent shared—needs to be treated with complete **confidentiality** and respect.

SELECTING AND USING EVALUATION METHODS

We have looked at a number of formal and informal methods of evaluation, information that can be mind-boggling considering that we have reviewed only a very small number of the many available commercial instruments. Selecting an appropriate method will depend on how the results are to be used. We will briefly examine some suggested methods in terms of three purposes of evaluation: gaining information (1) about children, (2) for program planning purposes, and (3) for parent feedback.

Information about Children

Effective teaching depends on knowing as much as possible about the children in the class. A variety of data-gathering methods can be used as follows:

- Ongoing observation can provide valuable insight into all children, their functioning as part of the class, and their growth in all developmental areas.
- A screening test coupled with parent inteviews might help with those children who, on the basis of your observations, seem to have problems.
- A developmental assessment can be given to children whose performance on the screening test indicated a need for further evaluation. Periodic reassessment may be appropriate.
- You may decide that a referral to an outside professional (e.g., psychologist, speech pathologist, or doctor) is needed.

Information for Program Planning

One of the main purposes of assessment is to help direct program development. Once you have an idea of strengths and areas that need attention, both for individual children and for the group as a whole, you can plan a prescriptive curriculum (Hendrick, 1986; Wright, 1983). Some useful data-gathering methods include the following:

- Information from observations can provide excellent programming direction.
- Checklists and rating scales allow you to evaluate the functioning of the group of children on tasks that you identify as important. You may, for instance, discover that the majority of your 3-year-olds are not able to hold scissors effectively.

Information for Parent Feedback

All forms of evaluation provide information to share with parents. It is important to examine the child's strengths, not just areas that may be problematic, and it is vital that all information be as accurate, realistic, and unbiased as possible. Data carefully collected over a period of time and thoughtfully evaluated provide the basis for good parent-feedback conferences.

PARENTS AND PROFESSIONALS

Sharing Evaluations with Parents

The results of tests, observations, and other measures provide valuable information that can be shared with parents. As you read this information, you might also briefly review the discussion of parent conferences in Chapter 5, for the methods described are important to sharing evaluation results. We should expect that any evaluation that teachers administer to the child is used because the teachers expect it to offer relevant insights. Thus, if this information is important to teachers, it will also be important to parents who certainly have a right to know how their child is performing (Wortham, 1990).

There are a number of points to keep in mind when sharing evaluation results with parents. In all instances, tests or other evaluation information should never be given in isolation, out of the context of the child's overall nature. As we will continue to stress throughout this book, children cannot be divided into separate developmental compartments. Thus, to tell parents that their 4-year-old daughter is performing below (or, for that matter, above) the norm in fine motor skills is only part of the picture. It is equally important to tell them that their child has excellent social skills, that she shows leadership qualities, that she has a delightful sense of humour, that she seems to particularly enjoy sensory activities, and so forth. Such information does not rely just on the results of a developmental assessment, which yielded the fine motor score, but is reinforced by observations, anecdotes, and the teacher's reflections about this child.

Another point to remember when sharing evaluation results with parents is that you should be able to explain the measures that were applied. Some standardized tests are rather complicated to use, score, and interpret. Be sure that you understand what the test results mean and that you can explain them. It does not help a parent who asks, "What do you mean she scored below the norm?" to be told, "Well, I'm not exactly sure what 'norm' means." If your school uses any kind of standardized test, read its manual carefully, understand how the test was constructed, know how results should be interpreted and used, and be familiar with the terminology.

At the same time, it is also important to keep in mind and convey to parents that tests have their limitations. Consider the preceding discussion about the shortcomings of and concerns about tests and let parents know that these represent only part of the input used in evaluation. Also remind parents, as well as yourself, that young children are amazingly flexible and often will experience a quick change or growth spurt in their development that could suddenly modify the test findings. Do not present any evaluation results as the definitive answer about the child's abilities and functioning.

A similar point is that each child is individual and unique, and test results will show a wide variety of profiles that fall within a normal range. It is reassuring to parents to be reminded that many factors affect a child's performance, particularly when parents compare the child with siblings or other children (Wortham, 1990). Keep in mind, however, that when you share test scores or other evaluation results, you should present only the child's scores, not the child's score in relation to other children's.

Finally, when sharing evaluation results with parents, also be prepared to defend the measures you used. A parent may well ask you, "Why did you give this test to my child?" Be able to answer such a question, because it is certainly logical and valid. You need to feel that the test provides valuable information and you should be able to specify how such information will be used. For instance, such measures should help plan relevant and appropriate learning experiences for the child (Wortham, 1990).

KEY TERMS

ABC analysis

anecdotal record

behavioural objective

Brigance Diagnostic Inventory of Early Development

checklist

confidentiality

content objective

criterion-referenced

Denver Developmental Screening Test (DDST)

Developmental Indicators for the Assessment of Learning—Revised (DIAL-R)

developmental objective

developmental test

Early Childhood Environment Rating Scale

event sampling

Family Day Care Home Rating Scale

formative evaluation

goal

Home Observation for Measurement of the Environment (HOME)

Infant/Toddler Environment Rating Scale

McCarthy Scales of Children's Abilities (MSCA)

non-verbal cue

norm-referenced

objective

KEY POINTS OF CHAPTER 7

GOALS

▲ 1. Goals should be based on an understanding of children and should reflect the program's underlying theoretical base.

OBJECTIVES

▲ 2. Objectives facilitate short-term planning and should be part of written lesson plans.

▲ 3. Developmental objectives specify which developmental domain will be enhanced by an activity.

▲ 4. Content objectives relate to the subject matter to be conveyed by the activity.

▲ 5. Behavioural objectives are written in very specific, observable terms and usually apply to an individual child.

EVALUATION

▲ 6. Observation is an unobtrusive way of gaining information about children.

▲ 7. An anecdotal record provides a "word picture" of an event or behaviour.

▲ 8. A running record provides a detailed account of everything that occurred during an extended period of time.

▲ 9. In the time-sampling method, a given behaviour is recorded only at specified intervals of time, such as every half-hour.

▲10. Event sampling is used to observe and record only when a specified behaviour occurs.

▲11. Good observations need to be objective but at the same time adequately descriptive. A collection of observations can then be combined and interpreted to better understand the child.

▲12. Checklists and rating scales are ways of checking whether a child or group of children engage in specific behaviours or skills.

▲13. Standardized or formal tests are more stringently developed and used, and they must meet specific criteria.

▲14. Screening tests are a quick way of identifying children who might be at risk, but such tests must be followed up with more thorough assessments.

▲15. Developmental tests are thorough assessments of children's development in all or several domains.

▲16. Intelligence tests measure intellectual functioning and are usually highly structured as to how they can be administered and interpreted.

▲17. In recent years, readiness tests have been increasingly used to determine whether children are prepared to enter a specific program such as kindergarten or first grade.

▲18. Early childhood professionals have raised some major concerns about the use and misuse of standardized tests, particularly when these lead to developmentally inappropriate practices.

▲19. Evaluation methods can provide valuable information about the children, give direction for program planning, and contribute feedback to share with parents.

KEY QUESTIONS

1. Review a lesson plan containing specific objectives. Do you see a relationship between the objectives and the planned activities? How do the objectives give direction to the teachers who carry out the activities?

2. With a fellow student, spend about fifteen minutes observing the same child. Each of you should write an anecdotal observation involving this child. Now compare your two observations. Do they describe the same behaviours, activities, and interactions? Do they convey the same "picture" of this child? If the two observations differ significantly, why? Are there some subjective elements in either observation that might contribute to this difference?

3. Design a checklist of ten items for a group of preschoolers to assess social development. How did you decide which items to include? What resources did you use to put this checklist together? If possible, observe a group of preschoolers and apply this checklist to several of the children.

4. Have you been tested with a standardized instrument? Recall how you felt about the testing situation and the questions asked. What emotional impact did the test have on you? How might young children feel about being tested? What can a tester do to help children perform to the best of their abilities?

5. Given the information from this chapter about the values and potential misuses of evaluation procedures, develop a set of criteria that might guide you, as an early childhood professional, in using assessments in the most effective way. What do you consider to be the three most important benefits of such testing? What should you avoid?

PROGRAMMING FOR THE WHOLE CHILD

As you know from Chapter 3, there is no one early childhood model that produces long-term positive gains in development. Rather, high-quality programs following several different approaches have been successful, and you might well want to select different components from different models when you design a program. In keeping with these results, this text is somewhat eclectic in approach, and does not subscribe to just one theoretical approach. Nevertheless, just as flour seems to be necessary for most chocolate cakes, some ingredients seem fundamental to a good early childhood program. Play, active involvement, and choice or self-selection are among the critical ingredients we will discuss in this chapter.

Play is the cornerstone of quality early childhood education programs, and is at the foundation of developmentally appropriate practice. The whole child will develop in a child-centred, play-based program or curriculum that is appropriate to the child's developmental level and individual history. While the child's cognitive skills might develop in a work-oriented, teacher-centred, hothousing program, good teachers would say "At what cost?" Teachers in quality early childhood education programs, whether they be for infants, toddlers, preschoolers, or school-aged children, want to see the child grow in all spheres of child development. They want to provide a program that encourages the development of the child—physically, cognitively, linguistically, socially, and emotionally. And they are willing to prepare, organize, and regularly evaluate an environment that is designed to encourage self-directed, active, play-based learning.

In this chapter, we will examine these basic components of high-quality, early childhood education programs:

1. Play, the child's way of learning about the world, is basic in early childhood education. We will discuss in this chapter different types of play and its place in the curriculum.

2. The program or curriculum in high-quality early childhood programs is *developmentally appropriate*:

   • The program is *age-appropriate* for the children it serves.

   • The program is adapted so that it is *individually appropriate* for each child it serves. Every child in the program is different, and the program is responsive to developmental, temperamental, familial, cultural, and ethnic differences.

   • The program does not foster bias or stereotypes.

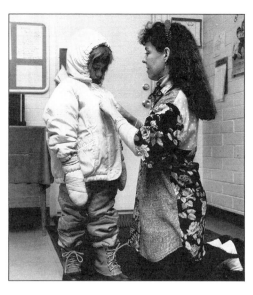

3. The teacher must plan the curriculum and organize the environment so that play-based, child-centred learning will occur. Whether a program operates full-day or part-day will have an impact on your planning, as will the ages and individual histories of the children you serve. Nevertheless, there are common elements in all programs as we will see:

- Children need time in a program—time to be alone, time to be with others, time to reflect, time to be noisy, time to be children. In planning a program, you will want to provide for time spent in self-directed activity, time indoors and outdoors, time with a group, time at meals and/or snack, and time napping in a full-day program. You will want to allow time to get snowsuits on and off, but you do not want a child to be idle when waiting for everyone else to get their snowsuits on or off—unless the child wants to be idle, of course. All of the child's needs for time vary with the developmental level and history of the child.

- Children need variety and choice in a program. Children need different experiences at different difficulty levels. Both self-selected and teacher-directed activities have value, but there must be a balance between them.

- Children need flexibility and predictability in a program. Again, striking a balance between versatility and stability is an ongoing challenge for the teacher.

- The program should be evaluated on a daily basis.

4. We will end by discussing the development of written plans, which vary considerably with the ages of the children in early childhood programs.

PLAY

One commonality of children across the world is their need to play, which we discussed briefly in Chapter 5. Through play, children come to know and understand their world. In play, children try out new skills and roles, they refine old ones, and they develop without really trying to do so. Play is a source of joy, learning, and absorption—and no one forces children to do it. So why do you need to be concerned about play? In part, because play is under attack in North America. David Elkind (1990), an eminent early childhood educator, who has raised so many concerns about the "hurried child," hothousing, and people's belief that "earlier is always better," comments:

> The major victim of the earlier is better ideology has been the play of infants and young children. ... Play is a bad word. Given children's sponge-like abilities to learn, the purported rapidity of brain growth, and the time-limited nature of this window of opportunity, play is extremely wasteful of time that might be put to more important and more long-lived activities. ... Childhood is a period for work, not for play (pp. 4–5).

Early lessons in almost everything become more and more prevalent, and the value of play is being questioned by more and more parents and members of the public. This places additional demands on teachers in early childhood education programs. They not only have to decide what to include in their programs and why, but they have to be able to give cogent reasons for their practices to others. Far too frequently, teachers have adopted play-based program models *without knowing why the approach was valid,* and

then they have been unable to articulate the reasons why they have play as a central feature in the curriculum (Monighan-Nourot, 1990). Teachers in play-based programs need to be familiar with the research on play and its effectiveness.

THEORIES OF PLAY

Theories of play have proliferated over several centuries (Berlyne, 1969; Bruner, Jolly, & Sylva, 1976; Gilmore, 1971; Rubin, 1982; Rubin, Fein, & Vandenberg, 1983), and Canadians have been among the leaders in play research for a number of decades. In fact, three of the authors in the foregoing list of references—Berlyne, Gilmore, and Rubin—have been based at Canadian universities (the first two—both of whom worked with Piaget in Geneva as well—at the University of Toronto, and Rubin at the University of Waterloo). Most authors (e.g., Rubin et al., 1983) agree that early play theories fall into four categories:

1. *The Surplus Energy Theory*—Play is a mechanism for burning off excess energy.

2. *The Relaxation and Recreation Theories of Play*—Play meets an adult's need for relaxation after a hard day's work.

3. *The Practice Theory of Play*—Play allows children to practise adult activities.

4. *The Recapitulation Theory of Play*—Children are the link in the evolutionary chain between animals and adults. In play, children go through—or recapitulate—all the steps humans passed before reaching their current evolutionary stage.

Roots of these theories can be found in 20th-century play theories, but the early theories all have been subjected to serious criticism and are lacking in a number of ways (Rubin et al., 1983). More recent theories of play have placed less emphasis on why people play, and more on the actual *process* of play.

A comprehensive review of recent theories of play is beyond the scope of an introductory text. However, the views of Freud, Piaget, and Vygotsky on play merit consideration, especially because they have had considerable influence on early childhood education.

Freud's Theory of Play

Play had release and wish-fulfilment functions for Freud. Play allowed the child a release from the real world and the opportunity to express impulses and wishes that were too dangerous in the real world. In that sense, play was cathartic as it permitted children to relieve frustration and express their emotions. Play therapy evolved from the Freudian view of play and it still is a common and powerful tool in therapeutic and hospital settings.

Piaget's Theory of Play

One of Piaget's (1951) earlier works, *Play, Dreams, and Imitation in Childhood*, concentrated on play, including that of his own children. Piaget saw play as pure assimilation (see Chapter 2 on Piaget to refresh your memory about the terms he uses). In play, the child assimilates a person, an event, or an object into current schemes or ways of thinking. Piaget also noted that play changed with age. In the sensorimotor stage of development, play is physical, not symbolic. **Practice play** is the term Piaget used to describe the repeated actions of the infant. Whether sucking, banging, or dropping an object, the infant repeats the behaviour that once was difficult and takes pleasure in controlling the behaviour. As children enter the preoperational stage, **symbolic play** becomes possible as the child can mentally represent objects, events, and people. **Pretend play** is common during this period, and it becomes more social in nature, progressing from solitary to social pretend play. Games with rules become possible once concrete operations are achieved, and the rules become more complex as the child's cognitive capacities become more advanced.

Vygotsky's Theory of Play

Vygotsky (1976; Rubin et al., 1983), a Soviet psychologist, died before he completed work on his theory of mental development. However, his work on play in preschoolers has had a significant impact on research involving pretend play. Like Freud, Vygotsky saw play "as the imaginary, illusory realization of unrealizable desires" (p. 539), but he also saw it as a form of conscious or mental activity that was not present in infants and animals. Like other aspects of mental development, play initially demands action, but later it becomes imagination: "The old adage that child's play is imagination in action can be reversed: we can say that imagination in adolescents and schoolchildren is play without action" (p.539).

Imaginary play does not emerge until around 3 years of age, according to Vygotsky, as younger children are too constrained by reality. For example, a child of 2 years will not and cannot say "I am standing up," if the child is really sitting down. Similarly, the child cannot say "It is snowy," if looking out the window on a sunny, summer day. A word or an action cannot be separated from the real object or action. As the child approaches 3 years, however, thought becomes possible without objects and actions, and words can be freed from objects and reality. The child can talk about standing while sitting, and about snow while in the sun. What facilitates this change is the ability to use one object (e.g., a stick) for another (e.g., a horse), or one action (e.g., stomping feet on the floor) for another (e.g., being a train).

WHAT IS PLAY?

Definitions of play have abounded over the years, and the most satisfactory ones seem to focus on play as an attitude. Children and adults enter into play with an attitude—or *psychological disposition* or *set*, as the psychologists call it— that is different from their attitude when they work or study. That attitude distinguishes play from other forms of activity; a child who is playing has different intentions than one who is not. Rubin and his colleagues have outlined six characteristics of play that theorists from different perspectives agree upon:

1. Play is *intrinsically motivated*; it comes from within the child, and is not induced by needs for food or company, by social demands, or by promises of rewards.

2. In play, children focus on means, not ends. In play, the end-product is not important, whereas it is in enjoyable work.

3. Play is different from exploration; play occurs with familiar objects, while exploration occurs with unfamiliar ones. In exploration, a child says "What can this object do?", but in play, the question becomes, "What can I do with this object?"

4. Play is an "as if" activity; it involves pretending and has non-literal qualities.

5. Play has *no externally imposed rules*, whereas games do.

6. Play requires *active involvement*, whereas daydreaming does not.

PLAY IN INFANCY

Teachers working in settings that include infants and older preschoolers will tell you that your role in play differs substantially with the age of the child. In a preschool setting, for example, extended periods of time are allotted for self-directed play, whereas infants play for much shorter periods of time. Younger infants also spend much of their day involved in caregiving routines, like feeding and changing. Play with infants often evolves during these caregiving sequences. The infant in the sensorimotor period of development also needs abundant opportunities to actively explore the environment—looking, smelling, tasting, banging, moving, listening, and shaking. Of course, arranging the environment so that sensorimotor play will occur is the responsibility of the caregiver. Teachers also are important facilitators of infant play, and they will be more likely to initiate play sequences with the very young than they would be with preschoolers.

To date, most studies of infant play have been descriptive in nature (Rubin et al., 1983). Most play during the first year is with single objects; the infant applies a sensorimotor action to the object. This type of play diminishes rapidly between 7 and 18 months, dropping from 90 percent of all play sequences to 20 percent. Symbolic play with objects (e.g., drinking from an empty cup) shows a marked increase between 11 and 18 months in a wide variety of settings and cultures.

The games parents play with infants also have been the subject of a number of investigations (Rubin et al., 1983). Parents initiate a number of play sequences (e.g., peek-a-boo, tickling, hiding, etc.), and infants coo, smile, and laugh in return. In the first few months of life, play is more likely to involve tactile, visual, auditory, and motor stimulation as opposed to toys. However, infants as young as 2 months respond to a responsive toy and try to maintain the stimulation. There is some suggestion that the language used in parent–infant game sequences introduces turn-taking conversational rules and social interaction.

The quality of play changes rapidly in the second year, and sensorimotor schemes are used less frequently. Pretend play with objects like toy cups, spoons, and pillows becomes more frequent. These sequences also come to involve others rather quickly; rather than self-feeding, the toddler will feed a doll, a parent, or a caregiver. Initially, this form of play involves an isolated event, but complex sequences soon emerge. These sequences are related to familiar activities, like cooking, feeding, phoning, and changing. Substitute objects, rather than realistic objects, usually enter into play around 18 or 19 months, but the substitute needs to have some similarity to the real object for some months to come. Around 2 years, the toddler uses substitute objects more freely and they contribute to an increase in the diversity of pretend play sequences. Pretend play becomes more social in the third year as the following section indicates.

PLAY IN THE PRESCHOOL AND EARLY SCHOOL YEARS

Mildred Parten (1932) provided one of the landmark studies on play. Her work, still considered valid today (Sponseller, 1982), categorized young children's social play. She found that between 2 and 5 years children move from being asocial in their play to being associative. Although children at later ages engage in earlier forms of play, particularly solitary play (Hartup, 1983a), their play is typically more complex than it was when they were younger. Parten's six categories of social play are outlined below.

1. **Unoccupied behaviour** involves a child who moves about the classroom going from one area to another, observing but not getting involved.

   Sebastian wanders to the blocks and watches several children work together on a structure. After a few seconds he looks around, then walks over to the art table, where he looks at the finger-painting materials briefly but does not indicate a desire to paint. He continues to wander, going from area to area, watching but not participating.

2. In **solitary play** the child plays alone, uninvolved with other children nearby. Children at all ages engage in this type of play, although older children's solitary play is more complex (Almy, Monighan, Scales, & Van Hoorn, 1984; Rubin, 1977).

   Soon Yi works diligently at building a sand mountain, not looking at or speaking with the other children who are involved in other activities around her.

3. **Onlooker play**, quite common among 2-year-olds, involves a child who stands nearby watching others at play, without joining in.

   Rajeef stands just outside the dramatic play area and watches a group of children participate in doctor play, using various medical props.

4. Children engaged in **parallel play** use similar materials or toys in similar ways, but do not interact with each other.

   Clarissa alternates red and blue Legos on a form board while Daniel, sitting next to her, uses Legos to build a tall structure. They seem influenced by each other's activity but do not talk to each other or suggest joining materials.

5. In **associative play**, increasingly evident as preschoolers get older, children interact and even share some of their materials, but they are not engaged in a common activity.

    Several children are in the block area working on a common structure. Jolynne runs a car through an arch she has built at one side of the structure; Arlen keeps adding blocks to the top, saying, "This is the lookout tower," while Akira surrounds the structure with a "fence."

6. **Cooperative play**, typical of older preschoolers, is the most social form of play and involves children playing together in a shared activity.

    On arriving at school one day, the children find an empty appliance box in their classroom. At first they climb in and out of the box, but then a few of them start talking about what it might be used for. Jointly they decide to make it into a house, and their discussion turns to how this could be accomplished. While continuing to discuss the project, they also begin the task of transforming the box, cutting, painting, and decorating to reach their common goal. It takes several days, but the children together create a house.

    Other researchers have viewed play from a different perspective. For instance, Sara Smilansky (1968) proposed play categories based on children's increasing cognitive abilities and measured by how children use play materials. This view is complementary to Parten's classifications because it focuses on a different aspect of play. Smilansky's categories include the following:

1. **Functional play** is characteristic of infants' and toddlers' repetitive motor play used to explore what objects are like and what can be done with them.

    Clark picks up a block, turns it, and looks at it from all sides. He bangs it on the floor, then picks up another block with his left hand and bangs the two blocks together. He alternates striking the blocks against each other and on the floor.

2. **Constructive play** involves creating something with the play objects.

   Asma uses blocks to construct a tower. Her activity now has a purpose.

3. In **dramatic play** the child uses a play object to substitute for something imaginary.

   Stephen takes four blocks, puts one on each of four plates placed around the table, and says, "Here is your toast for breakfast."

4. **Games with rules** involve accepted, prearranged rules in play. This stage is more typical of older children.

   In kindergarten, Ajake and a group of peers play the game "Blockhead," agreeing on the game's rules.

Rubin (1977, 1982) has combined Parten's and Smilansky's categories in a series of studies. This approach, diagrammed in Exhibit 8-1, is sometimes adopted by teachers rating the types of play occurring in their program.

EXHIBIT 8-1 PLAY RATING SHEET USING RUBIN'S COMBINATION OF SMILANSKY'S AND PARTEN'S CATEGORIES

TYPE OF PLAY	SOLITARY PLAY	PARALLEL PLAY	GROUP PLAY
Functional play			
Constructive play			
Dramatic play			
Games with rules			

Research on pretend play has consistently found that this type of play increases with age in middle-class children from intact families, and it becomes more interactive with age. However, solitary pretend play decreases between 3 and 5 years, and then increases again around age 6 (Rubin et al., 1983). Parallel pretend play remains frequent throughout the preschool years. A number of studies (Rubin et al., 1983; Shefatya, 1990) have suggested that pretend play is delayed and/or less mature in children from lower-class backgrounds. Some of these studies have not been well controlled, and the differences may not be as great as once was suspected. Nevertheless, across several cultures, children who have parents with less formal education engage in less pretend play than children who have parents with more formal education. Children who watch a great deal of television also are less likely to engage in pretend play, and there is some suggestion that divorce reduces the occurrence of pretend play, especially in boys. Large toys that fit with pretend play themes (e.g., a horse and a car) seem to produce more pretend play, as do more creative playgrounds.

There are some fairly pronounced and persistent sex differences in play (Rubin et al., 1983). Boys are more active than girls, more likely to play "superhero roles," and more likely to engage in rough-and-tumble play. In fact, the rough-and-tumble play differences have been noted across six different cultures. Domestic toys like dolls and stoves are still preferred by females, while boys like vehicles, blocks, and construction materials.

Rubin and his colleagues (1983) and Smilansky (1990) also have reviewed the extensive literature on the effects of play on development, but the literature is clouded with methodological difficulties. The evidence suggests that problem-solving, story-making, classification skills, and scores on intelligence tasks are positively correlated with pretend play. Tutoring in pretend play also has been investigated (Rubin et al.,

1983; Smilansky 1990), and found to lead to both an increase in pretend play in the class, improvement in related cognitive skills, and an increase in social participation. As peer interactions are significant influences on cognitive development, the increase in social participation may have far-reaching effects.

Smilansky (1990) notes that twelve independent studies, conducted over a sixteen-year period, have shown positive benefits from adult intervention into pretend play. The interventions were meant to improve and extend the play, not to make it adult-dominated. Subsequently, she conducted a survey of 120 preschool and kindergarten teachers in the United States and Israel to see if these results affected educational practices. While 100 percent of the teachers had a playhouse corner in their programs, 90 percent of the teachers did not expect all children to play there during the week and none of the teachers assessed the children's play in that area. In fact, none of the teachers remembered any course that covered pretend play, and 90 percent of them did not think pretend play helped prepare children for school. Moreover, 50 percent of the teachers never intervened in pretend play, and another 30 percent only encouraged and facilitated pretend play. This gap between research and practice concerned Smilansky, who maintains that the cognitive learning potential of pretend play is being overlooked in many classrooms. Other teachers "believe that provision of a proper setting and environment plus encouragement is sufficient for the child to grow. They look on intervention in socio-dramatic play activity with suspicion" (p. 40).

She recommends a fundamental change in attitudes, and points to teacher education as the force that can lead to such a change. With knowledge about the importance of pretend play, and appropriate assessment and intervention techniques, teachers are likely to make much greater use of this untapped resource. Wright (1983), for example, demonstrated that changes in the theme of the dramatic play area (e.g., from a house to a store, hospital, hairdresser and barber shop, etc.) led to increased use of the centre, especially by older children. A study by Marcotte and Young (1992) in Hamilton, Ontario, also found that a switch in the pretend play centres theme was associated with a substantial increase in language use in the centre.

Smilansky (1990) and Rubin et al. (1983) have documented many studies that have demonstrated the value of play in the life of the young child. Teachers who are aware of this literature are able to defend play-based programs, and resist the downward push for academics. In so doing, they defend developmentally appropriate programs, which we will turn to at this point.

DEVELOPMENTALLY APPROPRIATE PROGRAMS

By the mid-1980s, the "earlier is better" ideology had led to the establishment of increasingly academic kindergarten programs in many parts of the United States. The National Association for the Education of Young Children (NAEYC) opposed this move to direct instruction and maintained that play-based programs in which children were active learners were more developmentally appropriate (Williams, 1992). To support their position, they produced and subsequently expanded *Developmentally Appropriate Practice in Early Childhood Education Programs Serving Children from Birth through Age 8* (Bredekamp, 1987). The document has generated considerable discussion. It has also generated a number of changes to more **developmentally appropriate practices**, even at the elementary school level (e.g., Scales et al., 1992; Smith, 1991). The document is as relevant in Canada as it is in the United States. A full discussion of the policy is beyond the scope of this text, but it is likely to be covered in advanced courses on early childhood education. Nevertheless, the key points merit our attention.

Just what does the policy paper say? The concept of developmental appropriateness has two components: *age appropriateness* and *individual appropriateness*. The concept of age appropriateness probably is already somewhat familiar, especially if you have studied child development or developmental psychology. Bredekamp (1987) offers this definition of age appropriateness:

> Human development research indicates that there are universal, predictable sequences of growth and change that occur in children during the first nine years of life. These predictable changes occur in all domains of development—physical, emotional, social, and cognitive. Knowledge of typical development of children within the age span served by the program provides a framework from which teachers prepare the learning environment and plan appropriate experiences (pp. 3–4).

The concept of individual appropriateness is perhaps less familiar:

> Each child is a unique person with an individual pattern and timing of growth, as well as individual personality, learning style, and family background. Both the curriculum and adults' interactions with children should be responsive to individual differences. Learning in young children is the result of interaction between the child's thoughts and experiences with materials, ideas, and people. These experiences should match the child's developing abilities while also challenging the child's interest and understanding (pp. 3–4).

The policy continues with many examples of both appropriate and inappropriate practices for early childhood programs for 0- to 8-year-old children. The policy also comments on play. "Children's play is a primary vehicle for and indicator of their mental growth. ... Therefore, child-initiated, child-directed, teacher-supported play is an essential component of developmentally appropriate practice" (p. 4). Later NAEYC publications include *Developmentally Appropriate Practice in Early Childhood Programs Serving Infants (1989)* and *Developmentally Appropriate Practice in Early Childhood Programs Serving Toddlers* (1989). They deal with the special needs of the very young.

INDIVIDUALLY APPROPRIATE ANTI-BIAS, MULTICULTURAL PROGRAMS

Within the concept of individual appropriateness is the notion that teachers should be responsive to each child's familial background. In multicultural, multilingual countries like Canada and the United States, that statement has far-reaching implications for the teacher. While an early childhood program will include knowledge and experiences from the dominant culture, an individually appropriate program will balance the program with knowledge and experiences from the other cultures. Moreover, non-dominant cultures, languages, and practices will always be dealt with respectfully, and will be reflected in the program.

Some Canadians think that problems like racism and cultural bias are more of a U.S. problem, where the history of slavery and black oppression has been long and troubled. However, as any of you know, racism is becoming more and more of a problem in Canada, especially in large, multi-ethnic communities. Moreover, Canadian history is also tainted with racial prejudice, as the sections on the Yukon and the Northwest Territories in Chapter 4, for example, clearly demonstrate. The fact that we still have so few early childhood education programs for our aboriginal peoples and no clear policy for funding such programs points to our ongoing need for improvement.

The concepts of *anti-bias education* and *multicultural education* (Derman-Sparks & Ramsey, 1993) will be apparent in every high-quality educational program. An anti-bias program actively confronts—or proactively avoids—prejudice, stereotypes, and the "isms" and phobias, including racism, sexism, and homophobia. Teachers confront problems rather than sweep them under the proverbial carpet. The diversity of children in the program and their families is respected and reflected in the program, the day-to-day environment, staffing, and all activities. Ruth Armstrong, from Nee Gawn Ah Kai Day Care in Manitoba, describes how an ECE program can be responsive to aboriginal children in A Canadian Professional Speaks Out.

COMPONENTS OF THE EARLY CHILDHOOD PROGRAM

Most early childhood programs contain some fairly standard elements. How these components are arranged and how much time is allocated to them reflects the ages and individual histories of the children, and the teachers' philosophy and goals. It would be absurd for an infant program to allocate large blocks of time for self-initiated play, but

A CANADIAN PROFESSIONAL SPEAKS OUT

Native Child Care

The smells of bannock baking, the thumping of drums in the background, the happy sounds of children playing in the tipi. These are some of the things you might see at a Native child care centre.

Traditional Native culture depends on the extended family to provide child care when the immediate parents are not able to. With the urbanization of many aboriginal families, group child care has become a necessary reality. It is important, therefore, for early childhood educators working with Native children to provide culturally appropriate child care to children within the comfort zone of parents and grandparents. Within this comfort zone may lie the need for continuation of language and traditional child-rearing practices.

What are these traditional child-rearing practices? Many of them are the same as those we would wish to teach all children, regardless of culture: building self-esteem, independence, and a respect for others and the environment. However, instilling self-respect for being a Native person should also be strived for.

Early childhood educators can offer activities involving traditional Native crafts such as beading or willow-weaving, but having an Elder teach the craft, with stories or legends to accompany the teaching, can pass on the culture and traditions while strengthening the family bonds. Reinforcing the "material" aspects of culture such as drums, tipi, and bannock, can only serve

to create awareness of the culture and its continuity in our urban setting.

Language facilitation is of utmost importance in any early childhood setting. However, when the language becomes second to English, which is most commonly used in education or in work situations, it has a distinct possibility of becoming lost within the shuffle. For many Native families, speaking the language, whether it be Cree, Ojibwe, MicMac, or Shushwap, creates a familiarity and a sense of belonging. Urbanization has rapidly depleted the use of Native language and created a feeling of conformity for those who are forced to use English. It is therefore important that the languages be kept sacred, taught, and used within the family and the child care setting.

Working within an aboriginal child care environment, I can understand the areas that parents are most concerned with and wish to see offered to their children while in the setting. These areas include language, culture, and tradition, and the importance of contributing to society through meaningful employment or education. As early childhood educators, we must go back to the basics and offer all children experiences to strengthen self-esteem so that they will have a desire to further their goals and aspirations beyond the preschool level.

Ruth Armstrong
Director, Nee Gawn Ah Kai Day Care Inc.
Winnipeg, Manitoba

this would be a standard feature in developmentally appropriate preschool and primary programs.

The philosophy and goals of the program should reflect a respect for the child's growing independence, increasing decision-making skills, and ability to draw what is valuable from the day's experiences. The teacher facilitates play, structures the environment, and supports children's choices. The teacher offers group activities for older children, but recognizes that some children are not yet ready for them. The teacher also keeps groups small and has faith in children's ability to learn and flourish in a well-planned environment.

Let us now examine standard components of the early childhood programs for preschool and school-aged children. (If you intend to specialize in infant care, you will need to consult additional resources listed in Chapter 5.) Exhibit 8-2 lists some elements you will find in most early childhood programs; of course, these can be arranged in a great variety of ways.

EXHIBIT 8-2 COMPONENTS OF THE EARLY CHILDHOOD SCHEDULE

Activity time
Large-group activity
Small-group activity
Outdoor-time activity
Routines—Eating, clean-up, resting, washing, toileting, and transitions

ACTIVITY TIME

The largest block(s) of time each day should be reserved for planned activities from which the children can select. In many programs, **activity time** is also called self-selected learning activities, free play, play time, learning centre time, or other similar names suggestive of the fact that children make choices about the activities in which they engage. Many of the activities we will discuss in the next few chapters would be offered during this period. A wide variety of well-planned activities should reinforce and support the objectives and theme of the curriculum. Each day's activities should also provide multiple opportunities for development of fine and gross motor, cognitive, creative, social, and language skills.

In a part-day preschool program, there will usually be only one lengthy activity time block; an all-day child care program will typically have at least one such block in the morning and one in the afternoon. Such time blocks should include at least 45 minutes, and can be as long as two hours, to allow children ample time to survey the options, select an activity, get involved in it, and bring it to a satisfactory conclusion. Many children will, of course, participate in more than one activity, but others will spend all of their time with one activity.

Increasingly larger time blocks will be required as children mature and as their attention span increases. Thus, in a class of 5-year-olds, most of the day will consist of activity time, and children will select from the stimulating, age-appropriate activities available.

A recent study confirms the importance of an adequately long time block for self-selected play. Christie, Johnsen, & Peckover (1988) compared 4- and 5-year-olds' social and cognitive levels of involvement in play during 15- and 30-minute free play periods. They found that when the play period was longer, children engaged in more mature play. More specifically, in the longer play period, children engaged in considerably more group play than parallel or solitary play; in the shorter period, there was more onlooker and unoccupied behaviour. During the longer play period, there was significantly more constructive play, in which objects are used to make something.

Beginning teachers often are concerned that they are not active enough during activity time or free play, but being a careful listener and observer is not being idle. Try to think of it as an opportunity to respond to child-initiated learning opportunities. When you are simply looking and listening, you are learning more about the developmental status of the children you observe. When play becomes unproductive, however, or someone is wandering aimlessly, you are ready to guide children into productive activities and help them resolve disagreements. At other times, you engage in quiet, informal conversations with children, but you do not distract busy players. Your relationships with the children are strengthened, and their self-esteem is enhanced because you let them discover solutions to their problems, rather than provide them.

When planning the activity time block, you also should consider safety and adequate supervision. Some activities require close attention by an adult, while others can be carried out relatively independently by the children. Such activities as cooking and woodworking require constant teacher attention. Water and sand play, other sensory activities, messy media, and blocks also need to be monitored on an ongoing basis.

For each activity time block, it is important to consider the balance between activities that should be closely supervised and those that are more self-directed, particularly in relation to the number of adults available in the class. It can be easy to lose sight of safety needs in an effort to provide a wide variety of interesting and stimulating activities.

LARGE-GROUP OR CIRCLE ACTIVITIES

Most programs include one or more times when all of the children and teachers gather together. **Large-group time**, or *circle time*, which originated with Froebel, can be used for many purposes. Some teachers tend to use it in the same way day after day, and others use such times to meet various objectives. Some programs have several group times, each serving a different purpose, for example, stories, music and movement, and sharing time when children bring something special from home to share with their peers.

Group times help the teacher meet a wide variety of objectives. For instance, they provide an excellent opportunity to introduce new topics and explore new materials, or to probe the children's comprehension of concepts and information (Essa & Rogers, 1992). They can also be used for discussions, stories and books, songs, finger plays, movement, socialization, poetry, games, dramatizations, sharing, relaxation exercises, planning and review, calendar or weather, and a host of other activities often carried out with the whole group (McAfee, 1985).

From interviews with and observations of early childhood teachers, McAfee

(1985) found that the most popular and frequently observed circle activity was reading of books or stories. In verbal interviews, teachers indicated that music activities were carried out almost as often as book and story activities, but in actual classroom observations McAfee found music was used only about one-third as often as reading activities. Sharing time or "Show and Tell" was observed quite regularly, whereas other types of activities were seen relatively infrequently or not at all.

Group times are usually teacher-initiated and -led, although teachers always seek children's input. In fact, older preschoolers enjoy and are very competent in leading group activities, for instance, "reading" a familiar book, leading songs, and moving the group into transitions. Such opportunities to take over group leadership should, of course, never be imposed and should be conducted as the child chooses.

When guiding large-group (as well as small-group) activities, it is important to remember how children learn and what constitutes developmentally appropriate group activities. Children, as active learners, will gain more from activities that allow for their input, include active involvement, and encourage flexible problem solving. Asking children to provide answers for which there is a "right" or "wrong," "correct" or "incorrect" response does not support their developmental needs and their growing self-esteem.

SMALL-GROUP ACTIVITIES

With infants and toddlers, the group size must be very small for most activities. For preschoolers and school-aged children, who usually are in larger groups, some programs include a **small-group activity time** during which five or six children work with one teacher for a short period. This can be handled by staggering small groups throughout the program day or by having each teacher take a small group during a designated small-group time block. Usually such times focus on specific concepts and materials and are geared to the abilities and interests of the children in the group (Hohmann et al., 1979; Wright, 1983). Children are often grouped by developmental level for small-group activities, although Hohmann and colleagues recommend that small groups represent a cross-section of the classroom population to promote cross-learning. In a small-group setting, the teacher has an opportunity to pay close attention to each individual child. As you might expect, careful planning is crucial for successful small-group activity times. Children should also be able to choose not to attend small-group activities.

OUTDOOR ACTIVITY

A large time block for outdoor play should be part of the daily schedule. Some adults think of outdoor play merely as a time for children to expend excess energy and for teachers to take a rest. But outdoor time contains far too many valuable opportunities for learning and development to be dismissed in this way, as the open model schools have so aptly demonstrated. When you think of outdoor play as an integral part of the early childhood experience, it becomes natural to allocate a large period of time for it, whenever the weather permits. Keep in mind that outdoor time requires planning in the same way that indoor activity does, and that it involves the same kinds of teacher–child interactions.

Just as during activity times, the teacher's role when outside includes setting up a stimulating environment, providing for each child's individual needs, guiding children's behaviour, providing a variety of experiences, taking opportunities to teach concepts, and encouraging exploration and problem solving. In addition, some unique safety concerns require special attention in an outdoor play area. An important skill that you, as the teacher, should develop is the ability to scan, to keep an eye on the entire outdoor play area. It is particularly important to pay attention to the fronts and backs of swings, slides, climbing equipment, tricycles, and other wheeled toys, and the area in and around the sandbox.

Time for outdoor play may be affected by the weather, although the weather should never be used as an excuse for not going outside. Children do not catch cold from playing outside in the winter. Children thoroughly enjoy the snow, if they are properly clothed. Nevertheless, there are times in most areas of Canada when frostbite will be a concern. Similarly, extended periods in the sun are also becoming more of a concern.

If inclement weather does prevent the children from enjoying outside time, alternative activities should be made available inside so children can expend energy and engage in large motor activity. Many schools have a selection of large motor equipment, such as tumbling mats or indoor climbing apparatus, to use on rainy days. If this equipment is in a relatively restricted space, teachers should allow small groups of children to use it throughout the day rather than have the entire group involved at one time.

ROUTINES

Routines are regular, predictable behaviours that are repeated every day—or almost every day—in early childhood programs. They include arriving and departing, cleaning up the play room and the playground, transitions, and personal care routines. How you approach personal care will vary greatly with the children's ages, but will include eating, resting, washing, and toileting. Routines can provide valuable learning experiences, and they are also important for children's well-being. While routines are regular behaviours, it is important to remember that their timing should never be carved in stone.

Clean-up

With infants and toddlers, the teachers usually tidy up as required and ensure that the playroom remains an attractive setting that invites play. With age, children are more likely to put toys away after they are finished with them. Older children also are quite willing to assist in tidying up large toys, like blocks. Children also enjoy helping to put outdoor toys in the storage shed.

Meals and Snacks

Sharing food provides a unique opportunity for socialization and learning; thus, almost every program includes at least one snack, if not several meals. A three-hour program usually includes a snack time around the halfway point of the day, and many children are ravenous at that point. The timing of meals, however, should be dictated by the children's needs, not by a rigid schedule. If it appears that some children get to school having had breakfast several hours before or not having eaten breakfast at all, then an early morning meal should be provided. An alternative, particularly if children's arrival at school is staggered over several hours, is to have snacks available for a period of time and allow children to eat as they feel the need to refuel.

Timing of lunch will depend on the ages of the children, the length of time they are at the centre, and when morning snack was served. Younger preschoolers may need lunch at 11:30 a.m. and be ready for a nap by noon. How much time is allocated for each of these meals will depend on the children in the group and the type of meal; generally, however, 15 to 20 minutes for snacks and 20 to 30 minutes for lunch is adequate. Most children can comfortably finish a meal in this period of time.

Nap or Rest

In full-day programs, children should have time for sleep or rest during the middle of the day, usually sometime after, though not immediately following, lunch. Allocating one to two hours for this time is usually enough (see Chapter 15 for a more detailed discussion). Also be aware of your local regulations for rest time, because some jurisdictions include specific requirements.

Transitions

Those times between activities are as important as the activities themselves. Failing to plan how children will get from one area to another—from group to the bathroom to snack, or from activity time to putting on coats to going outside—can result in chaos. We will discuss transitional techniques in more detail in Chapter 15 in the context of group guidance.

GUIDELINES FOR PROGRAM PLANNING

These components of the early childhood day—activity time, large-group activities, small-group activities, outdoor activity, clean-up, meals, nap or rest, and transitions—can be combined in your program in a wide variety of ways. Let's examine some guidelines that will help in planning an effective program.

ALTERNATING ACTIVE AND QUIET TIMES

Children need time both to expend energy and to rest. A useful rule in planning is to look at the total time in terms of cycles of activity and rest, boisterousness and quiet, energy and relaxation. Categorize the descriptions of time blocks listed in your daily schedule in terms of active times (for example, activity time, outdoor play, large-group activities that involve movement) and less active times (for example, story, small-group activities, nap, snack).

In applying this guideline, think about providing the opportunity to be physically active after quiet times and to slow down after active involvement. Also consider the total consecutive time that children are expected to sit quietly. If you planned to have children sit at a large-group activity from 10 to 10:20, then move into a small-group activity from 10:20 to 10:35, and then have snack until 11:00, you would be courting chaos, if not disaster. Young children need periods of activity, and that plan has children shifting from one relatively inactive period to another for a full hour. Similarly, when children have been engaged in active exploration, a quieter time should follow. However, do not expect children to move immediately from very active involvement, such as outdoor play, to being very quiet, such as nap time. For such times, plan a more gentle transition that helps children settle down gradually.

BALANCING CHILD-INITIATED AND TEACHER-INITIATED ACTIVITIES

In quality early childhood programs, most of the day consists of large time blocks in which children can make decisions about the activities in which they will participate and how they will carry them out. Most programs also include times when teacher-directed group activities are available. Most of the day's activities should, however, be child-selected and allow children to move from activity to activity at their own pace (Miller, 1984). Typically, activity time and outdoor time accommodate child initiation, whereas small-and large-group times involve teacher initiation. Some functional activities, such as snack, meals, and nap, also require some teacher direction, but meal and snack times also include opportunities for children to make choices.

Developmentally appropriate programs emphasize child-initiated, child-selected, and teacher-supported activities. When young children are allowed to decide how they will spend their time, they develop qualities such as autonomy, judgment, independent decision making, social give-and-take, initiative, exploration, and creativity. In addition, children develop a reasonable amount of compliance, they understand the rules of group behaviour, and they accept the authority and wisdom of their teachers in safety-related issues. Generally, if teachers convey respect for and trust in the ability of children to make appropriate decisions, children will reciprocate with enthusiastic participation in teacher-initiated, developmentally appropriate activities that engage their interest. Teachers who trust the children's abilities, of course, also allow children to leave group activities that do not interest them.

ACTIVITY LEVEL OF CHILDREN

By nature, young children are active and must have many opportunities for expending energy. Some children, however, are more active than others. And, on average, boys are more active than girls (Maccoby & Jacklin, 1974). Occasionally, you will find a group in which a large portion of the children are particularly active. If this occurs, a schedule that has worked for you in the past may not serve as well because the needs of the children are different. In such a case, adjusting the schedule as well as the classroom arrangement and the types of activities planned will help the class run more smoothly. You might, for instance, carry out traditionally indoor activities outside and plan either a longer or an added outdoor time block.

If you have a disproportionate number of boys in your program, you may find that you need to provide more opportunities for active play. Sometimes female teachers are threatened by the high activity level, but the research does show that boys need more of this type of play.

DEVELOPMENTAL LEVEL OF CHILDREN

As children get older, their attention span noticeably increases; thus, your daily schedule should reflect the group's ages and developmental levels (Miller, 1984). For older preschoolers, plan longer time blocks for small-group and large-group activity times. On the other hand, younger preschoolers require added time for meals and nap. With even younger children, you may also want to schedule regular times for toileting, for instance, before going outdoors and before nap. And with infants, you would want to check diapers and have bottles available before going outdoors.

The length of time you devote to large-group activities can be problematic. The time allocated to such activities will depend on the ages and attention spans of the children, but it will also depend on the length of time they have been in the program and on their activity level. At the start of the year, five minutes may be long enough for young preschoolers, but they may want to participate in a large-group activity for fifteen minutes later on. Children entering kindergarten, with previous experience in an early childhood program, may be interested in spending twenty minutes in a group, whereas children new to a group experience may lose interest after five minutes. Children of all ages can, of course, sit for a longer period of time if the activity captivates their interest; but, generally, a well-paced, shorter group time is more rewarding for all. As the program year progresses, reassess the length of group time and adjust it according to the children's interest.

No matter how long or short the attention spans are in your group, it is important to remember that young children need to be *actively involved in problem solving*. A group time that just entailed listening to the teacher would not be a source of learning for young children.

GROUP SIZE

Group size may also influence your planning. A general rule of thumb is to keep groups as small as you can. If you happen to be in a province or territory that does not have group size regulations—or has less than ideal ones—try to arrange the program so that the children are in smaller groups as much as possible. For example, while one group is outdoors, another group is indoors. When some children are involved in self-selected activities, offer a music activity or read a story for those who are interested.

FAMILY GROUPINGS

Of course, if you are in a program that has family groupings, the mix of ages will influence the length of your group activities and your program planning. You will also need to provide either a wider range of activities or variants of the same activity so that there is a selection of developmentally appropriate materials.

ARRIVAL OF CHILDREN

How children arrive and leave the centre—whether over staggered periods of time or at about the same time—has to be taken into account in planning. In most full-day programs, the early morning period, until most or all of the children are at the centre, and the late afternoon period, when children start leaving for home, require some special considerations. The arrival or departure of children makes carrying out teacher-initiated activities difficult because the teacher and other children are interrupted frequently and because the arriving or departing children will not get the full benefit of the teacher-led activity. Thus, self-selected activities, in which children can control engagement and disengagement, should be available during such times.

SEASONAL CONSIDERATIONS

In geographic locations where the weather varies considerably from season to season, you may want to adjust the schedule according to the time of year. For instance, during winter in northern Alberta and the Yukon, it would be difficult to keep to a schedule that contains three outdoor time blocks when each involves helping children get into their snowsuits, boots, mittens, and hats and then getting them out of such clothing at the end of the outdoor time. At the same time, a lengthy outdoor time is inappropriate when the temperature is well below freezing. Yet once spring arrives and the temperature is balmy, the schedule should allow for longer outdoor time. The weather can certainly affect your schedule, so a flexible approach and attitude are important when working with young children.

WASTED TIME

Keep in mind that children spend most of their waking hours in an early childhood program. It is, therefore, particularly important to assure that their daily experiences are meaningful. Davidson (1982) observed time use in child care centres and found that, when considered cumulatively, a considerable amount of time each day—often well over an hour—was wasted. She found wasted time particularly during routine activities such as lunch, nap, transitions, and special or unexpected occasions. Wasted time, Davidson suggests, can lower self-esteem, encourage children to behave inappropriately, and make it more difficult for them to learn to value and use time wisely. Davidson found that the causes for ill-used time included poor organization, inadequate equipment or space, not enough teachers for the number of children, lack of respect for the children, and inappropriate activities.

One clarification should be made. The wasted time described by Davidson revolves around times that force inactivity on children. Children, however, may *choose* times when they refrain from activity, stand at the periphery to observe, or seem to be daydreaming. Such times represent a self-selected rest from activity, rather than imposed inactivity.

Some realities of early childhood programs (for instance, a less than ideal number of teachers, too large a group size, and/or inadequate space) are beyond the teacher's control. Nevertheless, teachers who are caring and concerned about the needs of the children and plan an age-appropriate program are on the right track. Additional attention and sensitivity to times in the schedule during which waiting and inactivity could occur will help improve the program. Moreover, how you handle these routines can make a major difference. For example, snowsuit time can be a time for conversation, singing, and developing self-help skills. Children who wake up early from a nap could look at a book with an adult or by themselves if they are old enough. Lunch time often is rich with opportunities for socialization and conversation, as well as learning about foods and enjoying them.

DEVELOPMENTALLY APPROPRIATE SCHEDULES

Obviously, the schedule in a program will vary with the children's ages, their developmental histories, and the length of the day. Infants and toddlers have unique needs that do not readily adapt to scheduling, as any parent or teacher who has been with them knows. Moreover, only in rare cases do they have predictable schedules. While time must be allocated for feeding, changing, and sleeping, the very young will always be somewhat unpredictable in their needs. Familiar teachers need to respond to them in a consistent manner, and realize that the child's schedule one month will change in short order.

Programs for older preschoolers and school-aged children are more likely to have a schedule in mind. Obviously, the outline of the day for a two- or three-hour preschool program will differ from that of a nine- to eleven-hour child care centre program. But it is not only the difference in the number of hours but also *the needs of the children* that distinguish schedules for these two types of programs. A Closer Look (p. 211) reviews a typical day for two children—one in a preschool program, the other in child care—to illustrate the point that different programs must consider different concerns.

In planning the course of a typical day in an early childhood program, teachers typically include the components outlined in Exhibit 8-3. There are times for

EXHIBIT 8-3 PLANNING FORMAT

Plans for: (Date) Theme or project (if any):					
ACTIVITIES	**PHYSICAL**	**SOCIO-EMOTIONAL**	**COGNITIVE**	**LANGUAGE**	**ANTI-BIAS/ MULTICULTURAL**
Monday 1. 2. 3.					
Tuesday 1. 2. 3.					
Wednesday 1. 2. 3.					
Thursday 1. 2. 3.					
Friday 1. 2. 3.					

self-selection, times for group activities, times for routines, and times for transitions. Children and their parents are greeted when they arrive and bade farewell at the end of the day. Both the indoors and outdoors are used whenever possible, and there is a balance between quiet and active times, between group and individual times. The teachers know their responsibilities, and thus ensure that no area of the program is unsupervised. However, they are in no way rigid about their schedule.

A Closer Look

David and Rita

David's parents enrolled him in a 9 to noon preschool program sponsored by the city recreation department so that he could have an enriching social and learning experience. He typically gets up at 7, eats breakfast with his parents before his father leaves for work, plays alone or with his younger sister Tina for an hour or so, then gets dressed. At 8:45 David's mother drives him to the nearby recreation centre, where he spends the morning in play and activities. At noon he goes home and eats lunch with his sister and mother. While Tina takes her nap, David and his mother often read or play together. After David's sister awakes, they pass the afternoon with errands, a trip to the grocery store, playing, watching television, or visiting a neighbourhood friend. Dinner is served around 6, and is followed by a television show on some evenings, a bath with Tina, a story read by David's father, and bed by 8.

Rita, who lives with her mother and two older sisters, has been at her child care centre since she was 6 weeks old because her mother has always worked. Rita gets up at 6:30, gets dressed with help from one of her sisters, and is out of the house by 7:15. Sometimes she does not eat breakfast because she is not hungry yet; sometimes she munches on a piece of toast in the car. On the way to the child care centre, they drop off Rita's sisters at a neighbour's house, where they stay until it is time to go to their elementary school. Rita arrives at the child care centre, which is sponsored by a church near her mother's workplace, by 7:45. Her day is spent in planned activities, play, meals, and nap at the centre until her mother picks her up around 5:30. They pick up her sisters, sometimes stop at the grocery store or at a restaurant, then get home around 6:30. While dinner is being prepared and after dinner, the girls watch television. After a bath, Rita is usually in bed by 9.

David's preschool program and Rita's child care centre serve different functions and meet different needs for these two children. David's preschool experience is an interlude in his day, most of which is spent at a fairly leisurely pace in his home with his family. It offers what cannot be provided by his family—opportunities for social interaction with peers, development of group skills, exposure to stimulating new ideas and activities, and group guidance from knowledgeable adults.

Rita, on the other hand, spends relatively little time at home, and often that time is busy and rushed. Rita's program also provides many opportunities for socialization with peers and for learning. But the child care centre, where Rita spends the majority of her waking hours, by necessity must also meet more of her physical requirements, for instance, for food and rest. It must also contribute more to her emotional well-being by providing a nurturing climate in which she feels warmth, security, and recognition as a unique individual, not just a member of the group. In many ways, the child care centre replaces rather than augments part of Rita's home experience. Thus, when setting a schedule, whether for a preschool or a child care program, the central concern must be for the needs of the children.

A flexible daily schedule does provide security, because it gives the day a predictable order. Children need predictability, and they soon know the usual sequence of activities. Thus, you can say to a child, "I know you are anxious for your mother to come. After we finish cleaning up, we will go outside. Later, when we come back inside, we will read a story, and then your mother will be here." The child can relate to this temporal time-frame because he or she is familiar with the schedule.

A schedule is simply an outline of a typical day that can be changed when children's interests and needs point to a need for change. For example, if children want to watch a large cement truck that comes into view just as the group was about to go indoors, the teachers extend the outdoor period. If new materials are attracting considerable attention, activity time is extended. If it has been raining relentlessly for two weeks and today is a beautiful, sunny day, plan to spend a large portion of the day outside so everyone can enjoy the nice weather. Similarly, if despite your best efforts the children are restless and uninterested in your group activity, shorten the time rather than allow a negative situation to develop. In other words, use cues from the children—and your judgment—to adapt the schedule if it will improve the flow of the day and better meet the needs of the children. You might also ask the children what changes in the schedule they would suggest. Their insights will surprise you! And if the chickens start to hatch when you are about to read a story, always forget the story!

You will make appropriate age adjustments in your typical day. For example, you will extend the number of choices available for older children, who also are able to make some transitions as a group. With school-aged children, you also will have more teacher-initiated activities and they will usually last for a longer period of time. The materials you select will be developmentally appropriate as well. You may read a short story to an infant, but read the same story and sing a song with several toddlers. Preschoolers who have some experience in the program may want to sing four songs after a more complex story, but on some days they will not. Kindergarten and primary-level children may spend even longer times with the group.

Some large early childhood centres present special challenges because they have multiple classes that share some common facilities. This can place some constraints on your flexibility, but still allows for some latitude. It may not be possible, for example, to make substantial alterations in the time allocated for outside play when groups rotate the use of the playground. Meal times are more regular if groups share a common dining room, but exchanges of meal times can be arranged if you have a special activity. Moreover, the self-contained parts of the program, such as activity or group time, can still be adapted freely.

As teachers, you will review the day's events and make adjustments on a regular basis. You will realize that schedules have to be tailor-made by teachers who know the needs of the children in their care. While the main scheduling consideration for child care centres is the needs of the children, the schedule must also take your needs into account. Early childhood teachers spend long and difficult hours working with their young charges, a job that can be both tiring and energizing, frustrating and rewarding. As a complement to the schedule you develop for the children, you need a schedule that provides rest, rejuvenation, and planning time for the adults. When the needs of the adults are considered, the children's needs will be better met, and teacher burn-out is less likely to occur.

WHAT IS CURRICULUM?

Unfortunately, quality early childhood education programs do not come in ready-made, hand-delivered packages. They entail a great deal of teacher time—time planning activities and organizing the environment so that child-initiated, play-based, teacher-supported learning will occur. The amount of planning and the terms used vary somewhat with the age of the children in the program.

Most people and texts (e.g., Almy, 1975; NAEYC, 1992; Maxim, 1989; Shimoni et al., 1992) prefer to avoid the term **curriculum** when describing programs for infants and toddlers. However, the word curriculum comes from the Latin word describing the race course a chariot followed. If you think of curriculum as the *course of the day* for children in a program, then the term is appropriate for all ages. Programs for infants and toddlers are carefully planned, the environment is carefully and safely structured, and teachers in these settings have a knack for using many diverse opportunities for learning. However, the very short attention spans and more demanding caretaking needs of infants and younger toddlers in the sensorimotor stage of development mean that extended periods of self-directed play are out of the question.

The longer attention spans and reduced caretaking needs of preoperational preschoolers and pre- and concrete-operational school-aged children require different forms of program planning. Consequently, people are more likely to use the term curriculum when discussing programs for preschool children. **Lesson plan** almost always creeps into the terminology when school-aged children are being discussed. Notwithstanding the variations in terminology, quality early childhood education settings have developmentally and individually appropriate programs and/or curricula that have been carefully planned and regularly evaluated by their teachers.

In the following sections, we will consider some of the elements of the early childhood program or curriculum. Some ingredients will be found in all programs, regardless of the children's ages. Caring, warm adults who welcome parent involvement in a developmentally appropriate program are taken as givens. Choice, variety, and challenge in an anti-bias program are also basics. But young children also need the sense of security that a predictable, yet fully flexible, program can offer. Finally, young children—especially children in full-day programs—also need time, time to do what comes naturally, time to pause and reflect, time to be alone, and time to be with others. If the program has all of these ingredients, the environment will also have children and adults who are enjoying each day; you will hear sounds of delight, joy, pleasure, and humour from both children and teachers who approach each day with enthusiasm.

ELEMENTS OF THE CURRICULUM

The early childhood curriculum is the result of both long-range and short-term planning, and the children's developmental levels. Long-term planning is patently inappropriate for infants and toddlers. In contrast, in late August, a kindergarten teacher might outline what he would like to accomplish over the year, and then revise and refine the outline upon meeting the children in the program.

Curriculum has to be integrally related to several important factors—program philosophy, goals, objectives, and evaluation—as we will discuss (Langenbach & Neskora, 1977). These elements form a cyclical pattern: program philosophy guides goals and objectives; these, in turn, lead to development of content and activities; content and activities are evaluated on an ongoing basis; and, returning to the starting point, goals and objectives are reassessed and adjusted as needed, starting the cycle anew (Lawton, 1988).

Program Philosophy and Curriculum

Curriculum takes its direction from the overall philosophy of your program. For instance, underlying beliefs and values about how children learn will have an impact. Another factor shaping the curriculum will be reliance on a particular theorist's works. For instance, programs derived from the theory of Jean Piaget will focus on developmentally appropriate cognitive tasks, whereas programs based on behaviourist theory may rely more on a direct instructional approach. Montessori programs will have equipment and activities, some of which you are unlikely to find in a Piagetian or behavioural program.

Finally, the children in your program and your assumptions about how best to meet their specific requirements will also affect the curriculum. For instance, you might increase the language component of your program if you have children from low-income families. You would also adjust your program if you think that some children in your program have special needs, including a need for positive socialization experiences, for an improved self-concept, or for cognitive stimulation.

Goals and Objectives and the Curriculum

Out of the program's philosophy comes a set of broad goals, which are then translated into more specific objectives. These provide the basis for the curriculum, elevating activities above a utilitarian rationale, such as "but we have to keep the kids busy!" As we discussed in Chapter 7, goals and objectives are designed both to promote and facilitate growth in developmental areas and to convey specific content related to the curriculum. Objectives, in turn, give direction to the activities that are planned to implement the daily curriculum.

Evaluation and the Curriculum

A curriculum has to be closely matched to the needs of the children in the program. For this reason, evaluation is an important element in curriculum development. It is important to evaluate, on an ongoing basis, whether the topics and activities of the curriculum are appropriate and meaningful for the children. This can be done informally, by observing the children's engagement in activities and reviewing their comprehension of concepts. If your assessment leads you to question aspects of the program, then modify or change the objectives and the curriculum as needed. (Chapter 7 discusses evaluation in more detail.)

CHILDREN'S DEVELOPMENT AND CURRICULUM

You know from our earlier discussion of developmentally appropriate practice and individually appropriate, anti-bias, multicultural programs that what you include in the curriculum must be directly related to the children in your program. A curriculum that does not fit the comprehension level, abilities, needs, and interests of the children is meaningless. To plan an appropriate program requires knowledge about the age group of your class, about family characteristics and backgrounds, and about the individual variations among the children in the class.

A valuable guide in developing curriculum is the NAEYC's brochure, discussed earlier—*Developmentally Appropriate Practice in Early Childhood Programs Serving Children from Birth through Age 8* (Bredekamp, 1987). This resource provides a philosophical rationale as well as specific and pragmatic information on appropriate and inappropriate practice when working with young children.

CURRICULUM CONTENT

What, then, is appropriate in an early childhood curriculum? What interests the children in your program? What is relevant to them? What is developmentally relevant, assuming that during the early years children are developing a predictable set of capacities (Hohmann et al., 1979)?

Perhaps the best way to define what is appropriate in a curriculum is to say that it should be derived from the children's life experiences, based on what is concrete, and tied to their emerging skills. Consider that young children have been part of their physical and social world for only a very short time. They have so much to learn about the people, places, objects, and experiences in their environment. When you give careful consideration to making the elements of the environment meaningful and understandable to children, you need not seek esoteric and unusual topics. Children's lives offer a rich set of topics on which to build a curriculum, including learning about themselves, their families, and the larger community in which they live (Essa & Rogers, 1992).

Children as the Focus of Curriculum

The most crucial skills with which young children can be armed to face the future are feelings of self-worth and competence. Children are well equipped for success if they are secure about their identities, feel good about themselves, and meet day-to-day tasks and challenges with a conviction that they can tackle almost anything. The curriculum can foster such attributes by contributing to children's self-understanding and providing repeated reinforcement and affirmation of their capabilities, individual uniqueness, and importance.

Self-understanding comes from learning more about oneself—one's identity, uniqueness, body, feelings, physical and emotional needs, likes and dislikes, skills and abilities, and self-care. Children enjoy learning about themselves, so a focus on children as part of the curriculum can and should take up a significant portion of time. It is important, however, to ensure that planned activities are age-appropriate so they contribute to both self-understanding and positive self-esteem. Infants will enjoy playing patty-cake, for example. Two-year-olds are still absorbed in learning to label body parts; thus, activities that contribute to sharpening this language skill are appropriate. Older preschoolers, on the other hand, are more interested in finer details. For example, they enjoy examining hair follicles under a microscope or observing how the joints of a skeleton move in comparison with their own bodies. Still older children are interested in processes like digestion and respiration, when presented in a concrete way.

The Family as the Focus of Curriculum

The family is vitally relevant to children and provides another rich basis for curriculum topics. We can help children build an understanding and appreciation of the roles of the family, similarities among families, the uniqueness of each family, different family forms, the tasks of families, and relationships between family members. Similarly, an examination of the children's family homes, means of transportation, food preferences, celebrations, parental occupations, and patterns of communication also provide appropriate curriculum topics. You might invite family members to come into the classroom and share special knowledge and talents. Alternatively, children as well as teachers might bring photographs of their families to share.

A curriculum focus on the family contributes to children's feelings of self-esteem and pride. They can share information about something central to their lives, while at the same time expand their understanding of the family life of the other children. While such learning strengthens children's emerging socialization, it also contributes to cognitive development. Teachers help children make comparisons, note similarities and differences, organize information, and classify various aspects of family structure.

The Community as the Focus of Curriculum

The open schools have aptly demonstrated that children's awareness of their world can particularly be expanded through the community. Older toddlers and preschoolers have had experience with numerous aspects of their community, especially shopping, medical, and recreational elements. School-aged children know even more about it. The community and those who live and work in it can certainly extend the walls of your program and offer a wealth of learning opportunities and curriculum material.

From the community and the people who work in it, children can learn about local forms of transportation; food growing, processing, and distribution; health services, including the role of doctors, nurses, dentists, dental hygienists, health clinics, and hospitals; safety provisions such as fire and police departments; communications facilities, including radio and television stations, newspapers, telephone services, and libraries; and local recreational facilities, such as parks, zoos, and museums. Children can visit an endless variety of appropriate places through field trips. (In Chapter 15, we will discuss field trips in more detail.) In addition, community professionals can be invited to visit your class and share information and tools of their professions with the children.

You can help children begin to build an understanding of the community as a social system by focusing on the interrelatedness of the people who live and work in your area. For instance, people are both providers and consumers of goods and services; the dentist buys bread that the baker produces, and the baker visits the dentist when he has a cavity.

In addition, the larger physical environment of the area in which you live provides a setting worth exploring with the children in your class. Your approach will differ, depending on whether your community is nestled in the mountains, by the ocean, or in the midst of rolling prairies. Most young children living in Saskatchewan, for instance, will not have experienced the ocean. It is difficult to convey what the ocean is like to someone who has never seen it, and this is particularly true for children who rely on concrete, first-hand experience. Therefore, it makes little sense to plan a unit on "the ocean" when it is more than a thousand miles away. Instead, focus on what is nearby and real in the environment, on what children are familiar with and can actually experience. If it is harvest time in Saskatchewan, you may choose a unit on farming, whereas you may choose shellfish as a topic in Nova Scotia during lobster season. If you are visiting a barn with horses and pigs, you will not select tender fruit farming as a topic.

PLANNING THE CURRICULUM

In some programs, especially those with infants and toddlers, long-term plans and objectives are inappropriate. Short-term objectives, however, are reasonable. With older preschoolers and school-aged children, your plans and objectives may cover a longer time span. Flexible long-term objectives also are appropriate at the primary school level. Teachers try to plan their programs so that the whole child is challenged every day. Quite frequently, the only effective way of making sure you do this is to develop global plans for each week and more specific ones for each day. (And quite often, your instructors insist that you have a written plan!) Exhibit 8-4 presents one of many possible formats for a weekly plan. A more detailed plan can be developed for each day.

Daily plans describe each activity planned for that day, objectives for activities, and the time-frame within which they are carried out. In addition, a daily plan can give information about which teacher will be in charge of the activity, in what part of the classroom each activity is to be carried out, and what materials are needed. Plans can take many forms, but they should be complete enough so that any teacher can pick one up and know for any given day what activities are planned and why they are planned. Exhibit 8-4 shows a sample lesson plan.

Each plan may be part of a project or theme and, as such, related to broader goals and objectives. But each plan should also be a whole in itself by providing a balanced day for the children. Within each plan there should be provision for activities that meet needs in all developmental domains—gross and fine motor, cognitive, social, and emotional. There should be activities that promote creative expression. Communication should be woven throughout activities, so children exercise receptive and expressive language, as well as a variety of non-verbal means of communication. And there should be opportunity for exploring new topics in a variety of ways through multiple activities, in a leisurely, unrushed manner.

While beginning teachers find planning time-consuming, they also find that written plans are useful as they help to organize thinking about objectives, materials, and evaluation. Written plans are also helpful when teachers work in teams, and when unexpected illness necessitates a supply teacher. Plans for older children who are working on themes also keep parents informed about what the child has been experiencing, discussing, and investigating. But plans are like schedules—flexibility is critical. You may need to abandon your plan completely, or you may need to revise it as you go along. With older preschoolers and school-aged children, you probably will also want to consider using projects and themes in your program. We will discuss them in the next section.

EXHIBIT 8-4 A SAMPLE LESSON PLAN

Class Name: Three-year-olds: Half-day program
Unit: Senses: Focus on touch
Unit Objectives: The children will develop an awareness that objects feel differently and that there are different textures.

TIME BLOCK	ACTIVITY	CONTENT OBJECTIVES	DEVEL. OBJECTIVE	TCHR	AREA	MATERIAL
9–9:15 Circle	Discussion: "How does it feel?" Pass around objects for children to feel and discuss their texture.	Explore and name textures: hard, soft, smooth, rough	L, P, S, C			Apple, sandpaper, velvet, wood block, etc.
9:15–10:10 Activity Time	▪1. Finger painting: with corn syrup	Explore and label sticky, smooth	P, Cr, FM			Paper, syrup, food colours
	▪2. Texture matching	Explore and match textures	P, FM, C, L			Texture samples
	Sensory bin: popcorn		P, FM, S			Popcorn
	▪3. Cooking: applesauce	Note difference: hard apples/soft applesauce	P, FM, L, S, C			Ingredients
	Dramatic play: focus on how objects feel/textures: blankets, stuffed animals	Experience various textures	S, P, M, L, C			Props
10:10–10:20 Clean-up	Focus: on textures as items are put away		M, P, L, C			
10:20–10:35	Applesauce, apple slices, apple juice, crackers	Compare different textures	P, L, FM, C, S			
10:35–10:50 Small Group	▪4. Feely box: Objects of different textures	Identify items by feel: name textures	P, C, L, FM, S			Feely box, objects
10:50–11:35 Outside	▪5. Foot painting	Experience that feet can feel	P, GM, L			Paper, paint, water, towels
11:35–11:50 Large Group	▪6. Puppetry: select two puppets and have them talk with children about how different things feel	Review concepts related to sense of touch and and different sensations	L, C, S			Puppets
11:50–12:00	Prepare to go home; talk to parents					

Developmental objective codes:

C = Cognitive	GM = Gross motor	P = Perceptual	Cr = Creative
L = Language	S = Social	FM = Fine motor	

SOURCE: E.L. Essa and P.R. Rogers. (1992). *An early childhood curriculum: From developmental model to application.* Albany, NY: Delmar Publishers.

THEMES AND PROJECTS

Themes and projects, which can be traced back to the open model and to Dewey in North America, provide a unifying element around which activities are planned (Katz & Chard, 1992). While **theme** and **project** are often used to mean the same thing, themes are generally less specific than projects. You might have a theme titled "Spring," but that does not provide much information on what you will do. A related project would be more specific, for example, "What happens in the garden—or fields, or the ranch, or fisheries—during spring?" (**Unit** is often used to mean theme. However, unit also is used to describe a series of teacher-initiated, prearranged lessons on specific topics. As such, a unit would be more appropriate at the upper limits of the early childhood years, especially if provincial or territorial directives require teachers to cover certain topics.)

A project or theme can last any length of time, from a day or two to a month or more. The interest-value and relevance of the topic to the children should dictate how much time is spent on a theme. Furthermore, the length of a project or theme should be flexible so you can spend more time if the topic intrigues the children or cut it shorter if the children seem ready to move on.

Planning a project or theme should begin with a careful consideration of your objectives and the children's interests. What is it that you want the children to learn about the topic? What concepts, skills, and information can this project convey? Most important, are these relevant, age-appropriate, and of interest to the children, and will the children enjoy them? Children have to be the starting point for planning, and, after about age 3, they can be involved in the planning. Check with them when you are planning, find out what their ideas are, and incorporate them into your plan. For instance, if you are planning a project on "How You Make Bread," you might hope to cover the following topics:

- Bread is baked at the bakery.
- The baker is the person who bakes bread.
- Many loaves of bread are baked at the bakery (mass production).
- Bread is made up of many ingredients.
- Bread is taken by trucks to grocery stores, where it is sold to people such as those in the children's families.
- Different bakeries make different types of bread (e.g., Rajeev's baker makes chapati and puri; Rana's baker makes pita bread; Maria's baker makes tortillas; and Albino's baker makes crusty corn bread).

A project usually begins with an introduction in which the theme is initially presented, and often this is a field trip. Early on in a project, you will want to focus on the children's familiarity with the subject or closely related areas, and adjust your plans to fit with their existing knowledge. Thus, if you plan a theme on the topic "bread", you can discuss, for instance, types of bread with which the children are familiar, the food group to which bread belongs (if you have already spent time discussing nutrition and the four basic food groups), the process of baking (for those children who have helped their parents make bread), and the different ways in which bread is used in meals.

New ideas and activities can be introduced logically and sequentially. New material should always be presented first in a concrete manner. While field trips are frequent starting points, concrete experiences also can be brought into the classroom through objects or guests. In the case of the bakery unit, you may want to plan a field trip to the local bakery at the beginning of the unit so the children can see how bread is made; on the other hand, some in-class experiences with bread baking can be a wonderful preparation for a trip to the bakery. Alternatively, Rajeev's and/or Maria's mother and father may agree to help the children make chapatis and tortillas. In either case, *it cannot be emphasized enough that any new concept should begin with the concrete, with first-hand experience.*

Once children have had a chance to observe and learn through first-hand experience, they can begin to assimilate this information through subsequent activities. After the field trip, children should have opportunities to factually represent what they observed by talking about and dictating accounts of the visit to the bakery, drawing pictures of what they saw on the field trip, and otherwise recalling and replicating their visit. This factual recounting allows children to fix the experience in their minds.

Children can begin to use new information in creative ways once it has been integrated into their existing memory and experiential store. They can play with the information through such activities as art, dramatic play, puppets, or blocks. This element of the project offers a wide variety of possibilities that children can approach in their unique ways.

PARENTS AND PROFESSIONALS

Parent Involvement in the Curriculum

As we indicated in this chapter, the curriculum should reflect the backgrounds, needs, and interests of the children. One excellent resource, as you plan the curriculum for your group of children, is their parents. Frequent parent–teacher communication and an open policy that conveys the school's emphasis on the importance of the family can encourage parents to be part of the early childhood program. Parent involvement in the curriculum can take many forms.

Most parents are interested in what their children are involved in each day. The overall curriculum, the units, and the daily lesson plans should be available for the parents' review. A school newsletter might be the place to share information about the overall curriculum and philosophy early in the year. Lesson and unit plans can be posted in a prominent place, for instance, just outside the classroom door or on a parent bulletin board, where parents can look at the activities and objectives. Parents appreciate knowing what activities their children engaged in during their day at school, something that is often a topic of conversation between parent and child on the way home from school.

Parents can also be called on to participate in the curriculum. As we discussed in Chapter 5, there are many areas in which their expertise and input can greatly enhance the program. Parents can provide information about special family, cultural, religious, or ethnic customs, celebrations, foods, or dress. They can visit the classroom to share occupational information or special skills. A parent who makes pottery, weaves baskets, plays an instrument, or knows origami will contribute a fascinating element to the classroom.

Some parents may be particularly interested in the direction and content of the curriculum and may want to offer suggestions or ideas. These should be welcomed and incorporated into the program, as appropriate. If, however, the values of a parent seem to be at odds with the program's philosophy, the teacher or director ought to convey that; although she or he respects the parent's views, the school has its own approach founded on child development principles and research. A parent who disagrees with the program's direction has the option of placing the child in another school if the parent is unhappy with that program.

Finally, a project is ended through a summarizing component. Younger children may enact baking in the bakery they have made in the housekeeping area. Older children may have individual and group projects they would like to share with others. Visitors also may be invited to see the children's creations—and to taste them. Usually, the teacher also evaluates the children's response to the project and makes notes about changes for future years.

ACTIVITIES

The smallest element of curriculum planning is the activity, the actual play in which the children will be involved. It is important to be aware of the objectives of a given activity as well as to think through how the activity will be carried out so that the children will gain the knowledge and skills you would like them to acquire. The lesson plan in Exhibit 8-4 describes that day's activities in some detail. Would you, walking into the classroom for which that lesson plan was developed, be able to assume responsibility for some of the activities?

STAFF PLANNING

It is helpful if the staff members who work with the same group of children can plan together. Working as a group ensures that all teachers are familiar with objectives and activities, because they took part in their development. It can also lead to greater commitment to the program because everyone's ideas were incorporated. The teachers' personal investment in the curriculum can contribute to the overall cohesiveness of the program.

KEY **POINTS OF CHAPTER 8**

PLAY

▲ 1. Play provides many opportunities for children to learn, to practise skills, stretch thinking abilities, work through emotions, socialize, and be creative.

▲ 2. There are a number of theories and definitions of play. Theorists seem to agree that there are six characteristics of play.

▲ 3. Play in infancy differs from the play of older children.

▲ 4. Play can be categorized by its social characteristics (six types) and its cognitive characteristics (four types).

DEVELOPMENTALLY APPROPRIATE PROGRAMS

▲ 5. Quality early childhood education programs are developmentally appropriate: they are age-appropriate and individually appropriate.

▲ 6. Quality programs confront bias and reflect multiculturalism.

COMPONENTS OF THE EARLY CHILDHOOD PROGRAM

▲ 7. The program varies with children's ages, but there are some common components in most early childhood programs.

▲ 8. One of the largest time blocks in the early childhood schedule for preschoolers and school-aged children is activity time, during which children select from a variety of developmentally appropriate activities.

▲ 9. Large-group times, when teachers and children gather together, can serve a variety of purposes and include many types of activities.

▲10. During small-group activities, a teacher usually presents a concept to a few children, ensuring that the activity matches their abilities and interests.

▲11. Large time blocks should also be set aside for outdoor activities.

▲12. Other important components that must be considered in scheduling include clean-up, meals, nap, and transitions.

GUIDELINES FOR PROGRAM PLANNING

▲13. In planning a schedule, it is important to balance times when children are active and when they are quiet.

▲14. There should also be a balance between child-initiated and teacher-initiated activities to allow children enough time to make decisions and exercise their growing autonomy.

▲15. The activity level of the children is another consideration in making scheduling decisions.

▲16. The age of the children will have a significant impact on the program. Infants have very limited attentional skills and multiple caretaking needs. Older children have longer attention spans and are more competent with some routines.

▲17. Creative scheduling can provide an effective way of working with large groups of children.

▲18. The schedule also needs to take into account whether children all arrive at school at the same time or whether, as in most child care centres, their arrival is staggered over a period of time.

▲19. In locations where the weather gets very cold or very hot in winter or summer, the schedule may need to be adjusted to include less outdoor time.

▲20. Teachers must be sensitive to times when children have to wait unnecessarily. Wasted time can affect children in negative ways.

DEVELOPMENTALLY APPROPRIATE SCHEDULES

▲21. Schedules will always vary with the age of the children.

▲22. A good schedule takes into account not only the needs of the children but also those of the teachers.

▲23. Young children need the security of a predictable schedule, but the schedule should never be rigid. For instance, activities can be prolonged if the children are engrossed or shortened if they are inattentive.

WHAT IS CURRICULUM?

▲24. Early childhood professionals view curriculum as dealing with the "whole child," rather than only one facet such as intellectual development.

▲25. Curriculum involves consideration of the program philosophy, goals and objectives, and evaluation.

KEY TERMS

activity time

associative play

constructive play

cooperative play

curriculum

developmentally
    appropriate practice

dramatic play

functional play

games with rules

large-group time

lesson plan

onlooker play

parallel play

practice play

pretend play

project

small-group activity time

solitary play

symbolic play

theme

unit

unoccupied behaviour

▲26. Particularly important is the match between the children's developmental levels, abilities, needs, and interests and the curriculum. This involves understanding child development principles and knowing the characteristics of individual children in the group.

▲27. Relevant curriculum for young children is derived from the children's life experiences and can revolve around the children themselves, their families, and the community.

PLANNING THE CURRICULUM

▲28. Planning also varies with the ages of the children in the program.

▲29. Projects and themes are useful with older preschoolers and school-aged children.

▲30. Daily lesson plans, by specifying activities and objectives, provide the working document from which the program is run.

KEY QUESTIONS

1. Visit an early childhood program and observe the children at play. Look for examples of the types of play we discussed in this chapter. Do you see a relationship between age and type of play?

2. Observe the dramatic play area in an early childhood centre and record the types of play you see. Also watch to see if there is any teacher involvement in the play. Do you agree or disagree with what you saw? Relate your observations to Smilansky's concerns.

3. Visit an early childhood program and look at its program. What elements are included? Does the program seem developmentally appropriate by taking into account the needs of the children? Does it provide the kind of balance discussed in this chapter? Would you change anything in this program? Why or why not?

4. Using your knowledge of how children learn best, consider the issue of child-initiated versus teacher-initiated activity. Do you think there should be more time for children to make decisions and exercise independence, or do you think more teacher control is important? Note that there is no general consensus of this issue. Discuss it with others in your class and consider both sides.

5. You probably know children like Rita (see A Closer Look in this chapter), ones who spend most of their day in a child care centre. How are the needs of these children met? In what ways can the schedule take the children's needs into consideration?

6. What are your memories of your earliest school experiences? What kinds of activities were involved? Can you glean from your recollections what type of curriculum your preschool or child care or kindergarten teacher might have been following?

7. What are some of the unique features of your community? Which would interest young children? Think of several ways in which your community can be the basis for relevant learning for preschoolers.

THE PHYSICAL ENVIRONMENT

Today, many young children spend the bulk of their waking hours in an early childhood program, often in one room for nine or ten hours every weekday. They spend some time in the outside play area and occasionally go on excursions into the community, but, by and large, most time for many young children is spent in a relatively confined space.

From research we know that the physical environment affects children's behaviour (Thomson & Ashton-Lilo, 1983). In fact, some theorists propose that **place identity** should be considered part of self-identity, because it contributes to a definition of who the person is. Place identity is integral to self-identity because it is within the environmental context that children's needs are met, that they develop mastery and competence, and that they gain control over the physical world (Proshansky & Fabian, 1987). It is, therefore, extremely important to consider physical environment, its arrangement, and its contents.

1. First we will discuss how the physical environment affects both children and adults.

2. Next we will explore the importance of the indoor environment, focusing on how to use it to most effectively support the development of young children.

3. We will also examine the outdoor environment and how to maximize its potential.

4. Occasionally the environment must be adapted to meet the requirements of children with special needs, as we will consider.

5. We will look at criteria for selecting developmentally appropriate equipment, with particular emphasis on the role of computers in early childhood programs.

6. Our last section will examine criteria for selecting appropriate materials for use in early childhood programs.

EFFECTS OF THE PHYSICAL ENVIRONMENT

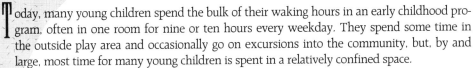

Take a moment to think about a place where you enjoy spending time. What is it about this place that makes it enjoyable? What are its appealing features? Is it because this place is relaxing and soothing, stimulating and exciting, thought-provoking and

challenging, orderly and methodical, comfortable and homey, colourful and bright? Now think about a place that you do not particularly like, and consider why it is unappealing to you. It may be that this place is boring, messy, stark, disorganized, dark, or uninviting. Think about spending all day in each of these places. What feelings and attitudes does this idea evoke? How do you think you will act and react in each place? Can you draw some conclusions about how and why the environment affects you? According to researchers (Kounin & Sherman, 1979), when children are in a particular **behaviour setting** they behave in a manner appropriate to that locale, following what might be viewed as unspoken rules.

> It is apparent that preschoolers behave "schoolish" when in a preschool. They are diligent creatures who spend 95% of their time actively occupied with the facilities provided and they deal with the facilities appropriately. They do all of these things in a sort of unwritten private contract between themselves and the setting they enter; teachers and peers infrequently exert any pressure to either enter or leave these settings (p. 146).

Such research underscores the importance of providing an environment that supports development and learning. If children's engagement in activities is to a large measure prompted by the environment, then it is incumbent upon teachers to provide the most appropriate setting possible.

The quality of the environment has an impact on the behaviour of children as well as adults who spend their time in that space (Kritchevsky, Prescott, & Walling, 1977). "Arrangement, organization, size, density, noise level, even the color of the classroom directly and indirectly invite a range of behaviors from children and teachers" (Thomson & Ashton-Lilo, 1983, p. 94).

EFFECT OF THE ENVIRONMENT ON CHILDREN

The early childhood environment should support the development of children. It has a direct effect on how children behave toward each other. Positive peer interaction is promoted when children are not crowded, when an ample number and variety of items are available, and when socially oriented materials are provided. Classroom arrangement and careful selection of materials also foster cognitive development by providing opportunities for children to classify, find relationships, measure, compare, match, sort, and label (Weinstein, 1987). The environment also enhances both fine and gross motor development through a range of appropriately challenging equipment and materials.

Children's growing sense of independence is supported when they can confidently and competently use equipment and when space and materials are arranged so they can see what is available and make autonomous choices. At the same time, children develop a sense of responsibility when the environment makes it clear how and where materials are to be returned when they finish using them. Children are more productively involved in activities when the purpose of classroom spaces is clearly defined and when materials are developmentally appropriate (Phyfe-Perkins, 1980; Thomson & Ashton-Lilo, 1983). Children are also more likely to follow classroom rules when the environment reinforces these; for instance, if it is important for reasons of safety that children not run inside, classroom furnishings should be arranged in a way that makes walking, rather than running, natural.

The environment also enhances children's self-esteem when it is designed with their needs and development in mind, when it provides space for personal belongings, and when it promotes competence by allowing children to function independently (Weinstein, 1987). In addition, the environment should convey a sense of security and comfort through a friendly, warm, and inviting atmosphere; and through "soft" elements such as beanbag chairs, carpeting, or sling swings (Jones & Prescott, 1978; Weinstein, 1987).

EFFECT OF THE ENVIRONMENT ON TEACHERS

When the environment is set up to maximize children's development, prevent problem behaviours, and promote appropriate behaviours, teachers' well-being will be indirectly supported. More directly, teachers' jobs are made more pleasant if they work in aesthetically pleasing surroundings, if they have a designated space where they can relax and plan, and if their needs are generally taken into consideration (Thomson & Ashton-Lilo, 1983). Both personal comfort and professional needs should be supported (Harms & Clifford, 1980). Environmental factors such as pleasant temperature, light, colour, sound absorption, ventilation, and spatial arrangement can facilitate or hinder staff in carrying out their jobs (Jorde-Bloom, 1988). Thus, a carefully arranged environment can help prevent teacher burn-out by supporting teachers' goals for the children and by making the work site a pleasant place to be.

ARRANGING THE INDOOR ENVIRONMENT

As we consider the indoor environment, we must take into account both its fixed features—for instance, size and shape of the room, placement of windows and doors, built-in features such as shelves and storage spaces—and its movable or semi-fixed features, such as arrangement of furnishings and materials, colour, and texture (Phyfe-Perkins, 1980).

FIXED FEATURES

Room size will, to a large extent, dictate how many children and how much material can be housed in the space. Minimal standards governing the maximum number of children allowed in an area is prescribed by licensing regulations. As you know from Chapter 4, at least 2.75 m² per child of indoor space is required in Canada, but up to 5 m² is mandatory in some locations. Some experts recommend as much as 9 to 10 m² per child (Spodek, 1985). Although the research on the effects of crowding is not clear-cut (Phyfe-Perkins, 1980; Smith & Connolly, 1980), Phyfe-Perkins concludes that "crowding of children which provides less than 25 square feet per child [2.3 m²] for an extended period of time should be avoided. It may increase aggressive behaviour and inhibit social interaction and involvement" (p. 103).

The shape of the room has an impact on arrangement and supervision. A rectangular room seems more adaptable than a square one, and an L-shaped room poses more problems for supervision (Mayesky, 1990). To some extent, room arrangement will be affected by the amount of natural light available through windows. For instance, colour used during art activities is enhanced by clear, bright light; thus, it is desirable to locate the art area near windows. Areas in which children need to attend to close detail, such as the book or language centre, should also be located in a well-lit place. All areas of a room should be well lit, and places not reached by natural light should be provided with adequate electric lighting.

Building materials have an effect on acoustics. Some rooms are constructed with sound-absorbing ceiling, floor, or wall materials, whereas others seem to reverberate with noise. If the room's noise level hinders rather than enhances the children's participation in activities and the communication process, added features such as drapes, carpets, and corkboards can help eliminate much of the noise.

Because many young children's activities are messy, it is important to have water accessible, preferably in the room. Sensory activities, the art centre, and cooking projects should be placed near the water source. If there is no running water in or adjacent to the room, an alternate arrangement, for instance, a bucket with soapy water and paper towels, should be close at hand, but, of course, it will have to be changed frequently.

Rooms with built-in storage units, should be arranged to best utilize these units. Shelves that are placed at child level should hold materials the children use every day, for instance, blocks, manipulatives, or art implements. Besides built-in storage, easily reachable portable units should be added as needed. If built-in storage space is above the children's reach, such shelves can be used for teacher materials or items not used every day.

MOVABLE FEATURES

More than a room's fixed features, it is the movable elements that allow you to arrange a well-planned, developmentally appropriate environment for children. Placement and grouping of equipment and furnishings communicate many messages. They convey the purpose of spaces, set limits on behaviour, indicate how many children can comfortably use an area, establish boundaries, invite possible combinations of play through juxtaposition of areas, and encourage quiet or active involvement. Research has provided some guidelines for maximizing the effective use of space.

Phyfe-Perkins (1980), in a review of studies that examine the effect of physical arrangements on children's behaviour, proposes some helpful principles:

- Children in full-day care need privacy; thus, places where children can be alone should be provided in the environment.
- Soft areas such as beanbag chairs, pillows, or rugs allow children to snuggle and find comfort if "adult laps are in short supply" (p. 103).
- Small, enclosed areas promote quiet activities as well as interaction among small groups of children.
- Physical boundaries around areas can reduce distraction, which, in turn, increases attention to activities.
- Large spaces allow for active, large-group activities that are more boisterous and noisy.
- Clearly organized play space and clear paths can result in fewer disruptions and more goal-directed behaviour.

Elizabeth Prescott (1987), one of the leading researchers on effective environments for young children, suggests that recurring guidance or curriculum problems can quite often be resolved by rearranging the classroom. She advises teachers to examine classroom pathways from a child's eye level to ensure that they are clearly defined, that all areas have a path leading to them, and that they are not obstructed.

If, for example, you find that children hardly ever use an area, maybe there is no clear path leading to it. At one child care centre, the little-used science table had been placed against the wall behind the door. When it was relocated to a more readily accessible place, the children's interest in science increased dramatically and science became a more important part of the curriculum. Similarly, Wright (1983) describes several

physical changes to the environment at the UWO program that led to mo
play. For example, moving the dramatic play area away from the entry are
children into more private types of play early in the day and more active, so
later.

LEARNING CENTRES

Indoor space is often organized into **learning centres** (also called interest or activity areas), which combine materials and equipment around common activities. Learning centres can include art, manipulatives, dramatic play, sensory experiences, blocks, music, science, math, computers, books, language arts, woodworking, cooking, and a variety of other areas that fit the unique interests, developmental needs, and characteristics of a group of children and teachers (Essa & Rogers, 1992).

Learning centres allow children to make choices from a range of available, developmentally appropriate activities. A curriculum based on learning centres can be considered responsive to the children because it is designed to meet and respond to their specific needs and experiences (Myers & Maurer, 1987). Yet, although learning centres and their activities are planned, structured, set up, and facilitated by teachers, the children determine how to engage in and carry out the activity (Spodek, 1985).

One useful tool in arranging a room into learning centres is to draw a scale model of the classroom, with fixed features such as doors, windows, and built-in furnishings marked. You can then pencil in furniture until you find a workable arrangement. A more time-consuming method that allows extensive spatial experimentation is to make scale models of the furniture and manipulate these on your classroom drawing. Commercial classroom planning guides are also available, which include room layouts and a wide variety of scaled equipment cutouts (one such guide is available from Environments, Inc., P.O. Box 1348, Beaufort, SC 29901). Exhibit 9-1 offers some suggested guidelines to keep in mind when arranging a classroom.

SAFETY

It is also important to be aware of safety considerations when arranging and equipping an early childhood classroom and a playground (Click & Click, 1990). Building codes, fire regulations, and the child care legislation spell out *minimum* requirements. But beyond these, additional measures can protect children from foreseeable accidents. Clearly marked emergency exit routes should be posted and familiar to teachers and children alike, and regularly inspected fire extinguishers and smoke detectors should be in each room. Fire-retardant carpets, fabrics, and furnishings should be used.

Walls and other surfaces should be painted with lead-free paint. Any potentially hazardous substance, such as medicines and cleaners, should be safely stored. Electrical outlets should be covered. Sharp edges should be eliminated from all furniture. Any lightweight equipment should be anchored so it cannot be knocked or pulled over during vigorous play. In addition, when the classroom is carefully arranged with clearly defined learning areas and paths, the number of accidents will be minimized.

Often, unseen environmental pollutants can also pose a hazard to young children (Noyes, 1987). Because of their immature bodily systems and small size, young children are much more vulnerable than adults to inhaling and absorbing pollutants. In recent years, we have become more aware of the dangers of asbestos, lead, pesticides, and other invisible chemicals. You may wish to consult Noyes (1987) for suggestions on how to reduce air pollution.

ES FOR ORGANIZING CLASSROOM SPACE

nt should reflect the program's
gram's aim is to foster indepen-
g, self-help skills, positive self-
 action, and more child-initiated
activities, this should be pro-
rrangement.

dren's ages and developmental
As children get older, provide more choices, a
more complex environment, and greater opportunity
for social play. For young preschoolers, it is best to
offer a simple, uncluttered, clearly defined classroom
with space for large motor activity.

3. Any environment in which children as well as adults
spend blocks of time should be attractive and aesthetically pleasing. Thought and care should be given to
such factors as the arrangement of furnishings, use of
colours and textures, and display of artwork. Plants
and flowers added to the classroom can enhance its
attractiveness.

4. If children are encouraged to make independent
choices, then materials should be stored at a level
where children can easily see, reach, and return them.

5. If children are to develop self-help skills, toileting
facilities and cubbies for coats and boots should be
accessible to them. Access to learning materials also
contributes to development of self-help skills.

6. If the program supports a positive self-concept in children, then there should be individual places for children's belongings, for their projects or art to be
saved, and for their work to be displayed.

7. If development of social skills and friendships is
encouraged, then the environment should be set up to
allow children to participate in activities with small
groups of other children without undue interference
or disruption.

8. If children are to have many opportunities to select
and direct their own activities, then the environment
should be set up to offer a variety of activity choices.

9. There should be places for children to be alone if they
so wish. Quiet, private spaces can be planned as part
of the environment, for instance, a corner with large
pillows, a cozy spot in the library area, or a designated rocking chair with cushions.

10. There should be "soft" places in the environment
where children can snuggle and find comfort.

11. An environment set up into learning centres should
have clearly marked boundaries that indicate the
space designated for each given area. Storage shelves
and other furnishings can be used to define the
edges.

12. Paths to each area should be clear and unobstructed.
Children are less likely to use areas that are hard to
reach.

13. A pathway to one area should never go through
another activity centre. This only interferes with ongoing play and can cause anger and frustration.

14. Doorways and other exits should be unobstructed.

15. Quiet activities should be grouped near each other,
and noisy ones should be placed at some distance
from these. The block area should not be next to the
book area, for example.

16. Group those activities that have common elements
near each other to extend children's play possibilities.
Blocks and dramatic play are often placed next to
each other to encourage exchange of props and ideas.

17. Provide areas for individual, small-group, and large-
group activities by setting up different-sized centres.

18. Some areas require more space than others. Block
play, for instance, is enhanced by ample room to build
and expand block structures.

19. The sizes of various learning centres will, to some
extent, convey how many children can play in each
area and how active that play should be. Small, cozy
areas set natural limits on the number of children and
the activity level, whereas large areas send the opposite message.

20. Decrease noise level by using carpeting or area rugs
in noisy centres such as the block area.

21. Place messy activities near a water source.

22. Place activities that are enhanced by natural light near
windows. Ensure that all areas are well lit, however.

23. Place tables and chairs in or near centres where tabletop activities are carried out. For instance, tables
should be placed in the art and manipulative areas but
are not needed in the large block centre. Tables scat-
tered through the room can take on an added use during snack time.

24. Consider multipurpose uses for space, especially
where room size is restricted. When your room allows
for a limited number of areas to be set at any one
time, some of these might be used for more than one
activity. For instance, the area designated for large-
group activities might also be the block area, music
centre, or place set aside for large motor activity.

25. Some learning centres may not be part of the classroom on a daily basis. Such centres as woodworking,
music, or cooking may be brought into the classroom
on a less frequent schedule or may be rotated with
other areas for specified periods of time.

26. Be flexible in use of space and open to rearranging it.
As children mature and their interests change, so
should the centre. Also, if repeated problems arise, try
solving these by rearranging the environment.

27. Safety should be an overriding, primary concern in
setting up an environment for young children.

In addition, be aware of the children's safety at all times. Clothing can be hazardous. Long scarves, for example, have been responsible for the accidental deaths of several Canadian children in recent years. Skirts can be a problem on climbers, as can shoes without proper treads. Hooks and strings on clothing also can cause accidents.

ARRANGING THE OUTDOOR ENVIRONMENT

Just as the indoor space is arranged with care and thought, considering the children's needs and developmental levels, so should the outdoor environment be carefully designed. Steen Esbensen (1987), from the University of Quebec at Hull, who comments in A Canadian Professional Speaks Out, has prepared an excellent outdoor planning resource, *The Early Childhood Playground: An Outdoor Classroom*, which you

 ## A CANADIAN PROFESSIONAL SPEAKS OUT

Playing Outdoors: Time, Space, and a Positive Attitude

In the mid-1990s close to 200 000 young children between 6 months and 5 years of age will attend an early childhood program in Canada. Some of these children will spend up to 12 000 hours of the first five years of their lives in the care of early childhood educators or other private care providers. This is more than the collective time that they will spend in school for the next twelve years. Increasingly, young children spend their early years in day care centres, family day care homes, or alternative care arrangements. Some travel great distances to the child care centres, others remain close to home in the residential community. What they have in common, however, is that the physical space in which they live has largely been built based on standards established in the 1960s that may not respond to the needs of the 21st century.

Standards for outdoor play areas in North America range between 20 and 25 m² per child in licensed day care centres. These requirements have remained unchanged and relatively unchallenged since the early 1960s. In 1984 the Child Welfare League of America (CWLA) recommended that 60 m² of space per child be available for outdoor play. Unfortunately, the minimal outdoor space required by licensing standards is often waived and many centres do not have space readily accessible for children to play outdoors. Experience and research have shown that the CWLA recommendation is legitimate; unfortunately, in most cases, land is no

longer available and children and early childhood educators are forced to spend the majority of their time indoors. In 1991, the Canadian Institute of Child Health undertook a National Survey of Day Care Centres to assess the types of physical activity programs available. Almost 50 percent of respondents reported that they had no outdoor gross motor play activity area and a significant number (60 percent) reported that children spend less than 10 percent of time in structured outdoor gross motor play and 36 percent of respondents spend less than 10 percent of time in free outdoor gross motor play.

Playing outdoors in all seasons has to become an integral part of the daily lives of young children. Research evidence confirms that regular physical activity started early in childhood is essential to building healthy and vigorous adults.

Playing outdoors requires a positive attitude toward the importance of play, and early childhood educators have a critical role to play in changing attitudes and professional practice, which has more often than not neglected the outdoor play experience. In addition to attitude, time and space are essential ingredients to making outdoor play experiences possible for the children of the next century. Hopefully it will not be too late to secure some high-quality outdoor play experiences for young children growing up in day care centres.

Steen B. Esbensen
Université du Québec à Hull
Hull, Québec

will want to consult if you are planning for the outdoors. Like the teachers in the British open model, Esbensen sees the outdoors as an extension of the classroom, not just a place "to blow off steam" and exercise large muscles. It should provide opportunities that enhance socialization, cognitive and language development, sensory exploration, creative expression, and an appreciation of nature. It should also be aesthetically pleasing.

Unfortunately, too often outdoor areas are literally set in concrete, leaving little room for versatility and rearrangement. Most early childhood playgrounds come equipped with either traditional structures such as metal swings, slides, and climbers or with more contemporary **playscapes**, which combine a variety of materials and allow for a range of activities. Such equipment must meet standards of safety and developmental appropriateness. Beyond the immovable components of the outdoor space, however, various elements can enhance and expand children's play, as we will discuss.

FIXED OUTDOOR PLAY STRUCTURES

In the early decades of this century, when the playground movement took root in this country, outdoor play areas were generally equipped with swings, slides, seesaws, and sandboxes, not so different from many playgrounds today (Eriksen, 1985). But design of play structures has also come a long way from such traditional, single-purpose pieces of equipment. Through the efforts of child development specialists, professional playground architects, and commercial equipment developers, far more creative and versatile play structures are now available.

Many of today's **creative playgrounds** contain equipment constructed of such materials as tires, cargo nets, railroad ties, telephone poles, large cable spools, barrels, and drainage pipes. A European variation is the **adventure playground** in which children use a wide range of available "junk" materials to create their own environments (Frost & Henniger, 1982). In fact, research has shown that children engage in a wider variety of social interactions, greater language usage, and more originality on innovative rather than on traditional playgrounds (Hayward, Rothenburg, & Beasley, 1974). Where traditional structures were primarily constructed of metal, which could become dangerously hot or very cold during weather extremes, new equipment materials include a variety of treated wood surfaces and "space-age plastics" (Frost & Wortham, 1988).

Just because equipment is contemporary, however, does not necessarily make it developmentally appropriate or safe (Frost & Klein, 1979). Some guidelines can help ensure that outdoor equipment provides suitable play space for young children.

- Because large structures are relatively fixed in the function they serve, they should be complex in design. For example, while encouraging a wide range of motor skills, they might also provide some open spaces underneath for dramatic play (Frost & Wortham, 1988).

- Play equipment should provide graduated challenges, offering activities that allow for safe risk taking for children of different ages and developmental levels (Moore, Goltsman, & Iacofano, 1987). An outdoor play area used by a range of children could, for instance, include one gently sloped and one taller, more steeply angled slide; balance beams of different widths; or steps as well as ladders leading to raised platforms.

- Play structures should promote social interaction rather than competition among children. Wide slides, for example, encourage two or three children to slide down together; tire swings invite several children to cooperatively pump; and added props encourage dramatic play. At the same time, there should also be provision for privacy if children want to be alone.

- A final, important factor is the safety of outdoor play equipment. Equipment should be securely anchored to the ground and in good repair with no sharp edges, broken or splintered elements, loose nuts and bolts, or openings that could trap a child's head, fingers, hands, or feet. Swing seats should be made of lightweight material. Climbing heights should not exceed the reaching height of the children (Frost & Henniger, 1982; Frost & Wortham, 1988). The surfacing material under swings and climbers should cushion children when they fall. In some parts of the country, spiders and other insects like to nest in play equipment, such as tires; thus, frequent safety checks should be carried out. Tires can also trap water, which then stagnates and attracts mosquitos in some areas of Canada; drilling drainage holes into the bottoms of tires eliminates the problem.

FLEXIBLE OUTDOOR PLAY COMPONENTS AND SEASONAL CONSIDERATIONS

Although not many adjustments can be made with the large equipment, the outdoor environment still can be arranged to enhance and support children's development. By adding equipment and materials, capitalizing on the natural features of the play space, and creating interest areas, the outdoor play space can be made more exciting and flexible.

A variety of movable large equipment components can be added to the outdoor area. When large crates, sawhorses, ladders, ramps, balance beams, tires, pulleys, hollow blocks, or cardboard boxes are provided, children will find a variety of creative ways to incorporate these into their play. Such movable components give children the opportunity to structure and arrange their own environment.

An outdoor play area should also take advantage of all available natural features—physical contours, plants, and surfaces. A small hill, for example, can let children experience gathering momentum as they run or roll down, or it can be used as the site for a tunnel. A large, grassy area is ideal for large-group movement, ball toss, or parachute activities.

Trees provide shade; shrubs and flowers add to the aesthetic and sensory pleasures of the yard. A flower, vegetable, or herb garden that the children help tend can provide a meaningful science experience, and often attracts parent volunteers. Multiple surfaces such as fine sand for digging, cement on which to ride tricycles, pea gravel or wood shavings under large equipment, grass to sit on, dirt to make mud with, textured paving stones to touch with hands or bare feet—all add to making the outdoor area a good learning environment.

The playground should also accommodate all indoor curriculum areas, for instance, art, music, science, or story time. "The good contemporary playground contains nooks and crannies, amphitheatre areas, tables, benches, and so on for full exploration of these subjects" (Frost & Wortham, 1988, p. 26). Woodworking, sand, water, and other sensory activities are also portable and very suitable additions to the outdoor environment. An outdoor area can also be enhanced by creating defined learning centres that are more permanent, similar to those used indoors. One school used this approach in its outdoor area, as A Closer Look (p. 234) describes.

Of course, in winter, children are unlikely to want to paint or read stories outdoors! In fact, outdoor play during the cold months needs to be very active. Sleds, toboggans, and shovels are a source of delight, as long as you have snow. During the cold days, when there is no snow, however, teachers have to be more innovative.

A CLOSER LOOK

A Playground for Learning

St. Elizabeth's Child Care Centre, in a metropolitan community in northern California, serves a large population of children from low-income families. Several years ago, one of the staff members was particularly interested in transforming the original blacktop playground—with its traditional swings, slides, and jungle gyms—into a more exciting and flexible outdoor area that would enhance and extend learning. She devised a plan that, through extensive fundraising and cooperative efforts of staff, parents, and the community, eventually became a reality.

This new outdoor area now includes multiple, well-defined learning centres. Included in this carefully and aesthetically landscaped space are an amphitheatre for storytelling and dramatic play; a fenced animal care area for rabbits; a covered art area; a "freeway" network of paths for riding toys; an extensive sand area; a woodworking centre; a "meditation garden" or quiet area surrounding a shady willow tree; a boat-shaped centre with props and equipment for housekeeping dramatic play as well as a car engine with which children can tinker; a five-opening drainage pipe tunnel; and many places that can be used to climb, swing, and build. Storage spaces are provided wherever materials and props are needed.

Building materials throughout the area were selected and arranged to provide various textures, multiple sizes, and aesthetic appeal. Equipment was selected to encourage children to observe and classify, make comparisons, and note similarities and differences. Movable equipment such as planks and tires were added to promote problem-solving skills. In addition, this outdoor play area is a delight to the senses, with its dwarf-tree fruit orchard, vegetable garden, strawberry patch, raised herb garden for easy sniffing, and flower beds, all of which children and teachers help tend. This playground has a wide range of activities to engage children, activities that promote all areas of development. Through the imaginative planning of one teacher and the efforts of the many people who helped make it a reality, this playground has enriched the play of many young children (Essa, 1981).

Not all early childhood programs have the luxury of such an exciting playground, because each school is unique in its approach as well as limited by space, weather, funding, and other resources. All playgrounds have the potential to be improved, however, through added movable props, enhancement of natural features, and arrangement of learning centres.

Walks, searches, and other large-muscle activities are enjoyed. Older children also like a trip to the local arena or pond.

ADAPTING THE ENVIRONMENT

Increasingly, early childhood programs are integrating children with disabilities into their facilities. It is important when children are mainstreamed to provide a suitable environment in which all of the children can experience appropriate challenges and successes. Children with disabilities "need to play ... but, because of personal, social, and physical barriers, it is more difficult for these needs to be fulfilled" (Frost & Klein, 1979, p. 220). Some suggested adaptations for children with physical and visual disabilities follow.

Children with severe physical limitations need specialized equipment, such as special chairs, to maximize their participation in activities. Children who rely on wheelchairs or walkers for mobility need wide paths and entries to learning centres. Activities and shelves should be easy to reach. Similarly, outdoor activities and equipment must be accessible through such modifications as wide, gently sloped ramps with handrails; raised sand areas; or sling swings that provide secure body support.

Children with visual impairments require a consistent, uncluttered, and clearly arranged environment that they can recognize through touch. Landmarks such as specific equipment or furniture, and a sensory-rich environment with varying textures, can help children with visual impairments orient themselves inside or outside (Frost & Klein, 1979).

The environment should always be responsive to all children. Each child is unique, and the play environment should be versatile enough to provide a rich variety of sensory stimuli, opportunities for independent choice, and a range of experiences for all. A sensitive staff and a responsive environment can help make the early childhood experience of children with disabilities as beneficial as possible.

DEVELOPMENTALLY APPROPRIATE EQUIPMENT

Early childhood **equipment** refers to furniture and other large items that represent the more expensive long-term investments in an early childhood facility; **materials** refers to the smaller, often expendable items that are replaced and replenished more frequently. Because it is expensive, equipment needs to be acquired carefully. Exhibit 9-2 lists basic equipment that should be included in a classroom for preschool-aged children.

CRITERIA FOR SELECTING EQUIPMENT

Some important questions to ask when selecting equipment include the following:

- Does this piece of equipment support the program's philosophy?
- Is the equipment appropriately sized for the children?
- Is the equipment safe?
- Is the equipment durable?
- Is there room for this equipment?
- Can the equipment be constructed rather than purchased?
- Is the equipment aesthetically pleasing?
- Is the equipment easy to clean and maintain?

COMPUTERS

Over the past decade, early childhood programs have been investing in the purchase of computers and software for children's use. A growing number of people have achieved **computer literacy**; in other words, they are knowledgeable about and capable of using a computer. It is often argued that young children are entering a world in which familiarity with computers will be a prerequisite for effective functioning; therefore,

EXHIBIT 9-2 BASIC EQUIPMENT AND MATERIALS FOR A PRESCHOOL CLASSROOM

A classroom of 16 to 20 young children should include, but not be restricted to, the following pieces of equipment:

EQUIPMENT	MATERIALS
BASIC FURNITURE	
▪ 3–4 tables that each seat 6–8 (round, rectangular, or both) for meals and activities, as needed ▪ 24–28 chairs ▪ 1 rocking chair ▪ 16–20 cubbies, one for each child, to store personal belongings	▪ Beanbag chairs, pillows ▪ Bulletin boards
DRAMATIC PLAY CENTRE	
▪ 1 small table ▪ 2–4 chairs ▪ 4 appliances ▪ 1 large mirror ▪ 1 ironing board ▪ 4–6 dolls, different ethnic groups, both sexes ▪ 1 doll bed or crib	▪ Dress-up clothes, both men's and women's ▪ Empty food containers ▪ Set of dishes, pots/pans ▪ Telephones ▪ Doll clothes, blankets ▪ Dramatic play kits with props for selected themes
ART CENTRE	
▪ 2 easels, two-sided ▪ 1 storage shelf for materials	▪ Variety of paper, paints, crayons, scissors, glue, collage materials, clay
BLOCK CENTRE	
▪ 1 set unit blocks, 250 to 300 pieces, 12 shapes ▪ 1 set hollow blocks ▪ 1 set cardboard blocks ▪ 3–6 large wooden vehicles	▪ Various props, including animals, vehicles, people, and furniture
MANIPULATIVE CENTRE	
▪ 1 storage shelf with individual storage bins	▪ Wide variety of puzzles, pegboards, construction toys, parquetry, beads, lotto, and other games
SENSORY CENTRE	
▪ 1 sand and water table ▪ Plastic bins	▪ Variety of props such as deep funnels, hoses, measuring cups, water-wheels, scoops, containers, shovels
LANGUAGE CENTRE	
▪ 1 bookshelf ▪ 1 large flannel board ▪ 1 tape recorder ▪ 1 puppet theatre	▪ Wide variety of books ▪ File of flannel-board stories ▪ Writing materials ▪ Variety of puppets
SCIENCE AND MATH CENTRE	
▪ Animal homes such as aquarium or cages	▪ Animals ▪ Plants, garden supplies ▪ Wide variety of natural materials found in nearby environment ▪ Variety of scientific instruments such as microscopes, magnifiers, magnets, thermometers

EQUIPMENT	MATERIALS
	▪ Variety of math materials such as attribute blocks, Cuisinaire rods, items to sort, classify, or seriate, calendars, timers ▪ Variety of old mechanical objects to take apart, such as clocks, watches, cameras, or locks
MUSIC CENTRE ▪ 1 record player ▪ 1 set rhythm instruments ▪ 1 Autoharp ▪ 3–4 tonal instruments such as xylophones or bells ▪ Storage unit for instruments	▪ Variety of records/tapes ▪ Props for movement activities, such as scarves or streamers
WOODWORKING CENTRE ▪ 1 woodworking bench with vise ▪ 1 set tools ▪ 1 tool storage unit	▪ Soft wood scraps ▪ Thick Styrofoam sheets ▪ Variety of nails, screws
OUTDOOR EQUIPMENT ▪ Gross motor equipment that allows children to slide, climb, swing, hang, balance, crawl ▪ 8–10 wheeled vehicles: tricycles, wagons, scooters ▪ A play house or other space for quiet or dramatic play	▪ Sensory materials such as fine-grained sand and access to water (inappropriate weather) ▪ Movable equipment such as crates, planks, cardboard boxes, and tires ▪ Balls, ropes, parachute

NOTE: This suggested equipment and materials list is by no means exhaustive. Many other items could and should be added, selected to suit the program, children, and staff. Consult the discussion of activities in Chapters 10 through 14 for additional suggested materials.

exposure to computers and development of some basic computer skills should be part of early childhood programs.

Various concerns have been raised about the developmental appropriateness of using computers with young children (Barnes & Hill, 1983). However, research shows

that young children are quite competent in using the symbols of computers appropriately (Clements, 1987). When computers first became widespread in early childhood education, an often-heard concern was that their use would be at the expense of peer interaction. This fear has been dispelled by a number of studies that document the positive effects of computers on socialization and cooperation (Essa, 1987; Swigger & Swigger, 1984; Ziajka, 1983). Another concern has been that the computer could decrease participation in other activities, although research has shown that it augments rather than replaces other centres (Essa, 1987).

The computer should be viewed as neither good nor bad but rather as a tool, similar to the many other educational resources used by children. It is the wisdom of teachers—who structure the conditions and setting in which computers are used and who select the software—that makes such activities relevant and worthwhile (Clements, 1987; Haugland & Shade, 1990).

Acquiring a computer for children's use must also be accompanied by purchasing **software**, the set of "instructions" that direct the computer to perform an activity (Davidson, 1989). Software, which is usually stored on a disk that is inserted into the computer, is available through a variety of commercial sources. More and more software packages for young children are being developed and put on the market, too often offering a confusing choice to a novice software buyer. Haugland and Shade (1990), in assessing more than 100 software packages, suggest using the following criteria for judging developmental appropriateness.

1. *Age appropriateness*—The concepts taught and methods presented show realistic expectations of young children.

2. *Child control*—The children, as active participants, not the computer, decide the flow and direction of the activity.

3. *Clear instructions*—Verbal or graphic directions are simple and precise. Written instructions are not appropriate.

4. *Expanding complexity*—Software begins with a child's current skills, then builds on these in a realistic learning sequence.

5. *Independence*—Children are able to use the computer and software with a minimum amount of adult supervision.

6. *Process orientation*—The intrinsic joys of exploring and discovering are what engage children on the computer. Completed work is not the primary objective and extrinsic rewards are unnecessary.

7. *Real-world model*—Objects used in software are reliable models of aspects of the world.

8. *Technical features*—Children's attention is better held by high-quality software, with colourful, uncluttered, animated, and realistic graphics, realistic sound effects, and minimal waiting times.

9. *Trial and error*—Children have unlimited opportunity for creative problem solving, exploring alternatives, and correcting their own errors.

10. *Transformations*—Children are able to change objects and situations and see the effects of their actions.

DEVELOPMENTALLY APPROPRIATE MATERIALS

In addition to the more expensive furnishings and equipment, an early childhood classroom requires a rich variety of play and learning materials. These include commercially purchased items such as puzzles, crayons, or Legos; teacher- or parent-made games and manipulatives; commercial or teacher-assembled kits that put together combinations of items for specific dramatic play themes or flannelboard stories; and donated scrap materials for art or construction activities. Review the recommended basics for an early childhood program listed in Exhibit 9-2.

One special category of learning resources, **Montessori equipment**, stands out because of its specific attributes and prescribed use.

These materials are available, through special catalogues, for use in Montessori programs. Montessori items are of high quality and cost. The Montessori philosophy does not recommend the materials for non-Montessori schools, but many eclectic programs use them. You may want to review the discussion of Maria Montessori's program and its contemporary counterparts in Chapter 3.

CRITERIA FOR SELECTING MATERIALS

More than ever before, a great selection of early childhood materials is commercially available. Toy and variety stores, as well as catalogues, display variously priced toys and games that often promise to fully educate or entertain young children. In selecting learning and play materials, some specific criteria must be met to assure their suitability for young children.

- *Developmentally appropriate*—Materials should match the stage of development of the children. Infants need toys that are responsive to sensorimotor actions, mobiles to see, and bright, durable books and pictures. Toddlers and very young preschoolers just mastering language and locomotion will benefit from play items that encourage vocabulary building, promote a sense of balance, exercise fingers, and feed their burgeoning sense of independence. Older preschoolers, on the other hand, need materials that utilize their more refined skills in all areas of development. All preschool materials, however, should actively involve children, be interesting, and be safe.

- *Active*—Young children need materials that they can act on. They quickly get bored with items that require no action on their part. All early childhood materials should promote active involvement and exploration.

- *Open-ended*—Among the most popular and most frequently used materials are open-ended toys, ones that can be used flexibly and do not dictate how they are to be used. Not all materials in the early childhood program will be open-ended (puzzles, for instance, have only one outcome), but the majority should be.

- *Feedback-oriented*—As children interact with materials, they should receive feedback on the success of their actions. A completed puzzle tells the child that the pieces have been fitted together correctly; when the "bridge" stays up, the child knows that the blocks were stacked successfully; when there is a place setting for each of the four children at the table in the housekeeping area, they know that they have matched children and dishes appropriately.

- *Multipurpose*—Materials or combinations of materials should suggest many possibilities for play. Children's problem-solving skills and imaginations will be enhanced by multipurpose materials. Children of different skill levels should be able to use materials successfully.

- *Safe and durable*—Items purchased for children's use should be sturdy and constructed from high-quality material. Preschoolers should not be given toys that require electricity. All materials should be checked regularly for loose parts, sharp edges, splinters, or chipping paint.

- *Attractive and aesthetically pleasing*—Materials should be appealing and inviting. Colour, texture, and appearance should be considered when choosing materials in the same way you consider them when redecorating a kitchen.

- *Not stereotyped*—Materials should encourage a sense of equality and tolerance rather than reinforce sexist, racial, or cultural stereotypes.

• *Diverse*—A wide variety of materials that cater to different interests and that meet all developmental needs is necessary. There should be ample materials to develop fine and gross motor skills, to exercise cognitive processes, to promote language use, to encourage socialization, to provide outlets for emotional needs, and to invite creativity. Although variety gives children divergent ways through which they can develop skills, there should also be more than one of some items. This is particularly important with infants and toddlers. However, younger preschoolers, who have not yet mastered the art of sharing, especially need the assurance of multiples of some items.

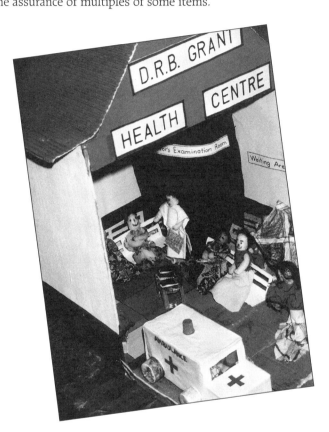

TEACHER-MADE MATERIALS AND RESOURCES

Some of the best early childhood materials are not purchased commercially but are ones that an energetic teacher or parent constructs. Homemade toys often are tailored to fit the specific interests or needs of the children. Many resource books offer excellent suggestions and instructions for games and materials that enhance cognitive concepts, fine or gross motor skills, and language development (Baratta-Lorton, 1979; Debelack, Herr, & Jacobson, 1981; Linderman, 1979).

Teachers also can develop and organize classroom resource materials to facilitate planning and programming. One helpful resource is the dramatic play kit, which contains a collection of props for common dramatic play themes. Contained in individually labelled boxes, such as painted 24-bottle beer cases, dramatic play kits can include some of the following items:

- *Health theme*—bandages, empty syringes, hospital gowns, stethoscope, bandages, empty medicine vials, and similar items donated by local doctors, hospitals, and other health care providers.
- *Bakery theme*—rolling pins, cookie cutters, baking pans, muffin liners, aprons.
- *Self-care theme*—small mirrors, combs, toothbrushes, hair rollers, empty shampoo bottles, and other cosmetic containers.
- *Grocery store theme*—empty food containers, cash register, tape register tapes, bags, play money.
- *Plumbing theme*—taps, connectors, lengths of ABS piping, plugs, wrenches, hardhat.

Another helpful resource is a flannel-board story file. If you keep the flannel-board pieces for each story in an envelope, then they will be readily available when you and the children wish to use them. A similar collection of favourites can be put into a song and fingerplay file. One way to do this is to type the most frequently used songs and fingerplays on file cards, laminate them, punch holes in the upper-left corners, alphabetize the cards, and connect them with a key ring. Newly acquired songs or fingerplays can be added at any time.

Numerous community resources can be tapped for useful materials. Often, their scraps can be an early childhood teacher's treasures. Home-decorating businesses may be able to contribute colour chips and wallpaper or drapery samples. Printing companies may be able to provide trimmings from paper of different colours, sizes, textures, and weights. Carpet salesrooms may make available carpet squares or the heavy inner rolls from carpeting. Businesses that receive copious computer printouts may be able to provide computer printout paper for art and writing projects. Lumber companies are usually willing to share scraps of softwood or wood shavings. Travel agents may have old travel posters and brochures to contribute. It is a good idea to canvas your community for possible resources.

PARENTS AND PROFESSIONALS

Parents' Role in the Early Childhood Environment

Parents can be active participants in matters related to the early childhood environment. To begin with, parents' choice of a preschool or child care centre can be viewed as part of an environmental decision. Early childhood facilities, as part of a larger environment, contribute to and reflect the total character of their community. Often, children's programs mirror the community's purpose and ethnic or cultural characteristics. For instance, there are distinct differences in an inner-city centre, an employer-supported program located on the premises of a factory, a suburban child care facility for dual-income parents, or a bilingual preschool in a predominantly immigrant community. By enrolling their children in their community's early childhood facilities, parents lend support to the wider community (Berns, 1989).

In addition, parents can contribute in a variety of ways to selecting, modifying, or maintaining various aspects of the environment. Some programs have advisory or policy-making parent councils that may be involved in decisions about major purchases or construction. Parents also often have a strong commitment to their children's program and are willing to spend a few weekend hours helping to paint, clean, varnish, or construct. Many parents contribute to their child's centre by making learning materials or contributing throwaways that children can use for creative activities. As in all areas of the early childhood centre's functioning, parents can be a tremendous resource in matters related to the environment.

KEY POINTS OF CHAPTER 9

EFFECTS OF THE PHYSICAL ENVIRONMENT

▲ 1. Because children's engagement in activities depends on the environment, teachers need to provide the most appropriate setting possible for learning.

▲ 2. The environment can help promote or discourage positive peer interaction, independence, and self-esteem in children.

▲ 3. An appropriate environment must also take the needs of teachers into account.

ARRANGING THE INDOOR ENVIRONMENT

▲ 4. Fixed features of a room—such as its size and shape, placement of doors and windows, built-in storage, and water access—must be considered when arranging the indoor space.

▲ 5. An early childhood classroom is made more flexible and can meet the needs of young children by thoughtful arrangement of its movable features such as furniture and equipment.

▲ 6. One effective way of arranging the indoor environment is through organized learning centres that combine materials and equipment around common activities.

▲ 7. Safety should be of primary concern as teachers arrange and equip the classroom.

ARRANGING THE OUTDOOR ENVIRONMENT

▲ 8. The traditional metal swings and slides of many playgrounds are being replaced by more contemporary playscapes.

▲ 9. Guidelines help the early childhood teacher evaluate the safety and developmental appropriateness of outdoor equipment.

▲10. The outdoor environment can be made more flexible by adding movable equipment, by including indoor curriculum activities such as painting or woodworking, and by taking advantage of natural features such as slopes and shady trees. Special consideration has to be given to winter activities.

ADAPTING THE ENVIRONMENT

▲11. There are a variety of ways to adapt the outdoor environment so that children with disabilities can enjoy its use.

DEVELOPMENTALLY APPROPRIATE EQUIPMENT

▲12. Equipment needs to be carefully evaluated to ensure its appropriateness for young children.

▲13. Computers are becoming more prevalent features of early childhood classrooms; in addition, a considerable amount of software has been developed for the use of young children. Software must be carefully evaluated for appropriateness.

DEVELOPMENTALLY APPROPRIATE MATERIALS

▲14. A wide variety of developmentally appropriate learning materials are available commercially; in addition, many programs also include teacher- or parent-made materials.

▲15. Materials need to be carefully selected to ensure that they are developmentally appropriate.

▲16. Teachers may develop classroom resource materials, for instance, dramatic play kits, a flannel-board story file, or a song and fingerplay file.

▲17. Community resources can provide a variety of interesting materials for early childhood programs.

KEY TERMS

adventure playground

behaviour setting

computer literacy

creative playground

equipment

learning centres

materials

Montessori equipment

place identity

playscapes

software

KEY QUESTIONS

1. Talk to two or three children who are 4 or 5 years old. Ask them what they like about their classroom and playground. Are the features they mention ones that you consider particularly interesting and noteworthy? What do their answers tell you about these children's interests, attitudes, and needs in relation to the environment?

2. Spend some time in an early childhood classroom and attune yourself to the environment. What do you like? What do you dislike? How would it feel to work all day in this setting? What changes could make this a more pleasant or accommodating environment for adults?

3. Observe a group of children in an outdoor environment. What kinds of activities are the children involved in? Which developmental needs are being met? If you see little involvement in activities that promote one or several areas of development (for instance, social, language, cognitive), what changes or additions could be made to bring these about?

4. Browse through one of the many catalogues that advertise early childhood materials and equipment. Evaluate several of the items in the catalogue according to the criteria outlined in this chapter for selecting equipment and selecting materials. What conclusions can you draw about selecting developmentally appropriate items for young children?

5. If you have access to a computer and early childhood software, try out one early childhood activity on the computer. After you have mastered the activity, evaluate the software according to the criteria presented in this chapter. What do you think young children will learn from the activity? What feature(s) do you think might be appealing, unappealing, or frustrating to preschoolers?

THE HOW OF EARLY CHILDHOOD EDUCATION—CURRICULUM

We will now turn our attention to the "how" of early childhood education as it applies to teachers and children. In Part 4, we will examine the following aspects of the early childhood program that deal with curriculum:

- Chapter 10, "Creative Development through the Curriculum," will look at ways to enhance children's creativity by providing an accepting, open atmosphere in which children are free to experiment and create.

- Chapter 11, "Physical Development through the Curriculum," will consider the many ways in which movement, the senses, health, and safety are promoted through the early childhood curriculum.

- We will then look at various aspects of enhancing children's thinking in Chapter 12, "Cognitive Development through the Curriculum."

- In Chapter 13, "Language Development through the Curriculum," we will focus on the many informal as well as more formal ways in which communication is encouraged in the early childhood program.

- We will end with a look at how the program strengthens socialization in Chapter 14, "Social Development through the Curriculum."

CREATIVE DEVELOPMENT THROUGH THE CURRICULUM

"The preschool years are often described as a golden age of creativity, a time when every child sparkles with artistry" (Gardner, 1982, p. 86). One of the most rewarding joys of working with young children is watching them approach experiences with that spark of freshness and exuberance that opens the door to creativity. Each of us possesses some measure of creativity—some more, some less. This is especially true of young children. Unfortunately, there is a danger of their creativity being stifled through increasing pressure to conform to adult expectations (Mayesky, 1990). In this chapter, we will examine creativity in some detail:

1. We will begin with a definition and discussion of some of the characteristics of creativity. Research on the different functions of the two sides of the brain is relevant to this discussion.

2. Both the teacher's attitude and the physical environment are important in encouraging creativity in young children.

3. One of the early childhood curriculum areas in which creativity can especially flourish is art.

   - We will consider several theoretical views of the process of art.
   - We will look at many types of art activities and materials that are appropriate in the early childhood classroom.
   - Aesthetic appreciation is another element of art that can be begun in the early years.

4. A second broad curriculum area that fosters creativity is music. We will consider listening to music, singing, playing musical instruments, and creative movement.

5. We will end this chapter by examining some factors that discourage and decrease creativity, including television.

WHAT IS CREATIVITY?

Creativity has been defined in a number of ways. Most definitions include such concepts as originality, imagination, divergent thinking (seeing things from different viewpoints), and the ability to create something new or to combine things in novel but meaningful ways. Creativity is more likely to occur when the person possesses traits such as curiosity, flexibility, and interest in investigation and exploration.

J.P. Guilford (1962), not satisfied with the limited definition of intelligence imposed by tests that measure it by a series of single, "correct" answers, developed a new way of looking at intelligence that includes some of these traits. In Guilford's structure of the intellect, **divergent thinking** is differentiated from **convergent thinking**, both of which are involved in the creative process. Divergence, by one definition, is "the making in the mind of many from one," for instance, by elaborating on a topic as in brainstorming, whereas convergence is defined as "the making of one from many," through narrowing down many ideas to a single, focused point (Hampden-Turner, 1981, p. 104).

One trait often associated with creative thinking is **fluency**, the ability to generate many relevant ideas on a given topic in a limited time. Five-year-old Michelle wonderfully displayed fluency when she was confronted with a sheet of paper containing twenty circles and asked to draw as many different items from these circles as she could in two minutes. After using some of the circles to make the more conventional face, balloon, ball, sun, orange, and flower, she then created an ashtray, glass, light bulb, and pencil eraser as they would be seen from the top. She had used all but one row of the circles when the teacher told her that she needed to finish in a few seconds. Michelle, after a moment's thought, drew two parallel lines under the remaining row of circles, connected them with crosshatches, then put boxes on top of the circles, creating a quick but recognizable train.

Another measure of creativity is **flexibility**, ability to adapt readily to change in a positive, productive manner. Three-year-old Ramon showed flexibility when another child accidentally knocked water on the lines that he had carefully painted in different hues of water colours. After a fleeting look of dismay crossed his face, Ramon surveyed his picture and declared, "Look, the water made new colours!"

A third trait related to creativity is **sensitivity**, a receptivity to external and internal stimuli. Creative people have a heightened awareness of their world, and often experience through their senses what others miss (Lowenfeld, 1962). The creative child will more likely be the one who points out that a cloud looks like a speeding motorboat, appreciatively sniffs the aroma of freshly sawed wood at the woodworking activity, or delights in the softness of the soapy water when blowing bubbles.

CREATIVITY AND THE SPLIT BRAIN

The human brain has two distinct hemispheres, or sides, interconnected by a complex stem of nerves. It has long been recognized that the two sides of the brain serve different functions, but recent research has provided more information to substantiate this (Hampden-Turner, 1981). This division or **lateralization** is very apparent in studies on adults, and research shows that although the young child's brain is still very malleable, there is an innate predisposition toward different functions in the two sides of the brain (Brooks & Obrzut, 1981). Research on the **split brain**, as we shall see, is relevant to understanding creativity.

The left half of the brain, the analytical side in most right-handed individuals, specializes in language and in logical, deductive thinking. In the same individuals, the right hemisphere is more concerned with processing spatial thinking and visual-motor skills, and it uses a holistic, intuitive approach associated with creativity (Brooks & Obrzut, 1981; Silver, 1982). In some left-handed individuals, the lateralization is reversed; for example, the right hemisphere specializes in language and the left in spatial-analytic tasks. As a society, we tend to value the verbal and analytical skills more highly. We see this attitude reflected in our educational system. Research has also shown that people have a preferred mode of thinking that favours one hemisphere over the other, and this mode is established early in life (Silver, 1982).

Yet the complex crossover of nerve fibres between the two hemispheres shows their strong interrelationship and tells us that we need both sides of the brain for all areas of functioning (Silver, 1982). In fact, optimum brain functioning seems to be the result of full development of both hemispheres of the brain (Brooks & Obrzut, 1981).

What such research about the brain tells us is that from a neuropsychological standpoint, it is equally as important to incorporate elements that encourage creativity as it is to promote more academic skills in programs for young children. Children need a wide variety of experiences in their environments, experiences that encourage right- as well as left-brain development (Brooks & Obrzut, 1981). As we shall discuss in the following section, activities and materials that promote divergent thinking, problem solving, spatial-perceptual tasks, and visual thinking contribute to development of the whole child.

AN ENVIRONMENT THAT ENCOURAGES CREATIVITY

In our earlier definition of creativity, we examined some traits characteristic of the creative process. The early childhood setting should provide an environment in which these traits are encouraged and valued. Such an environment, however, goes far beyond providing materials for artistic expression. The creative environment is made up not just of the physical arrangement, but is permeated by an attitude of openness, acceptance, and encouragement. We will examine both of these aspects—the attitudes that promote creativity and the physical parameters of such an environment.

ATTITUDES THAT ENCOURAGE CREATIVITY

Creativity, as we have seen, is related to flexibility, divergent thinking, and openness to new ideas. Young children's minds strive toward making sense of their world by organizing information and input. Once they become familiar with and master new concepts, they are free to use these in various ways. If we use what we learn in only one way, we are limited and rigid in our approach. Flexible or creative thinking is a mental set that can be encouraged in an open classroom atmosphere. A creative environment promotes new perceptions of and responses to the world.

Creativity has to be nurtured; it does not happen on its own. The teacher plays an important role in fostering creativity by providing a variety of materials and encouraging imaginative use of them. When children are allowed creative expression, each will produce a different outcome. The teacher's acceptance of each child's work and unique responses gives children the opportunity to learn that people feel and think differently, and to value this difference.

Creativity, however, does not always result in a product, although we traditionally tend to think of the picture, the story, or the dance as the creative product. But it is the *process*, not the product, that is important for young children—and the younger they are, the more this applies. All too frequently, you see adults imposing their desire for a finished product on young children. Infants and toddlers are not inclined to take paintings home! And preschoolers may have painted a beautiful picture in red, yellow, and blue that they then cover with black paint! By the time they are school age, however, many children will want a completed product to take home.

If you watch young children involved in creative activities, you will better understand why the process is so valuable. In the process, the child can

- experiment ("What will happen if I put this block across the top of these two?");
- enjoy the sensory experience ("Squishing the play dough between my fingers feels nice!");
- communicate ("I'm a bird!");
- relive experiences ("I'll tell the 'baby' she has to go to bed because that's what big people always tell me"); and
- work out fears ("I'll be the doctor, and my dolly will be the baby who gets the shot!").

As children mature, as their motor and perceptual skills improve, and as they plan ahead more, their creative efforts may well result in purposeful products. But young preschoolers are much more involved in the process of creative experiences. For children between 0 and 4 years, any end product is usually secondary to the enjoyment of doing the activity. Elizabeth Wood, an ECE instructor at Nova Scotia Community College (Cumberland Campus) comments further on the importance of the artistic process in A Canadian Professional Speaks Out (p. 250).

The teacher, by encouraging children to solve problems, also fosters creativity. By helping children think through different alternatives and find various solutions, the teacher expands their creative capacity. The teacher, however, is a facilitator rather than the one who comes up with answers or solutions. Divergent thinking involves the opportunity to go off in different directions and to explore various strategies. The teacher's acceptance of children's suggestions and willingness to try these tells them that they are capable of worthwhile ideas.

Another way of accepting and encouraging children's creative work is through uncritical acknowledgment. Well-intentioned praise ("I like your picture") can stifle

A CANADIAN PROFESSIONAL SPEAKS OUT

Creative Art: An Expression of the Inner Self

Young children come to our day care centres as avid participants in the discovery of their world. They are curious, excited, and creative when they arrive at our door. It is our responsibility and challenge, as child care professionals, to ensure they maintain these positive qualities.

Our child care facilities should provide programs that meet the social, physical, emotional, and intellectual needs of the young child. Such a program enables each child to develop to his or her fullest potential, feeling confident and willing to take risks. Having opportunities to participate in creative art activities enhances all areas of development in a relaxed, positive atmosphere. Through creative activities, children grow socially as they share materials and ideas. Fine and gross motor skills are developed as they manipulate a variety of art media. Intellectually, children learn about spatial awareness, colours, textures, and problem solving. The children learn to express their emotions in a positive manner and gain confidence in their capabilities.

As adults we must learn to appreciate the uniqueness of each child's artistic presentations. We should share in their joy as they utilize paints, crayons, clay, and other art media to produce original works of art. Frequently, as adults, we are tempted to try to channel the child's art by providing predesigned crafts or gifts, colouring sheets, glue and paste activities, or stencils for them to complete. These types of activities stifle imaginative thought and rob the children of the freedom to express their own ideas. According to Piaget's stages of intellectual development, children do not perceive the world as adults do. Neither are they developmentally capable of representing their world in an artistic form determined by adult standards. Robert Schirrmacher believes that as the creative process blossoms within each child, "the emphasis is on the making and doing rather than on the finished product." The making and doing of creative activities comes naturally from within the child, and adults do not need to impose their ideas on them.

The child care professional plays an important role in the development of the children's creativity. One of our greatest creative resources is the environment. By providing daily access to an art centre with a variety of art media, children are given the freedom to explore the materials and create as they desire to do so. The materials in the art centre should be changed frequently to maintain interest and stimulate creative thought.

In addition to the art centre, the adult needs to plan a variety of sensory experiences for the children. As they participate in the experiences, they will acquire information that will then be expressed through their artistic representations. An effective creative art program encourages children to portray their perceptions of the world in a variety of ways. Only through an open-ended approach will we create an atmosphere where children will become creative, confident people who are willing to risk sharing their ideas and feelings.

Elizabeth Wood,
Early Childhood Studies
Nova Scotia Community College, Cumberland Campus

---

creativity because it imposes a value judgment, or becomes meaningless when it is repeated to every child. Rather than evaluate, compare, or try to read meaning into non-representational art, a teacher can remark on the process ("You glued the squares on first, then you glued circles over them"); recognize the work that has gone into the picture ("You've really worked hard on this sculpture!"); or comment on its design qualities ("You're using lots of big circles!") (Schirrmacher, 1986).

It is also important in setting an appropriate climate for creativity to provide enough time for children to get involved in and complete their projects. When the time set aside for child-selected activity is short, children tend not to get very involved (Christie, Johnsen, & Peckover, 1988), thus missing opportunities to engage in creative activity. Children may continue to pursue a creative project over a period of time, as A Closer Look illustrates.

A Closer Look

The Garden

Last May, Martha's class became intrigued when a landscaping firm began work across the street from their school. Sensing the children's interest in this activity, Martha contacted the head of the company and asked whether they could observe and ask questions. The class walked across the street each day to watch and note the progress. They witnessed the transformation of a lot, which had contained a small, scraggly lawn surrounded by beds of weeds, into an attractive garden. The surface was cleared, earth was moved to create mounds and hills, shrubs and flowers were planted, decorative rocks were added, and a small birdbath was placed in one corner. The two men who worked on this project enjoyed the children's interest and answered their questions.

A week later, when the new garden was in place, several children asked Martha whether they could also make such a garden. "Of course," she answered, then asked them how they would go about it. A lively discussion ensued about where to plant their garden. The question of what to put in the garden was also explored. The children wanted lots of plants, rocks, and a statue just like the one Alison described from her neighbour's garden.

They considered what tools they would need to make the garden. Because they decided that they could not use "big tools" such as the bulldozer, they chose shovels and rakes. Where to get the plants was another question. Perry thought that it would be hard to get bushes like the ones planted across the street. Molly reminded everyone that they could plant seeds like they did on their windowsill earlier in the year. Ollie thought they could dig up things from other gardens and transplant them in their garden. The children decided that they would each ask their parents to help them find one plant for the garden.

The next day they began their work. Martha, with the help of some of the parents, provided a variety of tools. The children dug, raked, watered, and moved earth in buckets from one area to another. As they encountered problems—for instance, a big rock just below the surface that they could not move—they tried different approaches and talked about how to deal with the problems. Having watched the project across the street, the children realized that they would have to prepare the soil before putting in the plants. Some of the plants came to school on the first day, but these were left in the classroom and watered carefully until the garden was ready. Within a few days, plants and seeds were put into the earth and the children decorated their garden with rocks and pine cones.

The children also made pictures and wrote stories about their garden. Marissa wanted to make a picture as big as the garden was going to be, and soon several children joined her in making a mural containing flowers, trees, birds, butterflies, the sun, and children working and playing. Martha provided books and catalogues about gardens and plants in the reading area, which the children used to learn about and get new ideas for their own garden. With Martha's help, they read seed packages and gardening books for descriptions of the plants they were putting into their garden. Martha helped them develop a chart on which they marked the sizes of their plants now and measured and marked how large the plants would grow. For three weeks the children were engrossed in learning about gardening through observation, first-hand experience, and direct problem solving.

A PHYSICAL ENVIRONMENT THAT ENCOURAGES CREATIVITY

The physical setting can support creativity through provision of and access to a wide range of **open-ended materials**, that is, materials that lend themselves to various uses. Children have to make choices about how to use open-ended materials, and to employ their imagination in doing so because these materials do not dictate a single outcome. Furthermore, each time they use the materials, they can do so in a unique way. In fact, *children do not need a different art activity each day.* When a different set of limited materials is provided every day, children never get the chance to explore in depth or experiment with common, basic materials (Clemens, 1991).

A well-stocked early childhood program will be full of open-ended materials. Examples include a wide variety of art materials, manipulatives, blocks, sensory materials, puppets, dramatic play props, musical instruments, and versatile outdoor equipment. (This is not to say that single-purpose materials—for instance, puzzles—are not important, but they meet different developmental needs and are not particularly suited to creative development.) One study demonstrated that children who were offered a large selection of art materials from which to choose, rather than provided with materials limited to a single project, produced significantly more creative artwork, as judged by a panel of artists (Amabile & Gitomer, 1984).

The physical arrangement of the room can also facilitate creativity. Clearly organized classroom areas let children know where they can engage in various creative activities, for instance, where they can build or where they might experiment with messy media. Classroom areas should be set up so that traffic flow does not interfere or disrupt ongoing activity.

At the same time, children should be able to move freely from one activity to another. When materials are organized and visible on accessible shelves, the children know what is available for their independent use. These materials should be attractively displayed and uncluttered so that children can see possible new combinations they might try. You may also want to label the materials available. Such orderly display also conveys a respect for the materials. Similarly, a display area also tells the children that their creative endeavours are valued and respected. Even though many children will not be interested in the finished product, it is also important to have an area where you can store the children's work.

The remainder of this chapter examines two specific classroom areas in which creativity is likely to flourish: art and music. This discussion is somewhat arbitrary, however, in that creativity can and should occur in every aspect of the early childhood program. One of the difficulties in writing a book such as this one is that some organizational decisions have to be made that place activities into categories that are not nearly as clear in reality as they appear to be in the book. Although art and music foster creativity, they also promote cognition, socialization, language, emotional release, sensory stimulation, and muscle development. Similarly, language, outdoor motor, or manipulative activities can be very creative (as we will try to point out in the ensuing chapters, where such activities have been placed). As you read on, then, keep in mind that good early childhood activities serve many purposes, meet many needs, and above all contribute to the development of the whole child.

ART

Art, in its broadest sense, encompasses the application of creative imagination to a unique product through a wide variety of modes. Art can result in a painting, a sculpture, a collage, a song, a dance, a novel, or a poem. In the context of early childhood education, art usually refers to the creative process as applied to two-dimensional graphic arts (painting, drawing, print making) and to three-dimensional modelling arts (using clay or play dough, creating sculptures).

Art has been part of early childhood education since its earliest beginnings. Young children seem to gravitate to art activities, where they can express themselves non-verbally; find satisfying sensory experiences; experiment with a variety of materials; and work in a free, uninhibited way not characteristic of many other aspects of their lives.

THEORIES OF ART DEVELOPMENT

You have probably observed a 4-year-old boy, crayon in hand, produce a house with door, windows, and chimney; an adjacent tree with curly, green circles atop a brown stem; and a person next to the house, his stick legs floating slightly above ground level and his head reaching the house's chimney. How did this child come to produce such a picture? What does the picture mean? Where did he learn the skills, since not so long ago his pictures were made up of scribbles? How was he able to translate the image of a house, tree, and person into a recognizable depiction? We will consider several theories that have been proposed to answer such questions and explain how children's art develops.

Cognitive Theories

Cognitive theories assume that children draw what they know. The more developed a child's familiarity with a concept or subject, the more detailed or sophisticated the drawing will be. Older children have had a greater number of experiences and more time in which to develop more sophisticated concepts; therefore, their artwork is recognizable.

Piaget discusses the evolution of children's drawings in terms of the developing concept of space (Cox, 1986). In the **scribbling stage**, between the ages of 2 and 4, the child experiments with marks on a page. As the child recognizes that these marks can represent real things, he or she begins to give them meaning. Cox tells how her daughter drew a shape, then, in surprise, exclaimed that it was a bird, noted that it needed an eye, and added a dot. In fact, recent research indicates that even very young children's seemingly random scribbles are gestural (as opposed to pictorial) representations. Winner (1986) relates how a 1 1\2-year-old used a marker to hop around the page, leaving marks and describing how the bunny goes hop-hop.

In the later **preschematic stage**, from about ages 4 to 7, the child does have a subject in mind when beginning a picture, but the actual product will be an inaccurate, crude representation of the real thing. It isn't until a later age, in the **schematic stage**, that the child's representations become more realistic and accurate. Children's art is also related to Piaget's concept of object permanence (Seefeldt, 1987), a recognition that objects continue to exist even when they are out of view. The child, in other words, can evoke a mental image is needed to represent the object in a drawing.

Developmental Theories

According to developmental theories, that children's art ability develops naturally, through a series of universal stages, and that adult intervention or direct teaching can, in fact, adversely affect this development. The teacher's role is to create a secure environment, make a wide range of materials available, and provide appropriate guidance to facilitate art, a view widely accepted by early childhood educators (Seefeldt, 1987). Gardner (1989) noted an interesting contrast to this approach that he observed during his stay in China, where art techniques are carefully taught to children. The Chinese view would suggest that before people can be creative, they have to achieve competence in using the techniques of the art, techniques that have been developed through long-established traditions that do not need to be reinvented or by-passed.

Researchers have proposed developmental stages of art. Rhoda Kellogg (1969), based on her collection of more than one million pictures drawn by 2- to 8-year-olds from around the world, formulated a series of age-related stages that describe children's artistic development. Two-year-olds use **basic scribbles**, twenty kinds of markings that form the "building blocks of art" (p. 15), the elements found in any artistic work. These include various straight and curved line patterns. In addition to examining basic scribbles, pictures can also be analyzed in terms of **placement patterns**, seventeen ways in which the total picture is framed or placed on the paper. By the age of 3, children begin to make six recognizable **diagrams** or shapes, specifically the rectangle, oval, triangle, cross, X, and odd-shaped (but deliberate) line. Kellogg considers that "developmentally, the diagrams indicate an increasing ability to make a controlled use of lines and to employ memory" (p. 45).

In children's art, diagrams are seldom found alone, but in **combines** (two diagrams put together), and **aggregates** (combinations of three or more diagrams). Soon diagrams, combines, and aggregates suggest objects (often a face) and thus the transition to **pictorialism** begins between the ages of 4 and 5. Kellogg characterizes early pictorial efforts as humans, animals, buildings, vegetation, and transportation. Kellogg concludes that these stages are universal, occurring naturally in all children. She advises teachers and parents neither to judge children's art nor provide instruction on how to draw specific objects. Exhibit 10-1 shows the drawings of children aged 2 to 5; these pictures illustrate Kellogg's progression in the development of children's art.

EXHIBIT 10-1
DEVELOPMENT OF CHILDREN'S ART

The development of children's art through the preschool years can be seen in these pictures. Older children demonstrate increasing sophistication as their pictures become more representational. Typical of 2-year-olds' art, Zena's and Ryan's works contain many of the basic scribbles (note circular, curved, and straight lines). Jessie's picture includes more deliberate strokes, which, in combination, suggest a face, as does 3-year-old Tommy's depiction. Jessica's work shows the emergence of shapes and combines, particularly triangular shapes. As he was scribbling, 3-year-old Bret saw a suggestion of Snoopy emerge; he added some details to enhance the image and named the picture "Snoopy." The older children's works show a much more deliberate approach. Note Loren's dinosaurs, a keen interest of his at age 4. Parker, a 5-year-old, has included realistic detail, such as the nest and bird in the tree. The subjects of the 4- and 5-year-olds' drawings are typical of those selected by preschoolers.

Zena, age 2   Ryan, age 2   Jessie, age 2

Tommy, age 3   Jessica, age 3   Bret, age 3

Loren, age 4   Christian, age 4   Matt, age 4

Soni, age 5   Diana, age 5   Parker, age 5

AGE CONSIDERATIONS

Art is generally not developmentally appropriate for infants and young toddlers who are at the sensorimotor stage. More basic sensory and exploratory experiences are age-appropriate, and some of them may resemble art activities. However, there are safety concerns with respect to the very young, who are more likely to put drawing materials in the mouth rather than on the paper. Consequently, all materials (e.g., markers), must be non-toxic. Similarly, toddlers do enjoy using large paint brushes with water outdoors, and this is a safe activity. Activities of this nature are also closely supervised.

TWO-DIMENSIONAL GRAPHIC ARTS

Young children, as they move from scribbles to gradually more representational depictions, most commonly create these pictures through graphic arts media. We will examine graphic arts in terms of drawing, painting, and print making.

Drawing

For older preschoolers and school-aged children, crayons, non-toxic marking pens, pencils, and chalk are the usual media for drawing. Each produces a different effect and provides satisfaction and enjoyment. Graphic arts are relatively neat—certainly less messy than painting—and may encourage a child, uncomfortable with messy media or reluctant to participate in more uninhibited art activities, to engage in art.

It is important that the drawing tools be appropriate for children. In an art centre where children have free access to materials, crayons are often a favourite, partly because most children are already familiar with them. Chunky crayons, especially in small pieces, are easier for younger preschoolers to hold. Crayons lend themselves to experimentation as children become more adept in using them: colours can be mixed, peeled crayons can be used sideways, and pressure in drawing can produce different colour effects. Because crayons can be easily controlled (the colours don't run as they do in painting), they facilitate the emergence of shapes, combines, aggregates, and pictorial representations as children move beyond scribbles.

Children also enjoy marking pens because of their vibrant colours and because they are easy to use. It is not necessary to press hard to get a result. Markers come with fine and large tips, allowing children to experiment with different effects. It is important to provide only markers with non-toxic, washable ink because marking pens tend to mark more than the paper; children's tongues, fingers, and clothing are often coloured.

Pencils and chalk provide good graphic art alternatives for older preschoolers. The thicker primary pencils with soft lead are best. Chalk offers a novel experience because the colours are soft, smearing and blending easily. Light-coloured chalk shows up well on dark paper. Children enjoy drawing with chalk on paper spread with various liquids such as water, buttermilk, or liquid starch; the effect intensifies and seals the colours. A squirt of hair spray can "fix" the picture more permanently. Chalk can also be used on sidewalks to draw easily removable pictures.

Children most often draw on paper, but a variety of other surfaces make for interesting variations. Cardboard, corrugated cardboard, sandpaper, wallpaper samples, wood, and fabric are some of the alternatives to butcher paper, newsprint, manila paper, or construction paper. Even varying the shape and size of the paper can encourage children to try different approaches in their artwork.

Most early childhood educators advise against providing children with dittoes or colouring books because they inhibit creative expression; are not developmentally appropriate because "colouring within the lines" requires fine motor control beyond the

abilities of young children; and serve as poor aesthetic models because the pictures are usually inferior artistic renditions (Mayesky, 1990).

Painting

Painting, with its fluid outpouring of bright colours, is an activity that delights young children. Because it is rather messy, painting is something most children do primarily at school. We will consider tempera and finger painting as two common applications of this art form.

High-quality tempera paints should be a staple in an early childhood program. Such paints come in premixed liquid, in dried blocks that are used like watercolours, or in less expensive powder form. Adding a small amount of liquid detergent to tempera paints makes clean-up of brushes and accidental spills much easier. A pinch of salt keeps the paint from spoiling and growing mould. Because tempera paints are fairly thick, they are best applied to large surfaces with large brushes or other tools. Children enjoy painting on the slanted surface of an easel as well as on a flat surface, such as the floor or a table, and an upright surface, for instance, against an outdoor fence. Painting with tempera paints involves use of large muscles (especially shoulders, arms, and back) as well as the small muscles of the hands.

Younger preschoolers can be overwhelmed if too many colours are available. Provide two or three colours at a time, preferably primary colours that the children can then mix to create additional shades. Then, as children get older, introduce variations and new shades of colour to revitalize their interest in painting. Even if you place paint in separate containers, each with its own brush, children will invariably mix colours. Keeping small amounts of clean, premixed paints and paper easily accessible promotes independence and allows children to paint when their interest is aroused. You will want to have a supply of aprons, smocks, and/or used men's shirts near paint areas to protect children's clothing. Plastic aprons that slip easily over the head encourage independence.

Finger painting is a multisensory activity that encourages uninhibited use of materials and emotional release. It can be done on large sheets of paper or directly on a clean table surface. Tabletop finger-paint creations can be saved by lifting the print on a piece of superimposed paper. Thickly mixed tempera paints are a good finger-painting medium, but a wide variety of other media lend themselves to this activity. Liquid starch and wallpaper paste mixed with tempera provide two differing consistencies. Whipped soap flakes (see soap flake recipe in Exhibit 10-2) makes another excellent finger-paint base to which colour can be added. Although for ethical reasons many teachers and programs object to the use of food as an art medium (Schirrmacher, 1990), non-toxic items like pudding and Jello are also widely used for infants and toddlers. Another food-based finger-painting activity is corn syrup and food colouring, which results in an acrylic-like picture (Essa & Rogers, 1992).

Quality is important when purchasing paint brushes because inferior products quickly frustrate and discourage young artists. Good bristles, when carefully cleaned and allowed to air dry after each use, will retain their shape and won't begin to fall out. Provide a variety of brush sizes. Fine-point brushes are good for water colours. Wide brushes for tempera painting will allow children to experiment with different-sized brush strokes. Even wider sizes, such as those used for house painting, can be used, for instance, if children "paint" the outside of the school building with water. Foam brushes provide a different experience. Alternative utensils such as toothbrushes, empty deodorant containers, cotton swabs, sponges, kitchen utensils, feather dusters, or string are often used.

Print Making

A final graphic art form we will discuss is print making, in which children dip into thick paint an object that will leave an imprint when pressed on a piece of paper. Print making is different from painting in that the utensil is not moved over the paper but leaves a single imprint with each application. Of course, many children mix painting with print making, moving the printing utensil over the paper like a brush or, alternately, leaving single imprints of the brush on the paper. A variety of print-making objects can be used, including sponges cut into shapes, cookie cutters, corks, different kitchen utensils, potatoes and other vegetables, and even body parts like a hand or a foot.

THREE-DIMENSIONAL MODELLING ARTS

When children use three-dimensional media, they produce artwork that has depth, height, and solidity in addition to colour and shape. Just like graphic arts, three-dimensional projects can be abstract or representational. Play dough and clay, collage, and woodworking are three examples of modelling art that we will examine more closely.

Play Dough

Teacher-made (and child-made) play dough that contains, in a common recipe, flour, salt, water, and a few drops of oil is a favourite of children and teachers (see Exhibit 10-2 for some suggested recipes). Well-made and airtight-stored play dough is soft and can be easily manipulated by small hands to provide a satisfying manual and sensory

EXHIBIT 10-2 ART RECIPES

1. **Uncooked Play Dough**
   Mix together:
   3 cups (750 mL) flour
   1 1\2 cups (375 mL) salt
   Stir in:
   1 cup (250 mL) water
   1\4 cup (50 mL) cooking oil
   food colouring or dry tempera paint

Knead ingredients together until well mixed. Add more water if too dry or more flour if too sticky. Store in an airtight container or plastic bag.

2. **Cooked Play Dough**
   Mix together in an aluminum pot:
   2 cups (500 mL) flour
   1 cup (250 mL) salt
   2 cups (500 mL) water
   1\4 cup (50 mL) oil
   1 tablespoon (15 mL) cream of tartar
   food colouring or Kool-Aid crystals (gives it a scent as well as colour)

Cook these ingredients over medium heat, stirring constantly, until they thicken. Place on a plate to cool enough to handle comfortably. Knead and then store mixture in an airtight container.

3. **Cornstarch Dough**
   In a pot, bring to a boil:
   3 cups (750 mL) salt
   1 cup (250 mL) water
   In a separate bowl, mix:
   1 1\2 cups (375 mL) cornstarch
   1 cup (250 mL) water

Add the cornstarch mixture to the boiling saltwater mixture and cook over low heat for several more minutes, until thick. Place on a plate and let the dough cool enough to handle comfortably. Knead well, then store airtight in the refrigerator.

4. **Peanut Butter Clay**
   Combine and knead:
   1 1\2 cups (375 mL) peanut butter
   1 cup (250 mL) powdered milk

5. **Soap Flake Finger Paints**
   2 cups (500 mL) soap flakes (not soap powder)
   water
   food colouring

In a bowl, gradually add water to soap flakes while beating with a rotary or electric mixer. The soap should be the consistency of beaten egg whites, holding soft peaks. Add food colour to make desired shade.

6. **Liquid Starch Finger Paints**
   Pour 1 tablespoon (15 mL) of starch on heavy paper; add liquid colour.

experience or to create shapes and sculptures. Children can punch, squeeze, roll, pull, stretch, and otherwise manipulate play dough; they can roll balls, pull out long snakes, twist snakes into coiled bird nests, and make human or animal

After children have had ample experience in using play dough with their fingers, tools such as rolling pins, cookie cutters, plastic knives, and other implements that shape or leave interesting imprints can be added. Play dough can be used directly on a table surface or on an oilcloth table covering, but individual, smooth-surfaced boards make cleanup much easier.

Clay

Potter's clay, which is purchased commercially, should be used in addition to, rather than instead of, play dough, because it offers a different experience. Adults use this natural clay to create sculptures and utensils, which are fired, glazed, or painted. Children's creations can also be preserved, but the cool clay should be used primarily for the sensory enjoyment it offers. As with play dough, it is very important to store clay in airtight containers. It will be necessary to add water periodically to keep the clay pliable. Sculpting can also be done with sand and water or with mud from a nearby river or lake bank.

Schirrmacher (1990) proposes four stages, not unlike the stages that typify the development of drawing, that children pass through in their experiences with clay and dough. Two-year-olds, in the "what is clay?" stage, explore the properties of clay in a multisensory way. They quickly move into the "what can I do with clay?" stage, where 3-year-olds start processing the material manually, rolling, pulling, and patting it. In the "look what I made!" third stage, 4-year-olds creatively combine their clay forms into crude representations, though these happen accidentally as often as they do purposefully. Finally, 5-year-olds move into the "know what I'm going to make out of my clay?" stage, in which they begin with a finished product in mind.

Collage

Collages are a creative combination of materials kept together by glue or some other binding material. Because they contain varied materials, collages can reinforce shape, texture, and colour awareness. An almost infinite variety of materials and techniques can be used in making collages. Some, especially those in which paper is glued to paper, may be almost two-dimensional, whereas others combine components into a three-dimensional sculpture.

Collages need a base, collage materials, and some kind of binding to hold these together. The base can range from various types of paper used to make lightweight collages to cardboard, mat board, Styrofoam sheets, or wood for heavier concoctions. It can be made of paper or plastic plates, meat or TV dinner trays, various commercial plastic packaging containers, milk cartons, or almost any other suitable material. Collage materials can include torn scraps of foil, tissue, construction, crepe, news, wall, or other types of paper; various fabric scraps and fabric trims such as rickrack and bias tape; yarn, string, and heavy thread; buttons, beads, and toothpicks; hardware items such as nuts, bolts, screws, or washers; leaves, twigs, shells, rocks, and other natural collectibles; and almost any non-toxic, small item that lends itself to the art activity. The binding material used to keep the collage together is usually white glue, but cellophane or masking tape, staples, pipe cleaners, string, toothpicks, straws, or any other material that ties or tacks items to the base and to each other might be suitable for some collages.

Various techniques can also be used for collages. The selection of materials can be provided by the children or by the teacher, who may have a specific theme-related product in mind, from available collage materials stored in the art area. If you encourage children to create collages freely, then it is important to provide a good variety of appealing and neatly organized materials. Boxes with dividers can help keep materials separated. The number of materials can be increased as children become more proficient at using materials, and items should be rotated or changed to stimulate new ideas and interest.

Cutting

Children can change the shape of collage materials by tearing or cutting paper or fabric. Most young children learn to use scissors through exposure and repeated practice. Appropriate preschool scissors that are safe but not blunt provide excellent fine motor experience. "Lefty" scissors should be available for left-handed children. Sometimes training scissors that have four finger holes (two for the child, two for the adult) help young children feel the motions involved in cutting.

Children usually begin scissor use by snipping sturdy paper, move on to cutting straight lines, and progress to cutting along curved and angular lines. Cutting out drawn shapes is an advanced skill that does not emerge until children have had many experiences manipulating and controlling scissors.

Woodworking

One of the most satisfying experiences for young children is to successfully saw a piece of wood in two, pound a nail into a tree stump, or combine two pieces of wood with a nail and hammer. Once children have experimented with and achieved some mastery in the use of tools, they use woodworking as the basis for three-dimensional creations as well. How often do we hear a child, who has just combined two crossed pieces of wood with a nail, enthusiastically declare, "See my airplane!"?

Successful and safe woodworking requires high-quality tools, appropriate instruction in using the tools, reasonable rules, and careful supervision. Woodworking tools

Exhibit 10-3 WOODWORKING TOOLS

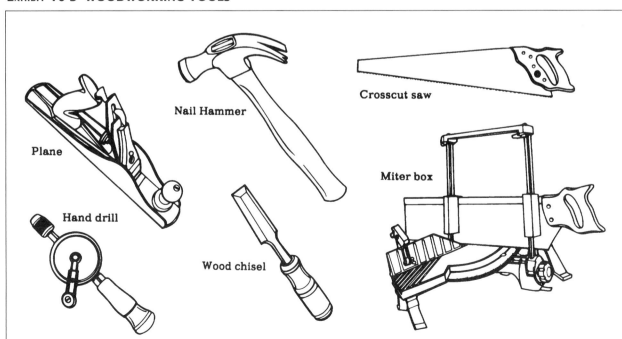

Plane

Nail Hammer

Crosscut saw

Hand drill

Miter box

Wood chisel

for children, which can be obtained through various early childhood equipment companies, are not toys. Basic tools should include well-balanced, small claw hammers weighing 225 to 340 grams; cross-cut saws, up to about 45 cm long; and well-made vises into which the wood can be securely clamped while children saw. Additional tools, once children have had plenty of practice with hammers and saws, can include braces and bits for drilling holes and rasps and planes for shaving the wood. Screwdrivers are generally too difficult for young children to master, and they end up being more frustrating than satisfying. Exhibit 10-3 shows some of the basic woodworking tools commonly included in early childhood programs.

In addition to the tools, it is important to provide a selection of softwood, such as pine, which can usually be obtained from the scrap pile of a local lumber wholesaler or carpenter. Nails with fairly large heads in a variety of lengths should also be made available. The teacher can guide children through the problem-solving process of selecting an appropriate nail length for the size of wood being nailed together.

It is very important to help children learn how to use tools appropriately, both for reasons of safety and to minimize frustration. To provide good leverage, hammers are best held with a firm grip toward the end of the handle rather than near the head; in this position, however, the swing of the hammer needs to be more accurate, because it takes greater eye–hand coordination to aim at the nail head from the further distance of the end of the handle. Before a piece of wood is sawed, it should be firmly clamped into the vise to allow the child to use both hands to manage the saw. For inexperienced sawyers, the teacher might want to begin the process by making a small notch as a starting point for sawing. For very young children, wood can be replaced by thick Styrofoam packing material, which is much softer and easier to saw.

Logical rules should be established and reinforced for woodworking activities to ensure safety and success. Such rules might include an understanding that the tools remain in the woodworking area, that only three or four children are allowed in the area at a time, or that the area can be used only if an adult is in attendance. Similarly, it is important that teachers provide attentive and appropriate guidance. This includes helping children learn how to use the tools, providing appropriate physical guidance as needed, reminding children of the rules, verbalizing the process, and encouraging problem solving.

Older preschoolers and school-aged children, who have gained proficiency in using the tools and purposefully made objects from wood, will be interested in added props. These should include round objects that suggest wheels, such as wooden spools, slices of large dowels, bottle caps, the metal ends from 355 mL frozen juice containers, film canister lids, and a variety of other items. Additionally, dowel lengths, knobs, handles, glue and collage materials, and paint and brushes can extend the woodworking activity in many ways.

AESTHETIC APPRECIATION

Aesthetics, an enjoyment and appreciation of beauty, is related to art in all its forms. Evans (1984) considers the inclusion of aesthetics in education as contributing to a "quality of life that is uniquely human" by exposing children to "sublime experiences"

(p. 74), that sense of wonder and enjoyment when we are touched by beauty. Aesthetics includes sensitivity and appreciation for both natural beauty and synthetic creations (Feeney & Moravcik, 1987). A teacher who is sensitive to beauty can help children find it in their surroundings.

One way that aesthetics can be included in the early childhood program is by introducing children to works of art, to "expose not impose" (Schirrmacher, 1990, p. 101). Feeney and Moravcik (1987) suggest age-appropriate ways of exposing children to fine art, for instance, displaying reproductions of artwork in the classroom and taking children on trips to local museums and galleries. From experience with her own children, later extended to her early childhood classroom, Wolf (1990) suggests that art postcards make an excellent vehicle for art appreciation because children can handle them easily. In addition, postcards provide the basis for other related activities such as matching, classification, and, later, learning about the artists.

As co-developers of the nationally recognized early childhood art appreciation program at the Toledo Museum of Art, Cole and Schaefer (1990) have detailed strategies for discussing works of fine art with young children. These involve the following four steps:

1. The first step, *description*, involves interactive dialogue between teacher and children to describe what the picture portrays. The teacher's questions encourage the children to look closely at the picture, examine details, and relate what they see.

2 In the *analysis* step, children relate the elements and qualities of the picture. The teacher might ask, "How do the colours get along? Are they quiet or noisy? Fighting or friendly?" or, "Find a line and follow it with your eyes. ... If it were on a playground, how would you play on it? Slide, swing, climb?" (p. 36).

3. The *interpretation* step invites children to stretch their imaginations by asking, for instance, "What kind of person do you think this man is? What might he say to you?" (p. 36).

4. Finally, in the *judgment* phase, children are helped to find personal meaning in the artwork by relating it to their own worlds. Questions encourage children to decide whether they would choose this piece for their homes or what elements of the work they like best.

Cole and Schaefer feel that this process not only promotes aesthetic appreciation but also fosters cognitive, language, social, and emotional growth. It involves logical and creative thinking, encourages appreciation and tolerance of others' viewpoints, and helps children put personal feelings into words.

MUSIC

Music is a powerful means of communication. It can be boisterous and joyful, wistful and sad, exuberant and exciting, or soothing and relaxing. Music can match as well as affect our moods. Children have a spontaneous affinity to music, which makes this a natural element to incorporate into the early childhood curriculum. We will look at the development of music during children's early years, then turn to a more careful examination of appropriate activities related to four components of music in the early childhood curriculum: listening to music, singing, playing instruments, and moving to music.

AGE CONSIDERATIONS

Infants clearly will not be involved in singing and playing instruments, but they love to listen to music and to be rocked in rhythm to the music. Sometimes they will move to it themselves, babble and coo to it, be soothed by it, and shake a rattle with it. They are comforted by a caregiver's singing, and also enjoy tapes and records. But they certainly have no interest in aesthetic appreciation activities! With development, infants' and toddlers' repertoire of responses increases, and you can involve them in very simple musical activities.

MUSIC AND CHILD DEVELOPMENT

From earliest infancy, music is welcomed in children's environments. Most infants have already had musical experiences before they arrive at an infant care program. By 2 years, children begin to gain some control over their singing voices and enjoy simple songs and finger plays, moving to music, and experimenting with simple rhythm instruments. Songs with simple physical actions are favourites of this age group. The 3-year-old, because of increasing motor control, attention span, memory, conceptual abilities, and independence, develops a larger repertoire of songs, begins to note comparisons in sounds, and associates special music with special movement.

Children who are 4 appreciate slightly more complex melodies, enjoy creating words and songs, and experiment with musical instruments. By ages 5 and 6, with continual refinement of abilities in all developmental areas, children begin to appreciate songs and dances that have rules, can follow specific rhythmic patterns, and may pick out simple, familiar tunes on musical instruments (Jalongo & Collins, 1985; Mayesky, 1990). Whereas the 2-year-old can sing an average of five different notes, by age 5 the child has expanded that ability to ten musical notes (Jalongo & Collins, 1985).

We are all aware that people have varying musical abilities. Mozart was writing musical scores and playing instruments brilliantly at a very early age; on the other hand, we also find individuals who seem to be totally tone deaf. Some children may have a special musical gift while others have talents in other areas. However, inclusion of music in the early childhood curriculum is not a matter of identifying and training special musical talent. Rather, it should promote appreciation and enjoyment of music in all its forms.

In fact, historically, music has been part of early childhood education, suggesting a long-standing recognition of its importance. Alper (1987), advocating music education as part of the early childhood curriculum, suggests that music teaches us about ourselves, moves us toward self-actualization, provides a historical link to the past, and facilitates learning. Music, as a process- rather than product-oriented activity, also allows for creative expression, develops children's aesthetic sense, and provides an enjoyable way of introducing concepts and skills (Bayless & Ramsey, 1982).

LISTENING

Listening is a prerequisite to understanding and using music. Children would not be able to identify environmental sounds, learn new songs, or move to the rhythm of music if they did not first listen. Children can be helped to develop attentiveness and sensitivity to all kinds of sounds, including music. Listening can be promoted in informal ways and through more formal listening activities.

The environment is full of sounds, which you can periodically bring to children's attention—the bird song, car horn, airplane drone, slamming door, or flushing toilet. By pointing out sounds, you are focusing children's attention on what often becomes mindless background noise.

In the midst of an activity, for instance, during circle time, you might occasionally suggest that the children close their eyes, listen carefully, and share what they hear. It is amazing how much sound there is in the silence! Listening should not be relegated to a once-a-year topic; it should be a frequent focus of activities. You can also provide good music as an integral part of every day by playing a record or tape during activity time or outdoor time. However, on some occasions, when the children are quite lively, for example, background music really becomes background noise and serves only to elevate the children's voice levels.

In planned, formal listening activities, the primary objectives will be to encourage and sharpen children's skills in listening to music. To help children understand the beat of the music, you can have them clap with the music. You might play very slow music and ask the children to listen to the tempo or speed, then move their bodies in the same tempo; repeat with a musical selection that has a fast tempo, then one that changes speeds, and discuss the difference with the children. Using a selection whose pitch ranges from high to low notes, you can ask the children to stand on tiptoe when the pitch is high and crouch close to the floor when the pitch is low.

You can also discuss the mood of music by asking children to describe how different selections make them feel. The same music can have different tone colour, depending on which instrument plays the piece; let children hear the same melody played by a piano, a xylophone, and a guitar, for instance, and discuss the differences. Children should be introduced to music from a wide variety of **genres**, including classical, popular, jazz, folk, country, and spiritual. Musical selections should certainly include those from the children's cultures.

SINGING

Children usually join readily in song. Many young children are not yet able to carry a tune, although a sense of pitch seems to come more easily to some youngsters (Alper, 1987). However, the main purpose of singing with young children should not be musical accuracy but enjoying and building a foundation for music appreciation. The early childhood program should encourage spontaneous singing and teach a repertoire of new songs.

When children feel relaxed and comfortable in an accepting climate, they will engage readily in spontaneous singing. A child may, for instance, sing a lullaby as he puts a doll in the cradle, expanding his play with a familiar element from his home life. Or a child may verbalize what she is doing, as 4-year-old Katrina did, chanting a made-up song that identified the items on the lotto cards she was laying out on the table. Some teachers who do not feel self-conscious about their voices model spontaneous singing throughout the day.

Teaching new songs to children is probably the most common music activity in early childhood programs. Children enjoy learning new songs and developing a growing repertoire of music. Early childhood songs have some common characteristics: they have distinctive rhythms, contain understandable lyrics, are often repetitive, stress enjoyment, and use a limited range of notes (Jalongo & Collins, 1985). When selecting a new song, be sure the lyrics are appropriate for young children, because many songs have words that rely on themes or humour more appropriate for adults than preschoolers. A child's voice range expands with age, controlled primarily by maturation; thus, songs that have too broad a range should be avoided. McDonald and Ramsey (1982) recommend a range that falls between the B below and the A above middle C on the piano keyboard.

Some appropriate guidelines can make group singing enjoyable for adults and children (Bayless & Ramsey, 1982; Jalongo & Collins, 1985; Mayesky, 1990).

- If you are going to teach a new song to children, know the song well first.
- Do not teach the words and music of a new song separately.
- Short, simple songs with repetitive themes can be taught by presenting the entire song at once, but longer, more complex songs can be taught in shorter segments.
- Musical accompaniment on a piano, Autoharp, or guitar or with a record or tape can help to reinforce words and melody when a new song is being taught. It is difficult, however, to sing, play an instrument, and observe the reactions of the children simultaneously.
- When you teach a song on a specific topic because it relates to a curriculum theme, do not abandon that song once you have finished the topic. The song has become part of the class repertoire and it should continue to be sung.
- Some children are reluctant to join in singing. Encourage *but never force* a child to participate.
- Singing should be an enjoyable experience. If the children are not enjoying it, you may need to teach some new songs, use varying techniques, add action elements, and/or use rhythm instruments as an accompaniment.

PLAYING MUSICAL INSTRUMENTS

From their earliest pot-banging days, children enjoy opportunities to make music. Children often use body parts, especially hands and feet, to keep rhythm. Instruments appropriate for the early childhood program fall into three categories: rhythm instruments, which have no pitch and are used for striking or scraping; melodic instruments, which present specific pitches; and accompanying instruments, which produce several tones together, particularly chords that accompany a melody (Alper, 1987). Opportunities to use good instruments, as well as to make rhythm instruments, should be available.

Rhythm instruments are the most common musical tools to which young children are exposed. Commercial sets of rhythm instruments may include several types of drums, rhythm sticks, pairs of wooden blocks, sand blocks that are rubbed against each other, tambourines, triangles, variously mounted bells, castanets, maracas, and cymbals. Each produces a distinctive sound, but, when played together with no ground rules, they can result in a rather deafening din.

It is important, therefore, to introduce rhythm activities properly. One way of familiarizing children with instruments is by introducing them, one at a time, and demonstrating how they should be used in a small-group activity. Each instrument can be played so children hear its distinctive sound and then passed around so all the children have the chance to handle it, examine it, and make sounds with it. It is often best to start small groups of children playing rhythm instruments to an appropriate record or song (one with a strong beat), calling their attention to the rhythm of the music and the unique sound that each instrument makes. Children should have the opportunity to select the instrument they prefer, trade instruments among the players, and try all of them.

Children can also make a variety of rhythm instruments, using assorted materials. Coffee cans, for instance, can be transformed into drums, while film canisters can be filled with rice and taped shut to make shakers or maracas. Such craft activities can help children become more familiar with what makes the sound in instruments, but they should not be considered "art" activities.

Some simple melodic instruments, such as xylophones and bells, can be included in the early childhood program. These allow children to experiment with different tones, discover ascending and descending notes, and begin to pick out simple tunes. Some schools have a piano in the classroom as well, a good addition if one of the teachers is skilled in playing this instrument. Children can make similar discoveries from a piano, but specific rules should be established to ensure that the piano is handled with care and respect. Colour-coded bells or piano keys and simple songs with colour-coded notes encourage children to play songs.

Accompanying instruments include the Autoharp, guitar, and ukulele. Teachers usually play these instruments during music activities and then store them in an out-of-the-way place until needed. If children are encouraged to try strumming, they should be familiar with the appropriate rules for each instrument's use.

MOVEMENT AND MUSIC

Small children seem to be in constant motion. Movement activities are a good way of combining this natural inclination with activities that stretch their imaginations, exercise muscles, contribute to formation of spatial and temporal concepts, and build respect for the uniqueness and ideas of others. As with all other aspects of music in the early childhood curriculum, movement activities occur spontaneously as well as in more planned ways.

Because young preschool children still learn very much in an active way, they often use body movement that imitates and represents elements of their environment to reinforce what they experience. For instance, children at the edge of a lake will unconsciously squat down in imitation of the birds on the water, seemingly assimilating through active movement what they are observing. Similarly, a child's head might turn round and round as she or he intently watches a spinning top.

Movement reinforces musical beat. Rhythmic movement in time to music begins to emerge around age 3, when children are better able to synchronize (McDonald & Ramsey, 1982). Children learn to keep time to music with ample practice. Clapping to music, marching in time to its beat, and taking small steps with short beats and long ones with long beats all reinforce children's emerging synchrony with music.

Creative Movement Activities

Children can also move with the mood of the music. Many lyric pieces invoke feelings of joy or sadness or reflectiveness or whimsy; they invite swaying, bending, rolling, swinging, twirling, or stretching. Asking children to move as the music makes them feel can result in a variety of creative dances. After children have had many opportunities to move their bodies to music, you can add various props to extend this experience. Such props can include scarves, ribbons, balloons, hoops, and streamers.

Another way that children can move creatively is by representing aspects of their environment that they have had an opportunity to observe. Nature provides many fascinating examples: sway like the trees in our play yard, fly like the butterfly we watched outside, walk like the pigs we saw at the farm, grow and open like the tulips on the windowsill that we planted and watered. Children can also be the popcorn they watched pop before snack, the fire engine they saw extend its ladder on the field trip, or the washing machine in which their parents do the laundry. They can make themselves into a ball or a long string. Wall mirrors can help children see what they are visualizing. What makes such activities creative is that all children have the opportunity to express themselves in their own unique fashion, not in a way modelled by a teacher. No particular rendition of a "tree" or "popcorn" is better than another; each represents a child's own feelings and concepts.

FACTORS THAT DECREASE CREATIVITY

A discussion about creative development should include a few words about the all-too-present factors in our society that often blunt children's creative impulses. As we have discussed, creativity depends on flexible, open, divergent thinking, which is encouraged in children through a flexible and open environment.

In the same way, however, creativity can also be diminished by socializing factors that narrow, stereotype, or limit ideas. An atmosphere that promotes racial, cultural, or sex stereotypes, for instance, imposes a narrow view of people that restricts potential. An environment in which the adult is always right and children are expected to do what they are told without asking questions is not conducive to creativity. When children are always shown how to do tasks, they will not have the opportunity to engage in problem solving and creative thinking. When adults laugh at a child's unique or unusual response, that child is discouraged from expressing other creative ideas.

TELEVISION AND CREATIVITY

One pervasive factor in children's lives that can affect creativity is television, and, increasingly, videotapes. On average, children spend more time watching television than they do engaging in any other activity except sleep (Huston, Watkins, & Kunkel, 1989). What children see—program content—as well as how much time they spend in front of the set can decrease creative thinking.

Programs on this medium tend to convey a very stereotyped view of people, one in which recognition and respect are accorded primarily to those who are white, male, young, and beautiful (Liebert & Sprafkin, 1988). Television also generally promotes the view that an effective way of solving problems is through violence, another narrow attitude that often does not model a variety of constructive problem-solving strategies.

PARENTS AND PROFESSIONALS

Some parents consider their children's creative development an important goal; others focus more on concerns about their children's pre-academic successes. It is, therefore, important to share with parents the school's philosophy about creativity, particularly in its broad sense of encouraging flexible, open thinking and problem-solving skills. Such information should be part of a philosophy statement that is given to parents when they enrol their children in the program. On an ongoing basis, you can let parents know which activities are planned and what you expect the children to gain from them. Similarly, a focus on creativity can continue to be reinforced individually, as you share with parents information about their child's interests and accomplishments.

Parents also enjoy seeing tangible evidence that their children are involved and productive at school. It is most often art products, which the child brings home in great stacks, that provide them with such confirmation. As the teacher, you can help parents appreciate their children's art in relation to the age-appropriateness of the work. It may be easy to dismiss children's scribbles as non-art and value only representational art products. Information on the development of children's art and the importance and sequence of all the stages can provide parents with insight into their children's work. Appropriate handouts, an article in the school's newsletter, an explanatory bulletin-board display, or books on children's art in the parent's library can all be good vehicles for conveying such information.

Even more disturbing are the results from a number of studies that have shown that frequent and consistent viewing of violent television programming is strongly related to aggressive behaviour (for example, Huesmann, Lagerspetz, & Eron, 1984; Joy, Kimball, & Zabrack, 1986; Singer, Singer, & Rapaczynski, 1984). As one author of a number of important studies concluded, "Aggressive habits seem to be learned early in life and, once established, are resistant to change and predictive of serious adult antisocial behaviour" (Huesmann, 1986, p. 129).

The amount of viewing time can also affect creativity. Creative learning is an active process, dependent on ample time spent exploring, investigating, manipulating, and reflecting. Television viewing is basically a passive occupation; thus, the more a child sits in front of the TV, the less time there is for active, self-directed play. If, in addition to home television viewing, children spend more hours in front of a TV at school, cumulative time in passive viewing can be considerable. On the other hand, some researchers feel that television is active in that children process what they see in relation to their own background and experience (Anderson & Lorch, 1983).

There are, certainly, worthwhile children's programs on television, ones that model and teach children positive, **prosocial behaviours**, especially children's programs on public channels, for instance, "Mr. Rogers' Neighborhood" and "The Barney Show." These programs provide high-quality, age-appropriate, sensitive fare for young children. "Sesame Street," while non-violent, has a very fast pace and is of questionable value (see Healy, 1991). Other programs, some of which are appropriate for preschoolers, are designed to promote appreciation of nature, aesthetics, and culture. Four rules can help assure that the positive values of television can best benefit young children.

1. Parents at home and teachers at school must carefully monitor the content so children watch only age-appropriate programs.

2. Television viewing should be allowed only in small doses.

3. Adults should watch television with children so discussion can take place.

4. Videos may be a better choice, if you cannot be with the children throughout the program. You can choose an age-appropriate, commercial-free video you know.

KEY POINTS OF CHAPTER 10

WHAT IS CREATIVITY?

▲ 1. A definition of creativity includes concepts such as originality, imagination, divergent thinking, novelty, fluency, flexibility, and sensitivity to stimuli.

▲ 2. Creativity is associated with brain functioning.

AN ENVIRONMENT THAT ENCOURAGES CREATIVITY

▲ 3. An open classroom atmosphere, where flexible and imaginative thinking are valued, will encourage creativity.

▲ 4. With creativity, the process as much as the product needs to be valued.

▲ 5. A variety of open-ended materials in the environment will encourage creativity.

ART

▲ 6. In its broadest sense, art involves the application of creativity to a unique product through a variety of modes.

▲ 7. Cognitive theory assumes that children draw what they know and that their drawings are reflected in a series of stages.

▲ 8. Developmental theories advocate that children's art develops naturally, through universal stages seen in children from all parts of the world.

▲ 9. Kellogg proposes age-related stages in children's art development, each marked by the emergence of unique elements in their art products.

▲10. Children's move from scribbling to representational art can be seen in their use of two-dimensional graphic art, which uses a wide range of media.

▲11. Stages in the development of children's art can also be seen in three-dimensional modelling arts such as sculptures from clay or play dough, collage, or woodworking.

▲12. An important aspect of early childhood education is aesthetics, fostering an appreciation of beauty in art and the environment.

MUSIC

▲13. Children develop an awareness of and response to music from a very early age, and the early childhood program should include many music activities to promote its appreciation and enjoyment.

KEY TERMS

aesthetics
aggregates
basic scribbles
combines
convergent thinking
diagrams
divergent thinking
flexibility
fluency
genre
lateralization
open-ended materials
pictorialism
placement patterns
preschematic stage
prosocial behaviour
schematic stage
scribbling stage
sensitivity

▲14. Music activities help sharpen children's listening skills.

▲15. Children enjoy learning new songs and singing spontaneously in a relaxed and accepting atmosphere.

▲16. Rhythm and melodic instruments provide another means of promoting music appreciation and enjoyment, and they should be part of any early childhood program.

▲17. Creative movement activities, with or without the accompaniment of music, provide a way to reinforce many concepts.

FACTORS THAT DECREASE CREATIVITY

▲18. Creativity can be stifled when stereotypes are imposed, when children are given few choices, and when they are always shown what to do.

▲19. Television viewing can decrease creativity. Both the content of television programs and the amount of time children spend watching television can have a negative impact.

KEY QUESTIONS

1. Which of your friends or acquaintances do you consider to be creative? What creative characteristics do they possess? Do they fit the definition of creativity presented in this chapter? How do they use creativity in ways other than the conventional sense (for instance, art or music expression)?

2. Observe a group of children. What expressions of creativity do you see? What factors in the environment or in the teacher's behaviour encourage or discourage creativity? Does any child in this group stand out as particularly creative? What characteristics does this child possess? Is your criterion for identifying a creative child different from one used to identify a creative adult?

3. Make a finger painting or collage with materials typically found in an early childhood program. How does this activity make you feel? What benefits can children gain from such activities? Do the same with a music activity, for instance, using rhythm instruments or dancing freely to music, and answer the same questions.

4. Look at children's artwork. Do you see an age progression from scribbles to shapes to representational pictures?

5. Watch a children's television program, for instance, a cartoon. What messages does this program convey to children? Does it promote stereotypes? If a child frequently watches programs such as this one, how might such viewing affect creativity?

PHYSICAL DEVELOPMENT THROUGH THE CURRICULUM

One of the major tasks of the early years is physical growth and development. At no other time in life is there such a rapid rate of change in size, weight, and body proportion as well as in increased control and refinement in the use of body parts (Allen & Marotz, 1989). Physical changes, which are readily observable, profoundly affect and are affected by all areas of development. As we have emphasized before, a child is a whole, not divisible into components such as physical, social, or cognitive areas, although to be able to manage the information, we do discuss development in such categories. This chapter will examine aspects of physical development and the activities that enhance it.

1. We will begin with a look at some theories that explain physical development.

2. Physical development is complex, involving a number of interrelated components.

- Body control involves mastering a number of skills important for movement and balance.
- Young children gain increasing manual control, the ability to use the hands effectively.
- Sensory-perceptual development involves children's increasing accuracy in interpreting information they gain through their senses.

3. We will discuss several early childhood activities that encourage and promote use of the large muscles of the body.
   - Physical fitness activities and outdoor play provide excellent opportunities for large-muscle development.
   - We will also consider the value of blocks and block play for young children.

4. Many manipulative materials and activities promote use and development of the small muscles of hands and fingers.

5. Because of the importance for young children of learning through the senses, we will consider activities that promote sensory exploration and discrimination.

6. A major aspect of physical development includes learning to care for the body, as we will discuss in relation to nutrition, health, and safety.

A DEVELOPMENTAL FRAMEWORK FOR MOTOR DEVELOPMENT

Before we begin discussing theories, we should clarify some terms commonly used in considering physical development. These include **gross motor development**—what is involved in control of the large muscles of the legs, arms, back, and shoulders needed for movements such as running, jumping, and climbing; **fine motor development**—the skills involved in use of the small muscles of the fingers and hands necessary for such tasks as writing, drawing, or buttoning; and **sensory-perceptual development**—which is involved in conveying information that comes through the senses and the meaning that it is given. This chapter will include all three aspects of physical development.

Traditionally, physical development has been considered from a **maturational theory** perspective. This viewpoint is based on information about when children reach developmental milestones in such functions as sitting, standing, and walking, tasks that are largely determined by the maturation of the nervous system (Wade & Davis, 1982). One of the earliest researchers to carefully observe and record the sequence of motor skill development was Arnold Gesell, whom we discussed in Chapter 2. His pioneering work through the Gesell Institute is still used extensively (Seefeldt & Haubenstricker, 1982). Most early research on motor development was descriptive, involving the use of observations and films to establish the average age at which children achieve various motor skills. Such information, however, does not explain the underlying process of motor development (Rarick, 1982).

In more recent years, Piaget's theory (as discussed in Chapter 2) has led to the **perceptual motor model** of physical development, a more integrative view proposing that motor behaviours are a prerequisite for and lead to cognitive abilities (Cratty, 1982). As you will remember from the discussion of Piaget's theory, the first level of development is the sensorimotor stage, in which the infant moves through a series of accomplishments, going from primitive reflexes to purposeful manipulation of the environment. In this early stage, covering approximately the first two years of life, the child learns through sensory input and body movement.

Repetition of certain motor patterns leads the child to form schemata, representations of experiences. In early infancy, children use their own body movement to create different schemata. At approximately 6 months, they begin to explore the effect of their actions on the environment. During the second year, they become active explorers, engaging in rudimentary problem solving to reach their goals (Mussen, Conger, Kagan, & Huston, 1990). As they enter the third year of life, children move into Piaget's second level of development, the preoperational stage. They can now mentally represent or think about objects and events that are not present in the immediate environment. This emerging ability derives from the sensory and motor learning of the first two years.

The implications of this view for early childhood education are that because young children learn through physical movement and interaction with the environment, they must be provided with numerous movement opportunities and experiences. Furthermore, this viewpoint also assumes that a child's academic performance can be improved by increasing the amount of motor activity, because cognition is predicated on motor experience (Cratty, 1982). The evidence for this second assumption is still being debated, as we will see later in this chapter.

INFLUENCES ON MOTOR DEVELOPMENT

In addition to internal influences suggested by the perceptual motor model, external factors also influence physical development (Keogh and Sugden, 1985). The early

childhood teacher is the facilitator of the environment that, in turn, should encourage and challenge children to explore, create, and discover. Through movement, in interacting with the environment, children engage in problem solving (Curtis, 1987). In other words, the environment, as set up by the teacher, provides materials, equipment, and activities that motivate, challenge, and stimulate the child. The child exercises his or her muscles while engaging in thinking, socialization, language, and creative development at the same time.

This view is consistent with the observations of extreme developmental delays in the infants and children who were in orphanages in the 1930s and 1940s, where marked deprivation was the rule (see Chapter 2; Skeels, 1966). The infants in these institutions were unable to move about and explore, left as they were in cribs shielded from view by sheets on the sides. While their basic needs for food and cleanliness were attended to, the interactions were rapid and without care. In this harmful psychological and social environment, the infants were unable to develop most primitive sensory motor schemes and their growth lagged. In a quality setting, teachers ensure that infants and toddlers are given a responsive environment to explore with their existing schemes.

Teachers who have physically challenged children in their classes must work even harder to ensure that these children have a responsive environment. In A Canadian Professional Speaks Out, Margaret Denison describes the efforts of a teacher to modify an ECE program for Cathie, a child with severe physical limitations.

 ## A CANADIAN PROFESSIONAL SPEAKS OUT

Integrating Children with Special Needs

> Successful integration is a continuing process rather than a discrete event. It includes the instructional and social integration of children who have handicaps into educational and community environments with children who do not have handicaps (Mott, Streifel, & Quintero, 1987, p. 5).

The process of integrating children with mild to severe physical and/or developmental challenges into the regular classroom is a reality for today's educators. In order to make integration a positive process for all students, a teacher must be aware of the exact nature of the handicap and the impact the handicap has on all areas of the child's development: cognitive, long-range, social and emotional, as well as physical. Therefore, a teacher should take steps to ensure that he or she has all the aforementioned information in order to facilitate interactions between the children with and without challenges.

For instance, the following information outlines the steps one teacher took to ensure the positive and successful integration of a child with Rett Syndrome. First, a definition of Rett Syndrome:

> Rett Syndrome (RS) is a very specific disorder which affects girls only. These children are born "healthy" and their psychomotor development is apparently normal up to 6–18 months of age. Then comes a devastating period of slowing down or stagnation, followed by regression. Girls and women with Rett Syndrome are mentally retarded, have severe gross and fine motor handicaps, epileptic seizures, some remaining autistic-like behaviours, communication disabilities, various kinds of stereotypic behaviours (Lindberg, 1991, p. 1).

Cathie, a 5-year-old girl with RS, was to be integrated into a junior kindergarten environment. Her teacher wanted to develop a successful educational intervention program for Cathie. Therefore, she first met with Cathie's parents and discussed her case history. Parents should be included in their child's education and act as tutors and advocates for their child. Cathie's parents transferred a wealth of knowledge to the teacher.

Next, Cathie's teacher, accompanied by one of the parents, observed Cathie at her nursery school and in her home. In so doing, the teacher became familiar with Cathie, her needs and desires. For example, the teacher learned how Cathie could walk with assistance, and how she could communicate with her eyes. Because she is nonverbal, Cathie uses eye pointing to indicate her needs.

The teacher was able to transfer information about Cathie's skills and communication abilities to other students in order to help them learn how to communicate with their new friend.

Next, Cathie's teacher, with the assistance of other professionals servicing her, developed an individual education plan. The education plan included introductory activities that were designed to facilitate interactions between Cathie and her peers. Games, including eye-pointing activities, were played during circle time. Physical proximity of simply placing a child with any type of challenge in a classroom will not automatically ensure integration occurs. The teacher must help the non-challenged students learn about the student's challenges and how they can help the student become part of their world.

A good individual educational plan must be continually assessed. First, Cathie's teacher developed a method for communicating between the home and school. She developed two journals: a home/school journal and a school journal. The home/school journal was used to record information about Cathie's general health and emotional state both at home and school. The school journal was used to record all the activities in which Cathie engaged for the purpose of aiding the teacher and teacher's assistant to evaluate Cathie's growth and development in her school setting. For instance, when the teacher recorded the number of times Cathie visited a particular centre and with whom she played, it was a means of learning about the activities Cathie enjoyed and why she enjoyed them. As a result, the teacher could concentrate on creating stimulating activities based on Cathie's personal needs and desires.

Finally, Cathie's teacher stressed the importance of continually evaluating the process of integration. Cathie was growing and so too must her educational plan grow and incorporate new activities.

In summary, successful integration policies may include: meeting the child's parents; developing and implementing an individual educational plan; collecting and assessing data; and evaluating the process of integration on a continual basis.

Margaret Denison
Junior Kindergarten
King George V School
Niagara South Board of Education

References

Mott, S., Striefel, S. & Quintero, M. (1987). *Preparing regular classroom students for mainstreaming: A literature review*. Utah State University. ERIC Document Reproduction Service No. ED 290 2951.

Lindberg, B. (1991). *Understanding Rett Syndrome*. Toronto, ON: Hogrefe and Huber Publishers.

COMPONENTS OF MOTOR DEVELOPMENT

As children start the preschool years, they have rudimentary movement ability and control, but by the time they enter middle childhood, their movements have become much more refined and competent. A number of movement components are part of this overall change in motor development.

BODY CONTROL

The preschool development of six important elements of body control—walking, running, jumping, hopping, throwing, and balancing—have been described by Keogh and Sugden (1985). Walking is the basic means of locomotion, self-movement from place to place; running, jumping, hopping, and throwing are fundamental play skills; and balancing provides one way of assessing postural control. All of these important skills become more accurate, controlled, and efficient during the preschool years.

Subtle changes in walking transform the toddler, whose concern is balance rather than efficiency, into the much more graceful preschooler. As the child gets older, legs and arms alternate, toeing-out decreases, stride becomes more consistent, heels and toes rather than the flat foot are used for landing and takeoff of each step, and feet are placed so they are more parallel. Mastery of stair climbing involves increasing skill in several factors such as moving from supported walking to walking alone, walking up before coming down, and stepping with both feet on each step to alternate stepping (Keogh & Sugden, 1985). By the time children are 4 years old, most are able to walk up and down stairs independently using alternating feet (Allen & Marotz, 1989).

Not just a faster version of walking, running makes the child airborne at moments, with both feet off the ground. By age 2, most children run, and by ages 4 to 6 they are quite skilled, increasing speed and control. Some of the changes involve a longer stride, a shift in the centre of gravity as the angle of the legs increases, increased flexion of the knees, and better synchrony between arms and legs (Keogh & Sugden, 1985). By age 4, many preschoolers can start, stop, and move around objects with ease while running (Allen & Marotz, 1989).

Jumping, during which both feet leave the ground simultaneously, seems to follow a consistent pattern in its development. The earliest form of jumping occurs when a toddler steps off a step to be briefly airborne. It isn't until the third year that the child leaves a step with both feet, executing a more accurate jump. Another way to view jumping is to observe children jump vertically off the ground, an achievement that usually occurs by their second birthday. The broad jump evolves around age 3, with length of jump increasing with age (Keogh & Sugden, 1985). By age 3 children jump in place with both feet, by age 4 most can jump over objects 12 to 15 cm high, and by age 5 they can jump forward on both feet 10 times in a row (Allen & Marotz, 1989).

Achievement of one-legged jumping or hopping generally emerges between ages 3 and 4, beginning with one hop, then increasing the number of hops. Early attempts at hopping usually end with both feet coming back to the ground for support, because children tend to propel their bodies too high by pushing too hard off the ground. Children are better able to hop forward than in place because the forward momentum helps them maintain their balance. Hopping becomes part of other movements such as galloping and skipping, tasks that appear between the ages of 4 and 5. Skipping appears to be mastered much more easily by girls than by boys (Keogh & Sugden, 1985).

The objective of throwing is to propel an object forward with accuracy and enough force so that it reaches the target. Before age 2, many toddlers execute an overhand throw, but with poor control and speed. By age 3, children become more accurate in throwing in a specific direction, and they can usually propel an object 1.5 to 3 metres. As they get older, children also become more efficient by rotating the body, stepping forward on one foot, and swinging the throwing arm to improve their throwing skills (Keogh & Sugden, 1985).

Development of balance is essential for children to acquire smooth coordination, which, in turn, leads to self-assurance and success in a variety of activities (Munro, 1986). By age 2, children can stand briefly on one foot, but not until after their third birthday can they maintain this posture for at least five seconds. Two-year-old children can walk, with steps astride, on a line on the floor; a few months later, they can walk backward in the same way. It isn't until about age 4 or 5 that they can walk heel-to-toe forward, then backward. These same steps on a balance beam are more demanding and are mastered at later ages (Keogh & Sugden, 1985).

A final indicator of increased movement control is moving slowly. Although preschoolers improve in their ability to speed up movements—walking, running, throwing, or riding a bicycle faster—executing these movements slowly is more difficult. Between ages 4 and 9, children show marked improvement in this form of body control (Keogh & Sugden, 1985).

MANUAL CONTROL

During the infant and toddler years, children develop basic grasping and manipulation skills, which are refined during the preschool years. The preschooler becomes quite adept in self-help, construction, and holding grips (Keogh & Sugden, 1985).

Self-help skills such as feeding, dressing, and grooming involve a variety of manual movements that are mastered during the early years. Between ages 2 and 4, children gain dressing skills of increasing difficulty, pulling on simple garments at the earlier age and learning most of the necessary skills by the later age. Most 4-year-olds can bathe, wash hands and face, and brush teeth quite competently, although some supervision is helpful (Keogh & Sugden, 1985). While 2-year-olds have some basic self-feeding skills, 3s use utensils with increasing competence. The 4s can use spoon and fork with dexterity, and 5s are mastering the use of the knife to spread or cut soft foods (Allen & Marotz, 1989).

Manipulative Activities

Many preschool manipulative materials are designed to encourage emerging construction skills. By age 2, children can build a tower of four to six small blocks, place pegs in a pegboard, and turn doorknobs. The 3-year-old can make a bridge with blocks, discriminate between and correctly place round and square pegs in a pegboard, and build a tower of nine or ten blocks (Allen & Marotz, 1989). As children reach ages 4 and 5, their constructions become more intricate and require more delicate manual dexterity and spatial relations.

Hand Grips

The most common tool use requiring a holding grip is writing or drawing. By age 1 1\2, children know how to hold a pencil or crayon, and by 4 they have a large repertoire of **holding grips**. Early grips include a **palmar grasp**, in which the pencil lies across the palm of the hand with the fingers curled around it and the arm, rather than the wrist, moves the pencil. Later developments involve variations of the **tripod grasp**, in which the fingers hold and the wrist and fingers move the pencil. Children will spend varying amounts of time in each of these stages.

Although we consider the development of holding grips to be age-related, it also seems to be affected by culture. In one study (Saida & Miyashita, 1979), researchers found that Japanese children achieve the most sophisticated grasp several months before British children do, a result partly attributed to the early mastery of chopstick use in eating. In addition, these researchers found that girls' grasp development is about six months ahead of that of boys.

Bimanual Control

Keogh and Sugden (1985) discuss one other emerging aspect of fine motor development, **bimanual control**. For many tasks we primarily use the dominant hand, but many manipulations require the use of both hands, each one assuming a different function. This is the case when tying shoelaces, holding an orange and separating it into segments, using a manual eggbeater, or manipulating a piece of paper with one hand so the other can cut out a shape. By age 4 or 5, children establish some stability in hand use requiring bimanual control, though little research has been conducted to study this function. Early childhood activities that promote bimanual control, such as dressing dolls and puppets, and/or using Montessori's dressing frames, should be included in the program.

SENSORY-PERCEPTUAL DEVELOPMENT

Closely intertwined with motor development are sensory and perceptual functioning. Sensory input involves the collection of information through the senses of sight, hearing, taste, smell, and touch and the kinesthetic sense; perceptual input involves attention to, recognition, and interpretation of that information to give it personal meaning. Thus, perception is a cognitive process.

The Senses

Because children first learn about their world through the senses, it is important to continue to include activities in the early childhood curriculum that involve all sensory modalities. Traditionally, education tends to encourage visual and auditory learning, often to the exclusion of the other senses, but the world, about which children are continually learning, is made up of more than sights and sounds. It has smells, tastes, and textures as well.

Early in life, children begin to discriminate with their visual sense, learning to recognize the familiar, forming preferences for increasingly more complex stimuli, and anticipating events from visual cues. Preschoolers continue to delight in exploring with their eyes. A rich and aesthetic early childhood environment should provide a wealth of opportunities that not only develop visual acuity but also encourage concept formation through exploration. An important integrative development is **eye–hand coordination**, the increasingly accurate use of the hands as guided by information from the eyes. Many early childhood materials, particularly manipulatives such as puzzles,

Duplos, and Legos, encourage, exercise, and refine eye–hand coordination.

The sense of hearing is one of the earliest functioning systems, present even before birth. By the time children reach the preschool years, they have achieved a highly sophisticated auditory skill in understanding language and using that understanding to communicate. Of course, the development of language is not only a function of hearing but also involves the perceptual ability to discriminate between discrete sounds and to focus on the relevant sounds to the exclusion of irrelevant ones. The early childhood environment provides a variety of auditory stimuli, but it should also provide many opportunities to focus on, discriminate among, and identify various sounds.

The taste sense is most identified with eating. To a great extent, it reflects learned preferences and socialization, although newborns appear to discriminate between and prefer certain tastes, such as sweet ones, to others, for instance, those that are bitter (Lamb & Bornstein, 1987). But taste is also instrumental in exploration, especially during the first year of life when children put objects in their mouths. Some young preschoolers continue to mouth some things, especially thumbs or other personally comforting objects, although not as indiscriminately as they do during infancy.

A variety of opportunities to explore new tastes through food experiences should be provided in the early childhood setting. In addition, a safe environment will ensure that anything that goes into children's mouths will not be harmful. At the same time, children will learn to discriminate between what is appropriate and what is inappropriate for putting in the mouth.

Smell, a sense in many ways tied to taste, is also present very early in life; newborns, in fact, have been shown to react favourably to the smell of bananas and with disgust to the smell of rotten eggs (Lamb & Bornstein, 1987). Children continue to show olfactory preferences, and they may reject a new food simply because of its smell or dislike a person because "he smells funny." Smell is an important sensory modality in learning to identify and discriminate among various common and uncommon odours, something the early childhood program can encourage and facilitate. Children enjoy matching familiar smells.

Whereas vision involves the eyes, hearing the ears, taste the mouth, and smell the nose, the sense of touch entails our largest organ, the skin. Touch can be soothing or irritating, pleasant or unpleasant, calming or exciting, and it can project a message of safety or danger. Sensitivity to tactile stimulation develops rapidly during infancy (Lamb & Bornstein, 1987), and, by early childhood, preschoolers gain a wealth of information through this sense. Touch tends to be underrated as a sense, but educators, at least back to Montessori's day, have recognized its importance as a learning avenue. Infants and toddlers like different tactile sensations, and explore much of the world through this avenue. Older children enjoy stroking different fabrics, mounding wet sand with their hands, or feeling tree bark. They also like feeling things with their feet—grass and sand, for example. School-aged children find sandpaper letters interesting, and footprints offer a novel way of painting. A variety of tactile experiences, along with opportunities to verbally discriminate between different textures, should be part of the early childhood program.

The Kinesthetic Sense

The body's **kinesthetic sense** provides knowledge about the body, its parts, and its movements. It also involves the "feel" of movement without reference to vision or verbal cues (Keogh & Sugden, 1985). All movement experiences add to children's growing understanding of what their bodies can do, their increasing control over their bodies, and their sense of self-confidence in their physical abilities. A child working with hammer and nail in the woodworking centre has to make kinesthetic judgments that go beyond visual perception of the location of and distance between nail and hammer; for instance, the child has to know how best to hold the hammer for an effective swing, how to position the body, how hard to swing the hammer, and how to hit the nail head rather than the fingers.

Perceptual Development

As children gain information about the world through the senses of sight, hearing, taste, smell, and touch and the kinesthetic sense, they become increasingly skilled in using this information. Perception involves selecting the important features of a complex environment, focusing on the salient aspects of those features, identifying those features, and discriminating them from others. All of these processes entail cognition, again pointing out the interrelatedness of all aspects of development.

Most often, perceptual information does not come from just one sensory mode but involves **multimodality** (Allen & Marotz, 1989). If, for instance, you bring a lamb onto the playground, the children will learn about it by seeing it and watching it move, listening to it say "baaaa," smelling its distinctive odour, and feeling its curly fur. All of this information, coming from the various sensory modalities, contributes to the children's concept of a lamb. From many sensory-perceptual experiences comes **sensory integration**, translation of sensory information into intelligent behaviour. Allen and Marotz (1989) provide an excellent example, that of a 5-year-old who sees and hears a car coming and waits on the curb for it to pass. The child is using what is seen and heard to control motor behaviour.

Perceptual Motor Skills

Over the years, a number of theorists and researchers have explored the relationship between motor skills, perception, and academic success. During the 1960s and 1970s, a number of programs focused on helping children with learning disabilities by improving the link between perception and movement. The developers of such programs feel that sensorimotor development (learning through movement and the senses) precedes and is the basis of perceptual and intellectual ability.

In one approach, that of Doman and Delacato (Delacato, 1964, 1966; Doman, Spitz, Zucman, & Delacato, 1960), specific exercises are intended to recapture the sequence of sensorimotor development and repeat motor patterns that may have been skipped (for instance, crawling). Considerable research examining the effectiveness of such programs, however, has provided no support for their claims that such activities improve academic learning (Wade & Davis, 1982). It has been recommended, therefore, that perceptual motor activities be encouraged for their own sake rather than because they might affect other areas of development (Cook, Tessier, & Armbruster, 1987).

We have briefly examined some developmental and theoretical issues related to gross motor, fine motor, and sensory-perceptual functions in young children. The rest of this chapter will look at some early childhood activities that enhance skill development in these areas. Again, keep in mind that this selection is somewhat forced because *almost all preschool activities involve motor and sensory-perceptual elements.* Similarly, the activities we will review also promote creativity, cognition, language, and social-emotional development.

GROSS MOTOR ACTIVITIES

This section examines gross motor activities, those that involve the large muscles of the body, in three areas. We will examine these activities in relation to physical fitness, outdoor play, and block usage.

PHYSICAL FITNESS

Gross motor exercise occurs in many early childhood activities. It should be emphasized that vigorous, active play is important not only to muscle development but also to the establishment of lifelong health habits (Seefeldt, 1984). Yet a recent large-scale survey found that preschool children, at least in the U.S., are not engaging in enough physical activity. (Poest, Williams, Witt, & Atwood, 1989, 1990). In addition, this study found that boys are more physically active than girls; children in preschools engage in more physical activity than those in child care centres; and children whose parents engage in exercise are more likely to do so as well. Physical fitness is concerned with overall health, specifically with the development and maintenance of an "adequate level of cardiovascular endurance, muscular strength, muscular endurance, flexibility, and body leanness" (Poest, Williams, Witt, & Atwood, 1990, p. 5). The sizable number of overweight North American preschool-aged children further attests to a need for physical fitness (see A Closer Look).

A CLOSER LOOK

Physical Fitness and the Overweight Child

When Nellie started at the child care centre at age 4, she weighed 36 kilograms or 80 pounds. It quickly became obvious that in addition to being overweight, Nellie sought out primarily sedentary activities and quickly dismissed any activity that involved more than minimal movement as ones she did "not like." Rosalie and Bob, her teachers, were very concerned about Nellie's health as well as her self-image. They decided that they needed a more accurate idea of just how much activity Nellie actually engaged in compared with the other children.

They devised an observation tool that was used over the next several days to measure the activity levels of Nellie and of Tiffany, another 4-year-old of average activity level, who was selected for purposes of comparison. Observations were recorded for a half-hour indoors, when the children were involved in self-selected activities, and for a half-hour outdoors. The observation sheet was a grid with 30 columns (one for each minute), in which a check mark was placed beside an activity listing each time the child engaged in that activity. Activities included sitting, standing, walking, running, involvement in a floor activity such as block building, lifting, bending, swinging, riding a tricycle, and climbing.

A comparison of the two children showed that Nellie spent almost 90 percent of her time sitting, both inside and outside, compared with Tiffany's 30 percent. While Tiffany engaged in a variety of ventures that required active movement, Nellie chose primarily tabletop art projects or manipulatives. Outside, Nellie usually found a place on the grass and talked to a teacher or watched the other children at play. This was not surprising because obese children have been found to be less active than their peers (Javernick, 1988). Talks between the teachers and Nellie's parents indicated that they were very interested in obtaining the staff's help to change Nellie's eating patterns and activity level. Rosalie and Bob, after considerable thought, decided to adopt a strategy that included recommended nutrition counselling for the family, limitation of Nellie's food intake at snacks and lunch, and hourly ten-minute exercise sessions for Nellie while she was at school. They had to be very ingenious in developing activities that would interest Nellie and encourage her to exercise. Nellie chased balloons, rolled hoops, flew kites, kicked balls, tumbled down a grassy slope, and engaged in a variety of other vigorous activities that were essentially unknown to her. Because Nellie had a teacher to herself for these ten-minute periods, she particularly enjoyed them.

Over time, Nellie's weight did stabilize with the added activity and decreased food intake. A year later, Nellie was still overweight, but her weight had not increased and she had gained almost 7 centimetres in height. She was also considerably more active than she had been when she started at the centre.

Javernick (1988) feels that teachers of young children often neglect gross motor development, giving it only lip service, and instead emphasize fine motor, cognitive, and social areas in the curriculum. A number of physical educators further express the concern that free play, which often includes various motor experiences, does not adequately meet the motor development needs of young children (Seefeldt, 1984; Skinner, 1979). They advocate that regular physical fitness activities (not organized sports!) be part of the early childhood curriculum. It is important to note, however, that no norms exists for what physical fitness in preschoolers should involve (Poest et al., 1990).

The term *physical fitness* often conjures up our own childhood experiences involving games and sports. Play, games, and sports have characteristics that are tied to developmental readiness and appropriateness (Coleman & Skeen, 1985). Play is free from time, space, and rule constraints, and reward is inherent in the play rather than dependent on winning. Play involves such activities as creeping, running, crawling, climbing, and throwing. Games are more structured than play. Although time limitations and rules can be altered to meet the needs of the players involved, games with rules are beyond the ability of most preschoolers. However, non-rule-based jumping and running games can be played.

Sports like football, track, or gymnastics are much more structured and are based on external rewards. Preschoolers do not have the physical, social, emotional, and cognitive skills to participate in sports and in many organized games. Instead, young children need to develop physical capabilities through many play experiences in which they can explore their outside world (Coleman & Skeen, 1985). *Competitive activities have no place in the early childhood program.* Because one child usually wins at the expense of the other participants, the self-concepts of those who do not win are affected negatively, and hostility and ill will are created.

The challenge to early childhood educators is to develop appropriate gross motor and physical fitness activities. Limited research has shown that specific, guided instruction of preschool children's motor skills can improve performance. In one study (Werner, 1974), 3-to-5-year-olds participated in physical education experiences related to locomotion and balance as part of their nursery school program. Follow-up tests showed that the children who participated in these experiences improved significantly, both in relation to their preprogram scores and over children who did not receive such training.

Motor skills that emerge during the preschool years, as discussed earlier in this chapter, should be the focus of such activities and could in fact provide an organizing structure similar to curriculum themes around which appropriate activities can be planned (Poest et al., 1990). Practice helps develop proficiency in motor skills beyond the rudimentary stage (Seefeldt, 1984). Javernick (1988) suggests some gross motor activity guidelines for teachers of young children.

- Motor tasks should be presented in ways that will interest children.
- Physical activities such as calisthenics, "adventurecises," or obstacle courses should be planned for each day.
- Music and movement activities should also be part of every day; many excellent children's records are available to enhance exercise and movement activities.
- Children should be allowed to make choices, for example, "Would you like to be a hopping bunny or an airplane?"
- The teacher must be an active participant in physical activity. Children are much more attracted to activities in which a teacher is enthusiastically involved.

- Outside time should not be treated as play time during which teachers are merely *passive supervisors.*

The research implies that early childhood teachers need to be more concerned with providing physical fitness as part of the daily program. Vigorous daily activities that are fun and enjoyable contribute to establishing a foundation for lifelong health habits and attitudes.

OUTDOOR PLAY

Uninhibited gross motor activity is most likely to occur during outdoor play. Children are not expected to control their voice and activity level and space is not constrained, as it often is indoors. As a result, children feel freer to run, jump, crawl, climb, hang, swing, shout. A variety of interesting and versatile equipment should be available in the outdoor play yard, as we discussed in Chapter 9, "The Physical Environment." Teachers should be actively involved in outdoor activities, and definitely should not view it as a time for teacher–teacher conversations.

The Benefits of Outdoor Play

The outdoor area and the time children spend outdoors should be integral parts of the early childhood program because of their many inherent values. Outdoor play is not just a time for children to expend excess energy while teachers take a break. Lovell and Harms (1985) summarize as follows: some of the educational and development objectives that well-planned outdoor activities in a well-designed, safe playground can meet

- Age-appropriate equipment should facilitate a wide range of gross motor activities at different levels of challenge, including balancing, throwing, lifting, climbing, pushing, pulling, crawling, skipping, swinging, and riding.

- Social skills such as sharing, cooperating, and planning together can be encouraged by such equipment as tire swings on which several children can swing together, wide slides, or movable equipment with which children can build new structures.

- Activities and equipment should also enhance development of concepts, for instance, understanding spatial relations (up and down, in and out, under and over, low and high) and temporal relationships (fast and slow; first, second, and next).

- Problem solving that involves both physical and social skills should be encouraged as children figure out how to move a heavy object or how to share a popular item.

- Children can learn about their natural world by observing and helping care for plants and animals, and by noting seasonal and weather changes.

- A variety of activities carried out outdoors, such as art, woodworking, or music, can enhance creative development.

- Children can try out and experience various adult roles through dramatic play, for instance, re-creating the fire house, gas station, or airport.

- In addition to stationary equipment, movable components such as planks, climbing boxes, and ladders allow children to create new and different possibilities to enhance their motor, social, language, cognitive, and creative development.

- Exploration and increasing competence help children develop positive self-image and independence.

Outdoor Activities

Although children enjoy the freedom of self-selected ventures while outside, the teacher should also provide and (again!) be actively involved in planned activities that enhance motor development. As preschoolers get older, they enjoy some noncompetitive games such as "Statues," "Red Light-Green Light," or "Mother May I," which involve both movement and control. Keep in mind, however, that races pitting children against each other, or girls against boys, are inappropriate. Setting up an outdoor obstacle course, which takes advantage of existing places to climb over, crawl through, or jump across, can be enjoyable and provide exercise. A parachute, with children grasping the edges, can be used to reinforce concepts such as up and down and over and under as well as to encourage cooperative effort. The teacher's and the children's creativity are the only limits to how the outdoor play area is used to enhance children's learning and development.

BLOCKS

Blocks are one of the most versatile and enjoyable materials found in early childhood classrooms. Blocks come in many shapes and sizes, are made of various materials, can be used alone or in combination with other items, and lend themselves to an almost infinite variety of play possibilities.

Benefits of Block Play

Blocks provide many opportunities for motor development. Children use both their large and small muscles during block play as they lift, bend, stretch, reach, turn, and manipulate and balance various types of blocks. In addition, blocks promote concept learning (big and little, tall and short, over and under); are a natural vehicle for learning about matching, similarities and differences, and classification; entail math and science concepts related to quantity, addition and subtraction, weight, and balance; develop vocabulary and visual memory related to shapes, sizes, and patterns; elicit creativity, problem solving, and role playing; encourage cooperative play; and are satisfying, giving a sense of accomplishment and self-worth. Blocks are certainly a versatile medium that meets many needs and provides many opportunities for development!

Stages of Block Play

As you observe young children using blocks, you will note differences in the type and complexity of such play among children. Children go through stages in their development of block play, stages related to age and experience, but certainly showing considerable individual variation. Young 2-year-olds often spend considerable time carrying blocks around, perhaps banging them together, and exploring their feel and weight. In the next stage, children's earliest constructions are either vertically stacked or horizontally laid-out blocks. The flat structure suggests a road, and often the earliest dramatic play with blocks involves small cars driving over such a road.

By 3 to 4 years, children begin putting blocks together into more deliberate constructions, for instance, enclosures, bridges, or decorative patterns. Enclosures can lead to dramatic play with animal, people, or furniture accessories as children make houses, farms, or zoos. Bridges often become a challenge for cars driving through, as children gauge and compare size, width, height, distance, and balance. Use of decorative patterns shows children's interest in symmetry, repetition of configurations, and exploration of various designs.

In the final stage, reached between 4 and 6 years, children engage in more representational constructions, naming their structures, building props for dramatic play, and making quite complex and elaborate edifices (*Blocks*, 1979; Reifel, 1984).

Each of these stages reflects children's increasing understanding of spatial concepts. Well before the age of 4, children have mastered basic spatial relationships such as *on*, *by*, and *in*. In the later stages of block building, they demonstrate more advanced spatial concepts as they manipulate space in symbolic representations of such structures as houses, farms, and other enclosures (Reifel, 1984).

Types of Blocks

The most common type are **unit blocks**, made of hardwood in standardized sizes and shapes. The basic unit is about 14 cm long, 5 cm wide, and 3.5 cm high (*Blocks*, 1979). Variations include the square or half unit, double unit, and quadruple unit, and there are a variety of triangular, cylindrical, arched, and curved units. (See Exhibit 11-1 for some examples of common unit block shapes.) Unit blocks should be made with precision to ensure mathematically exact relationships among the various units.

Large, hollow blocks have one open side and a slit for carrying. Hollow blocks are often accompanied by other equipment such as boards, ramps, sawhorses, ladders, and packing crates. Because of their size, hollow blocks encourage a different kind of dramatic play, one in which children can climb into the structures they build to drive the "car," pilot the "boat," or live in the "house." A variety of accessories can extend their

Exhibit 11-1 UNIT BLOCKS

Square or Half Unit	Roof Boards	
Unit	Intersection	
Double Unit		
Quadruple Unit		
Ramp	Half Roman Arch and Small Buttress	
Large Triangle and Small Triangle	Large Buttress	
Pillar and Half Pillar	Ellipse, Curve and Quarter Circle	
Unit Arch and Half Circle		
Large Column or Cylinder and Small Column or Cylinder	Side Road	
Small Switch	Large Switch and Gothic Door	

play as well. Hollow blocks are used as easily inside as they are outside. They are particularly good for large-muscle development because of their bulk and weight (*Blocks*, 1979; Cartwright, 1990).

Cardboard blocks, made of heavy corrugated cardboard resembling large, red bricks, are very useful objects of play for toddlers and young preschoolers. These sturdy blocks are lightweight and manageable for late 1-year-olds and 2-year-olds, whose motor skills and balance are not yet well developed. They are easily carried around by children in the first stage of block building, are readily stacked by children entering the second stage, and are generally not harmful if knocked over. These blocks are not particularly versatile for more complex block structures, however, because all the blocks are the same size and shape.

A variety of homemade blocks can also be added to your selection of construction materials. Relatively sturdy blocks, for instance, can be made of cylindrical oatmeal boxes and milk cartons. Wooden blocks can also be constructed by someone who enjoys carpentry, uses high-grade hardwood, is exact in cutting shapes, and sands and varnishes carefully. You might try visiting construction sites for an ample supply of free wood pieces that you then make into blocks, sand, and varnish.

Teachers' Role in Block Play

Teachers have to gauge their involvement in block play according to cues from the children. Observation may tell teachers that some children avoid the block area, while others frequently use blocks readily and creatively. Thus, teachers may need to encourage reluctant children to try block play and help the one who often uses blocks to extend his or her play. In some classes, blocks tend to be a male activity, and girls may be unwilling to engage in block play for this reason. In such cases, teachers need to support and encourage girls to try blocks, convey the fact that girls can be as effective as boys in constructions, value all the children's structures, and promote individuality rather than stereotyped views of people (*Blocks*, 1979).

In talking with children about their block constructions, it is better to use descriptive rather than evaluative comments. As we discussed in our last chapter in relation to children's art, judgmental statements tend to discourage and stifle children's creative efforts, because you convey an expectation about what the artwork should be like. Examples of what might be discussed include the names of the blocks used, where they are placed, how many are included, and how the blocks are balanced and connected. In doing this, you convey to the child that you have carefully looked at the construction, you may be promoting language development by using new vocabulary, and you will be encouraging the child to look closely at the work (*Blocks*, 1979).

Teachers can also encourage children's extension of block play into dramatic play. Blocks can help children re-create or act out experiences and take on the role of familiar people in their environment. A variety of props can encourage dramatic play. Wooden or plastic vehicles, animals, and figures of people are traditional block props, but other accessories can include items usually found in the dramatic play, woodworking, manipulative, sensory, or art areas. One alternative to extending block play is to combine the block area with the dramatic play area. Research on just what can happen when the divider between these two areas is removed showed that play with children of the opposite sex increased, as did appropriate use of block and housekeeping materials (Kinsman & Berk, 1982).

One aspect of block play is its relative impermanence. At clean-up time the blocks, which are "nonexpendable materials," usually have to be put back on the shelf. Yet ownership and permanence are very important aspects of activities in which children engage. Kushner (1989) provides some suggestions to help children achieve these.

Photographs can be taken of block constructions and posted, sent home, or mounted in classroom albums. Similarly, slides or videotapes of children's work can be shared at parent events. Sending home enthusiastically written notes about children's play can also give importance to a block activity. Children can also dictate stories about their block structures to verbally preserve what they created. Kushner also encourages teachers to rethink attitudes about clean-up by considering the appropriateness of preserving some block structures beyond the limited play time during which they were constructed.

FINE MOTOR ACTIVITIES—MANIPULATIVES

Fine motor development involves primarily the muscles of the hands and wrists, those needed in precise and small movements. Toys, which require some kind of manipulation with fingers and hands, can be categorized as **manipulatives**. Of course, manipulatives are the first toys to interest infants, but their appeal far outlasts infancy (Do you remember adults' fascination, if not addiction, to Rubik's cube?)

We will consider manipulative materials such as table toys, puzzles, beads, pegboards, and small blocks as they contribute to fine motor as well as other areas of development.

BENEFITS OF MANIPULATIVES

Manipulative toys enhance fine motor development because they require controlled use of hand and finger muscles. But they contribute much more. Manipulatives are sensory materials, involving visual and tactile discrimination; they require skill in coordinating the eyes with what the hands do. Manipulatives can reinforce a variety of concepts such as colour, shape, number, and size, as well as encourage one-to-one correspondence, matching, patterning, sequencing, and grouping.

Some manipulative toys such as puzzles are self-correcting, fitting together in only one specific way. Such toys allow children to work independently and know when they have achieved success. This helps build their sense of self-confidence. Because some manipulative materials have a definite closure point when the child completes the task, they also can contribute to children's growing attention span and the satisfaction of staying at a task until it is completed (*Table Toys*, 1979). One notable feature of Montessori materials (see Chapter 3) is their self-correcting nature, because many are designed with built-in feedback (Gettman, 1987).

Other manipulatives such as Duplos, Legos, and building logs are more open-ended, allowing children to work creatively. In a way similar to the development of art, children use open-ended manipulatives in stages, starting by fitting together and pulling apart pieces to explore their properties, moving on to more purposeful pattern and shape constructions, and finally creating specific, representational objects or structures.

TYPES OF MANIPULATIVES

Many materials and games could be classified as manipulatives, including commercial and homemade items. It is not easy to group manipulatives because different combinations of such toys share some properties, but they also have various differences.

Puzzles

These are among the most popular manipulative materials. Wooden or rubber puzzles are the most durable, but sturdy cardboard puzzles can extend the puzzle selection relatively inexpensively. Children find that puzzles appropriate for their developmental level are very satisfying. First puzzles for those just over 1 year might have three pieces at most, while slightly older toddlers and very young preschoolers should have only five or six pieces. In these simple puzzles, each piece should be a discrete inset or else it should be a simple fit-together picture. When toddlers and young preschoolers still have difficulty with manual control, pieces with knobs can help them avoid frustration.

Puzzles with an increasing number of pieces and complexity should be available as children's skill level improves. Many 5- and 6-year-olds have the dexterity and enjoy interlocking puzzles with 25 to 50 pieces. The 7- and 8-year-olds are even more formidable at times.

Larger puzzles are often completed cooperatively by older children. Puzzle pieces are easy to lose or intermingle, however, and some schools have found it helpful to write an identifying name on the back of each individual piece.

GAMES

A variety of games require manipulative skills and reinforce various concepts. Lotto, bingo, and picture dominoes, for instance, can encourage matching, sorting, and classifying by specific topics. Some board games such as Candyland and Hi-Ho Cherry-O are appropriate for older preschoolers, if the rules are simple and flexible and the game is played in a cooperative rather than competitive atmosphere.

Construction Toys

The selection and variety of commercial construction toys have increased considerably so that a wide assortment of choices is now available. Duplos, Bristle Blocks, magnetic blocks, and snap blocks are good beginning manipulatives for young preschoolers, allowing for easy grip and assembly. Many more complex materials with smaller pieces are available to provide a range of construction possibilities. Some come with different accessories such as small people, wheels, or vehicle bases, which can enhance play. It is best to avoid manipulative sets, such as a helicopter or car, that result in a single outcome. Children quickly lose interest after assembling the pieces a few times, whereas more open-ended materials can be used over and over in an endless variety of ways.

Small Blocks

It is possible to find a continuum of open-ended to structured small blocks. Wooden table blocks come in a variety of shapes, similar to the larger unit blocks, and lend themselves to many creative uses. Somewhat more structured are the variety of small block sets that are made up of houses, buildings, and accessories and with which children can build towns, farms, or cities. Playmats and carpets are available that provide the background settings on which such blocks can be used. Because of their angled shapes, **parquetry blocks** are more challenging to assemble into the form board, but they provide a unique perspective and some different pattern possibilities not achievable with the right angles of rectangles or cubes.

Miscellaneous Manipulatives

Many other kinds of manipulatives have value for young children. Children can string beads of different sizes and shapes, assembling them in an arbitrary order or following a preset pattern to reinforce matching and sequencing skills. Pegboards with various-coloured pegs can be used to create designs or follow patterns. Pegboards can be made or purchased in a variety of sizes, with large holes and pegs for very young preschoolers and smaller sizes for older children who have refined eye–hand coordination and manual dexterity. Lacing cards help children master a host of motor, perceptual, and cognitive skills.

SENSORY ACTIVITIES

Any activity involves a sensory component because we use sight, hearing, or touch almost all of the time. But some activities are specifically geared to enhance sensory awareness. Most young children seem to enjoy and become thoroughly immersed in such activities. We will briefly examine activities that are primarily for tactile enjoyment—specifically, water and sand play—and activities that sharpen sensory acuity.

WATER AND SAND PLAY

Water acts like a magnet to toddlers, preschoolers, and school-aged children who are drawn to this soothing and enjoyable medium. Water play should be considered a requisite activity for children between 1 and 8 years, not only because it is so appealing to children but also because of its many other values. At the youngest ages, it will require more supervision, but it is a favourite activity. Water play can take place indoors, at a water table or plastic bins placed on a table, or outdoors during warm weather. Water can be used with squeeze bottles, funnels, flexible tubes, and pouring containers; to wash dolls, doll clothes, or dishes; or to create bubbles with added liquid soap, straws to blow through, and various-sized bubble-making forms. Children enjoy the sensory stimulation of water but also learn about properties of water such as volume, buoyancy, and evaporation. They also learn to appreciate its importance as they provide water for plants and animals, and are exposed to mathematical concepts through pouring activities.

Sand play is another multipurpose sensory activity that fascinates and entices children. For safety reasons (e.g., eating sand, throwing it, and rubbing it in eyes are problems), it usually is not available in programs until the children are about 18 months. However, anyone who has sat on a sandy beach knows that younger toddlers and infants over 7 or 8 months also delight in sand play. If you can monitor the play closely, you might choose to provide sand on some occasions to the very young. Many schools provide an outdoor sand play area, but sand can also be provided indoors in a sand table. When available by itself, fine-grained sand lends itself to being manipulated, moulded, and smoothed. Added props such as containers, shovels, spoons, sifters, cars, and trucks expand the creative potential of sand play. For variety, some people change from sand to different types of grains (e.g., rice and corn) on occasion. Some simple rules about both water and sand play let the children know that these

materials need to stay in specified areas to protect the children, the classroom, and classroom materials.

SENSORY CONCEPTS

Sensory experiences can be pleasurable for their own sake, but they also provide many opportunities for concept development. Each sense is assailed by a range of stimuli, which children gradually learn to identify and discriminate among. Specific sensory activities can provide experiences and reinforcement for these tasks.

We tend to be most adept at identifying objects in our environment through visual cues, because we gather a majority of information through the eyes. But it is also important to be able to use the other senses. Consider the following examples of activities that help children in the task of object identification using a single sensory modality.

- *Touch identification*—Children use only the sense of touch when they put a hand into a feely bag or box and identify an object.

- *Sound identification*—Children listen to a tape or record of common environmental or animal sounds and identify them using only the sense of hearing. Similarly, during a walk children can be encouraged to listen for and identify the sounds they hear.

- *Smell identification*—Children identify common objects or foods, for instance, a flower or a cotton ball saturated with mint extract, using only the sense of smell. When an actual object is used, the child should not be able to see it so that smell is the only identifying criterion.

- *Taste identification*—While blindfolded, children are given a spoonful of common foods, which they identify using only the sense of taste.

In addition to using the various senses to identify objects, children also use sensory information to discriminate as they match, seriate, or classify sensory stimuli. Examples of activities that encourage refinement of sensory concepts are listed below.

- *Matching*—Children can match like objects using information from primarily one sense. Visual matching can involve colour, shape, or size, as well as pairs of objects or pictures that children match based on appearance. A collection of fabrics and sandpaper can provide opportunities for tactile matching. Pairs of sound cans (for instance, film canisters with a variety of objects such as rice, beans, or pebbles) can be matched using the sense of hearing, whereas small jars containing various distinctive smells can encourage smell discrimination.

- *Seriation*—A variety of objects can be seriated (placed in order along a dimension such as height, width, or colour) using cues from one sensory modality such as vision or hearing. Children can organize a collection of sticks from longest to shortest, seashells from smallest to largest, or colour paint chips from lightest to darkest. Similarly, sound cans can be placed in order from loudest to softest.

- *Classification*—Children can classify sensory stimuli in a variety of ways. They can group foods into such categories as sweet, sour, and salty; organize sounds as soft or loud, high or low, or into those made by household pets or farm animals; and classify objects by such visual cues as colour, hue, shape, size, sex, or any of a wide variety of dimensions.

The use and integration of more than one sense can also be promoted in a **cross-modal intersensory activity**. For instance, children can look at an object and then be asked to feel inside a box and pull out the object that matches the one viewed.

CARING FOR THE BODY

The early childhood program should help lay the foundation for good health habits. In addition to establishing routines and activities that emphasize the importance of physical exercise, the preschool or child care centre also can help children of all ages learn about appropriate nutrition, health, and safety concepts. Keep in mind, however, that not only infants and toddlers need adult assistance; preschoolers too are still very young and the adults in their lives ultimately are responsible for their health, safety, and well-being. Children learn by example and our practices, but we should never assume that such learning is enough. Children need our continued guidance because they do not have the maturity necessary for the enormous responsibility of self-care.

NUTRITION AND COOKING

Because food is a basic human need and so often provides great pleasure, nutrition education and cooking experiences should be an integral part of the curriculum. Nutrition concepts can be presented to children in an understandable manner, and they can be reinforced by hands-on cooking activities. The topic of nutrition could have been included in several places in this book; nutrition and cooking, although they promote understanding of a basic physical need, equally involve cognitive, language, creative, and social areas of development as well.

Nutrition

Nutrition education, attitudes toward food, and food behaviours are all of interest to older toddlers, preschoolers, and school-aged children. Of course, you would approach the topics in different ways at different ages, ensuring that the activities were appropriate for the young children in your care. The following list of nutrition-related concepts may help in planning activities (Herr & Morse, 1982, p. 154).

1. There is a wide variety of food.

2. Plants and animals are sources of food.

3. Foods vary in colour, flavour, texture, smell, size, shape, and sound.

4. A food may be prepared and eaten in many different ways—raw, cooked, dried, frozen, or canned.

5. Good foods are important to health, growth, and energy.

6. Nutrition is how our bodies use the foods we eat for health, growth, and energy.

7. Foods may be classified according to the following categories:

   • Milk

   • Meat and fish

   • Vegetables

   • Breads

- Dried peas, beans
- Eggs
- Fruits
- Pastas
- Cereals, grains, seeds
- Nuts

8. A good diet includes a wide variety of foods from each of the food categories.

9. Many factors influence eating, such as:

- Attractiveness of food
- Method of preparation
- Cleanliness, manners
- Environment, atmosphere
- Celebrations

10. We choose the foods we eat for many reasons, such as:

- Availability and cost
- Family and individual habits
- Taste
- Aesthetics
- Social and cultural customs
- Mass-media influence

The above concepts, as well as possible additional ones, can be presented to young children through appropriate activities to help them understand the importance of good nutrition. If you are in a full-day setting, where meals are a standard feature, you will probably discuss many of these topics informally while eating. The foregoing concepts begin to take into account the complexity of this topic while providing realistically appropriate concepts. You might have noticed that the seventh concept does not recommend the standard classification of foods into the four basic food groups. Herr and Morse (1982) explain that these groups require too many generalizations based on an abstract grouping of nutrients, which young children often are not able to understand. You will need to tailor nutrition concepts to the ages and ability levels of the children, your own knowledge about nutrition, and the depth with which you plan to approach the subject.

Herr and Morse (1982) recommend that nutrition be an integral part of the early childhood program, covered on an ongoing basis. Local and provincial marketing boards (e.g., egg, beef, and milk producers' boards) often have excellent photographs and activities available for teachers, free of charge. In some locations, they also have speakers who will visit an early childhood program—and an ECE course on nutrition. You might also want to contact the U.S. National Dairy Council. Older preschoolers and school-aged children often enjoy components of their excellent program, *Food . . . Early Choices*, featuring Chef Combo (National Dairy Council, 1980).

Cooking Experiences

Among the most enjoyable activities for young children are those that involve food preparation. Such activities are multisensory; involve children in a process they have observed but in which they may not have participated; teach and reinforce a variety of concepts related to nutrition, mathematics, science, and language; and are very satisfying because they result in a tangible (and delicious) end product (Cosgrove, 1991).

Some cooking activities are more appropriate than others and should be carefully selected to meet specific criteria and objectives. The following are guidelines to keep in mind when planning food activities:

- The activity should be matched to the children. Older infants might help poke some bread dough, for example, but they would not be able to knead it, whereas older children could. Heat, sharp utensils, and a need for precise fine motor control place age constraints on activities, so think of activities that do not require

them for younger children. Examples include tearing lettuce for a salad, plucking grapes from the stem for fruit salad, mixing yogurt and fruit in individual cups, or spreading tuna salad on crackers with a spoon. Older preschoolers and school-aged children have more refined muscle control and can follow more complex instructions. More involved recipes that might require use of knives, electrical appliances, and multiple ingredients can be planned.

- Safety is of utmost importance. Many cooking tools are potentially dangerous, and careful adult supervision is required. Some steps in cooking require that only one child at a time be involved with a teacher, for instance, flipping pancakes in an electric skillet or griddle. Other cooking activities may well require that the number of children be limited, for instance, to five or six at a time, so that the adult can supervise and observe all of the children adequately. The process can then be repeated with additional groups of children so everyone who is interested has the opportunity to participate. However, limitations in the number of children who can be involved at one time have to be thought out before the activity is presented to the children.

- The recipe should involve enough steps so that all of the children in the group make a significant contribution. Some recipes can be prepared individually by each child in single-serving sizes. Other recipes will require group cooperation. An appealing activity such as cooking should have enough ingredients and steps, for instance, five or six, so that each child in the group is an active participant. If children are making muffins, for instance, one child can break and stir the eggs while others add and stir in the butter, flour, milk, honey, nuts and raisins, and flavourings and leavening; then they can take turns stirring the dough.

- Children can be helped to understand the entire process. It is helpful to prepare a pictorial recipe chart (or use one that is commercially made) that shows ingredients and amounts, allowing children to experience measuring as well as mixing (see Exhibit 11-2 for an example). Point out the changes in ingredients as they are mixed with others, for instance, that the flour loses its dry powderiness

EXHIBIT 11-2   PICTORIAL RECIPE CHART FOR BANANA BREAD

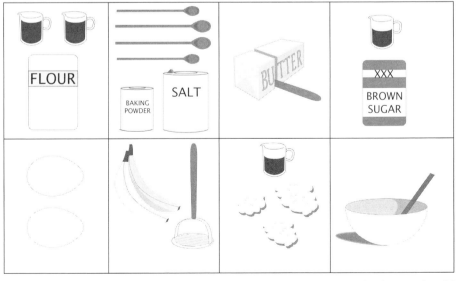

SOURCE: E.L. Essa and P.R. Rogers. (1992). *An early childhood curriculum: From developmental model to application.* Albany, NY: Delmar Publishers.

as it joins the liquids. Discuss and point out the effect of heat, which solidifies the semiliquid dough into firm muffins, for instance.

- The activity should focus on wholesome, nutritious foods. It is important to set a good example in the planned cooking activities to reinforce nutritional concepts. A wide selection of available cookbooks focus on healthy recipes, some of which are listed in Exhibit 11-4.
- The importance of hygiene and cleanliness must be stressed. Require that children as well as adults wash their hands before participating in cooking experiences. Make sure that cooking surfaces and tools are clean. It contributes to multisensory learning if you allow children to taste at various points during the cooking process; however, instead of letting children use their fingers for tasting, provide individual spoons or popsicle sticks.

EXHIBIT 11-4   **SELECTED COOKBOOKS THAT FOCUS ON NUTRITIOUS RECIPES**

Croft, K.B. (1971). *The good for me cookbook*. San Francisco, CA: R and E Research Associates.

Gooch, S. (1983). *If you love me don't feed me junk!* Reston, VA: Reston Publishing.

Goodwin, M.T., & Pollen, G. (1980). *Creative food experiences for young children*. Washington, DC: Centre for Science in the Public Interest.

Haney-Clark, R., Essa, E., & Read, M. (1983). *SHINE!: School-home involvement in nutrition education*. Reno, NV: Child and Family Centre, University of Nevada, Reno.

Harms, T., & Veitch, B. (1980). *Cook and learn*. Menlo Park, CA: Addison-Wesley.

Johnson, B., & Plemons, B. (1984). *Individual child portion cooking: Picture recipes*. Mount Rainier, MD: Gryphon House Press.

Katzen, M. (1977). *Moosewood cookbook*. Berkeley, CA: Ten Speed Press.

Wanamaker, N., Hearn, K., and Richarz, S. (1979). *More than graham crackers: Nutrition education and food preparation with young children*. Washington, DC: National Association for the Education of Young Children.

HEALTH

Young children get many messages about health needs and practices from what is expected of them, what they are told, and what adults model. School routines (discussed in Chapter 15) will set many expectations and structure the schedule to encourage and facilitate increasing self-care in toileting, cleanliness, and eating. But health information should also be conveyed as part of the curriculum. Discussions and activities can heighten children's awareness of such topics as the relationship between health and growth, the body's need for both activity and rest, temperature regulation through appropriate clothing, hygiene practices as part of disease prevention, the importance of medical and dental care, and health professionals and facilities that care for children in the community. In addition, if a child in the class has a specific allergy or a chronic illness, all of the children can be helped to better understand this condition by sensitively including the topic in the curriculum.

It was helpful in one preschool program, for instance, when the teacher discussed why Dorothea could not eat certain foods. The children became more sensitive to Dorothea's allergies and the restrictions it caused, and they saw that her special snacks were not a privilege but a necessity.

SAFETY

Young children begin to acquire safety information and precautions, although it is important to remember that adults must be responsible for ensuring children's safety by providing a safe environment and preventing accidents. Because toddlers and very young preschoolers may not process safety information accurately, it should be conveyed with a great deal of caution. Some 2-year-olds, or young 3-year-olds, may fail to understand the negative message in "don't do ..." or may get "ideas" from well-intentioned cautions (Essa & Rogers, 1992). Through curriculum topics, older preschoolers can gradually acquire information and learn some preventive precautions related to fire, electricity, tools, traffic, potential poisons, and strangers, as well as learn about community safety personnel and resources, and what to do in case of an accident.

 PARENTS AND PROFESSIONALS

Parental Values Concerning Physical Development and Care

Early childhood teachers and parents share responsibility for the development and care of young children in many areas that were formerly in the domain of the home. Today, children acquire many personal life skills and habits related to exercise, nutrition, health, and safety through their child care or preschool programs. Yet these areas are also very personal to parents, representing their own lifelong habits and practices. It is important, therefore, to share with parents the school's philosophy about helping children develop healthy patterns that include daily exercise, good nutrition, appropriate care for the body, and safety precautions. It is equally important to be open to parents' ideas and values concerning these topics.

One difference between home and school expectations that teachers of young children frequently cite is some parents' desire to have children sit quietly, learn academic skills, listen to the teacher, and do worksheets. In such an instance, it is particularly important that you, as an early childhood professional, provide appropriate developmental information and make readings available that clearly demonstrate that young children learn through an active rather than passive process. You may need to help parents share your concern and recognition that all aspects of children's development need to be furthered. Physical development is an integral part of the whole child; thus, all activities that promote fine motor, gross motor, and perceptual skills deserve prominence in the early childhood program.

KEY POINTS OF CHAPTER 11

A DEVELOPMENTAL FRAMEWORK FOR MOTOR DEVELOPMENT

▲ 1. Physical development involves gross motor, fine motor, and sensory-perceptual development.

▲ 2. The maturational perspective is concerned with those periods in which children reach developmental milestones.

▲ 3. The perceptual motor model considers that mastery of physical tasks is a prerequisite for cognitive development.

▲ 4. Motor development is influenced by internal factors—such as muscles and bones—and by external factors—for instance, location and social expectations.

COMPONENTS OF MOTOR DEVELOPMENT

▲ 5. In development of body control, preschool children gain mastery in walking, running, jumping, hopping, throwing, and balancing. Each requires complex skills.

▲ 6. Manual or hand control is seen through increasing competence in self-help skills, construction ability, holding grips, and bimanual control.

▲ 7. Children's earliest learning about the world is through the senses, that is, through seeing, hearing, tasting, touching, smelling, and feeling; this learning continues to be important throughout the early years.

▲ 8. The integration of information from the eyes with movement of the hands is referred to as eye–hand coordination.

▲ 9. The kinesthetic sense provides knowledge about the movement of the body.

▲10. Perception involves being able to select and pay attention to sensory information that is important and relevant.

▲11. Although a number of programs promote perceptual-motor activities to improve academic skills, research has not supported their effectiveness.

GROSS MOTOR ACTIVITIES

▲12. Research is finding that most young children do not engage in adequate physical activity; therefore, it is recommended that physical fitness activities regularly be included in the early childhood program.

▲13. Outdoor play provides one of the best opportunities for physical development, both through self-selected play and specific activities provided by the teacher.

▲14. Block play provides excellent opportunities not only for enhancing motor skills but also for all aspects of children's development.

▲15. Children's block play evolves through specific, age-related stages.

FINE MOTOR ACTIVITIES—MANIPULATIVES

▲16. Fine motor development is enhanced by manipulative materials such as puzzles, pegs, and small construction toys; in addition, such materials further other aspects of children's development.

SENSORY ACTIVITIES

▲17. Water and sand play, which promote tactile enjoyment, provide sensory stimulation and can promote learning of a variety of concepts.

▲18. Activities aimed at identifying an object by using a single sense, for instance, touch or smell, help children develop the use of all their senses.

KEY TERMS

bimanual control

cross-modal intersen-
  sory activity

eye–hand coordination

fine motor development

gross motor develop-
  ment

holding grip

kinesthetic sense

locomotion

manipulatives

maturational theory

multimodality

palmar grasp

parquetry blocks

perceptual motor model

self-help skill

sensory integration

sensory-perceptual
  development

tripod grasp

unit blocks

▲ 19. Sensory discrimination involves making distinctions between stimuli, for instance, distinguishing between sounds or matching a food smell with the picture of the food.

CARING FOR THE BODY

▲ 20. Young children can learn specific concepts about their need for nutritious foods and development of good eating habits.

▲ 21. Cooking activities can reinforce learning about nutrition as well as promote many other skills and concepts.

▲ 22. Young children begin to learn many concepts about health, caring for their bodies, and safety, topics that should be integrated into the early childhood curriculum.

KEY QUESTIONS

1. Observe preschoolers of various ages at play. What differences in physical development do you see as a function of age? What do these abilities tell you about appropriate activities and expectations?

2. Adults generally use their senses of sight and hearing far more than their other senses. Think about how and when you use information from the various senses. Does this suggest activities for young children that could enhance their sensory learning?

3. If you were asked to plan a physical fitness program for a group of preschoolers, what would you include? Would you plan different activities for 3-year-olds and 5-year-olds?

4. Select two different manipulative materials. What do you think children can potentially learn from each of them? Now spend ten minutes using each manipulative. Would you add any additional items to your lists?

5. Plan a cooking activity for preschoolers. How can this activity reinforce the nutrition concepts listed in this chapter?

COLUMBIA VALLEY
PUBLIC TELEVISION
ASSOCIATION
P.O. BOX 2712, INVERMERE, B.C. V0A 1K0
(604) 342-
NAME:
TITLE:

12

COGNITIVE DEVELOPMENT TH
THE CURRICULUM

Young children's thinking ability is quite amazing. Within just a few years of preschoolers have acquired an immense repertoire of information and cognitive s. A child, who two or three or four years before was a helpless baby responding to the environment mainly through reflexes, is now a competent, thinking, communicating, reasoning, problem-solving, exploring person. In studying children's cognition, you should be concerned more with the *process* of knowing than with *what* children know. In particular, we are interested in how children acquire, organize, and apply knowledge (Copple, DeLisi, & Sigel, 1982).

As in each of the chapters that focus on a specific area of development, we will consider some activities that are, by necessity, chosen somewhat arbitrarily. Although we will be highlighting science and math, keep in mind that virtually every activity involves **cognition.** Children actively learn, use problem-solving strategies, and construct new knowledge use from all activities, be they science and math or art, music,

movement, manipulatives, storytelling, or dramatic play. In no way does this choice imply that such development does not occur in other activities as well. With this caveat in mind, we will consider the following:

1. We will begin with a brief review of two influential theoretical views of cognitive development—behaviourism and Piaget's cognitive developmental theory—and then introduce some elements of cognitive theory that are relevant.

2. During the preschool years, children begin to acquire some specific cognitive skills.

   • We will consider five cognitive tasks—classification, seriation, number concepts, temporal concepts, and spatial concepts—and activities that can help children master them.

   • Children also acquire a considerable amount of information during their early years.

3. One of the early childhood curriculum areas we will consider is math.

4. We will also look at various appropriate aspects of science in the early childhood curriculum.

THEORETICAL FOUNDATIONS OF COGNITIVE DEVELOPMENT

Particularly in this century, a number of theories have attempted to explain the development of the intellect. One of the theories discussed in Chapters 2 and 3 that has influenced educational practices is behaviourism. A far more influential theory on early childhood education, however, is the cognitive developmental theory of Jean Piaget. Another noteworthy, recent theoretical framework that is quite compatible with Piaget's theory is provided by cognitive psychology.

BEHAVIOURISM

In our earlier examination of the influence of B.F. Skinner, we noted the foundation of behaviourism as the belief that learning is controlled by the consequences of behaviour. When those consequences are pleasant, a child is likely to repeat the behaviour, whereas a disagreeable consequence is more apt to result in the child discontinuing the behaviour.

Behavioural theory is used in early childhood education in both social and learning contexts. The DISTAR program discussed in Chapter 3 applies it to learning, but we have marked reservations about the developmental appropriateness of such a teacher-centred, work-oriented approach. In the social context, however, behavioural theory has more to offer early childhood programs. Behavioural modification, or **behaviour management,** is used to change a child's behaviour by systematically managing consequences.

PIAGET'S THEORY OF COGNITIVE DEVELOPMENT

Piaget offers a very different view of cognitive development, one based on allowing children to build concepts through direct teaching. He has given us a way to understand how children think, pointing out that their minds work in a way that is different from those of adults, and describing how their thinking develops. Over the past several decades, many early childhood educators have incorporated Piagetian principles in their programs to the point where today many of them are often considered common practice. We shall examine these principles later in this chapter when we review cognitive tasks.

To understand the rationale for some of these practices, it is important to recall Piaget's theory. Spend a few moments reviewing the section about Piaget in Chapter 2, which contains a basic overview of the process of learning through adaptation and organization of schemata as well as a brief examination of Piaget's stages of development. Here we will look closely at types of knowledge and characteristics of the preoperational period.

Types of Knowledge

Chapter 2 stated that one function of the mind is to categorize information into schemata. This is an active process by which the child continually finds relationships among objects (Furth, 1969). By physically manipulating and changing objects, the child constructs knowledge about the objects and their relationships. This is an important point. Knowledge is not something that is "poured" into the child by some external source, such as the teacher, but rather something that the child has to construct for herself or himself.

This is why Piaget's theory is also called **constructivist theory**. For example, a child trying to place a square block on the top point of a triangular one will, after some trials, construct an understanding of the relationship of these two blocks. By transforming the blocks into a new position, the child acquires knowledge (Forman & Kuschner, 1977). Because of this need to manipulate and transform materials in the environment, learning has to be an active, not a passive, process.

Piaget identified three types of knowledge. (Specific examples of their application will be discussed in the upcoming section on cognitive tasks.)

1. **Physical knowledge** involves learning about objects in the environment and their properties such as colour, size, weight, or shape. **Discrimination**, the ability to distinguish between different features, is the basic cognitive task involved in this type of knowledge.

2. **Logico-mathematical knowledge** concerns the relationships among objects as well as their relationships in time and space. This type of knowledge allows children to organize their environment to make sense of it.

3. **Social knowledge** is conveyed by people and defined by culture. It involves the many social rules, morals, and values children must learn to function in society (Charlesworth & Lind, 1990; Forman & Kuschner, 1977; Kamii & DeClark, 1985; Saunders & Bingham-Newman, 1984). We will discuss aspects of social knowledge in Chapter 13.

By about the age of 2, at the beginning of the preoperational period, children have acquired a new mental ability, **symbolic representation**. Young children are now able to use mental images to stand for something else. Preoperational children have a limited view of reality, one that comes from their own perceptions, which they rely on to understand what they see. As we all know, our eyes can fool us. As adults, however, we recognize the illusion of appearance—for instance, knowing through logic that although the ball of clay has been stretched out into a long sausage before our eyes, it contains no more or no less clay than it did before. But young children do not yet have that logical ability and rely on their perception, which tells them that it looks as if there is more (or less) clay now. This reliance on their own viewpoints contributes to children's **egocentricity,** the assumption that everyone experiences and sees the world as they do. Young children assume that other people can understand them and what they think because they believe that the viewpoint of others must match their own.

For preschool-aged children to begin to see experiences from a less egocentric point of view, they must have many opportunities to examine, manipulate, modify, transform, experiment, and reflect on objects. Piaget stressed the importance for children of **reflective abstraction**—the opportunity to think about and reflect on what they are doing—which is part of spontaneous, self-directed activity. Through reflective abstraction and active control over materials, children gradually learn to differentiate between what they perceive and reality.

Elkind (1986) cites one of Piaget's examples of reflective abstraction, that of a child arranging ten pebbles into a square, a circle, and a triangle. "What the child discovers, as a result of that activity, is that no matter how he or she arranges the pebbles, they still remain 10 in number" (p. 636).

Gradually, through many first-hand experiences in which they are able to act on objects, preoperational children move toward a more logical mode of thinking. They begin to use and refine the ability to classify and seriate objects (processes we will discuss later in this chapter), which allows them to organize information more logically. Most children do not reach the concrete operational period until they are in school.

Piaget's theory offers teachers insight into the growing abilities of young children to think logically. Through this insight come methods of working with young children that suggest that a well-structured environment, ample activities and materials from which children can actively learn, and understanding adults who encourage without interfering will facilitate cognitive growth in young children. Much of this approach is incorporated into many early childhood programs and accepted as developmentally appropriate practice today (Bredekamp, 1987).

COGNITIVE THEORY

Cognitive theory is concerned primarily with cognitive processes and shares a number of features with Piaget's cognitive developmental theory.

Both approaches try to identify children's cognitive abilities and limitations at different points in their development. Both also acknowledge that later cognitive abilities build on and grow out of earlier, more primitive ones. In addition, both theories consider that existing concepts have a great impact on the acquisition of new knowledge (Siegler, 1986).

But, as is true with behavioural theory, cognitive theory does not focus on stages of cognitive development. Instead, it emphasizes cognitive processes, like comprehension, memory, and reading, and then attempts to explain them. How does a child understand a story? Differently from an adult? How does a child remember a story or an event? How does memory change with age? In fact, toward the end of his life, much of Piaget's work also focused on these questions about cognition.

Some of the world's most influential cognitive psychologists are Canadians. For example, much of what we know about memory is due to Canadian theorists, especially Craik and Tulving from the University of Toronto.

Memory

Memory is divided into short-term and long-term components. **Short-term (or working) memory** provides limited capacity for remembering information temporarily, for instance,

a telephone number. **Long-term (or permanent) memory** refers to the vast store of information and knowledge that we hold for a long time. This stored information is organized so it can be readily retrieved and linked to new information. Children's ability to remember improves dramatically over the first years of life, but preschool children do not yet use memory as efficiently as do older children. School-aged children in the primary grades have made a number of gains, but they do not yet have the memory skills of adults.

A number of **memory strategies** are used to remember information, for instance, **rehearsal** (mentally repeating information over and over, which you probably do with phone numbers), **organization** (placing items to be remembered into logical categories), and **elaboration** (making up imaginary connections when there is no logical link among items).

Although preschoolers can learn to use such strategies, they are not very adept at this skill. It also takes preschoolers longer than older children or adults to retrieve information from both short-term and long-term memory stores. In addition, young children hold considerably fewer pieces of information in their working memories at one time than do older children (Mussen, Conger, Kagan, 1986 & Huston, 1990; Price, 1989; Siegler, 1983).

One aspect of memory that distinguishes older from younger children's thinking is **metamemory,** the ability to think about one's own memory. Older children, for instance, are more realistic in answering the question, "Do you forget?"; younger children often deny that they do forget. Young children are also not very good at estimating how many items they think they will be able to remember, unrealistically predicting that they can remember all of a large number of items. Also, the instruction to "remember what I tell you" does not improve preschoolers' memory when they are later asked to recall, whereas the word "remember" gives older children the cue to use some memory strategies (Daehler & Bukatko, 1985; Siegler, 1983; Siegler, 1986).

Cognitive theory provides some concepts useful in learning how children's cognitive development progresses. Specific consideration of how information is taken in, memory strategies, and metamemory helps us recognize young children's abilities and limitations. The activities planned for preschool children should be congruent with what we know about their abilities.

COGNITIVE TASKS

In addition to helping us understand how children think, theories of cognition also provide some insights into what cognitive skills children need to acquire. We know that developing sensorimotor knowledge is the main task of infants and young toddlers, who later will move toward representative thought and symbolic play, accomplishments that open a whole new world for both children and their teachers. The preoperational period (see Chapter 2) is a lengthy one, during which many cognitive skills are acquired. In this section, we will review some of those skills, including classification; seriation; number, temporal, and spatial concepts; and acquisition of information.

CLASSIFICATION

Classification is the ability to sort and group objects by some common attribute or property. To classify, a child has to note similarities and differences between objects. Classification involves two simultaneous processes, sorting (separating) objects and grouping (joining) objects (Charlesworth & Lind, 1990). For instance, in classifying beads, Liam groups the red beads at the same time that he sorts out the blue and yellow ones; Shanda groups the largest beads and sorts out all other sizes.

If we did not have the ability to classify, every object and experience would represent a separate, isolated piece of information in our minds. Classification allows us to deal "economically with the environment" (Lavatelli, 1970, p. 81). Although young children use perceptual judgment to classify, for instance, grouping items that look the same, true classification is a mental operation that goes beyond such sensory cues. True classification does not actually appear during the preoperational period, but innumerable preschool classification experiences contribute to its emergence.

Children classify spontaneously and frequently use themselves as a basis for social classification, separating boys from the girls, for example, or those who get to play with the blocks from those who don't. Of course, children can classify a group of

objects in many ways. Features such as colour, shape, size, material, pattern, and texture provide concrete attributes by which to group. Older preschoolers will use more abstract categories, such as the function of items (e.g., objects that are used in cooking); common features (e.g., things that have four legs); or association (e.g., galoshes and rain go together) (Charlesworth & Lind, 1990).

Because young children sort and group items naturally, the early childhood environment should provide a rich variety of objects and experiences that can be used for such activities.

- Many early childhood materials such as manipulatives, blocks, and science materials lend themselves to being classified.
- Less obvious items in the art, book, dramatic play, and sensory areas also have inherent properties that children will group and sort.

- In addition, teacher feedback should reinforce the value of children's sponta-neous classification activities. ("You put all of the green chairs around the round table and the blue chairs at the rectangular table!")
- Structured classification activities should also be part of the early childhood pro-gram. In large and small groups, and individually, children can be encouraged to find commonalities among people, objects, and experiences.
- Similarly, children can explore objects and describe their attributes, and articu-late similarities and differences.
- Older preschoolers can be encouraged to group items by two attributes. ("Put together the things that are round and hard.")
- Children can also be helped to compare subclasses by distinguishing between "all" and "some" (all of these are flowers, but some of these are daisies).

SERIATION

Seriation concerns the relationship among objects and the ability to place them in a logical sequence or order. Simple seriation involves concrete objects, for instance, arranging objects from longest to shortest or widest to narrowest. Sensory seriation can include ordering sounds from loudest to softest, tastes from sweetest to sourest, or colours from darkest to lightest. Seriation can also relate to time sequences, for example, what happened first, second, third, and so forth. As children engage in seri-ation activities, they use and are helped to acquire a vocabulary of comparative words ("this is the longest," "he is older," "I have more pudding," "your hair is lighter than mine," "my blocks are taller").

The early childhood environment should include many materials and experi-ences to encourage seriation.

- Unit blocks and a number of manipulatives such as nesting toys offer many opportunities for children to seriate because they are made in graduated sizes.
- Other materials—for instance, dolls, dishes, props for sand and water play, books, woodworking equipment, and nature collections—should be provided in a variety of sizes to prompt spontaneous ordering and comparison.
- Teachers can also encourage children to note and verbalize comparisons, between each other, between objects, and between sets of objects.
- Instructions in group activities such as "Simon Says" and "Red Rover" can be worded to encourage compar-isons (Hohmann, Banet, & Weikart, 1979).

NUMBER CONCEPTS

Number is an understanding of quantity, an awareness that entails increasingly more complex concepts. In its earliest form, number understanding involves gross comparison of quantity, identifying more and less. The young preschooler then begins to make more exact comparisons through **one-to-one correspon-dence**, pairing socks with shoes or plates with napkins. Preschoolers also acquire a large store of words to label their quantitative understanding, words such as big, small, more, less, tall, short, lots, few. By age 4, children understand that adding or taking away objects from a group changes the number. Not until after the preschool peri-od, however, are children able to distinguish the absolute number from arrangement, real-izing that despite perceptual changes, the number is still the same even if a group of objects is rearranged (Resnick, 1989; Saunders & Bingham-Newman, 1984).

One aspect of acquiring number concepts is counting. Young preschoolers often learn **rote counting,** reciting numbers by memory. Rote counting is different from **rational counting,** which occurs when the child says how many objects are in a group (Charlesworth & Lind, 1990). Be aware, however, that children do not necessarily have to apply the correct number names to count rationally. Children seem to understand the principle of counting and that number names are attached to each object in a group, even if they count "one, two, three, five, eleven, nine" (Gelman & Gallistel, 1978).

The good early childhood environment contains many opportunities to encour-age use of number concepts.

- Materials such as Unifix cubes, Cuisenaire rods, dominoes, number bingo, and other specific counting and math games can help children acquire number con-cepts.

- Children will also compare, count, match, add, and subtract when they are able to manipulate a wide variety of items actively.

- Being able to move objects around is essential to acquiring an understanding of numbers. Workbooks are an inappropriate way for children to gain number con-cepts (Charlesworth & Lind, 1990).

Although children must acquire number concepts through their own efforts, the teacher's role in facilitating this learning is very important. Constance Kamii (1982), one of the leading interpreters of Piaget's theory, suggests that teachers can encourage children to quantify objects logically through a careful choice of words, for instance, asking a child to "bring just enough cups" (p. 31). She encourages teachers to use everyday experiences, such as distribution of snack food, fair division of game pieces, or clean-up time, as a basis for using number concepts (Kamii, 1982). She also recommends group games as a way of encouraging numerical concepts, as children count people or objects, use game board counters, and learn about logical rules (Kamii & DeVries, 1980).

TEMPORAL CONCEPTS

Temporal concepts are concerned with the child's gradual awareness of time as a contin-uum. Infants in the sensorimotor period, not yet able to mentally represent events and experiences, live only in the now time-frame, in which before now and after now do not exist. During the preschool years, children become increasingly aware of temporal rela-tions, such as the order of events and the time relationship between cause and effect ("I hurt my knee because I fell off the climber," rather than "I fell off the climber because I hurt my knee"). Not until early adolescence, however, do children have a true idea of temporal relations (Hohmann et al., 1979; Saunders & Bingham-Newman, 1984).

Preschoolers' sense of time is still quite arbitrary and linked to concrete experi-ences. It would be meaningless to use conventional time measures (clock or calendar) to answer Mark's concern about how long until lunch or Serafina's question about when the field trip to the museum will be. Thus, saying "we will have lunch in a half-hour" or "the field trip is tomorrow" conveys very abstract information to young chil-dren. It makes much more sense to answer such questions in relation to concrete events, for instance, "we will have lunch after reading this story and washing hands, Mark" or "after school you will go home, Serafina, have dinner, and go to sleep; when you wake up tomorrow and come back to school, we will go on the field trip."

Older preschoolers begin to recognize that clocks and calendars help us mark time, although this understanding is still very imperfect. Nonetheless, adults should use conventional time measures in their conversations with children to begin exposing them to time-related vocabulary. In addition, concrete experiences with clocks and calendars should be provided. An actual clock alongside a pictorial clock on which key daily events are shown can help children make the connection between the hands on the clock and when snack, outside play time, group time, and other key activities occur. Similarly, a calendar on which the days of the week are accompanied by pictures representing home and school, interspersed with pictures of a child sleeping in bed can help make the passage of day and night or weekdays and weekends understandable.

In everyday experiences and conversations, temporal concepts can be strengthened.

- The daily routine reinforces a consistent time sequence (first comes group time, then activity time, next snack, and so forth) as well as intervals of varying lengths (group time is shorter than activity time).

- Children also need to be exposed to and frequently use temporal words such as before, after, start, stop, first, second, last, next, earlier, later.

- Discussing past occurrences and anticipating future ones gives children the opportunity to use **temporal sequencing**, placing a series of events into their order of occurrence. As an example, children might discuss the steps involved in coming to school in the morning (Essa & Rogers, 1992).

SPATIAL CONCEPTS

Spatial concepts relate to objects and people as they occupy, move in, and use space. Spatial concepts also concern the spatial relationships between people and objects, for instance, standing behind the chair, running toward the teacher, or putting the triangular block on top of the rectangular one. Actually, children are constantly experiencing

spatial concepts through their own body movement, their activities, and their physical proximity to others. Their earliest learning, during infancy, was based to a great extent on their motor activity, and this mode of learning continues through the preschool years.

A wide variety of experiences and equipment strengthen children's growing awareness of spatial concepts and relationships.

- Equipment that invites children to explore spatial possibilities is essential in an early childhood setting. Children need to position their bodies in many possible ways in relation to equipment; for example, they should be able to go over, under, around, through, into, out of, and across.

- Such experiences can also be structured through obstacle courses and games children invent. Stories that entail spatial concepts like "The Three Billy Goats Gruff" who walk *over* the bridge that the troll lives *under* also can be used. Similarly, "Harry by the Sea" (Zion, 1965) has led to some interesting games with autumn leaves going *on top of* a group of children.

- Active manipulation of objects, such as fitting things together or disassembling them, also strengthens children's spatial understanding. For one thing, children can explore manipulative items from all angles, seeing them from different points of view—from the front, back, side, bottom, or top.

- Puzzles, shape boxes, nuts and bolts, Tinkertoys, nesting blocks, pegboards with pegs, pots and pans with lids, dress-up clothes, woodworking, and collage materials are examples of common preschool materials and activities that reinforce spatial concepts (Charlesworth & Lind, 1990; Hohmann et al., 1979; Saunders & Bingham-Newman, 1984).

As is the case with their concept of time, young children's concept of space is viewed from a very subjective perspective. They rely on their own perceptions of where, in what position, how close, how far away, or near an object might be; conventional measures such as centimetres are meaningless. To say that it is three kilometres to the dairy means nothing; instead, saying, "we will be able to sing four or five songs in the bus, and then we'll be at the dairy" is much more concrete (Essa & Rogers, 1992). Be aware also that space and time are often closely related. For example, preschoolers see the distance between the building and the fence as closer if they run than if they walk, because they get to the fence more quickly.

Although preschoolers do not yet understand conventional measuring devices and units of measurement, they nonetheless measure space frequently. They gauge the relative sizes of blocks as they build structures, estimate how much more sand they need to fill the bucket, or judge whether their bodies will fit into the tunnel in the obstacle course.

- Teachers can help children verbalize measurement concepts by using words such as more, less, short(er), long(er), full, empty, double, or half.

- Activities such as making play dough, woodworking, and cooking can help children recognize the importance of accurate measurement and relative proportions.

- Older preschoolers and school-aged children also enjoy **mapping**, representing space through such media as marking pens or blocks. For instance, ask children to draw a picture of the route they took to get to school, to make a map with unit blocks of their walk around the neighbourhood, or to fill in special features on an outline map you have drawn of the classroom. A Closer Look describes such an activity.

ACQUISITION OF INFORMATION

While young children learn about the properties of objects, compare objects to discover what makes them similar and different, begin to understand quantity and number concepts, and start to develop a sense of time and space, they also learn a wide variety of facts and information. Some of this information emerges from repeated daily experiences; other items seem to peak children's interest and stick in their memories.

The day after she found an old innersole on a walk with her parents, 4-year-old Julie, for instance, told her teacher that she has a "pet paramecium." She made the

A CLOSER LOOK

Mapmaking

The children were taking a walk around the block. Teachers Ardith and Jason encouraged them to pay close attention to everything they saw on the way, including buildings, trees, stop signs, the parking lot next to the dentist's office, and other features. "Remember, when we get back we're going to make a map of our block. So we have to pay really close attention to everything we see," Jason told them.

The children discussed and described all sorts of features that, on previous walks, had gone unnoticed. Lynette, for instance, found a doghouse in the yard behind the brown house. Chad noticed a bed of tulips and daffodils along the side of the blue house.

When the children got back to their classroom, Ardith put out a large sheet of butcher paper as a starting point for the map. The children decided to start their map at the school. "Our school is on the corner, so we should put it right here," said James, pointing to the lower left-hand corner of the paper.

"Let's build the school," suggested Miriam, and got some blocks from the block area. She and James built the school with several unit blocks and enclosed it with a "fence" of connected, longer blocks.

"I want to put in the doghouse," said Lynette.

"Where is the brown house?" asked Ardith.

"Let's put it here," said Lynette, pointing next to the school.

"Is the brown house next to our school?" asked Ardith.

"No, it's on this side of the block," said Pradeep, pointing along the other side of the map.

Because the brown house was not on the map yet, Lynette decided to draw a picture of the doghouse. She got a piece of paper and crayons from the art shelf.

"Maybe we should think about what we saw in the order that we saw it on our walk," suggested Ardith. "What was the first thing we saw when we got past the playground fence?" The children discussed the various buildings and houses, and soon they began putting up more block structures as they recalled the spatial relationships of the various features.

Lynette finished her drawing of the doghouse and cut it out with the scissors. It was placed behind the brown house when that was put on the map. Chad wanted to paint the blocks for the blue house so it would be the right colour.

"I don't think we ought to paint our blocks, Chad. What else could you use to make the blue house?" Ardith asked.

After a moment's thought, Chad said he would find the materials for the house in the woodworking area. He found a piece of scrap lumber that was just the right size and painted it blue. Later, Chad and Melissa drew flowers on the butcher paper along the house's side. Stop signs, trees, cars, the snail that the children had seen along the side of the road, and the sign outside the dentist's office were all added to the map.

The teachers left the map out for several days. Children continued to add items to it, particularly things they noticed on following days on their way to and from school.

connection between seeing a picture of a paramecium, an elongated one-celled organism, and the shape of the innersole. Kim Lee, who is 5, is able to recognize pictures of and name more than a dozen kinds of dinosaurs. Elise, aged 3, tells the teacher, "I need an ice bucket to keep my milk cold at lunch." She had watched a movie on television the night before and was impressed by the ice bucket into which a bottle of wine was placed! Young children generally do not discriminate between esoteric and practical facts, collecting and storing much information. The early childhood curriculum allows us to select information and convey it to children.

As we discussed in Chapter 8, appropriate topics for curriculum development can revolve around children, families, and the community. These familiar subjects, which offer innumerable learning possibilities, can then be expanded and built on to help children gain additional information that has relevance in the context of their lives and experiences.

Acquisition of information, as well as of the concepts related to classification, seriation, numbers, time, and space, occurs in many ways in the early childhood program. Just about any activity in which young children engage involves one or several of these concepts. Although the acquisition of information and concepts is often associated with specific curriculum areas, especially math and science, it is not that easy to place them into discrete categories. *Children's thinking is ongoing and involves a constant taking in, sifting, connecting, and storing of experiences, concepts, and information.*

The following sections will examine math and science as separate curriculum areas. This is done to reinforce the importance of these subjects as vital parts of the early childhood curriculum, not to imply in any way that they are the major vehicles through which cognitive development is fostered. Remember also that math and science are as much a part of other activities (for example, blocks, cooking, woodworking, manipulatives, dramatic play, art) as they are separate activities. it is also important to note that the cognitive tasks we discussed earlier are an inherent part of both math and science. It is easy to see that the acquisition of number concepts is central to math. Classification, seriation, and temporal and spatial concepts are equally integral to both math and science. In addition, these concepts supply some of the tools required to carry out math and science endeavours, for instance, measuring, grouping, and comparing.

MATH

Adults often think of mathematics as an abstract discipline involving complex algebraic formulas and geometric calculations, yet the foundations of math are ground-

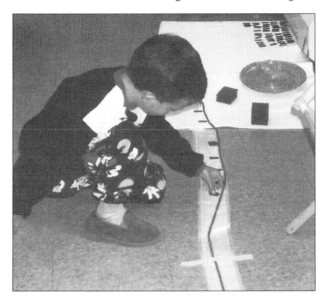

ed in concrete experience such as the exploration of objects and gradual understanding of their properties and relationships. The cognitive concepts we have just discussed—classification, seriation, numbers, time, and space—are all an integral part of the development of logico-mathematical and physical knowledge. Young children are continually involved in mathematical learning, which the early childhood environment and teachers must encourage. The suggested activities listed in the discussion of classification, seriation, numbers, time, and space all contribute to the gradual acquisition of math concepts.

Much of the previous discussion on cognitive tasks reflects what should be part of a math focus in the early childhood curriculum. Math for young children is not abstract. It is, rather, the provision of many materials that invite the child to handle, explore, compare, measure, combine, take apart, reconstruct, and transform in an infinite variety of ways. By acting on materials, children actively construct knowledge and gradually come to understand mathematical principles.

Central to this gradual understanding is the ability to conserve, recognize that objects remain the same in amount or number despite perceptual changes. As we have discussed before, preschoolers rely very much on their perceptions and think that because materials are rearranged or changed in form, their amount is also changed. Thus, Lisa may think there are more blocks when they are arranged on the floor in a "road" than when they are stacked on the shelf; Sylvester will tell you that now that the play dough ball has been made into three snakes, there is more play dough.

This reliance on the observable rather than on an internal understanding that materials do not change unless something is added or taken away is a characteristic of children in the preoperational period. It is through many experiences in arranging and transforming materials that children gradually move to the next period, in which they are able to conserve. Because preschool-aged children usually are not conservers, they need many concrete experiences on which to build the foundation to acquire this ability in their elementary school years.

The early childhood classroom should contain many materials that lend themselves to acquiring math concepts. These include blocks, sand and water implements, dramatic play props such as dishes and cooking utensils, a variety of manipulatives, art and woodworking materials, and a variety of other items that can be compared, grouped, counted, matched, or placed in a logical order. The class may also contain a specific math learning centre, in which materials designed to encourage and enhance math concepts are collected. Finally, many excellent children's books focus on or lend themselves to including math concepts. Such books should portray math ideas accurately, contain text and illustrations that appeal to young children, and have an appropriate amount of detail given the ages of the children (Harsh, 1987).

SCIENCE

Science is a natural endeavour for young children who are constantly exploring, asking questions, wondering why or why not, observing, touching, and tasting. It involves a growing awareness of self, other living things, and the environment through the senses and through exploration (McIntyre, 1984). Science is not so much a body of specific knowledge as it is a way of thinking and acting, an approach to solving problems (Charlesworth & Lind, 1990). For young children, science is "a reflective attitude toward an object of interest, even during play," a search for answers to interesting questions (Forman & Kaden, 1987, p. 141).

In viewing science as part of the early childhood curriculum, it is important to keep in mind our earlier discussions about the cognitive abilities and limitations of preschool-aged children. Science concepts need to be concrete and observable. A concept that is abstract and not within the realm of children's experience is not appropriate. Thus, topics like the revolution of planets and the nature of matter and energy are inappropriate for preschoolers (Smith, 1982) because they are abstract and non-observable. However, magnetism, simple electrical circuits, and simple machines like levers, pivots, and pulleys are observable, and therefore appropriate.

Science can be classified into two categories: biological science, which deals with living things, and physical science, which concerns non-living materials.

BIOLOGICAL SCIENCE

People, animals, and plant life provide fascinating subjects to discover and explore. Children have a natural interest in their own bodies and bodily functions; they also enjoy learning about and caring for animals and plants. In addition, there is the important interrelation between plant and animal life with respect to food. Each of these subjects provides a selection of appropriate topics to include in the early childhood curriculum.

The Human Body

Young preschoolers at age 2 or 3 are still learning the labels of various parts of their bodies, discovering the body's capabilities, and mastering skills in movement and dexterity. Older preschoolers, on the other hand, have a burgeoning awareness of the less visible parts of the body and want to know why a knee bleeds when someone falls down, where the food goes after it is eaten, or why the heart thumps after a person runs fast.

Children also become increasingly aware of their own growth, relishing the idea of being bigger than they were when they were babies. They are cognizant of each other's characteristics and note that children differ from each other in height, hair length, eye colour, and other ways. Below are some topics that can be incorporated into the curriculum to help children increase awareness of their bodies.

- Parts of the body and what they can and cannot do make an intriguing topic for movement activities. "Can you touch your knee with your fingers ... your ear with your elbow? Can you balance on your bottom ... on your little fingers?"

- The senses deserve exploration. Every action and activity involves the senses, although we are not always consciously aware of it. Specific activities that encourage children to attend to sensory messages, discriminate between various sensory stimuli, or enjoy sensory stimulation for its own sake should be planned. (See Chapter 11 for more discussion on this topic.)

- The concepts of growth and change captivate children. Baby pictures, growth charts, and visits from children's younger siblings can help strengthen these concepts.

- Comparison among children reinforces that each person is unique and that there are many differences among people.

- Care for the body through everyday self-help skills, as well as through activities that focus on the relationship of cleanliness and grooming to health, can be incorporated.

- Older preschoolers and school-aged children enjoy learning about the inner workings of their respiratory, circulatory, or digestive systems as long as such information is presented concretely. For instance, a "visit" from a skeleton can help teach the difference between bones and joints. Children can move as the skeleton "moves."

Animals

Any environment contains a variety of animals, for instance, domestic dogs and cats, the classroom gerbil, the sparrows and pigeons that hop in the trees or nest in the eaves of buildings, the horses and cows on nearby farms, the tigers and walruses in the city zoo, the starfish and sea cucumbers in the tide pools, the ants on the playground, the butterflies that flit outside the windows, or the snails that come out after the rain. Children can observe and learn about a wide range of animals in the immediate environment.

The animals that are part of your ecological system provide a rich variety of topics that can be included in the curriculum. If you live in Alberta, why discuss whales when you have not taken time to observe the mountain goats, elk, or cattle in your surroundings? Listed below are suggestions for how animals might be included in the curriculum.

- Classroom pets provide a natural way for children to learn about, observe, and care for animals.

- Take time to observe the animals around the school and neighbourhood.

- Animals can be temporary guests in the classroom.

- Plan field trips to nearby animal habitats such as a zoo, farm, aquarium, fish hatchery, or nature preserve. Visit more than once because there will be much more to see than can be observed on one trip.

- Discuss children's observations about animals.

- Keep records of the children's interactions with animals through photographs, children's pictures, and their stories.

- Through modelling, discussion, and reminders, help children develop a respect for all animal life.

- Children's exposure to animals through classroom pets, animals that visit the class, neighbourhood walks, or field trips should always precede representational activities.

Plants

Plant life surrounds us, whether through the vase of flowers in the classroom, the salad at lunch, or the tree in the play yard. Children can expand their understanding of the world by learning about plants, their function, needs, aesthetic value, and variety. As is the case in helping children learn about animals, children's increasing understanding about plants should focus on the plants in your environment. The following activities can help children increase their awareness of plants.

- Call attention to and encourage children to describe plants in the environment—the classroom fern, the maple outside the window, the apple tree across the street. Your enjoyment of plants can help children develop an appreciation for the beauty and variety of plant life.

- Observe and take photographs to record seasonal changes. Compare the photos and discuss the seasons in the context of the children's concrete observations and recollections.

- Help the children understand that plants need water, light, and soil. Note that the leaves droop if a plant does not get enough water, and celebrate as it perks up after an adequate watering. Compare the growth of similar plants on the windowsill and in a shady corner.

- Involve children in observing the growth of plants. Plant seeds in window boxes, pots, an outdoor garden plot, or individual containers that children can take home (grass and bean seeds grow very quickly). Keep a daily record of changes through photographs, measurements, or written records of the children's observations.

- If possible, observe a plant through the growth cycle, from seed to blossom to vegetable, fruit, or flower.

- Consider the plants we eat. Visit commercial farms and orchards or a neighbourhood garden to see how plants produce the foods we eat.

- Include frequent cooking activities in the curriculum to introduce children to new foods and to increase their understanding of familiar foods.

- Through concrete activities, convey the idea that food helps meet nutritional needs. (See Chapter 11 for a more detailed discussion of cooking and nutrition as part of the curriculum.)

PHYSICAL SCIENCE

Children are in constant contact with and take in information about the inanimate, physical elements of their world, and they acquire many scientific concepts. Patti finds the right length of block to create a bridge, applying an elementary law of physics, for example. Aiden mixes water with soil and, through basic chemistry, creates a new substance, mud. Kumalo notices that the black rock he found on the field trip is the same colour as the dark band along the face of the mountain. Through such experiences, children begin to construct knowledge about the world and the laws that govern it. We will consider how young children acquire knowledge of physics, chemistry, and meteorology, three examples of physical science.

Physics

Children encounter elements of physics—the relationship between matter and energy—through numerous materials and activities. Blocks, outdoor equipment, water

and sand, and manipulatives often present phenomena to be noted and problems to be solved. Children learn about force (throwing the ball hard makes it go further), gravity (cars roll faster down a steep incline), or inertia (a heavy object resists being moved but will move more readily when placed on rollers).

It is not particularly important that children label the laws of physics involved in their actions, although they do delight in acquiring a scientific vocabulary (the swing is a "pendulum" or the slide is an "inclined plane") (Ziemer, 1987). What is important is that children have many experiences in which their actions toward objects create movement, for instance, rolling on rollers, jumping, tilting, dropping, blowing, sucking, pulling, and swinging. Children thus experience how their actions affect objects, how they can vary their actions to vary the effect, and how different objects react to their actions (Kamii & Lee-Katz, 1982).

Chemistry

Chemistry deals with the properties, composition, and changes in substances, phenomena that children observe in everyday life. Sensory experiences help children learn about the properties of things around them. Children make intuitive comparisons that tell them that wood is different from metal, which is different from glass, which is different from plastic. They also learn that soap and water result in bubbles, water added to sand makes the sand mouldable, and chocolate mixed with milk makes chocolate milk.

Cooking activities are filled with examples of chemistry. Through many cooking experiences, children begin to generalize about how different foods react and are transformed through cutting, mixing, blending, heating, and cooling. For instance, when grapes, banana slices, and orange segments are mixed, they still look like grapes, bananas, and oranges; but when eggs, milk, and flour are mixed, they take on a totally new appearance as batter. When batter is baked, it becomes solid; when potatoes are boiled, they become soft; when eggs are boiled, they become hard. Water can be transformed from a liquid into solid ice after freezing and into elusive steam after boiling. Sugar or salt becomes invisible when stirred into water.

Meteorology

Children are certainly aware of and interested in the weather, an appropriate topic for discussion with young children. Mr. Jenkins encouraged the 4-, 5-, and 6-year-olds in his class to listen to the morning weather forecast and discuss it during the first group time. Throughout the day, then, the children validated what they heard through their own activities and observations. For instance, the children discovered that the wind can blow from different directions. The west wind predicted on the radio made their hair fly in their eyes when they faced the building, whereas an east wind blew their hair out behind them. Kites and streamers further reinforced the idea that the wind can blow from different directions. Storm predictions could be verified by noticing the clouds; they usually meant that the children would plan some alternate, indoor, large motor activities. The children decided what kind of outer clothing they needed. They checked the large outdoor thermometer and compared the level of the temperature line with the adjacent pictures of a shirt, sweater, jacket, and hat with mittens that were pasted at the appropriate temperature intervals.

PARENTS AND PROFESSIONALS

Parental Values Concerning Cognitive Development

As with all areas of the early childhood curriculum, it is very important to share with parents a clear statement of the school's philosophy about how to support and further children's cognitive development. Parents should be aware, for instance, that the program is built on the conviction that children learn best through concrete, hands-on activity; that children are able to select meaningful activities on their own; and that play and learning go together. Conversely, such a philosophy means that the program does not engage in abstract and developmentally inappropriate teaching practices that require the child to sit quietly and inactively.

Today's parents are bombarded by pressures to succeed, which includes having successful children as well. Thus, many well-intentioned parents feel a need to see evidence that their children are indeed learning in their early childhood program. For instance, parents may say to you, "But Marcia does nothing but play all day; when will she learn something?" or "Ron starts kindergarten next year; shouldn't he be learning to read?" or "I'm thinking of enroling Betsy in the school where my neighbour's son goes; he comes home with dittoes every day and Betsy only brings home paintings." How do you respond in a way that respects parental concerns but maintains the integrity of your program?

Conveying to parents your philosophy of how children best learn involves frequent explanation and supportive information. First, it requires that you, as the teacher, be secure in your understanding of how young children learn and acquire concepts; this will enable you to address parents' questions and concerns. It is also important to make information from experts, which supports your approach, available to parents. This might be done through a parent library, which includes such books as *Playtime Learning Games for Young Children*, by Alice Honig. In addition, you can distribute reprints of well-written articles to each family, prominently post short quotes on the parent bulletin board, invite an appropriate speaker to a parent meeting, or plan parent discussion groups with a knowledgeable facilitator. Let parents know about *Developmentally Appropriate Practice in Early Childhood Programs Serving Children from Birth through Age 8* (Bredekamp, 1987), which supports your approach. In other words, let them know that your work with the children is founded on and backed by research and theory.

One teacher dealt creatively with the questions some parents posed about what their children were learning. She videotaped the children one day during a half-hour of self-selected activities. Then, during a parent meeting, she followed the showing of the videotape by discussing how the children engaged in problem solving and concept formation through their activities. The parents were amazed at how much learning was going on!

Although it is important to convey your approach and philosophy to parents, it is also vital to recognize that parents are the most important elements in their children's lives. When parents share anecdotes and experiences with you, convey the value you place on the importance of their role as their child's primary teacher and mentor. Recognize parents' expertise and invite them to share it with all of the children. Also inform parents of special community events or exhibits that they might want to attend or visit with their children.

KEY POINTS OF CHAPTER 12

THEORETICAL FOUNDATIONS OF COGNITIVE DEVELOPMENT

▲ 1. The study of children's cognition is more concerned with how children learn than with what they know.

▲ 2. The influence of behaviourism on early childhood education has been particularly strong in direct-instruction programs, in which the teacher controls most aspects of learning.

▲ 3. Piaget's theory of cognitive development, which holds that children construct their own knowledge out of direct experiences, has been the most influential theory in early childhood education.

▲ 4. Physical knowledge involves learning about objects and discriminating between them.

▲ 5. Logico-mathematical knowledge means learning about the relationships between objects.

▲ 6. The preschooler, in the preoperational period, employs symbolic representation, the ability to use mental images to stand for something else.

▲ 7. Children who use preoperational thinking are egocentric and rely on perception rather than on logic.

▲ 8. Understanding preschoolers' thinking processes and limitations helps early childhood educators provide an appropriate environment for cognitive development.

▲ 9. Cognitive theory attempts to understand the cognitive processes involved in activities like understanding, remembering, reading, and writing.

▲ 10. Young children's memories are not as efficient as those of older children and adults.

COGNITIVE TASKS

▲ 11. Preschoolers begin to learn classification, the ability to sort and group objects by some similar characteristic.

▲ 12. Seriation helps children focus on the relationships among objects, as they place them in a logical order or sequence.

▲ 13. An understanding of quantity or number concepts involves more than rote counting; it concerns rational counting as well, the ability to correctly attach a numeral name to each item in a group of objects.

▲ 14. Preschoolers also begin to acquire temporal concepts, the sense of time as a continuum that includes the past, present, and future.

▲ 15. Spatial concepts are concerned with how objects and people occupy or relate to each other in space.

▲ 16. The early childhood program can help children acquire relevant information through an appropriate curriculum.

KEY TERMS

behaviour management

cognition

constructivist theory

discrimination

egocentricity

elaboration

logico-mathematical knowledge

long-term (or permanent) memory

mapping

memory strategy

metamemory

one-to-one correspondence

organization

physical knowledge

rational counting

reflective abstraction

rehearsal

rote counting

short-term (or working) memory

social knowledge

spatial concept

symbolic representation

temporal concept

temporal sequencing

MATH

▲17. The foundation of more abstract math concepts is formed in early childhood, as children explore concrete objects and understand their properties and relationships.

▲18. Children in elementary school acquire an essential concept, conservation—the recognition that objects remain the same even if they look different; learning conservation is based on numerous early childhood experiences in manipulating concrete objects.

SCIENCE

▲19. Science activities must be based on concrete, observable elements; children's environments provide many opportunities for such learning.

▲20. The biological sciences provide many fascinating topics for young children related to the study of the people, animals, and plant life in their environment.

▲21. There are many concrete possibilities for learning about the physical sciences, including physics, chemistry, and meteorology.

KEY QUESTIONS

1. Observe a young child for about twenty minutes. How does this child use cognitive skills? Note the many ways in which the child uses her or his thinking abilities, including evidence of problem solving, symbolic representation, memory, classification, seriation, time and space concepts, and number concepts.

2. Consider the people in the class for which you are reading this book. In how many different ways can you classify these individuals? Think of as many categories as possible. What does this exercise tell you about cognitive skill development in young children?

3. This chapter has considered only math and science as activities in which children use cognitive processes. How is cognition a part of other areas in the early childhood curriculum?

4. Think of a science class you have taken. What topics from this class might be appropriate concepts for young children? How do you modify information that you as an adult have learned so that it is appropriate for young children?

LANGUAGE DEVELOPMENT THROUGH THE CURRICULUM

Children's early development is particularly astounding when we consider the acquisition of language. Infants arrive in the world with no language, but within a year they are starting to converse. And they have done this without any direct instruction in one of the most complex cognitive tasks, and the one that is unique to humans. The toddler makes rapid gains in language and by the preschool years has acquired an enormous vocabulary, a fundamental grasp of the rules of grammar, and an understanding of the subtleties of the social aspects of communication. In addition, young children begin to develop the skills needed for the complex process of reading and writing, which they begin to tackle soon after they enter school.

These are truly amazing accomplishments. We know much about this language acquisition process, although language researchers certainly are far from understanding completely how children learn to communicate with such speed and accuracy (Gineshi, 1987).

As with each of the chapters dealing with how the curriculum supports children's development, the curricular aspects we discuss represent only some of the ways in which language development is fostered. Keep in mind that children's language is used and expanded in almost every early childhood activity in which they participate. In this chapter, we will look more closely at what we know about how language develops and how the early childhood curriculum can encourage and strengthen language development.

1. We will look at some theoretical views of language development.

2. We will also explore some components of language that can help us understand the complexity of all that children attain during their early years.

3. Because many early childhood programs include children who speak a language other than English, we will consider bilingualism and effective strategies for teaching children a second language.

4. The last half of this chapter will discuss the many components of the early childhood program that support and reinforce language learning.

   - Conversations and language play offer many spontaneous opportunities for language learning.
   - We will also consider some of the many types of planned activities aimed at enhancing language, and place particular emphasis on the story.
   - We will end by discussing emergent literacy, children's ongoing process of learning reading and writing.

THEORETICAL VIEWS OF LANGUAGE DEVELOPMENT

Theorists and researchers have applied a range of explanations to understand how the complex process of language acquisition develops in children. They often come to conflicting conclusions. The **behaviourist view of language development** sees language as mainly influenced by external factors such as the modelling and reinforcement of parents; the second, the **innatist view of language development**, considers inborn factors to be the most important component; a third position, the **interactionist view of language development**, stresses the interaction of language and environmental influences as most important (Bohannon & Warren-Leubecker, 1985; Lindfors, 1987; Owens, 1984).

BEHAVIOURIST VIEW OF LANGUAGE DEVELOPMENT

Earlier in this century, the prevalent view of how children learn language was that it is shaped by the environment. B.F. Skinner's classic text, *Verbal Behaviour* (1957), describes language acquisition as a learned behaviour, subject to the same rules of conditioning (see Chapter 2) as any other behaviour being learned.

According to this view, parents reinforce an infant's language development when they respond by smiling, cuddling the baby, and verbalizing. When specific syllables appear in the baby's babbling repertoire, especially ones that sound like "mama" or "dada," the delighted parents redouble their positive feedback to the baby. This behaviour serves as further reinforcement, encouraging the baby to repeat the sounds that brought such a response. Gradually, Reinforcement becomes more specific, contingent on increasing ability to produce adult-like language. Language becomes more complex because increasingly more complex language is reinforced (Lindfors, 1987). In addition, children learn that language helps them achieve their goals, and this further reinforces and strengthens language acquisition.

INNATIST VIEW OF LANGUAGE DEVELOPMENT

At the opposite end of the spectrum of language theories is the innatist view, which considers the capacity for language as inborn. Noam Chomsky (1972), one of the leading proponents of this view, hypothesizes that children are born with a linguistic structure that makes it possible for them to acquire language as quickly as they do during the preschool years.

Chomsky maintains that language development is largely innate or inborn, which is why some features of language are universal. He believes that every person starts life with a predisposition to understand the rules of grammar and meaning. Thus, children are "wired" to know without being taught that communication has meaning or that it can affirm, negate, question, and command. Beyond this innate **deep structure**, then, children have to learn the specific vocabulary and grammar of their language, what Chomsky calls the **surface structure**.

Because language is innate, it is linked to biological maturation and follows an internal clock, needing to emerge during the "critical age" for language acquisition (Lennenberg, 1967). Children who do not learn language in early childhood have a much more difficult time later, just as learning a second language later in life is not nearly as easy as acquiring it in the early years (Bohannon & Warren-Leubecker, 1985). Language, however, does not emerge automatically; rather, it is triggered by exposure to verbal communication in the environment.

INTERACTIONIST VIEW OF LANGUAGE DEVELOPMENT

A compromise between the behaviourist view, in which external environment is all important, and the innatist view, in which inborn factors are the key, is the interactionist view, which takes important elements from the other two theoretical extremes. Interactionists see many factors such as the social environment, maturation, biology, and cognition at play in the development of language. These elements interact with and modify each other (Bohannon & Warren-Leubecker, 1985).

There are two major approaches to this view—the **cognitive interactionist view of language development** and the **social interactionist view of language development**. As proponents of the former view, Piaget (1926) and other cognitive theorists considered that children's understanding of language is rooted in their cognitive development, requiring, for instance, the ability to represent objects mentally. Language is one way of expressing representational or symbolic thought.

Social interactionist theorists deem that language is intimately tied to social processes. Children's language development is guided by internal factors, but the critical fact is that it must emerge within the social environment provided by the parents. Furthermore, the social interaction that triggers language is a two-way operation, in which children cue their parents and parents, in turn, supply appropriate language experiences (Bohannon & Warren-Leubecker, 1985). Vygotsky (1962), one of the leading proponents of the social interactionist view, argues that the young child's primary social tool is language.

COMPONENTS OF LANGUAGE

Language is a complex system involving a variety of components. Included are learning as well as understanding words, knowing the rules for using words accurately, learning the rules for putting words together meaningfully, and obtaining a growing grasp of the appropriateness of what is being communicated. As each theory of language development indicates, children's early years are particularly crucial in the evolution of language skills. To better grasp the complexity of this task, we will take a closer look at some of these components related to meaning and rules of language.

LANGUAGE MEANING

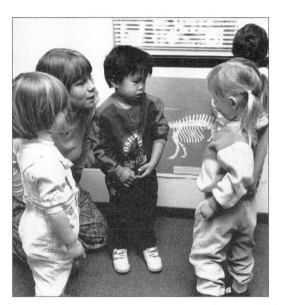

Vocabulary

One way of studying children's language development is to examine the rapid acquisition of vocabulary. For instance, one early study reported that between the ages of 2 1/2 and 4 1/2, children acquire two to four new words per day on the average (Pease & Gleason, 1985); a more recent report estimates that young children learn about ten words every day (Miller & Gildea, 1987). The 3-year-old has a vocabulary of 900 to 1000 words, the 4-year-old's vocabulary typically contains 1500 to 1600 words, and the 5-year-old has acquired a vocabulary of 2100 to 2200 words (Owens, 1984). Estimates of vocabulary size vary, but they are impressive when you consider that a young child has picked up such a large amount of information in such a short time.

Although vocabulary counts provide interesting figures, their use in understanding language development is limited. For one thing, it is difficult to determine whether a child really understands the words he uses. When Colin says, "We're going to Canada's Wonderland and we're going to stay there a million days," does he really understand the word "million"? While he clearly does not have a grasp of "million" as an absolute amount, he nonetheless knows that it has quantitative meaning (Lindfors, 1987). This is a case in which the study of semantics is relevant.

Semantics

Children learn the meanings of words in the context of their experiences. The study of **semantics** examines the understanding of word meanings. One significant part of semantics is a scrutiny of emotion-laden words; the most common examples are those connected to racism. In addition, name-calling depends on the negative impact of certain words. For instance, an "unloaded" word such as "red" simply refers to a colour, whereas labelling a person a "Red" makes this straightforward word derogative. The importance of this aspect of semantics in the handling of children is that they tend to hurt one another through such verbal attacks as name-calling.

In addition, word meaning is related to the **semantic network**, the interrelationship among words (Pease & Gleason, 1985). Fourteen-month-old Monica calls the family pet by its name, "Lucky," then applies the same word to other dogs and even some other four-legged animals she comes across. This **overextension** is typical of toddlers learning their first words, and it reflects their vocabulary limitations (Clark, 1978b).

As they get older, however, children narrow the meanings of words until they become closer to adults' meanings. Monica will gradually learn that Lucky is a dog, that dogs are animals, and that other creatures can also be called animals. Thus, the semantic network includes an increasing understanding of classification (see Chapter 12) through this relationship between the various words (Gleason, 1985; Moskowitz, 1982).

The meanings of some words, which adults take for granted, pose some problems for young children. For instance, they only gradually acquire an understanding of prepositions. It isn't until their third year that preschoolers comprehend the word *in*, followed by *on* and *under*.

More complex prepositions, for instance, *between* or *beside*, are not grasped until ages 4 to 5 (Clark, 1978a; Johnston & Slobin, 1979). Thus, when a teacher tells a group to "wait beside the sink to wash your hands," and Jimmy, aged 3, is under a table, the teacher must recognize that Jimmy may not be "not listening" but rather "not understanding." Young children also have difficulty understanding a sentence in which a sequence is not in its logical order (Goodz, 1982). Therefore, it is harder for preschoolers to understand "before you go outside put on your coat" than "put on your coat before you go outside."

LANGUAGE RULES

Morphology

As children acquire words and understand their meanings, they also learn rules that apply to these words; the study of such word rules is called **morphology**. A **morpheme** is a meaningful part of a word, and is the smallest unit of meaning. For example, the word "block" has one morpheme, whereas "blocks" has two morphemes—the noun "block" and the plural "s." Some examples of morphological word rules include verb tense, plurals, and the possessive form.

Researchers have identified a fairly predictable sequence in which children learn specific morphemes (Brown, 1973; deVilliers & deVilliers, 1973). Among the first such rules children learn are the present progressive form (-*ing* ending), the words *in* and *on*, and the regular plural (-*s* ending). Irregular verb forms and contractions (*isn't*, *we're*) are learned later. These morphemes are used when calculating a child's **mean length of utterance** or MLU (Brown, 1973), which is probably the best measure of language development in preschoolers (Dale, 1976).

Syntax

Rules also apply to combinations of words. **Syntax** involves the grammatical rules that govern the structure of sentences. Even very young children show a grasp of such rules in their construction of two-word sentences. A toddler is much more likely to say "my car" than "car my" or "more juice" than "juice more," indicating a sensitivity to conventional word order in sentences.

Whereas very young children often use simple nouns and verbs alone to convey meaning, older children elaborate on these to create increasingly more complex noun phrases and verb phrases as parts of longer sentences. In addition, somewhere between the ages of 2 and 4, children begin to combine more than one idea in one complex sentence rather than speak two simple sentences (Gineshi, 1987). Children also become progressively more adept at asking questions and stating negatives (deVilliers & deVilliers, 1979). Thus, their language, though limited in vocabulary, can take on infinite variety in its forms of expression. Careful analysis of how children learn grammatical rules indicates that they are not merely imitating what they have heard from adults, but that they are constructing a language system of their own (Gleason, 1985). An example of this is known as **over-regularization**. When children first learn a new morpheme, the past tense -*ed*, for example, they will apply it in all cases, including ones they have never heard used. The child will have *goed out*, *eated dinner*, and, with plural -*s* acquisition, seen *mouses*, *deers*, and *gooses*.

Pragmatics

One additional set of rules governs our system of language. That aspect of communication governed by the social context is called **pragmatics.** Children gradually learn the give-and-take rules of conversation. They learn that during certain times it is appropriate to remain quiet (for instance, when the teacher is reading a story), whereas at other times their verbal input is desired. They also come to understand that different forms of communication are expected in different situations. Depending on the conversational partner, children learn to use different words, apply different levels of formality, and give different types of responses to questions.

This ability to use language in socially appropriate ways is sometimes referred to as **communicative competence** and sometimes as **code switching**. Children acquire this skill very early in life, and are remarkably sophisticated. They will modify how they speak when they talk to a younger child, to a friend, to a visitor at school, or to the teacher; or when they assume the role of Superman, a parent, or a firefighter in role playing (Shatz & Gelman, 1973; Young & Shattuck, 1993). When describing new toys to an adult and to a 2-year-old child in their early childhood program, Canadian 3- and 4-year-olds from diverse backgrounds were found to speak more, speak at a faster rate, and use more syntactically complex speech with the adult listener (Young & Shattuck, 1993). When they spoke to the 2-year-olds, they lowered their MLU, spoke at a slower rate, said less, and were far more likely to use imperatives (e.g., "Do this!") than they were with the adults.

BILINGUALISM/MULTILINGUALISM

Canadian early childhood educators in some areas of the country have been familiar with the issue of **bilingualism** for a long time. However, with our changing immigration patterns, **multilingualism** in the program is now an issue, especially in some of our larger urban centres. Early childhood programs increasingly include children from other linguistic and cultural backgrounds, children who may speak only a language other than English, children who are in the process of acquiring English as a second language, and children who have grown up acquiring more than one language simultaneously.

In some programs, English-speaking children are also exposed to a second language, particularly if that language and culture are important parts of the community. Bilingualism and multilingualism, although often considered a matter of language learning, are intricately tied to cultural and social dimensions (Hakuta & Garcia, 1989). Awareness of and sensitivity to family values is particularly important in working with children learning English as a second language (Sholtys, 1989).

In general, young children have little difficulty acquiring more than one language and eventually speaking each of them with no interference from the other (Obler, 1985). In learning a second language, children follow a process similar to that used to

acquire the first language (Hakuta, 1988). In fact, common principles of learning are seen as the foundation for acquiring both languages (McLaughlin, 1984). Although bilingual children gain the elements of semantics, morphology, syntax, and pragmatics of two languages, they also have to acquire a sense of when it is appropriate to use each language. To function effectively in their multilanguage environment, bilingual children have become especially proficient code switchers, assessing their audience and shifting from one language system to the other with ease.

A distinction needs to be made between **simultaneous language acquisition** and **successive language acquisition**. A child who learns two languages at one time or a second language by age 3, is considered to be acquiring the languages simultaneously; learning a second language after age 3 is called successive acquisition (McLaughlin, 1984). At first, children who are learning more than one language simultaneously from the beginning are a little slower in acquiring vocabulary because each object or event has two words attached to it, but they soon catch up with children who are learning only one language (deVilliers & deVilliers, 1979). In addition, young simultaneous language learners tend to engage in some language mixing, but this is naturally followed by increasing awareness that the two languages are separate and different (Owens, 1984).

IMMERSION LEARNING

Immersion programs, developed in Quebec and exported to the rest of the world, use only the second language, and the children are treated as if they were native speakers of that language. Early immersion programs are offered for children as soon as they enter school. Middle immersion begins at the end of the early childhood years (usually when entering Grade 4), and late immersion programs begin around Grades 7 to 8. In **non-immersion programs**, both the native and second language are used, with a gradual shift from the former to the latter over time (Garcia, 1982). Teachers in non-immersion programs are most often bilingual, helping children begin to learn English while also furthering their native language.

Immersion students quickly become quite fluent in their new language, but it may be at a minor, short-lived cost. Research suggests that early immersion program graduates lag behind their non-immersion peers in their reading and writing skills, but they eventually catch up (Kelly, 1989).

Immersion programs are most likely to be found where large populations of children speak a language other than English, and in large urban centres. From the perspective of an English text, in Canada, most bilingual education programs are in French and some of the aboriginal tongues. However, in settings like Toronto and Vancouver, for example, Chinese language classes are numerous.

IMMIGRANT CHILDREN AND ENGLISH AS A NEW LANGUAGE

A single child or a few children from another linguistic and cultural background are often enrolled in an early childhood program, leaving teachers who are not familiar with the child's language to use their ingenuity in helping such youngsters learn English. More often than not, a less systematic approach is followed, taking cues from the child's reactions and apparent needs.

The following examples of Nina and Hoang illustrate why more than language has to be considered. When Nina came to Canada from San Salvador with her family, she was enrolled in a daily preschool program to help her learn English. Nina, an outgoing, friendly 4-year-old, quickly acquired a basic English vocabulary and, combined with non-verbal cues, soon communicated very effectively. Hoang, on the other hand, entered Canada as a refugee and experienced considerable hardships as well as a series of unsettling changes, including the recent death of his mother. He seemed to find his school program bewildering and rarely participated in activities, standing at the sidelines in sombre silence.

Although the approach to helping Nina acquire English involved encouraging peer interactions, exposure to stimulating activities, and a language-rich environment, Hoang's needs were clearly different. Before language learning could be addressed, his emotional needs had to be considered. After almost two months, Hoang began to establish a relationship with one of the teachers and gradually became involved in activities. Throughout this time of silence, Hoang had nonetheless been surrounded by language, and eventually it became clear that he had attended to much of what he heard. Once Hoang felt stability in his home and school life, his mastery of English progressed significantly.

Of course, immigrant children like Hoang and Nina also have other needs that are best met in anti-bias, multicultural ECE programs. Ruth Fahlman, from the West Coast Child Care Resource Centre, describes the challenges teachers must face in designing such programs in A Canadian Professional Speaks Out.

SECOND-LANGUAGE TEACHING STRATEGIES

Although there are no definitive guidelines for helping children learn a second language, some strategies can be helpful in this process (Saville-Troike, 1982; Sholtys, 1989). As you read this list, notice that many of these suggestions are equally important for all young children, not only those learning a new language.

- A new experience such as preschool can be bewildering to any young child, particularly if the child cannot understand the language. A friendly, consistent, supportive atmosphere can help make the child feel welcome and comfortable, which, in turn, will facilitate learning English.

- If someone who speaks the child's first language is available, enlist that person to help the child learn the routines and expectations, as well as the new language. If another child in the class speaks the language, interaction between the two should be encouraged, although certainly not forced.

- At the same time, encourage all of the children to talk to and include the child in activities.

- Use the child's name frequently, being sure to pronounce it properly when talking to the child.

- A non-English-speaking child should not be forced to speak, because the natural process of learning a second language usually entails a time of silent assimilation.

- Involve the child in the classroom through non-language activities, for instance, helping to set the table for snack, to help the child become part of the group.

A CANADIAN PROFESSIONAL SPEAKS OUT

Anti-Bias Education: A Personal and Professional Challenge for Early Childhood Educators

For many early childhood educators in Canada today, anti-bias education is a new and challenging topic. For some educators, anti-bias, human rights, and social justice concepts and goals may seem far removed from the ECE environment. For others, working with young children is both a vocation and an avenue for political action, "for making a better world."

Whatever our current personal perspective, it is important to consider that what we choose *to do* or *not to do* has consequences for children in their immediate environment and in the long term. Do we intervene effectively when children or adults reveal bias or prejudice? Do we select materials for our program that portray and reflect human similarities and differences positively? Do we introduce developmentally appropriate experiences for exploring individual and group rights and responsibilities? When making choices that relate to anti-bias ECE practice, we are challenged to examine our actions, and to clarify how these actions reflect our values and support our goals.

As we review our own practice, we are engaging in some of the processes that are, ultimately, at the heart of anti-bias education: namely, reflection, action, and evaluation. In turn, we can also encourage children to explore anti-bias issues by considering such questions as, "What do we think is important about sharing and getting along with everyone?" (reflection), "What can each of us do to take care of ourselves and treat each other fairly?" (action), and "What areas of our own behaviour do we want to improve?" (evaluation). Questions like these promote children's connection with issues such as respect, fairness, and inclusion, through action-oriented self-awareness, personal responsibility, and problem solving.

As we encourage these understandings and abilities in young children, we provide the foundation for their later consideration of broader social issues such as, "How do people share wealth and privilege, and get along without resorting to violence and war?", "What can individuals, organizations, and governments do to share more fairly and resolve differences more

effectively?", and, last, "How well are we, as a human family, dealing positively and creatively with our similarities and differences?" In considering these questions, we can see the links between the social challenges for children in the preschool environment and the challenges faced by society as a whole.

For early childhood educators, then, we return to consideration of how much or how little of an anti-bias approach we choose to implement within our programs. Some of us may feel that our knowledge is inadequate, or that we lack the skills for addressing issues such as stereotyping or discrimination. We may also have ambivalent feelings about exploring some areas or aspects of anti-bias with young children—perhaps we are comfortable talking about special needs, but feel less so about sexual orientation, or poverty, or religion. Such hesitations or concerns are valid and may be addressed through professional development and peer support. Yet when deliberating on the need to change our attitudes, knowledge, and practice, we should always consider the consequences of what we do or not do with children. Is not self-awareness, personal responsibility, and problem solving in the social sphere as important, or more important, than anything else we teach children? If we do not model how to reflect, act, and evaluate in relation to anti-bias issues, how and when will children learn these skills?

As individuals within a diverse society, and as educators guiding young children, it is important that we consider carefully our values and goals, and how they relate to anti-bias education. Many resources and options are now available for instructing developmentally appropriate anti-bias concepts and content within ECE settings. For early childhood educators committed to human rights and social justice goals, implementation of anti-bias ECE is one way to act on these values, thereby helping young children "begin well in the beginning" to identify with and protect the rights of the whole of the human family.

Ruth Fahlman
West Coast Child Care
Resource Centre
Vancouver, B.C.

- Language should be presented in a natural, meaningful way, in the context of the child's experiences and interests.

- Concrete objects or demonstration of actions should be paired with new words. For example say the word "milk" when helping the child pour it at snack.

- Repetition of new language learning is important, provided it is done naturally. Meaningless drill does not help. Consistently using the same wording each day, for instance, to signal classroom transitions, will help the child connect words and meaning more easily.

- When a child shares feelings or an idea verbally, such communication should be encouraged through uncritical acceptance. Correcting grammar or pronunciation tends to inhibit rather than foster language.

DIALECTS

Some children enter the early childhood program speaking a dialect of English. A **dialect** is a regional variation of a language different in some features of vocabulary,

grammar, and pronunciation. Many immigrants from the Caribbean speak a form of **Black English**, which is one of this country's dialects. The complex grammatical system of Black English has been studied extensively in the United States (Labov, 1970). What may appear to someone unfamiliar with Black English to be poor grammar actually represents a different set of grammatical rules (for instance, "we be here" or "I ain't finished"). It should be noted that certainly not all black Canadians speak Black English, and numerous other dialects exist, often developed as part of the culture of a given area or group. For example, Wallace Lambert (1977) of McGill University, a founder of immersion education, documented several distinct French dialects in Quebec. Additional French dialects are also found in New Brunswick.

It is important for teachers of young children who speak in dialect to recognize that they have language competence in the same way that all children do, having already acquired the morphology, semantics, syntax, and pragmatics of another form of English or French. An atmosphere of genuine acceptance and value of the children's language and culture, coupled with an environment in which standard English is spoken, can help them acquire the language that predominates in the larger culture of the country. In addition, children can be encouraged to gain skill in code switching, deciding which form of the language is appropriate in which situations.

LANGUAGE AND THE EARLY CHILDHOOD CURRICULUM

The following sections will examine several important aspects of language. First, we will discuss the informal, ongoing use of language that should be a natural accompaniment to whatever children are doing. We next will look at some specific activities that teachers plan to enhance language development. Finally, we will examine children's emerging literacy, their awareness that language extends to reading and writing, and how this is supported through integrated language experiences.

SPONTANEOUS LANGUAGE

Because language is used in almost everything children do, it must be central to the early childhood program. Children are constantly involved in communication—in listening, hearing, talking, interpreting, writing, and reading. All forms of language surround them as they interact with each other, with adults, with media, with activities, and with varied materials. Language activities do not need to be structured to teach language because preschool-aged children have already acquired an elaborate and complex language system. Rather, early childhood language experiences should emerge from natural and meaningful conversations and experiences between adults and children and among children. Such talk is used to inform, tell stories, pretend, plan, argue, discuss, express humour, and so on (Gineshi, 1987). Classrooms for young children, therefore, are not quiet. They are abuzz with language almost all of the time.

Almost every aspect of the early childhood environment and program facilitates language. For instance, the knowledgeable teacher, who values what children have to say and listens to them carefully, promotes language development. Similarly, a daily program (as we discussed in Chapter 8) that provides large blocks of time in which children can become immersed in activities and interactions fosters language usage. In addition, language growth is encouraged by a curriculum that introduces interesting and stimulating objects, experiences, and concepts, just as a classroom environment that is set up to invite small groups of children to work together promotes language.

Conversations

A natural way of using language is through conversation. In good early childhood programs, there is an almost constant, ongoing buzz of conversations between children and teachers and among children. For children, conversation is an art that takes time to develop, since it involves learning a number of elements such as how to initiate and end conversations, maintain coherent dialogue, take turns, and "repair" a conversation that breaks down (McTear, 1985). It is important, therefore, that there be many opportunities for children to practise their emerging conversational skills.

Equally an art is teachers' ability to engage in effective conversations with children. Dialogue between adults and small groups or individual children is essential in teaching preschoolers (Lay-Dopyera & Dopyera, 1987a). Unfortunately, research has found that there is generally little extended conversation between teachers and young children.

An in-depth study of one skilled teacher's conversational strategies revealed some significant differences between her approach with young children and that of other teachers (Rogers, Perrin, & Waller, 1987). For one thing, Cathy (the teacher) maintained an equalitarian relationship in her conversation; the number of words and length of sentences were relatively equal to those used by the child. In contrast, analysis of another teacher–child dialogue showed that the child used far fewer words and shorter sentences. Particularly important was Cathy's genuine interest in what the child was telling her. Cathy's interactions were based on the child's actions and interests and, more often than not, were in response to the child's initiation.

The most concrete finding of this study was Cathy's avoidance of "know-answer questions," questions to which the teacher already knows the answer (for instance, "what colour did you paint the sky?" or "how many cookies are on your plate?"). Such questions are answered by a simple response from the child and may be evaluated by the teacher. Children may fear giving a wrong answer and therefore avoid conversation with the teacher. Thus, teacher–child conversations should arise from natural situations and be based on genuine interest in what the child is doing.

Playing with Language

Another facet of language that teachers can use to enrich its use in the early childhood setting is children's language play. Once children have a good grasp of the principles of language and the correctness of a concept, they delight in confirming this by expressing the opposite, usually accompanied by much laughter and giggling (Geller, 1985). Expressions of humour through silliness, nonsense words or rhymes, and "dirty" words particularly enthral preschoolers. Children enjoy humour, and teachers can use it to capture and maintain children's attention, both in the stories they read or tell and in their conversations with children.

One basis for humour is children's increasing ability to recognize incongruity (Honig, 1988b). For preschoolers, this can involve changing the words of favourite rhymes ("Mary had a little bleep"), an absurd element in a picture (a cat's head on a goldfish's body), or calling a known object by an obviously inappropriate name.

Most riddles and jokes that depend on the double meaning of a word are too sophisticated for preschoolers, who do not yet have the cognitive skills to comprehend this level of linguistic incongruity. School-aged children, however, revel in them! Seven-year-old Caleb asks his family at dinner, "What did the dog say when he saw the top of the house?" His parents and younger sister Nancy, aged 4, laugh when he tells them, "Roof, roof!" Then Nancy decides to relate a riddle as well. "What did the kitty say when he saw the top of the house?" Nancy's answer—"Miaow, miaow!"—and her accompanying laughter indicate that she does not yet understand that words sometimes have double meanings, although she does understand that a joke is something funny that people enjoy sharing.

Children usually know when they are using a naughty word, and this is also a source of humour for them. "Bathroom language" is a particular favourite of many 4-year-olds, who can dissolve into fits of laughter as they recite such gems as "poo-poo-poo-poo." Usually, such language is best ignored. If it seems unduly disruptive, you might tell the children involved that bathroom language is restricted to the bathroom. Children also enjoy repeating adult swear words, usually unaware of their meaning but knowing that such words are somehow inappropriate. Let children know that swear words are not acceptable at school. This is particularly important if children use words that are intended to hurt others, for instance, racial, ethnic, or homophobic slurs.

EMERGENT LITERACY AND LANGUAGE ACTIVITIES

In a language-rich early childhood program, you will find language is part of every activity. You will hear it in the washroom, at the meal table, in the block centre, and on the playground. Language will permeate every activity. You will hear children talking to themselves, with their teachers, and with their peers. A quiet program is cause for concern. In addition to the ongoing use of language in the early childhood program, specific activities based on language use and elaboration are also incorporated. Such activities are often presented at large- or small-group times, enhancing not just language but listening skills, group social skills, creative thinking, concept formation, and other areas of development. The story is at the core of many of those experiences.

THE STORY SCHEMA AND STORY ACTIVITIES

Stories, in their various forms, are the most popular vehicle for language activities. Stories can be told or read by teachers, children, or both together; they can be enacted by children or with flannel-board pieces, puppets, or play dough; or they can come from the rich store of children's literature or from the children's own experiences. In this section, we will discuss how significant preschool experiences with stories are for development. Then we will briefly look at some of the ways in which stories can be used and presented. Later, in the section on emergent literacy, we will talk about literacy in a broader sense.

The Story Schema

As adults, you know that most simple stories have a regular, predictable structure—a beginning, a middle, and an end. The beginning, or "*once upon a time,*" section introduces the setting, the time, and the characters. In the middle, there is a complication—something unusual or unexpected happens. Then, in the end, or the "*lived happily ever after*" section, the complication is resolved or settled and the characters reach a more stable state. That simple structure is known as the **story schema**, and it has been the subject of fairly intensive research since the 1980s.

Both children and adults use the story schema to help them understand and remember stories. As long as stories follow that structure or schema, they are easy to understand and to remember. Experience with stories in the preschool years is critical for the development of the story schema (Young, 1987, 1993). In a series of studies in the greater Toronto area, it became clear that 4- to 7-year-old children from poverty

homes who had little experience with stories had great difficulty understanding them and remembering them. In contrast, children from more affluent homes who had story experiences were quite skilled at understanding and recalling stories. The differences between the two groups of children were marked. In fact, the 4-year-olds with story experience performed much better on a variety of tasks than did 6- and 7-year-old children without that experience. Even though the older children had far more experience in the world, their personal histories were such that they had no understanding of the story schema.

Subsequently, 4- to 7-year-old children from poverty homes, who were already in early childhood programs, were involved in an intervention or compensatory program that simply entailed listening to lots of schematic stories, like simple fairy tales and children's classics (Young, 1987, 1993). Other children just had the regular early childhood program, which did include stories, but not all the extra ones. The children who had the compensatory story program made rapid and significant gains, not only in their ability to understand and recall stories and in their understanding of the story schema, but also in their *language development.* The gains were greatest for the children who heard stories in a small group, but they were still substantial for ones in larger group settings. The 4-year-olds also gained more than the 6-year-olds, which is consistent with developmental theory.

By reading lots of stories in your program you are also helping children to learn about the story schema and to develop cognitive skills they will need throughout their lives. And you are contributing to significant cognitive growth through a developmentally appropriate activity.

Books

The most popular story activity in most early childhood programs is book reading. Because so many excellent books are available for young children, they provide a wealth of ways to contribute to language experience, reinforce concepts, entertain, stimulate thought, and offer emotional support. In selecting books, however, you need to consider the developmental appropriateness of the story and the children's histories.

Short, simple stories are suitable for infants and young toddlers, who will be interested in longer, more complex stories by the time they are 2. Older preschoolers will listen eagerly to quite lengthy stories. The complexity of the stories the children enjoy will continue to increase throughout the early childhood years.

Of course, children who have had experience with stories before they arrive at your program will enjoy longer stories than children without those experiences, because they already have some knowledge about the story schema and the joys of good stories. Preschoolers who come to the early childhood program having had happy experiences with books all of their lives approach book reading activities with enjoyment. Others may not have had many such opportunities and may need some individual, more intimate story reading time to help them acquire a greater appreciation for books.

Some techniques help engage children in the book reading process. For one thing, teachers play a vital role in how children respond to story reading. In a sense, they endorse the story through their enthusiasm, interest in the story, animation, and the use of their voices as tools in making the characters and action come alive. In addition, book reading—whether with a large or small group, or an individual child—should be interactive rather than a one-way endeavour. Younger children, in particular, should have opportunities to comment on and discuss the story and illustrations, speculate on what might happen next, and relate the story to their personal experiences. However, the story can get lost if there is too much discussion. Some—but not all—primary school teachers ask too many comprehension questions about stories; children need the opportunity to enjoy stories for their own sake. In the Toronto compensatory story program, children were not asked any questions about the stories they heard each day—but all questions they asked were discussed.

Many wonderful books are available for young children, spanning a wide range of appropriate and relevant topics. In general, stories that are well-structured, plot-driven, and follow a predictable sequence are best for preschoolers. Among these are storybooks on familiar topics and fairy tales and fables. Younger children enjoy wordless books and alphabet books, as well as rhymes. Older children enjoy informational nonfiction books, in addition to stories.

Books can also have a therapeutic function; for example, children going through a hospitalization experience enjoy hospital stories. Stories about new siblings, death, divorce, and so on take on a special relevance for children going through these crises (bibliotherapy is discussed in Chapter 17) (Machado, 1985).

Many books also revolve around themes that relate to the child's personal experiences and needs. Charles Smith (1989) suggests eight such themes that are common threads in high-quality children's literature.

1. *Becoming a goal seeker* is illustrated in books whose characters set goals and pursue their dreams.

2. *Confronting challenges courageously* is shown in stories in which the characters overcome their fears, for instance, the common fear of the dark.

3. *Growing closer to others* refers to stories in which kinship, love, kindness, and friendship are central.

4. *Coming to terms with loss and grief* includes books that deal with sadness, separation, and death.

5. *Offering kindness to others* revolves around books in which prosocial qualities such as sharing, generosity, and helping are central.

6. *Preserving an openness to the world* is a theme that focuses on awareness and exploration of the world.

7. *Becoming a social problem solver* includes books that emphasize awareness of the consequences of a person's behaviour and alternative solutions.

8. *Forming a positive self-image* is central in stories that reinforce each person's uniqueness.

A school should have a good selection of children's books in its own library, rotating them as curriculum topics as the children's interests change. In addition, the local community library can expand the available supply. Exhibit 13-1 lists guidelines for selecting children's books.

Poetry and Nursery Rhymes

In many early childhood programs, rhymes and poetry are a sadly neglected aspect of literature, perhaps because teachers have not had much exposure to them themselves. This is unfortunate, because appropriate rhymes and poems can broaden children's experiences and add a magical aspect to language activities (Andrews, 1988). The cadence of well-rhymed words, as is true with music, invites attention and

Exhibit 13-1 CRITERIA FOR SELECTING CHILDREN'S BOOKS

The books you select for children should meet the best standards, both for literary and artistic quality. Although more than 2000 children's books are published every year, the fact that a book is in print does not necessarily assure that it is good (Sword, 1987). There are some published guides to selecting high-quality children's books (for instance, the monthly *Bulletin of the Center for Children's Books,* the bimonthly *Horn Book Magazine,* or the American Library Association's *Notable Children's Books),* and resource persons such as children's librarians can prove extremely helpful. But it is also important to develop a sense of what constitutes a good book (Glazer, 1986). As you review books to read to children, apply the following guidelines (Glazer, 1986; Goodman et al. 1987; Machado, 1985; Sword, 1987).

OVERALL IMPRESSION

- The length of the book should be appropriate to the ages of the children. Although engrossing stories of increasing length should be presented as children get older, 5 to 10 minutes (not including discussion) is generally a good time limit for children over age 3.

- The amount of text per page should also be considered. Especially young preschoolers will find long text with few pictures difficult.

- The size of the book is important, particularly when you read to a group of children. Very small books should be kept for one-on-one reading sessions. Children do enjoy many of the new oversized books.

- The binding of a book is important if you are planning to buy it for the school library. Sturdy binding will ensure durability. Some schools prefer buying less expensive books such as paperbacks, which won't last as long but the cost is only one third or one fourth that of hardbound books.

TEXT ELEMENTS

- Read the book carefully and consider whether the plot or story line is coherent and interesting. The plot doesn't have to be complex, but it should be plausible and logical. The adventure of Max in Maurice Sendak's *Where the Wild Things Are* is a good example of a well-written plot that appeals to young children.

- The characters of the book should be distinctive and memorable, should not be stereotyped, and should provide children something with which they can identify. Children have no trouble remembering mischievous Curious George or spunky Madeline from their books.

- Many books revolve around a theme, for instance, friendship, emotional reactions, or exploration (Smith, 1989). If there is a theme, it should not sound like a sermon. A theme should also be relevant to young children's lives and worth sharing with them. Ann Scott's *On Mother's Lap* contains the common theme of jealousy over a new sibling, an experience with which many children can relate.

- As you review a book, pay close attention to the style of writing. Language should be simple but vivid and evoke appropriate mood and images. Because children delight in repetition and humour, look for some books that incorporate these elements. Children love to chime in the refrain of Wanda Gag's *Millions of Cats* as the old couple's acquisition of cats reaches the ludicrous stage with "hundreds of cats, thousands of cats, millions, and billions, and trillions of cats!"

ILLUSTRATIONS

- Above all, pictures should be aesthetic, complementing, and enlivening the words of the story. Many skilled artists' talents enrich children's books. Illustrators use numerous, effective ways to convey the story in pictures. As you browse through some children's classics, compare the whimsical characters of Dr. Seuss, the humorous pen-and-ink drawings of Maurice Sendak, or the impressionistic watercolours of Brian Wildsmith.

- Pictures should be placed adjacent to the text so the story and illustrations work in harmony.

involvement. Poetry's strongest appeal is its "singing quality" (Sutherland & Arbuthnot, 1986). Poems, like any literature, must interest children, speaking to a familiar experience or delighting with their nonsense and humour. Infants delight in sensorimotor rhymes like "Patty-Cake" and "This Little Piggy." Toddlers thoroughly enjoy listening to "Little Miss Muffet." Older preschoolers and school-aged children have broader interests. For instance, they can relate to Robert Louis Stevenson's poem, "Bed in Summer" (1985)—a child's complaint about having to go to bed when the sky outside is still blue—just as they enjoy the silly image of the "Mother Goose" cow jumping over the moon or Shel Silverstein's humorous poems.

Storytelling

Telling rather than reading a story from a book can be a more direct, intimate experience (Machado, 1985), and can stimulate children's imaginations as they visualize the story line and characters. The story can be original, pulled from a proficient teacher's imagination, or it can be a paraphrased version of a book or folktale. Of course, the teacher's skill in holding the children's attention through eye contact, voice variation, and dramatic pauses contributes considerably to storytelling.

Stories can also be told by children, either individually or as a group activity. In particular, older preschoolers, who are familiar with the story schema and have well-developed language fluency and vocabulary, enjoy making up original stories, which can be recorded in writing by an adult or tape-recorded if you wish to preserve them. Although storytelling can be prompted by showing children a picture or a wordless book, many children will tell much more elaborate stories without such guides (Hough, Nurss, & Wood, 1987). In fact, research links beginning reading skills and the development of literacy to opportunities for telling as well as listening to stories.

Flannel-Board Stories

A version of storytelling with props, flannel-board stories easily capture children's attention as they look forward to seeing what will be put on the board next (Machado, 1985). A flannel- or felt-covered board serves as a background, while felt, fabric, or pellon cutouts of characters are used to relay the story. A selection of favourite stories can be available for teachers' and children's use through a flannel-board story file (see the discussion of teacher-made materials in Chapter 9).

Flannel-board stories can be derived from a variety of sources including favourite books and poems, nursery rhymes, teacher-made stories, and stories based on the children's experiences such as field trips. A new flannel-board story can be presented during a group time, then the props left out so the children can retell the story in their own way later. In addition, a selection of familiar flannel-board stories can be placed in the language arts area of the classroom for children's everyday use.

Lap-Board Stories

Another variation of storytelling, which includes both children and the teacher, is lap-board stories (Essa & Rogers, 1992). Two elements are involved: the children, with the teacher's prompting, tell a story while the teacher creates the characters, props, and action of the story with play dough. Manipulating the play dough on a small board in her lap, the teacher "illustrates" the emerging story that the children tell. These depictions of the story, however, are not artistically formed but merely suggest what they represent (for instance, a ball of dough with two "ears" pinched into the top can be a dog). In fact, if the teacher pays too much attention to sculpting perfect forms, this tends to be too time-consuming and distracting in lap-board stories.

As the story emerges, the pieces can be moved around to show action, they can disappear by merging back into the larger play dough mass, and they can grow by adding more play dough. One group of preschoolers, who had watched two neighbourhood squirrels pick up some crackers the children had left outside, decided to retell what they had observed in a lap-board story. They were delighted to see the play dough "cookies" disappear as the hungry "squirrel" gobbled them up; in turn, the squirrel grew fatter with each cookie it engulfed. Children who participate in lap-board storytelling find the emerging play dough enactment a good stimulus to storytelling.

Story Enactment

Children respond with great enthusiasm to opportunities to enact favourite stories. Story enactment involves both language and social skills as children cooperate and share the roles of a given story. Schematic stories such as "The Three Little Pigs," "Goldilocks and the Three Bears," "Caps for Sale," and "Stone Soup" provide important elements such as repetitive dialogue, strong action lines, and familiarity. These stories can and should be adapted as needed. For instance, several children can play the role of Goldilocks while the teacher takes on the other roles, Papa Bear can cook the porridge, or a female hunter can save Little Red Riding Hood and Grandma (Ishee & Goldhaber, 1990). Variations from the theme are to be anticipated, and they should be welcomed. Often, they are a sign that the children know both the story schema and the story well enough that they can play with a story's theme.

Puppets

Another way to enact stories is to use puppets as the actors. A makeshift stage made from a table set on its side, or a more elaborate one with curtains, can provide the backdrop; alternatively, puppets can be used to enact a story without such a setting. A variety of commercial, teacher-made, or child-made puppets can help enact the story. Teachers can use puppets to convey a story during group time because children enjoy watching a lively puppet show. The puppets can be left out for the children to re-enact the story or to make up a different one later. Puppets can be an ongoing part of the language arts centre, however, inviting children to engage in puppetry at other times. Puppets allow children to project onto another character ideas and feelings that they might hesitate to express as their own. Puppets can also help a shy child by allowing that child to speak through an intermediary.

EMERGENT LITERACY

As we have seen, children learn to understand and express language in a natural way, through a process that begins very early in life. They also learn about the story schema without direct instruction. Similarly, preschool children also begin to form an understanding of reading and writing, something that has come to interest researchers and educators only relatively recently. The term **emergent literacy** acknowledges that learning to read and write (in other words, to become literate) is a dynamic, ongoing, emerging process. In fact, all aspects of language—listening, speaking, writing, and reading—are intertwined and develop concurrently, not sequentially (Teale & Sulzby, 1986). A Closer Look (p. 337) illustrates one teacher's strategies to encourage emergent literacy in her class.

Children develop an understanding of reading and writing through a supportive, literate environment, starting at home and continuing in the early childhood program. And this is done without formal instruction. If a young child is in a story- and

A CLOSER LOOK

Emergent Literacy

Mary was hired to teach a class of fifteen 5-year-olds in a school in which most of the children came from low-income families. Her first task was to get rid of the desks, both the small ones and the one intended for the teacher, and to set up a developmentally appropriate environment with learning centres. She particularly focused on providing a whole language environment. She carefully selected materials and arranged the room to reinforce language in as many ways as possible, also using day-to-day spontaneous conversations and planned activities.

As she found on the first day, many of the children came to school having had few or no experiences with art materials. From that very first day, she encouraged each child to draw many pictures, on any topic. "I remember one little boy who drew a line and said, 'It's a dog,'" Mary recalled. She wrote the word "dog" next to his line and encouraged him to make other pictures. "His picture was typical of this group's artwork in September," she said. In addition to the daily art, Mary posted labels around the room, talked about the labels, sounded them out, read many stories, had the children discuss and act out the stories, talked and encouraged the children to talk all the time, included letters and letter lotto games to allow the children to manipulate them, and generally enriched their environment with lots of written and oral language.

Mary also enlisted the help and support of the parents, who became very interested in what their children's teacher was doing. She talked with parents every day, showed them what the children were doing, and explained the importance of the children's work. She sent notes home and made phone calls to those parents she did not see. In addition, she put together a "writing suitcase," an old briefcase with a variety of writing and reading materials that the children took turns taking home.

By January, some of the children were drawing very detailed pictures and taking an interest in the letters of their names. One day, Lishana, after spending considerable time working on a complex picture that featured a lot of red, suddenly jumped up screaming, "I did it! I did it!" Mary went to Lishana to see what the excitement was about. She found, to her delight, the letters "i lik red" written at the top of the picture. "Obviously she had been thinking about what letters mean, and from that time on, she put letters into words. It clicked for her," explained Mary.

By the end of the school year, all fifteen children were writing often long and complex stories on their own. They continued to use invented spelling, to read many of the words in their environment and in books, and to use a lot of verbal language. According to Mary, "Given the right environment, these children could do a lot. They just blossomed!"

print-rich environment, the child will develop the foundations of literacy that are required for reading and writing.

Catherine Snow concludes that when parents read to their young children, these children's language is more complex than it is during other times of play. Furthermore, in the process of early reading, teachers and parents help their children acquire some of the basic rules of literacy, learning that books are for reading rather than manipulating or that

books represent a separate, fictional world (Snow & Ninio, 1986). Both home and school experiences with books provide children with further insights, for example, that print should make sense, that print and speech are related, that book language is different from speech, and that books are enjoyable (Schickedanz, 1986). Out of many experiences with the printed form of the language come the foundations for writing and reading.

Learning to Write

The beginnings of writing emerge early in life through a number of steps. Vygotsky (1978) traces the roots of writing to earliest infant gestures, described as "writing in the air." In late infancy, infants will try to copy a parent's list writing, and a toddler engages in more complex writing behaviours. During the preschool years, children become aware of the differences between drawing and writing, a distinction that is evident in their own efforts. By age 3, many children begin to use **mock writing**, a series of wavy, circular, or vertical lines that deliberately imitate adult writing and are distinctly different from drawing. Within the next couple of years, mock writing increasingly becomes a mixture of real letters and innovative symbols.

By late kindergarten or Grade 1, most children who have grown up in a pleasurable, literate environment and who recognize most or all of the letters of the alphabet begin to use **invented spelling** by finding the speech sound that most closely fits what they want to write (Atkins, 1984). Five-year-old Abby wrote, "I M GNG TO DRV MI KAR AT HOM" (I am going to drive my car at home) in one of her stories, which was accompanied by a picture of Abby atop a blue vehicle. Analysis of the errors seen in invented spelling indicates that children are trying to work out a system of rules, just as they did when, as toddlers, they were acquiring oral language. Because reading and writing are intertwined processes, such early attempts at spelling are soon replaced with more conventional forms as children repeatedly come across the same words in their reading (Atkins, 1984).

Learning to Read

When children read and write, they are "making sense out of or through print," although this sense does not require an understanding of a conventional alphabetic code (Goodman, 1986, p. 5). Eventually, children do acquire this understanding as they learn the consistent relationship between the letters of the alphabet and their use in the written form. Early literacy, however, is based on the growing awareness that print means something, for instance, that a stop sign indicates "step on the brake."

Some 2-year-olds already display such awareness, for example, pointing to a word in a book and saying, "That's my name" (Walton, 1989). By age 3, children clearly have substantial understanding of why and how print is used. Many 4-year-olds have developed the ability to recognize a variety of words when these are presented in their appropriate context, for instance, common labels and signs. Experiences in recognizing words in their environmental context help children learn about the process of reading and lead to eventual recognition of these words out of their context (Kontos, 1986).

Children actively seek to make sense of print in their environment by using a variety of strategies that they themselves invent (Willert & Kamii, 1985). Younger preschoolers' strategies focus on such clues as the first letter of a word ("That's my name," says Paul, "because it's got a 'P'"); looking at the shape of the word, such as its length or spacing if there is more than one word in a configuration; and using pictures as clues to help decipher accompanying words. As children get older and more experienced in acquiring reading skills, they use some additional strategies. Included are looking for familiar letters or combinations of letters in words; spontaneously and repeatedly practising the spelling and copying of words; and inventing a phonological system, similar to that used in invented spelling, to sound out words.

Implications

As the preceding discussions suggest, young children have a natural interest in the print environment around them, an interest most of them express through their own inventive attempts at writing and reading. This developmentally appropriate view of how children learn to read and write is far removed from some of the stereotyped notions of reading and writing as formal subjects best begun in first grade. Thinking of literacy merely as recognizing words or the sounds of letters "is as dangerous as it is erroneous" (Gibson, 1989, p. 30).

Yet, all too often, young children are placed into high-powered, rigid, formalized programs that focus on isolated skills involved in the reading process, rather than on the integration of all aspects of language. In fact, a statement expressing concern over this developmentally inappropriate practice was jointly prepared by a group of relevant organizations (International Reading Association, 1986).

Reading and writing emerge from many successful and enjoyable experiences with language, both oral and written. According to research, literacy best develops through meaningful context in an informal, supportive environment (Kontos, 1986). As Judith Schickedanz (1982), one of the leading authorities in children's emergent literacy, writes:

We need to abandon ideas and practices that assume early literacy development to be simply a matter of teaching children a few basic skills such as alphabet recognition or letter-sound associations. Much more is involved. Limiting children's reading experiences to contacts with bits and pieces of print isolated from meaningful contexts may actually prevent them from developing broader and more complex insights that are key to understanding what written language is all about (p. 259).

Promoting Literacy Development

Literacy, like oral language, emerges in a natural way that does not require formal teaching to prompt interest. What it does need is a language-rich environment to encourage its development. Literacy is best promoted in the context of a **whole language approach**, one in which high-quality oral and print language surrounds children, children can observe others using literacy skills, and they are encouraged to experiment with all forms of language. Such an approach integrates all forms of communication, including speaking, listening, writing, reading, art, music, and math (International Reading Association, 1986). The following suggestions for supporting literacy development come from a variety of sources:

- The aim of supporting literacy development in young children should be to enhance their desire to read and write by building on their intrinsic motivation to learn these skills (Willert & Kamii, 1985).

- A language-rich environment must contain many materials, opportunities, and experiences for planned and spontaneous interaction with language, both oral and written. This means providing appropriate materials and scheduled time blocks for children to pursue language activities (Machado, 1985; Teale & Martinez, 1988).

- A carefully selected library of high-quality children's books must be available for children to browse through or to ask a teacher to read.

- Stories should not just be read but should be discussed when the children want to do so. Children understand stories better when they have opportunities to ask and answer questions about the plot and characters of a story and relate the story to their own lives (Teale & Martinez, 1988; Walton, 1989).

- Children need many story-reading experiences to acquire the story schema. Knowing, for instance, how a story begins and ends and the story's sequence of events is important to literacy development (Jensen, 1985; Young, 1987, 1993).

- Books should be read more than once. Children are more likely to re-enact a book on their own if they have heard it at least three times (Teale & Martinez, 1988).

- Children should be encouraged to "read" to each other, whether or not they actually know how to read. Such activities promote emergent literacy (Teale & Martinez, 1988).

- If some children in the class seem to have had few one-on-one reading experiences at home, time should be set aside when a teacher can spend time reading to just one or two children (Jensen, 1985).

- Print awareness can be supported through books as well as through other forms of print in the school environment. Charts, lists, labels, and bulletin boards that surround children in the environment contribute to print awareness, as does a teacher who interprets, calls attention to, and gets the children's input when creating print (Goodman, Smith, Meredith, & Goodman, 1987; Schickedanz, 1986).

- Children gradually learn that there is a relationship between written and spoken words. When children read certain books frequently, they often become so familiar with the stories that they know which words correspond with which pages. Such experiences contribute to making the connection between speech and print (Schickedanz, 1986).

- Children should be provided with a variety of reading and writing materials to incorporate into their play. For example, paper, pencils, markers, and other implements in the art, language arts, dramatic play, science, and math areas should be included to suggest a link between the activities that go on in those areas and reading/writing.

- Given a supportive atmosphere, older children will engage in story writing. Although children may not be using conventional letters and words, their stories as well as the writing process are still full of meaning. The sensitive teacher must carefully attend to what children are conveying to understand that meaning (Harste, Short, & Burke, 1988).

- One way of promoting storytelling and writing is to include a "writing table" as an ongoing activity centre in the classroom (Bakst & Essa, 1990). The teacher writes down children's dictated stories but also encourages the children to write their stories.

- Stories should be shared, something that can be done informally as other children come to the writing table or more formally during a large-group activity. When their stories are shared, children develop **audience awareness,** an appreciation that their stories are a form of communication that should make sense to others (Bakst & Essa, 1990).

- Some children show little interest in reading and writing, perhaps because they have had little access to materials that promote these activities. One successful strategy to stimulate this interest is to provide a "writing suitcase" that the children can take home overnight or over a weekend. This suitcase can include such materials as various sizes and shapes of paper and notebooks; chalk and chalkboard, pencils, crayons, and markers; magnet, cardboard, or plastic letters and stencils; favourite picture books; scissors; and tape, glue, stapler, hole punch, and ruler (Rich, 1985).

PARENTS AND PROFESSIONALS

Parental Values Concerning Language Development

As we have seen from the various theoretical views of language development, parents are crucial in children's language learning. Their role as language facilitators and teachers reaches back to their children's earliest days of life. It is very important, therefore, that the teachers who are part of the lives of children recognize and acknowledge the importance of the parents' role. When children are in an early childhood setting, teachers and parents share the task of providing the experiences that will best promote continued language acquisition. As with all other aspects of children's development, their language learning is furthered when parents and teachers share goals, insights, and information through regular communication.

By the very fact that they do not set out to "teach" their young children language, parents consciously or unconsciously appreciate that language learning is a natural process that they promote through their modelling and interaction. They do not question that children will learn language (barring any special needs that might affect this development).

Yet, parents often do not have this same intuitive understanding of children's literacy learning, although they may well be providing many high-quality language experiences that will lead to competent, literate children. Some parents assume that learning to read and write begins in elementary school and is best left until the child reaches the appropriate age. Others, anxious that their children succeed in school, may seek formal reading and writing training in the preschool years to give their children a good start. It is important, therefore, that as an early childhood teacher you convey to parents your philosophy of a whole language approach to language and literacy development.

This can be done in a number of ways. Share with parents information through articles and books that point out the early beginnings of literacy development. You might, for instance, provide parents with a copy of the International Reading Association's (1986) statement, published in *Young Children*, which addresses appropriate and inappropriate early reading practices. Personalize information about literacy development by saving and discussing with parents their own children's work that contains contrasts between drawing and mock writing. Children's work can also be displayed attractively on a prominent bulletin board. Help parents recognize the many ways in which their children are engaged in reading and writing every day and how they, as parents, facilitate this. Also reinforce that the many activities they already engage in with their children—book reading, talking, shared time, outings, matching and sorting games, identifying food labels and road signs—contribute immensely to language, knowledge about the story schema, and literacy development. Below are some suggestions for enhancing this development, which you can share with parents (Mavrogenes, 1990).

- Provide an environment that conveys the value of literacy. Let children see their parents reading and writing. Make books, magazines, and newspapers an important part of the home. A literate environment need not be expensive when the community library or a lending library from the early childhood program is used.

- Make reading time with the child a special daily occasion. Read as well as discuss books.

- Give books as presents for birthdays and holidays.

- Make writing materials available to children. A special writing area with paper, pencils, markers, envelopes, memo pads, and forms from school, restaurants, or the doctor's office will encourage writing as well as incorporation of writing into pretend play.

- Help children write letters to friends and relatives or to the author of a favourite book.

- Write special word or picture notes to children and put these in their lunch boxes. Write out grocery lists and recipes with children to illustrate the usefulness of writing.

- Share with parents the titles of favourite school books that their children particularly enjoy.

Parents are reassured when teachers frequently reinforce the point that children are enthusiastic and active learners in all areas, including language and literacy. It is particularly important that teachers find ways to communicate this message to parents whose children are learning English as a new language. Usually, in such a case there is also a language barrier between teachers and parents. Teachers can meet this challenge by finding an interpreter to help in communication, by learning some words and phrases in the family's primary language and using these in combination with nonverbal messages, and by recommending English instruction for the parents, if this is appropriate.

KEY POINTS OF CHAPTER 13

THEORETICAL VIEWS OF LANGUAGE DEVELOPMENT

▲ 1. The behaviourist view of language development is that children's language learning is shaped primarily by the responses of parents.

▲ 2. The innatist view, voiced by theorists such as Chomsky, holds that children are born with a linguistic structure.

▲ 3. The interactionist view suggests that there is an interplay between inborn and environmental factors in children's language learning.

COMPONENTS OF LANGUAGE

▲ 4. Young children's vocabulary growth is quite astounding, estimated to average two to four new words every day.

▲ 5. Children's growing understanding of word meanings, including those that have an added emotional context, is called semantics.

▲ 6. Morphology refers to children's learning of rules about words, for instance, how to make a verb into the past tense or how to make a plural.

▲ 7. Learning the social rules of conversation is called pragmatics.

▲ 8. Code switching refers to children's ability to vary their language use as a function of the situation.

BILINGUALISM/MULTILINGUALISM

▲ 9. Children generally have little difficulty learning more than one language.

▲ 10. Different approaches to teaching a second language include immersing children in the new language without using the primary language and using both the new and old languages at the same time.

▲ 11. Some young children speak a dialect, which is a regional variation of the primary language.

LANGUAGE AND THE EARLY CHILDHOOD CURRICULUM

▲ 12. Because language is so integral to all parts of the early childhood program, much learning occurs spontaneously.

▲ 13. Effective conversations between teachers and children are responsive to the child rather than controlled by the teacher.

▲ 14. Once children have a good grasp of the principles of language, they begin to play with it through humour, nonsense words, rhymes, or "dirty" words.

▲ 15. Book reading is important for the development of the story schema and related cognitive skills of memory and comprehension. Good children's books on a variety of themes are available.

▲ 16. Poetry, nursery rhymes, storytelling, flannel-board stories, lap-board stories, story enactment, and puppets are variations of language activities that children enjoy.

▲ 17. Emergent literacy acknowledges that reading and writing are ongoing processes that begin early in life.

▲18. Young children engage in mock writing, which is distinctly different from drawing and scribbling.

▲19. Some older preschoolers may begin to use invented spelling by finding speech sounds that most closely fit what they want to write.

▲20. Reading also emerges gradually, as children increasingly make sense out of print.

▲21. A whole language approach surrounds children with high-quality oral and written language and encourages them to use language in all its forms.

KEY QUESTIONS

1. Listen to a young child's spontaneous language. What components of language do you note? Consider the child's understanding of the meaning of language as well as the child's grasp of language rules.

2. Talk to someone you know who learned English as a second language. What are this person's recollections about this learning process? What was most difficult, and what was easiest? What strategies or techniques were most helpful in this learning process? Talk with others in your class and compare the findings of those whose friends learned English at an early age with those who learned it later in life.

3. Observe a teacher of young children engage in spontaneous conversation with children. What techniques does she or he use? How are the children encouraged to interact with each other as well as with the teacher? Did you hear examples of language play or humour?

4. Read a book written for preschool-aged children. Does this book appeal to you? Do you think it will appeal to children? Is the story schematic? Evaluate this book according to the criteria outlined in Exhibit 13-1.

5. Examine some samples of children's artwork. Do you see examples of mock writing? Are letters included? Did the child write any recognizable words in invented spelling?

14

SOCIAL DEVELOPMENT THROUGH THE CURRICULUM

One major function of the early childhood program is to support the process of **socialization,** the means through which children become a functioning part of society and learn society's rules and values. Although socialization is a lifelong process that begins well before the child enters the early childhood program, it is particularly crucial early in life, when the foundation for later attitudes, values, and behaviours is laid.

Unquestionably, socialization begins with the parent–child and caretaker–infant relationships in infancy, where patterns of response, need fulfilment, and give-and-take have their roots. Children who do not come to an early childhood program until they are older already have had a lifetime of socializing experiences. They may have learned to trust or be wary of others, to meet new experiences enthusiastically or with caution, to care about others' feelings because their needs have always been considered, or to think of others as competitors for affection or resources.

Because socialization is such an important responsibility of the early childhood teacher, we will consider some of its facets in more than one chapter. This chapter will focus primarily on the development of social competence as it is encouraged through the curriculum; the following chapters discuss guidance techniques that facilitate the development of positive social skills. The term curriculum as used in this chapter does not refer solely to the planned activities of the day, but also includes all the elements in the environment that lead to conversations and activities that promote socialization. In this chapter, then, we will examine the following points:

1. We will begin with a look at some theoretical views of how socialization takes place.

2. Next, we will look at the development of social competence.

   - An important element in the development of social competence is peer interaction and friendships.

   - Children also develop gender role identity; we will consider non-sexist teaching strategies that promote positive gender attitudes.

   - Racial and cultural attitudes, as well attitudes toward people with disabilities, are also formed early in life; we will review guidelines that can help promote accepting attitudes toward others.

   - The foundations for moral development and positive social skills and behaviours are also formed during the early years.

3. We will end the chapter by looking at two types of activities that can promote positive social interaction: pretend play and cooperative games.

THEORETICAL VIEWS OF THE SOCIALIZATION PROCESS

In Chapter 2 we considered the work of Erik Erikson, whose psychosocial theory of young children's stages of development has had tremendous influence on early education. Although we will not review this theory in detail here, keep in mind Erikson's emphasis on the importance of providing infants, toddlers, and young children with a social environment in which they can trust people. In that setting, children can safely exercise their growing independence, and many opportunities to explore and experience competence are available. A good early childhood program is built on the premise that children's needs for trust, autonomy, initiative, and industry must be met. Judy Wainwright, an ECE instructor at Mount Royal College, outlines a program that aims to respond to each child's needs in a Canadian Professional Speaks Out.

During recent decades, another important view of how children become socialized has stemmed from the work of Jean Piaget. This approach centres on the idea that children construct all knowledge, including social knowledge. This contrasts with the behaviourist view that social knowledge is culturally transmitted (Edwards, 1986). Let us briefly examine these two ideas of how children acquire and assimilate an understanding of their social world.

THE CONSTRUCTIVIST VIEW OF SOCIALIZATION

In the Piagetian view of social development, social knowledge is acquired much in the same way as other knowledge (see Chapter 12). Children use their evolving **social cognition**, or understanding of other people's problems and how they feel, to organize and

A CANADIAN
PROFESSIONAL SPEAKS OUT

Tailoring Curricula to Ability and Interest

My desire for Canadian children enrolled in child care centres is that each child will receive quality, individualized care from educated, caring, and committed adults. Nice idea, you say, but hardly practical. I disagree. For many young children this idea is reality, and with some changes can become a reality for all children. From my perspective, theme planning and "recipe card" manuals should be discarded. Play experiences for children should be planned using playroom staff's educational expertise and information gathered through frequent, first-hand observations of each child's needs, interests, and abilities.

Let's suppose from recent observations and conversations with children, parents, and other playroom staff that Timothy is interested in dinosaurs, Rachel in colours, and Kent in changes. Michael had a new baby and needs to learn how to understand and express his feelings, positive and negative, about his sibling. Attiya is thrilled about her newly acquired skill of printing the letters in her name; Heather and Pam are frustrated that their block structures continue to tumble. Just as you were leaving the centre yesterday, Sharon's mother called to say that their family dog had been killed by a car. This is the information that forms the backbone of your upcoming daily play programs. For each child you develop a variety of play experiences for active and quiet play throughout the planned environment.

Here are some possible play opportunities that meet the individual needs of the children and more than likely will appeal to several others:

- At the easel, primary colours of paint, large pieces of paper cut in circles, and one-inch, long-handled brushes (Rachel, Attiya, Michael, Kent).

- Beside the sandbox, a box of dinosaurs, a variety of twigs and branches gathered from yesterday's walk in the nearly park, and a container of water (Timothy, Kent).

- On the manipulative table, three different types of paper, preschool pencils, erasers, rulers, crayons, stencils, and scissors. At a nearby table alphabet blocks with small people and animals (Attiya, Kent, Rachel, Michael, Sharon).

- At the science table, bean and onion seeds, soil, clear plastic cups for planting, watering can, and magnifying glasses with pictures of growing plants on the nearby bulletin board (Kent, Michael).

- In the dramatic play area, several stuffed baby zoo animals with appropriate foodstuffs, zookeeper shirts, hats, gloves, and cleaning supplies with a stack of hollow blocks that could be used to construct habitats (Michael, Sharon, Pam, Heather).

- Newborn babies, bottles, blankets, a carriage, and a cradle are available in the family area (Michael).

- The water table has clear water, and beside it are props for making bubbles (liquid soap, straws, tennis racquets, and plastic tubes with terry towel wrapped around one end) (Kent, Rachel, Michael).

- In the block area, several flat pieces of masonite are on the floor along with three large cardboard boxes (Heather, Pam, Kent).

- Added to the bookshelf are alphabet, dinosaur, plant, and animal books.

- For children who wish to join a group activity, there are scales for weighing and measuring people; conversations about growth of nails, hair, skin, and feet; and clothes of different sizes.

- When children arrive, Sharon's primary caregiver will be there to talk and support her in the playroom and is prepared to talk about her feelings about her dead pet at appropriate opportunities.

- Materials added to the outdoor playground will be sponges, chamois, cloths, brushes, buckets, and water for washing bikes, windows and equipment, woodworking materials, and some musical instruments.

- Throughout the day adults will interact with children as they self-select play experiences.

Using all knowledge and information available, early childhood professionals must trust their own judgment on what is best for each child and provide daily, numerous, real, first-hand play experiences that allow children to self-select from a wide range of opportunities to foster their own growth and development with supportive guidance from competent, confident adults. Children will feel valued and respected; learning opportunities will be individually and developmentally appropriate; and individual and group needs will be met in a responsive environment that recognizes the uniquenesss of each child in the playroom. The result will be quality care for each child.

Judy Wainwright
Mount Royal College
Calgary, Alberta

structure information about people and relationships in a way similar to the one used in organizing and structuring information about the physical properties of their world (Kohlberg, 1966). For instance, children classify the people they meet in relation to themselves and their own existing schemata, which have, of course, been shaped by their culture. As with all other learning, such understanding comes from the child's active involvement, not from passive transmission of information. As part of a complex world, children need to make sense of themselves and others. "Simply by being born into the human family, then, young children are challenged to understand self, others, social and moral relations, and societal institutions" (Edwards, 1986, p. 3).

THE BEHAVIOURIST VIEW OF SOCIALIZATION

In contrast to Piagetian theory, the traditional behavioural assumption is that children are taught about the social world when their responses are reinforced by the adults who shape their behaviour. **Social learning theory**, which is derived from but goes beyond traditional behaviourism, does not consider reinforcement as always necessary for social learning. From the social learning perspective, children also learn social behaviours through **observational learning**, by observing, noting the behaviour of, and imitating or **modelling** their behaviour on that of a **model**. Adults and peers can be models. Research has shown that particularly nurturant and warm adult models influence children's social behaviours (Yarrow, Scott, & Waxler, 1973). It is possible that children imitate those they like because they want to be like them. In addition, children are more likely to imitate models they observe being rewarded (Bandura, 1977).

DEVELOPMENT OF SOCIAL COMPETENCE

As increasing numbers of infants, toddlers, and preschoolers enter group care, these children experience increasingly intimate peer contact (Howes, 1987). By age 3 or 4, most children are part of a social world that is truly egalitarian, a world of peers who are equals (Moore, 1982). In this world, children are expected to share and cooperate, to learn the rules and expectations. As young children go through this process of becoming socialized to the peer society, they gain skill and competence in peer interaction, enter into friendships, develop gender identity, adopt racial and cultural attitudes, form a sense of morals and values, and acquire a host of prosocial behaviours.

The opportunity to develop multicultural, multiracial, and multi-economic acceptance will, to a large extent, depend on the integrative nature of the early childhood program. Although programs can help children learn about people from diverse backgrounds, many preschool and child care centres tend to be rather homogeneous, joining children from a common racial, cultural, and economic milieu.

PEER INTERACTION

Peer interaction is an essential ingredient in the process of childhood socialization, in fact, to the total development of the child (Hartup, 1983a). The early childhood setting offers an ideal opportunity for young children to develop social skills with peers. As with any skill, it is through practice in real situations that children develop competence in peer interaction. The many naturally occurring opportunities of day-to-day life allow children to be sympathetic and helpful to peers (Honig, 1982). These social skills include the many strategies children learn to help them initiate and continue social interactions, to negotiate, and to settle conflicts (Smith, 1982).

For young children who are just entering peer relationships, adult guidance—not interference—is important; as children get older and less egocentric, the presence of an adult becomes less necessary (Howes, 1987; Oden, 1982). The teacher, in facilitating social development, must, first of all, provide children with ample time and space, and appropriate materials, to facilitate social interaction. A child who has difficulty engaging in social play can be helped through sensitive teacher guidance, for instance, directing that child to a group with similar play interests or pairing the child with a more socially competent peer (Rogers & Ross, 1986).

Older children also provide excellent models for younger peers. In one study, the pretend play of 2-year-olds was characterized as much more cooperative and complex when they were paired with 5-year-olds than with fellow toddlers (Howes & Farver, 1987). This research supports the idea of providing children in early childhood programs with some opportunities for mixed-age interaction, something that Montessori did almost a century ago. It also provides support for the mixed-age programs we discussed in Chapter 3.

FRIENDSHIP

One special type of peer relationship is friendship, that close link between people typified by mutual concern, sharing, and companionship. Recent research points to the importance of early friendship to later emotional well-being (Flaste, 1991). Young children's concept of friendship is limited, primarily revolving around the immediate situation with little thought to the enduring nature of friendship. As children grow older, their friendships typically become more stable (Damon, 1983).

Preschoolers view friends in terms of their accessibility, physical attributes, and actions rather than their personality traits (Rubin, 1980). In other words, a friend is "someone you play with a lot," "someone who wears a Batman T-shirt," "someone who invites you to her birthday party," or "someone who isn't mean." Another insight into early friendship can be found in the often-heard question, "Are you my friend?" which can be translated to mean, "Will you play with me?" (Edwards, 1986).

Preschoolers expect friendships to maximize enjoyment, entertainment, and satisfaction in play (Parker & Gottman, 1989). Young children are focused on themselves, their own feelings and needs; not until later in childhood do they shift to a greater awareness of the needs and feelings of others (Rubin, 1980). Yet, as many observers have noted, young children are also surprisingly capable of caring about and giving emotional support to each other (Levinger & Levinger, 1986); for instance, observe the concern of onlookers when a child cries because he is hurt or distressed.

Trust is the basic foundation on which friendship is built. Children who are trustworthy, who share and cooperate, are more likely to be considered as friends by their peers. Trust in the peer relationship, however, does not simply emerge but is built on the sense of trust that children established early in life (as described by Erikson), when nurturing adults met their needs consistently. Teachers can help children develop a sense of trust, which can enhance friendships, through their support and guidance. More specifically, they can help children recognize their own needs and goals and those of others, develop more effective social skills (strategies will be discussed in more detail in the next chapter), recognize how their behaviour affects others, and become aware of their own social successes so they can be repeated (Buzzelli & File, 1989).

It is also wise to remember that friendships cannot be imposed or forced. To tell children, "we are all friends at school" or "go find another friend to play with" sends a

mixed message about the meaning of friendship. Young children will develop friendships based on trust and criteria meaningful to them. Teachers should respect their right to choose friends.

GENDER ROLE DEVELOPMENT

Research has shown that one of the most powerful determinants of peer interaction and friendship is the children's sex. If you work with young children, you will have observed that the majority of their playmate choices are of the same sex. This holds true in all cultural settings, not just in North America (Maccoby, 1990). Cross-sex friends are not uncommon; however, as they get older, girls increasingly choose to play with other girls and boys seek out other boys as play partners.

This **sex cleavage**, or distinct separation based on gender, begins to be evident before children reach age 3 (Howes, 1988). Children who are 4-years-old play with same-sex peers nearly three times as often as with children of the opposite sex; two years later, this preference has increased elevenfold (Maccoby & Jacklin, 1987). Children choose same-sex friends spontaneously, and attempts to change or influence their choices to encourage more cross-sex interaction have generally not been very successful (Howes, 1988; Katz, 1986; Maccoby, 1990).

Much speculation exists about the reasons for this sex cleavage. Eleanor Maccoby (1990), who has been involved in research on gender differences for many years, hypothesizes that girls avoid boys because they find it aversive to interact with unresponsive play partners. She speculates that girls generally dislike boys' competitive, rough-and-tumble play styles and, more important, find that they seem to have little influence over boys. The issue of influence becomes increasingly important during early childhood as children learn to integrate and coordinate their activities with those of playmates. In attempts to influence others, girls typically are more polite, whereas boys are much more direct. Over the span of the preschool years, boys increasingly disregard girls, and girls, in turn, increasingly avoid boys because their efforts to influence them are not successful.

How does this awareness of sex differences develop? Lawrence Kohlberg (1966) discusses a developmental process in the formation of sex-role attitudes. It begins with **gender identity**, when even very young children, often before their second birthdays, accurately identify and label themselves and others as boys or girls based on observable physical cues. Between the ages of 5 and 7, children acquire **gender stability**. Younger children do not yet realize that they will always remain the same sex; this sense of constancy emerges at about the same time as the development of such cognitive concepts as conservation, for instance, that the amount of clay in a ball does not change even if its shape is changed.

Another development in this process, evolving during the preschool years and becoming very pronounced by the time the child enters elementary school, is value of the same sex and whatever pertains to it. Children value the concrete symbols of their gender that confirm their maleness or femaleness, and they construct and adopt a rigid set of rules and stereotypes about what is gender-appropriate. This rigidity is consistent with a similar approach to other cognitive concepts. In acquiring same-sex values, children also form an identity with like-sex persons.

Guidelines for Non-Sexist Teaching

This rigidity, children's gravitation toward same-sex peers, and their engagement in gender-stereotyped activities is often troublesome to adults who want children to be broad-minded and tolerant of others. Despite many parents' and teachers' efforts to present non-sexist models to the children in their lives, these same children will often display highly sex-stereotyped behaviours and attitudes. Some guidelines can help the early childhood teacher lay the foundation for non-biased attitudes based on respect for each person as an individual.

- *Value each child as an individual.* Focus on the strengths and abilities of each child as a person, and help children recognize and value these characteristics.

- *Help children learn that gender identity is biologically determined.* Before they develop gender constancy, children may feel that it is their preference for boy or girl activities that makes them boys or girls. Reassure them that their bodies, not their activities, determine their sex (Derman-Sparks, 1989).

- *Be aware of possible gender biases in your own behaviour.* Studies have shown, for instance, that adults tend to protect girls more, react to boys' misbehaviours more, encourage independence more in boys, and expect girls to be more fearful (Honig, 1983).

- *Listen carefully to all children.* Adults tend to interrupt or speak simultaneously more with girls than with boys, suggesting that what girls have to say is less important (Honig, 1983).

- *Help children find the words to get their nurturance needs met.* Little boys are not as likely to ask for a hug or a lap to sit on as girls. Teachers can help all children find the right words to communicate their needs for affection (Honig, 1983).

- *Use language carefully, avoiding bias toward male identity.* The English language tends to assume male identity when sex is not clear. We generally say "he" when we don't know whether an animal, person, or storybook character is male or female, and this tricks children into thinking that "he's" are more important than "she's" (Sheldon, 1990).

- *Provide materials that show males and females in a variety of roles.* Puzzles, lotto games, posters, and photographs can portray males and females in non-tra-ditional roles. Dramatic play props can draw children into a variety of roles sometimes stereotyped as male or female.

- *Select children's books that portray non-sexist models.* Children's literature includes a range of characters from the very sex-stereotyped to the very non-sexist. A study of widely read children's books, including award-winning ones, showed that male and female roles are often distorted and stereotyped. Males appear far more often; females, when they are portrayed, tend to be shown as passive and dependent (Flerx, Fidler, & Rogers, 1976).

- *Plan a wide range of activities and encourage all children to participate.* Children will participate in and enjoy a variety of activities—cooking, woodworking, blocks, housekeeping, book browsing, sewing, sand and water, art—if they are well planned and the teacher's words or attitudes do not promote sex stereotyping.

- *Discuss obvious sex stereotyping with children.* Older preschoolers and school-aged children, especially if they have been around adults who are sensitive to using non-biased concepts and vocabulary, can engage in discussions about sex stereotypes in books, favourite television programs, or movies.

RACIAL AND CULTURAL AWARENESS AND ATTITUDES

Similar to their early recognition of gender differences, children also develop an awareness of racial variations at an early age. Although little research has been conducted to document this with children under the age of 3, many 3-year-olds and most 4-year-olds not only recognize racial cues, but also show racial preferences (Katz, 1983). Thus, children at a very young age already have a sense of racial difference. Preschoolers use the most readily visible physical differences as cues; skin colour in particular, as well as hair and eye colour, provide a basis for comparison and classification.

In a way similar to the process of acquiring gender identity, young children also do not seem to understand fully the permanence of race until they reach the stage of concrete operations (Piaget's stage that occurs during middle childhood). It may be somewhat more difficult for children to develop a sense of racial permanence because many youngsters have limited contact with people of other races. Some children, in fact, think that all people start out white but become darker through tanning, dyeing, or painting (Edwards, 1986).

A rather subtle variation in learning about different people arises when children begin to discover cultural differences. Family, neighbourhood, school, church, books, and mass media can introduce children to the fact that people meet their daily needs in different ways. All people need to communicate, but they may do so in different languages; all people need to eat, but they don't all eat the same types of foods; all people require clothing, shelter, and transportation, but they meet these needs in unique ways. *A focus on the similarities among people should be the basis of multicultural programming for young children.*

Although children's cognitive development steers them toward noting differences and classifying accordingly, society applies the comparative values that lead to stereotypes and prejudice. Children are bombarded with subtle and not-so-subtle messages about the worth of people. Parents, as the primary socializers of their children, seem the obvious transmitters of racial and cultural attitudes; yet, research has shown little relationship between children and their parents in this respect (Katz, 1982). A more plausible source of racial and cultural information may be television, movies, and books that, by their portrayals or by their omissions, imply superiority of some and inferiority of other groups.

In forming their own attitudes, young children continually strive to fit together the multiple and often contradictory sources of information about other people. This was poignantly illustrated to the author a number of years ago by 4-year-old Tory, an aggressive child with few friends. Tory stood at the edge of the playground, looking at Muanza, an affable, outgoing child from Kenya. Using a very derogatory term he had heard used about blacks, he said in a sad tone, "The _____ is my only friend." His use of this word stood in sharp contrast to his actual experience with Muanza.

Guidelines for Teaching about Race and Culture

The early childhood program is an ideal place to help children learn about themselves and others, learn to value and have pride in themselves, and learn to respect others. This involves conveying accurate knowledge about and pride in children's own racial and cultural groups, accurate knowledge about and appreciation of other racial and cultural groups, and an understanding of racism and how to counter it

(Derman-Sparks, Higa, & Sparks, 1980). One excellent resource for helping teachers of young children in this task is Louise Derman-Sparks's *Anti-Bias Curriculum: Tools for Empowering Young Children* (1989). This book sensitively and succinctly discusses and suggests strategies for helping children learn about and respect racial, gender, cultural, and physical differences and to promote anti-discrimination and activism. Derman-Sparks and Ramsey's 1993 article, *Early Childhood Multicultural, Anti-Bias Education in the 1990s: Toward the 21st Century*, would also be a useful resource.

The following guidelines, gleaned from various sources (Derman-Sparks, 1989; Derman-Sparks & Ramsey, 1993; Dimidjian, 1989; Edwards, 1986; Phenice & Hildebrand, 1988; Ramsey, 1982, 1987; "Suggestions for Developing Positive Racial Attitudes," 1980), can help you provide children with a developmentally appropriate understanding of other races and cultures.

- *When children bring up racial/cultural differences, discuss them honestly.* Help children recognize that there are differences between people, but that these differences do not make them superior or inferior to others.

- *Help children develop pride through positive racial/cultural identity.* Children's self-concepts are tied to feeling good about all aspects of their beings. Acknowledgment and positive comments about the beauty of different skin, hair, and eye colours is important to developing feelings about self-worth.

- *Help children develop positive attitudes about other races.* Children need accurate information about other races. Modelling acceptance and appreciation of all races is an important factor.

- *Help children see skin colour variations as a continuum rather than as extremes.* Colour charts to which children can match their own skin colour can help them recognize that everyone is a shade of brown.

- *Help children learn that darker colours are not dirty.* A common misconception among children is that they think that a child of a darker colour is dirty or unwashed. Be careful in your choice of words (do not say, "Wash that black dirt off your hands," for instance). Doll-washing activities, for instance, bathing an obviously dirty white doll and a clean black doll, can help begin to dispel this notion.

- *Post photographs of children and their families.* This can help children begin to acquire the concept of racial constancy as teachers point out similarities (as well as differences) between family members. Help dispel misconceptions about racial constancy as these come up spontaneously. Be prepared for questions if a child in your class was adopted by parents of a different race.

- *Ensure that the environment contains materials representing many races and cultures.* Books, dolls, pictures, posters, dramatic play props, manipulatives, puzzles, and other materials should portray people of all colours and cultures in very positive ways. This is particularly important if your class is racially/culturally mixed; it is also important, however, to expose children in homogeneous classes to different racial and cultural groups through the environment.

- *Discuss incidents of racism and racial stereotypes with the children.* Model anti-racist behaviours by challenging incidents of racism or racial stereotyping. Help children find alternative words if they use racial slurs in arguments with each other.

- *Focus curriculum material about cultures on similarities among people rather than on differences.* Children can identify with shared experiences engaged in by people of other cultures. All people eat, wear clothes, need shelter, share special occasions, and value family activities. Focusing on "exotic" aspects of a culture only points out how different these are and robs them of the shared human factor.

- *Avoid a "tourist" approach to teaching about cultures.* Do not teach children about other cultures out of context. For instance, avoid using only the holidays celebrated by other cultures or a one-shot "cultures" week to focus on this topic (i.e., Monday—Mexico, Tuesday—Japan, Wednesday—Africa, Thursday—Germany, and Friday—France). Also avoid using an ethnic cooking activity and a display of ceremonial clothing as the main components of these occasions. Such an approach is disconnected from everyday life, trivializes cultural diversity, and merely represents multiculturalism as a token gesture rather than as a genuine reflection of life around the world.

- *Make cultural diversity part of daily classroom activity.* Integrate aspects of the children's cultures into the everyday life of your class. Consider that the typical housekeeping corner in many early childhood classrooms conveys a single culture: a white, middle-class model. Many ways of life should be reflected throughout the classroom. For instance, you can include dolls of different races, post pictures showing different ethnic groups, introduce in the housekeeping cupboard food packages that reflect cultural preferences, or include home or cooking implements used by families of children from different cultures.

- *Convey the diversity of cultures through their common themes.* Read about different cultures to find out how various cultural groups meet their physical needs, engage in celebrations, and adapt to their environment. For instance, although Canadians and Americans carve pumpkins into jack-o'-lanterns at Halloween, other cultures also commonly carve fruits and vegetables on certain occasions.

- *Consider the complexity involved in celebrating holidays when their observance might be counter, even offensive, to some families' beliefs or cultures.* The celebration of Christmas could offend the non-Christian families with children in your program. Thanksgiving as a holiday might be an occasion of loss rather than celebration for Canadian aboriginal families. The celebration of holidays should not be avoided but should be considered carefully, taking into account the attitudes, needs, and feelings of the children, families, and staff. Holiday celebrations should focus on respect and understanding of cultural observances.

- *Do not single out a minority child in a way that would make that child feel "different."* Learning about a child's culture should be done in the context of learning about all of the children's cultures. Help such a child and the others in the class recognize that a particular culture is shared by many other people in the world.

- *Involve children's families.* Families are a prime source of information about cultural diversity. Invite parents to participate in the class and share ideas about how all of the children can learn more about their unique backgrounds. Particularly in child care centres, parents may not have the time to join the class, but they should always feel welcome.

SENSITIVITY TOWARD PEOPLE WITH DISABILITIES

Children can also learn to develop understanding, acceptance, and an attitude of helpfulness toward those who have special needs. More and more children with disabilities are **mainstreamed** into early childhood programs. In P.E.I., for example, direct funding to licensed centres for children with disabilities has been available since 1988, as Carolyn Simpson notes in A Canadian Professional Speaks Out. Consequently, the number of children with disabilities in the province's child care centres has risen quickly.

Children with special needs can benefit from a good mainstreamed program by experiencing success in a variety of developmentally appropriate activities, through contact with age-mates who can be both models and friends, and through exposure to the many opportunities for informal, incidental learning that take place in all early childhood programs (Deiner, 1983; Spodek, Saracho, & Lee, 1984). At the same time, children without disabilities benefit from mainstreaming by learning that children who are in some way different from them nonetheless have far more commonalities than differences (Karnes & Lee, 1979). Mainstreaming "provides children with the opportunity for positive experiences that build a good foundation for life-long learning about others. [It] is intended to decrease isolation from and prejudice toward those who are different" (Deiner, 1983, p. 14).

A CANADIAN PROFESSIONAL SPEAKS OUT

Mainstreaming in Early Childhood Education

Making the decision to utilize an early childhood program is often difficult for parents with children who have special needs. Matching the service to family needs can prove especially challenging. These parents must also match the quality and philosophy of services with other resources that may be required to meet their children's needs.

In Prince Edward Island, once the parent and ECE supervisor agree that this service will best meet the needs of the family, the supervisor can apply for funding under the Ministry of Health and Community Services (formerly the Department of Health and Social Services) for a Special Needs Grant. Prior to 1988 funding for specialized programming was available to families through either the Child Care Subsidy Program or Family Support Program; eligibility was determined by an income test. With the implementation of the Special Needs Grant in 1988, funding is now granted to licensed centres directly. The grant allows for a lower child–staff ratio and for the purchase of additional resources as required, thus enabling the centre to be in a better position to deliver a high-quality mainstreaming program.

The grant is individualized, and approval is based on an assessment of the child's needs, the appropriateness of proposed program activities, the availability of funds, and the agreement of the centre to administer any funds according to the policies of the Special Needs Grant.

Another strength of the program is its accountability. Centres are required to submit quarterly progress reports and salary reports, and to hold annual case conferences, the first being six months into the program, with the interdisciplinary team. As well, should this team decide that a child of school age would benefit from one year longer in the ECE environment, the Departments of Education and Health and Social Services have worked together to provide services for this child.

As a result of the Special Needs Grant, Island children and their families are receiving early education and intervention that may not otherwise have been possible.

Carolyn Simpson
Holland College
Charlottetown, P.E.I.

But integrating children with and without disabilities in and of itself does not assure interaction and acceptance. Mainstreaming has many potential benefits, but the benefits do not happen automatically. In other words, mainstreaming does not simply mean enrolling children with special needs in a preschool or child care program. Careful planning, preparation, modification, evaluation, and support are necessary for successful mainstreaming. Early childhood teachers, because they know a great deal about children and how best to work with them, have many skills needed for working with children with disabilities as well.

Children need accurate information about why a peer (or a teacher) looks, moves, sounds, or behaves differently. Children need the chance to express fears or misgivings and to ask questions. It is not unusual for children to be apprehensive about things that are unfamiliar and different or to worry that the disability could happen to them as well. Offering a simple, honest explanation will answer the child's concern and respect the person's disability (Derman-Sparks, 1989).

When a child with cerebral palsy was enrolled at one school, one student called her a "baby." The teacher explained, "Roberta cannot walk because there is something wrong with the muscles in her legs. She can get around on this scooter board by using her arm muscles. Would you like to ask Roberta if you can try her scooter board so you can see what it feels like?"

In addition to helping children accept and include peers with disabilities, the early childhood program can also incorporate into the curriculum activities that are specifically aimed at dispelling stereotypes and helping to build an accepting atmosphere. One such curriculum, *Including All of Us* (Froschl, Colon, Rubin, & Sprung, 1984), provides many excellent activities to meet these goals. A Closer Look describes how an activity led to the spontaneous involvement of one child; this incident, by the way, provided the teacher with a wonderful opportunity to build increased acceptance and involvement of this child.

MORAL DEVELOPMENT

One primary aim of socialization is for children to learn and internalize standards of what is right and wrong, in other words, to develop a conscience. **Moral development** is a long-term process to which many factors contribute. Children are surrounded by a social climate in which the actions of others convey degrees of fairness, consistency, respect, and concern for others. Children's observations of how others behave, how they are treated, and their own cognitive maturation contribute to their emerging sense of morality.

Children adopt a more mature set of standards if they are raised in an atmosphere of clearly set and enforced standards, support and nurturance, open communication in which the child's viewpoint is valued, and other-oriented reasons for expected behaviour (Maccoby & Martin, 1983). There is also evidence that the onset of the distinction between right and wrong may be an inborn trait, emerging by children's second birthday (Kagan, 1987).

Another factor with which children have to contend, especially in a diverse society such as ours, is that moral standards vary in different cultures. Some universal **interpersonal moral rules**—ones prohibiting harm to others, murder, incest, theft—are found across cultures. Other **conventional moral rules** are arrived at by general consensus and are more culture-specific, such as wearing clothes in public or chewing with your mouth closed. In addition, each society specifies some regulations that ensure orderly and safe functioning, for instance, stopping at red traffic lights. Implied in this differentiation is that some rules are more important than others. This is

A CLOSER LOOK

The "Sherman Hokey Pokey"

It was almost noon, the last group activity before the children went home, and the teacher played a favourite record, the "Hokey Pokey." The children stood in the circle and started singing and moving along with the record. Within a few minutes there was a lively collection of right hands, left hands, right feet, left feet, and other body parts being put in and out of the middle of the circle and little people turning themselves around.

Sherman, a 4-year-old with cerebral palsy, sat on the floor, rather than in his wheelchair along the edge of the circle. He put his hands and feet in and out of the circle along with everyone else. At the end of the first stanza when it came time to "turn yourself around," Sherman watched the other children, a slight smile playing on his face. The second time, he slowly scooted himself around on his bottom, and grinned broadly. The third time, Jason, who was standing next to Sherman, stopped to watch him, caught Sherman's eye, and then both of them laughed. By the time the directions were to "put your left foot in … and turn yourself around," Jason was sitting on the floor next to Sherman, and both of them were turning around on their bottoms, accompanying their actions and song with a lot of giggles.

At this point, Francesca, who was across the circle, noticed Sherman and Jason's variation on the old song. She also sat down and began to carry out the directions on her bottom. She called out to the teacher, "Look! I'm doing the Sherman Hokey Pokey, too!" As the song was halfway into its second round, more than half of the children were doing the "Sherman Hokey Pokey," and soon they were all on their bottoms. The children were delighted with this new version, but none more than Sherman. When his mother came to pick him up a few minutes later, he proudly told her, "I got to be the leader of everybody today!"

usually reflected in the classroom, where some transgressions, for instance, harm to others, are considered more serious than others (Edwards, 1986).

Piaget's View of Moral Development

Much of today's theoretical writing about moral development derived from Piaget's work on children's developing understanding of rules (1932). From his observations of children at play, Piaget formulated a stage theory of moral development that moves from an early childhood view in which rules are unchangeable and derived from a higher authority (for instance, God or parents) to the more mature perspective that rules are made by and can be changed through mutual consent of the players. Interestingly, even though young children see rules as inflexible, they also change them to suit their own interests; this is not a contradiction, but rather a reflection of their limited understanding of the nature and purpose of rules as a shared system.

Piaget also described young children as unconcerned with intentions, because they focus on the concrete and observable outcome. Thus, a preschooler will think that a child who breaks one plate while trying to get a forbidden cookie is less at fault than a child who accidentally breaks several plates while helping his mother set the table.

Kohlberg's Stages of Moral Development

Lawrence Kohlberg (1969) took Piaget's stage theory and developed a more elaborate framework for considering moral development based on why people make certain choices rather than on what those choices are (Edwards, 1986). He describes three levels, each divided into two substages, that relate to the person's view of social "conventions," hence the terms preconventional, conventional, and postconventional. Furthermore, these levels coincide with Piaget's cognitive developmental stages (Shweder, Mahapatra, & Miller, 1987), which we discussed in Chapters 2 and 12.

1. The **preconventional level of moral development** occurs approximately during the preoperational stage of cognitive development (about ages 2 to 7). Moral decisions are founded on personal preference and typify young children's egocentric thinking. External rewards and punishment determine right and wrong. Children will engage in behaviour because it is pleasurable or because they might risk punishment if they do not. By age 4, many children develop an understanding of reciprocity; doing something for another person can result in that person doing something for the child.

2. The **conventional level of moral development** coincides with the stage of concrete operations (approximately ages 7 to 12) and is more concerned with group approval and consensus.

3. The **postconventional level of moral development** dovetails with the stage of formal operations (reached by some adolescents) and is based on a higher moral sense of what is right and principled. Socially agreed-on values are accepted. However, these may be transcended if personal ethics, based on a universal morality, are violated. (Note that not all people reach this stage.)

William Damon's research (1977, 1983) further delineates young children's thought processes as they move through stages of moral development, especially as they relate to concepts of authority and fairness. His studies are based on interviews with children aged 4 and older.

- Four-year-olds base decisions on self-interest. Justification for a choice is simply, "I should get it because I want it."

- By age 5, children recognize the potential conflict between what they want and external rules, and they obey to avoid the consequences. They also begin to view authority as an obstruction to their own desires. Justification for their choices is based on visible external cues such as size or sex, for instance, "We should get more because we're girls."

- Over the next year, children show respect for authority because of the authority figure's social or physical power, which is considered almost as omnipotent. They also progress to a view of strict equality, where everyone gets the same amount when resources are distributed.

- Subsequent stages show more complex thinking, as children see authority figures in terms of special attributes that invest them with leadership qualities. Their view of fair distribution of resources increasingly considers more factors, for instance, looking at competing claims and at compromising.

Guidelines for Promoting Moral Development

Most of the early childhood years are spent in the preconventional level of moral development. The first signs that a child is entering the conventional level of moral development usually do not appear until age 7 or later. It is important to recognize children's abilities and limits in terms of moral reasoning and to guide them on the road to moral understanding. The following guidelines will help in this task (Edwards, 1986; Krogh & Lamme, 1985).

- *Use other-oriented reasoning with children.* For example, rather than state, "Our rule is that we don't run inside," say, "We don't run inside because we could hurt other children by bumping into them."

- *Use stories to promote thinking and discussion about moral issues.* Favourite children's stories often pose interesting moral dilemmas that, with teacher guidance, encourage discussion. Krogh and Lamme (1985) recommend such books as *The Little Red Hen* (Galdone, 1973), *Angus and the Cat* (Flack, 1931), and *Peter's Chair* (Keats, 1967) for this purpose.

- *Provide ample time for child-selected play and materials that promote cooperation.* Dramatic play, for example, allows children to take the viewpoints of others; equipment that requires more than one child to operate encourages cooperation.

- *Provide activities that help children become more aware of how the face conveys emotions.* Collages, masks, photos, acting out feelings, and "emotion puzzles" can strengthen this awareness.

- *Initiate thinking games that encourage children to seek multiple alternatives for social problems.* Puppets can enact a common social dilemma, for instance, one dealing with sharing, and children can generate alternative solutions to the situation.

- *Plan thinking games that deal with moral intentionality.* Children over the age of 4 can begin to differentiate between intended naughtiness and an accident that happened while a child was trying to help. Discuss the context of consequences in each instance.

- *Use any teachable moments that arise to encourage moral development.* For example, if you accidentally spill a large jug of juice, ask if that is better or worse then purposely spilling a small glass of juice.

• *Realize that not all cultures share the same values.* Communication with parents can help teachers find which values are important to families and help to reinforce these as appropriate with the children.

DEVELOPMENT OF PROSOCIAL BEHAVIOURS

Peer relations, friendship, gender role acquisition, racial and cultural awareness, and moral development are all part of an intertwined process that involves the emergence of a number of other related traits. Researchers have looked at how such social characteristics as nurturance, empathy, altruism, generosity, sharing, and tolerance evolve in young children. Children's social cognition will affect how they respond to others. With age comes greater comprehension, although a higher level of understanding will not ensure that children's responses will necessarily be appropriate. Other factors contributing to the emergence of prosocial behaviours include the modelling of the significant people in children's lives as well as the kinds of other-oriented values that have been stressed (Schickedanz, Hansen, & Forsyth, 1990).

An early childhood program in which adults model, emphasize, and value prosocial behaviours will facilitate development of such traits in children. Alice Honig (1988a), who considers a prosocial curriculum based on caring and kindness as a crucial goal of early childhood programs, has highlighted the importance of such behaviours.

Previous sections of this chapter presented activities and strategies that can help encourage developmentally appropriate and positive social attitudes and behaviours. In the context of a supportive atmosphere, understanding of child development, concern for children's needs, respect for their opinions, encouragement of their autonomy, support for their individuality, and provision of a stimulating program and environment, such activities will help promote positive socialization. Parents and Professionals offers suggestions for communicating with parents on these topics.

 PARENTS AND PROFESSIONALS

Reflection of Family Culture and Values

Communication with parents is particularly important in clarifying home and school values about socialization and about children's cultural and racial identities. Although the school is responsible for conveying to parents what values it tries to instil in the children through the curriculum and guidance techniques, the school also is responsible for obtaining similar information from parents about what they value for their children. Teachers need to be sensitive to the many variations among families of different cultures, and they must be particularly aware of their own attitudes and biases. It is easier to convey positive messages to a family whose parenting style and values you are familiar with and agree with than it is to understand and accept an approach different from your own.

Another reason that good parent–teacher communication is vital is to avoid making assumptions about children's home life based on cultural generalizations. There are wide variations within cultural groups. In addition, individual families' adaptation to Canadian culture will also affect their lifestyles and customs. One child care centre director, for instance, hired one of the parents to help with meal preparation. When this mother, who had recently come from Colombia, asked the director to explain the "tacos" on the menu, the director was taken aback, assuming that anyone from Central or South America would know what they were. As she quickly learned, Central and South America represent many countries with diverse and individual foods and customs.

Teachers can gain much information from parents about cultural and ethnic backgrounds and values. For instance, it is important to have the child's full name, the name the family uses, and its correct pronunciation. In some cultures such as the Vietnamese, the correct order in giving a name is last name first, followed by first and middle names (Morrow, 1989). Also, some Asian families give a child one name to be used in public and another to be used at home. It is important, therefore, to have accurate information about what name to use in speaking to the child.

Also gather information about the child's family, special friends, pets, or any other people or objects that are important. This will help facilitate discussions and provide ways of involving what is closest to the child. In addition, obtain information about holidays and other special cultural, religious, or family celebrations, including when they are observed, their purpose, and how the children are involved. This will help incorporate cultural activities that are meaningful (*Culture and Children*, 1985).

Some teachers may face an additional challenge if some of the families whose children are enrolled in the program speak a primary language other than English. In some communities with a large population from another culture, early childhood programs may have teachers who speak the language of this group and can either facilitate communication or provide a bilingual program. This is often not the case, however. It is important to help children, parents, and teachers communicate. One way is for teachers and even the other children to learn some common words and phrases that can help the child begin to integrate into the class. While children may quickly learn enough English to function effectively at school, their parents generally will not acquire the new language as rapidly, and communication with the school could be a problem.

Because communication between home and school is so important, the school can do several things. Finding an interpreter who can facilitate occasional parent–teacher meetings can be helpful. If there are older siblings, they are natural interpreters who can be asked to assist. You might also offer to locate an *ESL (English-as-a-second-language)* program, if the parents are interested in improving their acquisition of English. For everyday interaction, try to learn and use a few common words and phrases in the family's language; this can convey your desire and willingness to communicate. If nothing else, your quaint pronunciation attempts will bring a smile to the parent's face and create a sense of shared effort.

Finally, Derman-Sparks (1989), in *Anti-Bias Curriculum*, suggests that in addition to open communication in which values and ideas can be shared by parents and teachers, the school can provide accurate information to parents about the development of children's sexual, racial, and ethnic identities and attitudes. A series of parent group meetings can inform and invite discussion about such topics as gender identity and sexism, the creation of non-sexist environments, the development of racial identity and awareness, the creation of anti-racist environments, and evaluation of children's books for sexist and racial stereotypes. Such groups can help parents gain information about the school's philosophy, help teachers attain insight Into parents' values and attitudes, and provide parents with strategies for anti-biased socialization of children.

PRETEND PLAY

In Chapter 8, we discussed many of the values of pretend play. The development of positive social traits is fostered in a variety of preschool activities and learning centres, but it is perhaps most naturally facilitated in pretend play. In pretend play, children use symbols such as words, actions, or other objects to represent the real world; in pretend play, they expand this symbolic play to include other children (Fein, 1979; Smilansky, 1968).

Theorists and researchers have postulated a relationship between pretend play and the development of social competencies. For instance, through such play children have many opportunities to learn about social rules by taking on someone else's identity and enacting common situations, as well as by negotiating with peers when conflicts arise (Doyle & Connolly, 1989). Although research has found that not all children engage in pretend play (Christie, 1982; Smilansky, 1968, 1990), as you know, a number of programs have been successful in teaching young children how to do so.

The first of the series of pretend play training studies we discussed in Chapter 8 was carried out in Israel by Sarah Smilansky (1968). She helped children from deprived backgrounds learn skills required in role taking, use of symbols, social and verbal interaction, and persistence. The level of teacher intervention depended on the skills and needs of the children. If children had very limited skills, the teacher facilitated pretend play by participating in the children's play directly. As children became more adept, the teacher became less obtrusive, taking on the role of an outside observer who made suggestions to enhance play rather than being a participant.

In many cases, children assist peers who are not as skilled in entering pretend play. For instance, 4-year-old Felix most often engaged in onlooker behaviour during child-selected activity times, usually standing on the outskirts of social groups. On one day in November, Yasmine, age 5, deftly included Felix, who stood at the edge of the housekeeping corner observing a "family" group prepare dinner. The participants had assumed all the obvious roles, including that of family dog. The "mother," Yasmine, took Felix by the hand, led him to the play oven, and declared, "You can be the turkey." She helped Felix fit himself into the oven and closed its door. A few seconds later she opened the door, checked Felix's doneness by squeezing his thigh, and declared, "Turkey's done!" Everyone gathered around as the turkey was helped out of the oven. Felix's big grin testified to his delight at being assigned such an important role! (Appropriate comments were made later about children never getting into a real stove, fridge, and so on.)

Most young children engage in dramatic pretend play naturally; however, such play should also be purposefully encouraged and enhanced in all early childhood settings. Every early childhood classroom should have an area set aside and equipped for dramatic play. Most commonly, dramatic play props and children's engagement in dramatic play will centre on housekeeping because home-related roles and activities are most familiar to young children. Children re-create and enact what happens at home: meal preparation and consumption, bedtime routines, visitors, child rearing, even arguments. Home-related kitchen, living room, and bedroom items, as well as a selection of dolls, dress-up clothes, and mirrors, stimulate children's creative and social engagement in housekeeping play (see Chapter 9 for additional suggested dramatic play props). Materials for younger preschoolers should be realistic, whereas they should be more abstract for older preschoolers, to encourage pretending (Fein, 1982). Children can be further encouraged to broaden their concepts and dramatic play through displays and pictures of people of all ages and different ethnic groups engaged in common household activities.

Dramatic play can also revolve around any other theme familiar to the children—health care, shopping, and recreation are usually particularly relevant to young children because they invariably have visited the doctor, grocery store, or park. Children will also enact favourite book, television, or movie roles and stories. It is important, however, that children be thoroughly familiar with a topic through concrete, first-hand experience before they engage in dramatic play. Following a field trip, for instance, appropriate props in the dramatic play area can help children assimilate and integrate information from the trip.

COOPERATIVE GAMES

One prosocial goal that early childhood educators cite for young children is cooperation, the force that unites people into working together toward a common objective. In an effort to promote cooperation, there should be *no place in the early childhood program for competitive activities* in which all but one child end up as losers, even if they are called "second winners." Races, board games, musical chairs, and similar activities in which one child emerges as the winner only promote feelings of resentment, anger, failure, and lack of confidence. Yet, often such games can be easily adapted to keep the element of fun while eliminating competition. For instance, the game of musical chairs can be changed so that all the children share the decreasing number of chairs, until everyone is piled on (and around) the last chair, usually dissolved in gales of laughter!

Writers such as Terry Orlick (1978a, 1978b, 1982) have expressed concern over the destructive outcome of competitive games and have proposed as an alternative cooperative games in which no one is a loser and everyone is a winner. The rationale for cooperative games is not just the avoidance of situations in which most of the participants lose, but is much broader, extending to a general concern for the quality of life, emphasis on peace and harmony, and decrease in societal aggressiveness. Exhibit 14-1 contains a selection of cooperative games for preschool-aged children.

Activities involving two or more players can be considered cooperative if one or more of the following is involved: shared goals, joint decision making, shared ideas and materials, negotiation and bargaining, coordination of efforts to meet goals, and evaluation of progress toward goals (Goffin, 1987). Although Orlick recommends organized group games as a vehicle for promoting cooperation, this trait can be encouraged in more indirect and less structured ways as well.

Classroom space can be organized to encourage interactions, and ample time blocks can be allocated for child-selected play. Cooperative endeavours may well require more space and more time than activities in which children act alone. In addition, materials should be selected for their cooperative properties. Open-ended materials such as dramatic play props, blocks, water and sand, and puppets particularly promote cooperation. Teachers can also set up activities so that more than one child is involved. Instead of simply putting out beads and yarn as a fine motor activity, try laying long pieces of yarn across the table, with beads at each end, so that two children can work cooperatively on one yarn piece (Goffin, 1987).

EXHIBIT 14-1 COOPERATIVE GAMES

1. **"STICKY POPCORN"**
   Children begin by jumping or hopping up as they "pop." Because the popcorn is sticky, whenever a piece of popcorn touches another they stick together. Once stuck, they continue to pop together until all the popcorn kernels make one big popcorn ball.

2. **"MUSICAL HUGS"**
   With energetic music playing, children skip around the room. When the music first stops, children give a big hug to someone nearby. When the music starts again, pairs of huggers can skip together if they want. The next time the music stops at least three children hug together, and so on, until everyone is joined in one massive hug.

3. **"SHOE TWISTER"**
   The children each remove one shoe and place the shoes in a pile. While holding hands in a circle around the shoe pile, the children pick up someone else's shoe (the method for doing this is left up to the children's imagination). After locating the owners of the shoes, they exchange the footwear without breaking the circle.

4. **"BIG TURTLE"**
   Seven or eight children get on their hands and knees under a "turtle shell"—a tumbling mat, tarp, or blanket. Children have to work together to move without dropping the shell.

5. **"TOESIES"**
   With bare feet, pairs of children lie stretched out on the floor, toes touching. They try to roll across the floor while maintaining their toe touch.

6. **"BEACH BALL BALANCE"**
   Pairs of children try to hold a large ball between them without using their hands. They try to find as many different ways of doing this as possible (between their stomachs, knees, foreheads, hips, and so on). Next they try to walk without losing the ball.

7. **"LAP BALL"**
   The children sit close together in a circle and try to pass a large ball from lap to lap without using their hands. A less difficult version of "Lap Ball" and "Beach Ball Bounce" can be arranged by having four children each hold a corner of a towel and keeping a ball bouncing on the towel through cooperative effort.

8. **"ELBOW-NOSE REVERSE"**
   With the children in a circle, one child starts by pointing to her or his elbow and saying, "This is my nose." The second child passes this message to the next one, and so on. When the message has gone around the circle, a new confusing message is sent.

SOURCES: Orlick, T. (1978a). *The cooperative sports and games book.* New York: Pantheon Books. *Everybody wins: Non-competitive games for young people.* Copyright © 1983 by Jeffrey Sobel. Reprinted with permission from Walker and Company, 435 Hudson Street, New York, NY 10014, 1-800-289-2553.

KEY POINTS OF CHAPTER 14

THEORETICAL VIEWS OF THE SOCIALIZATION PROCESS

▲ 1. Socialization is the process through which children become functioning members of society, learning its rules and values.

▲ 2. An understanding of Erikson's theory is important for developing an appropriate social environment for young children.

▲ 3. The constructivist view of socialization holds that children gain social knowledge through the same process used in gaining other knowledge, by constructing it from their experiences.

▲ 4. Social learning theory suggests that children learn social behaviours through observation and imitation.

DEVELOPMENT OF SOCIAL COMPETENCE

▲ 5. The early childhood teacher facilitates development of positive peer relationships through guidance and by setting an appropriate environment.

▲ 6. Preschoolers begin to develop friendships, although early friendships are more concerned with the immediate situation than with long-term commitments.

▲ 7. Children tend to choose playmates of the same sex, a tendency that increases with age.

▲ 8. At a very young age, children identify themselves as boys or girls, although they do not realize until between the ages of 5 and 7 that gender is permanent and cannot be changed.

▲ 9. When teachers are sensitive to providing a non-sexist, non-stereotyped atmosphere, children will be more likely to develop attitudes based on respect for each person as an individual.

▲ 10. Children also develop an awareness of racial differences at an early age.

▲ 11. The early childhood curriculum should provide many opportunities for children to learn about themselves and others, to value their own and others' races and cultures, and to develop appreciation and acceptance of diversity.

▲ 12. In a similar way, the early childhood program should help children develop sensitivity toward those with disabilities.

▲ 13. Moral development is concerned with children's development of conscience through internalization of society's rules and standards.

▲ 14. To a great extent, young children's moral development is based on personal preference, but gradually evolves to consider the need for rules and the role of authority figures.

▲ 15. Prosocial behaviours are best promoted in an early childhood program that stresses caring and kindness.

PRETEND PLAY

▲ 16. Pretend play takes place when a group of children are jointly involved in symbolic or sociodramatic play.

▲ 17. Pretend play provides children with valuable opportunities to learn about themselves in peer relationships and to take on someone else's identity.

▲ 18. An appropriate classroom environment and the teacher's guidance will facilitate children's involvement in pretend play.

COOPERATIVE GAMES

▲ 19. Cooperation can be promoted in the early childhood environment through activities and games in which children work together toward a common goal.

▲ 20. There is no place in the early childhood program for competitive activities.

KEY TERMS

conventional level of
   moral development

conventional moral rules

gender identity

gender stability

interpersonal moral rules

mainstreaming

model

modelling

moral development

observational learning

postconventional level of
   moral development

preconventional level of
   moral development

sex cleavage

social cognition

social learning theory

socialization

KEY QUESTIONS

1. As we have discussed in this chapter, becoming socialized into society is a complex process. Which early childhood activities and teacher behaviours do you think contribute toward this goal?

2. What is your earliest recollection of a friendship? Can you recall why this friendship developed? How long did it last? What was special about this particular friend? What feelings does your recollection of this friendship evoke right now?

3. Observe a group of young children during a time when they can self-select activities. Note with whom they interact. How many of the children interact primarily with peers of the same sex? How many interact with peers of the opposite sex? Estimate the proportion of same-sex and cross-sex interactions.

4. Look around an early childhood classroom to assess how it promotes positive (or negative) attitudes toward other people in relation to sex, race, culture, or disabling condition. What recommendations can you make for setting up a non-biased classroom?

5. Some teachers appear to be biased in favour of one gender over the other, and this can create many difficulties for the less favoured sex. Examine your views on this, and discuss ways teachers can avoid gender bias.

6. Try one of the cooperative games listed in this chapter with a group of young children. What is their reaction?

Part

5

THE HOW OF EARLY CHILDHOOD EDUCATION—GUIDANCE

Another important part of the "how" of early childhood education is guidance, the principles that teachers use in directing the social behaviour of young children. In this section of the book, we will focus on the following topics:

- Chapter 15, "Guiding Routines and Group Activities," will look at two important aspects of the preschool day. Routines are those often overlooked but all-important elements such as meals and naps. Guidance suggestions for group activities are provided to help the teacher work effectively with the entire class as a whole.

- Chapter 16, "Guiding Behaviours" we will examine some general principles that are important in helping children meet appropriate expectations and discuss guidance techniques.

- In the final chapter of this section, "Helping Children Cope with Stress," we will turn to a topic that teachers of young children increasingly face.

15 GUIDING ROUTINES AND GROUP ACTIVITIES

In a well-managed classroom, children and teachers are involved, busy, happy, and organized, functioning smoothly and working within a flexible schedule and curriculum. Infants and toddlers will become familiar with the routines that are such an important part of their curriculum. Older preschoolers will learn what is expected and will come to behave according to those expectations. School-aged children who have had consistency in their lives will readily adapt to the group expectations; children with less positive experiences may need extra time. The classroom atmosphere is one in which the children are continually learning to be responsible for their own and the group's behaviour. Such a classroom does not just happen, however. Teachers set the stage through their guidance techniques.

Two guidance aspects of the early childhood program deserve special consideration—those parts of the day given over to routines such as meals or naps, and the times when all of the children participate in the same activity at one time as a group. Thus, this chapter will look at the following topics:

1. We will begin by discussing four routine times: arrival at school, meals, toileting, and sleep. All four have strong emotional significance for the child and need sensitive handling by the teachers.

2. We will also examine those important factors that affect group behaviour, particularly the developmental appropriateness of expectations and activities.

3. Forethought and planning can help ensure an orderly classroom during specific time blocks within the daily schedule, as we will also consider.

4. Transitions, those times when children move from one activity to the next, deserve special attention.

5. We will end this chapter with a look at occasions when the out-of-the-ordinary happens. These occasions may be planned (e.g., a field trip) or unplanned (e.g., an accident).

ARRIVAL AT SCHOOL

The first event of the day—the transition from home to school—must be considered carefully, because leaving their parents can be very difficult for children. One factor affecting the ease of arrival at preschool or child care is children's general enjoyment of school. Another consideration is the security of children's **attachment** to their mothers, which is related to the quality of the mother–child relationship; young children most distressed at separation often also show signs of anxious attachment (Fein & Schwartz, 1982). Feelings of **separation anxiety** are not uncommon in preschoolers, although they are more prevalent in younger children (Hinde, 1983). Other factors, particularly what happened at home as the child was getting ready that morning, also have an impact.

It is worth thinking through the arrival procedure and individual children's reactions and needs. Especially in a child care setting in which many children will be spending a large portion of their waking hours and where they arrive at different times of the morning, it is best to provide a low-key opening for the day. A few quiet activities, some soft music, and available teachers to ease anxiety or welcome enthusiastic children can help the day get off to a good start (adequate teaching staff are critical for such an enthusiastic welcome).

In any program, provision must be made for a teacher to welcome each child and parent individually. It is reassuring to a parent on parting from his or her child to know that someone is aware of and pleased about the child's presence at school. Similarly, children need to know that the teacher is glad to see them and is looking forward to mutual enjoyment during the day. This time also provides a chance for the parent to share with the teachers pertinent information that might affect the child's behaviour that day. Morning is not, however, a time for the teacher to bring up concerns with the parent.

MORNING HEALTH CHECK

Many schools use this early morning greeting as an opportunity to give each child a health check before the parent rushes off to work. This conveys their interest in the children's health as well as their concern that ill children not remain at school. A quick visual inspection of the child can tell you whether the child appears unusually listless, has dull or heavy eyes, is developing a rash, has a runny nose, or looks flushed. A hug or touch is an important part of a welcome for young children, and, at the same time, it lets you know if the child has unusually warm skin. If you suspect that a child is ill, discuss this with the parent and help find an alternative child care arrangement, if necessary.

THE NEW CHILD AT SCHOOL

The initial entry into an early childhood program often causes great anxiety for children. This experience can be traumatic, fraught with the unknown. It is difficult for a child to create a mental image of what school is, and without such an image the idea of school can be very frightening. Therefore, it is important for the child to have the chance to gradually become familiar with school, with the security of the parents nearby, rather than be thrust into a first day with no introduction or transition.

Ideally, a new child should visit the school with a parent before her or his first day. After this visit, the child can stay for a short period while the parent leaves briefly; this can help the child realize that she or he has not been abandoned. After that, the parent can be encouraged to stay a few minutes at the beginning of the first few days, as the child needs additional reassurance. If such an arrangement cannot be made because of parents' work schedules, urge the parents to allocate a little extra time at the beginning of those first few days.

One designated teacher should be available to welcome and spend some time with a new child. It is good for the child to have a reliable adult to turn to with questions or concerns. Other children, those who are veterans of the program, often help ease the new child into the centre. You might facilitate this by introducing the newcomer to another child who can show that child the classroom. As children get older, peers become increasingly more important in supporting separation from mother (Gunnar, Senior, & Hartup, 1984). For some children, a classroom pet can help ease the anxiety of the new school experience.

The first few days at school can be difficult for the new child, the parents, and the teachers. This experience can be even more disconcerting, however, when not just one new child but many or all of the children, starting a new school year, find themselves in unfamiliar surroundings. In such a case, it is best to encourage parents to stay with anxious children. Another approach is to plan a phased-in start to school, with only a few new children beginning at a time.

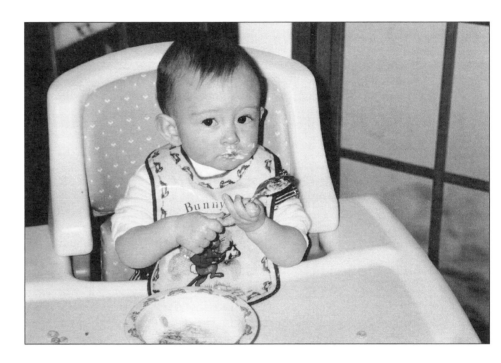

MEALS AND EATING BEHAVIOUR

Meals are an important element of the early childhood program because they fulfil a vital physiological need, as well as social and emotional needs. Care and thought must be given to menu planning, whether children will be eating a single, daily snack in a preschool program or breakfast, lunch, and two snacks in a child care program. Young children take in relatively few calories, yet they need a wide range of nutrients; thus, foods that maximize nutritional value should be selected. Meeting children's nutritional needs is particularly important because many of today's parents do not do so as reliably as did parents of past generations (Rothlein, 1989).

In A Canadian Professional Speaks Out, Barbara Elliott describes a multi-age grouping program at Confederation College in Thunder Bay that seems to facilitate group guidance and a family atmosphere during routines like mealtime.

A CANADIAN
PROFESSIONAL SPEAKS OUT

Multi-Ages in Group Care: Family-Style Care from Infancy to School Age

Historically, the family was the place where children were socialized to be part of society. We all have a vision of the ideal family setting as a place where adults and children live and learn together. Where mutual respect reigns supreme. Where the young learn from older members and older children learn about nurturing and caring for younger, more dependent little ones. Tolerance and compassion are natural. Working out solutions that involve many variables, including age and stage difference, are necessary to live in harmony. This is our goal in multi-aged group settings.

Deinstitutionalizing child care is a popular topic. "A prisoner of furlough" is how Donald MacDonald (1990) describes a child's life in an institution by day and a home by night and on weekends. Changing this setting to an environment that provides creativity, nurturance, and cognitive stimulation and encourages optimal growth and development is a challenge to all early childhood educators.

Defining early childhood education helps us plan the "perfect environment." Education, holistic in nature, represents the process of empowering children to develop capabilities of reasoning and judgment necessary to live in harmony with themselves, their family, and their immediate and global community. Living in harmony happens within trusting relationships and secure surroundings. Trusting relationships spring from unconditional acceptance. Acceptance promotes feelings of self-worth and self-respect, which is the precursor to social relationships that are meaningful and fulfilling. What kind of environment is likely to support this foundation for lasting satisfaction and lifelong learning?

A review of the literature that focuses on optimal space as well as a common-sense approach that acknowledges the traditional way children have adapted to space points to the value of homelike environments. Since adults always share the space, the design should accommodate the comfort of adults as well as children. This environment should be a place where adults and children live and learn together.

Physical space that looks like a home creates the desired anti-institutional effect. Space for children to be together and separate adds a necessary component. Just as in a family, the group car setting should recognize that an older child may want to go to a room alone or take a friend to another room to work on a project that a 2-year-old may not understand.

Certain times of the day are perfect for all ages to be together. Small groups are very important. A group of five to eight children ranging in age from 6 months to 6 years is wonderful family for lunch. Going outdoors can involve an older child helping a younger child get ready.

Since the early 1980s, multi-age group settings have served as a lab experience to the Early Childhood Education program at Confederation College. Currently, children as young as 4 months can share space with a 5-year-old or a school-aged child.

The curriculum is developed and adapted to meet the needs of a variety of ages. Space is available for individualized or age-specific play experiences. Routines such as mealtime, dressing, and toileting are often shared with other ages. This is similar to family life. Older children assist with younger children. Younger children use older children as models as they attempt to master new skills.

Children's cognitive skills may be enhanced as they work on problems with other children whose knowledge or abilities are similar but not identical. Opportunities for "cognitive conflict" that challenge but do not exceed children's capacities stimulate the thinking of each participant.

Mixed-age groupings also serve to relax the rigid curriculum with its narrowly defined age–grade expectations, which are inappropriate for many children.

As in a family, there are issues and problems to be resolved, which, in turn, lead to the development of strong problem-solving skills. The rewards of this model are quickly seen as children become more aware of the needs of others. The balance between having time with one's own age group or being by oneself completes the ideal environment for young children in group care.

Barbara Elliott
Confederation College
Thunder Bay, Ontario

Reference

MacDonald, Donald. (1990). *Architecture for kids: Deinstitutionalizing the design of child care centres.*

PROVIDING NUTRITIOUS MEALS THAT CHILDREN WILL EAT

Perhaps infants are the easiest children to feed! At least, before solid food is introduced, they do not have strong likes and dislikes. And they are easiest to feed if their nursing mother visits the program for feeding times, as many do when the centre is close to work. Finicky appetites develop in most children with the introduction of solid food. It is especially challenging to meet the nutritious needs of toddlers and preschoolers because these children often are extremely picky eaters. School-aged children tend to have developed a liking for more foods, so they are easier to please. Let's look at some guidelines that can be helpful in providing nutritious foods that children will eat.

- Provide variety.
- Take advantage of fresh seasonal fruits and vegetables.
- Offer simple foods.
- Introduce new foods carefully.
- Give special names to dishes sometimes; this adds to the fun of eating.
- Offer finger foods when possible.
- Limit sugar in the foods you provide.
- Provide healthy snacks that contribute to the daily nutrient intake.
- Time meals carefully.
- Vary the location of meals now and then.
- Be sensitive to children's cultural food preferences as you plan meals.

ENCOURAGING HEALTHY EATING HABITS

In any given class, you will find children who are vigorous eaters, enjoying whatever is served, and others who are picky and selective. Even individual children will vary considerably in appetite from day to day or meal to meal (Alford & Bogle, 1982). Let's look at some suggestions for encouraging the formation of good eating habits and for dealing with some eating problems.

- A relaxed, comfortable atmosphere is important to good eating.
- Teachers should sit and eat with the children during all meals.
- Children should never be forced to eat a food against their will, but they should be encouraged to taste all menu items.
- Food preferences and aversions are formed at an early age.
- Involve the children in mealtime.
- Children should be allowed to be as independent as possible at mealtimes.
- It is important to be aware of foods that put young children, especially those under the age of 3, at risk of choking.

PROBLEM EATING BEHAVIOURS

Some children are finicky eaters. Inborn as well as learned preferences seem to play a role in developing food habits (Trahms, 1989). In some cases, children are picky eaters because they have learned that such behaviour gets them attention (Essa, 1990). By not focusing on children's eating behaviour in your conversations, you take away that attention while directing it to something more pleasant. You are, in essence, giving children responsibility for their eating behaviour. As you converse with the children, you might talk about how crunchy the orange carrot sticks are, but not focus on the child who refuses to eat those carrots. Peers can also influence children's food choices (Birch, 1980a), as can repeated exposure to a new food (Birch, Marlin, & Rotter, 1984).

Overweight children pose a special concern because of long-range social and health problems associated with obesity (American Academy of Pediatrics, 1985). It is very likely that obese children will become obese adults, so early intervention is crucial (Garn & Clark, 1976; Pipes, 1989b).

You can monitor the food intake of overweight children and help them serve themselves reasonably sized portions. Also encourage children to eat slowly, perhaps put their forks down between bites, because overweight preschoolers chew their food less and eat too quickly (Drabman, Cordua, Hammer, Jarvie, & Horton, 1979). Encouragement to increase activity level is also important for overweight children.

TOILETING

Toileting is important because it helps children become more independent and establishes habits of good hygiene. Toileting takes on particular significance in groups of toddlers and young preschoolers, who are in the process or have recently mastered bowel and bladder control. Even with older preschoolers, it is good to remind ourselves that these children were still in diapers just a couple of years ago!

Before toileting becomes a matter-of-fact routine of life, young children may go through a period when they are especially interested in the acts of urinating and defecating as well as everything that surrounds them. With young preschoolers who are just mastering bladder control, periodically ask children if they need to go to the bathroom. Be particularly aware of signs such as wiggling or holding, which indicate a need to urinate. Reassure children who fear losing an activity if they go the washroom that their places at the play dough centre and block area, for example, will be there where they return.

TOILET ACCIDENTS

In a group of very young children, toilet accidents are inevitable. Children who have just recently mastered bladder and bowel control may not yet have the timing worked out, perhaps getting caught up in play and not leaving an activity quickly enough to get to the bathroom. Older preschoolers will also have periodic accidents, which should not be a cause for concern or shame. It is critical that teachers handle toilet accidents gently and sensitively.

Children will react differently to toilet accidents. For some, an accident will be embarrassing and upsetting, whereas for others it will be, at most, a minor irritant. *In neither instance should a child ever be lectured, shamed, or chastised for a mishap.*

Accidents should be handled in a matter-of-fact manner that does not call attention to the child and conveys acceptance of the accident as "no big deal."

Every school should have a supply of extra underwear, pants, and socks available in case of accidents. For a group of younger children, parents might be asked to bring several changes of clothing for possible mishaps. (Remember to ask parents to label them.) A Closer Look relates the case of a 4-year-old child whose sudden accidents baffled both her parents and her teachers.

BATHROOM FACILITIES

It is beneficial to children if toilets and sinks are child-sized and easy to reach. If only adult facilities are available, sturdy, wide steps should be placed in front of toilets and sinks to promote independence. Children should also be able to reach toilet paper, soap, and towels with ease. Having to overreach can cause accidents.

Bathrooms adjacent to the classroom are easiest to supervise, and children are less likely to have accidents when they can go on their own when they need to. Children should not be taken to the bathroom in large groups; such a procedure only promotes pushing, shoving, frustration, and even toilet accidents.

Some centres and most elementary schools have separate washrooms for girls and boys. However, open toileting has been a tradition in most early childhood programs, not just for convenience, but because it allows children to learn about anatomical and toileting differences in a matter-of-fact way. One parent cooperative preschool, located in an elementary school, used the girl's washroom at a time prearranged with the school for two reasons: (1) it was more convenient for supervision, and (2) the 2- and 3-year-olds did not receive mixed messages about their anatomy.

TOOTHBRUSHING

Especially in child care centres, toothbrushing supplies are often located in the bathroom. Wet toothbrushes should not be stored in a closed cabinet, but in an out-of-the-way place where they can air out after each use. Each child should have an individual, clearly marked brush; disposable paper cups can be used for rinsing. Once they are around age 2, the children can dispense the toothpaste, preferably from a pump, with supervision. It is important for establishing good hygiene habits that children be allowed to brush their teeth after meals. As toothbrushing often occurs after toileting, it is important to ensure that the children are supervised to ensure handwashing before toothbruhing.

SLEEP AND REST TIMES

Infants and young toddlers spend a considerable period of time napping. But older children need rest too. When children spend all day at a child care centre, a rest or nap time should be an important part of the day. Not all children need a nap, especially as they get older, but for children who are on the go all day, a time to slow down is important. According to Dr. Richard Ferber (1985), director of the Center for Pediatric Sleep Disorders in Boston, most but not all children sleep eleven to twelve hours at night by age 2, with a one- to two-hour nap after lunch. Most children continue to take naps until at least age 3, though some children still nap until they are 5 and others stop at age 2.

A CLOSER LOOK

Shirley's "Accidents"

When Shirley was 4, her parents, Dan and Alene, decided to get divorced. For the first time in her life, Shirley's father did not live at home with her. About a month after Dan moved out, he was involved in an accident at work. Alene got a phone call early one Saturday morning that Dan was in the emergency room of the local hospital. She and Shirley went immediately to the hospital.

Since they had left home in a hurry, Shirley and Alene had not had breakfast. After two hours of waiting with Dan for X-ray results, Alene decided to find her way to the hospital cafeteria. The emergency room receptionist told them how to get there by going through the hospital building. On the way, they passed a number of rooms in which patients were visible. In one particular ward, one patient could be seen with one arm and one leg raised in traction. Shirley slowed her steps and stared. "Why is he like that?" she asked her mother. "I guess he was in an automobile accident," Alene replied. A couple of hours later, Shirley and Alene were able to take Dan, now with a cast on his broken arm, back to his apartment.

About a week later, Shirley had her first toileting accident at school. "I forgot to go potty," she told one of her teachers. The teacher took her to the bathroom, found some extra pants and underwear for her, and helped her change. Two days later, Shirley had another accident; thereafter the rate increased so that within a week, she was having two to four accidents a day. The teachers talked with Alene, who indicated that Shirley was waking up wet at night and had begun to have bowel accidents as well. A parent–teacher conference was quickly scheduled to explore possible causes and solutions. At this meeting, Alene and the teachers agreed that Shirley was undoubtedly reacting to the stress of the divorce.

Their agreed-on strategy was to be matter-of-fact about the accidents while the teachers, Alene, and Dan would all try to be reassuring and understanding with Shirley. About a week later, the toileting accidents decreased and then disappeared.

Not long after, Shirley was gone from school for a week while she and her mother visited relatives. When they returned, Alene met with one of Shirley's teachers to relay some news. While they were out of town, Shirley had asked her mother one day, "Mommy, are you going to have an audiovisual accident, too?" Taken aback, Alene asked Shirley what she meant. The story, when it emerged, was that Shirley had been worried that her mother, who worked in the university's audiovisual department, would have an "audiovisual accident" like the man who was "tied up at the hospital" and then not be able to live at home. Daddy had an accident and now was not at home; the man at the hospital had an audiovisual accident and could not live at home because he had to be tied up; Mommy worked in audiovisual so she might have an accident too and have to stay at the hospital; then who would take care of Shirley?

"Is that what you've been worried about, Shirley?" asked Alene. Alene explained to Shirley what an "automobile accident" is and they talked about the fact that she would not leave Shirley.

As Alene told the teachers, "It sure is easy to jump to conclusions. We all decided that Shirley was upset about the divorce. Yet, in her complicated mind, she had put together a story that none of us could have guessed at!"

CHILDREN WHO DON'T NEED TO SLEEP

A variety of arrangements can be made for those children who do not take a nap in the middle of the day. In some programs, children are asked to lie on a cot quietly for a period of relaxation; if this is not handled punitively, children can enjoy a short period of rest and quiet. In other centres, children who do not sleep are allowed to engage in a quiet activity, such as book browsing, while they are on their cots. Non-sleepers are usually placed apart from those who are expected to fall asleep, so they are not disturbed. Some children, when they lie down in a relaxed atmosphere, will eventually fall asleep. Those who don't can get up after about a half-hour and move into an activity apart from the sleepers. Another alternative is to have a quiet time, in which non-nappers, rather than lie down, participate in a period of individual, restful activity, for instance, book browsing or playing quietly with manipulatives.

NAP GUIDELINES

Sleep, which is a natural part of the body's daily rhythm, requires that the body and mind be relaxed and at ease. If children are anxious or wound up, they will have a difficult time falling asleep. Thus, the way you prepare for nap time and set up the environment will either facilitate or hinder sleep.

Children should not be expected to move directly from a high-energy activity, such as outdoor play, into nap; rather, a transition is needed to let children slow down gradually. A predictable pre-nap routine that is followed every day is as important as the nap itself (Ferber, 1985). One teacher takes children for outside play after lunch, and then inside for a "wind-down activity" such as a story or relaxation exercises. She has found that this routine simplifies nap time. Others suggest that a leisurely ten-minute period be set aside for children to go to the bathroom, get a drink of water, take off shoes and tight clothing, get a favourite stuffed animal and blanket, and settle down on cots. The lights are dimmed, and drapes or shades are drawn. Cots are spaced far enough apart, and friends who enjoy talking are separated, to facilitate sleeping. Once all the children are settled down, a teacher may read a story or play a story record, sing softly, or lead the children in relaxation exercises. Bob Munsch, the renowned and much-loved Canadian children's author, got his start telling stories to the children in the sleep room at the University of Guelph's child care centre.

After these preliminaries, the teachers move from child to child, gently rubbing backs, whispering a soothing word, or stroking children's hair. Children who need a midday nap will fall asleep in an conducive atmosphere in which lighting is dim, the temperature is comfortable, the room is relatively quiet, and the teachers convey a gentle, soft mood. Because sleeping children would need extra help to move out of the building in case of an emergency, it is especially important that teachers be aware of exits and alternative escape routes.

Children should not sleep for too long; an hour or two suffices for most preschool children, although younger children and infants of course need more. Some children need time to wake up gradually, so an unstructured transition in which children can join the class at their own pace is helpful. An afternoon snack, to which children can move as they are ready, often helps provide that transition.

PROBLEM SLEEPERS

Occasionally you will encounter children who consistently resist sleep, even though they need the rest. A few children have genuine sleep problems, stemming from such conditions as chronic middle ear infection, the use of certain medications, and some cases of brain damage. For other children, falling asleep represents a letting go, where anxieties and fears can surface, and their sleep reluctance comes from a need to avoid such scary thoughts. Most children's difficulty in falling asleep, however, results from poorly established sleep habits and routines (Ferber, 1985).

Three-year-old Becky had a very hard time going to sleep, both at home and at school, and engaged in a variety of disruptive stalling techniques to avoid nap time. Often, by late afternoon she was grumpy and tired, and she invariably fell asleep in the car on the way home or "crashed" in the classroom around 4:00 p.m. Her teachers eventually decided that it was not worth trying to make Becky nap with the other children because she prevented everyone from sleeping when she was in the nap room. Instead, once the other children had fallen asleep, one teacher would sit with Becky in the rocking chair and quietly read her a story. This seemed to work about three days out of the week, when Becky would fall asleep on the teacher's lap and then be put down on her cot.

FACTORS THAT AFFECT GROUP BEHAVIOUR

Each of the previously discussed routine elements of the child's day is important and needs careful consideration as you decide how best to guide the group of children in your care. We will now turn to another aspect of guidance, those times of the day when all the children participate together in a common activity. Although it is important to consider each child as an individual within that group, some factors can facilitate group guidance.

THE PHYSICAL ENVIRONMENT

For one thing, it is important to examine the physical environment in relation to group behaviour. Are several children running in the classroom, for instance, although the rule is "walk inside, run outside"? Perhaps too much open space invites children to run. Critically examine room arrangement in relation to group behaviours. (See Chapter 9 for more detail on this topic.)

DEVELOPMENTALLY APPROPRIATE EXPECTATIONS

Another important factor in setting expectations for the group is the developmental level of the children. Carefully examine activities, the daily schedule, and materials to be sure they are appropriate to the ages of the children. Frequently refer to NAEYC's *Developmentally Appropriate Practice in Early Childhood Programs Serving Children from Birth through Age 8* as a guide (Bredekamp, 1987). If your expectations are either too simple or too complex for the children's abilities, behavioural problems are likely to ensure.

Also keep in mind that although developmental guidelines help you identify appropriate expectations for the age of the children, each child is an individual and will conform to some but not to other developmental milestones. You may also have children in your class who have special needs and in some ways do not fit the profile for their age group. Be sensitive to their unique needs and characteristics, make alternate arrangements when necessary, but help them fit into the group as smoothly as possible.

CONVEYING EXPECTATIONS

Young children are exuberant and active, so you may find times when their voices or activity levels get too high. Shouting instructions to "quiet down!" or "settle down!" will only add to the confusion, but whispering softly helps. Move from small group to small group and speak in a soft, slow voice. Children will quiet their pitch so they can hear you. You will find the noise level quickly reduced by your modelling.

You might want to let the children know that it will be "shout time when we go outside." Similarly, an elevated activity level, if it seems unproductive, also can be reduced by a quiet voice, dimmed lights, or soft music that induces relaxation rather than agitation.

As individual children quiet or settle down, let them know with a smile or nod that you appreciate it. Teachers will frequently praise the behaviour of one compliant child publicly in the hopes that others will behave similarly because they also want to be acknowledged. Hitz and Driscoll (1988), however, report that praise given in this manner can lead to resentment and anger. "Teachers of preschool-age children ... may get away with blatant manipulation and fool themselves into thinking that it works. But eventually most children come to resent this type of control" (p. 10).

RULES

Another way of encouraging good behaviour from the group is by letting the children know just what is expected. You probably need only one rule: *you may not hurt yourself, others, or the things around you.* Children should know what the limits are and why they are set.

GROUP GUIDANCE AND THE DAILY PROGRAM

In Chapter 8 we discussed some guidelines for program planning. The actual sequence and timing of activities, as well as their length, will have a bearing on group guidance. *There must be a logical rhythm and flow to the sequence of daily activities that relates to the developmental level of the children.* If children are expected to sit quietly for several activities in a row, they will tend to find unacceptable ways to release some of the energy that is pent up during this overly long period; if too many boisterous activities are scheduled one after another, the children may tire or get too keyed up. Boredom sets in when activities last too long and frustration is evident when activities are not long enough. Let's look at some specific aspects of the program in relation to group guidance techniques. At certain times, careful forethought and planning can make the difference between a chaotic and a well-ordered classroom.

ARRIVAL AND DEPARTURE TIMES

Morning arrival can be a difficult time because much is going on. Children, parents, and staff are starting a new day for which information needs to be shared. If parents bring the children to school individually (rather than children arriving in a group by bus), one teacher needs to be available near the door to exchange greetings and a few words with arriving children and parents.

If you have only one teacher present at arrival time, as is the case with some smaller programs, it would be helpful to have a few, simple, self-directed activities available for the children who arrive early. Puzzles and other manipulative materials serve well for this purpose. With only one teacher present, you may also have to make some areas "off limits."

If you have more than one teacher present at arrival time, the second teacher, in a program for children over 3, could ask each child to think about what they would like to do, with whom, and how they will do it. This strategy also works with 2-year-olds, if you help them with the choices.

Of course, with infants and toddlers, independent choices and activities as described for older children are entirely inappropriate. Consequently, you must have adequate staffing to handle greetings and care simultaneously.

Departure at the end of the day should be handled similarly. If all parents come for their children at about the same time or if the children go home by bus, a group activity works well. If children are picked up over a period of time, some selected activities that are easy to clean up and disengage from should be made available. Manipulative materials, book browsing, table games, or outdoor play are examples of appropriate activities. When a parent arrives, the child can finish and put away the activity while a teacher chats for a few moments with the parent. The transition from school to home, as well as from home to school, will be much smoother if you plan carefully.

ACTIVITY TIME

A good part of the day will be scheduled for activities that children select from several planned by the teachers or from the classroom learning centres. Children have the opportunity to engage in a decision-making process at these times (Hohmann, Banet, & Weikart, 1979). Some group guidance principles can help keep activity time blocks running smoothly.

One of the main guidance problems during activity time can arise from the grouping and distribution of children among activities. What if ten children want to participate in the water play activity, eight more are in the housekeeping area, and only one chooses to do the art project you planned so carefully? Chances are problems will develop at the water table and in dramatic play. How can you avoid such a situation?

Several methods can help you control the number of children who go to a given classroom area. Some of these methods strictly control the number of children; others have the added bonus of accentuating the decision-making process for youngsters. The former methods are more appropriate for younger preschoolers, whereas the others should be used with children over the age of 3 1/2.

One way to establish limits is to post happy faces in a conspicuous place at the entrance to each learning centre. The number of happy faces corresponds with the number of children who can be in a given area at one time. The number of children can also be limited by the availability of materials and equipment in an area. Thus, five chairs around the art table indicates how many artists can work at one time; four hard hats set the limits in the block area; and so forth. With older children, you may want to involve them consciously in decision making through some type of planning board (Baker, 1982). You might adopt medallions, individual symbols, or work cards. Medallions are simple necklaces (for instance, a string with a symbol) that children put on if they want to play in a given area. The symbol can be colour-coded (for instance, red for science) or have a pictorial representation of that area on it (for instance, a book for the library). The number of medallions kept on a board by each area limits the number of children in that area. Individual symbols are similar in function, but rather than being coded for an activity, they are coded individually for each child.

Work cards are somewhat more complex than medallions or individual symbols. Children select cards according to where they wish to work. Work cards are usually pictorial representations (photo or drawing) of the learning centres. These work best with 4- to 8-year-olds.

If you try using medallions, individual symbols, or work cards and you find yourself spending practically all your time reminding children how the system works and none of your time in the actual learning activities, it is time to re-evaluate. Perhaps the children are not ready for such a system. You may want to put your system away for a month and then try again. Or you might need to start gradually and use the system for a small part of each day until the children catch on to what is expected. Or perhaps you need to provide more concrete instructions, a flannel-board story, or rehearsals to clear up any confusion about how the system should work.

MEALS

Breakfast, lunch, dinner, or snack can pose group guidance problems if these times are not carefully planned. What happens before, during, and after a meal will directly affect group control, not to mention digestion.

Before the children sit down to eat, tables should be set and the food ready. Children should be involved in this process. It provides an excellent opportunity for young children to be engaged in a practical activity that builds self-concept, self-confidence, social competence, eye–hand coordination, and cognitive skills. Special helpers can assist in setting the table; putting out a plate, napkin, and silverware for each child; pouring juice or milk; and passing food.

Once the children have washed their hands and are ready to sit down, waiting should be kept to a minimum. Children, especially toddlers and young preschoolers, should not have to wait for everyone to be seated. And infants should never wait. With older preschoolers, in whom patience is beginning to develop, it is possible for them to wait one or two minutes until all the children at their table are seated. If, for some reason, the children are at the table and have to wait for more than a minute, initiate a song or finger play to keep the youngsters occupied until they can eat. Waiting for any prolonged period, especially quietly with hands folded in their laps, only frustrates children.

Children should not have to wait until everyone is finished eating. They should be able to engage in a self-directed, quiet activity such as book browsing or move individually to the next activity. The staff should be distributed according to where the children are. As more children finish eating, clear their plates (if they are old enough), and move to another area, so should more of the staff move. One staff member should stay with the eaters until all are finished and then clear away all food and utensils (unless there is a separate kitchen staff that does this).

GROUP TIMES

One of the most rewarding as well as most difficult parts of the preschool day occurs when children participate in teacher-initiated group activities. Good guidance is particularly important at group times because the success of such activities may well depend on your ability to keep the group attentive. This is no simple task because you are trying to move children gradually from their egocentric focus toward some specific social behaviours, ones that will be particularly important when they start elementary school. The control you maintain over the group will to a great extent depend on the environment and activities you provide for group times.

The physical environment within which group activities are conducted has to be carefully thought out. It should be relatively free from distractions so the children focus on the activity. If, for instance, a shelf of attractive materials competes for the children's attention, a simple covering of butcher paper or fabric can be used during group activities. Also, if children cannot see you or are crowded, they will respond with frustration or lose interest in the activity. Therefore, arrange the group seating with thought. A carpeted area and a circle or semicircle work best; children should be physically comfortable. If there is something to look at such as a book or flannel board, make sure all children can see it.

Sometimes, the children gradually creep closer and closer until you have a knot of little people sitting in no designated order. This may happen particularly with a group of younger preschoolers. Some things can be done to help children stay on the edge of the group area. You might simply outline the area, or you may use carpet samples for each child to sit on.

The timing of group activities is also important. Remember the discussion in Chapter 8 about the length of group times. Be aware of the developmental abilities of your group to sit quietly and pay attention. Begin the year with relatively short group times and lengthen these as the children are able to sit for increasingly longer times. You may plan several short group times at the beginning of the year and fewer longer ones later in the year.

A stimulating, longer group activity is sometimes fine, but as a rule don't expect children to sit quietly and attend for extended periods. It may also happen that although the group as a whole can pay attention for a certain period of time, one child lacks the maturity of the rest. In such a case, provide that child with a quiet alternative away from the group, rather than punishment, as the child is not developmentally ready.

You should plan a clear beginning, a middle part that presents your activity or is action-oriented, and a gradual ending for the circle, but children should be free to leave when they are ready. This means you may not have the entire group with you for some circles. Remember to have visual aids or real objects to keep the children's interest.

It is also important to be prepared for whatever you plan to cover during group time. If you try to "wing it," you may well lose the all-important sense of pacing. Several group guidance techniques help keep the children's attention while you are reading or telling a story.

If you see a child's attention wavering, you might try saying, "And do you know what happened next, Amy?" to gently bring Amy back to the group. To involve children in the story process, plan enough time to stop every so often to ask the children questions or to have them find something in a picture. Another way to heighten interest in a story is to periodically substitute the names of some of the children in the group for those of the characters in the story.

When you are using finger plays and songs during group activity, keep in mind that some of these excite and others quiet children. Have a repertoire of songs and finger plays on hand to use as a stimulant or a relaxant, as needed. Children should learn an increasingly larger number of songs and finger plays as the year goes on. Remember, young children enjoy and need repetition, so when you introduce a new song, give the children enough time to learn it thoroughly, then continue to use it periodically thereafter.

Songs and finger plays serve an excellent group guidance function at the beginning and end of group time. Don't wait for everyone to be seated before you start. You can also end your group with a familiar song or finger play.

One more group activity, a favourite of many teachers, is **Show-and-Tell** or "sharing time," which is often used to allow children to share something special and personal with their classmates. Such an activity can be tiresome and difficult, or it can provide a rich learning experience for all of the children (Oken-Wright, 1988).

Show-and-Tell gives children a chance to be in the limelight as well as to practise talking before a group. But Show-and-Tell has to be planned and carried out carefully. As with other preschool activities, you should keep in mind the attention span of the group. Show-and-Tell has to be handled skilfully by the teacher so that children who do not have many possessions are as valued as those that do. One alternative to Show-and-Tell, especially for young preschoolers and children from disadvantaged homes, is to select for each day, a "special child" who shares something from home. Remember to find a safe storage area for the children's personal treasures. And be sure to express strong interest in the child's treasured item.

TRANSITIONS

A very important though often neglected part of the day's schedule is not the daily activities, but rather what happens in the gaps or transitions between them (Alger, 1984). *Transitions have to be thought of as part of the routine, a part that provides many opportunities for children to learn.* Learning certainly takes place as children have to cooperate and be considerate of each other during toileting before lunch;

classify, seriate, match, and organize during clean-up; or bend, lift, stretch, and pull in putting outdoor toys into storage before coming back inside.

A beautifully planned day can fall apart if no thought is given to transitions between activities. Children should always be aware of upcoming transitions. You might use a song, chant, or flick of the lights as a transitional signal. Even before you announce the end of an activity, however, and the transition to the next, give children a warning so they can finish activities. For older preschoolers, a longer warning will be needed. As a rough guide, allow one minute of warning for each year of age (two minutes for 2-year-olds, three minutes for 3). "In a few minutes, it will be time to put your blocks away so we can get ready for snack." This is the first warning, to be followed within a few minutes by the cue that signals a transition time.

Try to involve children in cleanup; they are usually willing helpers. Clean-up will, of course, be facilitated by an orderly, well-thought-out environment (see also Chapter 9), where every item has a logical place. Sometimes you may have to devise games to encourage assistance with cleanup, especially for reluctant helpers, until they accept it as part of the routine. Suggestions to "drive your truck into the garage" or "swim like a fish to the sink and get the sponge to wash this table" can help encourage clean-up participation.

Sometimes a transition needs to be used to limit the flow of children to the next activity. For instance, you may have snack following group activity, with hand washing between the two. Sending twenty children at one time to a bathroom with two sinks is asking for problems. A familiar song or finger play is a good device for controlling the flow of children. For example, sing "Five Little Monkeys" using five children as participants at one time, and send each "monkey" to the bathroom as it "falls off the bed."

The position of teachers, as in the previous example of moving children from group to bathroom to snack, is another important factor in smooth transitions. Plan them carefully.

Children spend a considerable part of their day involved in transitions. In an analysis of time spent in various activity categories in five different early childhood settings, Berk (1976) found that children spent from 20 to 35 percent of their total time in transitions. Because the teachers involved in this study ranked transitions low in relation to other activities, Berk suggests that teachers need to consider transitions a legitimate part of the curriculum.

THE UNUSUAL SITUATION

A regular program and routine are essential to help young children work comfortably in their environment; they need the security and regularity. But sometimes the unusual or unexpected comes along. It is important that children be able to handle deviations from the usual since life is full of the unexpected. Unusual situations can be grouped into two categories—the planned and the unplanned. How should you handle them?

PLANNED UNUSUAL SITUATIONS

These include such changes from the regular routine as special events, special circumstances that you know about ahead of time, and field trips. Children can be prepared for expected changes, although it is advisable not to prepare them too far in advance to avoid undue anxiety or disappointment if they become ill. Also keep in mind that children's time sense is not the same as adults'; a week can seem like an eternity! When you prepare children, tell them exactly what will happen during the special event. If Santa Claus is coming tomorrow, tell the children that they will sing some songs for Santa and then they will each have a chance to sit on Santa's lap if they would like. A calendar that refers to the special coming event can help older preschoolers "see" the time span in a concrete way.

If you can anticipate a special circumstance that will involve a change—for instance, if you will be away from school for a few days next week and a substitute teacher will be taking your place—prepare the children. Discuss your upcoming absence and reassure the group that you will still be their teacher, even if you are gone for a few days. If possible, have the substitute teacher visit your class so the children have a concrete idea of who Mrs. Clarito is.

Field Trips

This is probably the most common example of a planned unusual event, and some of the principles we just discussed also apply here. Children should be well prepared ahead of time so they know what to expect. Permission slips should be obtained; informing the parents about the trip encourages discussion at home. Review with the children the schedule for the field trip, the return time ("we'll get back just before lunch"), the transportation arrangements, and the transportation rules. Review safety rules with the children, if necessary using role play or a flannel-board story to cover key points that the children need to know before leaving. Before leaving, also put a name tag on each child's outer garment with the child's name and the school's name and phone number.

If you are going by car, assign children and adults to a specific car in which they must go and return. This prevents a child being left behind accidentally because everyone assumes she is in the other car. Be familiar with the child safety restraint laws of your province and follow these carefully on car trips. Before and frequently during the trip, count heads. It is also advisable to get extra adult supervision for field trips (parents are often willing to go along and help) because any environment outside the school will be less familiar and less controlled, and therefore less safe. Also be certain that all staff—and all volunteers—are familiar with the policies you follow on trips.

Walks

Similar to field trips but with some different guidelines are walks. When you take the group on a walk, you again need to inform the children of expectations. A buddy system works well with older children. Children are paired off, and each partner assumes responsibility for the other by holding hands. An adult at the beginning and end of the line is essential on a walk, and any additional adults can walk in between. An alternate arrangement is to have each adult in charge of a small group of children, but enough adults must be available for this to work. With younger children, you may want to use a rope and have the children hold onto it at intervals; knots tied in a smooth, long rope can indicate handholds. With the very young toddlers, a rope with individual harnesses is necessary.

UNPLANNED UNUSUAL EVENTS

There are times when the totally unexpected occurs. A fire drill or a real fire, a serious accident involving a child, or any other emergency can throw the class into an agitated state or even panic. Although you cannot foretell unplanned unusual events, you can prepare the children for these situations with some discussion and practice. As with planned unusual happenings, you can role play, present a flannel-board story, use puppets, or otherwise pose hypothetical problem situations so children know what may happen and what they are to do.

Emergency procedures should be thought through so that teachers as well as children know what to do. A written policy for handling emergencies should be visibly posted. Such a policy statement can be written in another language if some of the parents or staff are not native English speakers. One example of a carefully planned emergency procedure is fire drills, which are legislated in much of Canada. It can also be helpful to have by the exit an "emergency pack" that includes a class list, phone numbers, a flashlight, and a couple of favourite books in case there is a wait.

Another type of emergency situation that is helped by forethought occurs if a child is seriously injured. One teacher should stay with the child while another moves the rest of the group away. Discuss ahead of time who will be responsible for which tasks. When an emergency is settled, discuss it with the children so they can express their concerns and feelings and be reassured.

The unexpected does not always have to be a dire emergency. Less serious occurrences such as broken glass, spilled paint, or a minor injury can still be disconcerting to children. If children realize that the teacher's attention must be focused temporarily on the calamity, they can take responsibility for being self-directed if they have been prepared to do so.

The teacher should set the stage by verbalizing what is happening: "Usually we get ready for snack at this time. But because this window was broken, we will have to take care of the broken glass first. So instead of snack right now, we get to do something else. Jenny, get the 'Goldilocks' flannel-board pieces and all of you help Jenny tell the story." When adults are organized—even in unexpected situations—know what to do, and do not panic, children will respond in a similarly calm manner, particularly if they have been prepared for unexpected events.

PARENTS AND PROFESSIONALS

Parental Concerns about Routines

As with all areas of the early childhood program, the school's philosophy about meals, toileting, nap or rest, and group guidance should be shared with parents. An exchange of information between teachers and parents helps provide a consistent set of expectations for children.

To help children achieve a balanced diet, parents and teachers need to cooperate. One way to further this goal is for the school to post a detailed menu of all meals and snacks served. The school may also compile and distribute a "cookbook" of healthy alternatives for snacks and lunches.

Some families have particular restrictions or preferences in their dietary habits, and these need to be honoured. Moslem and some Jewish families do not eat pork, for instance, so children from these religious backgrounds should not be served luncheon meats or hot dogs made of pork. Some families are vegetarian because of religious, ethical, or health reasons; the school will need to make special provisions to furnish appropriate meals for vegetarian children or make arrangements with the family to provide alternative foods.

Parents may convey concerns about their children's eating patterns, and the teacher's advice and informed responses can be very reassuring. One frequent parental concern involves lunch box meals, particularly if food items remain uneaten. Teachers can share the school's philosophy about meals, suggest alternative menu items, and discuss appropriate serving sizes for preschoolers, depending on the circumstances.

Toileting, especially if children take home plastic bags with wet or soiled clothing, can be a cause of concern for parents. If toilet mishaps seem to be happening too frequently in relation to the child's age, explore potential causes with the parents. Check with parents about possible stressful events in the child's life and assure them that toilet accidents are not uncommon among young children. Share the school's non-punitive attitude toward accidents. Your matter-of-fact perspective can be reassuring.

Parents may also express concerns about naps, particularly as they affect evening bedtime. Some children, if they sleep too long during the day, are not ready for sleep at night until quite late. This puts a burden on parents who want their children in bed at a reasonable time. It may take some coordination to meet the needs of the child, the family, and the school, but effective parent–teacher communication is the important ingredient in reaching such a goal. Parents may also seek your advice in dealing with their children's nighttime sleep problems. Your advice or recommendations for further readings can help parents establish a consistent and pleasant bedtime routine and recognize factors that can disrupt sleep patterns.

KEY POINTS OF CHAPTER 15

ARRIVAL AT SCHOOL

▲ 1. Some young children experience separation anxiety on leaving their parents.

▲ 2. A well-thought-out procedure for arrival, particularly when children don't all arrive at the same time, will help get the day off to a good start.

▲ 3. A morning health check conveys an interest in the child's health, sends a subtle though strong message that ill children do not belong at school, and gives the teacher a few moments to greet each child and parent individually.

▲ 4. A number of strategies can help the new child adjust to the early childhood program.

MEALS AND EATING BEHAVIOUR

▲ 5. It is challenging but important to provide nutritious, healthy foods for meals and snacks eaten at school because these must be considered part of the child's daily intake of nutrients.

▲ 6. Some specific mealtime guidelines can help encourage children, including finicky eaters or those who are overweight, to form good eating habits.

TOILETING

▲ 7. Occasional toileting accidents should be expected in a group of young children and should never be considered a cause for punishment or shame.

▲ 8. Child-sized toilets and sinks can help decrease falls and facilitate independence.

▲ 9. Bathrooms should be adjacent to the class and easy to supervise if possible.

SLEEP AND REST TIMES

▲10. A nap or rest time is important for children who spend all day in a child care centre.

▲11. A consistent pre-nap routine and a relaxing atmosphere will facilitate sleep.

FACTORS THAT AFFECT GROUP BEHAVIOUR

▲12. Group guidance can be facilitated by such factors as a well-set-up environment, schedule, activities, materials, and expectations that are appropriate for the developmental level of the children. When expectations are inappropriate, frustration or boredom are likely to result.

▲13. Children are most apt to follow rules if there are few of them and if they understand the reasons for these rules.

KEY TERMS

attachment

separation anxiety

Show-and-Tell

GROUP GUIDANCE AND THE DAILY PROGRAM

▲14. When children arrive and leave over a staggered period of time, it is a good idea to provide a selection of activities that are self-directed, easy to clean up, and easy to disengage from.

▲15. Problems may arise during activity time if too many children flock to one activity; several methods can be used to control the number of children who engage in a particular activity at one time.

▲16. Pleasant mealtimes result when children help set up, when they are not required to wait, when there is relaxing conversation, and when they know what clean-up is expected after they finish eating.

▲17. Effective group activities require careful planning and preparation, as well as forethought concerning seating arrangement.

TRANSITIONS

▲18. Children best respond to upcoming transitions, such as clean-up time, if they know what to expect; therefore, a warning a few minutes before the change will help them be prepared for it.

▲19. Teachers need to think through how children will move through activities and where the adults should be stationed to provide appropriate assistance where it is needed.

THE UNUSUAL SITUATION

▲20. Careful planning and forethought are important to ensure safety and enjoyment on field trips and walks.

▲21. Children cannot be prepared for all unexpected or emergency situations, whether these be fire drills, a broken window, or an injury; but some specific teacher strategies can help them respond calmly.

KEY QUESTIONS

1. Observe children arriving at school with their parents. What differences do you note in the ways in which they leave their parents?

2. A 3-year-old in your class consistently refuses to go to sleep during nap, but then almost always falls asleep later in the afternoon. What strategies might you use in such a situation?

3. Ask three teachers what rules they set for young children in their classes. Are there similarlities among the rules listed by the different teachers? Are there differences? Which rules seem reasonable and understandable to preschoolers? Do any of the rules seem inappropriate?

4. Observe a preschool class during transitions between activities. What strategies does the teacher use? Do these strategies reflect a sense of preparedness and forethought? Did the transitions go smoothly or were there some problems? How could these transitions be improved?

5. You are going to take a group of children on the first field trip of the year. How will you and the other staff members prepare for this trip? How will you prepare the children?

16

GUIDING
BEHAVIOUR

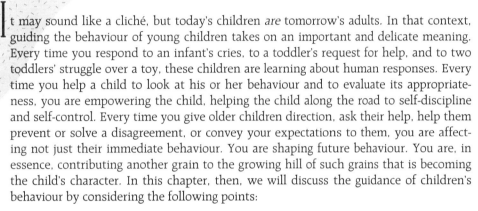

It may sound like a cliché, but today's children *are* tomorrow's adults. In that context, guiding the behaviour of young children takes on an important and delicate meaning. Every time you respond to an infant's cries, to a toddler's request for help, and to two toddlers' struggle over a toy, these children are learning about human responses. Every time you help a child to look at his or her behaviour and to evaluate its appropriateness, you are empowering the child, helping the child along the road to self-discipline and self-control. Every time you give older children direction, ask their help, help them prevent or solve a disagreement, or convey your expectations to them, you are affecting not just their immediate behaviour. You are shaping future behaviour. You are, in essence, contributing another grain to the growing hill of such grains that is becoming the child's character. In this chapter, then, we will discuss the guidance of children's behaviour by considering the following points:

1. We will first look at certain terms related to guidance and discipline.

2. We will then examine the kinds of behaviours we expect of children, and how to select a personal guidance approach.

3. We will discuss where to draw the line between behaviours that fall within the normal range and behaviours for which professional help should be sought.

4. Next, we will consider some factors that in both subtle and direct ways affect the way children behave, and that may lead to problem behaviours.

5. We will then consider a variety of guidance techniques and when these are used most effectively.

6. We will end the chapter with an in-depth look at two specific behavioural concerns: aggression and shyness.

IMPORTANT DEFINITIONS

We will be using the word guidance throughout this chapter. Before continuing, let's briefly examine this word and differentiate it from some other related ones. Webster's dictionary defines **guidance** as "the act of directing ... to a particular end." This implies, as we discussed earlier, that guidance is an ongoing process and that techniques must

be appropriate for the kind of people you want children to grow up to be. Guidance is also related to **discipline**, which, for too many adults, connotes a reaction to a misbehaviour by the child who did not follow the rules (Morrison, 1988). The word discipline, however, comes from the Latin word meaning learning or teaching, and, in early childhood education, we need to focus on this positive aspect of discipline. **Positive discipline**, or guidance, helps children achieve self-discipline (Gordon & Browne, 1993); it is an empowering force, not a negative one.

Undoubtedly, you will meet parents who equate **punishment** with discipline. But punishment has a whole series of difficulties associated with it. For example, it emphasizes what the child should not do, without giving any indication of what the desired behaviour is; it is a one-time rather than an ongoing occurrence; it focuses on obedience rather than on development of self-control; it undermines self-esteem; and it makes a decision for the child rather than allowing the child to think through a solution (Gordon & Browne, 1993). In addition, physical punishment may, in fact, increase undesirable behaviours such as aggression (Maccoby & Martin, 1983; Patterson, 1982) because it models the very behaviour it is intended to discourage. Early childhood experts discourage punishment because of its *long-term ineffectiveness* in changing behaviour. Children will also learn to dislike and avoid those who punish them (Sheppard, 1973). Positive discipline has none of these difficulties, and it preserves the child's self-esteem.

WHAT BEHAVIOURS DO WE EXPECT OF YOUNG CHILDREN?

Parents and early childhood educators in general hope to help develop children who are friendly, sociable, responsible, helpful, cooperative, and considerate, and who acquire a conscience (Moore, 1982). Such a range of behaviours, however, does not emerge without thoughtful and consistent guidance from parents and teachers.

Among the qualities of children that parents and teachers often value is an ability to care about others, to share willingly, to be altruistic and empathetic, and to be understanding of the needs of others. Such prosocial behaviours are most likely to appear in children who live in a nurturing environment, where understanding and caring are modelled, where responsibility is expected, and where **inductive reasoning** is used (Mussen & Eisenberg-Berg, 1977). Induction involves an approach in which adults help children see, through logic and reasoning, the consequences of their behaviour for other people.

One aspect of prosocial qualities in children appears to be development of self-control. This, in turn, leads to self-regulation, in which the child's judgment about the situation dictates the response (Kopp, 1982). Internal rather than external control is critical, for it means that the child does what is right, not because she or he might be rewarded (or punished), but because she or he knows this action is the morally responsible thing to do. Development of inner control, a long process tied to the gradual evolution of ego strength and moral judgment, is fostered through many opportunities for the child to make decisions and to experience the consequences of those decisions (Kamii, 1984). Of course, one would not expect to see any signs of inner control in the very young. Nevertheless, it is during those earliest years that the foundations for self-regulation are constructed.

A climate in which such opportunities are offered is *child-centred and nurturing, respectful of the child's growing autonomy*. Adults in the child's world are careful to use inductive reasoning, focusing on explanations that stress the rights and feelings of others rather than on punitive admonitions or restrictions (Honig, 1985b; Maccoby & Martin, 1983). Thus, the child is told, "It really makes Ingrid feel unhappy and hurt when you tell her nobody likes her," rather than "Don't you say that, you selfish brat!"

In an article titled, "Obedience Is Not Enough," Constance Kamii (1984) differentiates between **morality of autonomy**—based on an inner sense of integrity—and **morality of obedience**—based on doing what one is told to do. To achieve morality of autonomy, children need, from an early age, many opportunities to develop a sense of personal values. The development of values comes from the opportunities to exchange viewpoints with others and opportunities to make decisions.

An interaction style between adult and child, in which *the child is given a reason for what the adult expects*, has also been shown to produce children who are socially competent; have positive interactions with peers; and are self-controlled, assertive, self-reliant, generally happy, and explorative (Baumrind, 1967). The adult engages in verbal give-and-take with the child, provides opportunities for decision making, and is consistent in setting and enforcing rules and expectations (Baumrind & Black, 1967).

Research supports the fact that the process of child rearing and child caregiving is tied to the characteristics that the child displays. A consistent, loving, firm, reasonable, inductive environment helps children become morally responsible, considerate of others, independent, and assertive. These findings give direction to early childhood settings, which are partners with parents in the process of child rearing.

SELECTING GUIDANCE TECHNIQUES

But where will you begin? What approach or approaches to guidance should you use? Some guidelines may help you select an approach to working with young children. First, try to think through your own values and expectations as they relate to the care of infants and young children. Do this in the context in which you were reared, because your own background will affect your views. If you were raised in a family that used firmness and fairness, you will most likely bring your own experiences to the task of guiding young children. If your family was authoritarian—you were expected to follow rules because someone bigger than you said these were the rules—then you will need to examine whether you carry this attitude into your work.

Self-understanding is very important in working with young children; if you acknowledge your strengths and identify areas you might want to change, you will emerge with a more solid foundation. As you examine your own values, keep in mind your aim in working with the children whose parents have entrusted them into your care. As was stated at the beginning of this chapter, guidance is a long-term process, contributing to the evolution of children into adults. If the aim is to develop caring, competent, self-directed adults, this process begins early in life. What matters is that the guidance principles applied are in line with the desired outcome.

Good early childhood educators generally follow an **eclectic approach** to guidance, and, in so doing, hope to empower the child with self-discipline and problem-solving skills. Developing a personal style of guidance takes time, and it may well change over the years of your professional involvement and development. What is important is that you are comfortable with the guidance approach you use because it is effective and supports children's development in a positive, nurturing manner.

WHAT IS THE DIFFERENCE BETWEEN NORMAL AND CHALLENGING BEHAVIOUR?

If you view guidance as an ongoing process that contributes to the socialization of the child, it is easier to consider a solution to a problem behaviour as a change that has a far-reaching impact, rather than as a stopgap measure to make your class run more smoothly. Although many children go through temporary periods in their early years that can be difficult for the adults around them, children pass through these without too many residual effects. The negative stage of many toddlers, for instance, often dissolves within a few months into a period of cooperation. But some behaviours persist and may become more problematic as children get older.

Problem behaviours are one of the greatest challenges facing teachers of young children. Remember that all children misbehave at some time; it is normal for them to test the limits. Some children, although they misbehave, can easily be rerouted by the adults around them. Other children have diagnosed deficits, and knowing the diagnosis gives you some direction about handling the problem behaviours. For instance, a child with diagnosed *hyperactivity*, known as **attention deficit-hyperactivity disorder (ADHD)**, has particular needs that can be readily identified—but not so readily met, as Don Shattuck, a psychologist with the Welland Separate School Board, notes in A Canadian Professional Speaks Out (p. 394). And then some children totally frustrate all their teachers' attempts to deal with them. Teachers can go through a series of up-and-down feelings about their own competence as they try to cope with such children in the classroom.

But which behaviours are normal, and which should send up a red flag? The following guidelines can help you make that distinction.

- Know the developmental stages of the children in your class, particularly as they relate to social, emotional, and moral development. Many children of a given age go through a phase that will most likely pass. For instance, the tendency of 4-year-olds to blur the line between truth and fantasy does not predict a life of dishonesty and pathological lying.

- Realistic expectations for the age group, tempered with a recognition of individual variations among children, are important. However, if a child appears extremely immature in relation to her or his peers—for instance, a 4-year-old who acts more like a 2-to 3-year-old in social behaviour—the child may be developmentally delayed, particularly if other areas of development also are delayed.

- Look for signs of possible medical causes for problem behaviours. As we will discuss later in this chapter, a chronic infection, allergy, nutritional deficiency, or sensory deficit can profoundly affect behaviour. If, in addition to disruptive social behaviour, the child frequently rubs the eyes, winces when urinating, or appears unduly clumsy, consider a possible link between the social behaviour and an underlying health problem.

- When the behaviour of a child in your class is out of hand so frequently that you feel there are too many negative experiences between you and the child, *it is probably time to bring in professional assistance to help you deal with the situation.* Consulting an outside professional is particularly appropriate if other teachers, who are generally very effective in dealing with children, share your experience and feel as baffled and frustrated by this child as you do. Griffin (1982) suggests that if a child is so frequently disruptive and not able to get

PARENTS AND PROFESSIONALS

Working With Parents to Solve Behaviour Problems

Parents often seek out teachers' advice or support when they deal with their children's misbehaviours. It is, however, important to keep in focus the concept of guidance as an ongoing, positive process and to convey this philosophy to parents. Let parents know that your approach to guiding children is primarily concerned with helping them develop inner control and self-direction rather than merely dealing with problems. Many adults think of working with children in terms of discipline; however, you can help parents see guidance more broadly by framing your philosophy in terms of laying a foundation for lifelong patterns of creative problem solving, positive interactions, and concern for the needs of others.

When parents approach you about a behaviour they find troubling—or you approach them—it is important that effective communication, based on mutual understanding, take place. It is critical to recognize that a child cannot be viewed in isolation, solely within the context of the hours spent at school. What happens during the other hours, the people with whom the child interacts, the quality of those interactions, and the overall quality of the lives of those other people all affect the child. Thus, to understand the child well, you must also get to know the other important people in the child's life; the most basic way to do this is through frequent, informal, positive contacts (Herrera & Wooden, 1988). Individual families have unique characteristics, including their way of guiding their children. Many factors, such as the way the parents themselves were raised, and their culture, will have an impact. Knowing the family and having a trusting relationship will be beneficial if a behaviour becomes a concern.

Morgan (1989) recommends that when parents bring up concerns about their child's behaviour it is helpful for you, as the teacher, to keep certain points in mind. For instance, never forget the depth of the emotional investment parents have in their children, and acknowledge underlying feelings, such as anger, defensiveness, or frustration. One underlying message may be a parent's need for reassurance that he or she is a good parent; whenever appropriate, provide sincere feedback. Also recognize that parents may have different values and beliefs about appropriate guidance, for instance, in relation to spanking. Acknowledge the parent's view in a non-judgmental manner, while stating your philosophy. If suitable, you may use such an opportunity to help the parent explore an alternative method of guidance. Finally, clarifying a parent's misconception about child development can be reassuring and can help parents see a child's behaviour in better perspective.

---

along in the early childhood program without continuous help, that child needs professional, one-to-one help that cannot be given in a group school setting.

- As teachers, we generally notice acting-out children because they force our attention to their behaviour. But also be alert to the extremely withdrawn child who stays away from social interactions, is reluctant to participate in activities, avoids eye contact, or refuses to talk. Many children are shy, but extreme withdrawal might signal a deeper problem.

A CANADIAN
PROFESSIONAL SPEAKS OUT

Attention Deficit-Hyperactivity Disorder (ADHD)

Attention deficit-hyperactivity disorder (ADHD) is the technical term for what you may know as *hyperactivity*. The hyperactive child—or the child with ADHD—is the one who seems always on the go, always moving or talking, and bouncing from one activity to another. These children are often doing things they should not, seemingly oblivious to rules or the possibility of danger. They butt into others' activities, do not seem to listen to instructions, and are constantly getting into trouble for something they have said or done.

Obviously, these children show a wide range of problematic behaviours and are not simply overactive. This is why the condition is not technically known as hyperactivity. There are two other aspects to this syndrome that are frequently even more problematic. First, these children have *trouble paying attention*. They cannot concentrate on their work for long periods and often do not finish their assignments. They have trouble listening to instructions and seem easily bored. Second, they are often *very impulsive* and act without thinking. Running into the street and other risky behaviours are always a concern. Further, saying and doing the wrong things at the wrong times makes it difficult to be liked. If others do not like you, it is hard to like yourself, and not having friends makes it hard to learn social skills. Not surprisingly, then, ADHD children often have low self-esteem, may be easily frustrated, and many show signs of depression and anxiety. For some reason, a large percentage also have learning disabilities, in spite of average intelligence. As well, middle-ear infections, allergies, and asthma seem to appear more frequently than with most children.

Attention deficit-hyperactivity disorder is relatively common. How common is unclear, but probably about 5 percent of children have the disorder in varying degrees, usually boys, with some being much more affected than others. The cause or causes are unknown. Genetics may play a role; bad parenting does not, although this may make the problem worse. Elevated lead levels in children, and alcohol and nicotine use during pregnancy are correlated with ADHD symptoms, but their importance is not known. Popular opinion to the contrary, sugar or food additives have not been shown to be a problem.

Ritalin, a stimulant medication not unlike the caffeine in coffee, has been shown over and over to be a relatively safe and effective medication in the treatment of ADHD. Unfortunately, it only partially relieves some of the symptoms. Although most of these children make successful adult adjustments and their symptoms sometimes diminish with age, there is no cure. For the ECE teacher, however, it is important to know that there are a number of behavioural techniques, some of which are discussed in this book, that can be very helpful for an ADHD child. If you become an early childhood educator, you will meet ADHD children. When you do, seek help from professional people and follow their advice. Few of these children meet caring, helpful adults. Try to be one.

Don H. Shattuck
Welland County Separate School Board
Welland, Ontario

- A child whose behaviour changes suddenly and drastically may be signalling a problem requiring attention. You should feel concerned about the generally happy, outgoing child who suddenly becomes antisocial, or the active, assertive child who inexplicably becomes withdrawn and passive, particularly if the changed behaviour persists for more than a few days. Your first source of information, of course, is the child's parents. But if they too are baffled, a more thorough search for the cause of the change is in order.

- Finally, if you notice unexplainable bruises, abrasions, cuts, or burns on a child, consider the possibility of child abuse. Other forms of abuse—verbal and sexual abuse and/or neglect—do not leave physical scars but are just as damaging. An abused child usually also exhibits behavioural symptoms of the problem. If you have reason to suspect child abuse, speak to your supervisor or director so the concern can be followed up by notifying the appropriate authority. (We will discuss this issue further in the next chapter.)

When a competent teacher finds that a particular child's behaviour is just beyond that teacher's capacity to cope, it is time to look beyond a teacher's own resources. Getting professional help is not a sign of weakness, but rather of your strength in being able to recognize the limits of your professional expertise. Just as you would have a physician, not yourself, prescribe medication, there are times when a psychologist, psychiatrist, or other appropriate professional should be asked to help with a challenging behaviour. These community professionals also have a share of responsibility for the care and guidance of young children in your community.

FACTORS THAT AFFECT CHILDREN'S BEHAVIOUR

In dealing with children's behaviour, it is important to examine all potential factors that might be affecting that behaviour. All kinds of subtle influences undoubtedly contribute to behaviour, for instance, the weather (Essa, Hilton, & Murray, 1990; Faust, Weidmann, & Wehner, 1974). But behaviours also have more identifiable causes, some external, others internal. Particularly when you are concerned about a behaviour, it is wise to give careful thought to what might be triggering it. We will now examine some of the factors that can affect children's behaviour.

CLEAR-CUT GUIDELINES

Children generally abide by rules that are logical, simple, and few in number. There is no need to overwhelm children with too many rules. In Chapter 15, we suggested that the rule be that children cannot hurt themselves, others, or things.

Sometimes children's behaviour is a function of not understanding what is expected. When a child engages in a behaviour that you see as a problem, do not jump to the conclusion that the child is misbehaving deliberately. The child may simply be acting out of ignorance or may not understand your expectations. For example, by their second week in school, 4-year-old twins Trevor and Teddy seemed constantly to be testing the preschool program limits. One day they climbed over the 6-foot chain-link playground fence. Another time they were each swaying in the tops of two trees on the playground; on yet another day, they were found exploring and sampling the contents of the refrigerator in the school's kitchen.

The teachers were disconcerted by what they *perceived* as the boys' constant misbehaviour. It occurred to one teacher that Trevor and Teddy may not have understood the expectations. Indeed, in talking to their mother, the teacher found that the type of exploration the boys engaged in at school was encouraged at home. The teacher decided to talk to the boys about the school rules, which no one had reviewed with them as relative newcomers to preschool. Once the children discussed these with the teacher, they agreed that the rules made sense. They channelled their abundant energy into more acceptable activities with the help of the staff, who made greater efforts to inform the boys of their expectations.

Gartrell (1987) might place Trevor and Teddy's behaviour into the first and second levels in his classification of three levels of mistaken behaviour. The first, the **experimentation level**, is the mildest form of mistaken behaviour; at this level, children try to figure out how things work and what the consequences might be. Gartrell identifies the second as the **social habit level**, in which the child erroneously thinks the behaviour is appropriate, it has been acceptable in another context, or peers respond positively to it. The **deep emotional needs level** is the third, reflecting a more

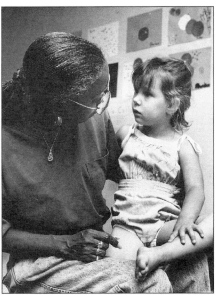

troubled cause and possibly erupting in extreme behaviours. Gartrell suggests that understanding the child is vital to effective intervention.

HEALTH AND RELATED PROBLEMS

Children often react in unacceptable ways because their bodies are not functioning well or are sending messages of discomfort or pain. When children do not feel well, they cannot be expected to behave normally. Think how most adults become very irritable when they are ill. Children are no different. In fact, children have fewer resources to control their behaviour when they don't feel well (Essa, 1990), and sometimes problem behaviours emerge when they do not feel well.

Some children are also affected by environmental or food **allergies**, which can change their behaviour in unpredictable ways. Miranda, aged 3, for example, had a severe sensitivity to all milk and corn products. Her child care teachers were very careful to avoid giving her any food with even a small amount of milk or corn. Inadvertently one day, Miranda ate some crackers that had cornstarch in them. The effect was swift and dramatic; this very competent preschooler was suddenly transformed into a uncontrollable whirlwind bouncing through the class. Certainly Miranda was not able to control her disruptive behaviour, but the adults around her had the power to control her diet so such episodes would not occur.

Some children have an undetected **sensory deficit** that may be affecting their behaviour. Could the clumsy child who is unwilling to try anything new have a vision deficit? Might the child who is often distractible and seems to ignore what you tell him have trouble hearing? Three-year-old George, for example, was uncooperative and inattentive at school, but his mother reported he would sit for long periods at home while she read to him and where he complied with her requests. At the suggestion of the director, George's mother had his hearing tested. It turned out that he had a severe hearing loss resulting from frequent ear infections, a situation that was remedied when tubes were inserted in his ears. George then became an entirely different child, attending, responding to adults and children, and becoming involved in activities; he could hear and interpret specific sounds in the group setting rather than hear only undifferentiated noise as he had before the tubes were inserted.

Nutrition, both the quality and the quantity of food, is another factor that can affect children's behaviour (Lozoff, 1989). A child who comes to school hungry or malnourished may be irritable or listless, may not work to potential, and/or may misbehave. Studies have linked nutrition to behaviour and learning (Barrett, 1986; Van Heerden, 1984). Canadian children from all social strata are at risk for malnutrition and undernutrition—some do not get proper nutrients because of costs, others subsist on a diet high in sugar, fats, additives, and empty calories.

INDIVIDUAL TEMPERAMENT

To a large degree, children's personalities are moulded by their environment, but research has also shown that children are born with a certain **temperament** (Thomas & Chess, 1969), which we discussed in Chapter 5. Thomas, Chess, and Birch (1968) found that the children they studied could be classified into three general categories: easy, slow to warm up, and difficult. They concluded that the largest group in their sample—40 percent—were classified as easy children, whereas 15 percent belonged to the slow-to-warm-up category, and 10 percent to the difficult category; 35 percent of the children did not fit neatly into any of these categories.

Easy children, from their earliest days, follow a regular cycle in sleeping, eating, and eliminating; are readily adaptable to change; have a reasonable attention span; display a moderate level of activity; are not overly sensitive to stimuli; and have a generally happy disposition. Difficult children, on the other hand, show opposite traits such as irregularity, intensity in reactions, an inability to adapt, and a high activity level, and they are often out of sorts. Slow-to-warm-up children fall in between these two extremes.

It is not easy to deal with difficult children because they often defy all attempts to pacify or engage them. "When children are difficult, less confident adults will doubt themselves, feel guilty, and be anxious about the child's future and their relationship" (Soderman, 1985, p. 16). Thomas and Chess (1969) encourage parents to accept a difficult child positively by seeing his or her traits in terms of self-assertion. Soderman advises teachers to deal with difficult children through respect, objectivity, environmental structure, effective limits, positive interaction, patience, and cooperation with colleagues and parents, all characteristics of sensitive, effective teachers. She further warns against inappropriate reactions such as ignoring the difficult behaviours, coercing compliance, shaming, labelling, or punishing.

As you pursue your early childhood teaching career, you likely will be entrusted with one or more temperamentally difficult children. Many beginning (as well as veteran) teachers have found this to be a real test of their self-confidence. Keep in mind that consistent, positive guidance skills and ingenuity can help channel the child's energy, perhaps into a leadership role, rather than into that of an unhappy outcast. Rely on your teaching strengths, examine and acknowledge your own feelings, and then continue to view each child—whether easy or difficult—as an individual worthy of your respect and support.

THE CHILD'S FAMILY

A child's behaviour may be a reaction to stress or change at home. Statistics tell us that a large number of young children will experience their parents' divorce, enter a single-parent family where there will most likely be financial as well as emotional stresses, or experience reconstitution of a family as one of their natural parents remarries (Halpern, 1987). Such major changes, even when parents are very sensitive to and mindful of the needs and feelings of their youngsters, are invariably upsetting to children who cannot fully understand what is happening. Other changes, such as a new baby in the family, a visit from grandparents, a parent away on a business trip, the death of a family member or pet, or moving to a new house, can also trigger behavioural responses. (These topics are discussed further in Chapter 17, in which we will examine stress and young children.)

It is important to maintain frequent and open communication with parents to find out what is happening at home. If you know, for example, that Eddie's parents are heading toward a divorce, you can better understand his sudden angry outbursts. You cannot put Eddie's family back together, but you can convey to him that you understand his distress and are there for him. If Eddie hits out at other children, you can let him know that you do not condone his behaviour and will take measures to stop it, but that you do acknowledge his pain.

Behaviour problems have also been linked to parenting style. Patterson, DeBaryshe, and Ramsey (1989) proposed a developmental model of antisocial behaviour. Poor parental discipline and monitoring can lead to **child conduct disorders** in early childhood; in middle childhood, such parenting practices may result in rejection by peers and academic failure; finally, in later childhood and adolescence, poor parenting can lead to affiliation with a deviant peer group and delinquency. Antisocial behaviour is more likely to develop in children of families with a history of antisocial behaviour and stressors such as unemployment, marital conflict, and divorce. The authors, in summarizing the literature on intervention efforts, conclude that intervention at adolescence produces short-lived results. *But intervention at earlier ages has proven to be more effective.*

A Closer Look provides insight into a disturbing family-based problem: drug-exposed babies and children. These drug-exposed infants and children pose many challenges for the early childhood profession.

A CLOSER LOOK

The Plight of Drug-Exposed Children

Just a few years ago the media began to reflect a concern about "crack babies," children born of mothers who had taken crack cocaine during pregnancy. Now, many of these babies are in their preschool and early elementary school years, and the focus of attention has turned to how these youngsters will function in the school environment. Some early childhood teachers have already experienced drug-exposed children who have been mainstreamed into their classrooms.

Over the years, many children exposed prenatally to drugs have been born. Stories of newborns suffering withdrawal symptoms are not new. Research has documented tremors, irritability, oversensitivity to stimuli, and other problems in infants whose mothers took a variety of illicit drugs. But one problem in studying this population of children is that it is difficult to tell what drugs or combination of drugs their mothers took, when during the pregnancy these children were exposed, how frequently they were exposed, and the quantity to which they were exposed. To complicate matters, many of the mothers had inadequate prenatal nutrition and no prenatal care.

Once they are born, drug-exposed babies are often taken away from addicted mothers and placed in foster care, subjecting already vulnerable children to a host of potential social risk factors. Thus, many unknown variables make it difficult to generalize about children who were exposed to drugs prenatally. There are no prototypes of drug-exposed children.

In recent years, several early childhood programs have been developed specifically to work with this group of children. Two such programs in California have concluded that the children do best in a high-quality early childhood environment.[1] The preschool program provides a secure base for children who are attached insecurely, according to one administrator. The focus of these programs is not on the children's history but on their current needs, which, most often, involve social-emotional and language problems.

Although there are no long-term studies to document the success of these children, staff members are very positive about the prognosis for those they have served. Several youngsters have moved into regular kindergarten classrooms, while others have required some limited special education services; none has required full special education placement. The staff feel that the children they have worked with would be best served in mainstreamed early childhood programs. Furthermore, they are very concerned that these youngsters not be stuck with a label that will follow them through their school years.

Other experts are not as optimistic, however. Many are particularly concerned about unexpected emotional swings that some drug-exposed children have demonstrated; such outbursts often result in unpredictable aggression. Although most children who react aggressively do so in response to some external provocation, the aggression of some drug-exposed children tends to come with no warning and often for no apparent reason. Some see this as a symptom of neurological damage. One child development expert feels that it is irresponsible to mainstream children who are so unpredictable. Unless a full-time aide is provided, the teacher should not be expected to add "just one more child" to the class.

The question of how to help children who were exposed to drugs before birth and often end up in unstable care once they are born is a difficult one to answer. As those who work with these youngsters in special programs indicate, the children can be helped, but the social service delivery system so often enmeshes them in a cumbersome and inconsistent bureaucracy. Some of the conflicting opinions and concerns about this group of children may be resolved as more research continues to follow their progress.

[1]From conversations in May 1991 with Mary Ann Nielsen, Assistant Superintendent, Diagnostic Center for Neurologically Handicapped Children, California State Department of Education, and Carol Cole, early childhood special education teacher with the Los Angeles Unified School District.

SOME GUIDANCE TECHNIQUES

Keep in mind that your attitude toward your job and toward children, your skill as a teacher, your ability to be consistent as well as flexible—and a good sense of humour—all contribute to setting the tone for the classroom. A respect for all children and a willingness to get to know each child as an individual are basic ingredients in positive guidance. So is a sense of partnership with the children ("me with the children") rather than a "me against them" attitude. There is no doubt that you, the teacher, are central to establishing a productive, lively, happy environment for children of all ages.

We have discussed guidance from the viewpoint of what kinds of adults we would like children to grow up to be, within the context of some different philosophical approaches, and as it is related to and distinguished from some other terms. Before we turn to some specific techniques that can help you better deal with children's behaviour, remember that behaviour management focuses on observable traits that can be *noted and measured*, such as crying, hitting, or whining, not on unobservable qualities, such as jealousy, insecurity, or separation anxiety. When a behaviour is a problem and needs to be changed, you carefully measure it (e.g., the number of aggressive incidents are counted) and quantify it, perhaps using a graph (Essa, 1990). If, for example, Edward has been hitting other children frequently, it is more accurate to know that after two weeks of a behaviour management program he has decreased his rate of hitting from an average of five times a day to two times a day than to conclude that the program is not working because Edward is still hitting.

THOROUGH AND CREATIVE PLANNING

Remember, when children are engrossed in meaningful activities that they find rewarding and interesting, they are much less likely to misbehave. Good curriculum is integrally tied to your guidance approach ("Good Discipline," 1987) and will in itself provide a key preventive technique.

PREVENTION

It is much easier on you, as the teacher, as well as on children if problems are prevented before they occur. Prevention is an excellent guidance technique because you step in to stop a potential problem before tempers flare. One way to use preventive guidance is to keep an eye on as much of the group as possible; both inside and on the playground, position yourself with your back to a wall or fence where you can watch the majority of the children, even though generally you are with an individual child or a small group. Prevention is particularly important at the beginning of the school year, when you set expectations for the rest of the year.

Also know what triggers certain children's problem behaviours. If Solomon tends to hit others when he gets frustrated, be available when you see him trying a difficult puzzle; if Rana cries when she does not get to be "Mommy" in housekeeping play, be available to guide children's role selection if needed; if Jarrod hits children when the room is crowded, ensure that he has more space; if Shaheen has a difficult time sharing, watch the block area when Andy approaches it. You are not stepping in to solve the children's problems but to be available to guide them if needed in learning problem-solving skills.

REDIRECTION

Another way to prevent potential problems is by redirection. For instance, distract Sylvia if she is about to kick over the block tower by steering her to the water table, or provide Yusuf with an alternative toy to replace the one he is about to snatch from

Richie. Redirection works particularly well with very young preschoolers whose self-control is just emerging and who do not yet have the verbal and social skills required for sharing. Sensitive teachers can help 2-year-olds develop these attributes over time and through many positive interactions. However, redirection should not be used routinely with older preschoolers, who need practice in handling social situations effectively (Essa, 1990).

Distraction through humour is used very effectively by some teachers ("Laughing," 1988). Many potential "me-against-you" situations in which a heavy hand is needed can be avoided by using the light touch—distraction to something interesting and fun, directions in the form of a jingle or song, or a joke, *not* at the child's expense, of course (p. 41). Distraction works particularly well with younger children; most toddlers readily change focus when distracted.

Humour helps prevent power struggles because the teacher and children are joint participants in a fun-filled friendship. Telling a child, "Now ... let ... me ... see ... you ... walk ... slow ... slow ... like ... a ... turtle" will be more effective than saying, "How many times do I have to tell you not to run in the classroom?"

POSITIVE REINFORCEMENT

Positive reinforcement is perhaps the most widely used application of behaviour management, but it is one that teachers frequently forget to use in abundance. You use it every time you smile at the children who are playing cooperatively in the dramatic play area, gently touch the head of the child who is engrossed in putting together a puzzle, or say thank you to the children for helping to clean up after snack; such subtle social reinforcers come naturally to most teachers. In behaviour management, reinforcers are often used systematically to encourage specified behaviours. If Julio gets positive attention every time he hangs up his coat, he is more likely to repeat the behaviour.

Behaviourists may resort to more powerful reinforcers such as food, toys, tokens, or privileges to reward a child, but only if that child does not respond to social reinforcement (e.g., Blanco, 1982; Lexmond, 1987; Sheppard, 1973; Zlomke & Piersel, 1987). Reinforcement, because it follows the behaviour ("Everyone who helps in clean-up will get a special sticker") needs to be distinguished from bribes ("If I give you a special sticker, will you help clean up?").

To be effective, it is important that reinforcement immediately follow the behaviour, although the frequency of reinforcement will vary. When you first attempt to help a child acquire a new behaviour (for instance, Julio hanging up his coat when he comes inside), the reinforcement must be applied every time the behaviour appears; however, once the child is on the way to remembering to hang up his coat, the reinforcement schedule can be decreased gradually until eventually Julio is reinforced for this behaviour about as frequently as the other children (Patterson & Gullion, 1971).

While positive reinforcement can be a powerful tool, ineffective praise, for example, general or gratuitous statements such as "Good job!" or "Good boy!" can actually be counterproductive (Hitz & Driscoll, 1988). Rather than foster positive self-concept and autonomy, ineffective praise can lower self-confidence and lead to dependency because the teacher has placed herself or himself in the position of telling children what is right or wrong (Kamii, 1984). Ineffective praise can also decrease motivation by making the reward rather than the activity the goal. When praising one child's appropriate behaviour is used to encourage the others to follow suit, children may react with anger and resentment because they feel manipulated.

Instead, it is recommended that you use **effective praise** or encouragement, which focuses on the activity and process, allows children to evaluate their own work, and discourages competition. Below are some examples of encouragement, as proposed by Hitz and Driscoll (1988, p. 12):

- Denise played with Jimmy at the sand table. They experimented with funnels for more than twenty minutes.

  Encouraging statement: "You and Jimmy played together for a long time at the sand table."

- Sue seldom talks in the group, but today she told a short story about Halloween.

  Encouraging statement: "That was a very scary story you told. It gave me goosebumps."

- Daniel just finished a painting. He comes to you, the teacher, and says, "Look at my painting, isn't it beautiful!"

  Encouraging statement: "You look happy about your painting. Look at all the colours you used."

ATTENTION

Reinforcement is a form of attention, but attention is more than reinforcement. All human beings need acknowledgment of their existence, affirmation of their linkage to others, acceptance of their membership in the human race. Sometimes we communicate through nurturance, caring, gentleness, sensitivity, and tenderness; we do this not because we are reacting to a desired behaviour, as in reinforcement, but simply because we are responding to a human need.

Reinforcement is given conditional on the child responding in a specific way, but children also need **unconditional attention**. Such attention makes an enormous difference to a child. Unconditional acceptance and response begin in earliest infancy and lay the foundation for feelings of trust. As a result, many children, receiving such attention in ample supply at home and in infant and toddler care programs, have strong, trusting relationships in their lives. By 3 years, these children are full of independence and openness to new experiences. Other children, whose foundation for trust is not as firmly established or has been shaken by a disruptive experience such as divorce, may seem unduly demanding; they may constantly seek your attention, possibly through misbehaviour.

Most often, a child who engages in a lot of attention-getting behaviour is expressing a need for attention. It is not wise to provide attention when a child expresses that need through some form of misbehaviour; that only reinforces the child's mistaken notion that the main way to get attention is to do something unacceptable. Such attention is generally negative and will not help the child feel good about herself or himself. Two kinds of attention should be provided instead. One is reinforcement of appropriate behaviours, as we have already discussed. The other is unconditional attention.

Unconditional attention tells the child that you value *her*, as a person in her own right, not just because she behaves as you want her to behave. You can give unconditional attention in a number of ways, such as greeting children at the beginning of the day with *genuine* statements such as, "Good morning, Jenny! I'm so glad to see you!" During the day, teachers also provide such attention when they smile at, hug, cuddle, or soothe a child or when they respond to the child who requests help or attention.

One mechanism for providing unconditional attention to a child who particularly seems to need extra attention is **special time** (Essa, 1990). The teacher sets aside just a few minutes a day, or even two or three times a week, just for the child. This one-on-one time is not conditional on the child behaving in a particular way (for instance, "If you ..., then we will spend special time") but is unconditional, not at all tied to the child's behaviour. The teacher conveys the message, "I want to spend time with just you because you are you." The teacher can ask what the child would like to do for special time and then follow up on that suggestion, whether it is going for a short walk, reading a book, or playing a game; the specific activity is less important than the teacher's undivided attention during this time together.

Such a time investment can have great payoffs. Early childhood educators who have used special time with children who seem to be seeking extra attention have found that these children seem to feel better about themselves and greatly decrease their acting-out behaviour. Some schools also recommend this method to parents (Keele, 1966), with the result that children whose parents regularly spend a few minutes using an individual time formula in one-on-one interaction seem much more self-assured and secure.

MODELLING

Modelling, advocated by social learning theorists, is effective because research has told us that children are likely to imitate those they admire and like. Observational learning occurs frequently in the classroom, and we use it when we model politeness, friendliness, or caring, although modelling is not a simple cause–effect phenomenon. Certain conditions, for instance, children seeing a model being reinforced, will more likely result in imitation of the behaviour (Bandura, 1977).

SHAPING

Shaping is another behavioural technique, perhaps used more frequently with children who have special needs. A behaviour is broken down into smaller steps, and **successive approximations** to the desired behaviour are reinforced until the final behaviour is achieved (Peters, Neisworth, & Yawkey, 1985; Sheppard, 1973). Thus, each time children come closer to the goal or target behaviour, they are reinforced. For instance, to increase a child's attention to any given activity when that child remains at one task for an average of only three minutes, the time required for reinforcement is increased gradually, moving from three minutes to five minutes to eight minutes to ten minutes to fifteen minutes (Peters et al., 1985).

CUING

Cuing is a technique used to help children remember what is expected. Thus, teachers may use a specific cue such as a bell to tell children that it is time to come in from outside play, or a specific song to signal a transition time, as we discussed in Chapter 15. It may suffice for the teacher to catch a child's eye and give a nod of the head to remind the child of what is expected.

IGNORING

Just as positive reinforcement strengthens behaviours, withdrawing it, through **ignoring** or **extinction**, can weaken and eliminate behaviours. We often inadvertently reinforce a negative behaviour by our reactions: frowning when a child shouts in the classroom; repeatedly saying, "Stop shouting, you are disturbing everyone!"; or taking the child aside and sitting with her or him until she or he promises to stop making noise. Each of these reactions tells children that they have successfully attracted our attention. Ignoring can extinguish the behaviour, if it is persistent and complete. But ignoring is not always the best method to use, especially when aggression is involved (Essa, 1990; Morrison, 1988). Aggressive behaviour must be dealt with more firmly and quickly for the safety of all involved.

Ignoring works well for annoying behaviours that are clearly a bid for your attention. Persistent and repeated instances of whining, pouting, baby talk, crying as a means of getting attention, tantrums (for older infants, toddlers, and younger preschoolers), and deliberately creating annoying noises are some examples of behaviours that can be changed through ignoring.

In all of these instances, let the child know clearly that you will not respond to the attention-getting behaviour. Then, be certain you provide attention when the child asks you a question without whining or requests your interaction without pouting so the child knows that appropriate behaviour can be rewarding.

For ignoring to be effective, all teachers in the class have to agree to use ignoring consistently. It is counterproductive if you remove attention from the child who throws a tantrum and another teacher goes to the child and attends in the old ways. Sometimes, when you ignore a behaviour that formerly gained your attention, the child will redouble his or her efforts and increase the behaviour to regain the old response; thus, the behaviour gets worse before it gets better (Peters et al., 1985). Ignoring, therefore, should not be tried for a day or two and then deemed a failure.

Ignoring works only if your attention, as the teacher, is the main source of reinforcement for the behaviour. If the child is getting reinforcement from other sources, such as the children, ignoring will probably not work. Does David look at you or another adult before he throws the blocks across the room? If he does, your attention is what he is most likely expecting for his efforts. If, however, other children laugh every time he engages in the behaviour, and this brings out a little smile on his face, ignoring probably won't be very effective.

One well-intentioned teacher decided to try ignoring to stop 3-year-old Bunny (who had three teenaged brothers) from swearing. Unfortunately, the result was that several children started using Bunny's choice vocabulary and the problem multiplied. The teacher failed to note Bunny's delighted reaction to the vocabulary expansion of the other children!

TIME-OUT

Although consistent ignoring should gradually eliminate an undesirable behaviour, psychologists (e.g., Blanco, 1982; Lexmond, 1987; Zlomke & Piersel, 1987) recommend, on rare occasions, when the behaviour is serious, **time-out** as a method for speeding up the removal of reinforcement that maintains the behaviour. Consistent time-out can be effective in eliminating undesirable behaviours, but it should be used *sparingly*, only for situations in which the removal of the child is the best response, and *only in conjunction with a program of positive reinforcement.*

Time-out is usually carried out in an identified location, often a chair in the place in the classroom that has the least chance of offering stimulation and opportunities for reinforcement. If the child engages in a behaviour such as hitting, the teacher matter-of-factly takes the child to the time-out area, calmly explains the reason for being removed, then leaves the child there for about two minutes. As a teacher, you would say: "You hit Letisha. Hitting hurt her. What is our rule at school? You can't hurt yourself, others, or things. It's time to sit here until I get you." After two minutes or less, the teacher gets the child from the time-out area and helps that child find an activity in which to engage.

One variation of this is **self-selected time-out** (Essa, 1990). This procedure gives children the responsibility of removing themselves from the class if they sense that they are about to lose control. Another variation is **time-away**. If Theomoor hits someone in the block area, you might choose to tell him, "It's time to talk with me now." Then, while he has time-away from the block area, you would ask him or review (at younger ages) why he was removed from the block area, discuss the rule about hurting people, and say he can return when he can play without hitting. Time-away allows the child to get away from the overstimulation of a particular activity for a few minutes rather than be removed from the room.

While time-out can be a powerful technique, it has been subject to overuse and abuse in most of Canada. For this reason, every reviewer for this text, all of them recognized Canadian experts in early childhood education, expressed some concern about the inclusion of this approach in an introductory text. They cited the many abuses of time-out they have seen in the field. If you remember this unanimous concern and use the technique only after all else has failed, you should avoid the regular pitfalls. As Peters, Neisworth, and Yawkey (1985, p. 126) note, "Time-out must not be used to get rid of the child, but to weaken specific behaviour." Moreover, time-out should be used when a child engages in a behaviour consistently, not for one-time occurrences. It is also most effective when used very infrequently and for very short durations, two to three minutes at most (Blanco, 1982; Lexmond, 1987; Zlomke & Piersel, 1987). Time-out also must be paired with ample attention for appropriate social interactions or it will not work (Blanco, 1982; Lexmond, 1987; Risley & Baer, 1973; Zlomke & Piersel, 1987).

Blanco (1982) notes that time-out, which entails removal from others, is totally inappropriate for children who are frightened of being alone. It is a punishment in these circumstances, not a removal from reinforcement. It also should not be used with very young children.

Time-out and time-away, used for no more than two minutes, can allow children to regain their composure when they lose self-control. *It should be re-emphasized that time-out should not be overused. It should also never be considered the primary method of disciplining children. Finally, it must always be paired with positive reinforcement for positive behaviours, and with empowering guidance techniques.* In fact, psychologists typically use time-out as a technique to deal with very serious behaviour problems, as the other behavioural techniques, including positive reinforcement, unconditional attention, prevention, redirection, ignoring, and discussing, are more effective and less intrusive than this procedure.

DISCUSSION

Talking about behaviour can be effective with some children, especially older preschoolers and school-aged children. Older children often respond well to such discussion, particularly if they have adequate verbal skills, the budding ability to look at themselves, and the motivation to change a behaviour that makes them unhappy. Infants and toddlers, in contrast, are quite unlikely to benefit from discussions. In essence, the teacher and child form a partnership: The child agrees to try to make some behavioural changes while the teacher promises to support the child and be there to help or remind.

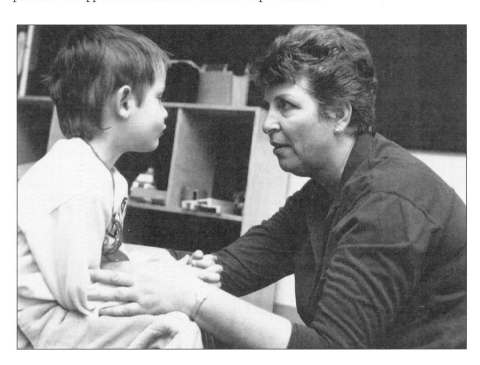

DEALING WITH SPECIFIC BEHAVIOURS: AGGRESSION AND SHYNESS

The early childhood teacher will encounter many challenging behaviours in his or her career, but it is beyond the scope of this book to examine them all. We will, however, discuss aggression as an example, with two specific examples, because it is probably the one behaviour that most concerns and ignites adults' emotions. Then we will examine one example of a shy child.

AGGRESSIVE BEHAVIOUR

Children who exhibit **aggression** deliberately hurt others. It is their intent to hurt that makes the act aggressive, not just the fact that someone was hurt, although the unobservable "intent" is difficult to pin down (Caldwell, 1977). Because of this difficulty, intention is generally just one criterion in the definition of aggression; others include what went before the act, its form and intensity, the extent of injury, and the role of both victim and perpetrator (Parke & Slaby, 1983).

One thing that makes dealing with aggression so difficult is an ethical dilemma: the potentially conflicting needs of the total group for a reasonably safe and peaceful environment and the child's need for appropriate guidance (Feeney, 1988). Countless teachers who cope with aggressive behaviours each day have used many approaches to decrease it; these methods often prove effective, although equally often they do not. Some guidelines for dealing with aggressive behaviours follow.

- *Under no circumstances should aggression be acceptable.* The classroom rule, discussed in Chapter 15, was that children cannot hurt themselves, others, or things. Stating such a rule lets everyone know the behaviour is not condoned and will be dealt with.

- *Aggression should never be ignored.* When an adult does not respond to an aggressive act, the child is given the subtle message that the adult approves of the behaviour (Caldwell, 1977; Morrison, 1988).

- *Prevention through vigilance is important in handling aggression.* Watch the child you know is aggressive and be prepared to prevent trouble, to mediate an argument, or to restrain the child who is raising a fist.

- *When the child is not being aggressive, it is important to take time to work on acceptable alternative behaviours.* Some children who engage in aggressive behaviours also exhibit good prosocial skills, indicating that they perhaps participate in more social interactions of all kinds (Caldwell, 1977). Channel them toward using their more positive skills. Children with few social skills, however, need to be taught more systematically how to play with others, how to share, and how to be gentle. Model and coach appropriate social responses (Parke & Slaby, 1983).

- *The child who acts aggressively must be provided with positive attention.* Aggressive behaviour often is a child's method of gaining adult attention. To eliminate the aggressive behaviour, you must systematically reinforce the child's appropriate behaviours and provide unconditional attention.

- *Environmental factors that may contribute to aggression should be minimized.* Crowding, for example, may heighten aggressive behaviour. Try to control group size (e.g., only four children at the woodworking table) and position a teacher next to a child who reacts to crowding during circle time, for example. Crowding is a greater problem if there is not enough play equipment to keep all the children busy (Parke & Slaby, 1983). Adequate equipment can help to minimize frustration and aggression. Finally, another environmental problem that can lead to aggression is not giving children enough time to expend physical energy and/or expecting them to sit passively for too long. Inclement weather can be a particular problem. Indoor activities that facilitate active play on these days help to keep aggressive behaviours in check.

Let's now look at two examples of children who act aggressively and how their teachers dealt with their aggression. In each example, a different approach proved effective. This underscores the need to examine carefully what factors might be affecting the behaviour and to be flexible, creative, and open when dealing with behaviour problems. No two children and no two situations are alike.

BRENDA

Brenda was ninth in a family of eleven children, used to jockeying for position and attention and to helping herself get what she wanted. She had good verbal skills, and her teachers considered her to be outgoing. Brenda often resorted to hitting another child who was playing with a toy she wanted, if a snack was not passed to her quickly enough, or if someone got to a tricycle she wanted before she reached it. Teachers talked with Brenda about the unacceptability of hitting, stressed that it hurt others, and encouraged her to use words to ask for what she wanted. Teachers tried to prevent hitting incidents whenever they could, and Brenda was willing to verbalize what she wanted when a teacher was with her to guide her behaviour. But after two months, Brenda was still hitting others when a teacher was not there to discourage the behaviour.

The teachers felt that Brenda understood what the expectation was, but chose to ignore it. As one said, "Brenda continues to get what she wants, and she is also getting our attention because we spend time talking with her after she has hit someone." They decided to try systematic time-out. They also discussed the importance of ample positive feedback to Brenda when she appropriately asked for a toy, shared, and took turns.

On the day they were going to start, the senior teacher took Brenda aside and explained to her in simple terms what would happen from now on if she hit. Within the first hour, Brenda hit Jack because she wanted to use the blue paint he was using. A teacher went to Brenda, took her by the hand to the designated time-out chair, and said, "You hit Jack and I cannot allow you to hurt other people. You need to sit here until I tell you that you can get up again." Brenda sat quietly in the chair for two minutes.

After two minutes, the same teacher took her out of time-out and helped her find another activity. She did not discuss Brenda's hitting with her because it was clear from the previous two months' experience that Brenda understood why she should not hit. That same day, Brenda was placed in time-out three more times for hitting. The next day Brenda again spent four times in time-out, but on the third day, she was there only twice. After that, she hit only occasionally over the next two weeks, and then ceased hitting all together.

Brenda had learned during her first few years of life that hitting was an effective way of getting something she wanted as well as getting attention. Systematic time-out worked well in Brenda's case because it helped her unlearn this behaviour by removing her from the enjoyment of the activity and taking away the teacher's attention. At the same time, Brenda was also helped to learn more appropriate social skills. For example, she learned to ask other children if she could have a turn with a toy and received lots of praise for that.

PETER

Time-out was not effective for 5-year-old Peter, who had engaged in aggressive behaviours over the almost three years he had been at his child care centre. The teachers had tried a variety of techniques, but Peter still persisted in hitting others when his quick temper was roused. One day, working at an art project, he said to teacher Liz who was sitting next to him, "The other kids don't like me because I hit them." Liz, after a moment of reflection, used an **active listening** technique, saying, "You are concerned because your friends don't like you when you hit them." "Yeah," responded Peter, "I don't like hitting." Liz suggested that she and Peter discuss what he might do to stop hitting other children and that she, as his friend, would help him change the behaviour.

Later, during outdoor time, when the other teachers could cover for her, Liz and Peter went for a walk to talk about his desire to stop hurting others. Peter conveyed a fear that he couldn't stop himself. Liz, in turn, asked him if he could tell when he was getting so mad that he would soon want to hit. Peter thought about this, then indicated that he did feel "funny and tight inside" when he was getting mad. Liz suggested that Peter be alert to this "funny, tight" feeling and seek out Liz immediately when he felt that way. She promised to help him work out the problem. She also promised to help him protect his rights, because he was concerned that he might lose a turn or a toy by coming to talk to her.

Over the ensuing months, Peter made a definite attempt to curb his aggression, although for some time not always successfully. He learned increasingly to seek out Liz and tell her when his anger was rising. She, in turn, went with him back to where the problem had occurred and mediated a verbal solution. Other children sensed Peter's attempts and were amazingly supportive of him, joining in congratulating him for successfully solving his problems. Peter had the maturity and motivation to change his behaviour, and with the help of a sensitive teacher and the other children he was able to learn the necessary social skills.

SHYNESS

Most children experience shyness at some times in their lives, although some children can be characterized as basically shy whereas others are generally outgoing (Honig, 1987). Evidence suggests that shyness is perhaps more influenced by hereditary factors than any other personality trait (Plomin & Daniels, 1986), and physiological differences have been found between children who are shy and those who are outgoing (Garcia Coll, Kagan, & Reznick, 1984).

These findings do not, however, rule out environmental factors, because children of shy parents also tend to be shy, whether or not they were adopted (Plomin & Daniels, 1986). A cultural effect is also indicated, evidenced in one study in which young Chinese children were consistently rated as more inhibited whether they attended full-time child care or were at home with their mothers full time (Kagan & Reznick, 1986). Thus, the reasons for shyness are not easy to pinpoint. It is important, however, to identify children who are shy and provide assistance in social assimilation if this is called for.

Children who are shy, because they feel inhibited and fearful in social situations, often have less opportunity to learn and practise social skills. Their self-concepts suffer because they are ignored, and this reinforces their feelings of isolation. Honig (1987) proposes many excellent suggestions for helping children who are shy:

- Observing the shy child trying to join others in play can provide insight into ineffective social strategies. From there, the teacher might identify some social skill words and phrases that she can teach the child as an entry into social situations. The teacher can also role play how to join others.
- Small social groups, rather than large ones, are easier for the shy child to handle, and there is also evidence that children who are shy may play more effectively with younger playmates.
- The teacher's consistency, nurturance, and acceptance will help the shy child feel more secure. In such an environment, the child can be safe enough to take some social risks.
- **Bibliotherapy** can also help the child, as the teacher selects books that focus on children who are shy and how they find friends (to be discussed in more detail in the next chapter).

Let's now examine one example of a shy child, and how her teachers helped her participate more fully in their programs.

FEMYA

Femya's mother told the child care staff that she had always been a shy child, reticent around people she did not know, and finding it hard to get involved in anything unfamiliar. She cried during her first days at school, even while her mother stayed, because she knew she would soon be leaving to start her new, part-time job. Since then, although she adjusted to being at the centre, she still found it difficult to be part of activities and almost never joined other children in play. She observed often from the sidelines, her thumb in her mouth.

The beginning of the day seemed hardest for Femya, and it often took her an hour to get involved in any activity. She related well to Andrea, one of the assistants, who was more successful than the others in inviting Femya to enter into play. She felt most comfortable with quiet activities such as art, manipulatives, and books, and she rarely participated in dramatic play or played with blocks. She never spoke during group activities.

Over the months, Femya continued her quiet presence. On her fourth birthday, she brought a special toy to share with the class. Her dilemma was written on her face; she was torn between wanting to share and having to speak before the group. She finally showed the toy without any accompanying explanation. Later, Andrea encouraged Femya to talk to another child, who came up to her to ask if he could play with the toy. The two played quietly together for ten minutes.

At times Femya played alongside Alycia, an outgoing, even-tempered, 3-year-old. Andrea created opportunities for Femya and Alycia to work together, occasions that became very successful. Alycia announced that "Femya is my special friend," and Femya, in turn, became more relaxed and spontaneous in playing with Alycia. Sometimes on weekends Femya visited Alycia's home or she came to her house.

By the time she was 5, Femya was still basically a quiet, shy child, but she was much more involved in the class. She was most comfortable with only a few children and felt secure enough to talk when there were no more than four or five in a group. She still preferred quiet activities, although she did not completely avoid more boisterous ones. The teachers were careful not to force her into an activity she was not ready to enter; they were successful by being gentle and supportive.

All the techniques we discussed in this chapter have merit and have proved their effectiveness. They are effective for dealing with most behaviour situations. Remember, however, that each child is a unique individual and may not fit into a "formula approach."

KEY POINTS OF CHAPTER 16

IMPORTANT DEFINITIONS

▲ 1. Although the word *discipline* often has negative connotations, the terms *guidance* and *positive discipline* are more concerned with the ongoing process involved in raising children.

▲ 2. Punishment as a technique is discouraged because it is ineffective in the long run.

WHAT BEHAVIOURS DO WE EXPECT OF YOUNG CHILDREN?

▲ 3. Prosocial behaviours have to be nurtured in an atmosphere of acceptance, in which inductive reasoning is used and children are helped to take the rights and feelings of others into consideration.

▲ 4. An eclectic approach to guidance allows you to select those features of various approaches that work best for you.

WHAT IS THE DIFFERENCE BETWEEN NORMAL AND CHALLENGING BEHAVIOUR?

▲ 5. All children misbehave at times; the early childhood educator, considering available information, distinguishes between normal behaviours and those that merit concern and intervention.

▲ 6. An understanding of developmental stages, coupled with a recognition of children's individual differences, helps the teacher distinguish between normal and problem behaviours.

▲ 7. Some children's challenging behaviours may be caused by medical factors that require treatment.

▲ 8. Children who are continually disruptive and unmanageable may need professional, one-to-one help.

▲ 9. Although children who act out are easily recognized, it is also important to be aware of very withdrawn children who avoid the social interactions of the early childhood program.

▲10. When children's behaviour inexplicably changes, and this changed behaviour persists for more than a few days, there may be cause for concern.

▲11. Signs of child abuse should always be a cause for concern.

FACTORS THAT AFFECT CHILDREN'S BEHAVIOUR

▲12. Many times the causes of misbehaviour are not within the control of the child but come from some source beyond the child's ability to change.

▲13. Children need to understand what is expected of them; a few clear-cut and logical rules will help children comply with such expectations.

▲14. When children are not feeling well, they may respond with unacceptable behaviours; other physiological factors that can affect behaviour include allergies, sensory deficits, and poor nutrition.

▲15. Children are born with individual temperaments—some basically easy, others difficult—that affect how they respond to the world around them. Difficult children generally have a harder time complying with expectations; in turn, adults find it more challenging to deal with such children.

▲16. Children's misbehaviour may be a reaction to stress they are experiencing at home. A variety of family changes, including divorce, a new sibling, or a parent's job loss, can upset children because they sense their parents' distress.

▲17. Parenting style can also affect children's behaviour; poor parental discipline and monitoring have been shown to result in escalating antisocial behaviours.

SOME GUIDANCE TECHNIQUES

▲18. Reinforcement should never be given gratuitously or thoughtlessly. Rather, for praise to be effective it must be personalized to what the child is doing in a way that is encouraging.

▲19. Whereas positive reinforcement is given as a consequence for a desirable behaviour, unconditional attention is not linked to any particular behaviour. It conveys to children that they are valued by those around them as people in their own right.

▲20. Particularly for attention-seeking and annoying behaviour, ignoring can be an effective technique; however, any time a behaviour is ignored, the attention that is withdrawn through the ignoring has to be given at other times.

▲21. Time-out is a technique in which the child is removed for, no more than two to three minutes, from the stimulation and reinforcement of the class. *It should be used sparingly.*

▲22. Prevention is an excellent guidance technique in which the teacher steps in when noting a potential problem situation before the problem actually occurs.

▲23. Infants, toddlers, and younger preschoolers can sometimes be distracted from a potential problem situation, although this should not be used at the expense of helping children learn problem-solving techniques.

▲24. Some older preschoolers and school-aged children respond well to talking about their problem behaviour, particularly if they feel motivated to change this behaviour with help from the teacher.

DEALING WITH SPECIFIC BEHAVIOURS: AGGRESSION AND SHYNESS

▲25. Children who act aggressively deliberately hurt others.

▲26. Aggression should never be acceptable; teachers can use a variety of strategies to change aggressive behaviours.

▲27. Children who are shy may need the teacher's assistance to help them become assimilated into the social environment of the early childhood classroom.

▲28. Teachers can use a variety of strategies to help children who are shy acquire some effective social strategies.

KEY QUESTIONS

1. List the behaviours you think are desirable in young children. Then list the characteristics you like to see in adults. Compare the two lists. Are the qualities on your two lists similar? Do you see a link between your expectations of children's behaviours and the outcomes you find desirable in adults?

2. How would you characterize the way in which you were raised as a child? How might your growing-up experiences affect how you work with children? Try to find out whether you were an "easy," "difficult," or "slow-to-warm-up" child. Can your parents or others characterize you as one of these types of people? What are the implications for working with young children?

3. Consider several typical behaviour problems of young children. What guidance techniques would you use for these different problems? Do these suggested approaches vary according to the nature of the misbehaviour? Why or why not?

4. Organize a class discussion—or even a debate—on time-out. Try to identify situations where it would be an appropriate technique and situations where it would be inappropriate. Have you seen abuses of the technique in the field or in your community?

5. Interview several early childhood teachers. Ask them which behaviour problems pose the greatest challenge and how they respond to them. Is there a pattern in their responses? Do these teachers use different approaches for different types of problems?

6. Why is it important to consider the underlying cause of a child's misbehaviour? Consider the consequences for a child to be continually berated or punished for a behaviour that he or she is not able to control.

7. Talk to a teacher of young children and ask whether there are any children in the class whose parents have recently divorced. How did the divorce affect these children? Were there noticeable behaviour changes in the children? How did the teacher respond to the situation?

8. Observe a group of children and note any aggressive behaviour. What was the nature of the aggression? How did the victim of the aggression react? What did the teacher do? Was the teacher's action or reaction effective? Why or why not?

HELPING CHILDREN COPE WITH STRESS

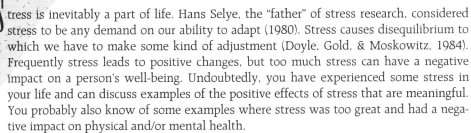

Stress is inevitably a part of life. Hans Selye, the "father" of stress research, considered stress to be any demand on our ability to adapt (1980). Stress causes disequilibrium to which we have to make some kind of adjustment (Doyle, Gold, & Moskowitz, 1984). Frequently stress leads to positive changes, but too much stress can have a negative impact on a person's well-being. Undoubtedly, you have experienced some stress in your life and can discuss examples of the positive effects of stress that are meaningful. You probably also know of some examples where stress was too great and had a negative impact on physical and/or mental health.

A variety of internal and external causes of stress are an inevitable part of life for young children as well. In this chapter, we will examine stress and young children by examining the following topics:

1. We will define stress and coping and look at the stages of stress.

2. A variety of possible sources for stress exist in young children's lives, as we will explore.

   • Family stressors, including divorce, poverty and homelessness, and fast-paced family life, can have a serious effect on children.

   • Child abuse and neglect, in addition to the potential for severe harm, is a serious source of stress for young children.

   • Health problems and dealing with death are other stressful occurrences for children.

   • Common fears may be a source of stress for children.

3. Children may have a wide variety of adverse reactions to stress, as we will discuss.

4. The early childhood teacher can use a number of effective techniques to help children cope with the stress in their lives. We will review several of these.

5. We will end the chapter with a critical examination of programs designed to teach young children self-protection from potentially harmful encounters.

DEFINING STRESS AND COPING

Stress has proved a difficult term to define, surrounded by "conceptual cloudiness" (Garmezy, 1984, p. 44) because researchers who study stress use the word in different ways. A broad definition, however, would include an environmental change that triggers the stress and some kind of resulting emotional tension in the individual that interferes with normal functioning (Garmezy, 1984). Yet stress is not in itself a negative force and, in fact, often provides the challenge and motivation to improve, grow, and mature. In her excellent two-part research review of stress and coping in children, Alice Honig (1986a, 1986b) points out that

> stress continues to mark the achievement of developmental milestones. How often an infant, on the verge of toddling, stumbles, lurches, falls, crashes, and recommences bravely. Not all stresses are harmful. The struggle to learn to walk is a good example of how some stresses can be perceived as challenges that impel a child to strive toward more mature forms of behaviour (1986a, p. 51).

Other stressful experiences can be more negative, however, requiring the child to deal with an emotional or physical situation that is unsettling, frustrating, painful, or harmful. More often than not, the child is helpless and unable to cope with this kind of stress (Arent, 1984). It appears to many professionals that the number and severity of childhood stresses have greatly increased over the past two decades. To add to this concern about increased stresses, "people who work with children report an uneasy sense that youngsters today have fewer sources of adult support, affirmation, and love than in the recent past" (Brenner, 1984, p. 1).

From our own experience, we are aware that stress causes emotional reactions, for instance, anxiety, fear, guilt, anger, and frustration in some cases, or joy, euphoria, and happiness in other instances. Behind these emotional responses are physiological, neurochemical reactions involving many bodily changes, such as in hormones, heart rate, blood flow, skin, and muscles (Ciaranello, 1983). It is important to recognize that stress is as much a physical as an emotional phenomenon because children often respond to stress in physical ways. The complexity of responses to stress has made its study a challenge to researchers and those who work with young children.

In response to stress, we use different **coping strategies** to ease the tension. Coping always involves mental and/or physical action and can take such forms as denial, regression, withdrawal, impulsive acting out, or suppression, as well as humour (Brenner, 1984) and creative problem solving. Coping reactions vary according to the stressful situation, and they depend on such inborn factors as temperament, the age and cognitive functioning of the child, and a variety of learned responses and social factors (Allen, 1988; Brenner, 1984). Children also begin to develop certain patterns of coping with specific stressors through **habituation** (i.e., becoming accustomed to it) and adaptation (Brenner, 1984). Some coping strategies are more effective and more socially acceptable than others; when a child uses aggression as a coping reaction to rejection by peers, we view such behaviour as less acceptable than if the child uses a problem-solving approach. Later in this chapter, we will discuss in more detail how to help children cope with stress.

STAGES OF STRESS

Alice Honig (1986a) has identified four stages of response to stress.

1. The *stage of appraisal* involves involuntary physical changes. For example, adrenaline may be released into the bloodstream or acid may be produced by the stomach. If stress persists, such responses can result in psychosomatic illness (not an "imaginary" illness, but a case of the mind and body working together to produce a physical problem).

2. The *stage of appraisal* is concerned with the cognitive process of evaluating and giving personal meaning to the stressful situation. The child's age and psychological makeup will affect this process.

3. The *stage of searching for a coping strategy* can include both adaptive and maladaptive responses. A child may, for instance, cry, throw a tantrum, ignore the situation, find a compromise, or find a substitute.

4. In the *stage of implementing coping responses*, children will react in different ways, depending on their personal experiences and resources. A child responding defensively may distort, deny, or respond with rigid and compulsive behaviours. Responding through **externalization** means tending to blame others rather than looking at using the child's own resources in coping. On the other hand, a child who uses **internalization** is more likely to accept responsibility for dealing with the stressor. With either internalization or externalization, it is not blame for cause of the stress but the responsibility for dealing with it that is at issue.

SOURCES OF STRESS IN CHILDREN'S LIVES

Today's children grow up in a complex world that contains a host of potential and actual stressors. A helpful framework for viewing sources of tension for children is the **ecological model** developed by such researchers as Urie Bronfenbrenner (1979). (This model was discussed in more detail in Chapter 5.) Stress sources as well as potential moderating influences within the social system (Doyle, Gold, & Moskowitz, 1984) can come from any of the interacting and overlapping systems. These systems can include the family (the microsystem); its interactions (the mesosystem); the family's social network, friends, school, and extended family (the exosystem); and the larger society, with its values and beliefs (the macrosystem).

Because stress is an individual's unique reaction to a specific event or circumstance, there is an infinite variety of possible stressors. Young children's stressors most often have their roots in the microsystem and mesosystem, and to some extent the exosystem; however, the larger macrosystem also affects young children as social forces and policies have an impact on their families. For purposes of discussion, we will focus on some common contemporary sources of stress, many of which have received the attention of researchers and theorists.

FAMILY STRESSORS

Children's security is anchored in their families. Ideally, this security is created by a caring family that provides a protected, predictable, consistent environment in which challenges and new experiences occur as the child is able to handle them successfully.

But families do not have such control over the environment and increasingly are caught up as victims of forces that produce enormous stress. Today's families face innumerable struggles—family violence, hostile divorces, custody battles, poverty, homelessness, unemployment, hunger, slum environments, neighbourhood gang wars, AIDS, drug and alcohol abuse—that can shatter their control and sense of security.

Divorce

One of the most common stressors that today's children face is divorce. It is estimated that 40 to 50 percent of the children growing up in this decade will experience their parents' divorce, live in a single-parent family for a period of time, and probably experience their parents' remarriage (Hetherington, Stanley-Hagan, & Anderson, 1989). Although divorce is stressful for everyone involved, it is probably most difficult for children, particularly young ones (Medeiros, Porter, & Welch, 1983).

Preschoolers in the midst of a divorce see what is happening from an egocentric viewpoint. They tend to attribute the departure of one parent to their own "bad" behaviour, in essence a punishment for something they did wrong (Brenner, 1984). Accompanying this anxiety is the worry that the other parent may also abandon them (Wallerstein, Corbin, & Lewis, 1988), a situation so stirringly depicted in the 1979 film *Kramer vs. Kramer.* Wallerstein (1983) has found that after a divorce preschoolers are likely to experience behavioural difficulties, such as sleep disturbances, irritability, increased sensitivity and heightened aggression.

Divorce is usually accompanied by a range of other occurrences that can have a profound effect on young children. Before the divorce there is often parental anger, discord, and open fighting, which can be very frightening to children. After the divorce, about 90 percent of children end up living with the custodial mother (Hetherington, Stanley-Hagan, & Anderson, 1989). Not only do the childen experience a shift from a two-parent to a single-parent arrangement, but often they also shift to a lower income bracket, have fewer resources, live in less expensive housing or with a transitional family (for instance, grandparents or mother's new friend), live with a parent who is stressed in new ways, and perhaps enter or spend more hours in child care (Hilton, Essa, & Murray, 1991). All these changes, on top of the loss of one parent, can be very traumatic.

Poverty, Homelessness, and Depression

Another area of stress on which increasing attention has been focused recently is the plight of children whose families lack adequate resources to meet basic needs. In Canada, one of five children live in poverty. Chronic poverty can interfere intrusively with effective parenting and may lead to insecure mother–child attachment (Honig, 1986a).

The number of homeless families with children in Canada is also increasing, as is the use of food banks. Such children tend to suffer health and emotional problems, developmental delays, nutritional defects, and irregular school attendance. The capacity for effective parent–child bonding is affected by the lack of privacy experienced by homeless families. Homeless children "are robbed of the most basic and essential element of childhood—reliable, predictable, safe routines" (Boxhill, 1989, p. 1). A small but growing number of public and non-profit organizations are starting to provide services, including child care, to homeless families and children.

In 1993, a series of teenage suicides, coupled with rampant substance abuse, in relocated Inuit communities like Davis Inlet received a great deal of media attention—but perhaps not enough professional and government attention. Many of the adolescents in these communities are depressed and have a sense of hopelessness as there is no promising future they can look forward to. Undoubtedly, the younger children in these communities are affected by the marked stress their elders are experiencing with these events.

Additional Stressors

We can easily recognize that experiences such as divorce, poverty, homelessness, and hopelessness can be grave sources of stress for young children. Children may also experience stress from family occurrences that to adults may not appear on the surface to be as stressful. For some children, for instance, the birth of a new sibling triggers regression to earlier behaviours, increased crying, and sleep problems (Honig, 1986a). Other stressors can include any event that causes a change, such as the death of a pet, relatives who are visiting, or a parent's prolonged business trip.

Fast-Paced Family Life

Some children, who at first glance might appear to be privileged, actually experience a great deal of stress. Many dual-income professional families, in which both parents work 60 or more hours a week to keep up with their medical, law, or executive jobs, produce a different kind of stress for themselves and their children. Parents are frequently rushed and beset by the constant need to make quick and important decisions. Their children are in the care of nannies, are enrolled in special schools, and attend ballet or tennis classes for tots.

Leisure time is spent at special resorts that are often more oriented toward adults than children. For example, one 5-year-old, Nina, was overheard discussing her recent vacation at Club Med. When looking at the child from a high-powered family, surrounded by abundant material possessions, keep in mind that this child is also involved in a fast-paced and stressful lifestyle, which can take its toll.

PARENTS AND PROFESSIONALS

Helping Families Cope with Stress

A stressed child usually comes from a stressed family. Although all families experience stress, the circumstances and their available resources for coping with stress will differ. Early childhood programs can function as important family support systems for parents of young children, although traditionally they have focused more on the child than on the family system (Powell, 1987b). Certainly from an ecological perspective, the child cannot be separated from the family (Weiss, 1987); thus, a good early childhood program includes a family support component.

As an early childhood educator, you can help families cope with life stressors, whether through your support, modelling, education, or referrals. Gestwicki, in her book *Home, School, and Community Relations* (1987), provides some helpful guidelines for teachers interacting and working with stressed parents:

- *Reassure parents*—Through empathy and caring, teachers can encourage parents and reassure them about such things as the amount of time needed to readjust after a divorce or the grief process. Suggested books for both children and adults can also provide reassurance.

- *Know available community resources*—Teachers' expertise is in working with children rather than in professional counselling; thus, their role with highly stressed parents is to provide emotional support, information, and a listening ear. Beyond that, they should refer parents to appropriate community agencies. It is important that early childhood teachers be aware of what is available in their own areas. Different communities have different services, for instance, family and children's service or United Way agencies. There are also mutual support groups such as Parents Without Partners, organizations for parents who have abused their children, and associations for parents of handicapped children. The yellow pages of the telephone directory often have appropriate listings under the heading "Social Services."

- *Be aware of legal agreements*—It is important to know both legal and informal agreements between parents, particularly when custody battles are involved. A written statement from every family listing authorized persons who can pick up the child should be on file as the events in the Canadian Professional Speaks Out section in Chapter 5 so aptly demonstrated.

- *Keep requests light*—It is important to be sensitive to the stress level of parents and not to ask an overwhelmed, single parent to bake two-dozen cookies for tomorrow's snack.

- *Be aware of your own attitudes and feelings*—It is sometimes easy to lay blame, be judgmental, or get angry at parents, especially when the teacher perceives them as inadequate. Teachers should examine their own attitudes and work especially hard to get to know the parents and their special circumstances so that true empathy can develop.

In addition to these suggestions, teachers can also assist parents through modelling positive guidance techniques, respect for children's ideas, and enforcement of reasonable limits. For some parents, it may be necessary to accompany modelling with verbal explanations and a discussion of alternatives (*Day Care, Families, and Stress*, 1985).

It is important to differentiate between a family that is coping adequately and continuing to carry out its family functions in the face of stress and a family that is in trouble and may require intervention. Some signs of a parent who may be at the breaking point include the following (*Day Care, Families, and Stress*, 1985):

- *Disorganized behaviour*—Parents frequently forget vital things, for instance, the child's jacket on subzero days or the child's lunch.

- *Frustration*—Parents have perpetually worried expressions, are unduly impatient with a slow child, threaten punishment, express lack of confidence in their parenting ability, or appear confused about how to handle the child.

- *Inability to accept help*—Parents get defensive and become verbally aggressive or walk away from a teacher who tries to discuss the child, perhaps in response to their own sense of guilt, failure, or inadequacy.

- *Concern more for themselves than for their child*—Parents seem more focused on their own problems and bring them up any time the teacher tries to talk about the child.

If you suspect that a parent is under so much stress that she or he is temporarily unable to cope, discuss your concerns with other teachers who interact with the parent, as well as with the director. A poorly functioning parent puts the child at risk. Your school's decision may be to contact a social service agency, which in turn may recommend that the child be temporarily removed from the home, that parental counselling be required, or that some other form of support be provided for the parent.

CHILD ABUSE AND NEGLECT

Stress is certainly an issue for children who are victims of abuse or neglect, although the more pervasive danger is that serious harm can befall them. Because young children are inexperienced and because they depend on adults to meet their needs, they are particularly vulnerable to abuse. Most often, although certainly not always, **child abuse and neglect** occur within the family. Garbarino (1990) identifies three basic causes of child abuse:

1. Our culture supports domestic violence by permitting a range of behaviours perpetrated by adults against children.

2. We have strong ideas about family privacy that reduce community responsibility for children, so that problems are viewed as "someone else's" rather than everyone's.

3. Family stresses stemming from social and economic factors often lead to parental feelings of inadequacy and frustration, which can explode into abuse against children.

Ray Helfer, one of the world's leading authorities on the subject, views child abuse and neglect as disruptors in the normal developmental process of children, with long-term repercussions. During childhood, youngsters begin to formulate and practise

many skills that are precursors to important adult skills; opportunities for such practice occur naturally, as part of normal development. Parents and other adults who interact with the child have a great impact on this process. When the normal course of development is disrupted through what Helfer terms "the world of abnormal rearing" (W.A.R.), serious developmental deficiencies occur. "Adults who are victims of the W.A.R. truly have 'missed out on childhood,' that is, missed learning many of those basic skills necessary to interact with others" (Helfer, 1987, p. 68).

Meddin and Rosen (1986) define child abuse and/or neglect as "any action or inaction that results in the harm or potential risk of harm to a child" (p. 26), including the following:

- *Physical abuse* is manifest in such signs as cuts, welts, bruises, and burns.
- *Sexual abuse* includes molestation, exploitation, and intercourse.
- *Physical neglect* involves such signs as medical or educational neglect and inadequate food, clothing, shelter, or supervision.
- *Emotional abuse* occurs through any action that may significantly harm the child's intellectual, emotional, or social functioning or development.
- *Emotional neglect* is considered inaction by the adult to meet the child's needs for nurture and support.

Physical marks or unusual behaviour may tell you that a child has been or is at risk of being abused or neglected, although it is not always easy to read such signs. Cigarette burns on a child's body are more recognizable as abuse, for instance, than a child's inability to sit for any length of time because of sexual molestation (Meddin & Rosen, 1986). Emotional abuse and neglect are particularly difficult to read because the behavioural symptoms could be the result of any number of causes. Exhibit 17-1 lists some physical signs of child abuse, while Exhibit 17-2 outlines some behavioural indicators of physical and emotional abuse that can help identify children who are being victimized. It is your skill as a careful observer, combined with your knowledge of child

EXHIBIT 17-1 PHYSICAL SIGNS OF CHILD ABUSE AND NEGLECT

- The child has bruises or wounds in various stages of healing, indicating repeated injuries.
- Multiple injuries are evident on two or more planes of the body, for instance, a head injury and bruises on the ribs, which are not likely to have happened in a single fall.
- Injuries are reported to be caused by falling but do not include the hands, knees, or forehead, the areas most likely to be hurt when a child attempts to break a fall.
- The child has oval burns left by a cigarette, shows doughnut-shaped or stocking-mark signs of being immersed in a hot substance, or has identifiable burn imprints of such items as an electric stove burner.
- A child's discomfort when sitting, which could be caused by sexual abuse.
- A child has sexual knowledge too sophisticated for the child's age, evident in conversations or through inappropriate play, which may indicate a victim of sexual abuse.
- A child is dressed inappropriately for the weather, for instance, wears sandals or no coat on a snowy day, which could be reason to suspect neglect.
- A child steals food because he or she does not get enough to eat at home, which may be another sign of neglect.

SOURCE: Adapted from N.J. Meddin and A.L. Rosen (1986). Child abuse and neglect: Prevention and reporting. *Young Children*, 41(4), 28.

EXHIBIT 17-2 BEHAVIOUR PATTERNS OF ABUSED CHILDREN YOUNGER THAN AGE 5

PHYSICALLY ABUSED CHILDREN
Expressiveness and apparent sense of self

- Bland affect, no tears, no laughter
- No curiosity/exploration
- Unable to play; no sense of joy
- Shows no affect when attacking another child
- Afraid of dark, being hurt, being alone
- Reluctant to try messy activities
- Aggressive, hyperactive, or withdrawn

Response to frustration or adversity—Withdraws or has tantrums

- Language and learning
- Lack of speech or delayed language development
- Delayed motor development
- Short attention span

Relationships with peers

- Grabs objects from others without trying to retain them
- Inept social skills
- Avoids or is aggressive toward peers
- Can't wait or take turns

Relationships with parents

- Shows no expectation of being comforted; no distress at separation
- Alert to danger
- Solicitous of parents' needs
- Constantly aware of parents' reactions

- May defy parents' commands
- Difficult to toilet train

Relationships with other adults

- Relates indiscriminately to adults in charming and agreeable ways; seeks affection from any adult
- Avoids being touched
- Responds negatively to praise
- Always seems to want/need more objects, attention, and so forth

EMOTIONALLY ABUSED CHILDREN
Expressiveness and apparent sense of self

- Comforts self through rocking and sucking
- Does not play
- Has difficulty sleeping
- Is passive and compliant or aggressive and defiant
- Rarely smiles

Language and learning—Speech disorders or delayed language development

Relationships with peers—Inept social skills

Relationships with parents

- Affectless, detached from parents or solicitous of them
- Fussy, unresponsive, irritable
- Watchful, yet avoids eye contact

Relationships with other adults

- Relates indiscriminately to adults in agreeable ways
- Seeks attention and always seems to want/need more

SOURCE: Adapted from A. Brenner (1984). *Helping children cope with stress.* Lexington, MA: Lexington Books, pp. 98–99, 101.

development, that can best provide clues about abnormal or unusual evidence that could indicate abuse or neglect (Meddin & Rosen, 1986).

Another source of information about whether a child has been or is at risk of being abused or neglected is the cues you might pick up from the child's parents. As you interact with parents informally, you might note whether parents convey unrealistic expectations for the child, seem to rely on the child to meet their own social or emotional needs, lack basic knowledge and skills related to child rearing, or show signs of substance abuse (Meddin & Rosen, 1986). Chronic family problems and frustrations stemming from unemployment, illness, and poverty often also result in child abuse and neglect. The majority of parents who abuse or neglect their children can be helped through intervention (Kempe & Kempe, 1978).

It is important to stress that it is your ethical as well as legal responsibility as a professional to report suspected child abuse or neglect to an appropriate children's aid society or agency. Every province and territory has regulations about professionals reporting suspected cases, and specific laws protect them from any liability for that report. A number of professional associations in different parts of the country also have guidelines for teachers to follow (e.g., provincial associations in B.C., Alberta, and Ontario have guidelines) that you may wish to consult.

It is not easy to make the decision to report a family for suspected child abuse or neglect. You may be aware of stress afflicting the family and be reluctant to add to it through your report; the evidence of abuse may not be clear-cut or the child may tell you that he or she fell rather than that he or she was hit. But it is your responsibility as an early childhood educator and caregiver to act on your concern and speak for and protect young children.

HEALTH STRESSORS

Another source of childhood stress derives from health-related problems. Children suffering from chronic asthma, facing a tonsillectomy, undergoing chemotherapy for cancer, or enduring the aftermath of a serious automobile accident experience stress. This stress is a combination of factors surrounding the physical problem—pain and discomfort—as well as of related elements such as fear of the unknown, limited understanding of what is happening, a strange environment populated by strangers, terrifying medical terms, and, perhaps most frightening, fear of being abandoned by the parents (Medeiros, Porter, & Welch, 1983). This last factor causes particular distress for young preschoolers facing hospitalization, because attachment and separation are important issues at this age. In addition, children who are seriously ill or face surgery are also aware of their parents' anxiety, and this adds further to their own stress (Rutter, 1983).

A parent's serious health problem, whether physical or mental, is also a source of stress for children. If a parent is hospitalized, the child's familiar routine is disrupted and the remaining parent or another adult fulfils some of the absent parent's functions. These changes produce stress, particularly if a new caretaker is involved. During the parent's convalescence, the child may also have to adapt to changes in the ill parent's personality, energy level, and preoccupation with health.

DEATH

Inevitably, as a teacher of young children, you will find a need to discuss and explain death, perhaps because the classroom parakeet was lying stiffly on the floor of the bird cage when the children arrived in the morning or because one of the children's relatives has died. Most young children encounter death, whether it is the death of a grandparent, friend, sibling, parent, family or classroom pet, or dead worm found in the backyard.

Preschoolers' Understanding of Death

Young children's understanding of death is a function of their cognitive development. Their "conceptualization of death ... is marked by a general immaturity, though death is by no means foreign to children of this age" (Smilansky, 1987, p. 43). Children in the preoperational stage of cognitive development do not yet have the mental ability to grasp fully the concepts involved in understanding death. This can lead to misconceptions based on the child's "magical or other pre-logical explanation" (Wass, 1984, p. 12) when they come face to face with death. Some preschoolers' reactions cited by Wass (1984) (from Schilder & Wechsler, 1934, and Anthony, 1972) include:

- "My grandfather died by eating too much dinner."
- "If people don't go for a walk, they die."
- "Boys don't die unless they get run over. If they go to a hospital, I think they come out living."

Smilansky (1987) describes five concepts involved in preschoolers' misunderstanding or partial understanding of death.

1. *Irreversibility*, an understanding that the dead cannot return to life, whether they have been buried or not, is not yet understood by many young children.

2. *Finality*, the fact that life processes end with death, is easier for young children to grasp in terms of tangible processes such as sight or hearing ("When you're dead, you can't hear any more") but less easy to grasp in terms of more complex processes such as sensation, thought, and consciousness.

3. *Causality of death*, such as illness or accident, is only partially understood by preschoolers, who may also think that people can die from a headache or because of sadness.

4. *Old age*, the fact that all people grow old, and the connection of aging to death, is difficult for young children to grasp because of their egocentric focus.

5. *Inevitability of death* is another difficult concept, because young children perceive that if death results from an illness or accident, all they have to do is avoid accidents and take care of themselves so they do not get ill.

Bereavement

Young children's limited understanding of death does not mean that they do not experience genuine grief at the loss of someone who was important in their lives. **Bereavement** is a natural process, an essential reaction to loss, which needs to be worked out and supported (Ketchel, 1986). Children's reactions to death will vary. Although some children will show no overt signs of mourning or may even seem indifferent to the death, others may react with anger, tantrums, and destructive rages. Children, like adults, pass through stages of mourning that include denial, anger, bargaining, depression, and, finally, acceptance (Kubler-Ross, 1969).

It is important that the adults in children's lives provide strong support and help in the mourning process. The early childhood teacher can offer such support by being willing to discuss the death, recognize and accept the child's feelings, and answer questions (Furman, 1982). This is particularly crucial for a child who has lost a parent, "the worst bereavement," because no other loss or separation is like it (Furman, 1982, p. 239).

A special example of death occurs when a young child in your class battles cancer unsuccessfully or is killed in an accident. Almost a year after the death of 5-year-old

Robbie, one of the children in the University of Oklahoma centre, there was still considerable discussion and expressions of grief by peers in his class. During his ten months of illness, chemotherapy, and hospitalizations, Robbie continued to see his friends and visited his class a few times. When Robbie died, the grief process involved the children, their parents, and the centre staff. Frequent discussions, prompted by questions or angry outbursts, continued. Some of the older children expressed anger that they had lost a good friend whom they would never see again, while the younger children sought frequent affirmation of the finality of Robbie's death ("Robbie won't be back because he is dead, right?"). Underlying many of the children's comments was a sense of their own vulnerability, the fear that they too might die. The staff and some of the parents also engaged in discussions, both to deal with their own fears and grief and to consider how best to help the children. Robbie's death was a painful experience, but also one that brought growth and understanding for everyone involved.

CHILDREN'S FEARS

Lisl's mother had gone to the apartment next door when the thunderstorm broke. Lisl was 5 years old, and the remembered boom of that thunderclap, while she was all alone, continued to frighten her for many years. Even long after Lisl learned about the physical workings of storms, thunder had the power to cause stress, to accelerate her heartbeat and make her mouth feel dry.

This early experience is not uncommon, and you can undoubtedly recall some generalized feeling of unease or a precise incident that caused a specific fear for you. Everyone experiences fear at some time because "fear is a normal emotional response to a perceived threat that may be real or imagined" (Sarafino, 1986, p. 15). Fear is an important self-protective response because it alerts us to danger. Children facing an unknown situation for the first time, for example, a visit to the dentist, will experience natural apprehension. In other instances, a fear can turn into a **phobia**, which is intense and irrational and stems directly from a specific event such as the thunderstorm just mentioned. A more generalized, vague feeling of uneasiness that cannot be traced to any specific source is labelled **anxiety**, and it is the most difficult form of fear to deal with (Sarafino, 1986). Overcoming phobias and anxieties often requires professional help, although teachers can support children as they struggle to understand the source of the fears and their feelings.

Preschool-aged children's cognitive characteristics influence the types of fears they experience. For example:

- Young children often confuse reality, dreams, and fantasy.
- Preschoolers often attribute human or lifelike qualities to inanimate objects.
- Concepts of size and relationship are just developing during the preschool years.
- The relationship between cause and effect is not yet well understood at this age.
- Young children are often helpless and not in control of what is happening around them.

These characteristics, reflecting incomplete or inaccurate understanding, combine to contribute to children's fears (Myers-Walls & Fry-Miller, 1984).

It is not always easy to recognize fearfulness in young children. Hyson (1986) gives three examples of children who are afraid of dogs: one child runs away from an approaching dog, another stands frozen in panic, a third constantly asks questions about and looks for dogs. The source of these three children's fear is the same, but their different reactions do not make it equally easy to recognize their fear. The third child's response, for instance, might be mistaken for interest or fascination rather than fear.

Although all people develop fears based on their unique experiences, some common fears of preschoolers can be identified. Pervasive fears for young children include abandonment and the unknown, apprehensions that commonly emerge when children deal with divorce, hospitalization, and death. Other frequent sources of fears are animals, the dark, doctors, heights, school, monsters, nightmares, storms, and water (Sarafino, 1986). Children have experienced such fears throughout time; in addition, modern society has created the source of some unique fears for children. Today's children worry not just about the dark or the "boogie man"; they also are victims of feelings of powerlessness and helplessness in an age of nuclear war, meltdown, and sophisticated missiles (Allen & Pettit, 1987). Canadian children who have had parents involved in the Bosnia-Herzegovina war in 1992 and 1993, for example, have renewed interest in young children's fears of war, as A Closer Look discusses. Canadian children in many locations, thanks to the pervasiveness of the media, also reacted with stress to the 1991 Desert Storm operation in Iraq, which television covered so graphically. Fears are powerful stressors for young children.

 ## A CLOSER LOOK

Young Children and War

In early 1991, when the United States engaged in war against Iraq, there was unprecedented media coverage of every aspect of this event. Adults in countries around the world were kept abreast of the latest developments almost as soon as they happened. Unfortunately, children also were exposed to this news. Much of the news conveyed anxiety, uncertainty, and unpredictability. Even very young children, not surprisingly, were affected by these feelings.

The United States media decided they must respond to children's fears about war, and Canadian children benefited from this media coverage just as they had been alarmed by the other aspects of the media stories. Major television networks broadcast prime-time programs aimed at providing understandable, factual answers to children's questions and apprehensions. Articles and features appeared in a variety of national and local newspapers, magazines, and journals. The magazine *Young Children* provided an article, co-authored by Fred Rogers (from "Mister Rogers' Neighbourhood"), on helping adults deal with children's concerns about war. While this wide-scale media focus on children and war was taking place, early childhood teachers dealt with issues of war and peace in their classrooms. We will consider one teacher's experiences with children's reactions.

During a group discussion soon after the war began, one child mentioned that she was afraid of the dark. The mention of a specific fear opened the door to further discussion. Mike said, "I'm afraid of bombs. What if one falls on my house?" Others also chimed in. They expressed various concerns on the same theme: What if a bomb hurts me … my family … my dog? The teacher allowed the children to share their fears, accepting their emotions as valid and genuine. They talked about the limited range that missiles could fly.

Discussion on the war continued in this class during the entire time of extensive media coverage. The children were particularly interested in labelling a "good team" and a "bad team." Words such as *kill* and *hate*, rarely heard in this class before, crept into the vocabulary. Music activities in which the children made up new verses to familiar songs began to take on a violent, war-related tone. School-aged children's artwork became very focused on war themes. Flags, missiles, bombs, and guns became prominent features. At the writing table, children wrote stories and made posters about the war. While the children's fears continued to surface in group discussions, a less self-focused concern also began to emerge. Many of the children expressed their wish that no one would be hurt.

Once the war ended and the television coverage stopped, the children's interest quickly disappeared. In retrospect, several important guidelines helped many parents and teachers help their young children cope with the war. These included the practical suggestions made by Rogers and Sharapan (1991) in the previously cited article in *Young Children.*

- Children need reassurance that adults will take care of them and ensure their safety. Such a message can be conveyed through verbal assurances as well as in non-verbal ways.

- An open environment allows children to share their concerns and anxieties without fear of being ridiculed or ignored.

- Adults who listen with empathy and understanding make it safe for children to discuss their feelings.

- An understanding of children's egocentric thinking helps adults accept children's fears. It is developmentally consistent that preschoolers will worry about a bomb hurting them or their families, even though the war is many thousands of miles away.

- Children's war play, like all play, may be one way that children can work through their concerns. The teacher, however, will want to ensure, through judicious supervision, that such play does not become overly scary.

Additional resources on this topic include *Who's Calling the Shots? How to Respond Effectively to Children's Fascination with War Play and War Toys* (Carlsson-Paige & Levin, 1990) and *Helping Young Children Understand Peace, War, and the Nuclear Threat* (Carlsson-Paige & Levin, 1985).

CHILDREN'S REACTIONS TO STRESS

Stress can result in a wide variety of reactions. The reaction will depend on the child as well as on the nature of the stressful event. Behavioural reactions have been classified into four categories (Blom, Cheney, & Snoddy, 1986) as follows:

1. *Feeling*—This category includes such reactions as crying, temper tantrums, shyness, fearfulness, loneliness, low self-confidence, sadness, anger, and depression.

2. *Thinking*—Such reactions may involve short attention span, distractibility, and confusion.

3. *Action*—Active reactions could include fighting, stealing, teasing, withdrawal, overdependency, impulsiveness, hiding, and running away.

4. *Body response*—Physical manifestations of stress might entail tics, hyperactivity, headaches, stuttering, loss of bladder or bowel control, clumsiness, nail biting, stomach complaints, and thumb sucking.

As we discussed in the chapter on guiding children's behaviours, it is important to consider what triggers a problem. The previous categorization indicates that children may respond to stressful events in a variety of negative ways. But behind the overt behaviour is often a stressor that precipitates the behaviour. Getting to the root of problem behaviours requires a thoughtful, observant teacher who gathers pertinent information and considers many factors when dealing with a child.

RESILIENT CHILDREN

It is important to be aware of what factors cause stress and that stress can result in a variety of undesirable or harmful behaviours. Yet, such a focus on the negative effects of stress should be balanced by considering that not all children respond adversely to stress. Some researchers have focused their attention on children who appear to be stable, healthy, outgoing, and optimistic in spite of incredibly stressful lives. They have been called **resilient children**, resistant, vulnerable but invincible, and superkids (Werner, 1984). Honig (1986b), however, cautions that although some children are incredibly resilient, "there are no super children who are impervious to all stresses in life" (p. 51).

Researchers have found some shared characteristics among resilient children. They tend to have an inborn temperamental character that elicits positive responses from adults, being cuddly, affectionate, good-natured, and easy to deal with as infants. They have established a close bond with at least one caregiver, enabling them to establish a basic sense of trust. As preschoolers they have been shown to have a marked independence, playing vigorously, seeking out novel experiences, showing fearlessness, and being self-reliant. They are highly sociable and often develop a close bond with a favourite teacher. In fact, they have been described as being adept at actively recruiting surrogate parents. In spite of poverty, abuse, a broken home life, and other chronic distress, resilient children grow up to feel in control of their destinies, loving, and compassionate (Werner, 1984).

An awareness of the "self-righting tendencies" of children under stress can help early childhood teachers focus on development of traits that contribute to such resilience. Werner (1984) suggests that to "tilt the balance from vulnerability to resiliency" (p. 71), teachers need to be accepting of children's individuality and allow them to be challenged but not overwhelmed; convey a sense of responsibility and caring and reward cooperation and helpfulness; encourage special interests as a source of gratification; model a positive outlook despite adversities; and encourage children to reach out to adults outside their family for support.

TECHNIQUES TO HELP CHILDREN COPE WITH STRESS

As an early childhood educator, you have the power to help children cope with some of the stresses in their lives, although you do not have the ability to change the source of most of their stressors. You cannot reconcile divorcing parents, make the new baby sister go away, change the rushed pace of hectic lives, or disperse the monsters in the closet. But you can help children develop some of the skills that will enable them to handle stress more effectively. As we will discuss, the kind of atmosphere you establish and your skills as a good communicator are part of a stress-reducing approach. We will also examine bibliotherapy, relaxation techniques, and play as they contribute to stress reduction in young children. In addition, you may want to consult Alice Honig's (1986b) invaluable list of suggested strategies for teachers to help children cope with stress.

A CONSISTENT, SUPPORTIVE ATMOSPHERE

A good early childhood program—one that is child-oriented, supports children's development, is consistent and predictable, provides experiences that are neither boring nor overly demanding, affords appropriately paced challenges, and is staffed by knowledgeable and nurturing teachers—is one important element in reducing children's stress. Establishing such a program allows you to provide direct help to stressed children. One underlying component of stress is that it results from something unknown and potentially scary over which the child has little control. Thus, a safe and predictable school environment, in which children can experience success and their actions are valued, will contribute to reduced stress.

The NAEYC publication, *Reducing Stress in Young Children's Lives* (McCracken, 1986), contains a collection of articles drawn from the journal *Young Children*. Many of the papers deal with helping children cope with stressful events in their lives and with ways of strengthening families. In addition, about half of the articles, under the heading "Making Sure We Don't Contribute to Children's Stress," focus on ensuring that the early childhood setting is developmentally appropriate. Similarly, a child care provider's guide entitled *Day Care, Families, and Stress* (1985), focuses much of its discussion on providing a well-thought-out program for young children.

These publications underscore the importance of the early childhood program's role in providing some elements of stability and security for young children under stress. The tentative results of a recent study support the basic premises of these publications. The researchers compared a developmentally appropriate and a developmentally inappropriate classroom and found significantly higher rates of stress in the children involved in the latter (Burts, Hart, Charlesworth, & Kirk, 1990).

COMMUNICATION

One of the most important ways that you, as a teacher of young children, can help eliminate stress is by how and what you communicate. Both the process (how you communicate) and content (what you say) of communication are important. Thus, it is important that someone share the child's concern, acknowledge how the child feels, and provide reassurance by hugging, holding, or rocking. Allen (1988) suggests that such responses are particularly important for very young children and for older children who are extremely distressed. Listening carefully to what children say and encouraging them to ask questions, express feelings, and discuss their perceptions are important in helping children deal with stress in their lives.

In addition to such responses, it is also important to give accurate and developmentally appropriate explanations and information to preschoolers old enough to understand. Vague reassurances such as "don't worry about the doctor" do not help the child develop control and alternative coping skills. On the other hand, information about what the doctor will do and what instruments will be used will help reduce the child's sense of helplessness (Hyson, 1986, p. 5).

Four-year-old Percy, whose parents were in the process of getting a divorce, spent most of his time at the child care centre involved in activities and play. But when he was confronted with minor frustrations, he would fly into angry outbursts, using abusive language, and unmanageable behaviour. Such conduct was quite different from Percy's former competent approach to life. His teacher, Ann, had been in close contact with Percy's mother and recognized his behaviour as resulting from stress. Ann did several things for Percy. She spent extra time with him, encouraging him to talk about his father, his fears, and his anxieties. She also tried to give Percy accurate information about the divorce, based on what she had learned from his mother. When Percy flew into one of his rages, Ann would immediately pick him up, take him away from centres of activity in the class, and hold him in her lap and rock him. This calmed him, and within five or ten minutes he was generally ready to return to an activity or sit quietly looking at a book.

BIBLIOTHERAPY

The term *bibliotherapy* refers to the use of books that deal with emotionally sensitive topics in a developmentally appropriate way, and that help children gain accurate information and learn coping strategies. Jalongo (1986) defines bibliotherapy as "using literature for the purpose of promoting mental health or the use of books in a therapeutic sense" (p. 42). Bibliotherapy provides a relatively comfortable form of dealing with difficult topics because book reading is a familiar activity for both teachers and children (Blom, Cheney, & Snoddy, 1986). Jalongo (1986, pp. 42–43) identifies three potential advantages of such books:

1. *Information*—It stimulates the adult–child exchange of ideas on significant topics.

2. *Relevance*—It encourages the child to make meaningful connections between school experiences and daily life.

3. *Acceptance*—It legitimizes the child's emotional responses to crisis situations.

Today, many books are available that deal with such issues as death, divorce, new siblings, separation, sexuality, handicapping conditions, hospitalization, and fears (*Day Care, Families, and Stress,* 1985; Jalongo, 1986). Books can help children replace a frightening mental image with a more realistic one by presenting accurate facts about a topic, for instance, helping children relieve the anxiety of facing the first day of school (Kleckner & Engel, 1988).

But, as Jalongo (1986) cautions, just because a book deals with a sensitive topic does not necessarily make it a good book for young children. In addition to the general guidelines for evaluating good children's literature presented in Chapter 13, crisis-oriented children's books also need to have settings and characters with which children can identify, accurately depict and explain the crisis situation, examine the origins of emotional reactions, consider individual differences, model good coping strategies, and display optimism (Jalongo, 1986). Exhibit 17-3 lists selected books for bibliotherapeutic use with young children.

EXHIBIT 17-3 SUGGESTED BIBLIOTHERAPEUTIC BOOKS

LOSS, DEATH, AND DYING

Burningham, J. (1984). *Granpa.* New York: Crown. **Ages 3–8.**
Buscaglia, L. (1982). *The fall of Freddie the Leaf: A story of life for all ages.* Thorofare, NJ: Charles B. Slack. **Ages 4 and up**.
Clifton, L. (1983). *Everett Anderson's goodbye.* New York: Holt, Rinehart & Winston. **Ages 3–8.**
DePaola, T. (1981). *Now one foot, now the other.* New York: Putnam. **Ages 4–8.**
Hickman, M.W. (1984). *Last week my brother Anthony died.* Nashville, TN: Abingdon. **Ages 3–8.**
Sharmat, M.W. (1977). *I don't care.* New York: Macmillan. **Ages 3–5.**
Wilhelm, H. (1985). *I'll always love you.* New York: Crown. **Ages 3–8.**

FAMILY-RELATED MATTERS

Alexander, M. (1979). *When the new baby comes, I'm moving out.* New York: Dial Press Books. **Ages 3–7.**
Baum, L. (1986). *One more time.* New York: Morrow. **Ages 4–8.**
Cain, B.S., & Benedek, E.P. (1976). *What would you do? A child's book about divorce.* New York: Saturday Evening Post. **Ages 4–7.**
Caines, J. (1977). *Daddy.* New York: Harper & Row. **Ages 4–8.**
Drescher, J. (1986). *My mother is getting married.* New York: Dial Press Books. **Ages 4–8.**
Galloway, P. (1985). *Jennifer has two daddies.* Toronto: Women's Educational Press. **Ages 3–8.**
Girard, L.W. (1987). *At daddy's on Saturday.* Niles, IL: Albert Whitman. **Ages 3–8.**
Lapsley, S. (1975). *I am adopted.* New York: Bradburg. **Ages 2 1/2 –6.**
Lasky, J., & Knight, M. B. (1984). *A baby for Max.* New York: Scribner. **Ages 4–7.**
Perry, P., & Lynch, M. (1978). *Mommy and Daddy are divorced.* New York: Dial Press Books. **Ages 4–8.**
Smith, P. (1981). *Jenny's baby brother.* New York: Viking Press. **Ages 3 1/2 –7.**
Stinson, K., & Reynolds, N. L. (1985). *Mom and Dad don't live together anymore.* Toronto: Annick Press. **Ages 3–5.**
Vigna, J. (1982). *Daddy's new baby.* Niles, IL: Albert Whitman. **Ages 4–7.**
Vigna, J. (1988). *I wish daddy didn't drink so much.* Niles, IL: Albert Whitman. **Ages 3–7.**

FEARS

Aylesworth, J. (1985). *The bad dream.* New York: Albert Whitman. **Ages 4–8.**
Bunting, E. (1987). *Ghost's hour, spook's hour.* New York: Clarion. **Ages 3–7.**
Dragonwagon, C. (1977). *Will it be OK?* New York: Harper & Row. **Ages 4–8.**
Howe, J. (1986). *There's a monster under my bed.* New York: Atheneum. **Ages 4–7.**

EXHIBIT 17-3 CONT'D

Jonas, A. (1984). *Holes and peeks*. New York: Greenwillow. **Ages 2–5.**
Jones, R. (1982). *The biggest, meanest, ugliest dog in the whole wide world*. New York: Macmillan. **Ages 3–7.**
Mayer, M. (1969). *There's a nightmare in my closet*. New York: Dial Press Books. **Ages 4–7.**
Robinson, D. (1981). *No elephants allowed*. New York: Houghton Mifflin. **Ages 4–7.**
Szilagyi, M. (1985). *Thunderstorm*. New York: Bradbury Press. **Ages 3–6.**
Viorst, J. (1972). *Alexander and the terrible, horrible, no good, very bad day*. New York: Atheneum Press. **Ages 3–6.**
Viorst, J. (1988). T*he good-bye book*. New York: Atheneum Press. **Ages 3–7.**

ILLNESS AND HOSPITALIZATION

Brandenberg, F. (1978). *I wish I was sick, too!* New York: Puffin. **Ages 3–8.**
Hautzig, D. (1985). *A visit to the Sesame Street hospital*. New York: Random/Children's Television Workshop. **Ages 2–7.**
Krementz, J. (1986). *Taryn goes to the dentist*. New York: Crown. **Ages 3–4.**
Rockwell, A., & Rockwell, H. (1982). *Sick in bed*. New York: Macmillan. **Ages 3–6.**
Rockwell, A., & Rockwell, H. (1985). *The emergency room*. New York: Macmillan. **Ages 2–5.**
Rockwell, H. (1973). *My doctor*. New York: Macmillan. **Ages 2–6.**
Rogers, F. (1986). *Going to the doctor*. New York: Putnam. **Ages 3–6.**
Wolde, G. (1976). *Betsy and the chicken pox*. New York: Random House. **Ages 3–6.**

FIRST DAY AT SCHOOL

Bram, E. (1977). *I don't want to go to school*. New York: Greenwillow. **Ages 3–6.**
Frandsen, K. (1984). *I started school today*. Chicago: Childrens Press. **Ages 4–7.**
Gross, A. (1982). *The I don't want to go to school book*. Chicago: Childrens Press. **Ages 5–8.**
Hamilton-Merritt, J. (1982). *My first days of school*. New York: Simon & Shuster. **Ages 4–6.**
Howe, J. (1986). *When you go to kindergarten*. New York: Alfred A. Knopf. **Ages 5–6.**
Oxenbury, H. (1983). *First day of school*. New York: Dial Press Books. **Ages 2 1/2 –4.**
Roger, F. (1985). *Going to day care*. New York: Putnam. **Ages 3–6.**
Wolde, G. (1976). *Betsy's first day at nursery school*. New York: Random House. **Ages 3–6.**

SOURCES: M. Cuddigan, & M.B. Hanson (1988). *Growing pains: Helping children deal with everyday problems through reading*. Chicago: American Library Association; *Day care, families, and stress*. (1985). Austin, TX: Child Development Program Division, Texas Department of Human Resources; M.R. Jalongo, (1986). Using crisis-oriented books with young children. In J.B. McCracken (Ed.), *Reducing stress in young children's lives*. Washington, DC: National Association for the Education of Young Children, p. 46; *The bookfinder: A guide to children's literature about the needs and problems of youth aged 2–15* (vol. 1). (1977). Circle Pines, MN: American Guidance Service.

RELAXATION TECHNIQUES

Older children, ones who are able to understand language fairly well, can be helped to reduce some of the physical tension associated with stress through guided relaxation exercises. Relaxation routines can easily be incorporated into the early childhood program, for instance, as part of movement activities or during rest or pre-nap time. Some programs schedule a regular relaxation period for specific exercises.

One approach to relaxation is to experience muscle tension followed by muscle relaxation (Humphrey & Humphrey, 1985). For instance, children can be instructed to make themselves stiff as a board, then to become as floppy as a Raggedy Ann or Andy doll. A more systematic approach, called **progressive relaxation**, asks children to tense and then relax various specified muscle groups. For instance, squeeze your eyes shut tightly, then relax; make fists with both hands, then relax; push your knees together

hard, then relax (Humphrey & Humphrey, 1985). A game such as Simon Says can be used to promote relaxation activities.

Imagery, a mental image that helps in the process of relaxation, can also be used effectively with young children. After children are lying in a comfortable position, they can be asked to "float like a feather" or "melt like ice." A poem or story read very slowly and softly can help children visualize an image in their own way.

PLAY AND COPING WITH STRESS

Play provides a natural outlet for children to cope with and work out stressors in their lives. Play furnishes a safe setting in which children can confront fears and anxieties, express anger, and find solutions to problems. Role playing or pretend play in particular allows children to re-enact frightening experiences, feel what it is like to take on the perspective or role of others, and make reality more acceptable (Allen, 1988). Taking on the role of the doctor by using a stethoscope or giving a doll an injection with an empty syringe can help dispel some of the fears associated with an upcoming visit to the doctor's office.

Another effective approach to decreasing fear is to increase understanding about something unknown. For instance, one study reported that children who used the game Hospital Windows, a medically oriented lotto game that helps children gain accurate information, increased their knowledge of health care concepts significantly, while decreasing their fear of medical equipment and procedures (Henkens-Matzke & Abbott, 1990).

Gunsberg (1989) notes that abused and neglected children often exhibit primitive and disorganized play behaviour, are disruptive, and are hostile toward, or avoid, adults. Gunsberg cites the case of a 4-year-old abused child whom the teacher engaged in a repeated, simple play episode. By structuring play that responded repeatedly and predictably to the actions of the child—that was contingent on the child's behaviour—the teacher helped her form a perception of a nurturing and attentive adult. Repeated, positive play experience was used not only to help the child develop more mature and effective play patterns but also to promote trust, a sense of control and power, and enjoyment.

SELF-PROTECTION PROGRAM

With increased social awareness and concern about child sexual abuse has come a host of programs aimed at teaching children self-protection techniques. Specially designed programs are usually presented to preschool groups by volunteer, law enforcement, or social agencies. They address such topics as the difference between "good" and "bad" touching and the child's right to say "no," and they present some specific protective techniques, including running away from a potential assailant and rudimentary karate moves.

Although such programs are well intentioned, their effectiveness has been questioned. In fact, a critical review of research evaluating child sexual-abuse prevention programs found little evidence that such programs for preschoolers actually meet their goals (Reppucci & Haugaard, 1989). These authors raise serious questions about the developmental readiness of young children for meaningful understanding of the concepts these programs teach. Furman (1987) raises a fundamentally important question about protecting children from abuse by pointing out that adults, not children, are responsible for providing protection. Young children are too inexperienced to be given such a serious responsibility. We need to protect them through our consistent and constant supervision, modelling of appropriate interaction with strangers, and teaching respect and ownership of the body through nurturing care.

KEY POINTS OF CHAPTER 17

DEFINING STRESS AND COPING

▲ 1. Stress has been defined in a variety of ways, but a definition usually includes the concept of an environmental change that brings about a response that interferes with normal functioning.

▲ 2. Stress is not necessarily negative; if it makes demands on children beyond their ability to cope, it can be harmful.

▲ 3. Children undergo identifiable stages of stress.

SOURCES OF STRESS IN CHILDREN'S LIVES

▲ 4. Many young children experience the divorce of their parents; divorce is one of the major sources of youngsters' stress.

▲ 5. A sizable number of Canadian families live in poverty; this includes a rapidly increasing number of homeless families. Poverty and homelessness are grave sources of stress for young children.

▲ 6. Children from affluent families, whose parents have a fast-paced, hectic lifestyle, also experience stress.

▲ 7. Children who are abused or neglected are beset by many sources of stress.

▲ 8. Early childhood educators need to be able to recognize potential signs of abuse. It is their ethical and legal responsibility to report suspected child abuse or neglect.

▲ 9. Children who suffer from chronic illnesses or experience a serious illness or accident are faced with many health-related stressors.

▲ 10. Although young children have a limited view of death, they nonetheless experience bereavement after the loss of a significant person in their lives.

▲ 11. Almost all young children experience some common fears, for instance, the unknown, abandonment, animals, the dark, or monsters.

CHILDREN'S REACTIONS TO STRESS

▲ 12. Responses to stress can take many forms; they can be manifested through emotional reactions, affect thinking processes, be reflected in aggression or withdrawal, or result in body responses such as loss of bladder control.

▲ 13. Some children, despite incredible stress, are stable and optimistic; such youngsters are called resilient children.

TECHNIQUES TO HELP CHILDREN COPE WITH STRESS

▲ 14. When children are stressed, it is particularly important to provide a supportive, stable, predictable, developmentally appropriate environment.

▲ 15. The teacher's communication, through understanding and acknowledgment of the child's feelings, can help a child cope with stress.

▲ 16. Some excellent children's books that deal with sensitive topics can help children gain accurate information and learn coping strategies.

▲ 17. Relaxation techniques and imagery can help children reduce some of the tension associated with stress.

▲ 18. Play is one important outlet for children as they attempt to assimilate and cope with stressful events.

SELF-PROTECTION PROGRAMS

▲ 19. A number of programs designed to help children protect themselves against abuse have been developed in recent years.

▲ 20. Research about the effectiveness of such programs has found little evidence that they actually meet their goals.

KEY QUESTIONS

1. What have been the most stressful events in your life? What were your reactions? How did you cope? What feelings did you experience? Can you think of a stressor in your life that has had a positive effect on you?

2. Talk to a teacher of young children and ask what types of family stressors are experienced by the children in the class. How do these stressors affect the children? How does the teacher help the children deal with their stress?

3. Check the procedures for reporting suspected child abuse and neglect in your local community. Which agency or agencies should be contacted? What procedure will be set in motion by such a report? What is the involvement of the person who makes the report?

4. Review several children's books, such as those listed in Exhibit 17-3, that deal with sensitive issues. How do these books address such topics as loss, divorce, or fear? Could a young child identify with the characters? Do the books offer alternatives to the child who is experiencing a similar stressor?

5. Observe a self-protection program presented for young children. What concepts are being presented? Are they appropriate for the cognitive and emotional abilities of young children? What do you think young children might learn from this program? Do you see any drawbacks or potential problems with this program?

Part

6

THE FUTURE OF EARLY CHILDHOOD EDUCATION

In Chapter 18 of this final section. "Issues and Dilemmas in Early Childhood Education," we consider the profession and the issues and challenges we face as we approach the 21st century. What problems must the profession confront? What does the future hold for early childhood education in Canada? How can we ensure the availability of affordable, high-quality child care for very young Canadians?

ISSUES AND DILEMMAS IN EARLY CHILDHOOD EDUCATION

Teachers are a critical ingredient in early childhood education. You can make the difference between a quality program and a mediocre one, as you know well by this stage in the text and your academic year. But as a teacher in ECE, you will face a number of issues and dilemmas that are of concern to all in the profession. Your commitment to bettering the profession and your advocacy for the field will benefit generations to follow.

In this chapter, we will look at the field of early childhood education and its future from the teacher's perspective. We will examine the following topics:

1. Although early childhood education presents teachers with exciting challenges, it also presents some issues and dilemmas.

   - Some problems faced by early childhood educators reflect historical trends.
   - Early childhood education faces some serious concerns, including teacher shortage, low pay, burn-out, and scarcity of men in the field.

- Through advocacy and empowerment of early childhood professionals, these issues are beginning to be addressed.

2. We will end the chapter by examining trends and drawing some conclusions about what the future holds for the field of early childhood education.

CURRENT ISSUES AND DILEMMAS

Early childhood education is, in many ways, a field of contradictions and extremes. Those who try to define it often find themselves in a dilemma, not clear on what to include and what to exclude. Where does a program fit that barely meets minimum standards, and what about the program that genuinely strives for excellence in meeting the needs of its children and families? Are the kindergarten teacher, the child care provider, the preschool master teacher, and the home care provider included? Are the preschool teacher who holds a master's degree in early childhood education and the high-school graduate who works in a child care centre equals in the same field? Can the child care provider who earns minimum wage and no benefits for the eight hours a day spent caring for children 50 weeks of the year be lumped together with the kindergarten teacher who earns a public school salary, often greater then $50 000, for ten months of teaching?

How can the teacher job description that calls for someone who "likes children" be compared with the one that requires a degree in early childhood education or child development? How can the lack of teacher training requirements in three Canadian jurisdictions be acceptable in light of educators' insistence that those who work with young children need specific training? In fact, is there a good reason to justify why some of you are enrolled in an academic program while others with no academic training may equally qualify for a position?

These questions and others are at the heart of the dilemma facing the early childhood profession. We will review some specific issues and look at some possible ways of addressing them. Although we will divide some of these issues into categories such as teacher shortage and low pay, these concerns are all interrelated.

A HISTORICAL PERSPECTIVE

It might be helpful to look a few historical issues in the field of early childhood education to gain a perspective on its current status.

Early childhood education today is inextricably linked to the role and status of women in North America. Between the mid-18th and mid-19th centuries, "womanhood was redefined, its image re-created and reimagined, its social function reviewed, its links to child rearing and socialization forged, and its authority over the moral and cultural development of the nation rationalized" (Finkelstein, 1988, p. 12). When, in the latter half of the 19th century, the kindergarten became firmly established as a Canadian institution, women had found their niche in an environment that was not quite domestic, yet not quite public either.

The early 20th-century pioneers of the early childhood movement, while building a scientific basis for child study, continued to see women as the guardians of the young, with a specialized role in upholding moral and cultural standards—a noble role that was held above concerns for economic and material comforts. Unfortunately, this legacy of "unselfishness" has followed early childhood educators to the end of this century, giving them a sense of the importance of their work, yet placing them in a low-paying profession with low status in the social structure (Finkelstein, 1988).

TEACHER SHORTAGE

Over the past several years, increasing attention has been focused on the shortage of qualified early childhood teachers. This shortage is partly caused by the high demand for child care as increasing numbers of mothers with children enter the workforce. In fact, Employment and Immigration Canada (1992) projections for the 1990s suggest that there will be approximately a 23 percent growth rate in the demand for preschool teachers. Yet, particularly in areas where there is low unemployment and a high cost of living, early childhood teachers are scarce. In addition, a decreasing number of people are entering the workforce as the "baby bust" generation—those born during the 1970s when the national birth rate declined—reaches maturity (Galinsky, 1989).

Teacher shortage, however, is only half the story. What is more serious is the high rate of turnover among early childhood teachers. According to *Caring for a Living.* (Canadian Child Day Care, 1992), the Canadian survey of early childhood teachers discussed in Chapters 1 and 6, the national teacher turnover rate is 26 percent. It ranges from a low of 16 percent in P.E.I. to a high of 84 percent in the Yukon. Although the data are not yet available, it is likely that the turnover rate varies with the type of facility. According to the recent National Child Care Staffing Study in the United States (Whitebook, Howes, & Phillips, 1989), the 1988 U.S. turnover rate was 41 percent. That figure, however, varied according to type of centre, ranging from a 74 percent annual staff change in chain, for-profit centres to a 30 percent rate in non-profit programs. Staff turnover in the United States nearly tripled between 1977 and 1988, jumping from 15 to 41 percent. Unless these high turnover rates can be halted, the

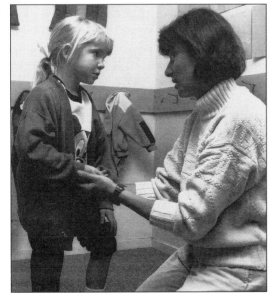

teacher-shortage problem is likely to continue. However, there is little doubt that the turnover rate must be viewed along with information on salaries.

TEACHER TURNOVER AND LOW PAY

High teacher turnover rates will continue to be a problem in early childhood programs in both Canada and the United States as long as wages remain low. Certainly, high turnover rates are not characteristic of kindergarten and primary level programs where the rate of pay is much higher—in fact, some teachers' federations are offering incentives for early retirement in an attempt to persuade aging teachers to leave the lucrative profession and create positions for young graduates in the teaching profession.

The staffing shortage in non-school-based early childhood programs would undoubtedly be much less of a problem if early childhood teachers were paid adequate salaries and if they received appropriate recognition and status. For most teachers of young children, however, monetary rewards are not equal to their professional training and value. Although there is wide variation in pay, early childhood teachers are generally paid poorly. *Caring for a Living* (Canadian Child Care, 1992) reported that the average salary for a senior teacher in Canada was $18 498 per annum, while assistants received an annual salary of $15 337. Administrative directors averaged $25 804 per year, while teacher supervisors earned $20 498. However, there was considerable variation in salaries across the provinces and territories. The average wage was as low as $5.57 per hour in Newfoundland (which is below Ontario's minimum wage of $6.35 per hour) and $6.23 in Alberta, and as high as $17.81 for an administrative director in the Northwest Territories (but remember Gillian Moore's discussion of costs in the territories in Chapter 6!). Only about 20 percent of the Canadian teachers surveyed were unionized, but these unionized workers had salaries that were 33 percent higher than those of teachers working in non-unionized settings. (In 1993 [Childcare Resource, 1993], the Canadian Union of Public Employees [CUPE] was organizing a unionization drive for Saskatchewan, but the outcome is not yet known. Similarly, the Public Service Alliance was encouraging unionization in the Yukon in 1993. This interest of a major Canadian union may have far-reaching implications for the field.)

Teachers in municipal, non-profit centres generally earned substantially more than teachers in non-profit and profit-making centres. For example, in Alberta, municipal teachers earned 26 percent more than teachers in non-profit centres and *63 percent* more than teachers in profit-making centres.

The low wages of Canadian early childhood educators still remain somewhat discouraging given that over two-thirds of the teachers surveyed had postsecondary-level diplomas or degrees. In contrast, only 41 percent of the national labour force has a comparable education. Historically, the profession has been dominated by females, and historically, predominantly female occupations are associated with low pay and low status. Moreover, over the years, females also have been less likely to protest their wages. However, this may be changing. In April 1993, for example, the Confédération des syndicats nationaux (CSN) organized a walkout of all unionized child care teachers in Quebec to support demands for a wage increase of $3.50 per hour (Childcare Resource, 1993).

Benefits are another issue of concern. Generally, early childhood programs sponsored by larger institutions such as municipalities, hospitals, school boards, or universities, benefit from the policies of their sponsoring agencies. In a similar way, employer-sponsored child care programs often also receive their company's benefits package. However, benefits are rare in smaller centres, especially profit-making ones.

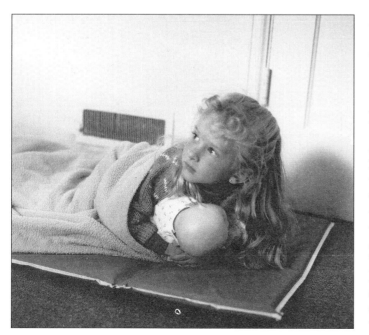

Canadian teachers' responses to *Caring for a Living* suggest that the high turnover rate in non-school-based early childhood programs is related to low wages. In the United States, Whitebook et al. (1989) found an inverse relationship between rate of pay and percentage of turnover. Those at the lower end of the pay scale changed jobs at twice the rate as those at the higher end. At the same time, however, they found that there was less turnover among teachers with early childhood training. In fact, the Canadian turnover rates are exceptionally high in the Yukon and the Northwest Territories (84 percent and 65 percent, respectively), where there are no training requirements. They are also high in Alberta (42 percent), which is just approaching its 1995 deadline for the implementation of teacher training requirements.

High staff turnover takes its toll in several ways. The National Child Care Staffing Study (Whitebook et al., 1989) found that in centres with a high turnover rate, children spent less time in social activities with peers and tended more to wander aimlessly. In addition, separation from parents becomes more critical when caregivers change frequently (Galinsky, 1989). Teachers also suffer when their co-workers change frequently because they have to assume the additional burden of orienting and training new staff (Whitebook, 1986).

Low pay feeds into a vicious cycle: poor pay causes qualified teachers to seek work elsewhere; as a result, jobs are often filled by unqualified staff; they, in turn, reinforce the low status in which early childhood education is held and negate the need for higher pay (Katz, 1984a). In a recent call for an "all-out effort to improve compensation and status," Marcy Whitebook (1986), director of the U.S. Child Care Employee Project under which the National Child Care Staffing Study was carried out, warned that child care could

> become a less and less attractive career choice despite the many inherently gratifying aspects of working with young children. The most likely and scariest prospect is that the pressure will build at a faster pace to lower standards for child care personnel—some of which are already frighteningly inadequate in many states—in order to fill teaching vacancies (p. 11).

Kyle (1992a) expressed similar concerns about teacher shortages in Ontario:

> There is also some concern that the [Ministry's] development of an options paper "to provide alternatives for determining equivalency" may result in the watering down of present training requirements in order to allow more semi-trained or untrained staff to work in child care centres (p. 444).

Semi-trained and untrained teachers might well solve the teacher shortage problem, and possibly reduce child care fees, but at what cost? While professionals with training command higher salaries, they also bring considerably more to their programs and enhance the quality of care young children receive.

LOW WAGES AND AFFORDABLE CHILD CARE

The low wages of early childhood teachers are inextricably related to the issue of affordable child care. Teachers' wages (and benefits if they receive them) constitute the largest expenditure in early childhood programs. However, that allocation varies considerably from one jurisdiction to another. In Newfoundland, for example, only 49 percent of a centre's budget is used for salaries, while that figure jumps to 78 percent and 80 percent for Manitoba and the Northwest Territories, respectively. (The average for Canadian programs is 69 percent.)

Of course, the fee parents pay for a program is directly affected by how much is allocated to salaries. The higher the teachers' cheques are, the greater the cost of the program. Teacher–child ratios and group size regulations have a similar impact on budgets and fees. The more children per adult, the lower the cost because fewer adults have to be hired. On the other hand, high child–adult ratios are associated with higher levels of teacher stress and decreased responsiveness to children (Phillips & Howes, 1987; Whitebook, Howes, Darrah, & Friedman, 1982).

Yet, the answer is not simply a matter of raising the cost of child care charged to parents. Although some families can afford to pay higher rates to ensure high-quality care offered by well-trained and well-paid professionals, many others cannot. Experts contend that the cost parents pay for child care includes a hidden subsidy—the low wages teachers receive (Willer, 1990).

Many professionals advocate aggressive lobbying for public support for child care. Some advocates maintain that only when teachers collectively insist on higher wages and benefits will there be sufficient economic impetus to force a solution to the problem.

As any additional costs would have to be borne by parents, unless they find public funds, parents will become more interested in the problem. If they cannot afford child care, parents will become involved in the political process. According to Morin (1989),

> common practice is to shield parents from the true cost of child care by having employees work at compensation levels that subsidize the cost to parents. Our advocacy efforts have been directed primarily toward increasing the supply of affordable care for parents, not to increasing compensation for employees (p. 19).

BURN-OUT

Teacher burn-out is another issue in the field, and it too is linked with teacher shortages, high turnover rates, low salaries, and the stress that arises as a consequence. Burn-out is complex, resulting from multiple causes. It is characterized by job dissatisfaction, stress, loss of energy, irritability, and a feeling of being exploited. The **burn-out syndrome** has been described as a feeling of exhaustion that results from too many demands on one's energy and resources (Mattingly, 1977).

Low salaries and minimum benefits contribute to burn-out, but so do other factors. Some of these, cited in research findings (Whitebook et al., 1982), include long

working hours, unpaid overtime, time spent outside working hours in curriculum planning or parent functions, expectations for maintenance duties, lack of breaks, the constant intensity of working closely with children, high child–adult ratios, and lack of power in the decision-making process.

Although burn-out is a final outcome for some of those who work in early childhood programs, many others find great job satisfaction, which balances some of these negative aspects. In Chapter 6, we noted that *Caring for a Living* (Canadian Child Day Care, 1992) found that "the nature of the work and the opportunity to make a difference in the lives of children is the silver lining" (p. 1) in the profession. Canadian teachers find their involvement with and their positive influence on young children very satisfying. They also enjoy the collegiality that accompanies their positions; over 85 percent of those surveyed are very happy with their colleagues. The opportunity for reflection and self-development, satisfying staff relations, job flexibility, autonomy, and staff interdependence have also been reported as positives in U.S. studies (Whitebook et al., 1982, 1989).

In the right setting, teachers can be highly satisfied with their positions—and even their salaries. A Closer Look (p. 444) describes two very different early childhood programs. The contrast between these two programs points out some of the reasons why some early childhood teachers experience burn-out, while others find their jobs highly satisfying.

A CLOSER LOOK

St. Peter's and Jack Sprat

A look at two early childhood centres in one community illustrates the two extremes of child care facilities that exist in North America: in one there is great satisfaction and stability, while in the other there is a high rate of teacher burn-out, which results in frequent staff turnover.

St. Peter's Child Care Centre is a church-sponsored facility begun by a group of interested parents in the 1970s. It has an active and supportive board made up of church, parent, and community professional representatives. Most of the staff have worked at St. Peter's for ten years or more, and the rare job openings tend to attract many applicants. Salaries are a little above the average for the community, but not as high as at some other centres.

The staff report high job satisfaction; they enjoy their work with the children, appreciate each other, and value their input into the decision-making process. The director meets weekly with the staff, discussing concerns and promoting group problem-solving strategies. She spends a good part of each day in the classrooms, with the staff and children. A child–adult ratio of 7 to 1, team teaching, flexible scheduling to accommodate the staff's personal needs, and response to staff requests for material and equipment also contribute to their level of satisfaction. One staff member summed up the feelings of her colleagues by saying, "I love this job and wouldn't trade it for the world. I work with a very special group of people whom I highly respect as well as really like. It's a pleasure to come to work. Each day is a challenge, and it's exhilarating. I suppose I could make more money at another job, but where else could I find this special combination of great people, little and big, and the chance to grow and develop personally as I have done in the twelve years I have been here?"

Jack Sprat, a privately owned child care program in the same community, suffers from constant staff turnover. Seven months is the longest any staff member has been at Jack Sprat. Most of the children have had as many teachers as the number of months they have been in the program. A director spends part of her time at this facility and part of her time at another one that belongs to the same owner. Each teacher has charge of a group of thirteen to seventeen children in isolated rooms, and there is little interaction between staff.

The owner subscribes to a monthly curriculum service and teachers are expected to follow this program, which involves letter and number recognition activities, dittoed exercises, and group discussions that focus on specific letters, numbers, names of the months, animals, and occupations. Each child is expected to complete a specific number of dittos each day. Teachers complain about feeling isolated, having no say over what they do with the children, being forced to carry out activities neither they nor the children enjoy, a lack of resources, an inability to request additional supplies, and a lack of support in dealing with the children.

The contrast between St. Peter's and Jack Sprat is underlined by the frequent teacher turnover in the latter and the almost total absence of staff changes in the former. St. Peter's places a priority on meeting the needs of children and staff, allows staff to participate in decision making, promotes communication and camaraderie among staff, and provides an atmosphere of mutual respect among teachers, administration, and children.

MEN IN EARLY CHILDHOOD EDUCATION

A somewhat different issue concerns the role of men in early childhood education. A 1992 study of Canadian early childhood teachers found that 98 percent of them were females; in the United States between 95 and 97 percent of practitioners are females (Seifert, 1988; Whitebook et al., 1989). There have been and continue to be male teachers who have a high commitment to the education and well-being of young children. For some children who grow up in single-parent homes without a father figure, a male teacher can fill a particularly special role.

Yet, men leave the field of early childhood education at an even greater rate than women do. Some male teachers who changed careers reported that they were subject to subtle prejudicial attitudes from parents, female co-workers, and administrators. They were considered not as good as women because they had never been mothers. Suspicion that was initially based on vague sex stereotypes was intensified during the 1980s by several highly publicized cases of sexual abuse involving male teachers in child care settings (Robinson, 1988). Similarly, the 1993 abuse trial of four male police officers, one unrelated woman, and a family (father, mother, and son) who operated an unlicensed child care facility in Martensville, Saskatchewan, again raised public suspicions about men in child care. While these are exceptional cases, they nonetheless have a deterrent effect on some men considering the child care field.

It is more likely that economic reasons prevent more men from entering the field of early childhood education, or cause them to more readily leave the field if they do spend some time as preschool teachers. Robinson (1988) found that 85 percent of his sample of male early childhood teachers were married with at least one child and were the major wage earners in their families. Low pay compelled them to look elsewhere for work. In part, men leave the field or do not enter it because they have more and better-paying career choices than women, not because of the nature of the job (Seifert, 1988). The absence of a substantial number of men in the field is undoubtedly a contributing factor to low salaries. Thus, it has been argued that "recruiting more men would enhance the professional self-image of early childhood education" (Seifert, 1988, p. 114).

EMPOWERMENT AND ACTIVISM

We have raised several urgent issues that face the early childhood profession. It is heartening that increasingly more effort is being devoted to solving to these issues. Articulate public statements, relevant publications, thoughtful research, and energetic political advocacy and lobbying are making an impact. There is no question that the needs of young children and families, the importance of high quality in child care, and the needs of early childhood teachers are becoming highly visible public matters.

Changes in the current realities of early childhood education can be brought about through joint political action and the empowerment of teachers (Dresden & Myers, 1989). Training for advocacy is being incorporated into some higher-education programs, so students learn how policies are made, how the political system operates, and how they can affect it (Lombardi, 1986). You may well be taking a course that covers advocacy as part of your program of study, something that probably would not have been part of the curriculum fifteen or twenty years ago.

What is clear is the resolve of professionals and organizations to push for change. Interest in and support for quality child care comes from many sectors both within and outside of the field of early childhood education, including parents, teachers, administrators, resource and referral agencies, related service providers, professional organizations, teacher trainers and educators, researchers, civic and religious groups, business

and labour organizations, volunteer service organizations, philanthropic organizations and foundations, and civic leaders. A coalition including members of such constituency groups can be a powerful force in beginning to address issues (Lombardi, 1990). However, the ultimate responsibility for enhancing the prestige—and the salaries—of early childhood educators lies with the members of the profession. As one of the reviewers of this text noted, some early childhood professionals "are quite apathetic and want other groups to plead their cause." In order to effect real change, professionals must be willing to commit their own time to lobbying efforts, and then, other groups—parents, for example—may join them.

The United States National Child Care Staffing Study (Whitebook et al., 1989) ends with five major recommendations for change and suggestions for achieving these. These recommendations are as relevant to the Canadian context as they are to the United States:

1. *Increase salaries*—To reach this goal, some of the recommendations are to establish salary levels that are competitive with jobs requiring comparable training and education; earmark government funds for salary enhancement; raise the minimum wage; and invest more public and private funds in child care to help low- and middle-income families.

2. *Promote education and training*—This goal can be reached by establishing a career ladder, as well as stipend programs to cover early childhood training costs.

3. *Adopt standards that will lead to higher-quality programs*—Such standards should establish national criteria for child–adult ratios, staff training, education, and compensation, and they should be required of recipients of any public funds.

4. *Develop industry-wide standards*—To increase the quality of early childhood programs, recommendations include a minimum allocation of a centre's budget for teaching-staff expenditures; a benefits package for all teaching staff; inclusion of time for curriculum preparation and staff meetings; and encouragement of staff to join a professional organization.

5. *Promote public education*—To educate the public about the importance of well-trained and adequately paid teachers, it is recommended that administrators, educators, professional organizations, and referral agencies participate in a concerted effort to promote this issue and its importance.

THE FUTURE OF EARLY CHILDHOOD EDUCATION

Up to this point, we have examined issues that Canadian early childhood teachers face as a profession. As we approach the end of the 20th century, we can look back and unravel some of the factors that have shaped the field as it exists today.

But what lies ahead? Are there more changes in store? Will unresolved social issues be addressed? Will early childhood education become an important force in considering these issues? Lacking the aid of a crystal ball, we might, nonetheless, try to predict what lies ahead by looking at current trends:

- From all economic and social indications, it is reasonable to expect that a high percentage of families will continue to have two parents in the workforce. Thus, while they are at work, dual-income families, along with working single parents, will continue to need care for their young children.

- At the same time, the increase in the percentage of women in the childbearing years will slow down as we approach the end of the century. Nonetheless, the actual number of children potentially requiring child care will still be higher by the year 2000 than it is today (Jones, Marsden, & Tepperman, 1990).

- Employment opportunities in early childhood education will continue to increase. Employment and Immigration Canada (1992) projects that child care will be one of the top ten high-demand occupations throughout the decade.

- The number of young children who live in poverty is also expected to increase (Halpern, 1987; Wash & Brand, 1990). However, recent economic and political realities in Canada have not made people optimistic about federal increases in funding for child care.

- Employer involvement in child care sponsorship has been one of the fastest-growing trends during the past decade. This interest is likely to increase as employers recognize the need to provide child care benefits for parent-employees to help maintain a productive workforce. A shift in type of program sponsorship, along with new job opportunities, is likely to accompany such a trend.

- All indications are that the number of positions for early childhood professionals will continue to rise because of the ongoing need of families for child care, projected expansion in publicly funded programs for children at risk, and increasing numbers of employer-sponsored programs. Yet there are and will continue to be grave concerns about the stability of the early childhood workforce. In no other industry is there such a high turnover of employees as in child care. Unless wages are attractive, this turnover is likely to continue.

- Professionals working with young children are realizing that teacher training programs for those specializing in early childhood education are fragmented in most Canadian jurisdictions. Programs for elementary school teachers often do not place a great enough emphasis on the early years, while programs for child care teachers do not place enough stress on school-related issues. More formal liaison mechanisms between programs and joint offerings are likely to increase.

An example of such a liaison is found in Ontario, where faculty from the early childhood education programs at Durham College (Oshawa) and Seneca College (Toronto) are involved in discussions with York University's education faculty about developing a degree program that emphasizes the early years and draws on the resources of all three institutions. In A Canadian Professional Speaks Out, Carolyne Willoughby, an ECE instructor at Durham College who spent part of the 1993/1994 school year on exchange with a junior kindergarten teacher, discusses some of the issues that arise when graduates from different early childhood training programs work together in the same class.

A CANADIAN PROFESSIONAL SPEAKS OUT

Team Teaching in Junior Kindergarten

In addressing the issue of a team teaching approach in junior kindergarten—each team consisting of an early childhood educator (ECE diploma from a community college) and a teacher (B.Ed. from a faculty of education) — a number of issues become apparent. First, the primary focus is quality education for the young child; however, one must ask if this includes a care element, given that a child can attend a junior kindergarten at the age of 3.8 years. Second, these two teachers are coming to this classroom with entirely different educational backgrounds; the ECE has the skills and knowledge to program for the young child, while the other has been trained to be a teacher. Third, in light of the difference in educational backgrounds, even though these two individuals will be expected to do the same job, there will certainly be a vast difference in the salaries that each will receive.

We must focus on the experience of the young child, who may be in the junior kindergarten in the morning with a teacher and a teacher's assistant and 23 other children, and, if he attends the school-based child care for the remainder of the day, he is with three ECEs and 23 other children. Because two different ministries have jurisdiction over these two settings, the child experiences two very different environments.

The issues of educational background and salary are closely linked and governed by collective agreements negotiated by the respective unions. In this situation the early childhood educator is not recognized as a qualified teacher and would therefore receive a salary significantly lower than the classroom teacher. A salary that recognizes level of education attained is important but not if it is at the expense of an individual doing the same job.

The entire field of education is currently experiencing a situation of diminishing resources while trying to accomplish more. The quality of education provided then becomes an issue. It also becomes evident that what needs to happen is to work smarter with the monies available and also to share the available resources between schools and institutions.

There are a number of projects throughout Ontario where a linkage has been created between a community college and a university to provide students with a more direct, cost-efficient means of achieving her or his educational goals. These projects will not only provide unique educational opportunities for students, but will also achieve the goals of partnering among educational institutions and the sharing of available resources.

In one such endeavour—the Partnership in Early Education Project—York University, Durham College, and Seneca College are investigating the development of an articulated B.Ed. program offering specialization in the early years. "It was envisioned that the proposed program would represent a collaborative delivery system of education for teachers of young children, blending the strengths of both the community college and the university. From the beginning of this project, there was a commitment to the belief that the certification of teachers of young children must adhere to general standards for teacher certification while at the same time allowing for necessary flexibility in the delivery of the preservice program."*

The concept of creating educational partnerships is to provide students with a broader educational base from which to make different career choices. However, it remains important to maintain the integrity of the ECE diploma to provide young children with quality caregivers.

Carolyne Willoughby
ECE Coordinator
Durham College
Oshawa, Ontario

*"Partnership in Early Education Project — Summary Report." June 15, 1993. Susanne Eden, York University, p. 1.

- As more children are in school-aged care, new issues emerge. The need for improved communication between child care facilities and elementary schools is becoming more urgent. Similarly, there will be a greater opportunity for teacher training programs to broaden their focus to incude non-school-based care in the curriculum. Leslie Nutbean, the director of an inner-city school-aged child care facility in Winnipeg, emphasizes some of the current challenges in A Canadian Professional Speaks Out.

A CANADIAN PROFESSIONAL SPEAKS OUT

Development of School-Age Curriculum for the Child Care Professional

The workforce depends on its workers having the appropriate knowledge to do the job right. Child care centres rely on staff who have received appropriate training from an accredited degree or certification program.

Postsecondary education is available both at the community college and university levels. Most of these programs are geared to the preschool child (12 weeks to 6 years). Child care professionals working with the school-age child, however, have found specific courses hard to find.

In the school-age child care field, teacher education backgrounds vary: education degree, youth worker certificates, recreation technicians, physical education, early childhood degrees, and social services. Colleges and universities lack the courses and curriculum for professionals working with the school-age child in a non-school setting. An accredited program must be formulated and implemented to meet the need of the school-age child care professional.

The problem is that no one will take on the responsibility of developing a curriculum because of the diversity of disciplines required. The education institution would have to bring together courses from several fields, namely, education, psychology, sociology, recreation, and social work. Along with consultation from the school age field, for example, bringing in experts from the school-age care community, this would help to develop a well-rounded and age-appropriate program.

Child care is becoming more and more important due to economic strictures placed on the family. Some changes will have to be made to keep up with the growth of this field and ensure quality care for all age levels.

Leslie A. Nutbean
Director, St. Matthew's Kids Korner
Winnipeg, Manitoba

- As we have discussed, stability of staff is an important element in the quality of early childhood programs because children's trust and attachment to the adults in their lives depends on that stability. As a result, there has been increasing concern about the interplay between the needs of children for quality care, the needs of parents for affordable child care, and the needs of early childhood professionals for appropriate compensation and status (Willer, 1987). This concern, expressed both within and outside the early childhood profession, will continue to be articulated. We can expect greater focus on, and increasing public awareness of, this issue in the future.

- As issues related to early care and education continue to occupy public attention, it becomes more and more apparent that our country lacks a cohesive and consolidated social policy within which to consider child and family matters. For instance, a wide variety of agencies initiate, license, administer, and evaluate varying programs for children and families, often relying on different philosophies, approaches, and regulations. Even within provinces, there are different regulations governing variables like teacher–child ratios, depending on which ministry is involved. But, at the same time, because of increased public attention, there also seems to be greater willingness to address such issues with more depth, integration, and forethought. It can be expected, therefore, that efforts to coordinate early childhood policies and approaches will continue in the future, and perhaps a national policy will eventually be a reality.

- Many programs for young children, compensatory education and kindergarten programs, for example, often are operated only part-day. Such scheduling is problematic for working parents who need full-day care for their children. This conflict may prevent youngsters who would potentially benefit from participating in such programs (Washington & Oyemade, 1985). Because limited funding is the major stumbling block to extending these programs to meet working parents' needs, this issue will continue to be raised.

- Within the early childhood profession, there is a continued focus on the pluralistic nature of our society and the shrinking world in which children are growing up. Many early childhood programs can be expected to focus more than ever on an unbiased curriculum that includes children and families from all cultural, ethnic, linguistic, and economic backgrounds, as well as children with disabilities. Special programs that preserve the culture of aboriginal groups also are likely to become more numerous. Sandra Beckman from Yukon College in Whitehorse outlines some child care issures for First Nations in A Canadian Professional Speaks Out.

 # A CANADIAN PROFESSIONAL SPEAKS OUT

Child Care Issues for First Nations

The First Nations people make up one-fifth of the Yukon's population. There are four First Nations band-operated day care centres in the Yukon, as well as a First Nations family day home in an isolated northern community. Caregivers in the rural communities as well as the larger centres understand the need to include language, heritage, values, and learning styles of First Nations people in the day care programs.

At Yukon College, our mission statement mandates all programs to incorporate a Native component as an integral part of courses, not just an add-on. The Council for Yukon Indians has developed a day care curriculum manual and curriculum resource guide entitled *Show Us the Way*, which is used in numerous day care centres and family day homes throughout the territory.

In a discussion of First Nations early childhood education, several points must be stressed:

1. A strong emphasis on verbal communication is vital; enriched programming is necessary to prepare First Nations children for our school system and increase success in postsecondary education.

2. There must be accessibility of child care training support for First Nations people wishing to enter the early

childhood field. In the Yukon, this means offering courses in the rural communities to enable single parents and/or parents of young children to further their education without leaving their home or family. Yukon College has addressed this need, offering early childhood courses to various rural communities each term. Distance education will enable us to reach even more students.

3. Training for child care workers and administrators must recognize and provide programming for fetal alcohol syndrome and fetal alcohol effects. Agencies providing funding and/or support staff are overburdened, and rural day care centres cannot acquire or afford staff specifically trained in this area.

4. Strong, clear cultural role models are necessary. The caregiver is the most powerful part of the curriculum, providing consistent patterns that value First Nations history and traditions. This is evident in the remote family day home, where the operator provides opportunities for the children to observe meat drying, berry picking, smoking fish, and snaring rabbits.

5. Programming must include involvement from parents, elders, and the extended family. The First Nations day cares are extensions of the community. Children develop a positive sense of identity, which

in turn leads to increased self-esteem when they have clear cultural role models and learn how their heritage is related to the present.

6. Each band-operated day care, as well as the family day home, stresses the need to introduce the traditional language to the children.

First Nations children in our child care centres need to be given the tools to adjust to non-Native environments, yet should have ample opportunity to preserve and maintain their cultural traditions.

The First Nations elders say the seed is the tree, the tree is the forest. Children are like the seeds of a tree. They contain not only the information of the one tree, but hold the potentiality of all the forests to come. To the parent(s), elder(s), and caregiver(s), each child is important. Although all children share some common characteristics, they believe each is a special being. It is the responsibility of the extended family, which includes the day care, to help each child reach his or her full potential.

Sandra Beckman
Yukon College
Whitehorse, Yukon

- Finally, because of recent legislation in some provinces, which ensures that young children with disabilities are included in early education, there will be continued efforts to integrate them into programs with other children. The parent groups representing children with disabilities are a powerful lobby, and they are likely to pressure provinces to enact legislation about integration.

As you complete your course, remember that you can make a difference to the field of early childhood education and enhance its status in Canada. Just as you can be a powerful influence on the development of the young children in your program, you can have a major impact on the development of the field in the 21st century. Finally, you also will have a major impact on the lives of the young children you teach and care for in your program, as well as on their families.

KEY POINTS OF CHAPTER 18

CURRENT ISSUES AND DILEMMAS

▲ 1. The history of women over the past two centuries is closely linked with the development of the field of early childhood education.

▲ 2. Low pay and poor benefits for early childhood teachers are directly tied to the cost of child care for parents.

▲ 3. Some early childhood teachers experience burn-out.

▲ 4. More than 98 percent of early childhood teachers are women, and male teachers leave the field at an even greater rate than female teachers do.

▲ 5. The issues and dilemmas facing early childhood education and its teachers are being addressed through vigorous advocacy and lobbying to help bring about change through political action and empowerment of teachers.

THE FUTURE OF EARLY CHILDHOOD EDUCATION

▲ 6. Economic and social factors point to a continued growing need for early childhood education. These include an expected increase in the number of women in the workforce, an increase in the number of children in poverty, and greater employer sponsorship of child care.

KEY TERM

burn-out syndrome

▲ 7. The need for qualified early childhood educators will increase, and provinces with minimal requirements for teachers in early childhood settings will be pressured to raise their standards.

▲ 8. The early childhood profession will continue to address issues related to quality care and the needs of staff.

KEY QUESTIONS

1. As a class, discuss teacher salaries, burn-out, and teacher turnover. Try to determine the best way of resolving these issues.

2. What would you do to encourage more men to enter early childhood education? In what ways would more male teachers be beneficial for young children in child care settings?

3. We have speculated about the future of early childhood education on the basis of current trends. What issues do you think the field will face in the future? What will the field look like in ten years?

GLOSSARY

ABC analysis An observational technique in which the observer records observations in three columns, identifying antecedent, behaviour, and consequence.

Absorbent mind Maria Montessori's term to describe the capacity of young children to learn a great deal during the early years.

Abstract thinking According to Jean Piaget, the ability to solve a variety of problems abstractly, without a need to manipulate concrete objects.

Academic materials *See* **Conceptual materials**.

Accommodation According to Jean Piaget, one form of adaptation that takes place when an existing concept is modified or a new concept is formed to incorporate new information or a new experience.

Active learning A teaching style in which children are active seekers of knowledge, not passive recipients of it.

Active listening Thomas Gordon's term for the technique of reflecting back to children what they have said as a way to help them find their own solutions to problems.

Activities Well-planned, self-selected learning opportunities, usually placed in activity centres, for children in an active learning program.

Activity centre (also called learning or interest area) An area in which materials and equipment are combined around common activities, such as art, science, or language arts.

Activity time The largest block(s) of time in the early childhood program day during which children can self-select from a variety of activities.

Adaptation Jean Piaget's term for the process that occurs any time new information or a new experience occurs.

Adventure playground A European innovation, a type of outdoor play area in which children use a wide range of available "junk" materials to create their own environment.

Aesthetics The enjoyment and appreciation of beauty, particularly related to all forms of art.

Aggregates Rhoda Kellogg's term for the step in the development of art in which children combine three or more simple diagrams.

Aggression Behaviour deliberately intended to hurt others.

Allergies Physiological reactions to environmental or food substances that can affect or alter behaviour.

Anal stage The second stage of development described by Sigmund Freud, occurring during the second 2 years of life, in which pleasure and conflict derive from bowel control and elimination.

Anecdotal record A method of observation involving a written "word picture" of an event or behaviour.

Anxiety A general sense of uneasiness that cannot be traced to a specific cause.

Assimilation According to Jean Piaget, one form of adaptation that takes place when the person tries to make new information or a new experience fit into an existing concept.

Assistant teacher (also called aide, helper, auxiliary teacher, associate teacher, or small-group leader). A person who works under the guidance of the head teacher in providing a high-quality program for the children and families in the class.

Associative play A category of play in which children interact to some extent and may share materials, but are not engaged in a common activity.

Attachment   The child's bond with the mother, established during the first year of life.

Attention deficit-hyperactivity disorder (ADHD)   Disorder characterized by short attention span, restlessness, poor impulse control, tendency to be distracted, and inability to concentrate.

Audience awareness   Children's growing awareness that their stories are a form of communication that should make sense to others.

Authority stage   The stage of parenting defined by Ellen Galinsky typifying parents of young preschoolers who are defining rules as well as their own parenting role.

Auto-education   *See* **Self-education**.

Autonomy vs. shame and doubt   The second stage of development described by Erik Erikson, occurring during the second 2 years of life, in which toddlers assert their growing motor, language, and cognitive abilities by trying to become more independent.

Back-to-basics movement   A movement that advocates a return to teacher/subject-centred education that stresses the basic subject areas.

Bank Street Model   An early childhood education program model, developed at the Bank Street College of Education in New York, that draws upon progressive education and the open education model seen in the British Infant Schools.

Basic scribbles   According to Rhoda Kellogg, the twenty fundamental markings found in all art.

Behaviour management   The behavioural approach to guidance, according to which the child's behaviour is under the control of the environment, which includes space, objects, and people.

Behaviour modification   The systematic application of principles of reinforcement to modify behaviour.

Behaviour setting   According to Kounin and Sherman, different environments elicit behaviours that are fitted to the setting; thus, children act "schoolish" at school.

Behavioural objective   An aim or goal, usually set for an individual child, that describes in very specific and observable terms what the child is expected to master.

Behaviourism   The theoretical viewpoint, espoused by theorists such as B.F. Skinner, that behaviour is shaped by environmental forces, specifically in response to reward and punishment.

Behaviourist view of language development   *See* **Behaviourisim**.

Bereavement   The grief over a loss, such as after the death of a loved one.

Bibliotherapy   The use of books that deal with emotionally sensitive topics in a developmentally appropriate way to help children gain accurate information and learn coping strategies.

Bilingualism   The ability to use two languages.

Bimanual control   The ability to use both hands in tasks for which each hand assumes a different function.

Black English   A term identifying the dialect that is spoken by some black childrenand that has a complex grammatical system of its own.

Board of directors   Policy-making or governing board that holds ultimate responsibility, particularly for not-for-profit programs.

Brigance Diagnostic Inventory of Early Development   A developmental assessment tool for children from birth to age 7.

British Infant School   Schools for 5- to 8-year-olds where the open model was developed.

Burn-out syndrome   A condition that is experienced by professionals as a result of undue job stress, and that is characterized by loss of energy, irritability, and a feeling of being exploited.

Canada Assistance Plan (CAP)   Canadian federal legislation that requires the federal government to share child care funding—only for those in need—with the provinces on a 50–50 basis.

Canadian Child Care Federation (CCCF)   National early childhood organization, founded by the federal government in 1987, that aims to improve the quality of child care in Canada by providing services to those in the field.

Canadian Childcare Advocacy Association (CCAA)   National early childhood organization, founded in 1983, that aims to make high-quality, affordable, non-profit child care accessible to all Canadians who need it.

Canadian National Child Care Study (CNCCS)   A federally funded study of child care in Canada.

CAP   *See* **Canada Assistance Plan**.

Caregiver   A term traditionally used to describe a person who works in a child care setting.

Casa dei bambini (children's house)   Montessori's first school in Rome, founded in 1907.

Centre-based program   A program for young children that is located in a school setting and usually includes larger groups of children than are found in home-based programs.

Checklist   A method of evaluating children that consists of a list of behaviours, skills, concepts, or attributes that the observer checks off as a child is observed to have mastered the item.

Child abuse and neglect   Any action or inaction that harms or puts a child at risk.

Child–adult ratio   The number of children for whom an adult is responsible, calculated by dividing the total number of adults into the total number of children. A high ratio means there are fewer children per teacher, while a low ratio means there are more children.

Child advocacy   Political and legislative activism by parents and professionals who urge consideration of social issues affecting children.

Child care centre   *See* **Centre-based program**.

Child care worker   *See* **Caregiver**.

Child-centred approach   An approach that allows children to self-select activities.

Child Development Associate (CDA)   An early childhood teacher who has been assessed and successfully proven competent through the national CDA credentialling program.

Child study movement   A movement that occurred in the 20th century in the United States when many university preschools were established to develop scientific methods for studying children.

Classical conditioning   A learning technique in which a stimulus that usually evokes a reflex is paired with one that does not usually evoke the reflex, until the latter eventually evokes the reflex by itself.

Classification   The ability to sort and group objects by some common attribute or property, for instance, colour or size.

Code of ethics   Agreed-upon professional standards that guide behaviour and facilitate decision making in work situations.

Code switching   The ability to switch appropriately from one language system to another.

Cognition   The process of mental development that is concerned more with how children learn than with the content of what they know.

Cognitive developmental theory   The theory, formulated by Jean Piaget, that focuses on how children's intelligence and thinking abilities emerge through distinct stages.

Cognitive interactionist view of language development   The view that children's language is rooted in cognitive development, requiring, for instance, the ability to represent objects mentally.

Collage   A type of art activity in which a creative combination of materials is assembled.

Colour tablets   In Montessori programs, two sets of wooden tablets of many colours that children match and sort by shades.

Combines   According to Rhoda Kellogg, a step in the development of art in which children combine two simple diagrams.

Communicative competence   A term that describes the ability to use language in socially appropriate ways.

Competency-based program   A program that gives paraprofessionals credit for the knowledge they acquire through experience, thereby facilitating in-service training of early childhood professionals.

Computer literacy   Familiarity with and knowledge about computers.

Conceptual materials   A Montessori classroom area that focuses on academic materials related to math, reading, and writing.

Concrete operations period   According to Jean Piaget, the period of development spanning approximately ages 7 to 11, when children do not depend solely on visual cues but can apply logic to explain physical tasks or operations.

Confidentiality   A requirement that results of evaluations and assessments be shared with only the parents and appropriate school personnel.

Conservation   The ability to recognize that objects remain the same in amount despite perceptual changes, usually acquired during the period of concrete operations.

Constructive play   Category of play involving creating something with play objects.

Constructivist theory   A theory, such as that of Jean Piaget, based on the belief that children construct knowledge for themselves rather than have it conveyed to them by some external source.

Content objective   The purpose or rationale for an activity that specifies that the activity is intended to promote specific subject matter.

Conventional level of moral development   According to Lawrence Kohlberg, the stage concerned with pleasing others and respect for authority.

Conventional moral rules   Standards, which are generally culture-specific, arrived at through general consensus.

Convergent thinking   The act of narrowing many ideas into a single, focused point.

Cooperative play   A category of play, typical of older preschoolers, in which children play together in a shared activity.

Coping strategies   Mental or physical reactions, which can be effective or ineffective, to help deal with stress.

Creative playground   Outdoor play area that uses innovative materials such as tires, telephone poles, nets, and cable spools.

Criterion-referenced   A characteristic of tests in which children are measured against a predetermined level of mastery rather than against an average score of children of the same age.

Cross-modal intersensory activity   The use and integration of more than one sensory modality, for instance, matching an object that is seen visually to an identical object that is selected through touch only.

Cuing   A technique used to help children remember what is expected by giving them a specific signal.

Curriculum   The master plan of the early childhood program that reflects its philosophy and into which specific activities are fit.

Daily living   Montessori classroom area that focuses on practical tasks involved in self-care and environment care.

Deep structure   According to Noam Chomsky, inborn understanding of underlying rules of grammar and meaning that are universal across all languages.

Denver Developmental Screening Test (DDST)   A quick test for possible developmental delays in children from infancy to age 6.

Developmental Indicators for the Assessment of Learning—Revised (DIAL-R)   A developmental screening test, for children ages 2 to 6, that assesses motor, concept, and language development.

Developmental objective   Purpose or rationale for an activity which specifies that the activity is intended to promote an aspect of physical, social, emotional, or cognitive development.

Developmental test   A test that measures the child's functioning in most or all areas of development, although some such tests are specific to one or two areas.

Developmentally appropriate practice   A term coined by the NAEYC to describe programs that match children's developmental and personal histories.

Diagnostic testing   Another term for screening, which might indicate that more thorough testing should be carried out.

Diagrams   According to Rhoda Kellogg, the stage in children's art when they begin to use the six recognizable shapes: rectangle, oval, triangle, X, cross, and deliberate odd shape.

Dialect   A regional variation of a language that differs in some features of vocabulary, grammar, and pronunciation.

Didactic   A term often applied to teaching materials, indicating a built-in intent to provide specific instruction.

Director   A label often used for the teacher in Montessori programs.

Discipline   Generally considered a response to children's misbehaviour.

Discovery learning   *See* **Active learning**.

Discrimination   The ability to distinguish among different features of objects.

Disequilibrium   According to Jean Piaget, the lack of balance experienced when existing mental structures and new experience do not fit exactly.

Divergent thinking   The act of expanding or elaborating on an idea, such as in brainstorming.

Dramatic play   Type of play in which children use play objects as a substitute for something imaginary.

Early childhood   The period between birth and 8 years of age.

Early childhood education   A term encompassing developmentally appropriate programs that serve children from birth through age 8; a field of study that trains students to work effectively with young children.

Early childhood education program model   An approach to early childhood education, based on a specific theoretical foundation, for instance, the behavioural, Piagetian, or Montessori view.

Early childhood educator   *See* **Early childhood teacher**.

Early childhood teacher   A specifically trained professional who works with children from infancy to age 8.

Eclectic model   An approach in which various desirable features from different theories or methods are selected.

Ecological model   A framework for viewing development that takes into account the various interconnected contexts within which individuals exist, for instance, the family, neighbourhood, or community.

Effective praise   A form of encouragement that focuses on children's activities rather than on teacher evaluation of their work; praise that is meaningful to children rather than general or gratuitous.

Ego   According to Sigmund Freud, the rational facet of personality that helps find appropriate ways of achieving the pleasure goals of the id and mediating between the id's demands and the superego's restrictions.

Egocentricity   A characteristic of young children whereby they see things from their own subjective perspectives.

Elaboration   A memory strategy that involves making up imaginary connections when there is no logical link among items.

Emergent literacy   The ongoing, dynamic process of learning to read and write, which starts in the early years.

Employer-supported programs   Provision by businesses of child care programs or support for child care costs incurred by employees' children.

Empowerment   Helping parents gain a sense of control over events in their lives.

Equilibrium   According to Jean Piaget, the state of balance each person seeks between existing mental structures and new experiences.

Event sampling   A method of observation in which the observer records a specific behaviour only when it occurs.

Externalization   When dealing with stress, the child blames others rather than using his or her own resources to cope with the stress (*see* **Internalization**).

Exosystem   According to ecological theory, that part of the environment that includes the broader components of the community (e.g., government agencies or mass media) that affect the functioning of the family.

Extended family   Family members beyond the immediate nuclear family, for instance, aunts and uncles, grandparents, or cousins.

Extinction   In behavioural theory, a method of eliminating a previously reinforced behaviour by taking away all reinforcement, for instance, by totally ignoring the behaviour.

Eye–hand coordination   Integrative ability to use the hands as guided by information from the eyes.

Family child care home   Care for a relatively small number of children in a family home that has been licensed or registered for that purpose.

Family involvement   The commitment of parents to the early childhood program through a wide variety of options.

Family systems theory   A view of the family as an ever-developing and changing social unit in which members constantly accommodate and adapt to each other's demands as well as to outside demands.

Feral children   Children who, lost or abandoned by their parents, were thought to have been reared by animals in the wild.

Fine motor development Development of skills involving the small muscles of the fingers and hands necessary for such tasks as writing, drawing, or buttoning.

Flexibility A measure of creativity involving the capability to adapt readily to change in a positive, productive manner.

Fluency A measure of creativity involving the ability to generate, in a limited time, many relevant ideas on a given topic.

Formal operations period According to Jean Piaget, the last period of development spanning approximately ages 11 to 15, characterized by sophisticated, abstract thinking and logical reasoning abilities.

Formative evaluation Ongoing assessment to ensure that planned activities and methods accomplish what the teacher intended.

For-profit program Privately owned early childhood program in which any monies left over after expenses goes to the owner or shareholders.

Functional play Category of play, characteristic of very young children, that is repetitive motor play used to explore what objects are like and what can be done with them.

Games with rules Type of play, usually engaged in by older children, in which there are accepted, prearranged rules.

Gender identity Identification with the same sex.

Gender stability The recognition by children aged 5 to 7 that gender is constant and cannot change.

Generativity According to Erik Erikson, the stage of human development in which the mature adult focuses on the care and nurture of the young.

Genital stage The last stage of development described by Sigmund Freud, beginning with the onset of puberty, during which adolescents become increasingly aware of sexuality.

Genre Category or type; in music, classical, jazz, or country.

Gifts A term used to describe the materials, such as blocks, triangles, and balls of yarn, that Froebel gave to his students.

Goal A general overview of what children are expected to gain from the program.

Golden beads Montessori manipulative materials that represent the decimal system in a concrete way. A single bead is one unit, while rows of ten and cubes of 100 and 1000 beads represent larger units.

Gross motor development Development of skills involving the large muscles of the legs, arms, back, and shoulders, necessary for such tasks as running, jumping, and climbing.

Group size A term that is used to describe the number of children together in a room in an early childhood setting, and that usually differs from the teacher–child ratio.

Guidance Ongoing process of directing children's behaviour based on the types of adults children are expected to become.

Head Start Comprehensive, federally funded early childhood program in the United States, designed for children from poverty backgrounds.

Holding grip Placement of the hands in using a tool for drawing or writing.

Home visit A one-on-one interaction between the teacher and the parent(s) of the child that takes place in the child's home.

Hothousing Term taken from horticulture in which plant growth is quickened by forced fertilization, heat, and light; refers to accelerated learning programs for young children.

Human development theory   A theory that describes what happens as individuals move from infancy through adulthood, identifying significant events experienced by all people and explaining why changes occur as they do.

Hurried child   Term coined by David Elkind to describe children who are rushed into academics and lessons or hothoused in other ways.

Hyperactivity   *See* **Attention deficit-hyperactivity disorder**.

Id   According to Sigmund Freud, a largely unconscious facet of personality that seeks immediate pleasure and gratification.

Ignoring   A principle of behaviour management that involves removing all reinforcement for a given behaviour in order to eliminate that behaviour.

Imagery   A relaxation technique in which a mental image such as "float like a feather" or "melt like ice" is invoked.

Immersion program   A program that involves teaching a second language to children by surrounding or immersing them in that language.

Inductive reasoning   A guidance approach in which the adult helps the child see, through logic and reasoning, the consequences of a behaviour on other people.

Industry vs. inferiority   The fourth stage of development described by Erik Erikson, starting at the end of the preschool years and lasting until puberty, in which the child focuses on development of competence.

Infant   In seven of the twelve provinces and territories, infants are defined as being between 0 and 18 months of age.

Infant school   *See* **British Infant School**.

Infant stimulation program   A compensatory program for infants at risk for developmental delays.

Initiative vs. guilt   The third stage of development described by Erik Erikson, occurring during the preschool years, in which the child's curiosity and enthusiasm lead to a need to explore and learn about the world, and in which rules and expectations begin to be established.

Innatist view of language development   The view that inborn factors are the most important component of language development.

Integrated curriculum   A program that focuses on all aspects of children's development, not just cognitive development.

Integrated day   In the integrated day, there are no lessons at prescribed times because subjects are integrated in activities offered throughout the day.

Interactionist view of language development   The view that language develops through a combination of inborn factors and environmental influences.

Interactionists   Interactionists think that children's development is determined by an interaction of inborn and external factors.

Internalization   When dealing with stress, the child accepts responsibility for dealing with the stressor (*see* **Externation**).

Interpersonal moral rules   Rules considered as universal, including prohibitions against harm to others, murder, incest, and theft.

Interpretive stage   Stage of parenting defined by Ellen Galinsky, typifying the parent of an older preschooler who faces the task of explaining and clarifying the world to the child.

Invented spelling   Used by young children in their early attempts to write by finding the speech sound that most closely fits what they want to convey.

Isolation of a single quality   A Montessori term used to describe how materials are designed to emphasize only one attribute, such as size—as opposed to colour and texture—for the pink tower.

Key experiences In the cognitively oriented curriculum, the eight cognitive concepts on which activities are built.

Kindergarten A German word, literally meaning "garden for children," coined by Friedrich Froebel for his program for young children.

Kinesthetic sense Information from the body's system that provides knowledge about the body, its parts, and its movement; involves the "feel" of movement without reference to visual or verbal cues.

Large-group time (also called circle, story, or group time) Time block(s) during the day when all children and teachers join together in a common activity.

Latch-key or self-care children School-aged children who, after school, return to an empty home because their parents are at work.

Latency stage The fourth stage of development described by Sigmund Freud, occurring during middle childhood, during which sexuality is repressed until adolescence.

Lateralization The division of the human brain, marked by a specialization in analytical and logical tasks in the left half and intuitive and creative functions in the right half.

Learning centre *See* **Activity centre**.

Lesson plan The working document from which the daily program is run, specifying directions for activities.

Locomotion Self-movement from place to place, as in walking.

Logical thinking According to Jean Piaget, the ability that begins to emerge around age 7 in which children use mental processes to solve problems rather than relying solely on perceived information.

Logico-mathematical knowledge One type of knowledge described by Jean Piaget, involving learning about the relationships among objects as well as their relationships in time and space.

Long-term (or permanent) memory In information-processing theory, the vast store of information and knowledge that is held for a long time.

Macrosystem According to ecological theory, the broadest part of the environment, which includes the cultural, political, and economic forces that affect families.

Mainstreaming The integration of children with and without disabilities in a school program.

Malting House School The name of Susan Isaac's famous nursery school in Cambridge, England, where open education was refined and exemplified.

Manipulatives Toys and materials that require the use of the fingers and hands, for instance, puzzles, beads, and pegboards.

Mapping A map-making activity involving spatial relations in which space is represented creatively through such media as marking pens or blocks.

Materials The smaller, often expendable items used in early childhood programs that are replaced and replenished frequently.

Maturation The nature side of the nature–nurture controversy emphasizes maturation, which is the unfolding of inherited potential.

Maturational theory Explanation of human development that depends on information about when children achieve specific skills.

McCarthy Scales of Children's Abilities An intelligence test, particularly used with children who are mildly retarded or who have learning disabilities.

Mean length of utterance (MLU) A measure that calculates the average length of a child's sentences.

Memory strategies   Various approaches used especially by older children and adults to help them remember information.

Mesosystem   According to ecological theory, the linkages between the family and the immediate neighbourhood and community.

Metamemory   The ability to think about one's own memory.

Microsystem   According to ecological theory, that part of the environment that most immediately affects a person, such as the family, school, or workplace.

Mixed-age grouping   Programs in which children of different ages, for instance, 3- to 6-year-olds, are together in one class.

Mock writing   Young children's imitation of writing through wavy, circular, or vertical lines, which can be seen as distinct from drawing or scribbling.

Model   In social learning theory, those whom children imitate, particularly because of some desirable feature or attribute.

Modelling   In social learning theory, the process of imitating a model.

Montessori equipment   Early childhood learning materials derived from and part of the Montessori approach.

Moral development   The long-term process of learning and internalizing the rules and standards of right and wrong.

Morality of autonomy   A sense of morality based on self-integrity.

Morality of obedience   A sence of morality based on doing what one is told to do.

Morpheme   A meaningful part of a word.

Morphology   The study of word rules, for instance, tense, plurals, and possessives.

Movable alphabet   Montessori-designed individual wooden letters that can be combined to form words.

Multilingualism   Ability to use multiple (more than two) languages.

Multimodality   Referring to information that depends on input from several of the senses.

Nanny   A caregiver who comes to the child's home and often lives there.

National Association for the Education of Young Children (NAEYC)   Largest American early childhood professional organization that examines issues associated with children from birth to age 8 and those who work with young children.

National Day Care Study (NDCS)   A study of child care availability in Canada summarized in the *Status of Day Care in Canada 1990* (National Child Care Information Centre, 1991).

Nature   Theorists in the nature camp believe that children's development follows an inborn plan, that is, it is largely determined by heredity.

Negative punishment   The removal of a pleasant stimulus.

Negative reinforcement   The removal of an unpleasant stimulus.

Non-immersion program   An approach to teaching a new language that involves using both the primary and second languages, with a gradual shift from emphasis on the first to the second.

Non-verbal cues   Some of the subtle cues of body language or voice inflection that can give an observer deeper meaning in a record of behaviour.

Norm-referenced   A test in which scores are determined by using a large group of same-age children as the basis for comparison, rather than by using a predetermined criterion or standard of performance.

Norms   A term used to describe what is usual, average, or customary in terms of development, behaviour, or expectations.

Not-for-profit program   Incorporated program or one sponsored by a public entity, such as a church or school, in which profits are put back into the program or returned to the sponsoring agency.

Nuclear family   The smallest family unit, consisting of a couple or one or two parents with children.

Number concept   One of the cognitive concepts young children begin to acquire, involving an understanding of quantity.

Nursery school   A term used to describe a half-day program for preschoolers that has an educational emphasis.

Nurture   Theorists in the nurture camp contend that children's development is affected primarily by external, environmental factors, not heredity.

Object permanence   Part of Jean Piaget's theory, the recognition that objects exist, even when they are out of view; a concept that children begin to develop toward the end of their first year of life.

Objective   An aim; a specific interpretation of general goals, providing a practical and directive tool for day-to-day program planning.

Observable behaviour   Actions that can be seen rather than those that are inferred.

Observational learning   In social learning theory, the process of learning that comes from watching, noting the behaviour of, and imitating models.

One-to-one correspondence   A way in which young preschoolers begin to acquire an understanding of number concepts by matching items to each other, for instance, one napkin beside each plate.

Onlooker play   Category of play involving a child who stands nearby watching others at play, without joining in.

Open education   A program that operates on the assumption that children, when provided with a well-conceived environment, are capable of selecting and learning from appropriate activities.

Open-ended materials   Early childhood materials that are flexible rather than structured and can be used in a variety of ways rather than in only a single manner.

Operant conditioning   The principle of behavioural theory whereby a person deliberately attempts to increase or decrease behaviour by controlling consequences.

Oral stage   The first stage of development described by Sigmund Freud, occurring during infancy, in which pleasure is derived from the mouth.

Organization   According to Jean Piaget, the mental process by which a person organizes experiences and information in relation to each other.

Overextension   Application of a word to a variety of related objects, especially used by toddlers.

Overregularization   A term that describes a child's overuse of grammatical rules. For example, the child who learns to add -s for the plural will use words like mouses, gooses, and sheeps for a short period after first learning the rule.

Palmar grasp   A way of holding tools in which the pencil or crayon lies across the palm of the hand with the fingers curled around it, and the arm rather than the wrist moves the tool.

Parallel play   Category of play in which children use similar materials but do not interact with each other.

Parent-cooperative   A program staffed by one professional teacher and a rotating staff of parents.

Parent education   Programs aimed at enhancing parent–child relations and improving parenting competence.

Parent–teacher conference   A one-on-one interaction between the teacher and the child's parent(s).

Parquetry blocks   Variously shaped flat blocks, including diamonds and parallelograms, that can be assembled into different patterns on a form board.

Perceived competence   Children's belief in their ability to succeed in a given task.

Perceptual motor model   A theoretical view of physical development that holds that motor behaviours are a prerequisite for and lead to cognitive abilities.

Personal control   The feeling that a person has the power to make things happen.

Phallic stage   The third stage of development described by Sigmund Freud, occurring during the preschool years, in which pleasure is derived from the genitals.

Phobia   An intense, irrational fear.

Physical knowledge   One type of knowledge described by Jean Piaget, involving learning about objects in the environment and their properties such as colour, size, weight, and shape.

Pictorialism   According to Rhoda Kellogg, the stage in the development of art in which children draw recognizable objects.

Pink tower   A set of ten pink wooden cubes, developed by Montessori, that vary from 1 cm³ to 10 cm³ and are used to build a tower.

Place identity   Considered part of self-identity because it relates to the environmental context within which a child's needs are met, competence is developed, and control over the physical world is gained.

Placement patterns   According to Rhoda Kellogg, a way of analyzing children's art by examining the seventeen ways in which the total picture or design is framed or placed on the paper.

Plan–do–review cycle   The heart of the cognitively oriented curriculum through which children are encouraged to make deliberate, systematic choices with the help of teachers by planning ahead of time, carrying out, then recalling each day's activities.

Planning time   In the cognitively oriented curriculum, the time set aside during which children decide what activities they would like to participate in during the ensuing work time.

Playscapes   Contemporary, often innovative playground structures that combine a variety of materials.

Pleasure principle   According to Sigmund Freud, the principle of maximizing what is pleasant and avoiding anything unpleasant, which motivates all behaviour.

Positive discipline   Synonymous with guidance, an approach that allows the child to develop self-discipline gradually.

Positive punishment   The addition of an unpleasant stimulus.

Positive reinforcement   The addition of a pleasant stimulus.

Postconventional level of moral development   According to Lawrence Kohlberg, the stage in which moral decisions are made according to universal considerations of what is right.

Practice play   A term used by Piaget to describe repeated actions, such as banging or playing patty-cake, that infants make.

Pragmatics   Rules that govern language use in social contexts.

Preassessment   A form of evaluation given before teaching a specific concept or topic to assess how much children know about it and to compare later how much they have learned.

Preconventional level of moral development   According to Lawrence Kohlberg, the stage during which moral decisions are made based on personal preference or avoidance of punishment.

Predictive validity   A term that means a test is a valid predictor of future events, such as school achievement.

Preoperational period   In Jean Piaget's theory, the second stage of cognitive development, approximately covering the preschool years, in which children are able to use various forms of mental representation but do not yet think logically.

Prepared environment   Maria Montessori's term to describe the careful match between appropriate materials and what the child is most ready to learn at any given time.

Preschematic stage   The stage in the development of art in which children have a subject in mind when they begin a picture, but in which the actual product will be an inaccurate, crude representation of the real thing.

Preschool   A term used to describe a setting for children who are not of elementary school age.

Pretend play   Children's dramatic or symbolic play that involves more than one child in social interaction.

Progressive education   A term used to describe the type of education advocated by John Dewey, who maintained that teachers should use the child's interests and that education should emphasize active learning through real experiences.

Progressive relaxation   A technique in which various specified muscle groups are tensed and relaxed systematically.

Project   Similar to themes because they provide a unifying element around which activities are planned, but projects are more specific. A theme might be titled "Spring," while a related project would be more specific, for example, "What happens at the fishery during spring?"

Prosocial behaviour   Positive, commonly valued social behaviour such as sharing, empathy, or understanding.

Psychoanalytic theory   The branch of psychology founded by Sigmund Freud that focuses on unconscious drives and the importance of the early years to later personality development.

Psychosocial theory   The branch of psychology founded by Erik Erikson, in which development is described in terms of eight stages that span childhood and adulthood, each offering opportunities for personality growth and development.

Punishment   An aversive consequence that follows a behaviour for the purpose of decreasing or eliminating the behaviour; not recommended as an effective means of changing behaviour.

Rating scale   An assessment of specific skills or concepts that are rated on some qualitative dimension of excellence or accomplishment.

Rational counting   Accurately attaching a numeric name to a series of objects being counted.

Reality principle   According to Sigmund Freud, the reality-based principle by which the ego functions to counter the pleasure-seeking goals of the id.

Recall time   In the cognitively oriented curriculum, the time when children review their work-time activities.

Reflective abstraction   According to Jean Piaget, part of a child's self-directed activity that allows the child to think about and reflect on what he or she is doing, leading to the development of new mental abilities.

Rehearsal   The term used to describe mentally repeating information over and over, which is commonly done with phone numbers.

Reinforcement   In behavioural theory, any response following a behaviour that encourages repetition of that behaviour.

Reliability   A measure of a test indicating that the test is stable and consistent; ensures that changes in score are due to the child, not the test.

Representation   According to Jean Piaget, the ability to depict an object, person, action, or experience mentally, even if it is not present in the immediate environment.

Resilient children   Children who, despite extremely stressful lives, appear to be stable, outgoing, and optimistic.

Respect for children   An unusual feature of Montessori's original program.

Restraining order   A court order that prevents someone from seeing someone else.

Rote counting   Reciting numbers from memory in the context of objects in a series, without attaching meaning to them.

Running record   A type of observation that provides an account of all the child's behaviour over a period of time.

Schemata (schema is the singular form)   According to Jean Piaget, cognitive structures into which cognitive concepts or mental representations are organized.

Schematic stage   Stage at which a child's representations become more realistic and accurate.

Screening test   A quick method of identifying children who might exhibit developmental delay; only an indicator that must be followed up with more thorough and comprehensive testing.

Scribbling stage   The stage in the development of art in which children experiment with marks on a page.

Self-care children   *See* **Latch-key children**.

Self-concept   Perceptions and feelings children have about themselves, gathered largely from how the important people in their world respond to them.

Self-correcting materials   Learning materials such as puzzles that give the child immediate feedback on success when the task is completed.

Self-education   A term used by Montessori to describe how a child educates herself or himself through activity in the prepared environment.

Self-esteem   Children's evaluation of their worth in positive or negative terms.

Self-help skills   Tasks involving caring for oneself, such as dressing, feeding, toileting, and grooming.

Self-selected time-out   A technique in which children are given the responsibility for removing themselves from the classroom if they feel they are about to lose control.

Semantic network   The interrelationship among words, particularly related to word meaning.

Semantics   Related to the understanding and study of word meaning.

Senior teacher   The person in charge of a class who is ultimately responsible for all aspects of class functioning.

Sensitive periods   Maria Montessori's term to describe the times when children are most receptive to absorbing specific learning.

Sensitivity   A term related to creativity that refers to receptivity to external and internal stimuli.

Sensorial materials   Learning materials in Montessori classroom area that help children develop, organize, broaden, and refine sensory perceptions of sight, sound, touch, smell, and taste.

Sensorimotor period   In Jean Piaget's theory, the first stage of cognitive development, covering approximately the first 2 years of life, in which the child learns primarily through movement and the senses.

Sensory deficit   A problem, particularly of sight or hearing.

Sensory education   A term used to describe the emphasis Montessori placed on education through the senses.

Sensory integration   The ability to translate sensory information into intelligent behaviour.

Sensory-perceptual development   Giving meaning to information that comes through the senses.

Separation anxiety   Emotional difficulty experienced by some young children when leaving their mothers.

Seriation   A relationship among objects in which they are placed in a logical order, such as from longest to shortest.

Sex cleavage   Distinct separation based on gender, evident in children at a very young age.

Shaping   In behavioural theory, a method used to teach a child a new behaviour by breaking it down into small steps and reinforcing the attainment of each step systematically.

Short-term (or working) memory   Cognitive theory uses the term to describe the limited capacity memory used for temporarily remembering information such as a telephone number.

Show-and-Tell   A common group activity in which children can share something special and personal with their classmates.

Simultaneous language acquisition   A child learning two languages at the same time or before the age of 3.

Small-group activity time   Time set aside for children to work with a teacher in a smaller group than usual.

Social cognition   Organization of knowledge and information about people and relationships.

Social interactionist view of language development   Theoretical view that considers language as closely tied to and dependent on social processes.

Social knowledge   According to Piaget, this knowledge is conveyed by people and defined by culture; it involves the many social rules, morals, and values children must learn in order to function in society

Social learning theory   Theoretical view, derived from but going beyond behaviourism, according to which children learn not just from reinforcement but from observing and imitating others.

Social reinforcer   In behavioural theory, a reward that conveys approval through such responses as a smile, hug, or attention.

Socialization   The process through which children become a functioning part of society and learn society's rules and values.

Software   The "instructions" that direct a computer to perform an activity, usually stored on a disk or directly in the computer; many such programs are available for young children.

Solitary play   Category of play in which a child plays alone, uninvolved with other children.

Sound boxes   Montessori equipment that includes two sets of cylinders, both of which are filled with various materials (e.g., rice, beans, and salt) and then matched by the sounds they make.

Spatial concept   A cognitive ability involving an understanding of how objects and people occupy, move in, and use space.

Spatial relationship   The relative positions of objects and people in space.

Special time   A method for spending a few minutes a day with just one child as a way of providing unconditional attention.

Split brain   The term that describes the brain as having two distinct sides or hemispheres, each with different functions.

Stage theory   Any theory that delineates specific stages in which development is marked by qualitatively different characteristics and accomplishments; each stage builds on the previous one.

Stanford-Binet Intelligence Scale   A widely used test that yields an intelligence quotient (IQ).

Story schema   A term used to describe the regular, predictable structure of simple stories.

Stress   Internal or external demand on a person's ability to adapt.

Successive approximations   Breaking a complex behaviour into smaller steps and reinforcing the child at each step as she or he comes closer to attaining the final behaviour.

Successive language acquisition   Learning a second language after the age of 3.

Summative evaluation   An assessment that follows a specific lesson or unit and determines whether the children have met the objectives.

Superego   According to Sigmund Freud, the facet of personality called the conscience, which is based on the moral norms of society as passed on by parents and other adults.

Surface structure   According to Noam Chomsky, specific aspects of language that vary from one language to another.

Symbolic play   A term used by Piaget to describe play by children who can mentally represent objects and therefore can pretend.

Symbolic representation   The ability acquired by young children to use mental images to stand for something else.

Syntax   Involves the grammatical rules that govern the structure of sentences.

Teacher–child ratio   *See* **Child–adult ratio**.

Team teaching   An approach that involves co-teaching in which status and responsibility are equal rather than having a pyramid structure of authority, with one person in charge and others subordinate.

Temperament   Children's inborn characteristics (e.g., regularity, adaptability, and disposition) that affect behaviour.

Temporal concept   Cognitive ability concerned with the child's gradual awareness of time as a continuum.

Temporal sequencing   The ability to place a series of events in the order of their occurrence.

Theme   Themes, such as spring or community helpers, for example, provide a unifying element around which activities are planned. *See also* **Project**.

Time-away   Technique in which the child is removed from an activity but not from the classroom.

Time-out   A technique in which the child is removed from the reinforcement and stimulation of the classroom.

Time sampling   A quantitative measure or count of how often a specific behaviour occurs within a given amount of time.

Toddler   In the majority of Canadian jurisdictions, toddlers are defined as being between 19 and 35 months of age.

Tonal bells   Two sets of bells (one brown, one white) that children in Montessori programs match by the sound they make.

Tripod grasp   A way of holding tools in which the pencil or crayon is held by the fingers; the wrist, rather than the whole arm, moves the tool.

Trust vs. mistrust   The first stage of development described by Erik Erikson, occurring during infancy, in which the child's needs should be met consistently and predictably.

Unconditional attention   A way of conveying acceptance to children by letting them know they are valued and liked; attention that is not given in response to a specific behaviour.

Unit blocks   The most common type of blocks, precision-made of hard wood in standardized sizes and shapes.

Units   A segment of the curriculum, based on a unifying theme, around which activities are planned.

Unoccupied behaviour   Category of play in which a child moves about the classroom, observing but not getting involved.

Validity   A characteristic of a test that indicates the test actually measures what it purports to measure.

Wechsler Intelligence Scale for Children—III (WISC-III)   An intelligence test for 6- to 16-year-olds that gives a verbal IQ score, a performance IQ score, and an overall IQ score. A score of 100 is average for the WISC-III.

Wechsler Preschool and Primary Scale of Intelligence—Revised (WPPSI)   An intelligence test, like the WISC-III, but for 3- to 7-year-old children.

Whole language approach   Strategy for promoting literacy by surrounding children with high-quality oral and print language.

Work time   In the cognitively oriented curriculum, the large block of time during which children engage in self-selected activities.

REFERENCES

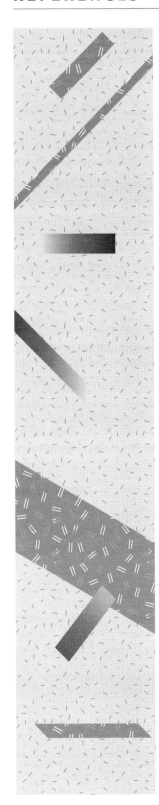

Alexander, N.P. (1986). School-age child care: Concerns and challenges. *Young Children, 42*(1), 3–10.

Alford, B.B., & Bogle, M.L. (1982). *Nutrition during the life cycle.* Englewood Cliffs, NJ: Prentice-Hall.

Alger, H.A. (1984). Transitions: Alternatives to manipulative management techniques. *Young Children, 39*(6), 16–25.

Allen, J. (1988). Children's cognition of stressful events. *Day Care and Early Education, 16*(3), 21–25.

Allen, J., & Pettit, R.B. (1987). Mighty Mouse and MX missiles: Children in a violent society. *Day Care and Early Education, 15*(1), 6–9.

Allen, K.E., & Marotz, L. (1989). *Developmental profiles: Birth to six.* Albany, NY: Delmar.

Almy, M. (1975). *The early childhood educator at work.* New York: McGraw-Hill.

Almy, M., Monighan, P., Scales, B., & Van Hoorn, J. (1984). Recent research on play: The teacher's perspective. In L.G. Katz (Ed.), *Current topics in early childhood education* (vol. 5, pp. 1–26). Norwood, NJ: Ablex Publishing.

Alper, C.D. (1987). Early childhood music education. In C. Seefeldt (Ed.), *The early childhood curriculum: A review of current research* (pp. 211–236). New York: Teachers College Press, Columbia University.

Amabile, T.M., & Gitomer, J. (1984). Children's artistic creativity: Effects of choice in task materials. *Personality and Social Psychology Bulletin, 10,* 209–215.

American Academy of Pediatrics. (1985). *Pediatric Nutrition Handbook* (2nd ed.). Elk Grove Village, IL: American Academy of Pediatrics.

Ames, L.B., Gillespie, C., Haines, J., & Ilg, F.L. (1980). *The child from one to six: Evaluating the behaviour of the preschool child.* London: Hamish Hamilton.

Anastasiow, N. (1988). Should parenting education be mandatory? *Topics in Early Childhood Special Education, 8*(1), 60–72.

Anderson, D.R., & Lorch, E.P. (1983). Looking at television: Action or reaction. In J. Bryant & D.R. Anderson (Eds.), *Understanding TV: Research in children's attention and comprehension* (pp. 1–33). New York: Academic Press.

Andrews, J.H. (1988). Poetry: Tool of the classroom magician. *Young Children, 43*(4), 17–25.

Anthony, S. (1972). *The discovery of death in childhood and after.* New York: Basic Books.

Arent, R.P. (1984). *Stress and your child: A parents' guide to symptoms, strategies and benefits.* Englewood Cliffs, NJ: Prentice-Hall.

Aries, P. (1962). *Centuries of childhood: A social history of family life* (R. Baldick, Trans.). New York: Alfred A. Knopf.

Arnett, J. (1987). *Caregivers in day care centers: Does training matter?* Paper presented at the biennial meeting of the Society for Research in Child Development, Baltimore, MD.

Atkins, C. (1984). Writing: Doing something constructive. *Young Children, 40*(1), 3–7.

Ayers, W. (1989). *The good preschool teacher: Six teachers reflect on their lives.* New York: Teachers College Press, Columbia University.

Baker, B.B. (1982). *The planning board: Ideas for construction and use with young children.* ERIC microfiche, #ED 233801.

Bakst, K., & Essa, E.L. (1990). The writing table: Emergent writers and editors. *Childhood Education, 66*, 145–150.

Bandura, A. (1977). *Social learning theory.* Englewood Cliffs, NJ: Prentice-Hall.

Banta, T. (1969). Research on Montessori and the disadvantaged. In R. Orem (Ed.), *Montessori and the special child.* New York: Putnam.

Baratta-Lorton, M. (1979). *Workjobs: Activity-centred learning for early childhood education.* Menlo Park, CA: Addison-Wesley Publishing Co.

Barnes, B.J. & Hill, S. (1983). Should young children use micro-computers: LOGO before LEGO? *The Computing Teacher, 10*(9), 11–14.

Barrett, D.E. (1986). Behaviour as an outcome in nutrition research. *Nutrition Reviews, 44*, 224–236.

Baumrind, D. (1967). Child care practices anteceding three patterns of preschool behaviour. *Genetic Psychological Monographs, 75*, 43–88.

Baumrind, D., & Black, A.E. (1967). Socialization practices associated with dimensions of competence in preschool boys and girls. *Child Development, 38*, 291–327.

Bayless, K.M., & Ramsey, M.E. (1982). *Music: A way of life for the young child.* St. Louis, MO: C.V. Mosby.

Baynham, P., Russell, L., & Ross, L. (1988). Wages and work experience survey of child care staff in an Ontario community. *The Canadian Journal of Research in Early Childhood Education, 2*(2), 159–164.

Becher, R.M. (1986). Parent involvement: A review of research and principles of successful practice. In L.G. Katz (Ed.), *Current topics in early childhood education* (vol. 6, pp. 85–122). Norwood, NJ: Ablex Publishing.

Bereiter, C. (1967). *Acceleration of intellectual development in early childhood.* Washington, DC: Department of Health, Education, & Welfare, U.S. Office of Education, Bureau of Research.

Bereiter, C. (1986). Does direct instruction cause delinquency? *Early Childhood Research Quarterly, 1*, 289–292.

Bereiter, C., & Engelmann, S. (1966). *Teaching disadvantaged children in the preschool.* Englewood Cliffs, NJ: Prentice-Hall.

Berk, L.E. (1976). How well do classroom practices reflect teacher goals? *Young Children, 32*(1), 64–81.

Berlyne, D. (1969). Laughter, humor, and play. In G. Lindzey & E. Aronson (Eds.), *The handbook of social psychology* (Vol. 3). Reading, MA: Addison-Wesley.

Berns, R.M. (1989). *Child, family, community: Socialization and support* (2nd ed.). New York: Holt, Rinehart and Winston, Inc.

Berrueta-Clement, J.R., Schweinhart, L.J., Barnett, W.S., Epstein, A.S., & Weikart, D.P. (1984). Changed lives: The effects of the Perry preschool program on youths through age 19. *Monographs of the High/Scope Educational Research Foundation, #8.* Ypsilanti, MI: High/Scope Press.

Bijou, S.W., Peterson, R.F., & Ault, M.H. (1968). A method to integrate descriptive and experimental field studies at the level of data and empirical concepts. *Journal of Applied Behaviour Analysis, 1,* 175–191.

Birch, L.L. (1980a). Effects of peer models' food choices and eating behaviours on preschoolers' food preferences. *Child Development, 51,* 489–496.

Birch, L.L. (1980b). Experiential determinants of children's food preferences. In L.G. Katz (Ed.), *Current topics in early childhood education* (vol. 3, pp. 29–46). Norwood, NJ: Ablex Publishing.

Birch, L.L., Marlin, D.W., & Rotter, J. (1984). Eating as the "means" activity in a contingency: Effects on young children's food preferences. *Child Development, 55,* 431–439.

Bjorklund, G., & Burger, C. (1987). Making conferences work for parents, teachers, and children. *Young Children, 42*(3), 26–31.

Blanco, R. (1982). *Prescriptions for children with learning and adjustment problems* (2nd ed.). Springfield, IL: Charles C. Thomas.

Blocks: A creative curriculum for early childhood. (1979). Washington, DC: Creative Associates.

Blom, G.E., Cheney, B.D., & Snoddy, J.E. (1986). *Stress in childhood: An intervention model for teachers and other professionals.* New York: Teachers College Press, Columbia University.

Bloom, B. (1964). *Stability and change in human characteristics.* New York: John Wiley.

Bohannon, J.N., & Warren-Leubecker, A. (1985). Theoretical approaches to language acquisition. In J.B. Gleason (Ed.), *The development of language* (pp. 173–226). Columbus, OH: Charles E. Merrill.

Borstelmann, L.J. (1983). Children before psychology: Ideas about children from antiquity to the late 1800s. In P.H. Mussen (Ed.), *Handbook of child psychology* (4th ed.). *History, theory, and methods* (vol. 1, pp. 1–40). New York: John Wiley.

Bowlby, J. (1951). *Maternal care and mental health.* Geneva: World Health Organization.

Boxhill, N.A. (1989, December). Quoted in S. Landers, Homeless children lose childhood. *The APA Monitor*, pp. 1, 33.

Bradley, R., & Caldwell, B.M. (1984). The relation of infants' home environments to achievement test performance in first grade: A follow-up study. *Child Development, 55*, 803–809.

Braun, S.J., & Edwards, E.P. (1972). *History and theory of early childhood education.* Worthington, OH: Charles A. Jones.

Bredekamp, S. (Ed.). (1987). *Developmentally appropriate practice in early childhood programs serving children from birth through age 8.* Washington, DC: National Association for the Education of Young Children.

Bredekamp, S. Quoted in E.R. Shell (1989, December). Now, which kind of preschool? *Psychology Today*, pp. 52–57.

Bredekamp, S., & Shepard, L. (1989). How best to protect children from inappropriate school expectations, practices, and policies. *Young Children, 44*(3), 14–24.

Brenner, A. (1984). *Helping children cope with stress.* Lexington, MA: Lexington Books.

Brigance, A.H. (1978). *Brigance Diagnostic Inventory of Early Development.* Woburn, MA: Curriculum Associates.

Briggs, B.A., & Walters, C.M. (1985). Single-father families. *Young Children, 40*(3), 23–27.

Briggs, D. (1975). *Your child's self-esteem.* New York: Doubleday.

Bronfenbrenner, U. (1971). Who cares for America's children? *Young Children, 26*(3), 157–163.

Bronfenbrenner, U. (1979). *The ecology of human development.* Cambridge, MA: Harvard University Press.

Bronfenbrenner, U. (1986). Ecology of the family as a context for human development: Research perspectives. *Developmental Psychology, 22*, 723–742.

Bronfenbrenner, U., & Crouter, A.C. (1983). Ecology of the family as a context for human development research perspectives. In P.H. Mussen (Ed.), *Handbook of child psychology* (4th ed.). *History, theory and methods* (vol. 1, pp. 357–414). New York: John Wiley.

Brooks, R.L., & Obrzut, J.E. (1981). Brain lateralization: Implications for infant stimulation and development. *Young Children, 36*(3), 9–16.

Brown, R. (1973). *A first language.* Cambridge, MA: Harvard University Press.

Bruner, J. (1980). *Under five in Britain.* Ypsilanti, MI: High/Scope Press.

Bruner, J., Jolly, A., & Sylva, K. (1976). *Play—Its role in development and evolution.* Markham, ON: Penguin.

Bullock, J. (1986). Teacher–parent conferences: Learning from each other. *Day Care and Early Education, 14*(2), 17–19.

Bundy, B.F. (1989). Effective record keeping. *Day Care and Early Education, 17*(1), 7–9.

Bundy, B.F. (1991). Fostering communication between parents and preschools. *Young Children, 46*(2), 12–17.

Burts, D.C., Hart, C.H., Charlesworth, R., & Kirk, L. (1990). A comparison of frequencies of stress behaviours observed in kindergarten children in classrooms with developmentally appropriate versus developmentally inappropriate instructional practices. *Early Childhood Research Quarterly, 5*, 407–423.

Bushell, D. (1982). The behavior analysis model for early education. In B. Spodek (Ed.), *Handbook of research in early childhood education* (p. 156–184). New York: Free Press.

Buzzelli, C.A., & File, N. (1989). Building trust in friends. *Young Children, 44*(3), 70–75.

Cairns, R.B. (1983). The emergence of developmental psychology. In P.H. Mussen (Ed.), *Handbook of child psychology* (4th ed.). *History, theory, and methods* (vol. 1, pp. 41–102). New York: John Wiley.

Cairns, R., Moore, C., Redshaw, D., & Wilson, T. (1992a). Addendum: Child care in the Northwest Territories, 1988–1990. In A. Pence (Ed.). (1992). *Canadian child care in context: Perspectives from the provinces and territories.* Ottawa: Statistics Canada & Health and Welfare Canada.

Cairns, R., Moore, C., Redshaw, D., & Wilson, T. (1992b). An historical overview of child care in the Northwest Territories. In A. Pence (Ed.), *Canadian child care in context: Perspectives from the provinces and territories.* Ottawa: Statistics Canada & Health and Welfare Canada.

Cairns, R., Moore, C., Redshaw, D., & Wilson, T. (1992c). An overview of child care legislation in the Northwest Territories. In A. Pence (Ed.), *Canadian child care in context: Perspectives from the provinces and territories.* Ottawa: Statistics Canada & Health and Welfare Canada.

Cairns, R., Moore, C., Redshaw, D., & Wilson, T. (1992d). A socio-geographic overview of the Northwest Territories. In A. Pence (Ed.), *Canadian child care in context: Perspectives from the provinces and territories.* Ottawa: Statistics Canada & Health and Welfare Canada.

Caldwell, B.M. (1968). The fourth dimension in early childhood education. In R.D. Hess & R.M. Bear (Eds.) *Early Education.* Chicago: Aldine Press.

Caldwell, B.M. (1971). Impact of interest in early cognitive stimulation. In H. Rie (Ed.), *Perspectives in child psychopathology.* New York: Aldine-Atherton.

Caldwell, B.M. (1973a). What does research teach us about day care? *Young Children, 29*, 197–208.

Caldwell, B.M. (1973b). Infant day care—the outcast gains respectability. In P. Roby (Ed.), *Child Care—Who Cares?* New York: Basic Books.

Caldwell, B.M. (1977). Aggression and hostility in young children. *Young Children, 32*(2), 4–13.

Caldwell, B., & Bradley, R. (1979). *Home observation of the environment.* Little Rock: University of Arkansas Press.

Canadian Child Day Care Federation (1991). *National statement on quality child care.* Ottawa, ON: Author.

Canadian Child Day Care Federation & Canadian Day Care Advocacy Association (1992). *Caring for a living: Executive summary.* Ottawa, ON: Author.

Canning, P., & Irwin, S. (1992). A socio-geographic overview of Nova Scotia. In A. Pence (Ed.), *Canadian child care in context: Perspectives from the provinces and territories.* Ottawa: Statistics Canada & Health and Welfare Canada.

Canning, P., Irwin, S., & Lewis, L. (1992). An overview of child care legislation in Nova Scotia. In A. Pence (Ed.), *Canadian child care in context: Perspectives from the provinces and territories.* Ottawa: Statistics Canada & Health and Welfare Canada.

Caplan, F., & Caplan, T. (1974). *The power of play.* New York: Anchor Press.

Carlsson-Paige, N., & Levin, D.E. (1985). *Helping young children understand peace, war, and the nuclear threat.* Washington, DC: National Association for the Education of Young Children.

Carlsson-Paige, N., & Levin, D.E. (1990). *Who's calling the shots? How to respond effectively to children's fascination with war play and war toys.* Philadelphia, PA: New Society Publishers.

Carrière, Y. (1992). A socio-geographic overview of Quebec. In A. Pence (Ed.), *Canadian child care in context: Perspectives from the provinces and territories.* Ottawa: Statistics Canada & Health and Welfare Canada.

Carter, D.B. (1987). Early childhood education: A historical perspective. In J.L. Roopnarine & J.E. Johnson (Eds.), *Approaches to early childhood education* (pp. 1–14). Columbus, OH: Merrill Publishing.

Cartwright, S. (1990). Learning with large blocks. *Young Children, 45*(3), 38–41.

Cartwright, C.A., & Cartwright, G.P. (1974). *Developing observation skills.* New York: McGraw-Hill.

Casler, L. (1961). Maternal deprivation: A critical review of the literature. *Monographs of the Society for Research in Child Development, 26* (2, Serial No. 80).

Cass, J.E. (1973). *Helping children grow through play.* New York: Schocken Books.

Cataldo, C.Z. (1987). *Parent education for early childhood: Child-rearing concepts and program content for the student and practicing professional.* New York: Teachers College Press, Columbia University.

Chafel, J.A. (1990). Children in poverty: Policy perspectives on a national crisis. *Young Children, 45*(5), 31–37.

Charlesworth, R., & Lind, K.K. (1990). *Math and science for young children.* Albany, NY: Delmar.

Chattin-McNichols, J.P. (1981). The effects of Montessori school experience. *Young Children, 36*(5), 49–66.

Chattin-McNichols, J. (1992). *The Montessori controversy.* Albany, NY: Delmar.

Child Care Resource Unit (1990). *Child care information sheets.* Toronto, ON: Centre for Urban and Community Studies, University of Toronto.

Childcare Resource Unit (1993, May). *What's happening in child care policy: A cross Canada overview.* Paper presented at the Canadian Child Care Federation's third National Child Care Conference.

Chomsky, N. (1972). *Language and mind.* New York: Harcourt Brace Jovanovich.

Christie, J.F. (1982). Sociodramatic play training. *Young Children, 37*(4), 25–32.

Christie, J.F., Johnsen, E.P., & Peckover, R.B. (1988). The effects of play period duration on children's play patterns. *Journal of Research in Early Childhood, 3,* 123–131.

Ciaranello, R.D. (1983). Neurochemical aspects of stress. In N. Garmezy & M. Rutter (Eds.), *Stress, coping and development in children* (pp. 85–105). New York: McGraw-Hill.

Cicirelli, V. (1969). *The impact of Head Start: An evaluation of the effects of Head Start on children's cognitive and affective development.* Athens, OH: Westinghouse Learning.

Clark, E.V. (1978a). Non-linguistic strategies and the acquisition of word meaning. In L. Bloom (Ed.), *Readings in language development* (pp. 433–451). New York: John Wiley.

Clark, E.V. (1978b). Strategies for communicating. *Child Development, 49,* 953–959.

Clarke-Stewart, A. (1988). The "effects" of infant day care reconsidered. *Early Childhood Research Quarterly, 3,* 293–318.

Clarke-Stewart, K.A. (1983). Exploring the assumptions of parent education. In R. Haskins & D. Adams (Eds.), *Parent education and public policy* (pp. 257–276). Norwood, NJ: Ablex Publishing.

Clarke-Stewart, K.A. (1984). Day care: A new context for research and development. In M. Perlmutter (Ed.), *Parent–child interaction and parent–child relations in child development: The Minnesota symposia on child psychology* (vol. 17, pp. 61–100). Hillsdale, NJ: Lawrence Erlbaum.

Clarke-Stewart, K.A. (1987a). In search of consistencies in child care research. In D.A. Phillips (Ed.), *Quality in child care: What does research tell us?* (pp. 105–120). Washington, DC: National Association for the Education of Young Children.

Clarke-Stewart, K.A. (1987b). Predicting child development from child care forms and features: The Chicago Study. In D.A. Phillips (Ed.), *Qualty in child care: What does research tell us?* (pp. 21–41). Washington, DC: National Association for the Education of Young Children.

Clarke-Stewart, K.A. (1988). Evolving issues in early childhood education: A personal perspective. *Early Childhood Research Quarterly, 3,* 13–19.

Clarke-Stewart, K.A., (1989). Infant day care: Maligned or malignant? *American Psychologist, 44,* 266–273.

Clarke-Stewart, K.A., & Fein, G. (1983). Early childhood programs. In P.H. Mussen (Ed.), *Handbook of child psychology* (4th ed.). *Infancy and developmental psychobiology* (vol. 2, pp. 917–1000). New York: John Wiley.

Clarke-Stewart, K.A., & Gruber, C. (1984). Daycare forms and features. In R.C. Ainslie (Ed.), *Quality variations in daycare* (pp. 35–62). New York: Praeger.

Clemens, S.G. (1991). Art in the classroom: Making every day special. *Young Children, 46*(2), 4–11.

Clements, D.H. (1987). Computers and young children: A review of research. *Young Children, 43*(1), 34–44.

Click, P.M., & Click, D.W. (1990). *Administration of schools for young children* (3rd ed.). Albany, NY: Delmar.

Clifford, Howard (1992). Foreword. In A. Pence (Ed.), *Canadian child care in context: Perspectives from the provinces and territories* (pp. xiii–xvii). Ottawa: Statistics Canada & Health and Welfare Canada.

Cochran, M. (1988). Between cause and effect: The ecology of program impacts. In A.R. Pence (Ed.), *Ecological research with children and families: From concepts to methodology* (pp. 143–169). New York: Teachers College Press, Columbia University.

Cohen, D.H., & Stern, V. (1978). *Observing and recording the behavior of young children* (2nd ed.). New York: Teachers College Press, Columbia University.

Cole, E., & Schaefer, C. (1990). Can young children be art critics? *Young Children, 45*(2), 33–38.

Coleman, M., & Skeen, P. (1985). Play, games, and sports: Their use and misuse. *Childhood Education, 61,* 192–198.

Coleman, J.S., et al. (1966). *Equality of Educational Opportunity.* Washington, DC: United States Government Printing Office.

Comenius, J. (1967). *The great didactic* (M.W. Keating, Ed. & Trans.). New York: Russell & Russell. (Original work published 1896 & 1910)

Cook, R.E., Tessier, A., & Armbruster, V.B. (1987). *Adapting early childhood curricula for children with special needs.* Columbus, OH: Merrill Publishing.

Copple, C.E., DeLisi, R., & Sigel, E. (1982). Cognitive development. In B. Spodek (Ed.), *Handbook of research in early childhood education* (pp. 3–26). New York: Free Press.

Cosgrove, M.S. (1991). Cooking in the classroom: The doorway to nutrition. *Young Children, 46*(3), 43–45.

Cox, M.V. (1986). *The child's point of view: The development of cognition and language.* New York: St. Martin's Press.

Cratty, B.J. (1982). Motor development in early childhood: Critical issues for researchers in the 1980s. In B. Spodek (Ed.), *Handbook of research in early childhood education* (pp. 27–46). New York: Free Press.

Critics Challenge. (1993, Feb. 24). Critics Challenge proposed program for pre-schoolers. *The St. Catharines Standard,* p. 8.

Culture and children. (1985). Austin, TX: Texas Department of Human Resources.

Curtis, S.R. (1987). New views on movement development and the implications for curriculum in early childhood. In C. Seefeldt (Ed.), *The early childhood curriculum: A review of current research* (pp. 257–270). New York: Teachers College Press, Columbia University.

Daehler, M.W., & Bukatko, D. (1985). *Cognitive development*. New York: Alfred A. Knopf.

Dale, P. *Language development* (1976) (2nd ed.). New York: Holt, Rinehart & Winston.

Damon, W. (1977). *The social world of the child*. San Francisco: Jossey-Bass.

Damon, W. (1983). The nature of social-cognitive change in the developing child. In W.F. Overton (Ed.), *The relationship between social and cognitive development* (pp. 103–141). Hillsdale, NJ: Lawrence Erlbaum.

Davidson, J.I. (1982). Wasted time: The ignored dilemma. In J.F. Brown (Ed.), *Curriculum planning for young children* (pp. 196–204). Washington, DC: National Association for the Education of Young Children.

Davidson, J.I. (1989). *Children and computers together in the early childhood classroom*. Albany, NY: Delmar Publishers Inc.

Day care, families, and stress: A day care provider's guide. (1985) Austin, TX: Child Development Program Division, Texas Department of Human Resources.

Debelack, M., Herr, J., & Jacobson, M. (1981). *Creating innovative classroom materials for teaching young children*. New York: Harcourt Brace Jovanovich Inc.

Deiner, P.L. (1983). *Resources for teaching young children with special needs*. New York: Harcourt Brace Jovanovich.

Delacato, C.H. (1964). *The Diagnosis and Treatment of Speech and Reading Problems*. Springfield, IL: Thomas Publishers.

Delacato, C.H. (1966). *Neurological Organization and Reading*. Springfield, IL: Thomas Publishers.

deMause, L. (Ed.). (1974). *The history of childhood*. New York: Harper & Row.

Derman-Sparks, L. (1989). *Anti-bias curriculum: Tools for empowering young children*. Washington, DC: National Association for the Education of Young Children.

Derman-Sparks, L., Higa, C.T., & Sparks, B. (1980). Children, race and racism: How race awareness develops. *Interracial Books for Children Bulletin, 11*(3–4), 3–9.

Derman-Sparks, L., & Ramsey, P. (1993). Early childhood multicultural, anti-bias education in the 1990s: Toward the 21st century. In J.L. Roopnarine & J.E. Johnson (Eds.), *Approaches to early childhood education* (2nd ed., pp. 47–70). New York: Merrill.

Desjardins, G. (1992). An historical overview of child care in Quebec. In A. Pence (Ed.), *Canadian child care in context: Perspectives from the provinces and territories*. Ottawa: Statistics Canada & Health and Welfare Canada.

deVilliers, J.G., & deVilliers, P.A. (1973). A cross-sectional study of the acquisition of grammatical morphemes in child speech. *Journal of Psycho-linguistic Research, 2,* 267–278.

deVilliers, P.A., & deVilliers, J.G. (1979). *Early language.* Cambridge, MA: Harvard University Press.

Dewey, J. (1897). *My pedagogic creed.* Washington, DC: The Progressive Education Association.

Dewey, J. (1900). *The school and society.* New York: McLure, Phillips & Company.

Dewey, J. (1902). *The child and the curriculum.* Chicago, IL: University of Chicago Press.

Dill, N. (1992). Addendum: Child care in Saskatchewan, 1988–1990. In A. Pence (Ed.), *Canadian child care in context: Perspectives from the provinces and territories.* Ottawa: Statistics Canada & Health and Welfare Canada.

Dimidjian, V.J. (1989). Holidays, holy days, and wholly dazed: Approaches to special days. *Young Children, 44*(6), 70–74.

Dinkmeyer, D., & McKay, G.D. (1976). *Systematic training for effective parenting: Parent's handbook.* Circle Pines, MN: American Guidance Services.

Doman, R.J., Spitz, E.B., Zucman, E., & Delacato, C.H. (1960). Children with severe brain injuries: Neurological organization in terms of mobility. *Journal of the American Medical Association, 174,* 257–262.

Douvan, E. (1990). Psychoanalytic theory of human development. In R.M. Thomas (Ed.), *The encyclopedia of human development and education: Theory, research, and studies* (pp. 83–88). New York: Pergamon Press.

Doxey, I. (1990). The Canadian child. In I. Doxey (Ed.), *Child care and education: Canadian dimensions* (pp. 3–12). Toronto: Nelson Canada.

Doyle, A.B., & Connolly, J. (1989). Negotiation and enactment in social pretend play: Relations to social acceptance and social cognition. *Early Childhood Research Quarterly, 4,* 289–302.

Doyle, A.B., Gold, D., & Moskowitz, D.S. (Eds.). (1984). *Children and families under stress.* San Francisco, CA: Jossey-Bass.

Drabman, R.S., Cordua, G.D., Hammer, D., Jarvie, G.J., & Horton, W. (1979). Developmental trends in eating rates of normal and overweight preschool children. *Child Development, 50,* 211–216.

Dresden, J., & Myers, B.K. (1989). Early childhood professionals: Toward self-definition. *Young Children, 44*(2), 62–66.

Dunst, C.J., & Trivette, C.M. (1988). Toward experimental evaluation of the family, infant, and preschool program. In H.B. Weiss & F.H. Jacobs (Eds.), *Evaluating family programs* (pp. 315–346). New York: Aldine de Gruyter.

Edwards, C.P. (1986). *Promoting social and moral development in young children.* New York: Teachers College Press, Columbia University.

Elkind, D. (1981). *The hurried child: Growing up too fast too soon.* Reading, MA: Addison-Wesley.

Elkind, D. (1983). Montessori education: Abiding contributions and contemporary challenges. *Young Children, 38*(2), 3–10.

Elkind, D. (1986). Formal education and early childhood education: An essential difference. *Phi Delta Kappan, 67,* 631–636.

Elkind, D. (1987a). The child yesterday, today, and tomorrow. *Young Children, 42*(4), 6–11.

Elkind, D. (1987b). *Miseducation: Preschoolers at risk.* New York: Alfred A. Knopf.

Elkind, D. (1988). The resistance to developmentally appropriate educational practice with young children: The real issue. In C. Warger (Ed.), *A resource guide to public school early childhood programs* (pp. 53–62). Alexandria, VA: Association for Supervision and Curriculum Development.

Elkind, D. (1990). Academic pressures—too much, too soon: The demise of play. In E. Klugman & S. Smilansky (Eds.), *Children's play and learning* (pp. 3–17). New York: Teachers College Press.

Employment and Immigration Canada (1992). *Labour market information.* St. Catharines, ON: Author.

Eriksen, A. (1985). Playground design: Outdoor environments for learning and development. New York: Van Nostrand Reinhold Co.

Erikson, E.H. (1963). *Childhood and society* (2nd ed.). New York: Norton.

Esbensen, S. (1990). Designing the early childhood setting. In I. Doxey (Ed.), *Child care and education: Canadian dimensions* (pp. 178–192). Toronto, ON: Nelson Canada.

Essa, E.L. (1981). An outdoor play area designed for learning. *Day Care and Early Education. 9*(2), 37–42.

Essa, E.L. (1987). The effect of a computer on preschool children's activities. *Early Childhood Research Quarterly, 2,* 377–382.

Essa, E.L. (1990). *Practical guide to solving preschool behaviour problems* (2nd ed.). Albany, NY: Delmar.

Essa, E.L., Hilton, J.M., & Murray, C.I. (1990). The relationship of weather and preschool children's behaviour. *Children's Environments Quarterly, 7*(3), 32–36.

Essa, E.L., & Rogers, P.R. (1992). *An early childhood curriculum: From developmental model to application.* Albany, NY: Delmar.

Ethics Commission. (1987). Ethics case studies: The working mother. *Young Children, 43*(1), 16–19.

Evans, E.D. (1975). *Contemporary influences in early childhood education* (2nd ed.). New York: Holt, Rinehart & Winston.

Evans, E.D. (1982). Curriculum models and early childhood education. In B. Spodek (Ed.), *Handbook of research in early childhood education* (pp. 107–134). New York: Free Press.

Evans, E.D. (1984). Children's aesthetics. In L.G. Katz (Ed.), *Current topics in early childhood education* (vol. 5, pp. 73–104). Norwood, NJ: Ablex Publishing.

Faust, V., Weidmann, M., & Wehner, W. (1974). The influence of meteorological factors on children and youths. *Acta Paedopsychiatrica, 40,* 150–156.

Feeney, S. (1988). Ethics case studies: The divorced parents. *Young Children, 43*(3), 48–49.

Feeney, S. (1988). Ethics case studies: The aggressive child. *Young Children, 43*(2), 48–51.

Feeney, S., & Chun, R. (1985). Effective teachers of young children. *Young Children, 41*(1), 47–52.

Feeney, S., & Kipnis, K. (1985). Professional ethics in early childhood education. *Young Children, 40*(3), 54–56.

Feeney, S., Christensen, D., & Moravcik, E. (1991). *Who am I in the lives of young children?* New York: Merrill.

Feeney, S., & Moravcik, E. (1987). A thing of beauty: Aesthetic development in young children. *Young Children, 42*(6), 7–15.

Fein, G.G. (1979). Play and the acquisition of symbols. In L.G. Katz (Ed.), *Current topics in early childhood education* (vol. 2, pp. 195–225). Norwood, NJ: Ablex Publishing.

Fein, G.G. (1982). Pretend play: New perspectives. In J.F. Brown (Ed.), *Curriculum planning for young children* (pp. 22–27). Washington, DC: National Association for the Education of Young Children.

Fein, G.G., & Clarke-Stewart, A. (1973). *Day care in context.* New York: John Wiley.

Fein, G.G., & Fox, N. (1988). Infant day care: A special issue. *Early Childhood Research Quarterly, 3,* 227–234.

Fein, G.G., & Schwartz, P.M. (1982). Developmental theories in early education. In B. Spodek (Ed.), *Handbook of research in early childhood education* (pp. 82–104). New York: Free Press.

Ferber, R. (1985). *Solve your child's sleep problems.* New York: Simon & Shuster.

Fernandez, J.P. (1986). *Child care and corporate productivity.* Lexington, MA: Lexington Books.

Finkelstein, B. (1988). The revolt against selfishness: Women and the dilemmas of professionalism in early childhood education. In B. Spodek, O.N. Saracho, & D.L. Peters (Ed.), *Professionalism and the early childhood practitioner* (pp. 10–28). New York: Teachers College Press, Columbia University.

Flack, M. (1931). *Angus and the cat.* New York: Doubleday.

Flanagan-Rochon, K.F. (1992a). Addendum: Child care in Prince Edward Island, 1988–1990. In A. Pence (Ed.), *Canadian child care in context: Perspectives from the provinces and territories.* Ottawa: Statistics Canada & Health and Welfare Canada.

Flanagan-Rochon, K.F. (1992b). An overview of child care legislation in Prince Edward Island. In A. Pence (Ed.), *Canadian child care in context: Perspectives from the provinces and territories.* Ottawa: Statistics Canada & Health and Welfare Canada.

Flanagan-Rochon, K.F., & Rice, C. (1992). An historical overview of child care in Prince Edward Island. In A. Pence (Ed.), *Canadian child care in context: Perspectives from the provinces and territories.* Ottawa: Statistics Canada & Health and Welfare Canada.

Flaste, R. (1991, April 28). Sidelined by loneliness. *New York Times Magazine*, pp. 14–15, 23–24.

Fleming, W.G. (1971). *Ontario's educative society* (Vol. 5). *Supporting institutions and services.* Toronto: University of Toronto Press.

Flerx, V.C., Fidler, D.S., & Rogers, R.W. (1976). Sex role stereotypes: Developmental aspects and early intervention. *Child Development, 67,* 998–1007.

Fogel, A. (1991). *Infancy: Infant, family, and society* (2nd ed.). St. Paul., MN: West Publishing.

Forman, G.E., & Kaden, M. (1987). Research on science education for young children. In C. Seefeldt (Ed.), *The early childhood curriculum: A review of current research* (pp. 141–164). New York: Teachers College Press, Columbia University.

Forman, G.E., & Kuschner, D.S. (1977). *The child's construction of knowledge: Piaget for teaching children.* Monterey, CA: Brooks/Cole.

Fowler, W. (1971). *Demonstration program in infant care and education: Final report.* Toronto, ON: Ontario Institute for Studies in Education, University of Toronto.

Fowler, W. (1972). A developmental learning approach to infant care in a group setting. *Merrill-Palmer, 18,* 145–175.

Fowler, W. (1973). *The development of a prototype infant, preschool and child daycare centre in Metropolitan Toronto: Year II Progress Report.* Toronto, ON: Ontario Institute for Studies in Education, University of Toronto.

Fowler, W. (1974, June). *From intuitive to rational humanism: The comparative effects of group and home care on infant development.* Paper presented at the annual meeting of the Canadian Psychological Association, Windsor.

Fowler, W. (1978). *Day care and its effects on early development: A study of group and home care in multi-ethnic. working-class families* (Research in Education Series, No. 8). Toronto, ON: Ontario Institute for Studies in Education, University of Toronto.

Fowler, W., & Khan, N. (1974, April). *A follow-up investigation of the late development of infants in enriched group care.* Paper presented at the annual meeting of the American Education Research Association, Chicago.

Frankenburg, W.K., Dodds, J.B., Fandal, A.W., Kajuk, F., & Cohr, M. (1975). *Denver Developmental Screening Test: Revised reference manual.* Denver: LADOCA Foundation.

Frazier, A. (1980). Making a curriculum for children. *Childhood Education, 56,* 258–263.

Friedman, D. (1989, August). A more sophisticated employer response to child care. *Child Care Information Exchange,* pp. 29–31.

Friesen, J. (1992). An overview of child care legislation in Manitoba. In A. Pence (Ed.), *Canadian child care in context: Perspectives from the provinces and territories.* Ottawa: Statistics Canada & Health and Welfare Canada.

Friesen, J., Humphrey, M., & Brockman, L.M. (1992a). Addendum: Child care in Manitoba, 1988–1990. In A. Pence (Ed.), *Canadian child care in context: Perspectives from the provinces and territories.* Ottawa: Statistics Canada & Health and Welfare Canada.

Friesen, J., Humphrey, M., & Brockman, L.M. (1992b). An historical overview of child care in Manitoba. In A. Pence (Ed.), *Canadian child care in context: Perspectives from the provinces and territories.* Ottawa: Statistics Canada & Health and Welfare Canada.

Froschl, M., Colon, L., Rubin, E., & Sprung, B. (1984). *Including all of us: An early childhood curriculum about disability.* New York: Educational Equity Concepts.

Frost, J.L., & Henniger, M.L. (1982). Making playgrounds safe for children and children safe for playgrounds. In J.F. Brown (Ed.), *Curriculum planning for young children* (pp. 48–55). Washington, DC: National Association for the Education of Young Children.

Frost, J.L., & Klein, B.L. (1979). *Children's play and playgrounds.* Boston: Allyn and Bacon, Inc.

Frost, J.L., & Wortham, S.C. (1988). The evolution of American playgrounds. *Young Children, 43*(5), 19–28.

Fullum, H. (1992a). Addendum: Child care in Quebec, 1988–1990. In A. Pence (Ed.), *Canadian child care in context: Perspectives from the provinces and territories.* Ottawa: Statistics Canada & Health and Welfare Canada.

Fullum, H. (1992b). An overview of child day care legislation in Quebec. In A. Pence (Ed.), *Canadian child care in context: Perspectives from the provinces and territories.* Ottawa: Statistics Canada & Health and Welfare Canada.

Furman, E. (1982). Helping children cope with death. In J.F. Brown (Ed.), *Curriculum planning for young children* (pp. 238–245). Washington, DC: National Association for the Education of Young Children.

Furman, E. (1987). More protection, fewer directions. *Young Children, 42*(5), 5–7.

Furth, H.G. (1969). *Piaget and knowledge: Theoretical foundations.* Englewood Cliffs, NJ: Prentice-Hall.

Galdone, P. (1973). *The little red hen.* New York: Seabury.

Galinsky, E. (1981). *Between generations: The six stages of parenthood.* New York: Times Books.

Galinsky, E. (1988). Parents and teacher-caregivers: Sources of tension, sources of support. *Young Children, 43*(3), 4–12.

Galinsky, E. (1989). Update on employer-supported child care. *Young Children, 44*(6), 2, 75–77.

Galinsky, E. (1990). Why are some parent/teacher partnerships clouded with difficulties? *Young Children, 45*(5), 2–3, 38–40.

Gallagher, J.M., & Coche, J. (1987). Hothousing: The clinical and educational concerns over pressuring young children. *Early Childhood Research Quarterly, 2*, 203–210.

Gamble, J. (1992a). An historical overview of child care in New Brunswick. In A. Pence (Ed.), *Canadian child care in context: Perspectives from the provinces and territories.* Ottawa: Statistics Canada & Health and Welfare Canada.

Gamble, J. (1992b). A socio-geographic overview of New Brunswick. In A. Pence (Ed.), *Canadian child care in context: Perspectives from the provinces and territories.* Ottawa: Statistics Canada & Health and Welfare Canada.

Garbarino, J. (1990, June). Child abuse: Why? *The World and I,* pp. 543–553.

Garcia C., Kagan, J., & Reznick, J.S. (1984). Behavioural inhibition in young children. *Child Development, 55,* 1005–1019.

Garcia, E.E. (1982). Bilingualism in early childhood. In J.F. Brown (Ed.), *Curriculum planning for young children* (pp. 82–101). Washington, DC: National Association for the Education of Young Children

Gardner, D. (1949). *Education under eight.* London: Methuen.

Gardner, H. (1982). *Art, mind, and brain: A cognitive approach to creativity.* New York: Basic Books.

Gardner, H. (1989). Learning, Chinese-style. *Psychology Today, 23*(12), 54–56.

Garmezy, N. (1984). Stressors of childhood. In N. Garmezy & M. Rutter (Eds.), *Stress, coping and development in children* (pp. 43–84). New York: McGraw-Hill.

Garn, S.M., & Clark, D.C. (1976). Trends in fatness and the origins of obesity. *Pediatrics, 57,* 443–456.

Gartrell, D. (1987). Punishment or guidance? *Young Children, 42*(3), 55–61.

Geller, L.G. (1985). *Word play and language learning for children.* Urbana, IL: National Council of Teachers of English.

Gelman, R., & Gallistel, C.R. (1978). *The child's understanding of number.* Cambridge, MA: Harvard University Press.

Genishi, C. (1982). Observational research methods for early childhood education. In B. Spodek (Ed.), *Handbook of research in early childhood education* (pp. 564–591). New York: Free Press.

Gersten, R. (1986). Response to "Consequences of three preschool curriculum models through age 15." *Early Childhood Research Quarterly, 1,* 293–302.

Gesell. A, (1923). *The preschool child: From the standpoint of public hygiene and education.* Houghton Mifflin.

Gesell, A. (1928). *Infancy and human growth.* New York: Macmillan.

Gestwicki, C. (1987). *Home, school, and community relations: A guide to working with parents.* Albany, NY: Delmar.

Gettman, D. (1987). *Basic Montessori: Learning activities for under-fives.* New York: St. Martin's Press.

Gibson, L. (1989). *Through children's eyes: Literacy learning in the early years.* New York: Teachers College Press, Columbia University.

Gilkeson, E., & Bowman, G. (1976). *The focus is on children: The Bank Street approach to childhood education as enacted in Follow Through.* New York: Bank Street College of Education.

Gilmore, B. (1971). Play: A special behavior. In R. Haber (Ed.), *Current research in motivation* (pp. 343–355). New York: Harper.

Gineshi, C. (1987). Acquiring oral language and communicative competence. In C. Seefeldt (Ed.), *The early childhood curriculum: A review of current research* (pp. 75–106). New York: Teachers College Press, Columbia University.

Ginsburg, H., & Opper, S. (1969). *Piaget's theory of intellectual development: An introduction.* Englewood Cliffs, NJ: Prentice-Hall.

Glassman, M. (1992a). An historical overview of child care in Newfoundland. In A. Pence (Ed.), *Canadian child care in context: Perspectives from the provinces and territories.* Ottawa: Statistics Canada & Health and Welfare Canada.

Glassman, M. (1992b). A socio-geographic overview of Newfoundland. In A. Pence (Ed.), *Canadian child care in context: Perspectives from the provinces and territories.* Ottawa: Statistics Canada & Health and Welfare Canada.

Glazer, J.I. (1986). *Literature for young children* (2nd ed.). Columbus, OH: Charles E. Merrill.

Gleason, J.B. (1985). Studying language development. In J.B. Gleason (Ed.), *The development of language* (pp. 1–35). Columbus, OH: Charles E. Merrill.

Goelman, H. (1988). The relationship between structure and process variables in home and day care settings on children's language development. In A.R. Pence (Ed.), *Ecological research with children and families: From concepts to methodology* (pp. 16–34). New York: Teachers College Press, Columbia University.

Goelman, H., & Pence, A. (1990). The Victoria and Vancouver research projects. In Doxey, I. (Ed.), *Child care and education: Canadian dimensions* (pp. 269–277). Toronto: Nelson Canada.

Goffin, S.G. (1987). Cooperative behaviours: They need our support. *Young Children, 42*(2), 75–81.

Goldfarb, W. (1943). The effects of early institutional care on adolescent personality. *Journal of Experimental Education, 12*, 106–129.

Good discipline is, in large part, the result of a fantastic curriculum! (1987). *Young Children, 42*(3), 49.

Goodman, Y.M. (1986). Children coming to know literacy. In W.H. Teale & E. Sulzby (Eds.), *Emergent literacy: Writing and reading* (pp. 1–14). Norwood, NJ: Ablex Publishing.

Goodman, K.S., Smith, E.B., Meredith, R., & Goodman, Y.M. (1987). *Language and thinking in school: A whole-language curriculum* (3rd ed.). New York: Richard C. Owen.

Goodwin, W.L., & Goodwin, L.D. (1982). Measuring young children. In B. Spodek (Ed.), *Handbook of research in early childhood education* (pp. 523–563). New York: Free Press.

Goodz, N.S. (1982). Is before really easier to understand than after? *Child Development, 53*, 822–825.

Gordon, A.M., & Browne, K.W. (1989). *Beginnings and beyond: Foundations in early childhood education* (2nd ed.). Albany, NY: Delmar.

Gordon, A.M., & Browne, K.W. (1993). *Beginnings and beyond: Foundations in early childhood education* (3rd ed.). Albany, NY: Delmar.

Gordon, I. (1967, June). *The young child: A new look.* Paper presented at the conference on The Young Child: Florida's Future, University of Florida.

Gordon, T. (1976). *P.E.T. in action.* New York: Peter H. Wyden.

Gottfried, A. (1984). Home environment and early cognitive development: Integration, meta-analyses, and conclusions. In A. Gottfried (Ed.), *Home environment and early cognitive development.* San Francisco: Academic Press.

Gould, R.L. (1978). *Transformations: Growth and change in adult life.* New York: Simon & Schuster.

Graue, M.E., & Shepard, L.A. (1989). Predictive validity of the Gesell School Readiness Test. *Early Childhood Research Quarterly, 4*, 303–315.

Greenberg, P. (1987). Lucy Sprague Mitchell: A major missing link between early childhood education in the 1980s and progressive education in the 1890s–1930s. *Young Children, 42*(5), 70–84.

Greenleaf, P. (1978). *Children throughout the ages: A history of childhood.* New York: Barnes & Noble.

Greenwood-Church, M., & Crozier-Smith, D., (1992). A socio-geographic overview of Alberta. In A. Pence (Ed.), *Canadian child care in context: Perspectives from the provinces and territories.* Ottawa: Statistics Canada & Health and Welfare Canada.

Griffin, E.F. (1982). *Island of childhood: Education in the special world of nursery school.* New York: Teachers College Press, Columbia University.

Griffin, S. (1992). Addendum: Child care in British Columbia, 1988–1990. In A. Pence (Ed.), *Canadian child care in context: Perspectives from the provinces and territories* (pp. 87–99). Ottawa: Statistics Canada & Health and Welfare Canada.

Grimsley, R. (1976). Jean-Jacques Rousseau. In P. Edwards (Ed.), *The encyclopedia of philosophy* (vols. 7–8, pp. 218–225). New York: Macmillan and Free Press.

Guilford, J.P. (1962). Creativity: Its measurement and development. In S. Parnes & H. Harding (Eds.), *A sourcebook for creative thinking* (pp. 151–168). New York: Charles Scribner's Sons.

Gunnar, M., Senior, K., & Hartup, W. (1984). Peer presence and the exploratory behavior of eighteen- and thirty-month-old children. *Child development, 55*, 1103–1109.

Gunsberg, A. (1989). Empowering young abused and neglected children through contingent play. *Childhood Education, 66*, 8–10.

Hakuta, K. (1988). Why bilinguals? In F.S. Kessel (Ed.), *The development of language and language researchers* (pp. 299–318). Hillsdale, NJ: Lawrence Erlbaum.

Hakuta, K., & Garcia, E.E. (1989). Bilingualism and education. *American Psychologist,* *44,* 374–379.

Halpern, R. (1987). Major social and demographic trends affecting young families: Implications for early childhood care and education. *Young Children, 42*(6), 34–40.

Hampden-Turner, C. (1981). *Maps of the mind: Charts and concepts of the mind and its labyrinths.* New York: Collier Books.

Harms, T., & Clifford, R. (1980). *Early childhood environment rating scale.* New York: Teachers College Press.

Harms, T., Clifford, R., & Padan-Belkin, E. (1983). *The day care home environment rating scale.* Chapel Hill, NC: Homebased Day Care Training Project.

Harms, T., & Clifford, R.M. (1980). *Day care environment rating scale.* New York: Teachers College Press, Columbia University.

Harms, T., Cryer, D., & Clifford, R. (1990). *Infant/toddler environment rating scale.* New York: Teachers College Press.

Harris, J.D., & Larsen, J.M. (1989). Parent education as a mandatory component of preschool: Effects on middle-class, educationally advantaged parents and children. *Early Childhood Research Quarterly, 4,* 275–287.

Harsh, A. (1987). Teach mathematics with children's literature. *Young Children, 42*(6), 24–27.

Harste, J.C., Short, K.G., & Burke, C. (1988). *Creating classrooms for authors: The reading–writing connection.* Portsmouth, NH: Heinemann Educational Books.

Hartup, W.W. (1983a). Peer interaction and the behavioural development of the individual child. In W. Damon (Ed.), *Social and personality development: Essays on the growth of the child* (pp. 220–233). New York: W. W. Norton.

Hartup, W.W. (1983b). Peer relations. In P.H. Mussen (Ed.), *Handbook of child psychology* (4th ed.). *Socialization, personality, and social development* (Vol. 4, pp. 103–196). New York: John Wiley.

Haskins, R. (1985). Public school aggression among children with varying day care experience. *Child Development, 56,* 698–703.

Haugland, S.W., & Shade, D.D. (1990). *Developmental evaluations of software for young children.* Albany, NY: Delmar.

Hautman, L., Read, M., & Greenwood-Church, M. (1992). An overview of child care legislation in Alberta. In A. Pence (Ed.), *Canadian child care in context: Perspectives from the provinces and territories.* Ottawa: Statistics Canada & Health and Welfare Canada.

Hayward, D., Rothenburg, M., & Beasley, R. (1974). Children's play and urban playground environments: A comparison of traditional, contemporary, and adventure playground types. *Environment and Behaviour, 6*(2), 131–168.

Healy, J.M. (1991). Ten reasons why "Sesame Street" is bad news for reading. *The Education Digest,* Feb., 63–66.

Helfer, R.E. (1987). The developmental basis of child abuse and neglect: An epidemiological approach. In R.E. Helfer & R.S. Kempe (Eds.), *The battered child* (4th ed., pp. 60–80). Chicago, IL: University of Chicago Press.

Hendrick, J. (1986). *Total learning: Curriculum for the young child* (2nd ed.). Columbus, OH: Merrill Publishing.

Henkens-Matzke, A., & Abbott, D.A. (1990). Game playing: A method for reducing young children's fear of medical procedures. *Early Childhood Research Quarterly, 5*, 19–26.

Herr, J., & Morse, W. (1982). Food for thought: Nutrition education for young children. In J.F. Brown (Ed.), *Curriculum planning for young children* (pp. 151–159). Washington, DC: National Association for the Education of Young Children.

Herrera, J.F., & Wooden, S.L. (1988). Some thoughts about effective parent–school communication. *Young Children, 43*(6), 78–80.

Hess, R.D., & Shipman, V. (1965a). Early blocks to children's learning. *Children, 12*, 189–194.

Hess, R.D., & Shipman, V. (1965b). Early experience and socialization of cognitive modes in children. *Child Development, 36*, 869–886.

Hess, R.D., & Shipman, V. (1968). Maternal influences upon early learning: The cognitive environments of urban pre-school children. In R.D. Hess & R.M. Bear (Eds.), *Early Education*. Chicago: Aldine-Atherton.

Hetherington, E.M., Stanley-Hagan, M., & Anderson, E.R. (1989). Marital transitions: A child's perspective. *American Psychologist, 44*, 303–312.

Hills, T.W. (1987). Children in the fast lane: Implications for early childhood policy and practice. *Early Childhood Research Quarterly, 2*, 265–273.

Hilton, J.M., Essa, E.L., & Murray, C.I. (1991). Are families meeting the nonphysical needs of their children? A comparison of single parent, one-earner and two-earner households. *Family Perspectives, 25*(2), 41–56.

Hinde, R.A. (1983). Ethology and child development. In P.H. Mussen, (Ed.), *Handbook of child psychology* (4th ed.). *Infancy and developmental psychobiology* (pp. 27–93). New York: John Wiley.

Hitz, R., & Driscoll, A. (1988). Praise or encouragement? New insights into praise: Implications for early childhood teachers. *Young Children, 44*(5), 6–13.

Hofferth, S.L., & Phillips, D.A. (1987). Child care in the United States, 1970 to 1995. *Journal of Marriage and the Family, 49*, 559–571.

Hohmann, M., Banet, B., & Weikart, D.P. (1979). *Young children in action: A manual for preschool educators*. Ypsilanti, MI: The High/Scope Press.

Honig, A.S. (1979). *Parent involvement in early childhood education*. Washington, DC: National Association for the Education of Young Children.

Honig, A.S. (1982). Prosocial development in young children. *Young Children, 37*(5), 51–62.

Honig, A.S. (1983). Sex role socialization in early childhood. *Young Children, 38*(6), 57–70.

Honig, A.S. (1985a). Research in review: Compliance, control, and discipline (Part 1). *Young Children, 40*(2), 50–58.

Honig, A.S. (1985b). Research in review: Compliance, control, and discipline (Part 3). *Young Children, 40*(3), 47–52.

Honig, A.S. (1986a). Stress and coping in children (Part 1). *Young Children, 41*(4), 50–63.

Honig, A.S. (1986b). Stress and coping in children (Part 2): Interpersonal family relationships. *Young Children, 41*(5), 47–59.

Honig, A.S. (1987). The shy child. *Young Children, 42*(4), 54–64.

Honig, A.S. (1988a). Caring and kindness: Curricular goals for early childhood educators. In G.F. Robertson & M.A. Johnson (Eds.), *Leaders in education: Their views on controversial issues* (pp. 58–70). New York: University Press of America.

Honig, A.S. (1988b). Humor development in children. *Young Children, 43*(4), 60–73.

Honig, A.S. (1993). The Eriksonian approach. In J.L. Roopnarine & J.E. Johnson (Eds.), *Approaches to early childhood education* (2nd ed., pp. 47–70). New York: Merrill.

Hough, R.A., Nurss, J.R., & Wood, D. (1987). Tell me a story: Making opportunities for elaborated language in early childhood classrooms. *Young Children, 43*(1), 6–12.

Howes, C. (1983). Caregiver behavior in center and family day care. *Journal of Applied Developmental Psychology, 4*, 99–107.

Howes, C. (1987). Social competency with peers: Contributions from child care. *Early Childhood Research Quarterly, 2*, 155–167.

Howes, C. (1988). Same- and cross-sex friends: Implications for interaction and social skills. *Early Childhood Research Quarterly, 3*, 21–37.

Howes, C., & Farver, J.A. (1987). Social pretend play in 2-year-olds: Effects of age of partner. *Early Childhood Research Quarterly, 2*, 305–314.

Howes, C., & Olenick, M. (1986). Family and child care influences on toddlers' compliance. *Child Development, 57*, 202–216.

Huesmann, L.R. (1986). Psychological processes promoting the relation between exposure to media violence and aggressive behaviour by the viewer. *Journal of Social Issues, 42*, 125–139.

Huesmann, L.R., Lagerspetz, K., & Eron, L.D. (1984). Intervening variables in the TV violence–aggression relation: Evidence from two countries. *Developmental Psychology, 20*, 746–775.

Humphrey, J.H., & Humphrey, J.N. (1985). *Controlling stress in children.* Springfield, IL: Charles C. Thomas.

Hunt, J.McV. (1961). *Intelligence and experience.* New York: Ronald Press.

Hunt, J.McV. (1968). Revisiting Montessori. In J.L. Frost (Ed.), *Early childhood education rediscovered* (pp. 102–127). New York: Holt, Rinehart & Winston.

Huston, A.C., Watkins, B.A., & Kunkel, D. (1989). Public policy and children's television. *American Psychologist, 44,* 424–433.

Hymes, J.L. (1981). *Teaching the child under six* (3rd ed.). Columbus, OH: Merrill Publishing.

Hyson, M.C. (1986). Lobster on the sidewalk: Understanding and helping children with fears. In J.B. McCracken (Ed.), *Reducing stress in young children's lives* (pp. 2–5). Washington, D.C., National Association for the Education of Young Children.

International Reading Association (1986). Literacy development and pre-first grade: A joint statement of concerns about present practices in pre-first grade reading instruction and recommendations for improvement. *Young Children, 41*(4), 10–13.

Irwin, S., & Canning, P. (1992a). Addendum: Child care in Nova Scotia, 1988–1990. In A. Pence (Ed.), *Canadian child care in context: Perspectives from the provinces and territories.* Ottawa: Statistics Canada & Health and Welfare Canada.

Irwin, S., & Canning, P. (1992b). An historical overview of child care in Nova Scotia. In A. Pence (Ed.), *Canadian child care in context: Perspectives from the provinces and territories.* Ottawa: Statistics Canada & Health and Welfare Canada.

Isaacs, S. (1933). *Intellectual Growth in Young Children.* New York: Schocken.

Ishee, N., & Goldhaber, J. (1990). Story re-enactment: Let the play begin. *Young Children, 45*(3), 70–75.

Izard, C. (1982). *Measuring emotions in infants and children.* New York: Cambridge University Press.

Jalongo, M.R. (1986). Using crisis-oriented books with young children. In J.B. McCracken (Ed.), *Reducing stress in young children's lives* (pp. 41–46). Washington, DC: National Association for the Education of Young Children.

Jalongo, M.R., & Collins, M. (1985). Singing with young children! Folk singing for non-musicians. *Young Children, 40*(2), 17–22.

Javernick, E. (1988). Johnny's not jumping: Can we help obese children? *Young Children, 43*(2), 18–23.

Jenkins, S. (1987). Ethnicity and family support. In S.L. Kagan, D.R. Powell, B. Weissbourd, & E.F. Zigler (Eds.), *America's family support programs: Perspectives and prospects* (pp. 282–294). New Haven, CT: Yale University Press.

Jensen, A.R. (1985a). Compensatory education and the theory of intelligence. *Phi Delta Kappan, 66,* 554–558.

Jensen, M.A. (1985b). Story awareness: A critical skill for early reading. *Young Children, 41*(1), 20–24.

Johnson, J. (1993). Evaluation in early childhood education. In J.L. Roopnarine & J.E. Johnson (Eds.), *Approaches to early childhood education* (2nd ed., pp. 317–336). New York: Merrill.

Johnson, L., & Joe, M.J. (1992). An historical overview of child care in Yukon. In A. Pence (Ed.), *Canadian child care in context: Perspectives from the provinces and territories.* Ottawa: Statistics Canada & Health and Welfare Canada.

Johnston, J.R., & Slobin, D.I. (1979). The development of locative expressions in English, Italian, Serbo-Croatian, and Turkish. *Journal of Child Language, 6,* 529–545.

Jones, C., Marsden, L. & Tepperman, L. (1990). *Lives of their own: The individualization of women's lives.* Toronto, ON: Oxford University Press.

Jones, E., & Prescott, E. (1978). *Dimensions of teaching—Learning environments, II: Focus on day care.* Pasadena, CA: Pacific Oaks College.

Jorde-Bloom, P. (1988). *A great place to work: Improving conditions for staff in young children's programs.* Washington, DC: National Association for the Education of Young Children.

Joy, L.A., Kimball, M.M., & Zabrack, M.L. (1986). Television and children's aggressive behaviour. In T.M. Williams (Ed.), *The impact of television: A natural experiment in three communities* (pp. 303–360). Orlando, FL: Academic Press.

Kagan, J. (1987). Introduction. In J. Kagan & S. Lamb (Eds.), *The emergence of morality in young children* (pp. ix–xx). Chicago: University of Chicago Press.

Kagan, J., & Reznick, J.S. (1986). Shyness and temperament. In W.H. Jones, J.M. Cheek, & S.R. Briggs (Eds.), *Shyness: Perspectives on research and treatment* (pp. 81–90). New York: Plenum Press.

Kagan, S.L., & Newton, J.W. (1989). For-profit and non-profit child care: Similarities and differences. *Young Children, 44*(6), 4–10.

Kamii, C. (1982). *Number in preschool and kindergarten.* Washington, DC: National Association for the Education of Young Children.

Kamii, C. (1984). Obedience is not enough. *Young Children, 39*(4), 11–14.

Kamii, C. (Ed.). (1990). *Achievement testing in the early grades: The games grown-ups play.* Washington, DC: NAEYC.

Kamii, C., & DeClark, G. (1985). *Young children reinvent arithmetic: Implications of Piaget's theory.* New York: Teachers College Press, Columbia University.

Kamii, C., & DeVries, R. (1980). *Group games in early childhood.* Washington, DC: National Association for the Education of Young Children.

Kamii, C., & Lee-Katz, L. (1982). Physics in preschool education: A Piagetian approach. In J.F. Brown (Ed.), *Curriculum planning for young children* (pp. 171–176). Washington, DC: National Association for the Education of Young Children.

Kaplan, P. (1991). *A child's odyssey* (2nd ed.). St. Paul, MN: West Publishing.

Karnes, M. (1969). *Research and development project on preschool disadvantaged children.* Washington, DC: U.S. Office of Education.

Karnes, M., & Lee, R.C. (1979). Mainstreaming in the preschool. In L.G. Katz (Ed.), *Current topics in early childhood education* (vol. 2, pp. 13–42). Norwood, NJ: Ablex Publishing.

Karnes, M., Shwedel, A., & Williams, M. (1983). A comparison of five approaches for educating young children from low-income homes. In The Consortium for Longitudinal Studies (Ed.), *As the twig is bent*. Hillsdale, NJ: Lawrence Erlbaum.

Katz, L.G. (1972). *Teacher–child relationships in day care centres*. ERIC document #046 494.

Katz, L.G. (1977). *Talks with teachers: Reflections on early childhood education*. Washington, DC: National Association for the Education of Young Children.

Katz, L.G. (1980). Mothering and teaching: Some significant distinctions. In L.G. Katz (Ed.), *Current topics in early childhood education* (vol. 3, pp. 47–63). Norwood, NJ: Ablex Publishing.

Katz, L.G. (1984a). The education of preprimary teachers. In L.G. Katz (Ed.), *Current topics in early childhood education* (vol. 5, pp. 209–227). Norwood, NJ: Ablex Publishing.

Katz, L.G. (1984b). The professional early childhood teacher. *Young Children, 39*(5), 3–10.

Katz, L.G. (1988). Where is early childhood education as a profession? In B. Spodek, O.N. Saracho, & D.L. Peters (Eds.), *Professionalism and the early childhood practitioner* (pp. 75–83). New York: Teachers College Press, Columbia University.

Katz, L.G. (1989). *Engaging children's minds: The project approach*. Norwood, NJ: Ablex Publishing.

Katz, L.G., & Chard, S. (1993). The project approach. In J. L. Roopnarine & J. E. Johnson (Eds.), *Approaches to early childhood education* (2nd ed.) (pp. 209–222). Columbus, OH: Merrill Publishing Co.

Katz, L.G., Evangelou, D., & Hartman, J.A. (1990). *The case for mixed-age grouping in early education*. Washington, DC: National Association for the Education of Young Children.

Katz, P.A. (1982). Children's racial awareness and intergroup attitudes. In L.G. Katz (Ed.), *Current topics in early childhood education* (vol. 4, pp. 17–54). Norwood, NJ: Ablex Publishing.

Katz, P.A. (1983). Developmental foundations of gender and racial attitudes. In R.L. Leahy (Ed.), *The child's construction of social inequality* (pp. 41–78). New York: Academic Press.

Katz, P.A. (1986). Modification of children's gender-stereotyped behaviour: General issues and research considerations. *Sex Roles, 14*, 591–602.

Keats, E.J. (1967). *Peter's chair*. New York: Harper & Row.

Keele, V.S. (1966). *Individual-time formula: The golden formula for raising happy, secure children*. Unpublished paper.

Kellogg, R. (1969). *Analyzing children's art*. Palo Alto, CA: Mayfield.

Kelly, F.J. (1981). Guiding groups of parents of young children. *Young Children,* 37(1), 28–32.

Kelly, J. (1989). *Early, middle, or late immersion?* Unpublished master's thesis, Brock University, St. Catharines, ON.

Kempe, R.S., & Kempe, C.H. (1978). *Child abuse.* Cambridge, MA: Harvard University Press.

Keogh, J., & Sugden, D. (1985). *Movement skill development.* New York: Macmillan.

Kersey, K. (1985). *Helping your child handle stress: The parents' guide to recognizing and solving childhood problems.* New York: Acropolis.

Kessen, W. (1965). *The child.* New York: Wiley.

Ketchel, J.A. (1986). Helping the young child cope with death. *Day Care and Early Childhood, 14*(2), 24–27.

Kids freed from carpet factories join protest against child labor. (1993, Feb. 16). *The St. Catharines Standard*, p. C10.

Kilpatrick, W.H. (1914). *The Montessori system examined.* Boston: Houghton Mifflin.

Kinsman, C.A., & Berk, L.E. (1982). Joining the block and housekeeping areas. In J.F. Brown (Ed.), *Curriculum planning for young children* (pp. 28–37). Washington, DC: National Association for the Education of Young Children.

Kleckner, K.A., & Engel, R.E. (1988). A child begins school: Relieving anxiety with books. *Young Children, 43*(5), 14–18.

Kohlberg, L. (1966). A cognitive-developmental analysis of children's sex-role concepts and attitudes. In E.E. Maccoby (Ed.), *The development of sex differences* (pp. 82–173). Stanford, CA: Stanford University Press.

Kohlberg, L. (1969). Stages and sequence: The cognitive development approach to socialization. In D.A. Goslin (Ed.), *Handbook of socialization theory and research* (pp. 347–480). Chicago: Rand McNally.

Kontos, S. (1986). What preschool children know about reading and how they learn it. *Young Children, 42*(1), 58–66.

Kopp, C.B. (1982). Antecedents of self-regulation: A developmental perspective. *Developmental Psychology, 18*, 199–214.

Kounin, J.S., & Sherman, L.W. (1979). School environments as behaviour settings. *Theory Into Practice, 18*(3), 145–151.

Kritchevsky, S., Prescott, E., & Walling, L. (1977). *Planning environments for young children: Physical space.* Washington, DC: National Association for the Education of Young Children.

Krogh, S.L., & Lamme, L.L. (1985). "But what about sharing?" Children's literature and moral development. *Young Children, 40*(4), 48–51.

Kubler-Ross, E. (1969). *On death and dying.* New York: Macmillan.

Kushner, D. (1989). "Put your name on your painting, but...the blocks go back on the shelves." *Young Children, 45*(1), 49–56.

Kyle, I. (1992a). Addendum: Child care in Ontario, 1988–1990. In A. Pence (Ed.), *Canadian child care in context: Perspectives from the provinces and territories.* Ottawa: Statistics Canada & Health and Welfare Canada.

Kyle, I. (1992b). An historical overview of child care in Ontario. In A. Pence (Ed.), *Canadian child care in context: Perspectives from the provinces and territories.* Ottawa: Statistics Canada & Health and Welfare Canada.

Kyle, I. (1992c). An overview of child care legislation, programs and funding in Ontario. In A. Pence (Ed.), *Canadian child care in context: Perspectives from the provinces and territories.* Ottawa: Statistics Canada & Health and Welfare Canada.

Kyle, I. (1992d). A socio-geographic overview of Ontario. In A. Pence (Ed.), *Canadian child care in context: Perspectives from the provinces and territories.* Ottawa: Statistics Canada & Health and Welfare Canada.

Labov, W. (1970). *The study of nonstandard English.* Urbana, IL: National Council of Teachers of English.

Lally, J.R., Mangione, P.L., & Honig, A.S. (1988). The Syracuse University Family Development Research Program: Long-range impact on an early intervention with low-income children and their families. In D.R. Powell (Ed.), *Emerging directions in parent–child intervention* (pp. 79–104). Norwood, NJ: Ablex Publishing.

Lamb, M.E., & Bornstein, M.H. (1987). *Development in infancy: An introduction.* New York: Random House.

Lambert, W. (1977). The effects of bilingualism of the individual: Cognitive and socio-cultural consequences, In P. Hornby (Ed.), *Bilingualism: Psychological, social and educational implications.* New York: Academic Press.

Langenbach, M., & Neskora, T.W. (1977). *Day care curriculum considerations.* Columbus, OH: Charles E. Merrill.

Larsen, J.M., & Robinson, C.C. (1989). Later effects of preschool on low-risk children. *Early Childhood Research Quarterly, 4,* 133–144.

Laughing all the way. (1988). *Young Children, 43*(2), 39–41.

Lavatelli, C.S. (1970). *Piaget's theory applied to an early childhood curriculum.* Boston, MA: American Science and Engineering.

Lawton, J.T. (1988). *Introduction to child care and early childhood education.* Glenview, IL: Scott, Foresman.

Lay-Dopyera, M., & Dopyera, J.E. (1987a). Strategies for teaching. In C. Seefeldt (Ed.), *The early childhood curriculum: A review of current research* (pp. 13–33). New York: Teachers College Press, Columbia University.

Lay-Dopyera, M., & Dopyera, J. (1987b). *Becoming a teacher of young children* (3rd ed.). New York: Random House.

Lazar, I., & Darlington, R. (1982). Lasting effects of early education: A report from the Consortium for Longitudinal Studies. *Monographs of the Society for research in Child Development, 47*(2–3, Serial No. 195).

Lennenberg, E.H. (1967). *Biological foundations of language.* New York: John Wiley.

Levinger, G., & Levinger, A.C. (1986). The temporal course of close relationships: Some thoughts about the development of children's ties. In W.W. Hartup & Z. Rubin (Eds.), *Relationships and development* (pp. 111–133). Hillsdale, NJ: Lawrence Erlbaum.

Levinson, D.J. (1978). *The seasons of a man's life.* New York: Alfred A. Knopf.

Lexmond, T. (1987). Temper tantrums. In A. Thomas & J. Grimes (Eds.), *Children's needs: Psychological perspectives* (pp. 627–633). Washington, DC: National Association of School Psychologists.

Liebert, R.M., & Sprafkin, J.N. (1988). *The early window: Effects of television on children and youth* (3rd ed.). New York: Pergamon Press.

Lillard, P.P. (1973). *Montessori: A modern approach.* New York: Schocken Books.

Lindauer, S.L.K. (1987). Montessori education for young children. In J.L. Roopnarine & J.E. Johnson (Eds.), *Approaches to early childhood education* (pp. 109–126). Columbus, OH: Merrill Publishing.

Lindauer, S.L.K. (1993). Montessori education for young children. In J. L. Roopnarine & J. E. Johnson (Eds.), *Approaches to early childhood education* (2nd ed.) (pp. 243–260). Columbus, OH: Merrill Publishing Co.

Linderman, C.E. (1979). *Teachables from trashables: Homemade toys that teach.* St. Paul, MN: Toys 'n Things Training and Resource Centre, Inc.

Lindfors, J.W. (1987). *Children's language and learning* (2nd ed.). Englewood Cliffs, NJ: Prentice-Hall.

Lombardi, J. (1986). Training for public policy and advocacy: An emerging topic in teacher education. *Young Children, 41*(4), 65–69.

Lombardi, J. (1990). Developing a coalition to reach the full cost of quality. In B. Willer (Ed.), *Reaching the full cost of quality in early childhood programs* (pp. 87–96). Washington, DC: National Association for the Education of Young Children.

Lovell, P., & Harms, T. (1985). How can playgrounds be improved?: A rating scale. *Young Children, 40*(3), 3–8.

Lowenfeld, V. (1962). Creativity: Education's stepchild. In S. Parnes & H. Harding (Eds.), *A sourcebook for creative thinking* (pp. 9–17). New York: Charles Scribner's Sons.

Lozoff, B. (1989). Nutrition and behaviour. *American Psychologist, 44,* 231–236.

Lutes, D. (1992). An overview of child care legislation in New Brunswick. In A. Pence (Ed.), *Canadian child care in context: Perspectives from the provinces and territories.* Ottawa: Statistics Canada & Health and Welfare Canada.

Lutes, D., & Gamble, J. (1992). Addendum: Child care in New Brunswick, 1988–1990. In A. Pence (Ed.), *Canadian child care in context: Perspectives from the provinces and territories.* Ottawa: Statistics Canada & Health and Welfare Canada.

Maccoby, E.E., & Jacklin, C. (1974). *The psychology of sex differences.* Stanford, CA: Stanford University Press.

Maccoby, E.E. (1990). Gender and relationships. *American Psychologist, 45,* 513–520.

Maccoby, E.E., & Jacklin, C.N. (1987). Gender segregation in childhood. In H.W. Reese (Ed.), *Advances in child development and behaviour* (vol. 20, pp. 239–288). New York: Academic Press.

Maccoby, E.E., & Martin, J.A. (1983). Socialization in the context of the family: Parent–child interaction. In E.M. Hetherington (Ed.), *Handbook of child psychology* (4th ed.). *Socialization, personality, and social development* (vol. 4., pp. 1–101). New York: John Wiley.

Machado, J.M. (1985). *Early childhood experiences in language arts* (3rd ed.). Albany, NY: Delmar.

Maier, H.W. (1965). *Three theories of child development.* New York: Harper & Row.

Maier, H.W. (1990). Erikson's developmental theory. In R.M. Thomas (Ed.), *The encyclopedia of human development and education: Theory, research, and studies* (pp. 88–93). New York: Pergamon Press.

Marcotte, R., & Young, R. (1992). *The effects of changing themes on children's play in the drama centre.* Unpublished manuscript, Brock University, St. Catharines, ON.

Mardell-Czudnowski, C.D., & Goldenberg, D.S. (1983). *Developmental Indicators for the Assessment of Learning-Revised (DIAL-R).* Edison, NJ: Childcraft Education.

Marshall, H.H. (1989). The development of self-concept. *Young Children, 44*(5), 44–51.

Mattingly, M. (1977). Introduction to symposium: Stress and burnout in child care. *Child Care Quarterly, 6,* 127–137.

Mauch, D. (1992a). Addendum: Child care in the Yukon, 1988–1990. In A. Pence (Ed.), *Canadian child care in context: Perspectives from the provinces and territories.* Ottawa: Statistics Canada & Health and Welfare Canada.

Mauch, D. (1992b). An overview of child care legislation in the Yukon. In A. Pence (Ed.), *Canadian child care in context: Perspectives from the provinces and territories.* Ottawa: Statistics Canada & Health and Welfare Canada.

Mauch, D. (1992c). A socio-geographic overview of the Yukon. In A. Pence (Ed.), *Canadian child care in context: Perspectives from the provinces and territories.* Ottawa: Statistics Canada & Health and Welfare Canada.

Mavrogenes, N.A. (1990). Helping parents help their children become literate. *Young Children, 45*(4), 4–9.

Maxim, George (1989). *The very young* (3rd ed.). Columbus, OH: Merrill Publishing.

Mayesky, M. (1990). *Creative activities for young children* (4th ed.). Albany, NY: Delmar.

Mayfield, M. (1990). *Work-related child care in Canada.* Ottawa, ON: Labour Canada.

McAfee, O.D. (1985). Circle time: Getting past "two little pumpkins." *Young Children, 40*(6), 24–29.

McCarthy, D. (1972). *Manual for the McCarthy Scales of Children's Abilities.* New York: Psychological Corp.

McCracken, J.B. (Ed.). (1986). *Reducing stress in young children's lives.* Washington, DC: National Association for the Education of Young Children.

McDonald, D.T., & Ramsey, J.H. (1982). Awakening the artist: Music for young children. In J.F. Brown (Ed.), *Curriculum planning for young children* (pp. 187–193). Washington, DC: National Association for the Education of Young Children.

McDonell, L. (1992). An historical overview of child care in British Columbia. In A. Pence (Ed.), *Canadian child care in context: Perspectives from the provinces and territories.* Ottawa: Statistics Canada & Health and Welfare Canada.

McDonell, L., & Griffin, S. (1992). An overview of child care legislation in British Columbia. In A. Pence (Ed.), *Canadian child care in context: Perspectives from the provinces and territories.* Ottawa: Statistics Canada & Health and Welfare Canada.

McIntosh, A., & Rauhala, A. (February 3, 4, 6–8, 1989). Who's minding the children? *The Globe and Mail.* Toronto, ON.

McIntyre, M. (1984). *Early childhood and science.* Washington, DC: National Science Teachers Association.

McLaughlin, B. (1984). *Second-language acquisition in childhood: Preschool children* (vol. 1, 2nd ed.). Hillsdale, NJ: Lawrence Erlbaum.

McMillan, M. (1919). *The nursery school.* London: J.M. Dent.

McMillan, M. (1930). *The nursery school* (rev. ed.). London: J.M. Dent.

McTear, M. (1985). *Children's conversations.* Oxford, UK: Basil Blackwell.

McWilliams, M. (1986). *Nutrition for the growing years.* New York: John Wiley.

Meddin, B.J., & Rosen, A.L. (1986). Child abuse and neglect: Prevention and reporting. *Young Children, 41*(4), 26–30.

Medeiros, D.C., Porter, B.J., & Welch, I.D. (1983). *Children under stress.* Englewood Cliffs, NJ: Prentice-Hall.

Meisels, S.J. (1986). Testing four- and five-year-olds: Response to Salzer and to Shepard and Smith. *Educational Leadership, 44*(3), 90–92.

Meisels, S.J., & Sternberg, S. (1989). Quality sacrificed in proprietary child care. *Education Week,* June, p. 36.

Miezitis, S. (1972). The Montessori method: Some recent research. *American Montessori Society Bulletin, 10* (No. 2).

Milkovich, G., & Gomez, L. (1976). Day care and selected employee work behaviours. *Academy of Management Journal, 19,* 111–115.

Miller, C.S. (1984). Building self-control: Discipline for young children. *Young Children, 40*(1), 15–19.

Miller, G.A., & Gildea, P.M. (1987, September). How children learn words. *Scientific American,* pp. 94–99.

Miller, L.B., & Bizzell, R.P. (1983). Long-term effects of four preschool programs: Sixth, seventh, and eighth grade. *Child Development, 54,* 727–741.

Miller, L.B., & Dyer, J.L. (1975). Four preschool programs: Their dimensions and effects. *Monographs of the Society for Research on Child Development* (Serial No. 162), nos. 5–6.

Mitchell, A., & Modigliani, K. (1989). Young children in public schools?: The only ifs reconsidered. *Young Children, 44*(6), 56–61.

Monighan-Nourot, P. (1990) The legacy of play in American early childhood education. In E. Klugman & S. Smilansky (Eds.), *Children's play and learning* (pp. 59–85). New York: Teachers College Press.

Montessori, M. (1965). *The Montessori method* (A.E. George, Trans.). Cambridge, MA: Robert Bentley. (Original work published 1912)

Moore, R.C., Goltsman, S.M., & Iacofano, D.S. (1987). *Play for all guidelines: Planning, design and management of outdoor play settings for all children.* Berkeley, CA: MIG Communications.

Moore, S.G. (1982). Prosocial behaviour in the early years: Parent and peer influences. In B. Spodek (Ed.), *Handbook of research in early childhood education.* New York: Free Press.

Morado, C. (1986). Prekindergarten programs for 4-year-olds. *Young Children, 41*(5), 61–63.

Morgan, E.L. (1989). Talking with parents when concerns come up. *Young Children, 44*(2), 52–56.

Morin, J. (1989). We can force a solution to the staffing crisis. *Young Children, 44*(6), 18–19.

Morrison, G.S. (1984). *Early childhood education today* (3rd ed.). New York: Merrill.

Morrison, G.S. (1988). *Education and development of infants, toddlers, and preschoolers.* Glenview, IL: Scott, Foresman/Little, Brown College Division.

Morrison, G.S. (1991). *Early childhood education today* (5th ed.). New York: Merrill.

Morrow, R.D. (1989). What's in a name? In particular, a Southeast Asian name? *Young Children, 44*(6), 20–23.

Moskowitz, B.A. (1982). The acquisition of language. In *Human communication: Language and its psychobiological bases: Readings from Scientific American* (pp. 121–132). San Francisco, CA: W.H. Freeman.

Mullen, S. (1992). A socio-geographic overview of Prince Edward Island. In A. Pence (Ed.), *Canadian child care in context: Perspectives from the provinces and territories.* Ottawa: Statistics Canada & Health and Welfare Canada.

Munro, J.G. (1986). Movement education: Balance. *Day Care and Early Education. 14*(2), 28–31.

Mussen, P.H., Conger, J.J., Kagan, J., & Huston, A.C. (1990). *Child development and personality* (7th ed.). New York: Harper & Row.

Mussen, P.H., & Eisenberg-Berg, N. (1977). *Roots of caring, sharing, and helping: The development of pro-social behaviour in children.* San Francisco: W.H. Freeman.

Myers, B.K., & Maurer, K. (1987). Teaching with less talking: Learning centres in the kindergarten. *Young Children, 42*(5), 20–27.

Myers-Walls, J.A., & Fry-Miller, K.M. (1984). Nuclear war: Helping children overcome fears. *Young Children, 39*(4), 27–32.

NAEYC (1989). *Developmentally Appropriate Practice in Early Childhood Programs Serving Infants.* Washington, DC: National Association for the Education of Young Children.

NAEYC (1989). *Developmentally Appropriate Practice in Early Childhood Programs Serving Toddlers.* Washington, DC: National Association for the Education of Young Children.

NAEYC Information Service. (1990). *Employer-assisted child care: An NAEYC resource guide.* Washington, DC: National Association for the Education of Young Children.

NAEYC position statement on standardized testing of young children 3 through 8 years of age (1988). *Young Children, 43*(3), 42–47.

Napier-Anderson, L. (1981). *Change: One step at a time.* Toronto, ON: Faculty of Education, University of Toronto.

National Child Care Staffing Study (1989). *Who cares? Child care teachers and the quality of child care in America.* Child Care Employee Project. Oakland, CA: Author.

National Child Care Information Centre, Child Care Programs Division (1991). *The status of day care in Canada 1990.* Ottawa: Minister of Health and Welfare.

National Council of Welfare (1988). *Childcare: A better alternative.* Ottawa, ON: Supply and Services.

National Council of Welfare (1990). *Women and poverty revisited.* Ottawa, ON: Supply and Services.

National Dairy Council (1980). *Food ... Early choices: A nutrition learning system for early childhood.* Rosemont, IL: National Dairy Council.

Nauta, M.J., & Hewett, K. (1988). Studying complexity: The case of the child and family resource program. In H.B. Weiss & F.H. Jacobs (Eds.), *Evaluating family programs* (pp. 389–405). New York: Aldine de Gruyter.

Neisworth, J., & Buggey, T. (1993). Behavior analysis in early childhood education. In J. L. Roopnarine & J.E. Johnson (Eds.), *Approaches to early childhood education* (2nd ed., pp. 113–136). New York: Merrill.

Neugebauer, R. (1988, January). How's business? Status report #4 on for-profit child care. *Child Care Information Exchange*, pp. 29–34.

Neugebauer, R. (1991, January/February). How's business: Status report #7 on for-profit child care. *Child Care Information Exchange*, pp. 46–50.

Northway, M. (1973). Child study in Canada: A casual history. In L. Brockman, J. Whiteley, & J. Zubek (Eds.), *Child development.* Toronto: McClelland & Stewart.

Noyes, D. (1987). Indoor pollutants: Environmental hazards to young children. *Young Children, 42*(6), 57–65.

Nykyforuk, J. (1992a). An historical overview of child care in Saskatchewan. In A. Pence (Ed.), *Canadian child care in context: Perspectives from the provinces and territories*. Ottawa: Statistics Canada & Health and Welfare Canada.

Nykyforuk, J. (1992b). A socio-geographic overview of Saskatchewan. In A. Pence (Ed.), *Canadian child care in context: Perspectives from the provinces and territories*. Ottawa: Statistics Canada & Health and Welfare Canada.

Obler, L.K. (1985). Language through the life-span. In J.B. Gleason (Ed.), *The development of language* (pp. 277–305). Columbus, OH: Charles E. Merrill.

Oden, S. (1982). Peer relationship development in childhood. In L.G. Katz (Ed.), *Current topics in early childhood education* (vol. 4, pp. 87–118). Norwood, NJ: Ablex Publishing.

Oken-Wright, P. (1988). Show-and-tell grows up. *Young Children, 43*(2), 52–58.

Orlick, T. (1978a). *The cooperative sports and games book: Challenge without competition*. New York: Pantheon Books.

Orlick, T. (1978b). *Winning through cooperation*. Washington, DC: Acropolis Books .

Orlick, T. (1982). *The second cooperative sports game books*. New York: Pantheon Books.

Owens, R.E. (1984). *Language development: An introduction*. Columbus, OH: Charles E. Merrill.

Parke, R.D., & Slaby, R.G. (1983). The development of aggression. In P.H. Mussen (Ed.), *Handbook of child psychology* (4th ed.). *Socialization, personality, and social development* (vol. 4., pp. 547–641). New York: John Wiley.

Parker, J.G., & Gottman, J.M. (1989). Social and emotional development in a relational context. In T.J. Berndt & G.W. Ladd (Eds.), *Peer relationships in child development* (pp. 95–131). New York: John Wiley.

Parten, M.B. (1932). Social participation among preschool children. *Journal of Abnormal and Social Psychology, 27*, 243–269.

Patterson, G.R. (1982). *Coercive family practices*. Eugene, OR: Castalia Press.

Patterson, G.R., DeBaryshe, B.D., & Ramsey, E. (1989). A developmental perspective on antisocial behaviour. *American Psychologist, 44*, 329–335.

Patterson, G.R., & Gullion, M.E. (1971). *Living with children: New methods for parents and teachers*. Champaign, IL: Research Press.

Pease, D., & Gleason, J.B. (1985). Gaining meaning: Semantic development. In J.B. Gleason (Ed.), *The development of language* (pp. 103–138). Columbus, OH: Charles E. Merrill.

Pence, A. (1990). The child care profession in Canada. In Doxey, I. (Ed.), *Child care and education: Canadian dimensions* (pp. 87–97). Toronto: Nelson Canada.

Pence, A. (1992). *Canadian child care in context: Perspectives from the provinces and territories* (pp. xiii–xvii). Ottawa, ON: Statistics Canada & Health and Welfare Canada.

Pence, A., Read, M., Lero, D., Goelman, H., & Brockman, L. (1992). An overview of the NCCS data for British Columbia. In A. Pence (Ed.), *Canadian child care in context: Perspectives from the provinces and territories* (pp. 65–86). Ottawa, ON: Statistics Canada & Health and Welfare Canada.

Peters, D.L. (1988). The Child Development Associate credential and the educationally disenfranchised. In B. Spodek, O.N. Saracho, & D.L. Peters (Eds.), *Professionalism and the early childhood practitioner* (pp. 93–104). New York: Teachers College Press, Columbia University.

Peters, D.L., Neisworth, J.T., & Yawkey, T.D. (1985). *Early childhood education: From theory to practice.* Monterey, CA: Brooks/Cole.

Phenice, L., & Hildebrand, L. (1988). Multicultural education: A pathway to global harmony. *Day Care and Early Education, 16*(2), 15–17.

Phillips, D.A. (1987). *Quality in child care: What does research tell us?* Washington, DC: National Association for the Education of Young Children.

Phillips, D.A., & Whitebook, M. (1986). Who are child care workers?: The search for answers. *Young Children, 41*(4), 14–20.

Phillips, D.A., & Howes, C. (1987). Indicators of quality child care: Review of research. In D.A. Phillips (Ed.), *Quality in child care: What does research tell us?* (pp. 1–20). Washington, DC: National Association for the Education of Young Children.

Phillips, D.A., Scarr, S., & McCartney, K. (1987). Dimensions and effects of child care quality: The Bermuda Study. In D.A. Phillips (Ed.), *Quality in child care: What does research tell us?* (pp. 43–56). Washington, DC: National Association for the m Education of Young Children.

Phyfe-Perkins, E. (1980). Children's behaviour in preschool settings: A review of research concerning the influence of the physical environment. In. L.G. Katz (Ed.), *Current topics in early childhood education* (vol. 3, pp. 91–125). Norwood, NJ: Ablex Publishing Corp.

Piaget, J. (1926). *The language and thought of the child.* London: Routledge & Kegan Paul.

Piaget, J. (1932). *The moral judgment of the child.* New York: Harcourt, Brace & World.

Piaget, J. (1951). *Play, dreams, and imitation in childhood.* New York: Norton.

Piaget, J. (1983). Piaget's theory. In P.H. Mussen (Ed.), *Handbook of child psychology* (4th ed.). *History, theory, and methods* (vol. 1, pp. 103–128). New York: John Wiley.

Pipes, P.L. (1989a). Between infancy and adolescence. In P.L. Pipes (Ed.), *Nutrition in infancy and childhood* (4th ed., pp. 120–142). St. Louis, MO: C.V. Mosby.

Pipes, P.L. (1989b). Special concerns of dietary intake during infancy and childhood. In P.L. Pipes (Ed.), *Nutrition in infancy and childhood* (4th ed., pp. 268–300). St. Louis, MO: C.V. Mosby.

Plomin, R., & Daniels, D. (1986). Genetics and shyness. In W.H. Jones, J.M. Cheek, & S.R. Briggs (Eds.), *Shyness: Perspectives on research and treatment* (pp. 63–80). New York: Plenum Press.

Poest, C.A., Williams, J.R., Witt, D.D., & Atwood, M.E. (1989). Physical activity patterns of preschool children. *Early Childhood Research Quarterly, 65,* 367–376.

Poest, C.A., Williams, J.R., Witt, D.D., & Atwood, M.E. (1990). Challenge me to move: Large muscle development in young children. *Young Children, 45*(5), 4–10.

Powell, D.R. (1986). Parent education and support programs. *Young Children, 41*(3), 47–53.

Powell, D.R. (1987a). After-school child care. *Young Children, 42*(3), 62–66.

Powell, D.R. (1987b). Day care as a family support system. In S.L. Kagan, D.R. Powell, B. Weissbourd, & E.F. Zigler (Eds.), *America's family support programs: Perspectives and prospects* (pp. 115–132). New Haven, CT: Yale University Press.

Powell, D.R. (1989). *Families and early childhood programs.* Washington, DC: National Association of the Education of Young Children.

Prescott, E. (1987). The environment as organizer of intent in child-care settings. In C.S. Weinstein & T.G. David (Eds.), *Spaces for children: The built enviroment and child development* (pp. 73–78). New York: Plenum Press.

Price, G.G. (1989). Mathematics in early childhood. *Young Children, 44*(4), 53–58.

Proshansky, H.M., & Fabian, A.K. (1987). The development of place identity in the child. In C.S. Weinstein & T.G. David (Eds.), *Spaces for children: The built environment and child development* (pp. 21-40). New York: Plenum Press.

Radomski, M.A. (1986). Professionalization of early childhood educators: How far have we progressed? *Young Children, 41*(4), 20–23.

Ram, B. (1990). *Current demographic analysis: New trends in the family* (Cat. No. 91-535E). Ottawa, ON: Supply and Services, Canada.

Ramey, D., Dorvall, B., & Baker-Ward, L. (1983). Group day care and socially disadvantaged families: Effects on the child and the family. In S. Kilmer (Ed.), *Advances in early education and day care* (vol. 3, pp. 69–132). Greenwich, CT: JAI Press.

Ramsey, P.G. (1982). Multicultural education in early childhood. In J.F. Brown (Ed.), *Curriculum planning for young children* (pp. 131–142). Washington, DC: National Association for the Education of Young Children.

Ramsey, P.G. (1987). *Teaching and learning in a diverse world: Multicultural education for young children.* New York: Teachers College Press, Columbia University.

Randall, V. (1992a). Addendum: Child care in Newfoundland, 1988–1990. In A. Pence (Ed.), *Canadian child care in context: Perspectives from the provinces and territories.* Ottawa: Statistics Canada & Health and Welfare Canada.

Randall, V. (1992b). An overview of child care legislation in Newfoundland. In A. Pence (Ed.), *Canadian child care in context: Perspectives from the provinces and territories.* Ottawa: Statistics Canada & Health and Welfare Canada.

Rarick, G.L. (1982). Descriptive research and process-oriented explanations of the motor development of children. In J.A.S. Kelso & J.E. Clark (Eds.), *The development of movement control and co-ordination* (pp. 275–291). New York: John Wiley.

Read, M. (1992). Addendum: Child care in Alberta, 1988–1990. In A. Pence (Ed.), *Canadian child care in context: Perspectives from the provinces and territories.* Ottawa: Statistics Canada & Health and Welfare Canada.

Read, M., Greenwood-Church, M., Hautman, L., Roche, E., & Bagley, C. (1992). An historical overview of child care in Alberta. In A. Pence (Ed.), *Canadian child care in context: Perspectives from the provinces and territories.* Ottawa: Statistics Canada & Health and Welfare Canada.

Reiber, J.L., & Embry, L.H. (1983). Working and communicating with parents. In E.M. Goetz & K.E. Allen (Eds.), *Early childhood education: Special environmental, policy, and legal considerations* (pp. 152–183). Rockville, MD: Aspen Systems Corp.

Reifel, S. (1984). Block construction: Children's developmental landmarks in representation of space. *Young Children, 40*(1), 61–67.

Reppucci, N.D., & Haugaard, J.J. (1989). Prevention of child sexual abuse: Myth or reality? *American Psychologist, 44*, 1266–1275.

Resnick, L.B. (1989). Developing mathematical knowledge. *American Psychologist, 44*, 162–169.

Rich, S.J. (1985). The writing suitcase. *Young Children, 40*(5), 42–44.

Richarz, A.S. (1980). *Understanding children through observation.* St. Paul, MN: West Publishing.

Riessman, F. (1962). *The culturally deprived child.* New York: Harper & Row.

Risley, T.R., & Baer, D.M. (1973). Operant behaviour modification: The deliberate development of behaviour. In B.M. Caldwell & H.M. Ricciuti (Eds.), *Review of child development research* (vol. 3, pp. 283–329). Chicago: University of Chicago Press.

Ritch, A., & Griffin, S. (1992). A socio-geographic overview of British Columbia. In A. Pence (Ed.), *Canadian child care in context: Perspectives from the provinces and territories.* Ottawa: Statistics Canada & Health and Welfare Canada.

Robinson, B.E. (1988). Vanishing breed: Men in child care programs. *Young Children, 43*(6), 54–57.

Rogers, C.S., & Morris, S.S. (1986). Reducing sugar in children's diets: Why? How? *Young Children, 41*(5), 11–16.

Rogers, D.L., Perrin, M.S., & Waller, C.B. (1987). Enhancing the development of language and thought through conversations with young children. *Early Childhood Research Quarterly, 2*, 17–29.

Rogers, D.L., & Ross, D.D. (1986). Encouraging positive social interaction among young children. *Young Children, 41*(3), 12–17.

Rogers, F., & Sharapan, H.B. (1991). Helping parents, teachers, and caregivers deal with children's concerns about war. *Young Children, 46*(3), 12–13.

Roopnarine, J., & Johnson, J. (Eds.). (1993). *Approaches to early childhood education* (2nd ed.). New York: Merrill.

Rothlein, L. (1989). Nutrition tips revisited: On a daily basis, do we implement what we know? *Young Children, 44*(6), 30–36.

Rothman Beach Associates. (1985). A study of work-related day care in Canada. In *Childcare: The employer's role* (pp. 58–138). Ottawa: Status of Women.

Rowland, T., & McGuire, C. (1968). The developmental theory of Jean Piaget. In J.L. Frost (Ed.), *Early childhood education rediscovered* (pp. 145–152). New York: Holt, Rinehart & Winston.

Rubin, K. (1977). Play behaviors of young children. *Young Children, 32*(6), 16–24.

Rubin, K. (1982). Early play theories revisited: Contributions to contemporary research and theory. In D. Pepler & K. Rubin (Eds.), *The play of children: Current theory and research*. Basel, SWITZ: Karger AG.

Rubin, K., Fein, G., & Vandenberg, B. (1983). Play. In P.H. Mussen (Ed.), *Handbook of child psychology* (4th ed.). *Socialization, personality, and social development*. (vol. 4, pp. 693–774). New York: John Wiley.

Rubin, Z. (1980). *Children's friendships*. Cambridge, MA: Harvard University Press.

Ruopp, R., Travers, J., Glantz, F., & Coelen, C. (1979). *Children at the center: Final report of the National Day Care Study*. Cambridge, MA: ABT Associates.

Rutter, M. (1983). Stress, coping, and development: Some issues and some questions. In N. Garmezy & M. Rutter (Eds.), *Stress, coping, and development in children* (pp. 1–41). New York: McGraw-Hill.

Saida, Y., & Miyashita, M. (1979). Development of fine motor skill in children: Manipulation of a pencil in young children aged two to six years old. *Journal of Human Movement Studies, 5*, 104–113.

Salvia, J., & Ysseldyke, J. (1991). *Assessment* (5th ed.). Boston: Houghton Mifflin.

Sameroff, A.J. (1983). Developmental systems: Contexts and evolution. In P.H. Mussen (Ed.), *Handbook of child psychology* (4th ed.). *History, theory, and methods* (vol. 1, pp. 237–294). New York: John Wiley.

Samuels, S.C. (1977). *Enhancing self-concept in early childhood*. New York: Human Sciences Press.

Sarafino, E.P. (1986). *The fears of childhood: A guide to recognizing and reducing fearful states in children*. NY: Human Sciences Press.

Saunders, R., & Bingham-Newman, A.M. (1984). *Piagetian perspectives for preschools: A thinking book for teachers*. Englewood Cliffs, NJ: Prentice-Hall.

Saville-Troike, M. (1982). The development of bilingual and bicultural competence in young children. In L.G. Katz (Ed.), *Current topics in early childhood education* (vol. 4, pp. 1–16). Norwood, NJ: Ablex Publishing.

Scales, B., Almy, M., Nicolopoulou, A., & Ervin-Tripp, S. (1992a). Defending play in the lives of children. In B. Scales, M. Almy, A. Nicolopoulou, & S. Ervin-Tripp (Eds.), *Play and the social context of development in early care and education* (pp. 15–31). New York: Teachers College Press.

Scales, B., Almy, M., Nicolopoulou, A., & Ervin-Tripp, S. (Eds.). (1992b). *Play and the social context of development in early care and education.* New York: Teachers College Press.

Scarr, S., Phillips, D., & McCartney, K. (1990). Facts, fantasies and the future of child care in the United States. *Psychological Science, 1*(1), 26–35.

Schickedanz, J.A. (1982). The acquisition of written language in young children. In B. Spodek (Ed.), *Handbook of research in early childhood education* (pp. 242–263). New York: Free Press.

Schickedanz, J.A. (1986). *More than ABCs: The early stages of reading and writing.* Washington, DC: National Association for the Education of Young Children.

Schickedanz, J.A., Hansen, K., & Forsyth, P.D. (1990). *Understanding children.* Mountain View, CA: Mayfield.

Schilder, P., & Wechsler, D. (1934). The attitudes of children toward death. *Journal of Genetic Psychology, 45*, 406–451.

Schirrmacher, R. (1986). Talking with young children about their art. *Young Children, 41*(5), 3–10.

Schirrmacher, R. (1990). *Art and creative development for young children.* Albany, NY: Delmar.

Schwarz, S., & Robison, H. (1982). *Designing curriculum for early childhood.* Boston, MA: Allyn & Bacon.

Schweinhart, L.J., & Weikart, D.P. (1985). Evidence that good early childhood programs work. *Phi Delta Kappan, 66*, 545–551.

Schweinhart, L.J., & Weikart, D.P. (1993). Changed lives, significant benefits. *High/Scope resource, 12*(3), 1, 10–14.

Schweinhart, L.J., Weikart, D.P., & Larner, M.B. (1986a). Consequences of three preschool models through age 15. *Early Childhood Research Quarterly, 1*, 15–45.

Schweinhart, L.J., Weikart, D.P., & Larner, M.B. (1986b). Child-initiated activities in early childhood programs may help prevent delinquency. *Early Childhood Research Quarterly, 1*, 303–312.

Sciarra, D.J., & Dorsey, A.G. (1990). *Developing and administering a child care centre* (2nd ed.). Albany, NY: Delmar.

Seaver, J.W., & Cartwright, C.A. (1986). *Child care administration.* Belmont, CA: Wadworth.

Seefeldt, C. (Ed.). (1987). *The early childhood curriculum.* New York: Teachers College Press.

Seefeldt, C. (1987). The visual arts. In C. Seefeldt (Ed.), *The early childhood curriculum: A review of current research* (pp. 183–211). New York: Teachers College Press.

Seefeldt, V. (1984). Physical fitness in preschool and elementary school-aged children. *Journal of Physical Education, Recreation, and Dance, 55*(9), 33–40.

Seefeldt, V., & Haubenstricker, J. (1982). Patterns, phases, or stages: An analytical model for the study of developmental movement. In J.A.S. Kelso & J.E. Clark (Eds.), *The development of movement control and co-ordination* (pp. 309–318). New York: John Wiley.

Seifert, K. (1988). Men in early childhood education. In B. Spodek, O.N. Saracho, & D.L. Peters (Eds.), *Professionalism and the early childhood practitioner* (pp. 105–116). New York: Teachers College Press, Columbia University.

Seitz, V., Rosenbaum, L.K., & Apfel, N.H. (1985). Effects of family support intervention: A ten-year follow-up. *Child Development, 56,* 376–391.

Selye, H. (Ed.). (1980). *Guide to stress research* (vol. 1). New York: Van Nostrand Reinhold.

Shatz, M., & Gelman, R. (1973). The development of communication skills: Modifications in the speech of young children as a function of listener. *Monographs of the Society for Research in Child Development, 38* (5, Serial No. 152).

Sheehy, G. (1976). *Passages: Predictable crises of adult life.* New York: Dutton.

Shefatya, L. (1990). Socioeconomic status and ethnic differences in sociodramatic play: Theoretical and practical implications. In E. Klugman & S. Smilansky (Eds.), *Children's play and learning* (pp. 137–155). New York: Teachers College Press.

Sheldon, A. (1990). "Kings are royaler than queens": Language and socialization. *Young Children, 45*(2), 4–9.

Sheldon, J.B. (1983). Protecting the preschooler and the practitioner: Legal issues in early childhood programs. In E.M. Goetz & K.E. Allen (Eds.), *Early childhood education: Special environmental, policy, and legal considerations* (pp. 307–341). Rockville, MD: Aspen Systems Corp.

Sheppard, W.C. (1973). *Teaching social behaviour to young children.* Champaign, IL: Research Press.

Shimoni, R., Baxter, J., & Kugelmass, J. (1992). *Every child is special.* Don Mills, ON: Addison-Wesley.

Sholtys, K.C. (1989). A new language, a new life. *Young Children, 44*(3), 76–77.

Shure, M.B., & Spivak, G. (1978). *Problem solving techniques in childrearing.* San Francisco, CA: Jossey-Bass.

Shweder, R.A., Mahapatra, M., & Miller, J.G. (1987). Culture and moral development. In J. Kagan and S. Lamb (Eds.), *The emergence of morality in young children* (pp. 1–83). Chicago: University of Chicago Press.

Siegel, A.W., & White, S.H. (1982). The child study movement: Early growth and development of the symbolized child. *Advanced Studies in Child Development and Behavior, 17,* 233–285.

Siegler, R.S. (1983). Information processing approaches to development. In P.H. Mussen (Ed.), *Handbook of child psychology* (4th ed.). *History, theory, and methods* (vol 1, pp. 103–128). New York: John Wiley.

Siegler, R.S. (1986). *Children's thinking.* Englewood Cliffs, NJ: Prentice-Hall.

Sigel, I.E. (1987). Does hothousing rob children of their childhood? *Early Childhood Research Quarterly, 2,* 211–225.

Silberman, C. (1990). *Crisis in the classroom.* New York: Random House.

Silin, J.G. (1985). Authority as knowledge: A problem of professionalization. *Young Children, 40*(3), 41–46.

Silver, R.A. (1982). Developing cognitive skills through art. In L.G. Katz (Ed.), *Current topics in early childhood education* (vol. 4, pp. 143–171). Norwood, NJ: Ablex Publishing.

Simons, J.A., & Simons, F.A. (1986). Montessori and regular preschools: A comparison. In L.G. Katz (Ed.), *Current topics in early childhood education* (vol. 6, pp. 195–223). Norwood, NJ: Ablex Publishing.

Singer, J.L., Singer, D.G., & Rapaczynski, W. (1984, Spring). Family patterns and television viewing as predictors of children's beliefs and aggression. *Journal of Communication,* 73–89.

Skeels, H. (1966). Adult status of children with contrasting early life experiences. *Monographs of the Society for Research in Child Development, 31*(3, Serial No. 105).

Skinner, B.F. (1957). *Verbal behaviour.* New York: Appleton-Century-Crofts.

Skinner, B.F. (1969). *Contingencies of reinforcement: A theoretical analysis.* New York: Appleton-Century-Crofts.

Skinner, B.F. (1974). *About behaviorism.* New York: Alfred A. Knopf.

Skinner, L. (1979). *Motor development in the preschool years.* Springfield, IL: Thomas Publishers.

Smilansky, S. (1968). *The effects of sociodramatic play on disadvantaged preschool children.* New York: John Wiley.

Smilansky, S. (1987). *On death: Helping children understand and cope.* New York: Peter Lang.

Smilansky, S. (1990). Sociodramatic play: Its relevance to behavior and achievement in school. In E. Klugman & S. Smilansky (Eds.), *Children's play and learning* (pp. 18–42). New York: Teachers College Press.

Smith, C.A. (1982). *Promoting the social development of young children.* Palo Alto, CA: Mayfield.

Smith, C.A. (1989). *From wonder to wisdom: Using stories to help children grow.* New York: New American Library.

Smith, D. (1991). Here they come: ready or not! In B. Scales, M. Almy, A. Nicolopoulou, & S. Ervin-Tripp (Eds.), *Play and the social context of development in early care and education* (pp. 51–61). New York: Teachers College Press.

Smith, M.M. (1990). NAEYC annual report. *Young Children, 46*(1), 41–48.

Smith, P.K., & Connolly, K.J. (1980). *The ecology of preschool behaviour.* Cambridge, England: Cambridge University Press.

Smith, P.K. & Connolly, K.J. (1981). *The behavioural ecology of the preschool.* Cambridge, UK: Cambridge University Press.

Smith, R.F. (1982). Early childhood science education: A Piagetian perspective. In J.F. Brown (Ed.), *Curriculum planning for young children* (pp. 143–150). Washington, DC: National Association for the Education of Young Children.

Snow, C.E., & Ninio, A. (1986). The contracts of literacy: What children learn from learning to read books. In W.H. Teale & E. Sulzby (Eds.), *Emergent literacy: Writing and reading* (pp. 116–138). Norwood, NJ: Ablex Publishing.

Sobel, J. (1983). *Everybody wins: Non-competitive games for young children.* New York: Walker.

Soderman, A.K. (1985). Dealing with difficult young children. *Young Children, 40*(5), 15–20.

Spitz, H. (1986). *The raising of intelligence: A selected history of attempts to raise retarded intelligence.* Hillsdale, NJ: Lawrence Erlbaum.

Spitz, R. (1945). Hospitalism.: An inquiry into the genesis of psychiatric conditions in early childhood (Part I). *Psychoanalytic Studies of the Child, 1,* 53–74.

Spodek, B. (1985). *Teaching in the early years* (3rd ed.), Englewood Cliffs, NJ: Prentice-Hall, Inc.

Spodek, B., & Saracho, O.N. (1982). The preparation and certification of early childhood personnel. In B. Spodek (Ed.), *Handbook of research in early childhood education.* New York: Free Press.

Spodek, B., Saracho, O., & Lee, R.C. (1984). *Mainstreaming young children.* Belmont, CA: Wadsworth.

Sponseller, D. (1982). Play and early education. In B. Spodek (Ed.), *Handbook of research in early childhood education* (pp. 215–241). New York: Free Press.

Stapleford, E.M. (1976). *History of the Day Nurseries Branch: A personal record.* Toronto, ON: Ontario Ministry of Community and Social Services.

Statistics Canada. (1985). *Women in Canada.* Ottawa, ON: Author.

Statistics Canada. (1993). *Labour force activity of women by presence of children.* Ottawa, ON: Author.

Stevens, H. (1992). A socio-geographic overview of Manitoba. In A. Pence (Ed.), *Canadian child care in context: Perspectives from the provinces and territories.* Ottawa: Statistics Canada & Health and Welfare Canada.

Stevenson, J. (1990). The cooperative preschool model in Canada. In I. Doxey (Ed.), *Child care and education: Canadian dimensions* (pp. 221–239). Toronto: Nelson Canada.

Stevenson, R.L. (1985). *A child's garden of verse* (M. Forman, Illus.). New York: Delacorte Press.

Suggestions for developing positive racial attitudes. (1980). *Interracial Books for Children Bulletin, 11*(3–4), 10–15.

Sutherland, Z., & Arbuthnot, M.H. (1986). *Children and books* (7th ed.). Glenview, IL: Scott, Foresman.

Swigger, K.M., & Swigger, B.K. (1984). Social patterns and computer use among preschool children. *AEDS Journal, 17*(3), 35-41.

Sword, J. (1987). Help! I'm selecting children's books. *Day Care and Early Education, 15*(2), 26–28.

Table toys: A creative curriculum for early childhood. (1979). Washington, DC: Creative Associates.

Teale, W.H., & Martinez, M.G. (1988). Getting on the right road to reading: Bringing books and young children together in the classroom. *Young Children, 44*(1), 10–15.

Teale, W.H., & Sulzby, E. (1986). Emergent literacy as a perspective for examining how young children become writers and readers. In W.H. Teale & E. Sulzby (Eds.), *Emergent literacy: Writing and reading* (pp. vii–xxv). Norwood, NJ: Ablex Publishing.

Thomas, A., & Chess, S. (1969). *Temperament and development.* New York: New York University Press.

Thomas, A., Chess, S., & Birch, H.G. (1968). *Temperament and behavior disorders in children.* New York: New York University Press.

Thomas, R.M. (1990a). *The encyclopedia of human development and education: Theory, research, and studies.* New York: Pergamon Press.

Thomas, R.M. (1990b). Basic concepts and applications of Piagetian cognitive development theory. In R.M. Thomas (Ed.), *The encyclopedia of human development and education: Theory, research, and studies* (pp. 53–56). New York: Pergamon Press.

Thomson, C.L., & Ashton-Lilo, J. (1983). A developmental environment for child care programs. In E.M. Goetz & K.E. Allen (Eds.), *Early childhood education: Special environmental, policy, and legal considerations* (pp. 93–125). Rockville, MD: Aspen Systems Corp.

Thorndike, R., Hagen, E., & Sattler, J. (1985). *Stanford-Binet Intelligence Scale* (4th ed.). Chicago, IL: Riverside.

Thornton, J.R. (1990). Team teaching: A relationship based on trust and communication. *Young Children, 45*(5), 40–43.

Tietze, W. (1987). A structural model for the evaluation of preschool effects. *Early Childhood Research Quarterly, 2,* 133–153.

Tire hazards, woodworking, and crib safety. (1986). *Young Children, 41*(5), 17–18.

Tizard, B., Mortimer, J., & Burchell, B. (1981). *Involving parents in nursery and infant schools.* Ypsilanti, MI: High/Scope Press.

Townson, M. (1985). Financing child care through the Canada Assistance Plan. In Status of Women, Canada (Ed.), *Financing child care: Current arrangements. A report prepared for the Task Force on Child Care, Series 1.* Ottawa: Status of Women, Canada.

Trahms, C.M. (1989). Factors that shape food patterns in young children. In P.L. Pipes (Ed.), *Nutrition in infancy and childhood* (4th ed., pp. 160–170). St. Louis, MO: C.V. Mosby.

Tribe, C. (1982). *Profile of three theories: Erikson, Maslow, Piaget.* Dubuque, IA: Kendall/Hunt Publishing.

Truemner, T. (1992). An overview of child care legislation in Saskatchewan. In A. Pence (Ed.), *Canadian child care in context: Perspectives from the provinces and territories.* Ottawa: Statistics Canada & Health and Welfare Canada.

Ulich, R. (1947). *Three thousand years of educational wisdom.* Cambridge, MA: Harvard University Press.

Ulich, R. (1967). Johann Heinrich Pestalozzi. In P. Edwards (Ed.), *The encyclopedia of philosophy* (vols. 5–6, pp. 121–122). New York: Macmillan and Free Press.

U.S. firms join forces to build daycare centres. (1992, July 10). *The Toronto Star,* p. D1.

Van Heerden, J.R. (1984). Early under-nutrition and mental performance. *International Journal of Early Childhood, 16*(1), 10–16.

Vandell, D.L., & Corasaniti, M.A. (1990). Variations in early child care: Do they predict subsequent social, emotional, and cognitive differences? *Early Childhood Research Quarterly, 5,* 555–572.

Vander Ven, K. (1986). "And you have a ways to go": The current status and emerging issues in training for child care practice. In K. Vander Ven & E. Tittnich (Eds.), *Competent caregivers—competent children: Training and education for child care practice.* New York: Hawthorne Press.

Vygotsky, L.S. (1962). *Thought and language.* New York: John Wiley.

Vygotsky, L.S. (1976). Play and its role in the mental development of the child. In J. Bruner, A. Jolly, & K. Sylva (Eds.), *Play—Its role in development and evolution* (pp. 537–554). Harmondsworth, UK: Penguin.

Vygotsky, L.S. (1978). The prehistory of written language. In M. Cole, V. John-Steiner, S. Scribner, & E. Souberman (Eds.), *Mind and society: The development of higher psychological process* (pp. 105–119). Cambridge, MA: Harvard University Press.

Wade, M.G., & Davis, W.E. (1982). Motor skill development in young children: Current views on assessment and programming. In L.G. Katz (Ed.), *Current topics in early childhood education* (vol. 4, pp. 55–70). Norwood, NY: Ablex Publishing.

Wadsworth, B.J. (1984). Piaget's theory of cognitive and affective development (3rd ed.). New York: Longman.

Walker, D.K., & Crocker, R.W. (1988). Measuring family systems outcomes. In H.B. Weiss & F.H. Jacobs (Eds.), *Evaluating family programs* (pp. 153–176). New York: Aldine de Gruyter.

Wallerstein, J.S. (1983). Children of divorce: Stress and developmental tasks. In N. Garmezy & M. Rutter (Eds.), *Stress, coping, and development in children* (pp. 265–302). New York: McGraw-Hill.

Wallerstein, J., Corbin, S.B., & Lewis, J.M. (1988). Children of divorce: A ten-year study. In E.M. Hetherington & J. Arasteh (Eds.), *Impact of divorce, single-parenting and stepparenting on children* (pp. 198–214). Hillsdale, NJ: Lawrence Erlbaum.

Walton, S. (1989). Katy learns to read and write. *Young Children, 44*(5), 52–57.

Wash, D.P., & Brand, L.E. (1990). Child day care services: An industry at a crossroads. *Monthly Labor Review, 113*(12), 17–24.

Washington, V., & Oyemade, U.J. (1985). Changing family trends: Head Start must respond. *Young Children, 40*(6), 12–18.

Wass, H. (1984). Concepts of death: A developmental perspective. In H. Wass & C.A. Corr (Eds.), *Childhood and death*. New York: Hemisphere Publishing.

Watson, J.B. (1925a). *Behaviorism*. New York: W.W. Norton.

Watson, J.B. (1925b). What the nursery has to say about instincts. In C. Murchison (Ed.), *Psychologies of 1925*. Worcester, MA: Clark University Press.

Watson, J.B. (1928). *Psychological care of infant and child*. New York: W.W. Norton.

Watson, J.B., & Rayner, R. (1920). Conditioned emotional reactions. *Journal of Experimental Psychology, 3*, 1–4.

Weber, E. (1971). *The English infant school and informal education*. Englewood Cliffs, NJ: Prentice-Hall.

Weber, E. (1984). *Ideas influencing early childhood education*. New York: Teachers College Press, Columbia University.

Wechsler, D. (1989). *Wechsler Preschool and Primary Scale of Intelligence-Revised*. San Antonio, TX: Psychological Corp.

Wechsler, D. (1991). *Wechsler Intelligence Scale for Children* (3rd ed.). San Antonio, TX: Psychological Corp.

Weikart, D.P., & Schweinhart, L.J. (1987). The High/Scope cognitively oriented curriculum of early education. In J.L. Roopnarine & J.E. Johnson (Eds.), *Approaches to early childhood education* (pp. 253–267). Columbus, OH: Merrill Publishing.

Weikart, D.P., & Schweinhart, L.J. (1993). The High/Scope curriculum for early childhood care and education. In J.L. Roopnarine & J.E. Johnson (Eds.), *Approaches to early childhood education* (2nd ed., pp. 195–208). Columbus, OH: Merrill Publishing.

Weinstein, C.S. (1987). Designing preschool classrooms to support development. In C.S. Weinstein & T.G. David (Eds.), *Spaces for children: The built environment and child development* (pp. 159–185). New York: Plenum Press.

Weiss, H. (1987). Family support and education in early childhood programs. In S.L. Kagan, D.R. Powell, B. Weissbourd, & E.F. Zigler (Eds.), *America's family support programs: Perspectives and prospects* (pp. 133–160). New Haven, CT: Yale University Press.

Werner, E.E. (1984). Resilient children. *Young Children, 40*(1), 68–72.

Werner, E.E. (1986). Resilient children. In H.E. Fitzgerald, & M. G. Walraven (Eds.), *Annual editions: Human development.* Sluice Dock, CT: Dushkin.

Werner, P. (1974). *Education of selected movement patterns of preschool children. Perceptual and Motor Skills, 39,* 795–798.

West, S. (1988). *A study of compliance with the Day Nurseries Act at full-day child care centres in Metropolitan Toronto.* Toronto, ON: Ministry of Community and Social Services.

White, B. (1968). Informal education during the first months of life. In R.D. Hess & R.M. Bear (Eds.), *Early Education.* New York: Aldine-Atherton.

Whitebook, M. (1986). The teacher shortage: A professional precipice. *Young Children, 41*(3), 10–11.

Whitebook, M., Howes, C., Darrah, R., & Friedman, J. (1982). Caring for the caregiver: Staff burnout in child care. In L.G. Katz (Ed.), *Current topics in early childhood education* (vol. 4, pp. 211–235). Norwood, NJ: Ablex Publishing.

Whitebook, M., Howes, C., & Phillips, D. (1989). *Who cares? Child care teachers and the quality of care in America: Executive summary, National Child Care Study.* Oakland, CA: Child Care Employee Project.

Willer, B. (1987). Quality or affordability: Trade-offs for early childhood programs? *Young Children, 42*(6), 41–43.

Willer, B. (1990). Estimating the full cost of quality. In B. Willer (Ed.), *Reaching the full cost of quality in early childhood programs* (p. 55–86). Washington, DC: National Association for the Education of Young Children.

Willert, M.K., & Kamii, C. (1985). Reading in kindergarten: Direct vs. indirect teaching. *Young Children, 40*(4), 3–9.

Winner, E. (1986). Where pelicans kiss seals. *Psychology Today, 20,* 24–35.

Wolf, A.D. (1990). Art postcards—Another aspect of your aesthetics program? *Young Children, 45*(2), 39–43.

Women's Bureau (1970a). *Women in the labour force: 1970 facts and figures.* Ottawa, ON: Information Canada.

Women's Bureau (1970b). *Working mothers and their child care arrangements* (Cat. No. L38–2970). Ottawa, ON: Queen's Printer.

Women's Bureau (1990). *Women in the labour force* (1990–1991 edition). Ottawa, ON: Supply and Services.

Woodrich, D.L. (1984). *Children's psychological testing: A guide for nonpsychologists.* Baltimore, MD: Paul H. Brookes.

Wortham, S.C. (1990). *Tests and measurement in early childhood education.* Columbus, OH: Merrill Publishing.

Wright, M. (1983). *Compensatory education in the preschool: A Canadian approach. The University of Western Ontario preschool project.* Ypsilanti, MI: High/Scope Press.

Yarrow, L.J. (1961). Maternal deprivation: toward an empirical and conceptual re-evaluation. *Psychological Bulletin, 58,* 459–490.

Yarrow, M.R., Scott, P.M., & Waxler, C.Z. (1973). Learning concern for others. *Developmental Psychology, 8,* 240–260.

Young, R. (1981). *Association for Early Childhood Education, Ontario (AECEO) submission to the Minister of Education.* Toronto, ON: AECEO.

Young, R. (1987). *Bringing the "bedtime story" into inner city classrooms.* Toronto, ON: Queen's Park, Ontario Ministry of Education.

Young, R. (1993). *The acquisition and use of knowledge about the story schema.* Manuscript submitted for publication, Brock University, St. Catharines, ON.

Young, R. (1993). *Child care in Canada: History, regulation, teacher training, scope, and parental needs.* Manuscript submitted for publication, Brock University, St. Catharines, ON.

Young, R., & Shattuck, D. (1993). *The communicative competence of inner-city children.* Manuscript submitted for publication, Brock University, St. Catharines, ON.

Ziajka, A. (1983). Microcomputers in early childhood education. *Young Children, 38*(5), 61–67.

Ziemer, M. (1987). Science and the early childhood curriculum: One thing leads to another. *Young Children, 42*(6), 44–51.

Zimiles, H. (1981). The Bank Street approach. In J.L. Roopnarine & J.E. Johnson (Eds.) *Approaches to early childhood education* (pp. 163–178). Columbus, OH: Merrill Publishing.

Zimiles, H. (1982). Psychodynamic theory of development. In B. Spodek (Ed.), *Handbook of research in early childhood education* (pp. 135–155). New York: Free Press.

Zion, G. (1965). *Harry by the sea.* New York: Harper & Row.

Zlomke, L., & Piersel, W. (1987). Aggression. In A. Thomas & J. Grimes (Eds.), *Children's needs: Psychological perspectives* (pp. 19–26). Washington, DC: National Association of School Psychologists.

SUBJECT INDEX

To the owner of this book

We hope that you have enjoyed *Introduction to Early Childhood Education,* and we would like to know as much about your experiences as you would care to offer. Only through your comments and those of others can we learn how to make this a better text for future readers.

School _____ Your instructor's name _____

Course _____ Was the text required? _____ Recommended? _____

1. What did you like the most about *Introduction to Early Childhood Education?*

_____

_____

_____

2. How useful was this text for your course?

_____

_____

_____

3. Do you have any recommendations for ways to improve the next edition of this text?

_____

_____

_____

4. In the space below or in a separate letter, please write any other comments you have about the book. (For example, please feel free to comment on reading level, writing style, terminology, design features, and learning aids.)

_____

_____

_____

_____

Optional

Your name _____ Date _____

May Nelson Canada quote you, either in promotion for *Introduction to Early Childhood Education* or in future publishing ventures?

Yes _____ No _____

Thanks!

FOLD HERE

Nelson

TAPE SHUT

0107077099-M1K5G4-BR01

MAIL ➤POSTE
Canada Post Corporation / Société canadienne des postes
Postage paid **Port payé**
if mailed in Canada si posté au Canada
Business **Réponse**
Reply **d'affaires**
0107077099 01

TAPE SHUT

Nelson Canada
College Editorial Department
1120 Birchmount Rd.
Scarborough, ON M1K 9Z9

PLEASE TAPE SHUT. DO NOT STAPLE.